Handbook of Research on AI Methods and Applications in Computer Engineering

Sanaa Kaddoura
Zayed University, UAE

A volume in the Advances in Computer and
Electrical Engineering (ACEE) Book Series

Published in the United States of America by
    IGI Global
    Engineering Science Reference (an imprint of IGI Global)
    701 E. Chocolate Avenue
    Hershey PA, USA 17033
    Tel: 717-533-8845
    Fax: 717-533-8661
    E-mail: cust@igi-global.com
    Web site: http://www.igi-global.com

Library of Congress Cataloging-in-Publication Data

Names: Kaddoura, Sanaa, 1986- editor.
Title: Handbook of research on AI methods and applications in computer
  engineering / Sanaa Kaddoura, editor.
Description: Hershey, PA : Engineering Science Reference, [2023] | "Topics
  1. Introduction to AI 2. Applications of AI in Cloud Computing and
  Distributed Systems 3. Applications of Artificial Intelligence in
  Gaming 4. Applications of Artificial Intelligence in Automobiles 5.
  Applications of Artificial Intelligence in Social Media 6. Applications
  of Artificial intelligence in Navigation 7. Applications of Artificial
  Intelligence in Robotics 8. Applications of Artificial Intelligence in
  Healthcare 9. Artificial Intelligence in self-modifying code 10.
  Intelligent Human-computer interaction 11. Artificial Intelligence in
  Healthcare 12. Artificial Intelligence in Surveillance and Image
  processing 13. Artificial Intelligence in Cybersecurity 14. Artificial
  Intelligence in Search engines 15. Artificial Intelligence in Automotive
   Industry 16. Role of Artificial Intelligence in Smart Cities and
  IoT"--Introduction. | Includes bibliographical references and index. |
  Summary: "Since artificial intelligence (AI) is a branch of computer
  science that focuses on assisting machines in finding human-like answers
  to complex problems, the goal of this book is to show how today's
  computer engineers and scientists can use artificial intelligence in
  real-world applications"-- Provided by publisher.
Identifiers: LCCN 2022039789 (print) | LCCN 2022039790 (ebook) | ISBN
  9781668469378 (h/c) | ISBN 9781668469385 (s/c) | ISBN 9781668469392
  (eISBN)
Subjects: LCSH: Engineering--Data processing. | Artificial
  intelligence--Industrial applications. | Computer science.
Classification: LCC T57.5 .A78 2023 (print) | LCC T57.5 (ebook) | DDC
  620.00285--dc23/eng/20221004
LC record available at https://lccn.loc.gov/2022039789
LC ebook record available at https://lccn.loc.gov/2022039790

This book is published in the IGI Global book series Advances in Computer and Electrical Engineering (ACEE) (ISSN: 2327-039X; eISSN: 2327-0403)

British Cataloguing in Publication Data
A Cataloguing in Publication record for this book is available from the British Library.

For electronic access to this publication, please contact: eresources@igi-global.com.

Advances in Computer and Electrical Engineering (ACEE) Book Series

Srikanta Patnaik
SOA University, India

ISSN:2327-039X
EISSN:2327-0403

MISSION

The fields of computer engineering and electrical engineering encompass a broad range of interdisciplinary topics allowing for expansive research developments across multiple fields. Research in these areas continues to develop and become increasingly important as computer and electrical systems have become an integral part of everyday life.

The **Advances in Computer and Electrical Engineering (ACEE) Book Series** aims to publish research on diverse topics pertaining to computer engineering and electrical engineering. **ACEE** encourages scholarly discourse on the latest applications, tools, and methodologies being implemented in the field for the design and development of computer and electrical systems.

COVERAGE

- Chip Design
- Computer Science
- Digital Electronics
- Algorithms
- VLSI Design
- Electrical Power Conversion
- VLSI Fabrication
- Applied Electromagnetics
- Programming
- Computer Architecture

IGI Global is currently accepting manuscripts for publication within this series. To submit a proposal for a volume in this series, please contact our Acquisition Editors at Acquisitions@igi-global.com or visit: http://www.igi-global.com/publish/.

Titles in this Series

For a list of additional titles in this series, please visit: http://www.igi-global.com/book-series/advances-computer-electri-cal-engineering/73675

Energy Systems Design for Low-Power Computing
Rathishchandra Ramachandra Gatti (Sahyadri College of Engineering and Management, India) Chandra Singh
(Sahyadri College of Engineering and Management, India) P. Srividya (RV College of Engineering, India) and
Sandeep Bhat (Sahyadri College of Engineering and Management, India)
Engineering Science Reference • © 2023 • 310pp • H/C (ISBN: 9781668449745) • US $270.00

5G Internet of Things and Changing Standards for Computing and Electronic Systems
Augustine O. Nwajana (University of Greenwich, UK)
Engineering Science Reference • © 2022 • 308pp • H/C (ISBN: 9781668438558) • US $250.00

Theory and Applications of NeutroAlgebras as Generalizations of Classical Algebras
Florentin Smarandache (University of New Mexico, USA) and Madeline Al-Tahan (Lebanese International Uni-
versity, Lebanon)
Engineering Science Reference • © 2022 • 333pp • H/C (ISBN: 9781668434956) • US $270.00

Antenna Design for Narrowband IoT Design, Analysis, and Applications
Balachandra Pattanaik (Wollega University, Ethiopia) M. Saravanan (Vel Tech Rangarajan Dr. Sagunthala R&D
Institute of Science and Technology, India) U. Saravanakumar (Muthayammal Engineering College, India) and
Ganesh Babu T R (Muthayammal Engineering College, India)
Engineering Science Reference • © 2022 • 261pp • H/C (ISBN: 9781799893158) • US $250.00

Handbook of Research on Advances and Applications of Fuzzy Sets and Logic
Said Broumi (Laboratory of Information Processing, Faculty of Science Ben M'Sik, University Hassan II, Casablanca,
Morocco & Regional Center for the Professions of Education and Training (CRMEF), Casablanca-Settat, Morocco)
Engineering Science Reference • © 2022 • 944pp • H/C (ISBN: 9781799879794) • US $435.00

Blockchain Technology and Computational Excellence for Society 5.0
Shahnawaz Khan (University College of Bahrain, Bahrain) Mohammad Haider Syed (Saudi Electronic Univer-
sity, Saudi Arabia) Rawad Hammad (University of East London, UK) and Aisha Fouad Bushager (University of
Bahrain, Bahrain)
Engineering Science Reference • © 2022 • 309pp • H/C (ISBN: 9781799883821) • US $270.00

701 East Chocolate Avenue, Hershey, PA 17033, USA
Tel: 717-533-8845 x100 • Fax: 717-533-8661
E-Mail: cust@igi-global.com • www.igi-global.com

Editorial Advisory Board

List of Contributors

Table of Contents

Detailed Table of Contents

Chapter 1

Sewit T. Yohannes, Zayed University, UAE
Simar Mansi, Beirut Arab University, Lebanon
Sanaa Kaddoura, Zayed University, UAE

Artificial intelligence (AI) has been a topic of high interest in this day and age. AI has emerged through the early nineties and continues to grow at an unprecedented rate. The idea of having machines that are able to process certain cognition to come to a decision without the intervention of humans is the ultimate idea that is being pursued. Though the stage in which AI is able to completely outperform humans in its cognitive skills is yet to be achieved, there has been remarkable progress towards that area. This chapter aims to provide a brief introduction about AI and the area covered under the topic. Various algorithms are used in programming AI on machines such as evolutionary algorithms, genetic algorithms, and swarm intelligence. AI encompasses machine learning, which will be further discussed in this chapter. Furthermore, the impact of AI on society and futuristic predictions the chapter reviews.

Chapter 2

Julia El Zini, American University of Beirut, Lebanon

The rise of deep learning techniques has produced significantly better predictions in several fields which lead to a widespread applicability in healthcare, finance, and autonomous systems. The success of such models comes at the expense of a trackable and transparent decision-making process in areas with legal and ethical implications. Given the criticality of the decisions in such areas, governments and industries are making sizeable investments in the accountability aspect in AI. Accordingly, the nascent field of explainable and fair AI should be a focal point in the discussion of emergent applications especially in high-stake fields. This chapter covers the terminology of accountable AI while focusing on two main aspects: explainability and fairness. The chapter motivates the use cases of each aspect and covers state-of-the-art methods in interpretable AI and methods that are used to evaluate the fairness of machine learning models, and to detect any underlying bias and mitigate it.

Artificial intelligence (AI) is a branch of cognitive science concerned with intelligent machines capable of doing tasks formerly accomplished by humans. It focuses on using computers to perform activities that require knowledge, perception, reasoning, comprehension, and cognitive talents. AI algorithms can be trained to exploit individual actions, preferences, opinions, and interests. They can educate machines to behave in human-like ways. Furthermore, AI can learn these habits much faster than humans. Artificial intelligence is used in various industries to automate and increase the efficacy of specific processes and excessively in social media. Organizations use social media to reach many people by assessing their general perception and learning about their feelings and reactions to brands and products through AI However, there is a knowledge gap in the literature when holistically exploring AI's role in social media, its application, challenges, and opportunities.

Chapter 4

Computers have become ubiquitous and play an important role in our lives. To be usable, any computing device must allow some form of interaction with its user. Human-computer interaction is the point of communication between human users and computers. AI is gradually being integrated into the human-computer interaction. Designing traditional human-computer interaction courses faces new challenges with breakthroughs in third-generation AI technology. New interaction scenarios between humans and computers, such as smart homes and self-driving cars, are constantly emerging. As AI systems become more widespread, it will be essential to understand them from a human perspective. This chapter will provide an overview to the AI-based intelligent human-computer interaction.

Chapter 5

The computer-based navigation system computes the object's position, speed, and direction in real-time. In the last decades, many researchers, companies, and industries have been working on improving the existing navigation system due to its vast application in military and civilian activities. Typically, navigation systems are based on integrating inertial navigation systems and global positioning systems using a Bayesian filter, like the Kalman filter. The limitations of the Kalman filter have inspired researchers to consider alternatives based on artificial intelligence. Recently, many types of research have been developed to validate the possibility of using artificial intelligence methods in navigation systems. This chapter aims to review the integration of artificial intelligence techniques in navigation systems.

    Tetiana Shmelova, National Aviation University, Ukraine
    Maxim Yatsko, Bees Airline, Ukraine
    Iurii Sierostanov, Bees Airline, USA
    Volodymyr Kolotusha, National Aviation University, Ukraine

The authors make an analysis of the International Civil Aviation Organization documents on applications of new technology for minimizing risk and improving safety in the aviation system. ICAO defined new approaches for effectiveness in aviation – application of artificial intelligence (AI) models for the organization of collaborative decision making (CDM) by all aviation specialists (pilots, air traffic controllers, engineers, etc.) using CDM models based on general information on the flight. The AI is presented in models of decision making (DM) in air navigation system (ANS) as expert systems. The effectiveness of ANS operators' decisions depends on the rational use of intelligent automation at all stages of aircraft flight in the form of intelligent decision support systems (IDSS), with hybrid intelligence (natural intelligence), and AI in DM. Models may be used in the education of aviation specialists and in IDSSs in real flight, especially in emergencies. The chapter presents some examples of CDM models in an emergency "engine failure in flight."

    Jana Saab, Lebanese University, Lebanon

In an aim to improve search engine results, AI interferes to boost it. Thus, this chapter investigates the impact of artificial intelligence on search engine. It includes the most advanced techniques of artificial intelligence that improve search engine optimization (SEO) rankings. In order not to fall in the hassle of having no ranking for your website, artificial intelligence can uplift a website position in the search engine. It is important to state that the growth of SEO has an integral role in digital marketing through AI. Moreover, the obtained results in research studies approve that the integration of artificial intelligence is vital for the progress of search engines.

    Rajab Ssemwogerere, University of Electronic Science and Technology of China, China
    Assadig Abdelrhman Sajo, University of Electronic Science and Technology of China, China
    Nambobi Mutwalibi, Islamic University in Uganda, Uganda
    Asha Khamis Mzee, University of Electronic Science and Technology of China, China

Artificial intelligence (AI) mimics or stimulates human behaviors or thinking to solve specific problems. It has been applied in the analysis of huge datasets and provides reliable outputs without human supervision in various online platforms, for example, information retrieval in search engines, digital assistants, voice assistants, digital marketing, personalized learning, social media, etc. This technology has provided many opportunities and challenges in line with strengthening the authenticity of the information provided via different search engines. This chapter reviews the current pieces of literature about the different AI algorithms used in the most popular metasearch engines and the application of artificial intelligence in these search engine contexts.

Tesfahiwet Abrham, Zayed University, UAE
Sanaa Kaddoura, Zayed University, UAE
Hamda Al Breiki, Zayed University, UAE

For the past decades, cyber threats have been increasing significantly and are designed in a sophisticated way that is tough to detect using traditional protection tools. As a result, privacy and sensitive personal information such as credit card numbers are being continuously compromised. Therefore, it is time to find a solution that can stand against the spreading of such threats. Artificial intelligence, machine learning, and deep learning could be among the top methods of detecting cyber threats. These methods could help to improve the detection technologies and engines for computer network defense. This chapter mainly focuses on artificial intelligence in cybersecurity. The main goal of this chapter is to highlight the drawbacks of the traditional security protection tools and discuss the improvements that has been made so far by applying artificial intelligence to solve the current cybersecurity problems.

V. Dinesh Reddy, SRM University, India
Yasaswini Desu, SRM University, India
Medarametla Sindhu, SRM University, India
Chilukuri Vamsee, SRM University, India
Neelissetti Girish, SRM University, India

Many recent studies on text-to-image synthesis decipher approximately 50% of the problem only. They failed to compute all the imperative details in it. This chapter presents a solution using stacked generative adversarial networks (GAN) to generate lifelike images based on the given text. The stage-I GAN creates a distorted images by depicting the rudimentary/basic colours and shape of a scene predicted on text illustration. Stage-II GAN ends up on generating high-resolution images with naturalistic features using Stage-I findings and the text description as inputs. The output generated by this technique is more credible than many other techniques which are already in use. More importantly, stack GAN produces 256 x 256 images based on the text descriptions, while the existing algorithms produces 128 x 128.

Viacheslav Shkuratskyy, York St. John University, UK
Aminu Bello Usman, York St. John University, UK
Michael S. O'Dea, York St. John University, UK

An earthquake is one of the deadliest natural disasters. Forecasting an earthquake is a challenging task since natural causes such as rainfall or volcanic eruptions disrupt data. Earthquakes can also be caused by human beings, such as mining or dams. Solar activity has also been suggested as a possible cause of earthquakes. Solar activity and earthquakes occur in different parts of the solar system, separated by a huge distance. However, scientists have been trying to figure out if there are any links between these two seemingly unrelated occurrences since the 19th century. In this chapter, the authors explored the methods of how machine learning algorithms including k-nearest neighbour, support vector regression, random forest regression, and long short-term memory neural networks can be applied to predict earthquakes and to understand if there is a relationship between solar activity and earthquakes. The authors investigated three types of solar activity: sunspots number, solar wind, and solar flares, as well as worldwide earthquake frequencies that ranged in magnitude and depth.

Chapter 12

  Suja A. Alex, St. Xavier's Catholic College of Engineering, India
  B. Gerald Briyolan, St. Xavier's Catholic College of Engineering, India

In the era of modern technology, blockchain is out of harm's way in making proceedings ample of its reliability trademark, and chiefly for its immutability, and it doesn't hang on any mediator network while any transaction happens. The use of this technology helped solve many problems in society by detecting the problem which happens in the industry sphere, similarly trust, unambiguously, security, and reliability of statistics processing. The objective of the article is to review the blockchain technologies with the focus of reviewing blockchain in artificial intelligence (AI) applications. With the exception of cryptocurrency, blockchain technology can also avail oneself of financial and social services and healthcare facilities, which is risk-free.

Chapter 13

  Ishraq Abdulmajeed, Jinan University, Lebanon
  Ghalia Nassreddine, Jinan University, Lebanon
  Amal A. El Arid, Rafik Hariri University, Lebanon
  Joumana Younis, CNAM, Lebanon

Artificial intelligence is one of the essential innovations made by scientists to simplify people's life. It allows intelligent computers to imitate human behaviors to accomplish specific tasks. Machine learning is a branch of artificial intelligence in which devices can learn from existing data to predict new output values. Machine learning is used in different domains, including human resources management. This chapter presents an application of machine learning in the human resources department. Machine-learning techniques help select the most suitable candidate for a job vacancy during recruitment stages based on different factors. Factors could include educational level, age, and previous experience. Based on these factors, a decision system is built using the binary classification method. The results show the effectiveness of this method in selecting the best candidate for a job vacancy, revealing the flexibility of the approach in making appropriate decisions. In addition, obtained results are accurate and independent of the dataset imprecision.

Artificial intelligence (AI) can address some of the most significant issues facing education today, innovate teaching and learning methods, and eventually quicken the fulfillment of SDG 4. However, these quick technological advancements carry with them several challenges that have thus far surpassed regulatory structures and policy discussions. The Education 2030 Agenda can be achieved with the help of AI technologies. AI has already been used in education, especially in various tools and assessment platforms that aid skill development. The goal is that as AI educational solutions continue to develop, they will help close gaps in learning and teaching and free up schools and teachers to accomplish more than before. To provide teachers the time and freedom to teach understanding and adaptability—uniquely human talents where computers would struggle— while AI can promote efficiency, personalization, and streamline administrative procedures. This chapter presents challenges and opportunities related to AI use in education and ends with recommendations.

Olive trees diseases harm the quality and the quantity of the harvest seriously, which causes considerable economic losses for farmers, and more importantly affects the national economy in its entirety. The aim of this investigation is to work out a recognizing pattern method, based on the analysis of the texture and supervised classification. It essentially detects and classifies olive tree diseases in order to provide the farmers with tools helping them not only to get informed of their trees' diseases, but also to know how to treat them effectively.

Artificial intelligence's (AI) learning, reasoning, problem-solving, and perception features have given a new horizon to the modern healthcare infrastructure. AI is demonstrating best practices in different domains of healthcare, such as efficient drug discovery processes, accuracy in disease diagnosis, assisted surgeries, efficient utilization of human resources, and many more. This chapter provides a comprehensive overview of AI in healthcare, its applications, and recent research studies with respect to disease prediction and information-processing healthcare applications. Associated technologies of AI healthcare applications have been discussed as the realization of concepts is not possible without considering these technologies. Furthermore, it is essential to present the ethical aspect of AI in healthcare, and discuss the ethical boundaries the ethical boundaries of the applications. AI is becoming inevitable for modern and future healthcare; however, certain challenges are associated with the realization of smart and intelligent healthcare infrastructure.

Chapter 17

S. Uma, Hindusthan College of Engineering and Technology, Coimbatore, India

Hospitals are experiencing an increase in patients due to the prevalence of chronic diseases and the growing elderly population. As a result, every day, a large volume of patient health data is generated, which must be stored and managed effectively. Artificial Intelligence (AI) has played a pivotal role in preventing, diagnosing, treating diseases and rehabilitating patients in the past few decades. Innovations and scientific breakthroughs have improved patient outcomes and population health as the healthcare industry has embraced the digital age. Hence, digital transformation is no longer an option, but rather an industry standard. Though, Biomedical engineering (BE) contributes to improving patient care quality, future healthcare applications will rely on AI enabled BE to solve complex healthcare issues. This book chapter uncovers the potential of AI and BE as a powerful tool for solving some of the most challenging issues of our age and brings comparable changes in scale to the renaissance, the Industrial Revolution in the healthcare sector.

Chapter 18

Lubana Isaoglu, Istanbul University-Cerrahpaşa, Turkey
Derya Yiltas-Kaplan, Istanbul University-Cerrahpaşa, Turkey

Quality of service (QoS) prediction has great importance in today's web services computing. Several researchers proposed methods to enhance the quality of service prediction. The most used one is collaborative filtering (CF), which can be categorized into three main categories: memory-based algorithms, model-based algorithms, and context-based CF algorithms. This paper proposes a model-based algorithm using the graph neural network (GNN) to predict the QoS values. To evaluate the performance of the proposed method, an experiment was conducted. The WS-dream dataset used in the experiment and the proposed method performance were compared with three baseline methods (User item-based Pearson correlation coefficient for QoS prediction-UIPCC, reputation-aware network embedding-based QoS Prediction-RANEP, and trust-aware approach TAP for personalized QoS prediction). The experiment results show that the proposed method, the GNN-based QoS prediction algorithm, performs better than memory-based and other model-based methods in terms of RMSE and MAE in most cases.

Chapter 19

Adeyemi Abel Ajibesin, American University of Nigeria, Nigeria
Doken Edgar, American University of Nigeria, Nigeria

Deep learning models being used to improve human life has been an ongoing domain of research. Violence, especially with the proliferation of arms, has been on the increase worldwide. Many tragedies have occurred right across the globe, leading to people losing their lives as a result of being shot at with guns. This research sought to use deep learning frameworks to detect rifles in images and assess their performance based on the metrics of accuracy and F1 score. The study used a combination of images from Google open images and other sources to form a dataset of 2105 images; 1857 of those was used to train YOLOv3 and RetinaNet models to detect rifles, using Darknet-53 and ResNet50 respectively as the backbone networks. The models were evaluated after training using a test dataset containing 248 images, both the training and evaluation of the models were carried out using scripts written in Python. The results obtained showed that YOLOv3 had better output in terms of accuracy, precision, recall, and, consequently, the F1 scored better than RetinaNet

Chapter 20

Mouna Afif, University of Monastir, Tunisia
Riadh Ayachi, University of Monastir, Tunisia
Yahia Said, Electrical Engineering Department, Northern Border University, Arar, Saudi Arabia
Mohamed Atri, College of Computer Science, King Khalid University, Abha, Saudi Arabia

Building new systems used for indoor sign recognition and indoor wayfinding assistance navigation, especially for blind and visually impaired persons, presents a very important task. Deep learning-based algorithms have revolutionized the computer vision and the artificial intelligence fields. Deep convolutional neural networks (DCNNs) are on the top of state-of-the-art algorithms which makes them very suitable to build new assistive technologies based on these architectures. Especially, the authors will develop a new indoor wayfinding assistance system using aging evolutionary algorithms AmoebaNet-A. The proposed system will be able to recognize a set of landmark signs highly recommended to assist blind and sighted persons to explore their surrounding environments. The experimental results have shown the high recognition performance results obtained by the developed work. The authors obtained a mean recognition rate for the four classes coming up to 93.46%.

Chapter 21

Sabitha E., SRM Institute of Science and Technology, Vadapalani Campus, Chennai, India

Healthcare applications in monitoring and managing diseases have undergone rapid development in medical sectors and play an important in observing and controlling diabetes mellitus (DM). DM is a chronic infection that is caused by extreme blood sugar level. The rapid increase of DM world-wide have the effect of gaining attention to predict DM at early stage. Consequently, various technologies have been used to diagnose diabetes at an early stage to avoid major health defects. The most satisfaction in disease prediction and classification methods has been achieved through AI techniques and algorithms in healthcare. The main of the objective of the study is to provide a detail review on DM, the increase of

DM around world-wide, datasets used in diabetic prediction, advance techniques and methods applied for disease prediction, and applications and its limitations used in diabetic prediction. The study also provides a detailed review on recent techniques and methods used in disease prediction, which guides the evolution of AI techniques and will provide a well-grounded knowledge of existing methods.

Chapter 22

Riadh Ayachi, University of Monastir, Tunisia
Mouna Afif, University of Monastir, Tunisia
Yahia Said, University of Monastir, Tunisia
Abdessalem Ben Abdelali, University of Monastir, Tunisia

Most actual intelligent vehicles (IV) are powered by a variety of sensors and cameras. Vision-based applications for IV mainly require visual information. In this paper, the authors introduce a pedestrian detection application used for pedestrian safety. The authors proposed a deep fully convolutional neural network (DFCNN) for pedestrian detection. The proposed model is suitable for mobile implementation. To do this, the authors propose to build lightweight blocks using convolution layers, and replace pooling layers and fully connected layers with convolution layers. Training and testing of the proposed DFCNN model for pedestrian detection were performed using the Caltech dataset. The proposed DFCNN has achieved 85% of average precision and an inference speed of 30 FPS. The reported results have demonstrated the robustness of the proposed DFCNN for pedestrian detection. The achieved performance was low computation complexity and high performance.

Chapter 23

Jayesh Soni, Florida International University, USA

Predictive maintenance has attracted many researchers with the increased growth in the digitization of industrial, locomotive, and aviation fields. Simultaneously, extensive research in deep learning model development to its deployment has made its way to industrial applications with unprecedented accuracy. The most crucial task in predictive maintenance is to predict the machine's remaining useful life, yet the most beneficial one. In this chapter, the authors address the problem of predicting the remaining lifecycle of an engine using its sensor data. The authors provide practical implementation of predicting the RUL of an engine by proposing a deep learning-based framework on the open-source benchmark NASA's Commercial Modular Aero-Propulsion System Simulation (C-MAPSS) engine dataset, which contains sensor information of around 100 engines with 22 sensors. The proposed framework uses the bi-directional long short term memory algorithm. The authors optimize hyperparameters using advanced deep learning frameworks.

Chapter 24

V. Dinesh Reddy, SRM University, India
Sai Vishnu Vamsi Senagasetty, SRM University, India
Krishna Teja Vanka, SRM University, India
Mohana Vamsi Dhara, SRM University, India
Rupini Durga Puvvada, SRM University, India
Muzakkir Hussain, SRM University, India

These days, it's becoming harder to feel safer when we go out at night. So, to tackle this security problem, the authors propose a night patrolling mechanism to detect objects in low light conditions. Images taken during the nighttime have difficulties with less contrast, brightness, and noise owing to inadequate light or insufficient exposure. Deep learning-based methods accomplish end-to-end, unsupervised object recognition using convolutional neural networks, which abolishes the requirement to describe and draw out attributes separately. Despite the fact that deep learning has led to the invention of many successful object detection algorithms; many state-of-the-art object detectors, like Faster-RCNN and others, can't carry out at their best under low-light situations. Even with an extra light source, it is hard to detect the features of an item due to the uneven division of brightness. This chapter proposes a deep learning algorithm called single shot detector, with Mobilenet v2 as the backbone to tackle the issues of object detection under low-light situations.

Chapter 25

Sankaragomathi B., Sri Shakthi Institute of Engineering and Technology, India
*Senthil Kumar S., Department of Computer Science and Engineering, Amritha University,
Cochin, India*

Musculoskeletal impairment can be caused by Avascular Necrosis(AN). Younger people are more likely to develop it, thus early intervention and fast diagnosis are essential. The femoral bones are typically affected by this condition, which results in fractures that change the geometry of the bones. It is difficult to retrieve the AN-affected bone pictures because of the many places where the fractures are located. In this work, a useful method for retrieving AN pictures using deep belief CNN feature representation is proposed. Preprocessing is first applied to the raw dataset. In this stage, the median filter (MF) is used to reduce image noise and downsize the image. Using a deep belief convolutional neural network, features are represented (DB-CNN). The representations of the image feature data have now been converted to binary codes. Then, using the modified-hamming distance, the similarity measurement is calculated. The images are then retrieved with a focus on the similarity values. The test results demonstrated that the proposed approach is superior to the other methods now in use.

Preface

Artificial intelligence (AI) is a technology that has been integrated into almost every activity of our day-to-day life, from chatbots on different websites to auto-recommendations to smart speakers like Alexa and Siri. The newest revolution of AI is ChatGPT released by OpenAI company while this book was being prepared. ChatGPT is an AI-based chatbot that specializes in dialogue trained with both supervised and reinforcement learning techniques. It is a large fine-tuned language model version of a model in OpenAI's GPT-3.5 family of language models.

Though there is a wide range of definitions of what AI is, AI has been termed as the technology that enables machines to perform tasks with some intelligence. The area of AI has broadened in terms of complexity and coverage of various aspects of activities. The concept has been around from as early as the1950s, and there have been many relevant innovations till now. AI was closely related to the concept of robotics in its early seasons of development. One test conducted on machines to measure how far they can resemble human cogitation is the tanning test. In different scenarios, these machines proved to succeed in the test, which convinced people that machines could think for themselves. The study of human cognition is still in progress, and the field of AI is advancing as much. There have been many advancements since AI's early stages, and now it is integrated into our daily life. AI has been outperforming humans in various fields but is confined to the area the AI is assigned to. However, superintelligence or general intelligence, where AI is holistically over-performing humans in diverse areas, is still being pursued.

The ethical aspect of AI has been under debate from the early times till now, and still, the discussion is put on what AI can do in the future. Most of those AI innovations perform the given tasks with excellence. However, if they are assigned a dangerous task, they could also perform it. Such ethical concerns are hard to predict and put regulations on. Though the public has relatively shifted from being skeptical about AI overtaking humanity in this age, the question remains unanswered.

One of the major subsections of AI that has been dominantly worked on is machine learning, which is often mistaken as equivalent to AI. Machines learn from a set of inputs given to them in terms of data and experience, known as machine learning. There are many categories within machine learning: supervised, unsupervised, and reinforcement learning methods. Many algorithms fit into those categories, and the book comprises diverse verities of those algorithms. Those algorithms are sets of steps the machine is given to follow to develop the targeted solution.

Conventional AI is applied in different fields of reasoning, learning, planning, and creativity, and some of it is discussed in the different chapters of this book. AI came in handy with the ever-growing big data collected from individuals for different reasons in terms of collection, sorting, and prediction. Some of the current fields of advancements are the diagnosis of different health complications of animals and plants, drug manufacturing, and surgery assistantship in the field of healthcare. They are organizing data and predicting user behavior on social media and advertising platforms to optimize services or products. In the area of aviation and automobile navigation, as well as monitoring. On creating optimal interaction with humans as business owners. And on ensuring AI security where AI is being used to secure the platforms of AI. Scientists have been catching different AI trends during different seasons. Some of the currently trending advancements in this field are advanced language modeling, in the augmented workforce, the metaverse or the environment that is created where digital reality is converging with the actual reality to some degree, low code AI where minimum coding is required to generate fully functioning AI, smart or autonomous vehicles, and creative AI where the technology is implemented in creating some art.

A wide range of AI trends is discussed in the chapters of this book, along with detailed explanations of the algorithms used to solve the presented cases. A summary of the content of each chapter follows:

Chapter 1, "Introduction to Artificial Intelligence," introduces the topic of AI along with the historical trend and progressions in this field. Some of the earliest inventions from the early nineteenth century are mentioned. The chapter also outlines the areas where AI has outperformed humans and the areas that have shown remarkable progress. Different categories and subcategories of AI are also discussed.

Chapter 2, "AI Accountability in Emergent Applications: Explainable and Fair Solutions," discusses using deep learning methods to create a fair platform for various fields such as healthcare and finance. The chapter describes how machine learning methods can be used to make a unbiased decision-making process. The chapter explains accountable AI focusing on two specific areas: explainability and fairness.

Chapter 3, "The Rising Trend of AI in Social Media: Applications, Challenges, and Opportunities," describes how the rising trend of AI has been applied in social media in cognitive science. AI learns about consumers' preferences for products through social media interactions. Areas of customer management and targeted advertisement are also discussed. The chapter aims to fill the gap in the knowledge area of AI's role in the social media field.

Chapter 4, "AI-Based Intelligent Human-Computer Interaction," talks about how the advancements in AI have made the interaction of humans with computers and other smart devices more dynamic, along with its challenges. How the trend of AI has impacted this interaction is thoroughly discussed. This chapter discusses how the interaction happens from the perspective of humans on various levels with different devices.

Chapter 5, "Artificial Intelligence in Navigation Systems," discusses the object's factors, such as the position and direction concerning the navigation system of objects. The chapter shows that the navigation system is based on calibrating the inertial navigation with the global positioning using a Bayesian filter. Other filters and navigation methods are also discussed in comparison. The input from the readings is processed through a neural network to achieve optimal results.

Chapter 6, "Artificial Intelligence Methods and Applications in Aviation," talks about the application of AI to reduce risk in aviation systems. Different civil aviation organization documents are considered to come up with realistic means of improving aviation safety. AI and hybrid intelligence solutions are presented to deal with the decision-making process of aviation systems and subdivisions. The model is targeted at optimizing the collaborative decision-making conducted by specialists.

Chapter 7, "The Impact of Artificial Intelligence on Search Engine: Super Intelligence in AI," talks about the role of AI in search engine optimization. This chapter shows how the ranking process takes place and how AI can uplift your product ranking on search engines. The chapter also details how information is retrieved and what is taken to be processed by the search engines. The chapter also shows natural language processing techniques used in processing search engines.

Chapter 8, "A Survey About the Application of AI in Search Engines: Opportunities and Challenges of AI," talks about how AI imitates and simulates human behavior to conduct specific tasks. This chapter discusses how big human interaction data is considered to project results in search engines and digital assistants. The chapter also discusses the challenges and opportunities presented concerning this area.

Chapter 9, "Artificial Intelligence Applications in Cybersecurity," talks about the increasing complexity of cybersecurity as AI advances exponentially. The chapter discusses the need for modern tools to oversee cybersecurity concerning various areas like intrusion detection and phishing attacks. The tools can be focused on detecting and preventing possible attacks. The chapter also talks about how deep learning can be used to tackle the discussed problem.

Chapter 10, "Text to Image Synthesis Using Multistage Stack GAN," discusses text-to-image analysis using stacked generative adverbial networks to create lifelike images from a given text. The process comprises two steps: in the first step, a distorted image is created and processed to become a high-resolution image in the second image. The image produced is 256 by 256, which is far advanced from the other algorithms' output, 180 by 180.

Chapter 11, "The Application of Machine Learning for Predicting Global Seismicity," discusses the relation of solar activities in relation with earthquakes. This chapter further shows how different machine-learning algorithms can be used to predict upcoming earthquakes and solar activities. The algorithms consider the input of sunspots number, solar wind, solar flares, and earthquake frequencies to predict the results.

Chapter 12, "Convergence of Blockchain to Artificial Intelligence Applications," talks about blockchain and its role in creating a trust-free platform that is implementable in various sectors. How blockchain transaction is performed within the context of AI is thoroughly discussed. The chapter focuses on how blockchain enables a decentralized and immutable environment suitable for financial and social services, complementing the security issues presented by AI and many technological platforms.

Chapter 13, "Machine Learning Approach in Human Resources Department," talks about the application of machine learning (ML) in managing the human resource department. ML is used to select the right candidates for specific job positions based on the inputs. The input is flexible per the job requirement, and the decision is made using the binary classification method.

Chapter 14, "Artificial Intelligence in Higher Education: A New Horizon," discusses the issues faced in education along with means of productivity enhancement methods. Regulatory structures and policy discussions are also taken into consideration. The chapter thoroughly discusses the opportunities and the challenges AI presents in the education sector; then, it gives recommendations on how optimal results could be reached.

Chapter 15, "Smart Farming: Automatic Detection and Classification of Olive Leaf Diseases," talks about how machine learning can easily classify diseases that occur on olives leaves. The pattern of the leaf's color or discoloration is taken as input to determine the state of the leaves. Then supervised classification takes place to classify the leaves accordingly. This help in the correct diagnosis and the correct prescription of solutions for the disease.

Chapter 16, "A Comprehensive Overview of Artificial Intelligence in Healthcare," discusses the various areas of AI implemented in the health sector, like correct diagnosis, drug discovery, and assisted surgeries. This chapter discusses how AI has played a cardinal role in various disease prediction and information-processing healthcare applications. The chapter also discusses the ethical boundaries and projects future predictions.

Chapter 17, "Potential Integration of Artificial Intelligence and Biomedical Research Applications: Inevitable Disruptive Technologies for Prospective Healthcare," discusses AI's critical role in the healthcare system. Many contributions of AI are discussed in different fields, and the role of biomedical engineering in improving the healthcare system is shown. The chapter also discusses how AI could be implemented in the future to have a more dynamic impact.

Chapter 18, "Using Graph Neural Network to Enhance Quality of Service Prediction," discusses how various algorithms have been implemented to create the quality of service predictions using three algorithms, mainly: memory-based algorithms, model-based algorithms, and context-based CF algorithms. Those algorithms' results are discussed to develop the most optimal and accurate means of prediction.

Chapter 19, "Rifle Detection and Performance Evaluation Using Deep Learning Frameworks," talks about using deep learning frameworks to detect rifles from images and their performances to reduce the risk of violence with the proliferation of arms. The images are taken from open google images and used for evaluation. The evaluation result is assessed based on the F1 score and the accuracy score of the results.

Chapter 20, "A Transfer Learning Approach for Smart Home Applications Based on Evolutionary Algorithm," discusses the use of deep convolutional neural networks on the new assistive technology that is implemented in assisting blind and visually impaired individuals integrating with smart building architecture. The chapter discusses using the aging evolution algorithm to assist individuals who are sighted and blind in exploring their environment. The accuracy of the recognition of the environment is discussed.

Chapter 21, "Artificial Intelligence Approaches in Diabetic Prediction," talks about the use of AI in predicting health complications, especially diabetes mellitus. The chapter discusses different means algorithms that could be used to classify health complications and discusses in detail how deep learning in a general and artificial neural network is used in creating accurate classification methods. The algorithm is also implemented in monitoring the disease.

Chapter 22, "Lightweight Neural Networks for Pedestrian Detection in Intelligent Vehicles," discusses the use of deep convolution neural networks to predict pedestrian positions sensed by intelligent devices. This is implemented by cameras of vehicles and CCTVs during daytime and nighttime. The chapter discusses other means of object detection and compares the proposed result with the attained results of alternative methods.

Chapter 23, "Towards Predicting the Life of an Engine: A Deep Learning Approach," discusses the application of deep learning to predict the life of an engine. Accurate prediction of the life might lead to correct maintenance and replacement of parts. The engines could be of different automobiles, and data is taken from different open-source engine datasets of diverse automobiles. The data is processed using a bi-directional long short-term memory algorithm.

Chapter 24, "Nighttime Object Detection: A Night Patrolling Mechanism Using Object Detection," talks about a patrolling mechanism that can detect objects that are in low light. The chapter used a deep learning model named mobilenet_v2 with a single-shot multibox detector working as an object detection model to identify objects at night accurately. This could be used as a more secure and reliable method of nighttime patrolling.

Chapter 25, "Identification of Avascular Necrosis or Osteoporosis Using Deep Belief Convolutional Neural Network," discusses the use of deep belief convolutional neural network to detect the presence and the degree of osteoporosis in the bones. The image of the bone scan is taken as input and processed to be classified into the correct category. This proposed method is better than existing approaches as it uses modified-hamming distance to compute similarity.

Many books are designed in the area of artificial intelligence. However, most of them are technical and require coding. This book presents recent research in different areas where AI can be applied. It opens the eyes of many researchers to the possibility of applying AI to many problems, no matter the area. AI is transforming the world. AI is revolutionizing every aspect of life despite its general lack of knowledge. It is a comprehensive tool that allows people to reconsider how we combine information, evaluate data, and use the ensuing insights to enhance decision-making. Our goal in providing this thorough overview is to explain AI to a group of decision-makers, opinion leaders, and interested observers while highlighting how AI is already changing the world and posing significant issues for society, the economy, and governance.

Sanaa Kaddoura
Zayed University, UAE

Acknowledgment

This work would not have been possible without the support of the authors and reviewers.

Special thanks to Ms. Fatima Al Husseiny, Ms. Amal Arid, and Dr. Ghalia Nassreddine for their support throughout the process. Also, thank my colleague Dr. Madeleine Al-Tahan for her continuous support. A special thanks to my brother Dr. Mustafa F. Kaddoura, for being with me step by step in this work. Without the support of colleagues and contributors, I would not be able to achieve this project.

Chapter 1
Introduction to Artificial Intelligence

Sewit T. Yohannes
Zayed University, UAE

Simar Mansi
Beirut Arab University, Lebanon

Sanaa Kaddoura
https://orcid.org/0000-0002-4384-4364
Zayed University, UAE

ABSTRACT

Artificial intelligence (AI) has been a topic of high interest in this day and age. AI has emerged through the early nineties and continues to grow at an unprecedented rate. The idea of having machines that are able to process certain cognition to come to a decision without the intervention of humans is the ultimate idea that is being pursued. Though the stage in which AI is able to completely outperform humans in its cognitive skills is yet to be achieved, there has been remarkable progress towards that area. This chapter aims to provide a brief introduction about AI and the area covered under the topic. Various algorithms are used in programming AI on machines such as evolutionary algorithms, genetic algorithms, and swarm intelligence. AI encompasses machine learning, which will be further discussed in this chapter. Furthermore, the impact of AI on society and futuristic predictions the chapter reviews.

INTRODUCTION

The term artificial intelligence is quite a popular term that has various impressions on various audiences around the globe. Some people see it as a great risk to develop machines that can learn and improve themselves. People directly link the idea of AI with robots and science fiction where the robots control the world and enslave humans. While on the other side people hope to have a much simpler reality where their chores and all hard work are managed by programmed intelligent machines.

DOI: 10.4018/978-1-6684-6937-8.ch001

The initial intention of many researchers and scientists was to have machines that can run on a certain level of intelligence to perform their activities. The definition of intelligence was one of the main controversial aspects of whether a machine can have its own intelligence or not. To replicate human intelligence the researchers tried to use children as their model as children do not know everything, to begin with, but keep learning new things as they grow (Zhang & Lu, 2021). Accordingly, even the current definition of AI is not explicitly stated. According to Dall'Anese (2020), some relate AI only to high-level machine intelligence while others consider other technologies to be a part.

Then what is artificial intelligence? AI is when a machine is made to simulate human consciousness in wholesome or particular matters. The AI advancements made until now are yet to portray an all-rounded human consciousness that responds to everything just like humans do, which is called general AI. However, there are various advancements in this technology to tackle particular events in human life by mimicking human intelligence; and this is referred to as narrow AI.

The technology has been around for some years now, though the advancement and dynamics of the field are escalating exponentially. One of the main concerns is can a programmed machine come to a state where it can think for itself and generate original work as humans do.

BACKGROUND

Artificial intelligence can be defined as the way machines are programmed to mimic the intelligence of humans to perform tasks that require humans by being independent or partially dependent. Though there were many studies and research on the topic in the previous years, intelligent machines started to be taken seriously during the 1950s starting from the Bomb, a machine, that was able to break the enigma code. While the idea of machines having the ability to think seemed ideal, the Turing test introduced by Alan Turing started proving a point. The Turing test is conducted by two individuals and a machine where one of the individuals tries to guess if he is conversing with a machine or a human. The Turing test is held every year and will be continuing until the intelligence of such a machine becomes a replica of human intelligence. Though there are no machines that completely pass this test, this was one of the tests that convinced people of the possibility of AI and how close it is to human intelligence.

Afterward, in 1955 Professor John McCarthy named the technology "the science and engineering of making intelligent machines". In the following year, 1956, he organized a research team at Dartmouth College and came up with the term Artificial Intelligence (Buchanan, 2005). In 1961 the Unimate robot became the first mechanical robot with a granted patent; it performed repetitive tasks that were performed by employees (Wallén, 2008). Then there was a major research and contribution in the area of algorithms the machines used which birthed the first chatbot named Eliza which was developed between 1964 and 1966 at MIT.

In 1966 the first electronic person was launched named Shakey stirred up predictions of super-powerful AI in the following 8 years (Wu, Liu & Wu, 2018). The robot was a general-purpose mobile robot with multiple sensors and cameras, and it was designed to make decisions after considering multiple input factors to perform a reasonable task (Wu, Liu & Wu, 2018). There was a dynamic improvement in computer vision and language processing.

While there was an increase in the attention and funding AI was receiving from various scientists, the WABOT project began in 1967 in Japan and was completed in 1972 (Liu et al., 2019). The WABOT-1 became the first full-scale intelligent humanoid robot (Liu et al., 2019). The robot had arms and legs and it could perform some of the simplest tasks like picking up a cup or just dancing to music.

The advancement in AI intimidated many organizations and individuals to put more resources and effort into developing further enhanced technologies. Despite the successful advancements however followed a season known as the AI winter, which was a season time when the scientists lacked funding for the AI innovations and experiments that were undergoing (Francesconi, 2022). The AI winter is also further classified as the first and the second AI winter however, various foundational ideas were presented instead of practical results (Francesconi, 2022).

Right after the AI winter season, the blossoming of AI began to soar radically. There were innovations and advancements in the field that were incremental and contributed to each other. In 1997 a unique purpose-built chess-playing computer was developed by IBM with the name Deep Blue which was the first machine to beat a human at a chess game in real-time. In the following year, 1998, an emotionally intelligent robot was developed by MIT which was named KISMET; this robot was able to detect human emotions and interact with them using different expressions. On 11th May 1999, Sony launched the first customer robot pet that resembles a dog. The robot developed its personality and skills over time.

Some robots were developed to ease human chores by replicating them intelligently. In 2002 Roomba, an autonomous vacuum cleaner was invented by the MIT roboticist, Colin Angle. The main feature of the robot is to navigate and clean a room.

In 2011 Apple integrated SIRI with its iPhone S4 release, a virtual assistant with a voice interface that receives vocal instructions. A similar virtual assistant, Alexa, was introduced by Amazon in 2014. Those virtual assistants have a wide range of functionalities to assist users with online-related activities.

In 2014 Eugene Goostman became the first AI to pass the Turing test. This AI was a chatbot with a background of a young 13years old Ukrainian kid, and the consistency of his broken English, as well as random strange responses with his background, convinced a third of the judges conducting the Turing test.

Up until now, there are countless advancements in various areas with greater quality. There are more autonomous robots that conduct various tasks that were conducted by humans and were thought irreplaceable like surgery and bartending. There is also a popular robot by the name of Sophia which was given Saudi Arabian nationality.

TYPES OF ARTIFICIAL INTELLIGENCE

Artificial intelligence is often categorized as weak and strong or as weak, general, and strong. Here we will consider the latter categorization.

Weak AI

Weak AI also known as narrow AI targets specific tasks, where the majority of AI advancements made to date lay. The term weak indicates the area to which the AI is applied rather than its strength (Kumar & Thakur, 2012). It includes google search and virtual assistants like Siri and Alexa. This area of AI has shown dynamic progress and notable accuracy throughout the years. Though those technologies are quite advanced and accomplish tasks much better than humans, they are confined to a certain field or area of expertise (Kumar & Thakur, 2012).

Strong AI

General AI or Strong AI is the artificial intelligence of machines that is aspired to be implemented in the future where the machine exhibits an all-rounded intelligence to tackle various incidents as its everyday task (Kumar & Thakur, 2012). Strong AI is intelligence that is at the level of human intelligence. This type of intelligence is not yet attained either in theoretical aspects or in practical implementations. However, when this type of AI is at hand, singularity is unavoidable.

Superintelligence AI

Superintelligence can be loosely defined as intelligence that outperforms human cognition in all aspects (Kumar & Thakur, 2012). In other words, a strong AI would be able to outperform humans in nearly every cognitive task. This is in its ideal stage and is the next step that is projected to be reached after the implementation of strong AI.

KNOWLEDGE-BASED SYSTEMS

A knowledge-based system (KBS) is a form of AI that uses human knowledge to guide the decision-making process of various systems. KBS uses data and information about certain systems as input and uses it as foreknowledge to make decisions or come up with new knowledge about the specific domain. KBS resembles a database containing a set of unrelated data inputs that are stored together, however, the KBS contains related information about a particular system (Irfan, 2019). The data that is initially provided is processed by an interface engine of the system; the engine system looks for important information to satisfy the request of the user. The engine system follows the heuristics that were initially set up in the system (Irfan, 2019). Then the results are shown to the user through a user interface (Irfan, 2019).

KBS is usually used interchangeably with the expert system, while the expert system is a type of KBS that goes after the decision-making process of humans after considering various factors. There are also some other types such as case-based reasoning, frame-based systems, intelligent tutoring systems, and rule-based systems (Leo Kumar, 2019). Case-Based Reasoning (CBR) relies on previous cases or information that was given to the system to solve new incidents (Leo Kumar, 2019). The next one is the Frame-Based System (FBS); where a system relates to various database frames in the form of abstracts to enlarge the knowledge base of the system (Leo Kumar, 2019). After that, object-oriented systems use a hierarchy of classes to categorize access and use of information in the knowledge base (Leo Kumar, 2019). Finally, the rule-based system depends on sets of rules, if-then conditions, that are provided by the user to converge to a specific result (Leo Kumar, 2019).

The knowledge-based system was designed to solve tasks that require human expertise and hence does not rely on a set of algorithms but on real-world knowledge heuristics to compute tasks (Ertel, 2018). This makes KBS unique since real-world problems do not have definitive solutions. Knowledge-based systems aid people with accelerated expertise by providing organized information on requested topics whereby the user can make decisions quickly with greater accuracy. Hence, KBS has been implemented in various sectors such as healthcare systems and engineering.

The KBS has three components: knowledge base, interface engine, and user interface. The knowledge base is an element of the KBS that has an organized set of information that is given to the system, the part that resembles a database. The knowledge can be in the form of if-then procedures or logical conditions (Ertel, 2018). The second part is the interface engine, the part that creates means of reasoning on the information provided by the knowledge base and comes to solutions or conclusions (Ertel, 2018). The last part is the user interface, the component that assists the communication of the user with the system (Ertel, 2018). The user inputs the facts through the user interface, and the results of the KBS are displayed through the interface.

The attributes of the domain are determined and translated into a comprehensible set of data that can be processed by the computer (Ertel, 2018). The reasoning procedures and the ways how the KBS will use uncertain knowledge are programmed, usually by the knowledge engineer. Then the system is set for dealing with requests generated from the users. Hence, the KBS is capable of dealing with uncertainty and gives reasoning for produced solutions; however, the system is confined to a specific topic and is hard to remodel (Ertel, 2018).

An instance of a knowledge-based system is Watson, a software that was developed by the collaboration of IBM with other universities. Watson was a machine designed to answer questions asked in the natural language. This machine won a competition held in a special edition of Jeopardy beating two human contestants, who were champions of previous years, in February 2011. This showed how natural language can be used along with the advancement of natural language processing, how knowledge can be portrayed, and comprehensible reasoning of attained decisions.

ALGORITHMS AND BIG DATA

For machines to be able to learn and predict they need to have a huge amount of information for knowledge and a set of parameters on which to base their decision. Those sets of parameters are referred to as algorithms. Some of the most used algorithms will be discussed below.

Evolutionary Algorithm

An evolutionary algorithm (EA) is a population-based metaheuristic algorithm that finds solutions to problems that are hard to compute by the polynomial-time algorithm (Ryerkerk et al., 2019). Evolutionary algorithms use biological evolutionary patterns to come up with optimum solutions by conducting mutation, selection, and cross-over (Ryerkerk et al., 2019). The sets of possible solutions serve as the population at the beginning of the evolutionary algorithm. Thereafter, there is a fitness function to determine the selection process of the initial population. Afterward, the selected population undergoes crossing-over and mutation to generate an optimum solution. The solution is then continuously assessed by the fitness function to determine its continuity. The survival of the fittest that occurs in the natural evolution process gets applied by discarding the inefficient solutions while keeping the most efficient solutions to contribute to the next generation. This process proceeds to iterate until there is a convergence to an optimal solution; then the termination occurs. If the iteration ceases to converge, the convergence can be determined by the present number of iterations that are allowed to take place or by fitness approximation. The steps can be shown in figure 1.

Figure 1. Steps of evolutionary algorithm

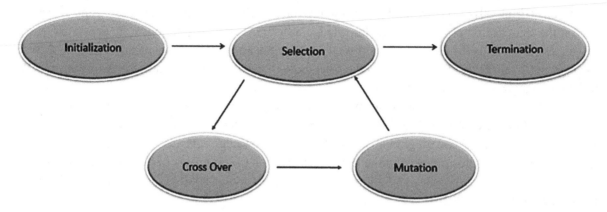

The EA faces computational complexity in finding the solution that satisfies the fitness function; hence, fitness approximation is used to assist in the convergence of the algorithm to the most optimal solutions (Maier et al., 2019). EA is used when a wide population is under consideration for optimal solutions considering that it can converge into a globally optimal solution. While the whole population is being considered for optimal solutions, the computation is conducted in parallel for every generation which saves a reasonable amount of computation power (Maier et al., 2019). According to Maier et al. (2019), EA is also used for the optimization of presented solutions because it can be easily linked to pre-existing models and can deal with constraints.

Evolutionary algorithms encompass various algorithms which are genetic algorithms and genetic programming which will be discussed below.

Genetic Algorithm

A genetic algorithm is an algorithm that undergoes a genetic evolution as the population breeds and evolves to approach a healthy population imitating natural selection of evolution. The genetic algorithm optimizes functions using heuristic optimization methods. Just like the procedure of natural genetics and evolution, the algorithm selects fit individuals to breed into a new generation from a set of possible solutions. Afterward, the new generation is subjected to genetic operations like mutation. The genes that are considered in the process are the input factors of the data reflecting the genes that are found in nature with representing various features.

The genetic algorithm uses several genetic operators: encoding schemes, initiation, crossover, mutation, and selection which can be shown in figure 2.

Figure 2. Procedures of genetic algorithm

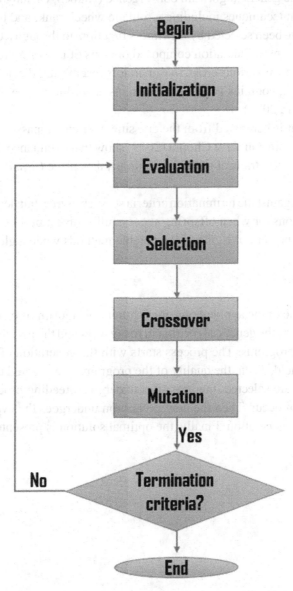

Encoding schemes refer to the process of encoding the data into a set of codes that can be used for genetic operations (Katoch, Chauhan & Kumar, 2021). Various encoding techniques are taken into consideration like binary, octal, permutation, and value encodings.

After the data is encoded, the genetic algorithm uses random initiation because the genetic algorithm is a stochastic optimization method (Katoch, Chauhan & Kumar, 2021). Hence, distinct individuals with random features are generated randomly.

Then the fitness function evaluates whether an individual solution will participate in the reproduction process by evaluating the weight of the individual. The process of the genetic algorithm keeps iterating until there is a consistent and optimal result over a certain number of generations; the fitness function plays a cardinal factor in the genetic algorithm convergence (Katoch, Chauhan & Kumar, 2021). There are various fitness selection techniques including a roulette wheel, rank, and tournament.

The individuals that have been selected by the fitness function go through a crossover function where they are combined to form a new generation composed of traits of two or more parents (Katoch, Chauhan & Kumar, 2021). There are various crossover operators resembling the actual crossover conducted between genes; the offspring contains genes of the parents according to the method of crossover used (Katoch, Chauhan & Kumar, 2021).

The new generation that is generated from the crossing over encompasses notable similarities with the parent generation. Lambora, Gupta & Chopra (2019) show that to enhance diversification in the new generation, mutation of specific traits at random locations takes place (usually one over the number of features of the gene).

The process is checked against the termination criteria set such as a certain level of fitness of offspring, a fixed number of generations, or when offspring successfully solve a problem. The genetic algorithm requires high computation power but is one of the notable methods when a global solution is required.

Genetic Programming

Genetic programming is one of the applications of evolutionary algorithms on computer programs. Genetic programming resembles the genetic algorithm in many ways and the individuals who are considered for the genetic operations programs. The process starts with the generation of a random population of programs about a certain field. Then, the quality of the programs is evaluated using certain parameters. When the fittest programs are selected, the programs undergo a breeding process where reproduction, crossing over, and mutation occur. Then the new generation undergoes the evaluation to select the fittest offspring from the new generation. Finally, the optimal solution is presented. The whole process is represented in figure 3.

Figure 3. Steps of genetic programming

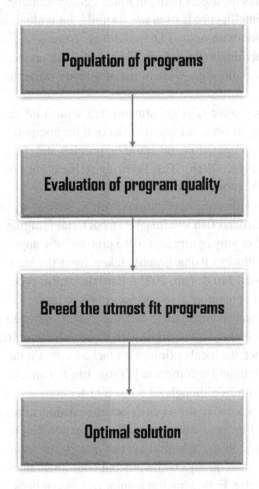

Genetic programming is represented in the form of a tree where the terminals represent the constants and variables while the operations are held at parent nodes. The Genetic operators used in breeding the programs of genetic programming are reproduction, crossover, and mutation.

Like the GA, the fit parents are qualified for further reproduction to form the next generation. Subsequently, the selected fit parents undergo crossover where the branch of a parent is replaced with another part of the other parent starting from a certain node. Then the new generation undergoes mutation on a certain node to create variation among the population.

Genetic programming assists in creating and discovering optimal algorithms and programs otherwise would require a lot of effort to generate.

Swarm Intelligence

Swarm intelligence is a biology-inspired algorithm pattern that aims to solve problems by following through with the decentralized and self-organized behavior of social insects in their societies (Brezočnik, Fister Jr & Podgorelec, 2018). The algorithm concludes after observing and considering the group behavior in response to a given matter. Insects individually are not smart considering their few numbers of brain cells; however, colonies of insects perform much better providing protection and food for their population. Likewise, swarm intelligence is used when similar individuals are not that powerful to come to a decision but in combination with many like individuals come to a certain solution that is optimal for the community and the individuals (Brezočnik, Fister Jr & Podgorelec, 2018). The self-organization of swarm intelligence enables exploring a wide range of options while the behavior of each individual is being considered.

Brezočnik, Fister Jr & Podgorelec (2018) indicates that swarm intelligence is commonly used for the optimization of existing algorithms and feature selection for computation. Feature selection from a dataset is a cardinal factor for computation and could be problematic if the dataset is multidimensional (Brezočnik, Fister Jr & Podgorelec, 2018). This is owing to the ability of swarm intelligence to solve NP-hard (Non-deterministic Polynomial-time) problems.

There are various swarm intelligence applications such as ant colony optimization (ACO), particle swarm optimization (PSO), artificial fish swarm (AFS), bacterial foraging optimization (BFO), and artificial bee colony (ABC). Ant colony optimization is a probabilistic approach to solving computational problems by finding better pathways using graphs; taken from the means ants discover the shortest pathway to find their food (Tang, Liu & Pan, 2021). Particle swarm optimization is an iterative means of experience-based solution improvements to a given problem by considering the quality of a certain attribute; designed after the manner birds and swarming insects optimize their search for food (Tang, Liu & Pan, 2021). Fish follows other fish as areas with more fish are nutritious, likewise, an Artificial fish swarm is a method by which the local optimum is reached to attain the global optimum by converging towards the area where solutions are compacted (Tang, Liu & Pan, 2021). AFS has features that are similar to that of genetic algorithms although AFS has a faster convergence rate and no crossing-over. Bacterial foraging optimization is one of the recently developed algorithms that is based on the behavior of E.coli bacteria characterized by fast convergence. The elements of a problem symbolized by bacteria in the community compete and cooperate to find the optimal global solution (Tang, Liu & Pan, 2021). Real bees are categorized into three groups by nature and coordinate intelligently within the group and as a whole to easily collect nectar. Following the natural process of bees, the Artificial bee colony is a stochastic method where bees gather their food by categorizing the solution indicators into groups to redirect toward the optimal solution (Tang, Liu & Pan, 2021).

This algorithm is scalable and flexible due to the shared control architecture through increasing complexity may lead to longer computations and unclear reasoning of how a solution is reached (Brezočnik, Fister Jr & Podgorelec, 2018). The swarm intelligence is prone to redundancy while observing community behavior which makes it a non-optimal solution as well as uncontrollable (Brezočnik, Fister Jr & Podgorelec, 2018).

Cognitive Science and Artificial Intelligence

Cognitive science can be defined as the study of mind and intelligence by considering various aspects such as psychology, AI, anthropology, neuroscience, and philosophy. Cognition deals with intelligence, memory, reasoning, understanding, emotions, and many topics related to how the mind operates (Fan et al., 2020).

Cognition is one of the most important topics for AI since the ultimate goal of AI is to develop machines that have the capability of processing information and responding as a human being would. The study of cognitive science has been quite controversial as many argue its unattainability. There has been a great advancement in the field of cognitive science since the emergence of AI; however, the argument remains to date.

Cognitive science is related to AI in two ways. The first one is studying cognitive science to replicate such intelligence on machine programs. Cognitive science is a study that has been going on and since it is not completely exhausted, how far AI can replicate is measured comparatively (Fan et al., 2020). Scientists and researchers focused on the cognition of children to design and improve their approaches to AI, studying how a newborn grows to learn about many new things and how the child responds to various impulses. The Turing test is one of the tests created to measure the cognition ability of AI in certain measures (Fan et al., 2020). The other one is to see how a machine has come to a correct conclusion and reverse engineer the procedures to understand the human mind furthermore or predict human decisions to a given motive (Fan et al., 2020).

MACHINE LEARNING

Machine learning is a subset of AI that is focused on the technology that enables the machine to learn patterns and create models from the experience the machine has been exposed to solve or improve certain tasks without being explicitly programmed for it. Machine learning deals with how machines can learn from a large dataset to comply and adjust with every use to overtake repetitive tasks that are conducted by humans. Machine learning is pivoted around the improvement of tasks concerning performance from attained experience.

Machine learning generally undergoes the following processes. First, the machine receives data from the outside world through measuring devices. Next, the data is cleaned and processed. Then, the dimension of the data is reduced into lower dimensions by selecting only the important features you want to consider. Although separation among clusters decreases as there is decreased as the dimension is reduced, features that are considered the need to be selected to avoid underfitting. Afterward, the model is learned concerning the preset induction algorithm and classification model on the machine to be able to make accurate predictions. Prior knowledge of data is the dividing factor for determining the algorithms and models that are going to be used. Finally, the model is tested in the prediction of some data to check how accurate the machine model is. And when the model is predicting accurately, we have a well-trained model that can predict random data in the future. The steps the random data undergoes in machine learning are shown in figure 4.

Figure 4. Typical machine learning procedure

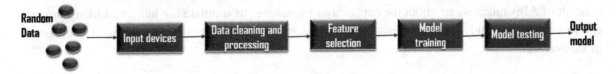

The classification model can be a lazy learning model like k-means clustering or eager learning like a decision tree and Naive Bayes. The lazy learning model inputs data and classifies the upcoming data according to the initial data that was taken. Some of the everyday classifications we see are the search recommendation, shopping recommendation, and YouTube recommendation we get saying people in your area also viewed. Hence, it has a short training time but a long prediction time. Eager learning on the other hand learns from every data that is being given instead of benchmarking data against previous ones. Since every data is taken under consideration to come up with a model, eager learning has more training time but a much shorter prediction time. Even after selecting the classification model that is most compatible with the data in use, insubstantial patterns are likely going to be found in the data which may lead to a dead end.

Machine learning is one of the areas that is thriving dynamically due to the huge amount of available data, improved computation power, and matured experience in the field by many scientists. However, there is confusion on what explicitly is covered under machine learning, AI, and deep learning. To provide a simplistic overview, figure 5 indicates machine learning is a subset of AI while deep learning is a subset of machine learning.

Figure 5. Classification of artificial intelligence

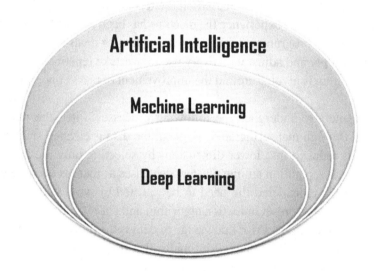

Artificial Intelligence vs. Machine Learning

Artificial intelligence and machine learning are commonly used as synonyms of each other; however, machine learning is a portion of AI that is focused on explicitly learning from a given data. While the concept of AI is much wider about the capability of machines to simulate the human thinking process and respond accordingly. Table 1 shows the comparison of machine learning and artificial intelligence in various areas.

Table 1. Artificial intelligence and machine learning comparison table

Artificial Intelligence	Machine Learning
AI enables machines to simulate human cognition.	Machine learning is a subset of AI that is set to learn from a given data
AI is set to perform any task performed by humans in a generic manner	ML is concentrated on performing redundant tasks performed by humans
AI is classified into weak/narrow, strong/general, and super AI depending on competence.	ML is classified into supervised, non-supervised, and reinforcement learning.
AI constitutes the learning process, self-modification, representation, reasoning, and language processing.	ML includes learning processes and self-modification.
AI is focused on optimizing the rate of success	ML is focused on having high accuracy, observing patterns, and having the right model
AI has a wide scope with the intention to create systems that can tackle various tasks.	ML has a relatively limited scope with the intention of tackling a specific task they are assigned to.
AI is implemented in chatbots, Siri, Alexa, Cortana, humanoid robots, etc.	ML is implemented on online recommendations from various search sites, social media recommendations, suggestions, etc.

TYPES OF MACHINE LEARNING

Machine learning is classified into supervised learning, and non-supervised learning based on data labeling on the training set. It is also sometimes classified as supervised learning, unsupervised learning, and reinforcement learning. From a supervised learning perspective, reinforcement learning is loosely supervised learning on optimized data. And from the unsupervised learning perspective, it is a way of directing unsupervised learning. The main difference between those machine learning types is data labeling and output determining factors. Further details will be discussed below.

Supervised Learning

Supervised machine learning is a type of machine learning that associates input with output to generate a pattern and be able to predict upcoming input (Mahesh, 2020). Supervised learning requires external guidance to converge to a conclusion from a set of data. Data is divided into training sets and test sets to evaluate the prediction capability of the generated model. The training data is constituted of a pair of input data and desired output data which is eventually going to be used to map new instances according to the setting of the training data.

Some instances of supervised learning include classification and regression. Classification is a process of grouping data into several classes according to distinct factors; for instance, predicting gender or ethnicity. One of the renowned methods of classification is K-nearest neighbors (KNN); which is one of the lazy algorithms that classify data according to a preset feature. KNN classifies new data concerning preset renowned clusters by assigning the new data to the closest clusters available.

While regression is the process by which the machine uses the training data to predict output; usually predictions can be projected into the future. An instance of regression is linear regression, an algorithm that finds the line that best fits the points of the given data to predict the results of upcoming data assuming they would be on the line.

Unsupervised Learning

Unsupervised learning is a method of machine learning that implements the categorization of the given data for the algorithm to make decisions on the given task. As the name indicates, there is no foreknowledge of the data to implement guidance. The main aim of unsupervised learning is to generate a model from the input pattern to make accurate predictions. In unsupervised learning, there is no preset desired result hence the categorization process is more liberal (Mahesh, 2020). This type of learning resembles the thinking process that occurs in the human brain much more than supervised learning. The human brain learns patterns from various inputs instead of restricting the learning process to previously correlated input and output.

Some examples of unsupervised learning are clustering and self-organizing maps. Clustering can be k-means clustering or hierarchical clustering. K-means clustering is a clustering technique that is most commonly used in statistics and data mining. First, the number of centroids is determined which is represented by k. Then the value of k will be used as the number of centroids to be plotted and the rest of the data is clustered onto the closest centroid to the point. When the clustering is done on the whole data, the centroid point is rearranged into the average spot of all the points within a cluster. This loop keeps going until there is no significant shift in the position of the clusters. Hierarchical clustering on the other hand is a clustering technique that assembles data according to similar features into a hierarchy of clusters. Hierarchical clustering does not require prior information on the number of clusters and results in clusters that are hierarchical in structure. Therefore, hierarchical clustering requires greater time complexity and is optimal for small-sized data.

Reinforcement Learning

Reinforcement learning is a method of learning based on experience and a set of interactions with the external environment to determine the rewarding activities as well as the detrimental activities to determine a set of rules (Mahesh, 2020). The program for Reinforcement learning is based on multiple trials hence, to implement this type of learning the set of options or trials must be limited. Reinforcement learning has three components: the agent, the environment, and the actions. The agent is the algorithm that notices its environment to make decisions. The environment is a simulation or set of activities that the agent decides while interacting. And the action is how the machine transitions from one state of the environment to the other. Gaming can be one of the instances where reinforcement learning can show its strength. A machine tries every scenario, since the set of scenarios is finite, and devises the optimal set of movements to outperform humans.

Common algorithms of reinforcement learning include state-action-reward-state-action (SARSA) and Q-learning. SARSA directs its agents with policies that indicate the tendency of a certain action to result in a reward. Q-learning on the contrary is not given any policy and directs itself to discover its environment.

Reinforcement learning is helpful in reasoning out decisions made as every activity is associated with an effect. However, reinforcement learning is not a real-world implementable algorithm due to the innumerable unprecedented random events that occur. Accordingly, most of the advancements in this field are theoretical rather than practical implementations.

Deep Learning

Deep learning is a branch of machine learning that uses artificial neural networks (ANN) to gain understanding in a manner that is similar to that of humans. The ANN is set to resemble how neurons are situated and organized in the human brain. Deep learning uses a multi-layered network of artificial newtons to predict the results of new data. These neurons have a weight that is dependent on the signal that is sent downstream. The neurons also have a bias that is used to adjust the output to the weighted sum of inputs depending on the range of the sent signal.

Based on model creation, deep learning can be classified into three: convolutional neural nets (CNN) which are used for image recognition, recurrent neural nets (RNN) used for audio and text recognition, and multi-layer perceptrons (MLP) mostly used for encoding databases and monitoring access data. Deep learning can also be classified by the machine learning in use. Those classifications include supervised deep learning, unsupervised deep learning, and hybrid deep architecture.

Deep learning has been in use overtaking the place of previously functioning old algorithms due to expanding magnitude of data. Deep learning performs well when there is high-quality data with the correct representation. One of the shortcomings of deep learning is its inability to give reasoning as to why a certain decision is made as a consequence of the multi-layered internal hidden nodes.

Artificial Intelligence and Society

AI has been one of the most controversial topics in society and the intellectual community. The idea that is associated with AI (like automation, machines, and robots) and the actual advancement of AI has drastically changed in the past decades and people have more understanding regarding AI. On the other hand, there are countless speculations and fantasies of AI due to science fiction movies and the unfathomable human imagination. With regards to AI, the fact that a machine can have its own intelligence and conduct activities after reaching certain decisions was quite vague. Now, however, researchers are looking into ways to optimize this intelligence of the machines.

The industrialization civilization has commonly been characterized into four sections namely industry 1.0, industry 2.0, industry 3.0, and industry 4.0 (Xu, L., Xu, E., & Li, 2018). Industry 4.0 is the current industry we are living in which is in its early stage. AI, big data, and smart factories are part of this industrialization. Every industrial revolution has affected society by simplifying the activities that were conducted by humans. The labor share percentages across the globe also declined gradually as one industrial revolution was relaying to the other (Xu, L., Xu, E., & Li, 2018). Simultaneously, various employment opportunities were created while low to medium-skilled jobs are becoming rare (Lu & Zhou, 2019).

Dall'Anese (2020) details that there is not enough evidence to determine what the impact of AI is on various factors of society and how it is affecting it. The main reasons for this include lack of enough gathered research with a broad audience and a lack of explicit definition of the term artificial intelligence.

Society was not welcoming of AI, and there was not much information regarding the topic. Although now there is hardly any area in human lives where AI has not been intertwined. Many of the unpleasant and tiresome tasks that were performed by people are now automated and simplified. An inevitable paradox is raised as the production of materials has been simplified and made more precise, and the expertise of people is no longer needed to add details or make sure that things are produced in a certain way (Ertel, 2018).

AI and Unemployment

One of the main aims of AI was to create an intelligent system by imitating human intelligence so that machines could simplify the tasks that were done by people. But what happens when the machines are far better in whatever activity they are assigned, and people are no longer needed for employment? This is one of the major intimidating factors of AI and the future. To predict the actual consequence of AI on the unemployment rate there has been a few analyses of the impact of recent AI advancements. According to Lu and Zhou (2019),

According to Ghobakhloo (2020), the jobs that can be automated are facing a gradual decline however there are also new job opportunities that are created due to industry 4.0 which includes AI. The effect of industry 4.0 in correlation with society has shown noticeable harm in two ways. The first one is employees being displaced by machines and the second one is increased demand for labor due to increased productivity. There has been a decrease in wages and more burnout deprived of the benefits of productivity (Ertel, 2018). The profit that is obtained from the increased productivity is retrieved by the owners and invested back into their business, enlarging their wealth furthermore. AI has influenced robust growth in world economics, however, the wealth created is not shared equally resulting in a greater wealth gap.

Dall'Anese (2020) points out that the efficiency of robots is not accurately predictable yet and hence, is insufficient evidence for employers to completely replace the tasks performed by employees with robots. Consequently, there will be time needed for employers to completely use machines instead of employees relying on the consistent results of AI. Likewise, the impact of machines eliminating job opportunities is yet to be seen.

Artificial Intelligence in UAE

AI in UAE seems to be heading in the right direction. According to the reports stated in the UAE Government portal, as of 2017, the UAE has been set to achieve the following goals as a part of the government plan. Some of the stated goals are the use of integrated digital systems in different services and solving different present and future challenges. The introduction and practice of AI in different sectors such as healthcare, education and energy, traffic, and even space have progressed exponentially; and the continuation of endeavor is one of the main plans of the UAE government (*UAE Strategy for Artificial Intelligence*, 2022).

To oversee such achievement, the UAE is the first country that has appointed a state ministry just for AI, Minister Omar Sultan Al Olama. According to the minister, Al Hammadi, the UAE has already started the journey toward growth in AI by launching different initiatives including the opening of a new graduate-level university, Mohammed Bin Zayed University of Artificial intelligence (MBZUAI). This aims to pursue the AI knowledge base on different research to improve and introduce new concepts regarding the use of AI (Khan, 2019). Furthermore, they aim to analyze the impact of AI throughout the years and embrace the change in the positive and leading implementation of AI in different sectors (Halaweh, 2018). With all this being the agenda of UAE regarding AI, the Think AI initiative was launched from the year 2017 to 2019, aiming to escalate the use of AI by many different people and businesses (Khan, 2019).

Alongside all the development and radical movement of AI and its influence, the UAE has embarked to assess the ethical aspect of AI and its involvement in almost every governmental sector (Ghandour & Woodford, 2019). According to the article, AI is challenging the societal, ethical, and legal aspects of different business activities which are disrupting the legal framework of almost every business. AI could be exploited and misused unless guided and framed by certain laws and monitoring the progress of AI. As useful as it is for AI to have the capability of deduction, prediction, and speed in processing, this could also mean the demeaning of human potential to make decisions and active involvement in different activities. As a solution to all this, the UAE has taken the matter into its hands to enforce some legal action on the inclusion and practices of AI services in different sectors and their approach to ethical values. The impact of AI is not only a local issue but international since the internet is making distance intangible; the UAE suggests for different countries take this initiative and prioritize it because it is no longer an assumption that AI will dominate in the digital world (Ghandour & Woodford, 2019).

The Vision of 2071

According to the UAE Cabinet (n.d), the five-decade plan which is the Vision of 2071 is a long-term plan that is aiming to align the government's and the country's initiatives in strengthening the technology, education, healthcare, and many other government sectors. The processes in achieving this goal comprise investing in the future generation such as teaching, training, and preparing youngsters for the different innovations that they are capable of developing since they are the future of the country (*News - UAE cabinet, n.d*). Alongside all this, embracing the rapid and swift changes that are happening around the world to have a clear plan and increase awareness is also one of the objectives of this vision that is already in action. This vision is not only about improving the quality of work but about handling the state of the country and future generations (Almarzooqi, 2019).

UAE's revolution of AI is heading in the right direction compared with the past UAE and other countries that are in use of AI currently. The leadership of the UAE and its ambition of creating a very well-organized and connected country with the help of AI is the mainstream of the development plan. If the plans go according to the progress, they are assumed to go by mitigating risk and having innovative ideas that are shaking the world, this plan will be beyond its estimation.

CONCLUSION

The role of AI in the progress and accomplishment of the 2071 vision is clear since AI is only in the starting stage of the digital revolution (Khan, 2019). The shift of the current technology to AI and replacing/encompassing the current systems with the use of AI will have a greater impact (Ghandour & Woodford, 2019). For example, the education system, the current education system, and healthcare have IoT (internet of things), sensors, and networks, the main ingredient that is missing here is the integration level. The ability to integrate different devices and draw enough knowledge to make decisions/predictions is the capability of AI. Considering the pace of AI development and practice the education system will change for the better given reasonable law enforcement and system monitoring, especially in the government sector (Khan, 2019).

AI-driven technology will take the full lead in solving different issues regarding tech-related services/businesses. According to Almarzooqi(2019), the UAE's overall performance will increase with the use of AI. The introduction of fully functioning surgical robots (equipment) and different kinds of recognition for personal/social identification along with well-coordinated system integration will ensure the development of the country technologically (Almarzooqi, 2019).

All these techniques and applications will shape the governmental sector's framework and leadership framework which benefits the country to achieve the country's desired vision that has been laid out.

REFERENCES

Almarzooqi, A. (2019). *Towards an artificial intelligence (AI)-driven government in the united arab emirates (UAE): A framework for transforming and augmenting leadership capabilities* [Thesis, Pepperdine University, USA] Proquest (2284210975). https://www.proquest.com/dissertations-theses/towards-artificial-intelligence-ai-driven/docview/2284210975/se-2

Brezočnik, L., Fister, I. Jr, & Podgorelec, V. (2018). Swarm intelligence algorithms for feature selection: A review. *Applied Sciences (Basel, Switzerland)*, *8*(9), 1521. doi:10.3390/app8091521

Buchanan, B. G. (2005). A (very) brief history of artificial intelligence. *AI Magazine*, *26*(4), 53.

Dall'Anese, D. (2020). *The impact of Artificial Intelligence on unemployment: a systematic literature review*. Università Ca' Foscari Venezia.

Ertel, W. (2018). *Introduction to artificial intelligence*. Springer.

Fan, J., Fang, L., Wu, J., Guo, Y., & Dai, Q. (2020). From brain science to artificial intelligence. *Engineering*, *6*(3), 248–252. doi:10.1016/j.eng.2019.11.012

Francesconi, E. (2022). The winter, the summer and the summer dream of artificial intelligence in law. *Artificial Intelligence and Law*, *30*(2), 1–15. doi:10.100710506-022-09309-8 PMID:35132296

Ghandour, A., & Woodford, B. J. (2019). Ethical Issues in Artificial Intelligence in UAE. 2019 International Arab Conference on Information Technology (ACIT), (pp. 262-266). IEEE. 10.1109/ACIT47987.2019.8990997

Ghobakhloo, M. (2020). Industry 4.0, digitization, and opportunities for sustainability. *Journal of Cleaner Production*, *252*, 119869. doi:10.1016/j.jclepro.2019.119869

Haenlein, M., & Kaplan, A. (2019). A Brief History of Artificial Intelligence: On the Past, Present, and Future of Artificial Intelligence. *California Management Review*, *61*(4), 5–14. doi:10.1177/0008125619864925

Halaweh, M. (2018). Viewpoint: Artificial Intelligence Government (gov. 3.0): The UAE leading model. *Journal of Artificial Intelligence Research*, *62*, 269–272. doi:10.1613/jair.1.11210

Irfan, M. (2019). A Review on Knowledge-Based Expert System. *The International journal of analytical and experimental modal analysis, 11*(4).

Katoch, S., Chauhan, S. S., & Kumar, V. (2021). A review on genetic algorithm: Past, present, and future. *Multimedia Tools and Applications*, *80*(5), 8091–8126. doi:10.100711042-020-10139-6 PMID:33162782

Khan, M. U. H. (2019). UAE's artificial intelligence strategies and pursuits. *Defence Journal, 23*(4), 19. https://www.proquest.com/scholarly-journals/uae-s-artificial-intelligence-strategies-pursuits/docview/2358556530/se-2?ac
countid=15192

Kumar, K., & Thakur, G. S. M. (2012). Advanced applications of neural networks and artificial intelligence: A review. *International journal of information technology and computer science, 4*(6), 57.

Lambora, A., Gupta, K., & Chopra, K. (2019, February). Genetic algorithm-A literature review. In 2019 international conference on machine learning, big data, cloud and parallel computing (COMITCon). IEEE.

Leo Kumar, S. P. (2019). Knowledge-based expert system in manufacturing planning: State-of-the-art review. *International Journal of Production Research, 57*(15-16), 4766–4790. doi:10.1080/00207543. 2018.1424372

Liu, G. H., Chen, M. Z., & Chen, Y. (2019). When joggers meet robots: The past, present, and future of research on humanoid robots. *Bio-Design and Manufacturing, 2*(2), 108–118. doi:10.100742242-019-00038-7

Lu, Y., & Zhou, Y. (2019). A short review on the economics of artificial intelligence. *Journal of Economic Surveys.*

Mahesh, B. (2020). Machine learning algorithms-a review. *International Journal of Science and Research (IJSR).[Internet], 9*, 381-386.

Maier, H. R., Razavi, S., Kapelan, Z., Matott, L. S., Kasprzyk, J., & Tolson, B. A. (2019). Introductory overview: Optimization using evolutionary algorithms and other metaheuristics. *Environmental Modelling & Software, 114*, 195–213. doi:10.1016/j.envsoft.2018.11.018

Ryerkerk, M., Averill, R., Deb, K., & Goodman, E. (2019). A survey of evolutionary algorithms using metameric representations. *Genetic Programming and Evolvable Machines, 20*(4), 441–478. doi:10.100710710-019-09356-2

Slowik, A., & Kwasnicka, H. (2020). Evolutionary algorithms and their applications to engineering problems. *Neural Computing & Applications, 32*(16), 12363–12379. doi:10.100700521-020-04832-8

Tang, J., Liu, G., & Pan, Q. (2021). A review on representative swarm intelligence algorithms for solving optimization problems: Applications and trends. *IEEE/CAA Journal of Automatica Sinica, 8*(10), 1627-1643.

UAE Cabinet. (n.d.). *News.* UAE Cabinet. https://uaecabinet.ae/en/details/news/mohammed-bin-rashid-launches-five-decade-government-plan-uae-centennial-2071

UAE Strategy for Artificial Intelligence. (2022, February 21). *UAE strategy for Artificial Intelligence - the official portal of the UAE Government.* UAE. https://u.ae/en/about-the-uae/strategies-initiatives-and-awards/federal-governments-strategies-and-plans/uae-strategy-for-artificial-intelligence

Wallén, J. (2008). *The history of the industrial robot.* Linköping University Electronic Press.

Wu, Q., Liu, Y., & Wu, C. (2018). An overview of current situations of robot industry development. In *ITM Web of Conferences* (Vol. 17, p. 03019). EDP Sciences. 10.1051/itmconf/20181703019

Xu, L. D., Xu, E. L., & Li, L. (2018). Industry 4.0: State of the art and future trends. *International Journal of Production Research, 56*(8), 2941–2962. doi:10.1080/00207543.2018.1444806

Zhang, C., & Lu, Y. (2021). Study on artificial intelligence: The state of the art and future prospects. *Journal of Industrial Information Integration, 23*, 100224. doi:10.1016/j.jii.2021.100224

KEY TERMS AND DEFINITIONS

Algorithm: A set of rules or steps that make a machine perform a certain task.

Artificial Intelligence: Is the ability of machines to perform task by simulating human behaviors.

Deep Learning: Is a section of machine learning that uses numerous receptors of different network levels to learn new scenarios.

Evolutionary Algorithm: Is an algorithm that follows the natural order of evolution, such as the survival of the fittest, to come up with the desired results.

Genetic Algorithm: Is an algorithm that is created after the structure of genetics and the inter-breeding of DNA.

Genetic Programming: Genetic programming is a programming that is patterned according to the style of genetic reproduction of cells.

Machine Learning: Is a section of AI that deals with the ability of a machine to learn for the set of experiences it has been exposed to.

Supervised Learning: Is part of machine learning that uses the input data to predict the output patter with the help of conditions set by the programmer.

Unsupervised Learning: Is part of machine learning that realistically resembles the human learning process by having the ability to learn from set of activities without having a specified outcome.

Chapter 2
Artificial Intelligence Accountability in Emergent Applications:
Explainable and Fair Solutions

Julia El Zini

ⓘ https://orcid.org/0000-0001-7499-8668

American University of Beirut, Lebanon

ABSTRACT

The rise of deep learning techniques has produced significantly better predictions in several fields which lead to a widespread applicability in healthcare, finance, and autonomous systems. The success of such models comes at the expense of a trackable and transparent decision-making process in areas with legal and ethical implications. Given the criticality of the decisions in such areas, governments and industries are making sizeable investments in the accountability aspect in AI. Accordingly, the nascent field of explainable and fair AI should be a focal point in the discussion of emergent applications especially in high-stake fields. This chapter covers the terminology of accountable AI while focusing on two main aspects: explainability and fairness. The chapter motivates the use cases of each aspect and covers state-of-the-art methods in interpretable AI and methods that are used to evaluate the fairness of machine learning models, and to detect any underlying bias and mitigate it.

INTRODUCTION

The popularity of AI systems is motivated by the rise of deep learning models which have demonstrated significant performance gains in a plethora of areas. However, such models are seen as extremely opaque models whose predictions are notoriously hard to explain. Accordingly, the emergence of deep models brings to the front the trade-off between their accuracy and their accountability. In high-stake areas, AI accountability is of critical importance. For instance, healthcare systems require fair treatment of individuals regardless of their skin color, gender, or sexual orientation. Insurance applications must explain

DOI: 10.4018/978-1-6684-6937-8.ch002

their decision-making system to engender users' trust. Additionally, autonomous driving systems should deliver acceptable safety standards and legal guarantees on the rights, duties, and responsibilities of the user. Consequently, there has been increased attention recently dedicated to studying and enforcing the accountability of such models. This research is manifested in developing methods to ensure the proper functioning of AI systems through their design, development, and deployment phases.

These concerns led The US Federal Trade Commission to issue new guidelines requiring AI systems to be open, explainable, and fair. Moreover, the General Data Protection Regulation (GDPR) of the European Union mandates transparency for algorithms and fair representation and treatment in AI systems. Whether or not they operate in the European Union, industries that develop and use data-driven systems are moving into ensuring these regulations. That being the case, data and algorithmic accountability witnessed explosive growth mainly nurtured by the invasive use of autonomous systems and the regulations imposed by legal institutions on data and smart processes. Governments started to make sizeable investments in responsible and accountable AI systems. Researchers are extensively engaged in the fields of accountability, fairness, and explainability (Gade et al., 2019; Mehrabi et al., 2021). This is reflected in developing methods to explain AI decisions and learned representations for different data types. Additionally, researchers are working on providing fairness definitions and bias detection methods in numerous applications. This is mostly accompanied by several techniques to neutralize learned representations and mitigate bias in decision-making systems.

Covering all aspects of AI accountability is beyond the scope of this book. However, the nascent subfield of accountability should be an integral part of the discussion on any emergent AI application. This chapter presents a comprehensive study of critical areas that are moving into adopting AI-based solutions and integrating accountability guarantees. These requirements entail a transparent decision-making scheme and fair treatment of individuals.

This chapter focuses on the two aforementioned accountability aspects: explainability and fairness in AI applications and their fundamental interconnection. Explainability requires a meaningful explanation of AI's logic in reaching a decision concerning their data. This explanation should be clear, concise, and easily comprehensible format. Fairness ensures that AI systems handle individual's data fairly. This requires that AI systems do not generate outcomes that could negatively impact marginalized groups. Even if AI systems are not created with detrimental goals, fairness ensures that these systems do not unintentionally learn historical and social discrimination from unfair datasets. This chapter discusses state-of-the-art methods of explainable AI on different modalities and applications while highlighting different notions of algorithmic fairness and its applicability in different settings.

To set the expectations of the reader, the next section highlights the importance of explainability and fairness with the current breakthroughs in AI, Deep Learning (DL) specifically. The section also categorizes explainable AI methods according to (1) whether explainability is introduced into AI models before or after design and (2) the type of representations or decisions they explain. This categorization underlines the interdependency between the explainability aspect of AI systems and the detection of any underlying bias. The third section is devoted to cover the need for explainable AI in emergent applications while briefly covering state-of-the-art methods and discussing a novel line of work within Explainable AI (ExAI), counterfactual explainability. Lastly, the fourth section covers the bias sources in AI systems, the important fairness definitions in the literature, and successful ways to neutralize models and mitigate bias before concluding with final remarks.

IMPORTANCE OF ACCOUNTABILITY

Explainability is an aspect of accountability that supports machine learning decisions with human-understandable facts (Adadi & Berrada, 2018). Traditionally, the predictions of decision trees, k-nearest neighbors, and linear models were supported with inherent model weights and if-then decision rules. However, the focus of researchers has shifted to neural networks due to their ability to approximate complex non-linear functions. Unfortunately, the advancements in the effectiveness of neural networks have coincided with an alarming increase in the complexity of their dynamics. Such networks do not possess the property of inherent explainability due to their architecture and back-propagation training mechanism.

Deep networks amplify the opacity aspect with their deep layers, complex non-linearity, and advanced architectures. This opacity is limiting wider adoption of deep networks in high-stake areas such as healthcare and criminology despite their spectacular performance. This can be explained by the fact that regulators are still hesitant in approving any decision that lacks human-understandable evidence and practitioners in critical areas cannot compromise the trustworthiness of their models for their performance.

Moreover, given their black-box nature, deep models could be learning social and historical biases and prejudices in an opaque manner. As an example, language models learn to associate occupations with genders which might lead to harmful stereotypical decisions (Bolukbasi et al., 2016). The amplification of social discrimination by AI systems became alarming as smart systems are increasingly used across all walks of our daily lives.

In this view, on 21 April 2021, the European Commission proposed the first legal framework on AI to address the risks posed by smart emerging techniques and models. The proposed AI Act requires machine learning models and systems to guarantee transparency, lawfulness, and fairness. This is achieved by establishing different mechanisms to guarantee responsible AI throughout different stages in the AI life cycle: from the design and data collection reaching to testing and deployment. Prior to that, the influential European Union legislation shaped global data privacy regulations through the general data protection regulation (GDPR). The GDPR employs a risk-based framework to regulate the use of personal data and AI systems. These regulations mainly encapsulate the principles of data minimization, fairness, transparency, explainability, integrity, and accountability to minimize any potential harm in the misuse of personal data and training algorithms.

Accordingly, there has been a surge of interest in the trustworthiness aspect of machine learning models. Their wider adoption requires guarantees for fair treatment of subjects while providing supporting evidence for their decisions in a human-understandable manner. Hence, literature is currently witnessing an explosion of research work on the explainability and fairness of deep learning models in different modalities. While fairness and ExAI techniques are fundamentally distinct, they share the need to understand the encoded knowledge of deep models in some contexts. Additionally, they are usually evaluated in similar real-world applications, mostly critical domains. For instance, a hiring system should support a rejection decision with actionable insights and should prove fair treatment regardless of the gender, religion, and ethnicity of the applicant. This chapter covers the two accountability aspects in parallel by categorizing ExAI methods while highlighting their intersection with fairness definitions. Then, real-world applications that profited from the growing literature on the accountability of AI systems are described.

Levels of Accountability

Explainability methods are categorized according to their mode of application (the *"when"*) and the knowledge type they are trying to interpret (the *"what"*).

The "When" of Explainability

Based on the explanation mode, i.e., whether explainability is performed on pre-trained models or before building the architecture, ExAI methods can be categorized into the following.

Post-hoc Interpretability

These methods operate on pre-trained models with predefined architectures by analyzing how they process inputs before producing a decision. When no assumptions are made on the model, the interpretability method is *model-agnostic*. If the method entails a particular architecture, the method is *model-specific*. LIME (Ribeiro et al., 2016) and SHAP (Lundberg & Lee, 2017) are two of the most famous post-hoc interpretability techniques with open-source and well-documented Python-based implementations. LIME approximates the predictor *locally* with a simpler one, a linear model mostly. The linear approximator is faithful to the original predictor, i.e., the predictions of both models are the same in the local neighborhood. The explanation is then inferred by the parameters of the approximator which are interpretable by design. LIME can be extended to images by using super-pixels and to text by using bag of words as interpretable input features.

Instead of approximating the input, SHAP relies on game theoretical concepts such as Shapley values. Shapley value is one fair way to distribute the total gain of a cooperative game to individual players. More importantly, Shapley value is the only distribution with certain desirable properties such as linearity, symmetry, and anonymity. Inspired by the Shapley value, (Lundberg & Lee, 2017) present SHAP, a novel unified approach to measure feature importance in machine learning models. SHAP can be extended to provide a global explanation in addition to individual local explanations.

Inherently Interpretable Models

A less popular line of work develops models, from the ground up, that provide supporting evidence while processing input by modifying the underlying /architectures and learning strategies. The most famous examples of inherent interpretability are linear models and decision trees. The parameters in the former models quantify the feature importance and the decision in the latter models is a sequence of human-understandable if-then rules. In more complex models, generative models are used with other architectures to learn to generate fine-grained explanations while making classification decisions (Liu et al., 2019).

Despite their simplicity, inherently explainable models do not leverage state-of-the-art existing deep networks. For instance, retraining deep models such as the BERT-like family (Kenton & Toutanova, 2019) and GPT models (Radford et al., 2019) with the explainability constraint can be computationally expensive. Retraining might not be feasible with strict privacy limitations or when training data is no longer available. On the other hand, explaining black box models in a post-hoc manner, rather than creating models that are interpretable in the first place, might perpetuate bad practices. Mainly, post-hoc explanations do not present a perfect fidelity to the model being explained. They could be an inaccurate representation of the original model in the feature space. Hence, the interpretability mode must be carefully chosen in high-stake areas such as criminology and law. Given that they harness the power of deep learning and the advancements in the training process and the use of transfer learning, post-hoc interpretability is gaining more interest within the ExAI community.

Practitioners should consider privacy concerns and contemplate the trade-off between explanation faithfulness and the exploitation of existing models before deciding on the interpretability mode in their applications.

The "What" of Explainability

Explaining machine learning models occurs on three different levels: prediction (local and global), learning, and training. ExAI methods are ergo categorized, according to their explanation type, into four parts.

Local Prediction

Local methods are *data-centric* approaches that try to answer the question *"why did the model predict y_1 on input x_1?"* These methods provide explanations in terms of input features that are crucial for a particular output on a specific testing instance. Predictive models in critical areas can employ these methods to augment their predictions with supporting evidence to engender users' trust.

Global Categorization

Like local methods, global methods are also *data-centric* approaches. However, they try to answer the question *"Why does the model predict an output y in general? What are the features that are crucial for the classification of this specific class/label?"* They provide insights into the important features of the entire class in a trained classifier. The explanation is provided as a human-relatable concept that is common in all instances of a certain class/label. These methods can help AI practitioners debug their models and understand the contrast between predictions.

Learned Knowledge and Characterization of Hidden Features

These methods are *network-centric* approaches that answer the question *"What is this neuron trying to learn? or How can the neuron's activation be qualitatively explained?"* They provide an interpretation of the internal state in terms of human-friendly concepts that apply across the entire dataset and go beyond per-sample features. In other words, they provide some matching between individual hidden units and a set of semantic concepts by studying how patterns are encoded in the hidden layers of a deep network. These methods are the main hope of rendering the black-box models less opaque by revealing their learned knowledge. They can also expose vulnerabilities, unintended correlations, and bias cases.

Learning Dynamics

These methods are *network-centric* approaches that study the whole learning process and provide higher-level insights such as: "When is the class-specific information formed? What is the effect of freezing or the order in which the training instances are fed to the network?". In addition to this, they study how different training regimes affect the performance of deep neural networks.

Explainability methods in the first three categories show great potential in converging to fairness evaluation. For instance, explaining why someone is denied a loan of their gender is a clear discrimination case. Similarly, when the label "criminal" is globally explained by race or some correlated features (neighborhood for example), the global explainability method is consequently hinting at a biased decision.

More importantly, understanding learned knowledge, particularly in pre-trained models, is extremely useful to detect and prevent biased predictions with deep learning. In NLP, researchers have shown that word embedding models can be contaminated by historical discrimination against marginalized groups (Brunet et al., 2019). Recent studies on sentiment analysis models (El Zini et al., 2022; Rhue, 2018) revealed a bias toward predicting negative emotions for people with dark skin and toxicity detection discriminates based on the individual's sexual orientation (Garg et al., 2019). The detection of such bias is only possible by virtue of advanced explainability techniques that can decipher the knowledge learned by deep models.

Accountability in Research Benchmarks

With the increasing surge of interest in the notion of AI accountability, several benchmarking frameworks, datasets, and metrics have been recently proposed to evaluate fairness and explainability techniques. Three common applications are widely used in the literature to assess AI accountability.

- **Credit scoring algorithms** play a crucial role in market economies. They make an informed decision on the bank's investment strategies and loan granting. More concretely, credit scoring algorithms predict the probability of defaulting on a loan or the probability of experiencing financial distress in the next few years. These predictions are used by banks when determining whether an applicant should be granted a loan to make the best financial decisions. To this end, the Give Me Some Credit dataset is introduced to help practitioners understand the factors that affect credit scoring and detect hidden biases against marginalized (Demajo et al., 2020; Pawelczyk et al., 2021)

- **The criminal justice system** is one of the main fields that have legal and ethical implications with the pervasive use of AI systems. In this context, a Correctional Offender Management Profiling for Alternative Sanctions (COMPAS) dataset is introduced to score the defendant's likelihood of reoffending, a phenomenon known as recidivism by judges and parole. Research has shown that black defendants are often labeled with a higher risk of recidivism and white offenders who re-offended within two years were mistakenly labeled low-risk officers (Flores et al., 2016). Hence, COMPAS is being extensively used with ExAI methods to explain the decision-making scheme of the AI-based prison sentencing model (Pawelczyk et al., 2021). COMPAS is also employed to evaluate the effectiveness of bias mitigation techniques (Sushina & Sobenin, 2020). The bias in criminal justice systems is extended to computer vision applications as studied in (Noiret et al., 2021). The study includes facial recognition systems, handwritings, footwear impressions, and motion penal systems.

- **Toxicity predictions in online comments** is a classification task where a textual input, a comment on social media platforms, is checked against toxic content. Often, toxic comments are hidden to prevent psychological harm. Jigsaw toxicity dataset (Dixon et al., 2018) is commonly used in the classification task (Georgakopoulos et al., 2018) as well as in the detection of unintended bias (Krishna et al., 2022). Classifiers predicting toxicity are shown to discriminate against minorities based on gender and sexual orientation. Such discrimination causes an increased silencing of minorities on social medial platforms.

Other examples include, but are not limited to, inferring gender from biographies, in predicting income, predicting the patient's likelihood of hospital re-admission and predicting the probability of passing the BAR exam for law students (Le Quy et al., 2022).

EXPLAINABLE AI IN EMERGENT APPLICATIONS

Explainability is an aspect of accountability that supports machine learning decisions with human-understandable facts (Adadi & Berrada, 2018). The following part of the chapter discusses particular cases where explainability is of great importance and covers ExAI methods with a special focus on counterfactual explainability.

The Need for Explainability

Integrating explainability in machine learning models is not limited to successful models that need to provide supporting evidence to gain the user's trust. Three scenarios where interpretation is useful regardless of the model's performance are highlighted next.

Models Exhibit Satisfactory Performance

In this case, these models need to engender users' trust for wider adoption. This aspect encourages practitioners to adopt AI systems in healthcare, university admissions, hiring systems, and insurance applications. Medical diagnosis applications is a perfect example where explainable AI is witnessing a surge of interest in the medical community (Tjoa & Guan, 2020). Relying on autonomous systems, with opaque logic, violates ethical principles of medicine. More importantly, AI algorithms are found to be biased against some ethnicities. For example, an algorithm that assesses the degree of illness based on healthcare costs discriminates against people of dark skin. Hence, physicians do not trust highly accurate automated systems that can detect diseases from clinical tests (Rajpurkar et al., 2018) unless these systems can support their claims with medically convenient evidence. Employing interpretability methods in medical applications implies their trustworthiness promoting a wider adoption by clinicians and practitioners. Examples of ExAI methods in medicine are numerous. (Karam et al., 2021) explain features learned by two transfer learning techniques on the wrist fracture detection task from MRIs. (Lucieri et al., 2022) utilize concept activation vectors to explain DL decisions on skin lesions with human-understandable concepts.

The benefits of explainability go beyond building trust within the medical community by encouraging data-driven medical education and improving medical practices through insights into interpretable clinical decisions. Accountable AI systems build on the physician-patient relationship that is founded on communication and trust and augment the capabilities of physicians while maintaining precision and accuracy. Hence, it could open the door for greater usage of AI in healthcare.

Models Fail to Match Human Performance

Several concerns regarding the failure of machine learning models have spurred the AI accountability field. The pressure exerted by AI and data regulators over vulnerabilities of such models directed researchers to investigate the failure and design proper debugging paths. This would be a building stone toward responsible AI, where smart systems can highlight specific components to blame in the case of erroneous decisions. Debugging systems can also reduce the strain on the bottleneck caused by developers juggling multiple methods to evaluate their algorithms.

Different approaches have been proposed in the literature to debug NLP systems (Gardner et al., 2020; Garg et al., 2019; Mokhov et al., 2014; Ribera & Lapedriza, 2019; Sharma et al., 2020). Mainly, these methods search for a contrastive example that highlights a potential vulnerability. These contrasts detect bias cases when perturbing sensitive features (for instance change the word "actress" to "actor" and observe the change in the model outcomes). Moreover, they can serve as debugging tools against semantic adversarial attacks by computing the model's robustness score. Such methods are generally associated with mitigation techniques through a custom augmentation technique to improve models' robustness and fairness.

Models Beat Human Performance

AI breakthroughs in complex cognitive tasks such as Chess and Go games redefined game strategies. It is not surprising that, recently, reinforcement learning agents were able to beat world champions in the Go game (Silver et al., 2016; Silver et al., 2017). Yet, the AI-winning strategy highlights unusual and creative moves which are intriguing according to human experts. In this view, these models can serve as a machine teaching framework for humans to make better decisions. Particularly, AI in gaming can teach strategies, and tactics to improve human performance and reasoning (Hind et al., 2019; Wells & Bednarz, 2021).

Explainable AI (ExAI) Methods and Modalities

After discussing the importance of ExAI on different levels, state-of-the-art ExAI methods on tabular, textual and imagery data are covered.

Gradient-based Methods

One of the first attempts at ExAI was carried out by (Baehrens et al., 2010) to rely on local gradients. Their work addresses the question of why a black-box model predicted a particular label for a single instance and what are input features that contributed the most to a particular outcome. The estimation of the local gradient induced a quantification of the importance of a data point in altering the predicted label where higher gradients implied more important features. Based on the gradient concept, (Shrikumar et al., 2017; Sundararajan et al., 2017) optimized the gradient-based approach and generalized its applications to cases where the computation of the gradients is problematic.

Gradient-based methods are also congenial to imagery applications where individual pixels can be seen as features. In computer vision settings, saliency maps are the common term used to identify relevant regions in an image and to provide a type of quantification of the importance of a pixel in classification.

Saliency Maps

Gradient computation has also attracted researchers to develop efficient and fast methods for saliency computation. One of the earliest saliency methods was proposed by (Simonyan et al., 2013). Their method, which falls under sensitivity, computes the gradient of the class with respect to the image pixels and assumes that salient regions are at locations with high gradients based on the assumption that high gradient locations are important for the classification since their perturbation has a great effect on the output of the network. Later, many popular methods relied on the backpropagation of the gradient from the deepest layers of a network and its projection on the image to derive a gradient saliency map (Patro et al., 2019; Springenberg et al., 2014; Zeiler & Fergus, 2014). These techniques are widely used to explain visual recognition and object localization outcomes where relevant pixels are masked or highlighted (mostly with different intensities) as in (Dabkowski & Gal, 2017; Mahendran & Vedaldi, 2016; Smilkov et al., 2017).

Input Perturbation

Instead of computing the gradient of the predictor with respect to an input feature, some approaches rely on perturbing the input and observing the impact on the predictor. Perturbation-based approaches construct explanations by analyzing the model's response to local changes in the input. (Zeiler & Fergus, 2014) suggest performing local perturbations by masking portions of the input. Once some portions are occluded, a sensitivity analysis of the classifier output is performed to reveal the image parts that are important for the classification. Perturbation-based approaches are also appropriate in computer vision settings. For instance, the prediction difference analysis method of (Zintgraf et al., 2017) samples within the pixel neighborhood to analyze the importance of an input feature. The relevance of a feature x is estimated by how the prediction of a class would change when all the features, except *x*, are used. Sensitivity analysis techniques are heavily used to interpret segmentation models in cardiac MRI (Ankenbrand et al., 2021), to study the model's sensitivity to foregrounds, backgrounds, and visual attributes (Moayeri et al., 2022), and to understand cancer therapeutics (Puniya et al., 2016).

Activation Maximization

Another category in ExAI methods stems from neuroscience. To understand brain function, one of the most fundamental questions that the researcher tries to investigate is *what types of stimuli excite neurons and drive them to fire?* In the ExAI field, Activation Maximization (AM) methods address this question by focusing on the preferred stimuli that provoke a neuron in deep networks to fire strongly. AM techniques are heavily applied in imagery settings: given an input image $x \in R^{H \times W \times C}$ and the parameters θ of a classifier, a neuron i/ in a layer l, finding the image that maximizes the activation $a_{i_l}(\theta, x)$ is formulated by (Erhan et al., 2009) as the following optimization problem $x^* = \arg\max_x a_{i_l}(\theta, x)$. Gradient ascent algorithms are then used to solve the optimization at hand.

Explainability in NLP

In natural language applications, some text-specific challenges hamper the application of general ExAI methods into NLP models due to the fusion of syntax and semantics in words, polysemy, and ambiguity. For instance, perturbation methods cannot be directly mapped to NLP due to the reliance of the latter models on embedding models that are opaque representations, as opposed to pixels or numerical value (El Zini & Awad, 2022b). Long-term dependencies, multi-lingual support, and learned stereotypes present additional challenges to ExAI techniques in NLP.

A great deal of ExAI techniques investigates the semantic and syntactical information learned by language models. In fact, several methods have been proposed to dissect the inner dynamics of transformers to better understand *how* they process input and *why* they do it so well. Such approaches can be the first building block in the process of making transformers trustworthy by rendering their inner workings understandable (Jawahar et al., 2019; Tenney et al., 2019). They can also engender users' trust by explaining the knowledge learned by transformers and their parameters (Clark et al., 2019; Raganato & Tiedemann, 2018) and by highlighting their limitations (Rogers et al., 2020).

Due to their design, attention weights are relatively more interpretable than the conventional deep networks' parameters. Visualizing the inner weights and hidden representations of transformers can render the predictions more explainable (Lee et al., 2017; Strobelt et al., 2018) (Vig, 2019). However, solely, attention weights are not able to provide the full transparency that responsible AI entails where further processing is needed when the task at hand is not a simple classification but a more complex task such as translation, question answering, and natural language inference (Brunner et al., 2019; Vig & Belinkov, 2019).

Counterfactual Explainability

Traditional ExAI methods address the reason behind a particular output or decision supporting an automated decision. While this aim is of great importance for some ExAI scenarios, other practical cases require highlighting causal relationships between input features and different possible outputs. As an example, a person whose loan got denied is not only interested in the reason behind the rejection of their application, but in the adjustment that they can make to their application to modify the bank's decision. Counterfactual explanations address this problem by providing the interpretation in terms of a causal relation like *If your income had been £45,000, you would have been offered a loan* instead of: *You were denied a loan because your annual income was £30,000.*

(Dhurandhar et al., 2018) argue that the contrastive aspect of explainability has foundations in philosophy and cognitive science and can be found in many human-critical domains such as health care and prison sentencing. Their Contrastive Explanation Method (CEM) solves an optimization problem to derive contrasts of a black-box classifier. (Laugel et al., 2017) compute this contrast by growing hyper-spheres around a particular point and computing the outcome until a contrastive example is found. Generative models (Joshi et al., 2019), uncertainty estimation (Antoran et al., 2020), and game-theoretical concepts (Rathi, 2019) are also used by researchers to derive contrastive explanations with different assumptions and specifications. Additionally, Variational Auto-Encoders (VAEs) are used to model the conditional subspace and extract latent features that are crucial to contrast the decision (Downs et al., 2020; El Zini & Awad, 2022a).

Selecting the appropriate contrastive method is a crucial aspect of a meaningful contrastive explanation. Depending on the input space, properties of the underlying machine learning model, and the goal of the user, some contrastive methods can be more suitable with proper guarantees. (Pawelczyk et al., 2021) survey these techniques in their python benchmarking framework, CARLA. CARLA presents a thorough quantitative and qualitative evaluation scheme that makes the choice of the appropriate method easier for practitioners. As an example, a user interested in the minimal change aspect of contrastive explanations might consider methods that yield low alteration costs. Applications where the goal is to detect bias cases might consider diverse counterfactuals to inspect sensitive data (gender, race…) in the provided contrast.

FAIRNESS

As the use of machine learning models continues to spread in our daily lives, the notion of algorithmic fairness is becoming increasingly urgent to integrate into these models. After several failures of AI systems that were offensive to minorities, there has been a surge of interest in detecting discrimination cases. A failure example is the Amazon hiring systems trained on a dataset of an already male-dominated workforce. Accordingly, the hiring algorithm learned historical discrimination against women and made sexist decisions (Köchling & Wehner, 2020). Another discrimination against people with dark skin is manifested in healthcare and facial detection systems (Ghosh, 2017). Shockingly, the Google Photos application mistakenly tagged two African people as "Gorillas" due to the lack of representative data during the training process[1].

These failures can be attributed to some prejudiced assumptions made during the design or development phases of their process or the data collection phase. This section investigates possible bias sources in AI that practitioners need to consider in the machine learning cycle. In this section, the techniques to evaluate the fairness of machine learning models are studied along with bias detection techniques in different modalities. Finally, mitigation techniques that machine learning scientists and engineers augment their models with to ensure that decisions are generalizable to different demographics are described.

Bias Sources in AI

Biased training datasets are the immediate reason behind the discrimination of machine learning models. (Birhane & Prabhu, 2021) highlight undesired bias cases in the ImageNet dataset that is widely used in computer vision applications. (Shankar et al., 2017), (Steed & Caliskan, 2021) and (Stock & Cisse, 2018) further highlight implicit stereotypical patterns, embedded social biases, and harmful depictions of categories in numerous datasets. Existing bias can be perpetuated by AI models when these models are oblivious to its consequences. For instance, Amazon's intention was not to down-rank female applicants. However, unaware of the potential harm, the AI system replicated the inequalities present in the training data. Similarly, healthcare applications are contaminated by biased clinical decision-making, discriminatory healthcare processes, and unequal access and resource allocation. Training on such datasets, without analyzing the impact on minorities and enforcing fair treatment, will lead to discriminatory behavior.

Another major reason for bias in AI is the lack of representative datasets when sampling or collecting data. In this case, the discrimination can be baked into data distributions and reflected thus in AI systems. This is known in the fairness community as sample, or population, bias which occurs when the data used to train the algorithm does not accurately represent the problem space of the model. Good illustrations can be found in computer vision applications and object detection systems trained on subsets of populations that, mostly, miss under-represented groups. For instance, a tool developed by (Buolamwini & Gebru, 2018) to classify 1,270 images of parliament members from European and African countries performs better on male than female faces. Additionally, due to the lack of diversity in its training process, the tool exhibits a substantial bias against darker-skin females where over one-third of the testing cases in women reported failures.

Algorithmic bias is another type of bias in AI. It occurs when algorithms miss underlying complexities in the data they consume and perpetuate existing discrimination. Correlations between attributes can cause the algorithm to learn incorrect causations, hence, making an unfair judgment. For instance, even when AI algorithms are not aware of sensitive data such as race, the correlation between neighborhood information and the individual's race can lead AI to understand a causal relation between neighborhood and assassination probability for example (Intahchomphoo & Gundersen, 2020). Similarly, language models are shown to exhibit genderial bias by inaccurately linking professions to genders where jobs such as "Computer Programmer" can falsely infer a male gender whereas "Homemaker" or "nurse" are linked to female (Bolukbasi et al., 2016).

Prejudicial bias occurs when training data content is influenced by stereotypes or prejudice within the population. More specifically, assumptions that are made based on personal experience, that is not necessarily generalizable, yield discriminatory treatment in AI systems. For instance, an algorithm that is exposed to annotated images of people at home might form some cultural cues about women being housekeepers. Consequently, such systems might not connect women to influential roles in business.

Lastly, measurement bias occurs when data collections are designed poorly. This type of bias occurs when the annotation process is performed by labelers that do not reflect the population (Dixon et al., 2018). Other examples are found in poor surveying strategies and incomplete collection techniques. As an example, object detection tools lack a good representative dataset as well with objects related to ethnicities: baseball caps, Asian conical hats, and kufis can be missed in the category "hat" (Kim et al., 2022).

Some researchers further attribute bias sources in AI to the under-representation of minorities in the workforce responsible for the design, implementation, and deployment of AI systems. Such imbalance in AI practitioners and designers can be the main reason behind overlooking some alarming bias cases in the data collection and training regimes.

Fairness Evaluation in AI Systems

Recent years have witnessed an outpouring of research on designing and implementing fair AI models. Such models do not all implement the same fairness definition. In fact, there are more than 21 mathematical definitions for fairness such as individual fairness, group fairness, and disparate impact (Narayanan et al., 2018).

One of the most intuitive definitions of fairness is Fairness Through Unawareness (FTU). FTU necessitates that the protected attributes are not explicitly used in the decision-making process for a classifier to be fair. Despite its simplicity, such a definition does not account for the cases where sensitive data is not used in the prediction process, but its dependents are. For instance, a system unaware of the information about race can infer such information from attributes such as *neighborhood* and *city* (Hajian et al., 2016). Additionally, the exclusion of sensitive attributes might compromise the performance of the predictor. Exclusion becomes more complex with non-tabular datasets such as text and image where a combination of words or pixels infers protected data (grammatical structures inferring gender, wardrobe inferring religion…). Individual fairness ensures that individuals that are proximate with respect to a distance measure have the same prediction. The distance measure needs careful selection and heavily depends on the application at hand.

Counterfactual fairness requires the prediction to remain unchanged if one or more of the protected attributes were perturbed. Evaluation methods that rely on counterfactual fairness perform input perturbations on sensitive data and observe the change in output. This technique is widely used in textual applications where sensitive words are substituted with their analogs in different groups and the change in prediction is monitored (Dixon et al., 2018; Ma et al., 2020; Pruksachatkun et al., 2021). Such perturbations successfully detected fairness violations in sentiment analysis models in Microsoft NLP and. Amazon APIs were substituting "brothers" with "sisters" and "uncle" with "aunt" in the passages "… favorites are the O'Reily brothers…" and "…. train to make their way to L.A. to see his uncle to lift the curse…" respectively altered the sentiment (positive ® negative and negative ® positive respectively).

Other definitions include but are not limited to demographic/statistical parity, equalized odds, equality of opportunity, and disparate impact. These fairness evaluation metrics are statistical in nature; where the privileged and underprivileged groups are required to have the same probability of being assigned to a favorable outcome (demographic parity), a true positive outcome (equality of opportunity), or a false positive rate (average odds) … Face recognition models, especially highly accurate ones, are the perfect example where such metrics unveil discrimination against people of color. For instance, a growing body of research is exposing a disparity in the error rates across different demographic groups in state-of-the-art facial detection models (Furl et al., 2002).

Bias Mitigation in Emergent Applications

While some researchers continue to revisit fairness definitions, others are focusing on techniques to ensure that AI models can adhere to them. Those techniques are often called "enforcing fairness constraints" which are achieved on different levels. First, debiasing strategies are established on the dataset levels and the encoded knowledge (He et al., 2019). In image detection datasets, face obfuscation and exclusion are proved effective in removing bias in ImageNet (Asano et al., 2021; Yang et al., 2022). In text, the Mixture of Experts (MoE) ensemble method can remove three types of bias, namely word overlap, length mismatch, and partial input heuristics (Liu et al., 2020).

Alternatively, training algorithms can be modified to maintain performance while reducing correlations between outcomes and protected data (Grgic-Hlaca et al., 2016; Kilbertus et al., 2017; Zafar et al., 2019). Other approaches rely on data augmentation to ensure proper representation of marginalized groups. This augmentation is mostly referred to as *contrastive augmentation* where some training instances are added to the dataset while perturbing sensitive info and keeping the prediction the same (Chuang et al., 2020; Lee et al., 2021; Zhao et al., 2018). Human-machine interaction is also shown to be a successful mitigation technique where human subjects identify discrimination cases to resolve (Fu et al., 2021; Sun et al., 2019).

As an example, the toxicity prediction in online commentaries is witnessing efforts to remove discrimination against some ethnicities and sexual identities. Many techniques are shown to be effective in diluting discrimination in the toxicity detection task. These techniques include data balancing (Dixon et al., 2018), multi-task learning (Vaidya et al., 2020), and ensembling frameworks (Halevy et al., 2021). Similarly, a great deal of researchers is moving towards debiasing implicit stereotypes learned by language models and word embeddings. This is mainly achieved through projections into neutral spaces (Bolukbasi et al., 2016; Ravfogel et al., 2020) and augmenting a contrastive layer to ensure fair decision-making schemes (Cheng et al., 2020; Shin et al., 2020).

CONCLUSION

This chapter aims at raising awareness of the accountability aspect of machine learning models to develop responsible and trustworthy AI systems. The importance of integrating accountability aspects in emergent applications is discussed while focusing on two aspects: explainability and fairness. Accountability is studied according to the *when* and the *what* of explainability. Explainability can be applied to existing pre-trained machine learning models in a post-hoc manner or it can be integrated with the design of inherently interpretable systems. While the former can save the computations needed to retrain explainable systems, the latter models can exhibit explanations that are faithful to the original predictions. Then, ExAI methods are categorized into four clusters based on what they try to explain. The first cluster explains individual decisions on a particular testing instance while the second cluster generalizes the explanation to a class label and derives common features globally important in the prediction process. The third cluster interprets the learned knowledge in machine learning models and maps it to human understandable concepts. The last cluster explains the learning regimes and interprets the good performance of state-of-the-art models. The interconnection between the first three categories of ExAI methods and some bias detection techniques is studied. This categorization leads us to discuss three important applications where AI accountability plays a vital role in research benchmarks.

Later, the chapter describes applications where explainability is needed on three different levels: (1) when the machine learning model exhibits satisfactory performance, (2) when it presents undesired failures, and (3) when it outperforms humans and can serve as a teaching mechanism. General explainability methods are then covered with a focus on gradient-based methods input perturbations and activation maximization, visual saliency maps, and interpretability techniques in natural language processing settings. Counterfactual explainability methods that compute alternative inputs to alter the model's decision to explain the outcomes are then described. Lastly, the chapter focuses on fairness in AI by summarizing the bias sources in AI systems and discussing fairness evaluation metrics and techniques in general settings, images, and texts. Finally, different mitigation methods are described based on the modality they operate in.

The nascent subfield of interpretable AI is the true hope of achieving the true potential of AI systems. Ensuring fair treatment of individuals regardless of their identities is paramount for the wider and safer adoption of AI systems. In this view, this chapter charts the path toward responsible AI practices in several areas by encouraging the design and implementation of interpretable models that are more inclusive of different cultures, traditions, and values.

REFERENCES

Adadi, A., & Berrada, M. (2018). Peeking inside the black-box: A survey on explainable artificial intelligence (XAI). *IEEE Access: Practical Innovations, Open Solutions*, 6, 52138–52160. doi:10.1109/ACCESS.2018.2870052

Ankenbrand, M. J., Shainberg, L., Hock, M., Lohr, D., & Schreiber, L. M. (2021). Sensitivity analysis for interpretation of machine learning based segmentation models in cardiac MRI. *BMC Medical Imaging*, *21*(1), 1–8. doi:10.118612880-021-00551-1 PMID:33588786

Antoran, J., Bhatt, U., Adel, T., Weller, A., & Hernández-Lobato, J. M. (2020). Getting a CLUE: A Method for Explaining Uncertainty Estimates. International Conference on Learning Representations.

Asano, Y. M., Rupprecht, C., Zisserman, A., & Vedaldi, A. (2021). PASS: An ImageNet replacement for self-supervised pretraining without humans. *Thirty-fifth Conference on Neural Information Processing Systems Datasets and Benchmarks Track (Round 1)*.

Baehrens, D., Schroeter, T., Harmeling, S., Kawanabe, M., Hansen, K., & Müller, K.-R. (2010). How to explain individual classification decisions. *Journal of Machine Learning Research*, *11*, 1803–1831.

Birhane, A., & Prabhu, V. U. (2021). Large image datasets: A pyrrhic win for computer vision? *2021 IEEE Winter Conference on Applications of Computer Vision (WACV)*. IEEE.

Bolukbasi, T., Chang, K.-W., Zou, J. Y., Saligrama, V., & Kalai, A. T. (2016). Man is to computer programmer as woman is to homemaker? debiasing word embeddings. *Advances in Neural Information Processing Systems*, 29.

Brunet, M.-E., Alkalay-Houlihan, C., Anderson, A., & Zemel, R. (2019). Understanding the origins of bias in word embeddings. *International conference on machine learning.* .

Brunner, G., Liu, Y., Pascual, D., Richter, O., Ciaramita, M., & Wattenhofer, R. (2019). On Identifiability in Transformers. *International Conference on Learning Representations*.

Buolamwini, J., & Gebru, T. (2018). Gender shades: Intersectional accuracy disparities in commercial gender classification. Conference on fairness, accountability and transparency.

Cheng, P., Hao, W., Yuan, S., Si, S., & Carin, L. (2020). FairFil: Contrastive Neural Debiasing Method for Pretrained Text Encoders. *International Conference on Learning Representations*.

Chuang, C.-Y., Robinson, J., Lin, Y.-C., Torralba, A., & Jegelka, S. (2020). Debiased contrastive learning. *Advances in Neural Information Processing Systems*, *33*, 8765–8775.

Clark, K., Khandelwal, U., Levy, O., & Manning, C. D. (2019). What Does BERT Look at? An Analysis of BERT's Attention. Proceedings of the 2019 ACL Workshop BlackboxNLP: Analyzing and Interpreting Neural Networks for NLP, .

Dabkowski, P., & Gal, Y. (2017). Real time image saliency for black box classifiers. *Advances in Neural Information Processing Systems*, 30.

Demajo, L. M., Vella, V., & Dingli, A. (2020). Explainable ai for interpretable credit scoring. *arXiv preprint arXiv:2012.03749*. doi:10.5121/csit.2020.101516

Dhurandhar, A., Chen, P.-Y., Luss, R., Tu, C.-C., Ting, P., Shanmugam, K., & Das, P. (2018). Explanations based on the missing: Towards contrastive explanations with pertinent negatives. *Advances in Neural Information Processing Systems*, 31.

Dixon, L., Li, J., Sorensen, J., Thain, N., & Vasserman, L. (2018). Measuring and mitigating unintended bias in text classification. Proceedings of the 2018 AAAI/ACM Conference on AI, Ethics, and Society, 10.1145/3278721.3278729

Downs, M., Chu, J. L., Yacoby, Y., Doshi-Velez, F., & Pan, W. (2020). Cruds: Counterfactual recourse using disentangled subspaces. *ICML WHI, 2020*, 1-23. doi:10.1145/3278721.3278729

El Zini, J., & Awad, M. (2022a). Beyond Model Interpretability: On the Faithfulness and Adversarial Robustness of Contrastive Textual Explanations. *Findings of the Association for Computational Linguistics: EMNLP.*

El Zini, J., & Awad, M. (2022b). *On the Explainability of Natural Language Processing Deep Models. ACM Computing Surveys.* CSUR.

El Zini, J., Mansour, M., Mousi, B., & Awad, M. (2022). On the Evaluation of the Plausibility and Faithfulness of Sentiment Analysis Explanations. IFIP International Conference on Artificial Intelligence Applications and Innovations, 10.1007/978-3-031-08337-2_28

Erhan, D., Bengio, Y., Courville, A., & Vincent, P. (2009). Visualizing higher-layer features of a deep network. *University of Montreal, 1341*(3), 1. doi:10.1007/978-3-031-08337-2_28

Flores, A. W., Bechtel, K., & Lowenkamp, C. T. (2016). False positives, false negatives, and false analyses: A rejoinder to machine bias: There's software used across the country to predict future criminals. and it's biased against blacks. *Federal Probation, 80*, 38.

Fu, Z., Xian, Y., Geng, S., De Melo, G., & Zhang, Y. (2021). Popcorn: Human-in-the-loop Popularity Debiasing in Conversational Recommender Systems. Proceedings of the 30th ACM International Conference on Information & Knowledge Management, .

Furl, N., Phillips, P. J., & O'Toole, A. J. (2002). Face recognition algorithms and the other-race effect: Computational mechanisms for a developmental contact hypothesis. *Cognitive Science, 26*(6), 797–815.

Gardner, M., Artzi, Y., Basmov, V., Berant, J., Bogin, B., Chen, S., Dasigi, P., Dua, D., Elazar, Y., & Gottumukkala, A. (2020). Evaluating Models' Local Decision Boundaries via Contrast Sets. Findings of the Association for Computational Linguistics: EMNLP 2020,

Garg, S., Perot, V., Limtiaco, N., Taly, A., Chi, E. H., & Beutel, A. (2019). Counterfactual fairness in text classification through robustness. Proceedings of the 2019 AAAI/ACM Conference on AI, Ethics, and Society

Georgakopoulos, S. V., Tasoulis, S. K., Vrahatis, A. G., & Plagianakos, V. P. (2018). Convolutional neural networks for toxic comment classification. *Proceedings of the 10th hellenic conference on artificial intelligence*

Grgic-Hlaca, N., Zafar, M. B., Gummadi, K. P., & Weller, A. (2016). The case for process fairness in learning: Feature selection for fair decision making. NIPS symposium on machine learning and the law,

Hajian, S., Bonchi, F., & Castillo, C. (2016). Algorithmic bias: From discrimination discovery to fairness-aware data mining. *Proceedings of the 22nd ACM SIGKDD international conference on knowledge discovery and data mining*

Halevy, M., Harris, C., Bruckman, A., Yang, D., & Howard, A. (2021). Mitigating racial biases in toxic language detection with an equity-based ensemble framework. In *Equity and Access in Algorithms* (pp. 1–11). Mechanisms, and Optimization.

He, H., Zha, S., & Wang, H. (2019). Unlearn Dataset Bias in Natural Language Inference by Fitting the Residual. Proceedings of the 2nd Workshop on Deep Learning Approaches for Low-Resource NLP (DeepLo 2019), .

Hind, M., Wei, D., Campbell, M., Codella, N. C., Dhurandhar, A., Mojsilović, A., Natesan Ramamurthy, K., & Varshney, K. R. (2019). TED: Teaching AI to explain its decisions. Proceedings of the 2019 AAAI/ACM Conference on AI, Ethics, and Society, Intahchomphoo, C., & Gundersen, O. E. (2020). Artificial intelligence and race: A systematic review. Legal Information Management, 20(2), 74–84

Jawahar, G., Sagot, B., & Seddah, D. (2019). What does BERT learn about the structure of language? ACL 2019-57th Annual Meeting of the Association for Computational Linguistics, 10.18653/v1/P19-1356

Joshi, S., Koyejo, O., Vijitbenjaronk, W., Kim, B., & Ghosh, J. (2019). Towards Realistic Individual Recourse and Actionable Explanations in Black-Box Decision Making Systems. *arXiv e-prints*, arXiv: 1907.09615. doi:10.18653/v1/P19-1356

Karam, C., El Zini, J., Awad, M., Saade, C., Naffaa, L., & El Amine, M. (2021). A Progressive and Cross-Domain Deep Transfer Learning Framework for Wrist Fracture Detection. *Journal of Artificial Intelligence and Soft Computing Research*, *12*(2), 101–120. doi:10.2478/jaiscr-2022-0007

Kenton, J. D. M.-W. C., & Toutanova, L. K. (2019). BERT: Pre-training of Deep Bidirectional Transformers for Language Understanding. Proceedings of NAACL-HLT, .

Kilbertus, N., Rojas Carulla, M., Parascandolo, G., Hardt, M., Janzing, D., & Schölkopf, B. (2017). Avoiding discrimination through causal reasoning. *Advances in Neural Information Processing Systems*, 30.

Kim, Z., Araujo, A., Cao, B., Askew, C., Sim, J., Green, M., Fodiatu Yilla, N. M., & Weyand, T. (2022). Improving Fairness in Large-Scale Object Recognition by CrowdSourced Demographic Information. *arXiv e-prints*, arXiv: 2206.01326.

Köchling, A., & Wehner, M. C. (2020). Discriminated by an algorithm: A systematic review of discrimination and fairness by algorithmic decision-making in the context of HR recruitment and HR development. *Business Research*, *13*(3), 795–848. doi:10.100740685-020-00134-w

Krishna, S., Gupta, R., Verma, A., Dhamala, J., Pruksachatkun, Y., & Chang, K.-W. (2022). Measuring Fairness of Text Classifiers via Prediction Sensitivity. Proceedings of the 60th Annual Meeting of the Association for Computational Linguistics (Volume 1: Long Papers), Laugel, T., Lesot, M.-J., Marsala, C., Renard, X., & Detyniecki, M. (2017). Inverse classification for comparison-based interpretability in machine learning. *arXiv preprint arXiv:1712.08443*. 10.18653/v1/2022.acl-long.401

Le Quy, T., Roy, A., Iosifidis, V., Zhang, W., & Ntoutsi, E. (2022). A survey on datasets for fairness-aware machine learning. *Wiley Interdisciplinary Reviews. Data Mining and Knowledge Discovery*, *12*(3), 1452. doi:10.1002/widm.1452

Lee, J., Shin, J.-H., & Kim, J.-S. (2017). Interactive visualization and manipulation of attention-based neural machine translation. Proceedings of the 2017 Conference on Empirical Methods in Natural Language Processing: System Demonstrations, .

Lee, M., Won, S., Kim, J., Lee, H., Park, C., & Jung, K. (2021). CrossAug: A Contrastive Data Augmentation Method for Debiasing Fact Verification Models. *Proceedings of the 30th ACM International Conference on Information & Knowledge Management*

Liu, H., Yin, Q., & Wang, W. Y. (2019). Towards Explainable NLP: A Generative Explanation Framework for Text Classification. *Proceedings of the 57th Annual Meeting of the Association for Computational Linguistics*

Liu, T., Xin, Z., Ding, X., Chang, B., & Sui, Z. (2020). An Empirical Study on Model-agnostic Debiasing Strategies for Robust Natural Language Inference. *Proceedings of the 24th Conference on Computational Natural Language Learning*

Lucieri, A., Bajwa, M. N., Braun, S. A., Malik, M. I., Dengel, A., & Ahmed, S. (2022). ExAID: A multimodal explanation framework for computer-aided diagnosis of skin lesions. *Computer Methods and Programs in Biomedicine, 215*, 106620.

Lundberg, S. M., & Lee, S.-I. (2017). A unified approach to interpreting model predictions. *Advances in Neural Information Processing Systems*, 30.

Ma, P., Wang, S., & Liu, J. (2020). Metamorphic Testing and Certified Mitigation of Fairness Violations in NLP Models. IJCAI, 10.24963/ijcai.2020/64

Mahendran, A., & Vedaldi, A. (2016). Salient deconvolutional networks. European conference on computer vision

Moayeri, M., Pope, P., Balaji, Y., & Feizi, S. (2022). A Comprehensive Study of Image Classification Model Sensitivity to Foregrounds, Backgrounds, and Visual Attributes. *Proceedings of the IEEE/CVF Conference on Computer Vision and Pattern Recognition*

Mokhov, S. A., Paquet, J., & Debbabi, M. (2014). The use of NLP techniques in static code analysis to detect weaknesses and vulnerabilities. *Canadian Conference on Artificial Intelligence*

Noiret, S., Lumetzberger, J., & Kampel, M. (2021). Bias and Fairness in Computer Vision Applications of the Criminal Justice System. *2021 IEEE Symposium Series on Computational Intelligence (SSCI)*

Patro, B. N., Lunayach, M., Patel, S., & Namboodiri, V. P. (2019). U-cam: Visual explanation using uncertainty based class activation maps. *Proceedings of the IEEE/CVF International Conference on Computer Vision*

Pawelczyk, M., Bielawski, S., van den Heuvel, J., Richter, T., & Kasneci, G. (2021). CARLA: A Python Library to Benchmark Algorithmic Recourse and Counterfactual Explanation Algorithms. *35th Conference on Neural Information Processing Systems (NeurIPS 2021) Track on Datasets and Benchmarks.* doi:10.24963/ijcai.2020/64

Pruksachatkun, Y., Krishna, S., Dhamala, J., Gupta, R., & Chang, K.-W. (2021). Does Robustness Improve Fairness? Approaching Fairness with Word Substitution Robustness Methods for Text Classification. Findings of the Association for Computational Linguistics: ACL-IJCNLP 2021.

, Puniya, B. L., Allen, L., Hochfelder, C., Majumder, M., & Helikar, T. (2016). Systems perturbation analysis of a large-scale signal transduction model reveals potentially influential candidates for cancer therapeutics. Frontiers in Bioengineering and Biotechnology, 4, 10

Radford, A., Wu, J., Child, R., Luan, D., Amodei, D., & Sutskever, I. (2019). Language models are unsupervised multitask learners. *OpenAI blog, 1*(8), 9.

Raganato, A., & Tiedemann, J. (2018). An analysis of encoder representations in transformer-based machine translation. Proceedings of the 2018 EMNLP Workshop BlackboxNLP: Analyzing and Interpreting Neural Networks for NLP, 10.18653/v1/W18-5431

Rajpurkar, P., Irvin, J., Bagul, A., Ding, D., Duan, T., Mehta, H., Yang, B., Zhu, K., Laird, D., & Ball, R. L. (2018). MURA Dataset: Towards Radiologist-Level Abnormality Detection in Musculoskeletal Radiographs. doi:10.18653/v1/W18-5431

Rathi, S. (2019). Generating Counterfactual and Contrastive Explanations using SHAP. *arXiv e-prints*, arXiv: 1906.09293.

Ravfogel, S., Elazar, Y., Gonen, H., Twiton, M., & Goldberg, Y. (2020). Null It Out: Guarding Protected Attributes by Iterative Nullspace Projection. Proceedings of the 58th Annual Meeting of the Association for Computational Linguistics, .

Rhue, L. (2018). Racial influence on automated perceptions of emotions. *Available at SSRN 3281765*

Ribeiro, M. T., Singh, S., & Guestrin, C. (2016). Why should i trust you?" Explaining the predictions of any classifier. Proceedings of the 22nd ACM SIGKDD international conference on knowledge discovery and data mining, .

Ribera, M., & Lapedriza, A. (2019). Can we do better explanations? A proposal of user-centered explainable AI. IUI Workshops, Rogers, A., Kovaleva, O., & Rumshisky, A. (2020). A primer in bertology: What we know about how bert works. *Transactions of the Association for Computational Linguistics*, 8, 842–866.

Shankar, S., Halpern, Y., Breck, E., Atwood, J., Wilson, J., & Sculley, D. (2017). No Classification without Representation: Assessing Geodiversity Issues in Open Data Sets for the Developing World. *stat, 1050*, 22.

Sharma, S., Henderson, J., & Ghosh, J. (2020). Certifai: A common framework to provide explanations and analyse the fairness and robustness of black-box models. Proceedings of the AAAI/ACM Conference on AI, Ethics, and Society, 10.1145/3375627.3375812

Shin, S., Song, K., Jang, J., Kim, H., Joo, W., & Moon, I.-C. (2020). Neutralizing Gender Bias in Word Embeddings with Latent Disentanglement and Counterfactual Generation. Findings of the Association for Computational Linguistics: EMNLP 2020,

Shrikumar, A., Greenside, P., & Kundaje, A. (2017). Learning important features through propagating activation differences. International conference on machine learning

Silver, D., Huang, A., Maddison, C. J., Guez, A., Sifre, L., Van Den Driessche, G., Schrittwieser, J., Antonoglou, I., Panneershelvam, V., & Lanctot, M. (2016). Mastering the game of Go with deep neural networks and tree search. *nature, 529*(7587), 484-489. doi:10.1145/3375627.3375812

Silver, D., Schrittwieser, J., Simonyan, K., Antonoglou, I., Huang, A., Guez, A., Hubert, T., Baker, L., Lai, M., & Bolton, A. (2017). Mastering the game of go without human knowledge. *nature, 550*(7676), 354-359.

Simonyan, K., Vedaldi, A., & Zisserman, A. (2013). Deep inside convolutional networks: Visualising image classification models and saliency maps. *arXiv preprint arXiv:1312.6034.*

Smilkov, D., Thorat, N., Kim, B., Viégas, F., & Wattenberg, M. (2017). Smoothgrad: removing noise by adding noise. *arXiv preprint arXiv:1706.03825.*

Springenberg, J. T., Dosovitskiy, A., Brox, T., & Riedmiller, M. (2014). Striving for simplicity: The all convolutional net. *arXiv preprint arXiv:1412.6806.*

Steed, R., & Caliskan, A. (2021). Image representations learned with unsupervised pre-training contain human-like biases. Proceedings of the 2021 ACM conference on fairness, accountability, and transparency, .

Stock, P., & Cisse, M. (2018). Convnets and imagenet beyond accuracy: Understanding mistakes and uncovering biases. *Proceedings of the European Conference on Computer Vision (ECCV)*

Strobelt, H., Gehrmann, S., Behrisch, M., Perer, A., Pfister, H., & Rush, A. M. (2018). S eq 2s eq-v is: A visual debugging tool for sequence-to-sequence models. *IEEE Transactions on Visualization and Computer Graphics*, *25*(1), 353–363.

Sun, W., Khenissi, S., Nasraoui, O., & Shafto, P. (2019). Debiasing the human-recommender system feedback loop in collaborative filtering. Companion Proceedings of The 2019 World Wide Web Conference, .

Sundararajan, M., Taly, A., & Yan, Q. (2017). Axiomatic attribution for deep networks. International conference on machine learning

Sushina, T., & Sobenin, A. (2020). Artificial Intelligence in the Criminal Justice System: Leading Trends and Possibilities. 6th International Conference on Social, economic, and academic leadership (ICSEAL-6-2019)

Tenney, I., Das, D., & Pavlick, E. (2019). BERT Rediscovers the Classical NLP Pipeline. *Proceedings of the 57th Annual Meeting of the Association for Computational Linguistics*

Tjoa, E., & Guan, C. (2020). A survey on explainable artificial intelligence (xai): Toward medical xai. *IEEE Transactions on Neural Networks and Learning Systems*, *32*(11), 4793–4813.

Vaidya, A., Mai, F., & Ning, Y. (2020). Empirical analysis of multi-task learning for reducing identity bias in toxic comment detection. Proceedings of the International AAAI Conference on Web and Social Media, 10.1609/icwsm.v14i1.7334

Vig, J. (2019). Visualizing attention in transformer-based language representation models. *arXiv preprint arXiv:1904.02679*. doi:10.1609/icwsm.v14i1.7334

Vig, J., & Belinkov, Y. (2019). Analyzing the Structure of Attention in a Transformer Language Model. Proceedings of the 2019 ACL Workshop BlackboxNLP: Analyzing and Interpreting Neural Networks for NLP, 10.18653/v1/W19-4808

Wells, L., & Bednarz, T. (2021). Explainable ai and reinforcement learning—a systematic review of current approaches and trends. *Frontiers in artificial intelligence, 4*, 550030. doi:10.18653/v1/W19-4808

Yang, K., Yau, J. H., Fei-Fei, L., Deng, J., & Russakovsky, O. (2022). A study of face obfuscation in imagenet. International Conference on Machine Learning, Zafar, M. B., Valera, I., Gomez-Rodriguez, M., & Gummadi, K. P. (2019). Fairness constraints: A flexible approach for fair classification. *Journal of Machine Learning Research, 20*(1), 2737–2778.

Zeiler, M. D., & Fergus, R. (2014). Visualizing and understanding convolutional networks. European conference on computer vision, .

Zhao, J., Wang, T., Yatskar, M., Ordonez, V., & Chang, K.-W. (2018). Gender Bias in Coreference Resolution: Evaluation and Debiasing Methods. *Proceedings of the 2018 Conference of the North American Chapter of the Association for Computational Linguistics: Human Language Technologies*, Volume 2 (Short Papers)

Zintgraf, L. M., Cohen, T. S., Adel, T., & Welling, M. (2017). Visualizing deep neural network decisions: Prediction difference analysis. *arXiv preprint arXiv:1702.04595*

KEY TERMS AND DEFINITIONS

Bias: Discrimination against a person or a group based with respect to the sensitive data during predictions (supervised learning).

Counterfactual Explainability: Explaining a particular output by an alteration on the input to change the prediction.

Inherent Explainability: Augmenting a model with explainability constraints, or generating explanations while processing the input.

Post-Hoc Explainability: Explaining a model after training in a black-box manner.

Sensitive Attribute: A feature that the person can be potentially discriminated against, e.g. gender or race.

Stereotypes: Inferring conclusions about someone based on correlations between sensitive attributes and some historic behavior people within the same group (not necessarily supervised learning).

ENDNOTE

[1]   https://www.businessinsider.com/google-tags-black-people-as-gorillas-2015-7

Chapter 3
The Rising Trend of Artificial Intelligence in Social Media:
Applications, Challenges, and Opportunities

Fatima Al Husseiny
https://orcid.org/0000-0001-8547-6929
Lebanese International University, Lebanon

ABSTRACT

Artificial intelligence (AI) is a branch of cognitive science concerned with intelligent machines capable of doing tasks formerly accomplished by humans. It focuses on using computers to perform activities that require knowledge, perception, reasoning, comprehension, and cognitive talents. AI algorithms can be trained to exploit individual actions, preferences, opinions, and interests. They can educate machines to behave in human-like ways. Furthermore, AI can learn these habits much faster than humans. Artificial intelligence is used in various industries to automate and increase the efficacy of specific processes and excessively in social media. Organizations use social media to reach many people by assessing their general perception and learning about their feelings and reactions to brands and products through AI However, there is a knowledge gap in the literature when holistically exploring AI's role in social media, its application, challenges, and opportunities.

INTRODUCTION

Machine learning (ML) is evolving with the enormous promise of making marketing more efficient while also being more human. Every functional marketing area and stage of the consumer journey is powered by cognitive systems, whether they are included in marketing software. AI-driven marketing uses models to automate, optimize, and augment data transition into actions and interactions to anticipate needs, forecast behaviors, and hyper-personalizing messaging. Modern marketers use user data to create hyper-individualized and hyper-contextualized brand messages, with each message building on

DOI: 10.4018/978-1-6684-6937-8.ch003

past customer encounters. These interactions are considered a tool to choreograph future meetings in a satisfying virtuous loop rather than as the end of a consumer journey. Successful ML-powered companies use semi-automated and real-time procedures to transform data into seamless customer interactions. These predictive and augmented experiences help companies develop deeper one-to-one relationships with customers, improve the Omni channel customer experience, and differentiate their products. Managers must examine marketing demands in terms of automation, optimization, and augmentation of the sought-after benefits of prediction, anticipation, and personalization when developing an AI strategy—balancing machine-inspired aims with projected benefits requires managers to do a strategic assessment of their company to restructure roles and responsibilities while clearly outlining the work division between people and computers.

SMEs have emerged in response to the rising pressure on enterprises to respond to changing needs of product and service customers (as well as competitiveness and stakeholder preferences). The answer comes in the wake of mounting pressure from the social, political, and economic arenas, which have seen a significant increase in the frequency and duration of product and service customers' online interactions and transactions thanks to technology's complementing role (Basri, 2020). Artificial intelligence (AI) has made significant advancements since its conception, particularly in the previous five decades (Duffett 2017).

Company owners are using artificial Intelligence to improve their marketing technology. It transforms how people think about marketing in various industries and practices. Considering the data presented in Forbes (Louis 2021), AI possesses immense marketing benefits:

70% of high-performing marketing teams claim to have a defined AI strategy, compared to 35% of their underperforming peer marketing teams. CMOS leads high-performing marketing teams to emphasize continuous learning and adopt a growth mentality, as 56% expect to embrace AI and machine learning in the coming year. Investing the time and dedicated effort required to learn new AI and machine learning skills pays well for enhanced social marketing performance and greater marketing analytics precision.

According to 36% of marketers, AI is expected to impact marketing performance this year significantly. A recent study mentioned that 32%of marketers and agency professionals used AI to develop commercials, including digital banners, social media postings, and digital out-of-home ads.

Today, high-performing marketing teams employ an average of seven specific AI and machine learning applications, with just over half planning to expand their use this year. High-performing marketing teams and CMOs invest in AI and machine learning to increase consumer segmentation. They're also concentrating on customizing channel experiences for each user.

AI Defined

Many scholars have been captivated by the potential of building intelligent computers for as long as computers have existed. As previous literature has revealed, the first hints in the direction of artificial intelligence stretch back even further. But, since the term intelligence is challenging to define, what does Artificial Intelligence mean?

The actual definition and meaning of the word intelligence, and even more so of Artificial Intelligence, caught the interest of many scholars and created debate resulting in a great deal of misunderstanding. For example, one dictionary has four definitions of Artificial Intelligence: In the realm of computer science, this is a field of research. Artificial Intelligence is concerned with creating computers capable of learning, reasoning, and self-correction like humans. The idea is that robots can be enhanced to have skills generally associated with human Intelligence, such as learning, adapting, and self-correction.

Regardless of which definition, AI has exceptionally high potential to drive market forces, especially with the rapid expansion of social media. In the figure below, artificial intelligence evolution has been tracked with its updates and growth features.

Machine Learning

Machine learning is a branch of research that focuses on two related questions: how can cutting-edge systems that optimize themselves based on experience be developed? And what fundamental statistical algorithmic-theoretical laws govern all learning systems, including machines, humans, and industries?

Machine learning research is critical for addressing these significant scientific and technological challenges and the highly functional system software produced and used in various applications (Zhang, 2020).

Machine learning is the technique that uses artificial intelligence to execute a task without having to program it directly. This comprises a wide range of algorithms and statistical models that allows systems to recognize patterns, make conclusions, and learn to do tasks without being given explicit instructions. Machine learning algorithms may yield data insights that improve industrial efficiency (Sadiku et al., 2021).

Deep Learning

The branch of computer learning known as deep learning is a subset of machine learning. It's a method that combines numerous processing layers made up of complex structures or multiple nonlinear transforms to achieve high-level data abstraction. Deep learning is a machine learning algorithm that characterizes learning data (Hao, 2019). Deep learning architectures can handle hierarchies of more abstract features, making them particularly effective for speech and image recognition and natural language processing (Sadiku et al., 2021).

BACKGROUND

AI technology allows agencies and professionals to specialize, collaborate, and develop creativity as machines evolve. Organizations now have a variety of methods for gathering client data. AI transforms how data is analyzed and processed to deliver essential customer insights. For good reasons, artificial intelligence is gaining traction in the digital marketing sector. The term "technology" is so vast that it incorporates various technologies. To put things in perspective, artificial intelligence refers to any technology that simulates human Intelligence. Semantic search, machine learning, and picture and voice recognition are all part of their scope. It's not uncommon to hear marketers gushing about the latest technologies and how they're being used. Most of these people don't shy away from discussing AI applications, which include high-security features like preventing data leaks (Basu, 2020). Marketers can gain a lot from incorporating AI into their digital marketing approach. AI is currently invading a new era in which it will help companies increase production, organizational efficiency, and profitability. A better understanding of consumer demands and behavior will assist firms in gaining, growing, and maintaining client loyalty. As technology becomes more affordable, AI technologies will become the most beneficial tool for digital marketers. Customers will be influenced by these tactics when selecting the best brands and goods for their needs. As a result, markets must incorporate such technologies to grow and match client expectations. Artificial intelligence technologies will revolutionize digital marketing in the future (Nair & Gupta, 2021).

In a nutshell, the most powerful technology available to humankind now is artificial intelligence, and ignoring it is the biggest mistake anyone can make due to its immense applications. Leaders of nations and organizations recognize the immensity of AI's opportunities and the risks of being left behind in the AI gold rush (Bernard & Mat, 2019).

UTILIZING AI IN DIVERSE APPLICATIONS

Fuzzy Logic

Fuzzy logic, like expert systems, is a rule-based method that extends Boolean logic to a multivalued scenario. Instead of directly using the precise input crisp value, the fuzzy sets consisting of various membership functions to a range of 0–1 are used first. The inference step aggregates the fuzzy input signals using fuzzy rules. Defuzzification is then applied to the inference result, considering the degree of satisfaction and producing a crisp value. As a result, with intricately designed principles, the crisp value is controlled in a fuzzy space that completes nonlinear mapping between the input and output. (Zhao et al., 2020). This allows for creating rules for how machines respond to information that accounts for different possible outcomes rather than a simple binary response (Sadiku et al., 2021).

Neural Networks

These are specific machine-learning systems made up of artificial synapses that mimic the brain's structure and function. They resemble the human brain in appearance. They're made up of artificial neurons that accept several inputs and output a single result. As synapses transfer data to one another, the network observes and learns, processing information as it goes through numerous levels (Sadiku et al., 2021). AI uses the concepts of neural networks to emulate the human mind. It thinks like a human and acts in the same way to solve problems. This is AI's one-of-a-kind quality (Verma et al., 2021).

Discussion

It would be accurate to claim that people live in a social media era, given that there are 3.81 billion (and growing) active social media users worldwide. According to various internet research, every intelligent phone user utilizes at least one social media program (Instagram, Facebook, Twitter, LinkedIn, Snapchat, etc.).

Social media has become a fantastic platform for companies to attract new customers or strengthen their bonds with current ones. It is no longer only about interacting with friends and family. Companies and individuals are adding incredible data to these platforms by sharing their ideas, images, and videos. This amount of data is growing dramatically with each passing year. AI significantly impacts how these platforms manage the flood of human information they receive. This area of computer science teaches machines how to think, feel, and act like people. The sizeable social networking company es is using

AI and machine learning, a subset of AI, in social media to manage various activities by making sense of user-generated data.

How Facebook Implements AI

Support vector machines, gradient-boosted decision trees, and various types of neural networks are among the machine learning algorithms used by Facebook. Internal "ML-as-a-Service" processes, open-source machine learning frameworks, and distributed training algorithms are among the infrastructure's components. Facebook uses a massive fleet of CPU and GPU machines for training models to support the requisite training frequencies at the required service latency. Facebook uses CPUs for machine learning inference across all essential services, with neural network rating services such as News Feed accounting for most of the total compute load (Hazelwood et al., 2018). Facebook does practically everything on its site, including offering content, face identification, suggesting friends, and using advanced machine learning to deliver adverts to users. To improve each user's experience, Facebook employs various AI techniques (Sadiku et al., 2021).

Facebook and Suicide Prevention Through AI

Facebook also employs artificial Intelligence to track how users interact with the Service, looking for signals that may be sad or in danger of harming themselves. This is done by checking for patterns in a user's posting behavior that match those of other posts that have previously been recognized as having suicidal indications. Users are not contacted directly by the social network at this time, as it prefers to put data at their fingertips promptly. However, it has investigated the idea of informing a user's "support network" of friends and family in the real world. However, this would undoubtedly have serious privacy issues (Bernard & Mat, 2019).

It's critical to remember that, as previously stated, Facebook algorithms are designed to assist Facebook in discovering content linked to suicide and self-injury to delete content that violates Facebook's policies and flag it for review by the Community Operations team. The algorithms are not meant to diagnose or treat mental health issues and do not perform clinical or diagnostic duties (Facebook, 2022).

How Instagram Implements AI

As of June 2018, the Facebook-owned social network Instagram, focusing on image and video sharing, had 1 billion active users, posting 95 million photographs daily. Recognizing that bullying, harassment, and abuse are all too common online, Instagram has announced that it will implement artificial intelligence (AI) to stop lousy conduct before it impacts people's lives (Bernard & Mat,2019).

Because of its rapid growth, marketing academics have been paying attention to Instagram, a relatively new social network service (SNS). One critical conclusion is that food-related images highly associated with female profiles can have considerable ramifications in marketing research and management—having a visual endorsement from geolocated consumers is a strong motivator for potential customers. The described marketing technique heavily relies on hashtags and curating high-quality photographs on dedicated accounts (Geru et al., 2018). Instagram introduced the Instagram algorithm, a new work method based on artificial Intelligence and extensive data. This Instagram algorithm attempts to improve Instagram's work system and prevent cheating by users using auto likes, follows, comments, and unfollows (Agung et al., 2019). Artificial Intelligence is used to identify and suggest pictures and images. Instagram's Explore page is the first place artificial Intelligence is used (Sadiku et al., 2021).

How Linkedin Implements AI

LinkedIn has become a standard tool for job seekers in many labor markets. Because labor-based databases make it easier to trace where enterprises are investing in AI or ML initiatives, recent work tracking AI investments has tended to focus on labor stocks and flows. Several studies have used large-scale online labor databases like CareerBuilder and LinkedIn to link the commercial value of I.T. and productivity benefits from technology (Rock, 2021).

LinkedIn uses Artificial intelligence to recommend connections, job openings, specific topics in your feed, and people you should follow. Its system suggests links, personalizes user messages and delivers employment recommendations tailored to their needs (Sadiku et al., 2021). LinkedIn does what Facebook has done for individuals' professional lives by keeping individuals in touch with friends and family. So, whereas Facebook generates money by selling data to company es so that they may promote items, LinkedIn makes money by recruiting users to join their ranks. Rather than categorizing users based on what movies or music they "enjoy," it considers looking at users' job abilities and experiences. The platform then employs Artificial intelligence, built into every function, to match users with opportunities or bring users to potential employers' notice (Bernard & Mat,2019). LinkedIn can track what happens in the recruitment process regarding gender, providing companies with statistics and insights on the effectiveness of their job advertising and InMail. In addition, LinkedIn Recruiter's top search results will be re-ranked to be more representative (LinkedIn Engineering, 2018).

How Twitter Implements AI

Every day, approximately 330 million Twitter users send hundreds of millions of tweets on social media. People worldwide love the Service for its ease of staying in touch with friends and celebrities and keeping up with the news. Unfortunately, because of the large number of people who use the site and its largely anonymous character, some of the information broadcast 24 hours a day, seven days a week, is bogus. Furthermore, other Service users may not always have your best interests. One of the ways the social media behemoth uses Artificial intelligence is to keep up with the massive task of protecting its users from people who would exploit it to propagate lousy material. Since the public's awareness of the dangers of fake news has grown, Twitter has taken a more proactive approach to find and removing offending accounts from its platform. Part of its plan is to create machine learning technologies that can identify the spambot networks that fake news peddlers and scammers use to give their voices the appearance of credibility. This enables it to discover and shut down around 10 million accounts weekly without waiting for user reports. It operates by detecting patterns in an account's behavior–for example, linking to recognized fake news sites–and comparing them to 186 patterns displayed by previously identified fraudulent or bot accounts. Once the account is flagged, it is put into read-only mode, preventing its owner from posting. Then Twitter requires the account owner to authenticate their identity as a real person by providing a phone number or valid email address. Because fake news, conspiracy, and fraud networks amplify their message by using hundreds or thousands of phony identities, it's sometimes impossible for the human running the network to do so (Bernard & Mat, 2019).

How Whatsapp Implements AI

WhatsApp chatbots, also known as intelligent assistants, allow humans and machines to communicate using natural language. There are numerous chatbot-building platforms and types available for various company es, including e-commerce, retail, banking, leisure, travel, healthcare, and so on. Whatsapp is portrayed in its functionality when it comes to fighting disinformation. An example of this functionality occurred with Maldita. Maldita has built a WhatsApp chatbot to automate and centralize its community interactions. The bot analyzes the material once a person sends a social media post to the WhatsApp number - a photo, a video, a link, or a WhatsApp channel spreading suspicious stuff. The user will automatically receive a link to the debunking article if Maldita has already produced a fact check on the given item (Observer France24, 2021).

How Youtube Implements AI

Machine learning or artificial Intelligence involves training algorithms on data to recognize patterns and conduct actions without human interaction (David, 2018). Approximately 1.9 billion people log on to YouTube monthly and watch over a billion hours of video. Every minute, 300 hours of video are uploaded to the platform by content creators. With such a large number of users, activity, and content, it's only natural for YouTube to deploy artificial intelligence to aid operations. Here are a few examples of how YouTube, owned by Google, now uses artificial Intelligence. Automatic removal of offensive content, new effects and background filters on videos, "Up Next" feature, and text prediction (Michael, 2019).

How Tiktok Implements AI

TikTok is a social networking program that allows users to create and share short videos. It is viral among youths and millennials. The software has been downloaded over one billion times worldwide, with India, the United States, Japan, South Korea, European countries, Brazil, and Southeast Asia among the top users. After WhatsApp and Messenger, it was the world's third most-downloaded app in the first quarter of 2019. TikTok uses artificial Intelligence in two ways. On the consumer side, the company's algorithms quickly learn individual preferences by capturing users' "likes" and comments and how long they watch each video. Because the clips are so short, TikTok's algorithms can create large datasets swiftly. Second, AI assists content creators in creating viral videos on the producer side. It makes video editing easier by suggesting music, hashtags, filters, and other upgrades currently trending or have proven popular in the area (Knowledge Insead Education, 2019).TikTok uses AI to determine which content best fits the user (audience). Consumers do not even need to enter their preferences when using the app. AI will compile an extensive customer behavior database (Duncan, 2019).

AI APPLICATIONS IN SOCIAL MEDIA

Social media has become an integral part of our daily lives. AI integration with social media has the potential to improve user interaction and communication in diverse ways. We've recently seen widespread digital revolutions and adoption of artificial intelligence (AI) and machine learning (ML) technologies to increase company growth and consumer pleasure. Artificial Intelligence has the potential to change the way brands market on social media platforms like Facebook, Instagram, and Twitter. It can automate several time-consuming operations associated with social media administration and large-scale social media monitoring. Social media marketers can use AI to get closer to their audience and learn about their preferences. This allows them to target their advertisements better as well as develop content.

The section below explores how social media networks are utilizing AI

Social Media Marketing

The digital revolution transformed social media into a company platform in the last decade. Social media platforms have grown tremendously in popularity and are becoming more advanced every day. How people interact with various social media platforms and social communities has evolved, and this growth is aided by artificial Intelligence. AI analyzes our prior behavior, web searches, and other factors that feed our timeline and sends notifications. For most of us, our first encounter with artificial intelligence was with chatbots, which were created to react to questions with predefined responses. From Indian Railways' Disha chatbot to Netflix's algorithm-backed recommendations, restaurant recommendations on Zomato and Swiggy to real-time traffic information on Google or Apple Maps, from intelligent cars and drones to Ola and Uber's dynamic pricing – AI is being used in digital marketing in a variety of ways. According to the Drift and Marketing Artificial Intelligence Institute's 2021 State of Marketing Artificial Intelligence Report, most marketers understand the importance of AI for the company, but 70% of respondents believe that a lack of training and education is a barrier to AI adoption in marketing(Capatina et al., 2020). Some brands have begun investigating virtual influencers' use of computing power, and artificial intelligence algorithms improve this power. Virtual influencers will become much more prominent on social media in the coming years. They can consistently represent and act on brand values while engaging with followers anytime (Appel, 2020). Many artificial intelligence-driven apps can dramatically improve how professionals use social media for marketing. They're also relatively inexpensive to execute.

Social Media Advertising

Over the past 25 years, digital advertising has progressed dramatically to revolutionize the whole advertising company and create a new field of academic research since the launch of the first banner in October 1994. If people consider interactive advertising to be the first phase of digital advertising and programmatic advertising to be the second, intelligent advertising will be the third phase. It's critical to remember that a new digital advertising phase always keeps the preceding stage's positive aspects while introducing innovative features. Because of its interactive character, digital advertising was sometimes referred to as interactive advertising in its early years. Interactivity and automation are two critical characteristics of programmatic advertising. Similarly, intelligent advertising keeps the interactivity and automation of digital advertising while adding new creative features (Li, 2019).

For example, Google Assistant, which was released in 2016, can pull data from all of the Google apps a user uses with a single login, such as Gmail, Search, Maps, Shopping, Photos, Calendar, Contacts, and more; and then use AI technologies like natural language processing and machine learning to carry out various tasks in response to the user's voice request or keyboard input. For Google Assistant to function, a single source of data is required (Rebecca, 2018).

Customer Behavior

Artificial Intelligence is the programming of computers to perform tasks that require human Intelligence, such as thinking, learning, problem-solving, and perception. As AI becomes more mainstream, more corporations and companies are using AI in their competitive strategy. Artificial intelligence applications span from voice-activated Google Assistants to Siri and Alexa, which use Natural Processing Language to transform your query into an answer, to Tesla introducing innovative automobiles, to YouTube providing data-driven results based on your activity and interests. Today, there is an ever-increasing amount of data available, and with data breaches on the rise, AI could be the answer. Furthermore, because customers' preferences and complexity are continually changing, firms can no longer rely on old company practices to achieve growth.

While new technologies have given customers more ways to interact with brands and company es, digital technologies have also allowed companies to automate their interactions with customers

Social Listening

Algorithms are increasingly being used by companies to track employee satisfaction. To undertake "sentiment analysis," companies use social analytics and continuous "social listening" to monitor what people say on internal and external social media (Schweyer, 2018). Social listening, or the recording, analysis, and assessment of posts, shares, and likes on social media to capture the mood and opinion of the media as a sort of real-time marketing research, is one of the most common current applications of real-time marketing. Furthermore, advertising and ad placement are now available in real-time: Real-time marketing as a digital marketing approach includes techniques like real-time bidding, comparable to an auctioneering principle for setting the price of advertising space, as well as recommendation marketing and dynamic pricing (Lies, 2019).

Automation

The distinction between automation and artificial intelligence is critical in assessing their possible workplace consequences. Automation is a broad term that refers to a group of technologies rather than a single technology, which explains why there is so much misconception about its link to AI Artificial intelligence, robotics, and software—three topics included in the automation report—can all be considered forms of automation. Consider machine operators, cooks, clerks, and delivery drivers. "Activities that appear to be relatively secure, on the other hand, include people management and development; applying expertise to decision making, planning, and creative tasks; interacting with people; and performing physical activities and operating machinery in unpredictable physical environments," according to the automation report. AI is also expected to have different demographic effects than other forms of automation (Brookings Education, 2020).

Competitive Analysis

Discovering and evaluating data sources to identify market opportunities, threats, and dangers is what competitive Intelligence is all about. And artificial Intelligence can transform this process. The process is more precise because a machine can interpret data points better than a human.

The more challenging the problem is to solve, the better AI will be at it. Competitive Intelligence will only become more critical as society becomes more computerized. Here's how you can apply artificial Intelligence in competitive Intelligence right now. Companies can use competitive Intelligence to make informed decisions about positioning themselves against competitors. It also offers information on new company prospects, the rising client wants, and the changing economy (Content Marketing Institute, 2022).

IDC(International Data Corporation) states that AI services will be used in 40% of digital transformation activities in 2019 and 75% of commercial applications by 2021. Organizations will have to rely significantly more on AI to enhance their performance and develop new services to improve productivity and generate new offerings (Wamba-Taguimdje, 2020). When taking such measurements, organizations are improving their strategic decisions for growth. According to our industry contacts, some corporations have made significant progress in this area, but these initiatives are kept secret and treated as a source of competitive advantage. At this point, it's critical to emphasize that the goal isn't to replace human decision-making in strategic decisions with AI (Stone, 2020).

Social Media Analytics

Given the enormous interest from the application's perspective and the associated unique technical and social science challenges and opportunities, research on social media has dramatically expanded in recent years. This study plan is multidisciplinary and has attracted the attention of researchers from all major fields. Social media research has generally focused on social media analytics and, more recently, social media intelligence from an information technology approach. Gohar F. Khan's "Social Media Analytics" definition is the most accurate. He defined social media analytics as "the art and science of deriving critical hidden insights from huge amounts of semi-structured and unstructured social media data to enable informed and intelligent decision-making" in his book Seven Layers of Social Media (Crimson, 2019).

Content Creation

Previously, technological advancements have caused conflict in the intellectual property system. Artificial intelligence is no exception. The author/inventor roles are expected to become less well-defined as AI becomes more advanced. It does not violate universally accepted legal concepts on the one hand. At the same time, the other provides a reasonable and proportionate incentive to human participants in the innovation process that ultimately leads to AI-generated output (Ballardini, 2019). The phenomenon of deep fakes, which might be regarded as a type of fake news, has emerged due to recent practical developments in Artificial Intelligence. "Deepfakes" is the phenomenon of creating realistic digital items, and a slew of films have sprung up on social media in the previous two years. Deepfakes can be easily manufactured and distributed online due to the low technical expertise and equipment necessary to develop them. Several essential qualities of digital media determine their nature and how they are used. Even though they are a continuation of traditional media, their capabilities make information copying and transmission incredibly simple. As a result, target audiences can be large masses without location, time, or content size restrictions (Karnouskos, 2020). Advertisements are necessary for brand promotion, and AI can create and promote internet advertisements. It can make or update Ads content based on a user's choices, likes, and dislikes. AI can show the appropriate advertisements to the right people at the right time. Advertisers will get a higher return on investment due to this (Nalini, 2021).

Image Recognition

Artificial intelligence (AI) advances have made it possible for image recognition, intelligent speakers, and self-driving cars. AI is defined as "a system's ability to interpret external data correctly, to learn from such data, and to use those learnings to achieve specific goals and tasks through flexible adaptation." (Andreas, 2019) According to the researchers, AI's capabilities in language processing, image recognition, and the widespread use of reliable tools and algorithms may access data from both internal and external sources. These features enable low-cost on-premise technologies and provide the foundation for improved dynamic attribution and online targeting (Vlačić, 2021).

ARTIFICIAL INTELLIGENCE OPPORTUNITIES

Artificial Intelligence in marketing is defined as AI programs that can process, analyze, and interpret vast amounts of data like people. Even though these methods are new, they have already had a significant impact on marketing techniques and campaigns used by the company.

Indeed, there are numerous ways to improve digital advertising and tactics; however, artificial intelligence-based marketing solutions can go much further in terms of in-depth data analysis on a broad scale. This technique allows for the exploitation of concealed Internet users' data in keyword searches, social media profiles, and other online data, all to provide a better offer and solution. This fantastic data gives marketers the ability to feed consumer profiles. Artificial intelligence-based solutions offer a comprehensive perspective of Internet users and potential consumers, which will mention in the section below the major ones.

Increased Audience Engagement

Artificial intelligence is revolutionizing how people operate in various industries. Customer service has long been a part of these industries, whether in retail, finance, manufacturing, or law. Experts predict it will be hard to identify the difference between a human and an artificial intelligence agent in the following years. The customer service revolution has been driven by more significant investment in the industry by substantial internet companies like Google, Microsoft, and Facebook.AI, which allows firms to gain a deeper understanding of their target audience and their preferences to enhance the customer experience (Sadiku et al., 2021).

In e-commerce contexts, communicating with clients using live chat interfaces has become an increasingly common method of providing real-time customer care. Customers utilize these chat services to get information (for example, product specifications) and help (e.g., solving technical problems). Because of the real-time nature of chat services, customer support has evolved into a two-way conversation with substantial implications for trust, satisfaction, repurchase intentions, and WOM intentions (Institute of Entrepreneurship and Development,2022).

Greater Efficiency

Marketers save time and energy by delegating time-consuming, repetitive, and mundane jobs to AI, allowing them to focus on tasks that demand human effort. AI has the potential to boost corporate productivity by 40% (Sadiku, 2021).

Marketing that targets people based on their general inclinations is more effective than traditional advertising. Additionally, with the advent of artificial Intelligence, marketers may now use tailored data to determine whether potential customers will be interested in purchasing before requesting any payment. AI helps companies analyze vast amounts of data and forecast each customer's purchasing behavior and decisions. This makes it possible to market to a specific audience with precision. Additionally, it helps to raise customer satisfaction levels. Besides, by using AI-driven tactics, marketers may easily convert a lead into a sale at the correct times to increase conversions (Bernard,2019).

Reduced Marketing Costs

(ROI). Time-consuming and labor-intensive tasks can be entirely or partially automated with AI It can assist a social media marketer in increasing income while lowering costs.AI can work with minimal human supervision once the algorithms and action points are in place. This aids in the reduction of marketing costs. Compared to human work, AI has speed and cost advantages (Sadiku et al., 2021).

Artificial Intelligence has a very tangible impact on marketing efforts, with some situations resulting in differences worth hundreds of millions of dollars, according to companies who utilize it. According to MIT Technology Review, UPS's EDGE program has the potential to save the company $200–$300 million annually. Numerous programs that draw enormous amounts of data from UPS's multiple operations make up the EDGE program. AI analyzes this data to reveal insights into how trucks are loaded to the best time to wash cars.

A McKinsey study suggested that the marketing and sales sectors would be most affected by AI Marketers will seek to anticipate this trend because AI is expected to have a similar worldwide impact to the steam engine (Yingrui, 2020).

Maximizing company profit is another crucial benefit of applying AI to the marketing sector. AI's capabilities in boosting sales volume include customized advice, one-to-one marketing, and specific cutting-edge and effective advertising methods like robocalls. These personally oriented functions will fully cater to clients' preferences, considerably elevating sales. The cost of labor, the significantly lower productivity of humans, and the losses brought on by human error outweigh the cost of AI systems by a large margin. This is because writing algorithms, paying technicians and experts, purchasing and maintaining machines, and other prices are much more expensive than developing and maintaining AI systems. Therefore, implementing AI in marketing can reduce production costs (Appen,2022).

Individuals will likely use the improved computing capacity to support existing communities or establish new ones online and offline. This might indicate a return to rural life and a reduction in metropolitan areas in various regions. People will stay in their "silicon lane" in other areas, possibly where the infrastructure is more robust, or there are more attractions. In either scenario, computational power will enable us to make previously impractical decisions about where and how people live and work. In the networked world of 2025, the trade-offs caused by distance will change (Krizanova et al., 2019). There is a connection between critical thinking abilities and online learning resources in the digital world. In other words, an individual in an online medium is driven by an interactive communication model facilitated by technology (Kaddoura &Al Husseiny, 2021).

Increased Security

Social networking platforms have access to an unfathomable amount of data thanks to the estimated 2.77 billion users of social networks worldwide. In 2019, the global reach of social networks was growing at an alarming rate. These numbers will increase with time. User-generated data is abundantly available on social media. It is a mammoth endeavor to extract valuable insights from this sea of data due to the nature of the data, which is primarily unstructured. While many critics of AI assert that this technology would lead to job losses, it is intended to improve Intelligence and analyze data efficiently to streamline operations and function effectively and efficiently (Marketing Artificial Intelligence Institute, 2021).

Competition-Minded Tool

AI is a tool that thrives on competition. Knowing what your competitors are up to is just as vital as establishing your company strategy in the company. Artificial intelligence has been assisting online marketers in tracking their competitors' online activities (Sadiku et al., 2021).

This is because machines are better at data analysis than people, not just because AI processes information more quickly. Once AI has this knowledge, it may be able to forecast which flavors will become more or less popular, giving you an advantage over your rivals. This is followed by establishing long-lasting entry barriers, which may be of significant concern for competition policy. Even more concerning, this behavior may lead to the data becoming fragmented within each industry, reducing both the inventive productivity and the spillovers to the deep learning GPT sector and other application sectors. This shows that one crucial factor influencing the likelihood of financial advantages from the development and use of deep learning is the proactive development of institutions and regulations that promote competition, data sharing, and openness (Gran, 2021).

ARTIFICIAL INTELLIGENCE CHALLENGES

Undoubtedly, the growing application of AI in our daily lives has divided viewpoints. This is also true in the field of marketing. Many people are concerned about the potentially intrusive nature of AI as privacy concerns come to the forefront. Furthermore, the widespread use of AI on social media platforms brought these issues to light.

Ethical Considerations

Industry, academic researchers, and the general public have demonstrated a significant interest in artificial intelligence use's ethical and social concerns.

How AI is built, but more importantly how it is used, is influenced by the strong social and technological interaction. Technology is rarely employed in a scientific setting or by persons who share the same demographic profile as those who created or tested it. Technologies enter a world that is already alive, influenced by economic and political systems, and based on history. "Even the fairest and most accurate algorithms can nevertheless be exploited to infringe on people's civil freedoms," writes Karen Hao of the MIT Technology Review. Because they are employed in the actual world, with all its flaws and issues, the most deliberately planned technologies can work in ways that are not just. It should be evident by now that people can't comprehend the implications and ethics of AI without first understanding the social milieu in which it exists. This necessitates a discussion of culture's significance. The concept of "culture" may appear simple and intuitive at first glance. However, when people try to define culture, they find that it is rather complicated. "Culture is one of the two or three most challenging words in the English language," observed the historian Raymond Williams (Hagerty, 2019).

The ethical considerations surrounding AI, such as autonomous surgical robots or military use (such as autonomous drones), will not be studied and discussed. While they may be helpful in marketing in some situations (due to data collected), they were not created to be useful for marketing operations (Hildebrand, 2018). You may rapidly request a ride using the Lyft chatbot on Facebook Messenger or Slack. Simply tell the bot your location, and the virtual robot will display you the driver's location, vehicle model, and even license plate (Digital Marketing Institute, 2017).

Artificial Intelligence and the Digital Divide

A user's personal and professional life has been affected by the digital change that has characterized the 21st century. Each individual uses technology regularly and owns at least one intelligent gadget. Consequently, it is challenging to envision an environment that does not use technology. A new generation is now enrolling in universities due to the quick rise in interactive technology use in early education, and the trend is still rising (Kaddoura & Al Husseiny, 2021). Technology is critical in any individual's daily interactions and decisions. Based on the theory of reasoned action, The relationship between action and attitudes is outlined in the notion of reasoned action. People's behaviors change when their beliefs do, whereas arbitrary social norms and personal opinions shape attitudes. Based on the technology acceptance model (TAM), perceived utility and usability are essential indicators of people's propensity to utilize technological systems. According to a study, students are ignorant of the advantages of switching to online exams. Students were accustomed to using traditional assessment techniques, so convincing them of the benefits of switching to online evaluation took some convincing. The participants did not see the online evaluation approach as a practical way to gather information (Itani et al., 2022).

The way people, communities, governments, and private actors perceive and react to climate and ecological change is likely to change due to automated decision-making and predictive analytics enabled by artificial Intelligence, as well as the rapid advancement of technologies like sensor technology and robotics. Several study domains connected to climate change and environmental monitoring already use techniques based on various artificial intelligence forms. Investments in these technologies' use in forestry, agriculture, and the extraction of marine resources appear to rise quickly (Word Economic Forum, 2022).

Artificial intelligence is more than a trendy term. It enables systems that filter spam emails, identify harmful information on social media, and even detect cancerous tumors. It also translates between other languages and powers facial recognition in intelligent phones and computers.

In contrast, urgent needs like those for food, healthcare, sanitation, and education frequently precede underdeveloped nations over any sizable investment in digital transformation. In this context, AI can potentially expand the already-existing digital divide between developed and developing countries (Alsheibani et al., 2019).

Importantly, neural networks are voracious data consumers and frequently need millions of instances to learn how to do a new task efficiently. In contrast to more straightforward machine learning models, they demand a complicated data storage infrastructure and contemporary processing technology. Developing countries typically cannot afford such expansive computing infrastructure.

Skills Gap

As new types of labor have significantly expanded, there has been a striking rise in adopting AI technology in enterprises. Despite the anticipated advantages of adopting AI, many firms still find it challenging to advance their adoption (Alsheibani. et al., 2019).

Artificial intelligence-driven digital transformation is now a significant change agent across several industries (Boguda & Shailaja, 2019). Depending on the degree of AI adoption, the study's hurdles can be divided into three categories, the striking variation in how barriers affected the firms surveyed., lack of internal management and implementation capabilities as well as an unclear company case for AI deployments were the critical obstacles found in all three settings.

Data Privacy Concerns

Illegitimate individuals could access sensitive personal information such as financial, tax, and health records. That would be humiliating and harmful. Due to privacy concerns, AI-enabled marketing automation platforms should draw a line between intuitive and obtrusive (Sadiku et al., 2021). The digital age has overturned many societal structures and customs developed over millennia. These prioritize fundamental principles, including respect for individual privacy, independence, and democracy. These are the founding principles of liberal democracy, whose influence in the latter half of the 20th century was unparalleled in human history. The end of the century saw the potential for significant technological advancements for human well-being. But soon, warning flags started to emerge. Social media was made possible by the internet, and it has severely and seemingly permanently reduced the value of privacy. The Internet of Things (IoT) has enabled widespread surveillance and control over our daily life while automating many tasks. The development of "Big Data" and data analytics is one outcome of the internet and IoT (Harvard Magazine,2019).

Artificial Intelligence and Fake News Spread

One of the most significant issues facing journalists today is the epidemic of fake news and misinformation. To both detect false information on the one hand and improve the quality and accuracy of news, intelligent software, particularly journalistic algorithms, has become essential (Graves, 2018).

Software like Factmata is developing skilled contextual artificial Intelligence to lessen false information and abusive content online. To combat the problems of disinformation and automatically verify internet rumors, Kalina Bontcheva2 (2018) set a method that enables journalists to examine the accuracy of news on social media platforms. According to the research done by Graves (2018), automatic fact-checking can assist journalists in locating and validating false material spread throughout the media landscape and in providing the best possible responses, as seen in the figure below (Brookings Education, 2020).

AI methods contribute to the online disinformation epidemic in two ways. First, AI techniques open new possibilities for producing or editing texts, images, audio, and video content. Second, the practical and quick spread of misinformation online is considerably facilitated by the AI technologies created and used by online platforms to increase user engagement. These latter methods primarily cause the challenge. This issue has numerous ethical concerns that must be carefully considered (Walorska, 2020).

CONCLUSION

The World Wide Web facilitated competition by utilizing many technological advancements that truly enable billions of people throughout various geographic locations to communicate whenever and wherever necessary by relying solely on the analog medium of electronic devices, which is the primary fuel that pushes the horizons of all 21st-century technologies in (Rydning et al. 2018). Artificial intelligence is predicted to alter marketing tactics and consumer behavior in the future significantly. The authors present a multidimensional paradigm for assessing the impact of AI that considers intelligence levels, task types, and whether AI is implanted in a robot, building on existing research and substantial interactions with practice (Bernard, 2019). The truth is that today's generation cannot imagine living without social media. Likewise, future generations won't either.

FUTURE PROSPECTS

Using cutting-edge models and cutting-edge algorithms is redefining the social media era. AI can monitor vast amounts of unstructured data or user comments to spot trends, generate sharp insights, or create recommendations that are specifically tailored to the user. While a person switches between millions of sites on many platforms, AI can comprehend user behavior and forecast future trends to suggest relevant topics. To increase the number of opportunities to contact specialized user domains and segments, AI easily do redundant duties. On social media sites, artificial Intelligence is becoming more and more popular. AI integration can help marketers, companies, and individuals increase the effectiveness and productivity of their social media efforts. The advantages of AI in social media may grow when machine learning models, sophisticated analytics tools, and deep learning networking algorithms are scaled. Figure 1. Recommends areas of research for future studies.

Figure 1. Future areas of research

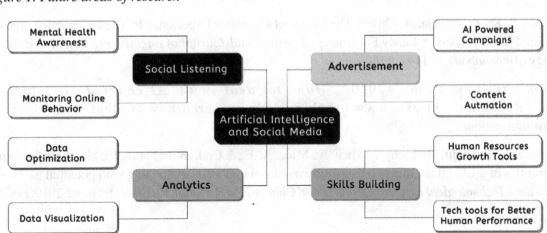

It is noteworthy that the future of AI in both marketing and digital marketing is showing promising results. As depicted in Figure 1. there are diverse research areas for future exploration. These areas are social listening, analytics, content creation, skills building, and advertisement, which will add value to the future of AI implementation in social media.

REFERENCES

Andreas,, K. & Haenlein, M. (2019). On the interpretation, Illustrations, and implications of artificial Intelligence. *Business Horizons, 62*(1), 15–25. doi:10.1016/j.bushor.2018.08.004

Appel, G., Grewal, L., Hadi, R., & Stephen, A. T. (2020). The Future of Social Media In Marketing. *Journal of the Academy of Marketing Science, 48*(1), 79–95. doi:10.100711747-019-00695-1 PMID:32431463

Appen. (2022). *How Artificial Intelligence Data Reduces Overhead Costs for Organizations.* From https://appen.com/blog/how-artificial-intelligence-data-reduces-overhead-costs-for-organizations/

Ballardini, R. (2019). AI-generated content: authorship and inventorship in the age of Artificial Intelligence. In *Online Distribution of Content in the EU* (pp. 117–135). Edward Elgar Publishing. doi:10.4337/9781788119900.00015

Basri, W. (2020). Examining the impact of artificial intelligence-assisted social media marketing on the performance of small and medium enterprises: Toward effective business management in the Saudi Arabian context. *International Journal of Computational Intelligence Systems, 13*(1), 142–152. doi:10.2991/ijcis.d.200127.002

Basu, P. (2020). Artificial Intelligence for digital transformation genesis, fictions, applications, and challenges. *Management Accountant., 55*(4), 1130–1141. doi:10.33516/maj.v55i4.68-72p

Bernard, M. (2019). The Amazing Ways YouTube Uses Artificial Intelligence And Machine Learning. *Forbes.* https://www.forbes.com/sites/bernardmarr/2019/08/23/the-amazing-ways-youtube-uses-artificial-intelligence-and-machine-learning/?sh=57356eca5852

Bernard, M., & Matt, W. (2017). Artificial Intelligence In practice. Wiley & SAS business series.

Boguda, S. K., & Shailaja, A. (2019). The Future of Customer Experience In The Information Age Of Artificial Intelligence-Get Ready For Change. *International Journal of Engineering Research & Technology (Ahmedabad), 8,* 1141–1150.

Brookings Education. (2020). *How to deal with AI-enabled disinformation.* Brookings https://www.brookings.edu/research/how-to-deal-with-ai-enabled-disinformation/

Capatina, A., Kachour, M., Lichy, J., Micu, A., Micu, A.-E., & Codignola, F. (2020). Matching the future capabilities of artificial intelligence-based software for social media marketing with potential users' expectations. *Technological Forecasting and Social Change, 151,* 151. doi:10.1016/j.techfore.2019.119794

Content Marketing Institute. (2022). *How AI Will Power the Future of Successful Content Marketing*. Content Marketing. https://contentmarketinginstitute.com/articles/ai-content-ma rketing-future

David, M. (2018). YouTube's AI is so good at finding offensive content that it needs more staff to keep up. *We Forum*. https://www.weforum.org/agenda/2018/04/ai-is-now-youtube-s-b iggest-weapon-against-the-spread-of-offensive-videos/

Digital Marketing Institute. (2017). *Grow Your Business With Social Bots*. Digital Marketing. https://digitalmarketinginstitute.com/blog/grow-your-busines s-with-social-bots

Duffett, R. G. (2017). Influence of social media marketing communications on young consumers' attitudes. *Young Consumers*, *18*(1), 19–39. doi:10.1108/YC-07-2016-00622

Facebook. (2022). *Suicide Prevention*. Meta. https://www.facebook.com/safety/wellbeing/suicidepre vention

Geru, M., Micu, A. E., Capatina, A., & Micu, A. (2018). Using artificial Intelligence on social media's user-generated content for disruptive marketing strategies in eCommerce. *Economics and Applied Informatics.*, *24*(3), 5–11.

Gran, B., Booth, P., & Bucher, T. (2021). To be or not to be algorithm aware: A question of a new digital divide? *Information Communication and Society*, *24*(12), 1779–1796. doi:10.1080/136911 8X.2020.1736124

Graves, L. (2018). *Understanding the promise and limits of Automated Fact-Checking*. Reuters Institute. https://reutersinstitute.politics.ox.ac.uk/sites/default/fil es/2018-02/graves_factsheet_180226%20FINAL.pdf

Hagerty, A., & Rubinov, I. (2019). *Global AI ethics: a review of artificial Intelligence's social impacts and ethical implications,* 1-27. Cornell University.

Hao, Z. (2019). Deep learning review and discussion of its future development. In *MATEC Web of Conferences*. EDP Sciences.

Harvard Magazine. (2019). *Artificial Intelligence and Ethics*. Harvard Press. https://www.harvardmagazine.com/2019/01/artificial-intellige nce-limita-tions

Hazelwood, K. (2018). Applied machine learning at Facebook: A data center infrastructure perspective. *IEEE International Symposium on High-Performance Computer Architecture (HPCA)*,620-629. IEEE/

Hildebrand, J. (2018). Amazon Alexa: What kind of data does Amazon get from me? | Android Central. *Aljazeera*. https://www.aljazeera.com/economy/2021/11/19/how-much-does-a mazon-know-about-you

Institute of Entrepreneurship and Development. (2022). *How is AI Transforming the Future of Digital Marketing?* From https://ied.eu/blog/how-ai-transforming-the-future-of-digita l-marketing/

Itani, M., Itani, M. A., Kaddoura, S., & Al Husseiny, F. (2022). The impact of the Covid-19 pandemic on online examination: Challenges and opportunities. *Global Journal of Engineering Education.*, *24*(2), 1–16.

Kaddoura, S., & Al Husseiny, F. (2021). Online learning on information security based on critical thinking andragogy. *World Transactions on Engineering and Technology Education*, *19*(2), 157–162.

Kaddoura, S., & Al Husseiny, F. (2021). An approach to reinforce active learning in higher education for I.T. students. *Global Journal of Engineering Education*, *23*(1), 43–48.

Karnouskos, S. (2020). Artificial Intelligence in digital media: The era of deep fakes. *IEEE Transactions on Technology and Society.*, *1*(3), 138–147. doi:10.1109/TTS.2020.3001312

Knowledge Insead Education. (2019). *The TikTok Strategy: Using AI Platforms to Take Over the World* Knowledge Instead. https://knowledge.insead.edu/entrepreneurship/the-tiktok-str ategy-using-ai-platforms-to-take-over-the-world-11776

Krizanova, A., Lăzăroiu, G., Gajanova, L., Kliestikova, J., Nadanyiova, M., & Moravcikova, D. (2019). The effectiveness of marketing communication and the importance of its evaluation in an online environment. *Sustainability*, *11*(24), 1–19. doi:10.3390u11247016

Li, H. (2019). Special section introduction: Artificial Intelligence and advertising. *Journal of Advertising*, *48*(4), 333–337. doi:10.1080/00913367.2019.1654947

Lies, J. (2019). Marketing intelligence and big data: Digital marketing techniques on their way to becoming social engineering techniques in marketing. *International Journal of Interactive Multimedia and Artificial Intelligence*, *5*(5), 134–144. doi:10.9781/ijimai.2019.05.002

LinkedIn Engineering. (2018). *An Introduction to AI at LinkedIn*. LinkedIn. https://engineering.linkedin.com/blog/2018/10/an-introductio n-to-ai-at-linkedin#:~:text=How%20do%20we%20use%20AI,helpful %20content%20in%20the%20feed

Louis, C. (2021). 10 Ways AI And Machine Learning Are Improving Marketing In 2021. *Forbes.* https://www.forbes.com/sites/louiscolumbus/2021/02/21/10-way s-ai-and-machine-learning-are-improving-marketing-in-2021/?s h=78133b2b14c8

Michael, A. (2019). Why Retail Is One Of The Leading Sectors Investing In AI. *Forbes.* https://www.forbes.com/sites/forbestechcouncil/2019/03/29/wh y-retail-is-one-of-the-leading-sectors-investing-in-ai/?sh=5 0914ae81b4b

Nair, K., & Gupta, R. (2021). Application of AI technology in the modern digital marketing environment. *World Journal of Entrepreneurship, Management and Sustainable Development*, *17*(3), 318–328.

Nalini, M. (2021). Impact of Artificial intelligence on Marketing. *International Journal of Aquatic Science*, *12*(2), 3159–3167.

Rebecca, J. (2019). *TikTok, Explained*. Vox. https://www.vox.com/culture/2018/12/10/18129126/tiktok-app-musically-meme-cringe

Rock, D. (2021). Engineering value: The returns to technological talent and investments in Artificial Intelligence. University of Pennsylvania, 1-72.

Sadiku, M. N., Ashaolu, T. J., Ajayi-Majebi, A., & Musa, S. M. (2021). Artificial Intelligence in Social Media. *International Journal of Scientific Advances*, *2*(1), 15–20.

Schweyer, A. (2018). Predictive analytics and artificial Intelligence in people management. *Incentive Research Foundation*, 1-18.

Stone, M., Aravopoulou, E., Ekinci, Y., Evans, G., Hobbs, M., Labib, A., & Machtynger, L. (2020). Artificial intelligence in strategic marketing decision-making: A research agenda. *The Bottom Line (New York, N.Y.)*, *33*(2), 183–200. doi:10.1108/BL-03-2020-0022

Verma, S., Sharma, R., Deb, S., & Maitra, D. (2021). Artificial Intelligence in marketing: Systematic review and future research direction. *International Journal of Information Management Data Insights*, *1*(1), 1–9. doi:10.1016/j.jjimei.2020.100002

Vlačić, B., Corbo, L., Costa e Silva, S., & Dabić, M. (2021). The evolving role of artificial Intelligence in marketing: A review and research agenda. *Journal of Business Research*, *128*, 187–203. doi:10.1016/j.jbusres.2021.01.055

Waleska, A. M. (2020). *Deepfakes and Disinformation. Friedrich Naumann Foundation for Freedom*. FNF.

Wamba-Taguimdje, S. L., Wamba, S. F., Kamdjoug, J. R. K., & Wanko, C. E. T. (2020). Influence of artificial intelligence on firm performance: The business value of AI-based transformation projects. *Business Process Management Journal*, *26*(7), 1893–1924. doi:10.1108/BPMJ-10-2019-0411

Zhang, X. D. (2020). *A matrix algebra approach to artificial Intelligence*. Springer Singapore. doi:10.1007/978-981-15-2770-8

Zhao, S., Blaabjerg, F., & Wang, H. (2020). An overview of artificial intelligence applications for power electronics. *IEEE Transactions on Power Electronics*, *36*(4), 4633–4658. doi:10.1109/TPEL.2020.3024914

KEY TERMS AND DEFINITIONS

Artificial Intelligence: AI does not have one standard definition. There are several definitions. Artificial Intelligence uses computers and other devices to simulate how the human mind makes decisions and solves problems.

Digital Divide: Refers to the widening gap between the affluent, middle-class, and those less fortunate in society who lack access to computers and the internet.

Social Listening: Social listening involves keeping an eye on your company's social media platforms for customer feedback, direct brand mentions, or discussions about particular keywords, subjects, competitors, or sectors.

Chapter 4
Artificial Intelligence–Based Intelligent Human–Computer Interaction

Pinaki Pratim Acharjya

ⓘ https://orcid.org/0000-0002-0305-2661

Haldia Institute of Technology, India

Subhankar Joardar

Haldia Institute of Technology, India

Santanu Koley

Haldia Institute of Technology, India

ABSTRACT

Computers have become ubiquitous and play an important role in our lives. To be usable, any computing device must allow some form of interaction with its user. Human-computer interaction is the point of communication between human users and computers. AI is gradually being integrated into the human-computer interaction. Designing traditional human-computer interaction courses faces new challenges with breakthroughs in third-generation AI technology. New interaction scenarios between humans and computers, such as smart homes and self-driving cars, are constantly emerging. As AI systems become more widespread, it will be essential to understand them from a human perspective. This chapter will provide an overview to the AI-based intelligent human-computer interaction.

INTRODUCTION

Human intelligence is the capacity for complicated cognitive feats to be performed and solved, as well as having a high level of motivation and self-awareness. Humans can learn, use logic, reason, notice patterns, make judgments, solve issues, and think thanks to intelligence. Humans have the cognitive skills necessary to observe the world, recognise good and true things, and engage in interactions with others and their environments through perception, comprehension, reasoning, and expression. Humans

DOI: 10.4018/978-1-6684-6937-8.ch004

are able to study works of classic literature and music, enjoy calming landscapes and works of art, and experience a vast world and a particular region. Then, students will be able to distinguish between them, understand what they mean, and express themselves through dialogue, writing articles, artwork, and any other means available. Humans are able to use their intelligence and interact differently because to these mechanisms. How human-machine interactions have changed through time is shown in Figure 1 below.

Figure 1. The Development of the Human-Machine Interaction over Time (Source: Xu, Dainoff, Ge, & Gao, 2021)

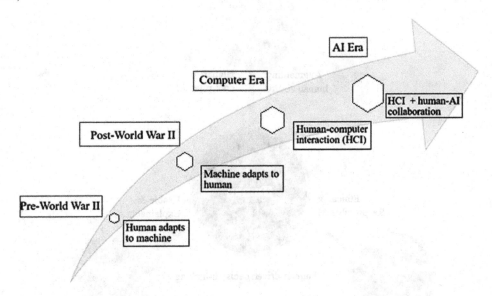

Artificial intelligence is a recent example of an emergent technology (AI) (M. N. O. Sadiku, 1989; R. O. Mason, 2003; S. Samoili, et.al, 2020; Zanzotto, F. M., 2019). Recently, artificial intelligence (AI) has gained widespread acceptance in a variety of sectors (Y. Mintz, et.al, 2019; A. N. Rames et al, 2004; Zhang, X., et.al, 2020; Yampolskiy, R.V., 2019; Yue, W., et.al, 2004), including virtual assistance, healthcare, and security. The field of human-computer interaction (HCI) has been combining AI and HCI (Zhou,J., et.al, 2018; Yang, F., et.al, 2020; Yang, Q., et.al, 2020) over the past few years in order to create an interactive intelligent system for user engagement. AI is being used in a variety of fields by employing various algorithms and utilising HCI to provide the user with transparency and build their trust in the computer.

Digitalization and the human-computer interaction are closely related concepts. In this study, it is referred to as HCI (A. Miller, 2019; T. Winograd, 2006; B. A. Nardi, et.al, 2009; M. Klumpp, et.al, 2019; Zhang, X. L., et.al, 2018). HCI is relevant in technical systems and software for a variety of reasons. For continued use, the perception and relationship between a human brain and a certain piece of software must be perfect and as clear as possible. Anything else won't be visible. This is a lively subject that emphasises the development of AI and HCI (M. Jeon, 2017; M. N. Posard, 2014; B. Dickson, 2017, T. Winograd, 2006; Zhou,J.& Chen, F.(2018) in addition to corporate digitization in general. AI has begun to make significant progress in a number of social concerns and has already helped with topics including agriculture and poverty, education, the environment, and health care. Simultaneously, AI has begun to expand its capacity to make crucial decisions in business, law, finance, and politics to support underprivileged communities in more effectively accessing and forecasting their health and welfare, diagnosing at-risk individuals more quickly and providing early intervention, and frequently finding

Figure 2. The Framework for Human-Cantered AI (HCAI) with Certain Design Objectives (Source: Xu, Dainoff, Ge, & Gao, 2022)

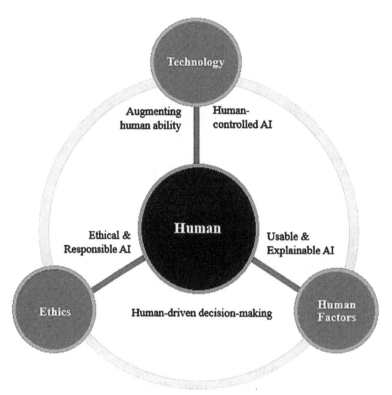

targeted solutions.

This study aims to demonstrate the connection between artificial intelligence and the interaction between humans and computers. The study will be carried out using a survey technique, and users of artificial intelligence will make up the sample. The employment of a machine between people and computers as a semiotic mechanism can be described in a descriptive manner while allowing for a great deal of generating capacity. The semiotic perspective can lead to a number of projects at the interface of AI and HCI (M. N. O. Sadiku, 2018; J. Chakraborty et.al, 2015; W. B. Rouse, 1977), both more theoretically and using current techniques. They can also take the shape of user-centered and evaluation-based tests on AI, model recognition, and data science-based systems, which are appropriate for both interaction design and processes.

LITERATURE SURVEY

This section is to provide an overview on the current state of the art research work of Human-Computer Interaction with AI. The aim includes the basic definitions and terminology, a survey of existing technologies and recent advances in the field, common architectures used in the design of HCI systems which includes unimodal and multimodal configurations, and finally the applications of HCI. This chapter will also offers a comprehensive number of references for each concept and methods.

The expression of the human face is one of the major research challenges. The major challenge is detection and reorganization of emotional states and improving computer to human communication. (Valstar, et.al, 2007) propose a hybrid technique where a Support Vector Machine (SVM) is used to segment the facial movements into temporal units. Then a Hidden Markov Model is used for classifying temporal actions. Using a particle system approach (Chang et.al, 2007) propose a framework, for using multiple cameras in pose and gaze estimation.

Another major research challenge is human body analysis. The following research has the potential to endow computers to see where humans are, what their gestures and motions are, and track them over time. (Oerlemans, et.al. 2007) propose a tracking system which uses the multidimensional maximum likelihood approach toward detecting and identifying moving objects in video. Their system has the additional novel aspect of allowing the user to interactively give feedback as to whether segmented objects are part of the background or foreground. The problem of large lexicon sign language understanding is explained by (Cooper, et.al, 2007) The method detects patterns of movement in two stages such that viseme classifiers and Markov chains. (Angelopoulou, et. al, 2007) are able to model and track nonrigid objects using a growing neural gas network. (Jung, et.al, 2007) uses a multi-cue method to recognize human gestures using AdaBoost and Fisher discriminant analysis. (Chu, et.al, 2007) finds 3D model of the human body from silhouettes using a particle filtering approach and infra-red cameras.

Apart from face and human body analysis, current research involving systems which are related to the complete human-computer interaction, thereby endowing computers with new important functionality. (State, et.al, 2007) had created a system where a virtual human can maintain exact eye contact with the human user, this can significantly improving the perception of immersion. An automatic kinematic model building method proposed by (Rajko, et.al, 2007) for optical motion capture using a Markov random field framework. (Vural, et.al, 2007) created a system for detecting driver drowsiness based on facial action units and classified using AdaBoost and multinomial ridge regression. (Thomee, et.al, 2007) used an artificial imagination approach to allow the computer to create example images to improve relevance feedback in image retrieval. (Barreto, et.al, 2007) use physiological responses and pupil dilation to recognize stress using an SVM.

In the area of interfaces, researchers are actively developing new systems. (Hua, et.al, 2007) presented a system for mobile devices for a visual motion perceptual interface. A tabletop interface using camera detected finger interactions was proposed by (Song, et.al, 2007). Interaction with a wall sized display was presented by (Stødle, et.al, 2007), whereby the user could interact with the system using arm and hand movements.

CURRENT RESEARCH WORK ON HCI WITH AI

In Human-Computer Intelligent Interaction, the three major domains of research are in the areas of face analysis, body analysis, and complete systems which integrate multiple modalities to give intuitive interaction to computers. Face and human body analysis includes modelling the face or body and tracking the motion and location. They are considered fundamental enabling technologies towards HCI.

(A. Dix, 2017) has proposed a study to examine current obstacles and the required architecture for isolation for cloud-based digital computer production. The three major broad fundamentals of HCI (human-computer interaction), like those of every professional area, are hypothetical concepts, a people community, and computers. Some common usability mistakes would be chosen for user testing or conventional usability principles because apple prioritises surface aesthetics above core usability. Despite the fact that apple is a clear target when it comes to poor usability. They also develop collectively in the areas of physical community automation or robotics and humanoid-robotic or automaton interaction. Carriages on Google Robotics or a self-sufficient arsenal Plans for social automaton or robotics for autonomous or self-directed simulated informal actors are advised.

(O. A. et.al, 2019) have dine a research on the impact of artificial intelligence (AI) and nanotechnology on humanoid computer collaboration examines the extent to which AI and nanotechnology develop the relationships between human and CPU machine or computers that are associated through proper coordination. Artificial intelligence (AI) and nanotechnology on Humanoid CPU Collaboration evaluates several significant advancements in how people interact with their processors, from the development of intellectual interfaces to the direct connection of the mind to computers. This study provides in-depth information on the development of collaborative humanoid computers and the myriad application domains that AI connects. Supercomputer science and other related fields, like as psychology and the humanities, are all represented in the multidisciplinary field of humanoid processor collaboration.

(Kim, et.al, 2019) have studied to determine the characteristics of an AI's connection sort and gender on a hominid's response to an artificial intelligence, such as buddy vs. servant and male vs. female relationships, artificial intelligence learning used a 2 into 2 among-subjects plans. Results show that the type of behaviour or relationship has a significant impact on warmth and enjoyment but not on capability. AI showed no gender differences in warmth, enjoyment, or capacity. The findings of this study suggest that anthropomorphism plays a crucial role in the relationship between AI and humanoids. After talking to the operating CPUs, participants judged a male-voiced processor as being more informed about expertise and CPU topics, whereas a female-voiced processor was viewed as being extremely informative on matters of hate or love and relationships.

(Pargman, et.al, 2019) have done one research work on the polyvocal negotiation in their study, as indicated, includes not only the vocal sounds of the researchers and doctors who attended the workshop, but also the vocal sounds of the scientists who will be working today in 2068. the voices of the beings, intelligent agents, and communities that are the targets, recipients, witnesses, and beneficiaries of advanced computer systems. We highlight the applications to an ineffable human nature where there is a naturally occurring consideration of sense (we may recognise a sensible person or a sensible activity), but where deriving the components of such sense is more difficult. While this sense can be mentioned, described, or carried to memory of their whole works, it may inevitably also be a sense that is equally difficult to describe as the sense. Understanding the relationship between people and developing technology specifically involves the interface between people and computers in all of its forms. The field of problem-solving known as human computer interaction is known for keeping a real and strong focus on constructive problems. The basis of human computer interaction is how predetermined solutions handle problems generated by diverse computer methods, interactions, and frameworks.

(Yun, Y., et.al, 2021) have proposed that in contemporary intellectual organisations like brain machine addition, humanoid action appreciation, somatosensory and telemedicine games, human computer interface continues to play a significant role. A decision provision system combines an information system with decision execution technology. A crucial technique in the system for providing decisions is the implementation of decisions using graphic humanoid computer interaction. Information mining gives a practical and doable solution for the project of the decision support system. DSS built on information mining may successfully anticipate and assess enterprise options. In this study, a graphic decision-execution system was calculated. Additionally, a thorough test demonstrated the viability of our proposed method. In order to rationalise, digitise, and programme the logic decision programme into the processor, the decision providing system relied on computer expertise. The intelligent decision-execution system encourages the production of both partially ordered and disorganised decisions. In a similar vein, we look at the fundamental structure of the decision-making mechanism. In addition, a system with a humanoid computer interface is created to provide feedback for changing the judgement.

(T. Yıldız, 2019) has done a study that how people acquire emotional indirect coordination with objects or materials, whereas direct emotional coordination develops with people. In the referential triangle created with the devices by the humanoid, artificial intelligence can be both a device and a companion at the same time. This essay argues that the social psychology research agenda should include this problematic assertion. Effective artificial intelligence (AI), which is developing as a fundamental tool, seems to have the potential to be a friend in the interim. What would happen if artificial intelligence improved our technology for abstraction? Will we respond to public signals from artificial intelligence (AI) as complexly as we already respond to community signals from people nearby? The current condition of learning that is focused on social cooperation is briefly discussed first in this agenda. After that, it is explained historically how human development and culture relate. This study attempted to explain the process predicted by this theory from ontogenetic and evolutionary viewpoints within the context of cultural learning. The referential triangle theory was offered as a significance of this argument.

(Gurcan, et.al, 2021) has done a research work by extending the revealed issues beyond a Polaroid, the subjects were studied in light of their changing points, capacities, and accelerations in order to provide a panoramic view that illustrates the escalation and contraction of trends through time. This framework illustrates how training in human computer interaction has progressed from apparatus concerned with schemes to person-cantered systems, showing its potential for developing into framework-aware adaptive organisations in the future. By looking at studies on human computer interaction conducted over the past 60 years, this learning provides a thorough understanding of dynamic organised systems. By providing a thorough understanding of the history of human-computer interaction and informing the field's future in exploring potential inquiry and application avenues in this busy field, the outcomes of this learning are expected to lead the way. Studies in the field of human computer interaction, both real and imagined, aim to produce communication and information technology for people and their needs. In 1976, NATO sponsored a workshop on human computer interaction and discussed the perception of user friendliness. By highlighting current issues, difficulties, and potential research openings, the analysis gives scientists a better understanding of the area. This study aims to investigate the research trends that have emerged over the past 60 years in the trainings for human computer interaction.

HUMAN-COMPUTER INTERACTION

The field of study known as HCI (human-computer interaction) examines how users interact with computers and the extent to which they have been designed to work well with people. HCI is now a topic of study (D. Aksu, et.al, 2017; G. Fisher. 1989; V. S. Moustakis, et.al, 1997; M. N. O. Sadiku, et.al, 2018; Y. Rogers, et.al, 2011) for a sizable number of big businesses and academic organisations. The ease of use of computers has not historically received much consideration from computer system developers, with a few notable exceptions. Many modern computer users contend that the "user-friendliness" of their products is still not sufficiently considered by computer manufacturers. The demand for the services that

Figure 3. Related Research Fields of HCI.

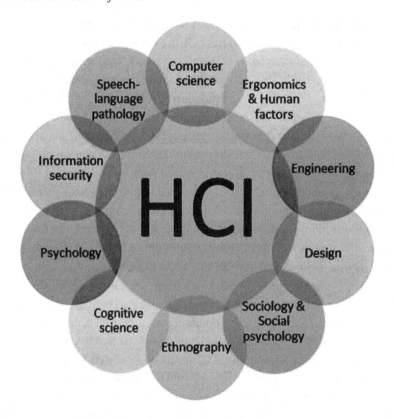

computers can provide has always outpaced the desire for ease of use, according to computer system developers, who contend that computers are extraordinarily complex things to design and manufacture. Diverse user conceptions or mental models about their interactions, as well as different methods of acquiring and retaining knowledge and skills, are significant HCI factors (D. A. Norman, et.al, 1986; A. Sears, et.al, 2007; J. Urquiza, et.al, 2017; Z. Obrenovic, et.al, 2004), for example, "left-brained" and "right-brained" people). Other factors include cultural and national variances.

The rapid evolution of user interface technology, which opens up new opportunities for interaction for which earlier research findings might not be applicable, is another factor to take into account while researching or developing HCI. User preferences also alter as they gradually learn new interfaces. The goal of HCI as a discipline is to establish a "natural" discourse between the user and the computer. In this type of dialogue, the user doesn't have to exert a lot of cognitive effort to interact with the machine (A. Newell, et.al, 1985; L. Guzman, et.al, 2020; Y. Yun, et.al, 2021). When we work hard to create a good human computer interface, we enable our users to use computers to address their issues. On the other side, poor user interfaces are nearly often the result of disregarding human computer interaction. Poor HCI results in poor usability, which raises the likelihood that a product will fail.

COMPONENTS OF HCI

The User

The term "user" can refer to a single person or a team of users. HCI examines (Y. K. Meena et.al, (2018); D. Bachmann et.al, 2018) their actions, interactions with technology, and wants and objectives. Their

Figure 4. Components of HCI.

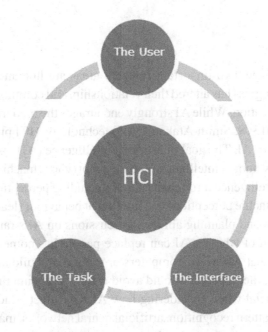

abilities and cognitive processes, as well as their personality, experience, motivation, and emotions, are important considerations. The finest user experience must be produced in the current, fiercely competitive market (B. K. Chadktaborty, et.al, 2017; A. Dix, et.al, 2004). It should come as no surprise that user-centered design—a method in which designers concentrate on users and their requirements at every stage of the design process—is crucial. Users are always involved in the design process from the very beginning for product teams that practise user centric design, and important design choices are assessed based on how well they serve users. Additionally, product teams strive to strike a balance between user and business demands.

The Task

The majority of the times, users who interact with computers have a task in mind that they want to complete. Simply said, a digital product is a tool that enables users to successfully complete this activity. For instance, adding an item to the shopping cart and making a purchase could both be tasks in an e-commerce context. One should consider the following things while considering goal-driven experience: How difficult or simple a task is for the user to complete, the knowledge necessary to interact with a product and the length of time needed to execute the procedure.

The Interface

It's crucial for designers to concentrate on establishing an appropriate hierarchy in design while building graphical user interfaces. The proper hierarchy facilitates user navigation and content consumption. The medium, the device, or the interfaces are essential elements of human-computer interaction. For instance, when users access your website from mobile devices, you might want to present only the most important details and resize the text to make it simpler to read on small screens for comfortable engagement.

AI AND HCI

In the intelligent information age, two important research areas are human-computer interaction and artificial intelligence. Their progress has altered their relationship, and common uses based on their close integration are also seen in education. While AI strongly encourages the modernization and advancement of HCI (A. Zahirovic, et.al, 2013; S. Smith-Atakan, 2006) technology, HCI provides research proposals and application requirements for AI. The goal of artificial intelligence (AI) research and development is to replicate, enhance, and grow human intelligence. To the point where machines can "think and act like people," it simulates human intelligence through machines, including perception abilities (visual perception, auditory perception, and tactile perception) and intelligent behaviour (learning ability, memory and thinking ability, and reasoning and planning ability). Discussions on AI's rapid progress have become very contentious. The question of whether AI can replace people has come to the forefront. The singularity concept which holds that AI-driven computers or robots can build and upgrade themselves or design more advanced AI than them. People should avoid either overestimating or underestimating AI. Maintaining objectivity is crucial when considering how AI will affect education. Intelligent control, natural language processing, pattern recognition, artificial neural networks, machine learning, intelligent robots, and other areas are among the primary AI study areas.

VARIOUS SECTORS OF HCI WITH AI

In the recent technological evolution, the future where technology is omnipresent, machines predict and anticipate human needs, robotic systems are an integral part of everyday life, and humans' abilities are technologically supported. Home, work, and public environments are anticipated to be smart, anticipating and adapting to the needs of their inhabitants and visitors, empowered with Artificial Intelligence (AI) and employing BigData towards training and perfecting their reasoning. Interactions in such environments will be not only conscious and intentional, but also subconscious and even unintentional. Users' location, postures, emotions, habits, intentions, culture and thoughts can all constitute candidate input commands to a variety of visible and invisible technological artefacts embedded in the environment. Robotics and autonomous agents will be typically embedded in such technologically enriched environments. Information will be communicated from one interaction counterpart to another 'naturally', while the digital world will coexist with and augment physical reality, resulting in hybrid worlds.

In this section, the sectors of each HCI are identified and challenges are also analyzed in terms of concepts and problem definition, main issues to identify the various state of the art sectors of HCI involved, as well as the associated emerging requirements, with the ultimate goal of offering to the HCI thought and inspiration towards identifying and addressing compelling topics for investigation and lines of research.

RESEARCH AREAS OF HCI USING ARTIFICIAL INTELLIGENCE

As interactive technologies pervade every life domain, HCI research is challenged to move beyond lab studies and expand to new fields and contexts, carrying out research "in the wild" (Crabtree, A., 2013). Research in public spaces, in particular, faces the dilemma of following typical procedures to inform participants and acquire their consent vs. studying the actual user experience and behavior, which can be influenced if participants are aware that they are being observed (Williamson, J. R., et.al, 2016; Fiesler, C., et.al, 2018). Similar ethical concerns about engaging participants in studies revolve around museums or research at the intersection of art and technology, where the distinction between research participants and event audience is not clear (Waycott, J., et.al, 2016).

Another point of caution for HCI research refers to involving vulnerable user populations, such as older adults, people with disabilities, immigrants, socially isolated individuals, patients, children, etc. Besides issues regarding participants' understanding of the study and giving their consent, there are

Figure 5. Some Research Areas of HCI using Artificial Intelligence.

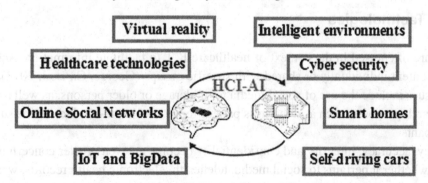

also concerns related to managing participants' misunderstandings, handling potentially erroneous and optimistic expectations about technology, and attending to problems that may occur when the technology does not perform as expected (Frauenberger, C., et.al, 2017).

The recent technological evolution has raised new issues related to the usage of online data in HCI research, such as the usage of data without subjects' consent. In this case, a fundamental question is if researchers are entitled to using data without consent, especially in cases that data are publicly available (Vitak, J., et.al, 2016; Kizza, J. M., 2017). Other open questions refer to what constitutes public data and what are the best practices for acquiring informed consent. Participant anonymity is also a challenging undertaking.

Online Social Networks (OSNs)

Privacy in OSNs is a major point of concern, and indicative of the discussion on privacy in all technological domains. Privacy can be defined as "a human value consisting of a set of rights including solitude, the right to be alone without disturbances; anonymity, the right to have no public personal identity; intimacy, the right not to be monitored; and reserve, the right to control one's personal information, including the dissemination methods of that information" (Beye, M., et.al, 2012).

Privacy concerns in OSNs include who can view one's private information, the ability to hide information from a specific individual or group, the degree to which other users can post and share information about an individual, data retention issues, the ability of the employees of the OSN to browse private information, selling of data, and targeted marketing (Kokolakis, S., 2017). Interestingly though, despite their privacy concerns, individuals reveal personal information for relatively small rewards, a phenomenon which is referred as the "privacy paradox".

Kokolakis (Brandtzæg, P. B., et.al, 2010) identifies a number of potential factors for this paradox, including that the use of OSNs has become a habit and is integrated into daily life, that the perceived benefits of participation outweigh observed risks, that individuals do not make information-sharing decisions as entirely free agents, and that privacy decisions are affected by cognitive biases and heuristics, as well as by bounded rationality and incomplete information. Privacy in OSNs becomes even more crucial when these are used by sensitive user groups for specialized purposes. Privacy and content sharing (and therefore sociability) constitute two conflicting fundamental features of OSNs, which however need to be perfectly joined, a challenge that designers of OSNs have to master (Denecke, K., 2015).

Healthcare Technologies

Social media are often used in the context of healthcare ICT to facilitate information exchange and to create media content individually or shared with specific groups (George, C., et.al, 2013). In this context, ethical issues include the use of social media for underage or older persons, as well as using social media for research purposes, such as to harness patient-reported data, to conduct online surveys, and to recruit participants.

Data privacy, accuracy, integrity and confidentiality become an even greater concern in the context of healthcare, whether it pertains to social media, telehealth, electronic health records, wearable health sensors, or any other eHealth domain (Fleming, D., 2009]. Additional ethical principles that should be addressed in the eHealth context include access for all to eHealth, anonymity, autonomy, beneficence and non-maleficence, dignity, no discrimination, free and fully informed consent, justice, safety, and value-sensitive design. Telehealth ethical concerns also extend to the impact that distant care may have on the healing relationship that is typically developed between patients and health providers, the loss of touch, and the danger that virtual visits may replace actual doctor visits in the name of cost/time effectiveness

(Kluge, E. H. W., 2011). With regard to patients' data, concerns pertain to the question of legitimacy of purpose, and the potential for data exploitation. Furthermore, an often neglected yet critical issue is that of liability, as patients become active participants in the delivery of healthcare, raising the issues of potential mistakes, misreports, or misinterpretations (Kizza, J. M., 2017).

Another aspect contained in all of the above technologies is the prevalence of persuasion techniques to change people's behaviour. While some objectives for the purposes of health (quitting smoking, weight maintenance, nutrition habits, exercise routines, etc.) are usually valuable and desirable, persuasive technologies could, in the wrong circumstances, be used to delude people or to persuade them to engage in undesirable behaviour. Mobile products (Marcus, 2015b) and social media are especially vulnerable to these distortions and need to be assessed as technologies develop and mature.

Virtual Reality

VR is a technological domain, in which – due to the illusion it creates – two major social and ethical themes are raised: (i) reactions and feelings of the user, such as over-attachment to virtual agents, or feeling out of control and behaving with hostility in the virtual environment and outside in the physical world, as well as (ii) the intentions of the VR environment creator, which may be obscure and dangerous for the user, e.g. by collecting information or inducing mental/psychological transformations without the user's knowledge (Mori, M., et.al, 2012). VR allows the user to step in a "reality", which can be entirely synthetic and a created digital environment, or it could be a suspended moment of an actual real-world environment. The synthetic environment could be modelled after the real world, a fantasy, or both. Most virtual realities do not fully cross over the uncanny valley (Ziegeldorf, J. H., et.al, 2014), but this is an issue that is expected to improve in the future.

A recent tangible example of attachment to virtual characters is the marriage of a man with a virtual character, which was asserted by the company producing the holograms with a marriage certificate, opening a wide discussion regarding the indisputable freedom of the individual, the role of technology in affecting free will, and the ethical dilemmas/responsibilities of technology creators and designers. Even more crucial than over-attachment to virtual agents is the concern of how social interactions may be reshaped in a VR context, leading for example individuals to opt out of societal engagements (which can have far-reaching implications on fertility rates, the economy, and existing social fabrics), or providing the option to virtually extend one's life beyond physical death.

IoT and BigData

The IoT paradigm is characterized by heterogeneous technologies, including smart objects that are interconnected and cooperate over the Internet infrastructure, enabling many new services and making buildings, cities, and transport smarter (Streitz, N., 2018). In this highly interconnected and heterogeneous environment, where any interactions may occur between humans, devices, and autonomous agents, new privacy and security threats are manifested. In particular, privacy will become even more important in the smart hybrid cities to come (Alterman, A., 2003). In the virtual world, people can use fake identities. This will be difficult or even impossible in the real world. Data existing about people in the virtual world are now complemented by and combined with real world data and vice versa. Public and private Closed Circuit Television (CCTV) cameras are taking pictures of people entering a shop or a restaurant with known locations, while face recognition identifies personal identities. Real objects that people are wearing, carrying, using, buying will be recognized by sensors in the environment because these objects are tagged. Increased instrumentation of vehicles in the context of autonomous driving affects privacy. Personal walking behaviour is transparent when carrying a Smartphone. Thus, it will become more and more difficult to avoid object and person tracking, and, the challenge of preserving privacy in the real/ hybrid world will be immense in IoT enabled environments.

BigData goes hand in hand with IoT, both being recent technological evolutions that will definitely constitute core components of future technologically augmented environments. BigData, due to the harvesting of large sets of personal data coupled with the use of state of the art analytics, outlines additional threats to privacy, such as automated decision making (when decisions about an individual's life are handed to automated processes), which raises concerns regarding discrimination, self-determination, and the narrowing of choices. For example, predictive analytics may hinder implications for individuals prone to illness, crime, or other socially unacceptable characteristics or behaviours. Other obscure possibilities are individuals (mistakenly) being denied opportunities based on the actions of others, the reinforcement of existing inequalities for vulnerable user groups (e.g. low-income consumers), as well as malevolent attempts and misleading offers to vulnerable individuals, such as seniors with Alzheimer or individuals with addictions. Responsible and fair data management and analysis is required from researchers to avoid inducing bias and discrimination.

Intelligent Environments

It is evident that ethics, privacy, and trust are topics that span all technological domains, for instance, biometrics in general pose the same threats to data privacy as any other user data (e.g. unwarranted identification and threats to the individual, undesired collection of personal data, and unauthorized access to personal information), however they also impose an additional moral dilemma because bio centric data has an impact on one's right to control the use and disposition of one's body (Boddington, P., 2017).

Likewise, intelligent environments invoke the same ethical concerns with other developing technologies, especially with those technologies that raise questions about how humans understand us and our place in the world (Anderson, S. L., 2008).In general, intelligent systems entail a number of risks, including users' identification based on collected data, permanence of personal/sensitive data, profiling and implicit deduction and attribution of new properties to individuals, use of data for monitoring, misinterpretation of data, public disclosure of confidential information, as well as collection of data and applying persuasion techniques without the user's awareness. Despite the potential of the system to acquire and retain large amounts of (personal) data, this collection should be limited.

When it comes to AI and autonomous agents, a fundamental ethical concern is that of responsibility: where does responsibility lie, what are the moral, societal and legal consequences of actions and decisions made by an AI system, and can an AI system be held accountable for its actions Ethical decision making in AI is a multi-disciplinary field of research that is called to provide answers to such dilemmas and safeguard our future. Moral decision-making by humans involves utilitarian considerations and moral rules, which often involve sacred values that may be acquired from past example cases and may also be culturally sensitive. As AI systems are constructed by humans, an approach is to integrate societal, legal and moral values into all the development stages of AI systems, so that AI reasoning takes into account these values, weighs their priorities when it comes to different stakeholders in various multicultural contexts, explains its reasoning and guarantees transparency. Asimov's three laws of robotics are often considered an ideal set of rules for machine ethics; however, there are arguments that show these laws may not be adequate (Dellot, B., 2017). An alternative approach advocates for shifting the burden of moral reasoning to autonomous agents, and enabling agents to behave ethically and to judge the ethics of other agents. Man-Machine Rules can help organize dialog around questions, such as: how to secure personal data, how ethical are chips embedded in people and in their belongings, what degrees and controls need to be taken into account for personal freedoms and risks, and whether consumer rights and government organizations will audit algorithms (Alaieri, F., et.al, 2016).

As autonomous intelligent agents will make increasingly complex and important ethical decisions, humans will need to know that their decisions are trustworthy and ethically justified (Weld, S. D., et.al, 2019). Therefore, transparency is a requirement, so that humans can understand, predict, and appropriately trust AI, whether it is manifested as traceability, verifiability, non-deception, or intelligibility. Intelligible AI, in particular, will further help humans identify AI mistakes and will also facilitate meaningful human control (Chen, J. Y. C., 2018). Nevertheless, depending on how the explanations are used, a balance needs to be achieved in the level of details, because full transparency may be too overwhelming in certain cases, while not enough transparency may jeopardize human trust in AI (Moallem, A., 2018).

Cyber Security

The issues discussed above mainly revolve around ethics and privacy, highlighting challenges and potential threats. Privacy, however, is coupled with cyber security, an issue that has become prominent for two main reasons. First, the transformation of our societies, through the expansion of digital technologies, offers more opportunities for cyber-criminal activity (Tragos, E. Z., et.al, 2018). It is not only public organizations and institutions, but also residential units that are now highly digitized (e.g. including surveillance cameras, IoT-connected home appliances and medical devices, home control and automation systems, etc.). It can be said that every aspect of human activity is managed, recorded, and tracked in the digital realm, even "in person" meetings. Second, cyber-attacks require few expenses; they are geographically unconstrained and involve less risk to the perpetrator than physical attacks.

Security is a challenging task, especially since the high number of interconnected devices raises scalability issues, making traditional security countermeasures inapplicable. In addition, as most of the current commercial IoT devices have limited on-board security features, they can constitute an easy target for hacking, blocking, altering their communication, changing their configuration, or sending them false commands (G. Riva, et.al, 2005). Overall, the main security threats involve data breach and privacy, as well as attacks against the devices or the software of both devices and servers.

Data anonymity and confidentiality are threatened by the connectedness of everyday things, which opens up possibilities for identification of devices through fingerprinting and the possibility to create huge databases with identification data (e.g. speech). At the same time, devices may manage sensitive information (e.g. user habits or health data), which entails privacy threats in the case of inventory attacks (by non-legitimate parties), as well as in lifecycle transitions of the devices. Additional privacy threats in the IoT context include: the possibility for advanced profiling through inferences by correlations with other profiles and data, exposure of private information through a public medium, as well as linking different systems such that the combination of data sources reveals (truthful or not) information that the individual had not provided and may not wish to reveal. Threats may also occur by malicious attacks against the sensors and activators of intelligent environments. For instance, attackers may steal information regarding the health status of a user who is being monitored and eventually identify when the user is at home or absent (M.T. Maybury, et.al, 1998). By attacking actuators, it may also be possible to control or tamper with house elements (e.g. doors and windows, air-conditioning, alarms, etc.), which not only causes physical security threats, but also decreases the reliability of the system and therefore the trust that users put in it.

The technological systems need to behave so that they are beneficial to people beyond simply reaching functional goals or addressing technical problems, by serving human rights and the values of their users, whether our ethical practices are Western, Eastern, Confucian, African or from a different tradition. The main concerns in this respect refer to privacy and the challenges it raises in the context of the new digital realm, to ethical issues as they appear in the various domains, and to cyber security.

Smart Homes

There is a direct connection between artificial intelligence and smart homes. After all, the goal of this product is to give users a more convenient and comfortable lifestyle. Smart homes (A. Kirlik 2006) include interactive techniques including language communication, computer vision, and gesture recognition, which make the human-computer interaction more difficult.

Modern intelligent homes exhibit prominent artificial intelligence traits that reflect linguistic interaction. Voice interaction, which is more natural, is gradually replacing the conventional mouse and touch screen actions. Data mining and the linking of content and services are where voice interaction will find its future worth.

New business models will emerge in the Internet of Things age using speech as its entry point. The functions for emotion recognition and gesture recognition must also be developed if you want to increase the overall intelligence of your house.

The smart home is currently in a phase of transition from mobile phone control to several controls combined. The primary way to control intelligent homes is still through a mobile app, but as AI technology advances, other ways to operate intelligent homes will emerge.

Self-Driving Cars

Particularly in the public press and in non-scientific debate, automated vehicles (Kopytko, V., et.al, 2018) are occasionally perceived as completely replacing a human driver. Although automated vehicles have seen some progress, no systems are yet capable of doing this. Instead, we contend that interactions between humans and automated systems in the context of automobiles should be seen as a partnership between the two. In other words, instead of a binary choice between the human and the system, the human actively participates in specific driving-related duties when appropriate.

Human-machine interaction has been a critical aspect of driving research for decades. After all, safe manual control of a vehicle requires well-designed interactions with the car, and with any devices that are built into or brought into the car. Interestingly, with the advent of automated driving, human-computer interaction (HCI) and, more broadly, the role of the human in the vehicle, remains an important aspect of vehicle design.

Similar to humans, automated systems and the environments in which they operate are also dynamic. First, as an instantiation of artificial intelligence, automated systems often learn from their environment, which can shape and change their responses over time? Second, automated systems are typically developed for use in specific contexts. In the case of automated vehicles, the Society of Automotive Engineers (SAE) has identified specific levels of automation for the functionality of the car, which can be used in specific "operational design domains," or contexts. However, the context in which a car is driving can change over time and space, and thereby the system's functioning and reliability can change over time and space. For example, adaptive cruise control might maintain the speed of a vehicle and a safe distance to cars in front of it on regular highways, under normal traffic and weather conditions. Yet what is safe might change with context: If there is suddenly heavy snowfall, the system might fail to act appropriately, and responsibilities that the car had (e.g., maintaining a safe distance to the car in front of it) might suddenly be transferred to the human.

RECENT ADVANCES IN HCI

The recent research advances in HCI, mainly intelligent and adaptive interfaces and ubiquitous computing. These interfaces involve different levels of user activity: physical, cognitive, and affection.

Intelligent and Adaptive HCI

Although the devices used by majority of public are still some kind of plain command/action setups using not very sophisticated physical apparatus, the flow of research is directed to design of intelligent and adaptive interfaces. The exact theoretical definition of the concept of intelligence or being smart is not known or at least not publicly agreeable. However, one can define these concepts by the apparent growth and improvement in functionality and usability of new devices in market.

Economically and technologically, it is very important that, to make HCI designs that provide easier, more pleasurable and satisfying experience for the users. To realize this goal, the interfaces are getting more natural to use every day. Evolution of interfaces in note-taking tools is a good example. First there were typewriters, then keyboards and now touch screen tablet PCs that we can write on using our own handwriting and they recognize it change it to text (Janssen, C.P., et.al, 2019) and if not already made, tools that transcript whatever we say automatically, so we do not need to write at all.

One important factor in new generation of interfaces is to differentiate between using intelligence (S.L. Oviatt, et.al, 2000; D.M. Gavrila 1999; L.E. Sibert, et.al, 2000) in the making of the interface (Intelligent HCI) or in the way that the interface interacts with users (Adaptive HCI). Intelligent HCI designs are interfaces that incorporate at least some kind of intelligence in perception from and/or response to users. A few examples are speech enabled interfaces (M. N. O. Sadiku, et.al, 2018) that use natural language to interact with user and devices that visually track user's movements or gaze and respond accordingly.

Adaptive HCI designs, on the other hand, may not use intelligence in the creation of interface but use it in the way they continue to interact with the users. An adaptive HCI might be a website using regular GUI for selling various products. This website would be adaptive -to some extent- if it has the ability to recognize the user and keeps a memory of his searches and purchases and intelligently search, find, and suggest products on sale that it thinks user might need. Most of these kinds of adaptation are the ones that deal with cognitive and affective levels of user activity.

Another example that uses both intelligent and adaptive interface is a PDA or a tablet PC that has the handwriting recognition ability and it can adapt to the handwriting of the logged in user so to improve its performance by remembering the corrections that the user made to the recognised text.

Finally, another factor to be considered about intelligent interfaces is that most non-intelligent HCI design are passive in nature i.e. they only respond whenever invoked by user while ultimate intelligent and adaptive interfaces tend to be active interfaces. The example is smart billboards or advertisements that present themselves according to users' taste.

Ubiquitous Computing and Ambient Intelligence

The latest research in HCI field is unmistakably ubiquitous computing (Ubicomp). The term which often used interchangeably by ambient intelligence and pervasive computing, refers to the ultimate methods of human-computer interaction that is the deletion of a desktop and embedding of the computer in the environment so that it becomes invisible to humans while surrounding them everywhere hence the term ambient.

The idea of ubiquitous computing was first introduced by Mark Weiser during his tenure as chief technologist at Computer Science Lab in Xerox PARC in 1998. His idea was to embed computers everywhere in the environment and everyday objects so that people could interact with many computers at the same time while they are invisible to them and wirelessly communicating with each other.

Ubicomp has also been named the Third Wave of computing. The First Wave was the mainframe era, many people one computer. Then it was the Second Wave, one person one computer which was called PC era and now Ubicomp introduces many computers one person era.

CONCLUSION

People are able to utilise the computing capacity of contemporary digital gadgets to their fullest potential thanks to well-designed user interfaces. HCI gives designers the ability to clearly communicate with machines. Consumers interact with other personas rather than intricate systems in these types of dialogues. The foundations of HCI must therefore receive special consideration when it comes to developing technologies.

The usability of human-computer interfaces is a major focus of HCI research, which aims to enhance human-computer interaction. It is a new field that has shown significant success. Stronger "marriages" between HCI and AI are now causing researchers to become more apprehensive. It is crucial to comprehend AI systems from a human perspective as they grow more and more commonplace. This will assist the designers in figuring out how to create interactions between people and machines that foster creative collaboration.

REFERENCES

Aksu, D., & Aydın, M. A. (2017). Human computer interaction by eye blinking on real time," *Proceedings of the 9th International Conference on Computational Intelligence and Communication Networks.* (pp. 135-138). 10.1109/CICN.2017.8319372

Alaieri, F., & Vellino, A. (2016). Ethical decision making in robots: Autonomy, trust and responsibility. *Proceedings of the 10th International Conference on Social Robotics (ICSR 2016)* (pp. 159–168). Springer, Cham. 10.1007/978-3-319-47437-3_16

Alterman, A. (2003). "A piece of yourself"': Ethical issues in biometric identification. *Ethics and Information Technology, 5*(3), 139–150. doi:10.1023/B:ETIN.0000006918.22060.1f

Anderson, S. L. (2008). Asimov's "three laws of robotics" and machine metaethics. *AI & Society, 22*(4), 477–493. doi:10.100700146-007-0094-5

Angelopoulou, A., Psarrou, A., Gupta, G., & Garcia Rodríguez, J. (2007). Nonparametric Modelling and Tracking with Active-GNG. In M. Lew, N. Sebe, T. S. Huang, & E. M. Bakker (Eds.), *HCI 2007. LNCS* (Vol. 4796, pp. 98–107). Springer.

D. Bachmann, F. Weichert, G. Rinkenauer (2018). Review of three dimensional human- computer interaction with focus on the leap motion controller. *Sensors,* vol-18(7), pp. 2194.

Barreto, A., Zhai, J., & Adjouadi, M. (2007). Non-intrusive Physiological Monitoring for Automated Stress Detection in Human-Computer Interaction. In M. Lew, N. Sebe, T. S. Huang, & E. M. Bakker (Eds.), *HCI 2007. LNCS* (Vol. 4796, pp. 29–38). Springer. doi:10.1007/978-3-540-75773-3_4

Beye, M., Jeckmans, A. J., Erkin, Z., Hartel, P., Lagendijk, R. L., & Tang, Q. (2012). Privacy in online social networks. In A. Abraham (Ed.), *Computational Social Networks: Security and Privacy* (pp. 87–113). Springer-Verlag., doi:10.1007/978-1-4471-4051-1_4

Boddington, P. (2017). *Towards a Code of Ethics for Artificial Intelligence.* Springer., doi:10.1007/978-3-319-60648-4

Brandtzæg, P. B., Lüders, M., & Skjetne, J. H. (2010). Too many Facebook "friends"? Content sharing and sociability versus the need for privacy in social network sites. *International Journal of Human–Computer Interaction,* vol-26, pp. 11–12, 1006–1030. . doi:10.1080/10447318.2010.516719

Chadktaborty, B. K. (2017). A review of constraints on vision-based gesture recognition for human-computer interaction. *IET Computer Vision, 12,* 3–15.

Chakraborty, J., Norcio, A. F., Van Der Veer, J. J., Andre, C. F., Miller, Z., & Regelsberger, A. (2015). The human–computer interaction of cross-cultural gaming Strategy. *Journal of Educational Technology Systems, 43*(4), 371–388. doi:10.1177/0047239515588163

Chang, C.-C., Wu, C., & Aghajan, H. (2007). Pose and Gaze Estimation in Multi-Camera Networks for Non-Restrictive HCI. In M. Lew, N. Sebe, T. S. Huang, & E. M. Bakker (Eds.), *HCI 2007. LNCS* (Vol. 4796, pp. 128–137). Springer. doi:10.1007/978-3-540-75773-3_14

Chen, J. Y. C., Lakhmani, S. G., Stowers, K., Selkowitz, A. R., Wright, J. L., & Barnes, M. (2018). Situation awareness-based agent transparency and human-autonomy teaming effectiveness. *Theoretical Issues in Ergonomics Science, 19*(3), 259–282. doi:10.1080/1463922X.2017.1315750

Chu, C.-W., & Nevatia, R. (2007). Real Time Body Pose Tracking in an Immersive Training Environment. In M. Lew, N. Sebe, T. S. Huang, & E. M. Bakker (Eds.), *HCI 2007. LNCS* (Vol. 4796, pp. 146–156). Springer. doi:10.1007/978-3-540-75773-3_16

Cooper, H., & Bowden, R. (2007). Large Lexicon Detection of Sign Language. In M. Lew, N. Sebe, T. S. Huang, & E. M. Bakker (Eds.), *HCI 2007. LNCS* (Vol. 4796, pp. 88–97). Springer.

Crabtree, A., Chamberlain, A., Grinter, R.E., Jones, M., Rodden, T., Rogers, Y. (2013). Introduction to the special issue of "The turn to the wild". *ACM Trans. Comput.-Hum. Interact.*, *20*(3), 1–13. . doi:10.1145/2491500.2491501

Cummings, M. L., & Britton, D. (2020). Regulating safety-critical autonomous systems: past, present, and future perspectives. In Living with Robots, 119-140.

Dellot, B. (2017, February 13). A hippocratic oath for AI developers? It may only be a matter of time. Retrieved from: https://www.thersa.org/discover/publications-and-articles/rsa-blogs/2017/02/a-hippocratic-oath-for-ai-developers-it-may-only-be-a-matter-of-time

Denecke, K., Bamidis, P., Bond, C., Gabarron, E., Househ, M., Lau, A. Y. S., & Hansen, M. (2015). Ethical issues of social media usage in healthcare. *Yearbook of Medical Informatics*, *24*(01), 137–147. doi:10.15265/IY-2015-001 PMID:26293861

Dickson, B. (2017). How artificial intelligence is revolutionizing human-computer interaction. Artificial Intelligence. https://thenextweb.com/artificialintelligence/2017/05/10/artificial-intelligencerevolutionizing-human-computer-interaction/

Dix. (2004). *Human-Computer Interaction* (3rd ed.). Pearson Education Limited.

Dix. (2017). Human–computer interaction, foundations and new paradigms. *Journal of Visual Languages & Computing*, *42*, 122-134.

Fiesler, C., Hancock, J., Bruckman, A., Muller, M., Munteanu, C., & Densmore, M. (2018). Research Ethics for HCI: A roundtable discussion. Extended Abstracts of the 2018 CHI Conference on Human Factors in Computing Systems (CHI EA '18) (p. panel05), Montreal QC, Canada. 10.1145/3170427.3186321

Fisher, G. (1989). Human-computer interaction software: Lessons learned challenges ahead. *IEEE Software*, *6*(1), 44–52. doi:10.1109/52.16901

Fleming, D. A., Edison, K. E., & Pak, H. (2009). Telehealth ethics. *Telemedicine Journal and E-Health: the Official Journal of the American Telemedicine Association*, *15*(8), 797–803. doi:10.1089/tmj.2009.0035 PMID:19780693

Frauenberger, C., Bruckman, A. S., Munteanu, C., Densmore, M., & Waycott, J. (2017). Research ethics in HCI: A town hall meeting. Proceedings of the 2017 CHI Conference Extended Abstracts on Human Factors in Computing Systems (CHI EA '17) (pp. 1295–1299). New York, NY, USA, ACM. 10.1145/3027063.3051135

Gavrila. (1999). The visual analysis of human movement: a survey. *Computer Vision and Image Understanding*, *73*(1), 82-98.

George, C., Whitehouse, D., & Duquenoy, P. (2013). Assessing legal, ethical and governance challenges in eHealth. In C. George, D. Whitehouse, & P. Duquenoy (Eds.), eHealth: Legal, Ethical and Governance Challenges (pp. 3–22). Springer. doi:10.1007/978-3-642-22474-4_1

Gurcan, F., Cagiltay, N. E., & Cagiltay, K. (2021). Mapping human-computer interaction research themes and trends from its existence to today: A topic modelling-based review of past 60 years. *International Journal of Human-Computer Interaction, 37*(3), 267–280. doi:10.1080/10447318.2020.1819668

Guzman & Lewis. (2020). Artificial intelligence and communication: A Human–Machine Communication research agenda. *New Media & Society, 22*(1), 70-86.

Hua, G., Yang, T.-Y., & Vasireddy, S. (2007). PEYE: Toward a Visual Motion based Perceptual Interface for Mobile Devices. In M. Lew, N. Sebe, T. S. Huang, & E. M. Bakker (Eds.), *HCI 2007. LNCS* (Vol. 4796, pp. 39–48). Springer. doi:10.1007/978-3-540-75773-3_5

Janssen, C.P., Boyle, L.N., Kun, A.L., Ju, W., and Chuang, L.L (2019). A hidden Markov framework to capture human-machine interaction in automated vehicles. *International Journal of Human—Computer Interaction, 35*(11), 947–955.

Jeon, M. (2017). Emotions and affect in human factors and human-computer interaction: Taxonomy, theories, approaches, and methods. In *Emotions and affect in human factors and human-computer interaction* (pp. 3–26). Academic Press. doi:10.1016/B978-0-12-801851-4.00001-X

Jiang, F., Jiang, Y., Zhi, H., Dong, Y., Li, H., Ma, S., Wang, Y., Dong, Q., Shen, H., & Wang, Y. (2017). Artificial intelligence in healthcare: Past, present and future. *Stroke and Vascular Neurology, 2*(4), 230–243. doi:10.1136vn-2017-000101 PMID:29507784

Jung, S., Guo, Y., Sawhney, H., & Kumar, R. (2007). Multiple Cue Integrated Action Detection. In M. Lew, N. Sebe, T. S. Huang, & E. M. Bakker (Eds.), *HCI 2007. LNCS* (Vol. 4796, pp. 108–117). Springer.

Kim, A., Cho, M., Ahn, J., & Sung, Y. (2019). Effects of gender and relationship type on the response to artificial intelligence. *Cyberpsychology, Behavior, and Social Networking, 22*(4), 249–253. doi:10.1089/cyber.2018.0581 PMID:30864826

Kirlik. (2006). *Adaptive Perspectives on Human-Technology Interaction.* Oxford University Press.

Kizza, J. M. (2017). Ethical and social issues in the information age (6th ed.). Springer. doi:10.1007/978-3-319-70712-9

Kluge, E. H. W. (2011). Ethical and legal challenges for health telematics in a global world: Telehealth and the technological imperative. *International Journal of Medical Informatics, 80*(2), e1–e5. doi:10.1016/j.ijmedinf.2010.10.002 PMID:21067967

Klumpp, M., Hesenius, M., Meyer, O., Ruiner, C., & Gruhn, V. (2019). Production logistics and human-computer interaction—State-of-the-art, challenges and requirements for the future. *International Journal of Advanced Manufacturing Technology, 105*(9), 3691–3709. doi:10.100700170-019-03785-0

Kokolakis, S. (2017). Privacy attitudes and privacy behaviour: A review of current research on the privacy paradox phenomenon. *Computers & Security, 64*, 122–134. doi:10.1016/j.cose.2015.07.002

Kopytko, V. Shevchuk, L. Yankovska, L. Semchuk, Z. Strilchuk, R (2018). Smart home and artificial intelligence as environment for the implementation of new technologies. *Path Sci., 4*, 2007–2012.

Mason, R. O. (2003). Ethical issues in artificial intelligence. Encyclopedia of Information Systems, 2, 239-258.

Maybury, M. T., & Wahlster, W. (1998). *Readings in Intelligent User Interfaces.* Morgan Kaufmann Press.

Meena, Lin, Dutta, & Prasad. (2018). Toward optimization of gaze-controlled human– computer interaction: Application to hindi virtual keyboard for stroke patients. *IEEE Transactions on Neural Systems and Rehabilitation Engineering, 26*(4), 911-922.

Mintz, Y., & Brodie, R. (2019). Introduction to artificial intelligence in medicine. *Minimally Invasive Therapy & Allied Technologies, 28*(2), 73–81. doi:10.1080/13645706.2019.1575882 PMID:30810430

Moallem, A. (Ed.). (2018). *Human-Computer Interaction and cybersecurity handbook.* CRC Press. doi:10.1201/b22142

Mori, M., MacDorman, K. F., & Kageki, N. (2012). The uncanny valley. *IEEE Robotics & Automation Magazine, 19*(2), 98–100. doi:10.1109/MRA.2012.2192811

Moustakis, V. S., & Herrmann, J. (1997). Where do machine learning and human-computer interaction meet? *Applied Artificial Intelligence, 11*(8), 595–609. doi:10.1080/088395197117948

Nardi & Kallinilkos. (2009). Human–computer interaction. In *The International Encyclopaedia of Communication.* John Wiley & Sons.

Newell, A., & Card, S. K. (1985). The prospects for psychological science in human-computer interaction. *Human-Computer Interaction, 1*(3), 209–242. doi:10.120715327051hci0103_1

Norman, D. A., & Draper, S. W. (1986). *New Perspectives on Human-computer Interaction.* CRC Press.

Obrenovic, Z., & Starcevic, D. (2004). Modeling multimodal human-computer interaction. *Computer, 37*(9), 65–72. doi:10.1109/MC.2004.139

Oerlemans, A., & Thomee, B. (2007). Interactive Feedback for Video Tracking Using Hybird Maximum Likelihood Similarity Measure. In M. Lew, N. Sebe, T. S. Huang, & E. M. Bakker (Eds.), *HCI 2007. LNCS* (Vol. 4796, pp. 79–87). Springer.

Okpe, O. A., John, O. A., Agu, E. O., & Obogo, O. A. (2019). The Impacts of Artificial Intelligence and Nanotechnology on Human Computer Interaction. *International Journal of Innovative Science and Research Technology, 4*(11), 803–808.

Oviatt, S. L., Cohen, P., Wu, L., Vergo, J., Duncan, L., Suhm, B., Bers, J., Holzman, T., Winograd, T., Landay, J., Larson, J., & Ferro, D. (2000). Designing the user interface for multimodal speech and pen-based gesture applications: State-of-the-art systems and future research directions. *Human-Computer Interaction, 15*(4), 263–322. doi:10.1207/S15327051HCI1504_1

Pargman, D. S., Eriksson, E., Bates, O., Kirman, B., Comber, R., Hedman, A., & van den Broeck, M. (2019). The future of computing and wisdom: Insights from human–computer interaction. *Future Generation Computer Systems, 113*, 102–434.

Posard, M. N. (2014). Status processes in human computer interactions: Does gender matter? *Computers in Human Behavior, 37*, 189–195. doi:10.1016/j.chb.2014.04.025

Rajko, S., & Qian, G. (2007). Real-time Automatic Kinematic Model Building for Optical Motion Capture Using a Markov Random Field. In M. Lew, N. Sebe, T. S. Huang, & E. M. Bakker (Eds.), *HCI 2007. LNCS* (Vol. 4796, pp. 69–78). Springer. doi:10.1007/978-3-540-75773-3_8

Rames. (2004). Artificial intelligence in medicine. *Annals of the Royal College of Surgeons of England, 86*, 334–338.

Riva, G., Vatalaro, F., Davide, F., & Alaniz, M. (2005). *Ambient Intelligence: The Evolution of Technology, Communication and Cognition towards the Future of HCI*. IOS Press.

Rogers, Y., Sharp, H., & Preece, J. (2011). *Interaction Design: Beyond Human-Computer Inrteraction*. John Wiley & Sons.

Rouse, W. B. (1977). Human-computer interaction in multitask situations. *IEEE Transactions on Systems, Man, and Cybernetics, 9*(5), 384392.

Sadiku, M. N. O. (1989). Artificial intelligence. *IEEE Potentials, 8*(2), 35–39. doi:10.1109/45.31596

Sadiku, M. N. O., Kotteti, C. M. M., & Musa, S. M. (2018). Human-computer interaction: A primer. *International Journal of Trends in Research and Development, 5*(3), 169–171.

Sadiku, M. N. O., Shadare, A. E., & Musa, S. M. (2018). Affective computing. *International Journal of Trend in Research and Development, 5*(6), 144–145.

Sadiku, M. N. O., Zhou, Y., & Musa, S. M. (2018). Natural language processing in healthcare. *International Journal of Advanced Research in Computer Science and Software Engineering, 8*(5), 39–42. doi:10.23956/ijarcsse.v8i5.626

Sadiku, M. N. O., Zhou, Y., & Musa, S. M. (2018). Natural language processing. *International Journal of Advances in Scientific Research and Engineering, 4*(5), 68–70. doi:10.31695/IJASRE.2018.32708 PMID:29500024

Samoili, López Cobo, Gómez, De Prato, Martínez-Plumed, & Delipetrev. (2020). *Defining Artificial Intelligence. Towards an operational definition and taxonomy of artificial intelligence*. Publications Office of the European Union.

Sears & Jacko. (2007). *The Human-Computer Interaction Handbook: Fundamentals, Evolving Technologies and Emerging Applications* (2nd ed.). CRC Press.

Shorten, C. (2018). *Machine learning vs. deep learning*. https://towardsdatascience.com/machinelearning-vs-deep-learning-62137a1c9842

Sibert, L. E., & Jacob, R. J. K. (2000). Evaluation of eye gaze interaction. Conference of Human-Factors in Computing Systems, 281-288.

Smith-Atakan, S. (2006). *Human-Computer Interaction*. Thomson.

Song, P., Winkler, S., & Gilani, S. O. (2007). Vision-based Projected Tabletop Interface for Finger Interactions. In M. Lew, N. Sebe, T. S. Huang, & E. M. Bakker (Eds.), *HCI 2007. LNCS* (Vol. 4796, pp. 49–58). Springer. doi:10.1007/978-3-540-75773-3_6

State, A. (2007). Exact Eye Contact with Virtual Humans. In M. Lew, N. Sebe, T. S. Huang, & E. M. Bakker (Eds.), *HCI 2007. LNCS* (Vol. 4796, pp. 138–145). Springer.

Stødle, D., Bjørndalen, J., & Anshus, O. (2007). A System for Hybrid Vision- and Sound-Based Interaction with Distal and Proximal Targets on Wall-Sized, High-Resolution Tiled Displays. In M. Lew, N. Sebe, T. S. Huang, & E. M. Bakker (Eds.), *HCI 2007. LNCS* (Vol. 4796, pp. 59–68). Springer. doi:10.1007/978-3-540-75773-3_7

Streitz, N. (2018). Beyond 'smart-only' cities: Redefining the 'smart-everything' paradigm. *Journal of Ambient Intelligence and Humanized Computing*, 1–22. doi:10.100712652-018-0824-1

Thomee, B., Huiskes, M. J., Bakker, E., & Lew, M. (2007). An Artificial Imagination for Interactive Search. In M. Lew, N. Sebe, T. S. Huang, & E. M. Bakker (Eds.), *HCI 2007. LNCS* (Vol. 4796, pp. 19–28). Springer.

Tragos, E. Z., Fragkiadakis, A., Kazmi, A., & Serrano, M. (2018). Trusted IoT in ambient assisted living scenarios. In A. Moallem (Ed.), *Human-Computer Interaction and Cybersecurity Handbook* (pp. 191–208). CRC Press. doi:10.1201/b22142-10

Urquiza-Fuentes, J., & Paredes-Velasco, M. (2017). Investigating the effect of realistic projects on students' motivation, the case of human computer interaction course. *Computers in Human Behavior*, *72*, 692–700. doi:10.1016/j.chb.2016.07.020

Valstar, M. F., & Pantic, M. (2007). Combined Support Vector Machines and Hidden Markov Models for Modeling Facial Action Temporal Dynamics. In M. Lew, N. Sebe, T. S. Huang, & E. M. Bakker (Eds.), *HCI 2007. LNCS* (Vol. 4796, pp. 118–127). Springer. doi:10.1007/978-3-540-75773-3_13

Vitak, J., Shilton, K., & Ashktorab, Z. (2016). Beyond the Belmont principles: Ethical challenges, practices, and beliefs in the online data research community. *Proceedings of the 19th ACM Conference on Computer-Supported Cooperative Work & Social Computing (CSCW '16)* (pp. 941–953). ACM. 10.1145/2818048.2820078

Vural, E., Cetin, M., Ercil, A., Littlewort, G., Bartlett, M., & Movellan, J. (2007). Drowsy Driver Detection Through Facial Movement Analysis. In M. Lew, N. Sebe, T. S. Huang, & E. M. Bakker (Eds.), *HCI 2007. LNCS* (Vol. 4796, pp. 6–18). Springer. doi:10.1007/978-3-540-75773-3_2

Waycott, J., Munteanu, C., Davis, H., Thieme, A., Moncur, W., McNaney, R., & Branham, S. (2016). Ethical encounters in human-computer interaction. *Proceedings of the 2016 CHI Conference Extended Abstracts on Human Factors in Computing Systems (CHI EA '16)* (pp. 3387–3394). ACM. 10.1145/2851581.2856498

Weld, S. D., & Bansal, G. (2019). The challenge of crafting intelligible intelligence. *Communications of ACM*. Retrieved from: https://arxiv.org/abs/1803.04263

Wesche, J. S., & Sonderegger, A. (2019). When computers take the lead: The automation of leadership. *Computers in Human Behavior*, *101*, 197-209.

Williamson, J. R., & Sundén, D. (2016). Deep cover HCI: The ethics of covert research. *Interactions*, *23*(3), 45–49. doi:10.1145/2897941

Winograd, T. (2006). Shifting viewpoints: Artificial intelligence and human-computer interaction. *Artificial Intelligence, 170*(18), 1256–1258. doi:10.1016/j.artint.2006.10.011

Xu, W., Dainoff, M. J., Ge, L., & Gao, Z. (2021). From Human-Computer Interaction to Human-AI Interaction: New Challenges and Opportunities for Enabling Human-Centered AI. *ArXiv.* https://doi.org/10.48550/arXiv.2105.05424

Xu, W., Dainoff, M. J., Ge, L., & Gao, Z.(2022). Transitioning to Human Interaction with AI Systems: New Challenges and Opportunities for HCI Professionals to Enable Human-Centered AI, International *Journal of Human–Computer Interaction, 39*(3), 494-518.

Yampolskiy, R.V. (2019). Predicting future AI failures from historic examples. *Foresight, 21*, 138-152.

Yang, F., Huang, Z., Scholtz, J., & Arendt, D. L. (2020). How do visual explanations foster end users' appropriate trust in machine learning? *Proceedings of the 25th ACM International Conference on Intelligent User Interfaces*, 189-201. 10.1145/3377325.3377480

Yang, Q., Steinfeld, A., Rosé, C., & Zimmerman, J. (2020). Re-examining whether, why, and how human-AI interaction is uniquely difficult to design. In *CHI Conference on Human Factors in Computing Systems (CHI '20), April 25–30, 2020, Honolulu, HI, USA*. ACM. 10.1145/3313831.3376301

Yıldız, T. (2019). Human-computer interaction problem in learning: Could the key be hidden somewhere between social interaction and development of tools? *Integrative Psychological & Behavioral Science, 53*(3), 541–557. doi:10.100712124-019-09484-5 PMID:30826986

Yue, W., Dong, S., Wang, Y., Wang, G., Wang, H., & Chen, W. (2004). Study on human-computer interaction framework of pervasive computing. *Chinese Journal of Computers, 27*, 1657-1664.

Yun, Y., Ma, D., & Yang, M. (2021). Human–computer interaction-based Decision Support System with Applications in Data Mining. *Future Generation Computer Systems, 114*, 285–289. doi:10.1016/j.future.2020.07.048

Yun, Ma, & Yang. (2021). Human–computer interaction-based Decision Support System with Applications in Data Mining. *Future Generation Computer Systems, 114*, 285-289.

Zahirovic. (2013). The Encyclopedia of Human Computer Interaction: The Interaction Design Foundation (2nd ed.). Academic Press.

Zhang, X., Khalili, M. M., & Liu, M. (2020). Long-term impacts of fair machine learning. *Ergonomics in Design, 28*, 7-11.

Zhang, X. L., Lyu, F., & Cheng, S. W. (2018). Interaction paradigm in intelligent systems (in Chinese). *Sci Sin Inform, 48*, 406–418. doi:10.1360/N112017-00217

Zhou, J., & Chen, F. (2018). 2D Transparency Space— Bring Domain Users and Machine Learning Experts Together. In Human and Machine Learning: Visible, Explainable, Trustworthy and Transparent. Springer International Publishing.

Ziegeldorf, J. H., Morchon, O. G., & Wehrle, K. (2014). Privacy in the Internet of Things: Threats and challenges. *Security and Communication Networks, 7*(12), 2728–2742. doi:10.1002ec.795

Chapter 5
Artificial Intelligence in Navigation Systems

Ghalia Nasserddine
iD https://orcid.org/0000-0001-9434-2914
Jinan University, Lebanon

Amal A. El Arid
iD https://orcid.org/0000-0001-5712-2138
Rafik Hariri University, Lebanon

ABSTRACT

The computer-based navigation system computes the object's position, speed, and direction in real-time. In the last decades, many researchers, companies, and industries have been working on improving the existing navigation system due to its vast application in military and civilian activities. Typically, navigation systems are based on integrating inertial navigation systems and global positioning systems using a Bayesian filter, like the Kalman filter. The limitations of the Kalman filter have inspired researchers to consider alternatives based on artificial intelligence. Recently, many types of research have been developed to validate the possibility of using artificial intelligence methods in navigation systems. This chapter aims to review the integration of artificial intelligence techniques in navigation systems.

INTRODUCTION

A navigation system is a computing system that assists in navigation. Usually, these systems can be implemented entirely on vehicles or other transportation machines. In addition, they can be located elsewhere and control the machine by utilizing radio or other transmission signals. In certain circumstances, a fusion of these methods can be used (Duffany, 2010).

Nowadays, navigation systems use Global Positioning Satellites (GPS) to point the machine or vehicle's location. They compare the associated location with the desired destination and guide along the right road (Hasan, Samsudin, Ramli, Azmir, & Ismaeel, 2009). GPS navigation systems are usually combined with stored map information to choose the optimal road based on the shortest path algorithm.

DOI: 10.4018/978-1-6684-6937-8.ch005

This technique successfully gets to the destination in a reasonable time. It is also faulted tolerant because it can spontaneously relocate the destination in case of error (Huang, Tsai, & Huang, 2012). The major inconvenience of using GPS in navigation systems is satellite signal blockage in urban areas where position errors may range from 100 to 300 m (Grewal, Andrews, & Bartone, 2020). GPS is usually integrated with an inertial measurement unit of three accelerometers and three gyroscopes to overcome this problem. These inertial sensors are inside the vehicle to provide its position, velocity, and heading angle. This overall system is inertial navigation (INS) (Britting, 2010). In addition, the Kalman filter (KF) is used to extract the location from GPS, INS, and map information. Recently, the limitations of KF have inspired researchers to consider alternative methods by combining artificial intelligence (AI), INS, and GPS (Al Bitar, Gavrilov, & Khalaf, 2020).

Artificial intelligence (AI) represents the ability of digital systems or robots to act like humans and perform tasks related to intelligent beings. According to John McCarthy (2019), the father of AI, artificial intelligence is defined as *the science and engineering of making intelligent machines and brilliant computer programs*. Additionally, the word artificial in AI stands for human-created; the word intelligence represents the power of thinking. Therefore, AI is a machine with thinking power (Jokanoviж, 2022).

Recently, AI techniques such as neural networks (NN) and multilayer perceptron (MLP) have been used in INS (Haid, et al., 2019). In (Zhang & Xu, 2012), the authors have proved that position and velocity update architecture based on two MLP networks can manipulate INS data and provide the location for east and north directions.

This chapter is composed of four sections. The different techniques used in navigation systems are presented in the following section. Later, the different AI systems are described, followed by exciting research on AI techniques in the navigation sector afterward. Finally, a conclusion about the importance of using AI in navigation systems is represented.

NAVIGATION SYSTEMS

The navigation system is a computer-based system embedded in a vehicle or any mobile device that delivers a real-time value of its current location. Recently, many researchers have focused on developing navigation systems due to their importance in civilian and military applications. Modern navigation systems using different electronic sensing devices (sensors) have been developed since the 1960s. These systems combine independent navigation sensors such as inertial measurement units, Doppler radar, and radio position fixed devices to collect the available information to produce a continuous position of the navigated object. Nowadays, microprocessors are integrated with current navigation systems to produce more accurate results (Hasan, Samsudin, Ramli, Azmir, & Ismaeel, 2009). Figure 1 shows the basic structure of navigation systems. The information collected by inertial navigation system (INS) sensors is combined with the position given by the global positioning system (GPS) receiver using a Kalman filter (KF) to give an accurate estimation of the object's position. Usually, a digital map and estimation position are combined to give the object's current position using a map matching technique.

Figure 1. the main structure of a navigation system

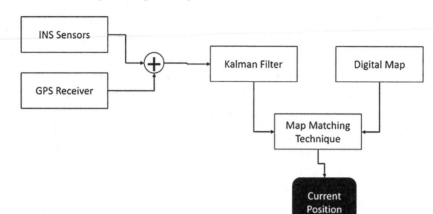

Inertial Navigation System Sensors

INS comprises two primary sensors (Liu, et al., 2018):

- Motion sensors are also called accelerometers: An accelerometer is a sensor used to measure proper acceleration that represents the rate of change of velocity of an object in its instantaneous rest frame according to three dimensions (see Figure 2). Proper acceleration differs from coordinate acceleration, which is acceleration in a fixed coordinate system. Accelerometers are used in many applications like navigation systems, aircraft, and missiles.
- Rotation sensors are also called gyroscopes: Gyroscopes are sensors usually used for measuring or maintaining orientation and angular velocity according to the three-axis (see Figure 2). They are used in many systems like compasses, aircraft, vehicles, ballistic missiles, and orbiting satellites.

Figure 2. INS sensors: (A) Gyroscope (B) Accelerometers

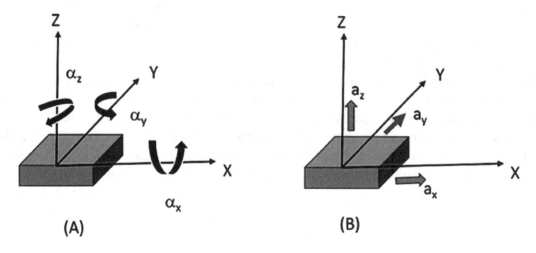

Global Positioning System Receiver

The GPS receiver uses satellite signals delivered by the GPS systems to compute its position (see Figure 3). It was produced by the U.S. Department of Defense (DoD) for military purposes. In 1980, GPS technology became available to civilian users. It is a standard technology embedded in cars, boats, cell phones, mobile devices, and even personal heads-up display (HUD) glasses. In order to give an accurate position, GPS receivers should collect information from three to four satellites. The collected information includes the exact position of the satellite sender and transmission time. Indeed, three satellites are enough to compute the x and y coordinates of the receiver. However, an additional satellite is required to compute the receiver's altitude. Usually, when satellites are available, the GPS accuracy can vary from 5 meters to 30 centimeters. In order to improve this accuracy, many new technologies have been used, such as DGPS or Kalman filters (Santerre & Geiger, 2018).

Differential Global Positioning System

The Differential Global Positioning System (DGPS) is an improved GPS navigation system that delivers better location accuracy. The position accuracy can be around 1–3 centimeters for the best implementations of the DGPS. DGPS uses a based station that is located at a known location. This based station is used to measure the errors in the GPS signals. Usually, it contains a radio station and sends corrections to users in the "local" area (dashed circle in Figure 3). The corrections are typically sent every few seconds (Chung, 2020).

Figure 3. A DGPS system

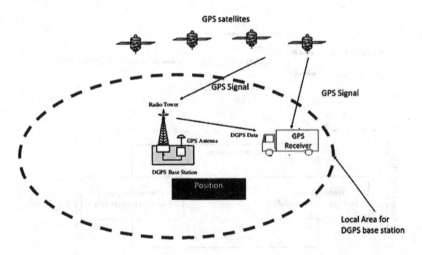

Error Sources of GPS

The primary sources of GPS positional errors (Ayhan & Almuslmani, 2021) are:

- Atmospheric Interference is caused by the delay of the GPS signal as it passes via the Earth's atmosphere. The troposphere and the ionosphere cause this delay.
- The GPS receiver causes calculation and routing errors. It usually occurs by its clocks or internal noise.
- Ephemeris (orbital path) data errors are computed as the variances between the position of the actual satellite and the one computed using the GNSS navigation message (Lihua & Wang, 2013).
- Multipath effects: A multipath error is produced when receiving GPS signals reflected from ground surfaces or other objects around a receiver. It may lead to a positional error produced by the computation of the range between the satellite and receiver (Lei, Liang, Tang, & Zhou, 2021).

Kalman Filter

Kalman Filter (FK) is an algorithm generally used to estimate particular states of a dynamic object by using the data given by a set of sensors. A state of an object or dynamic system is a set of variables that characterizes this object at a specific time. In a navigation system, the state of an object is all variables that define the object's current position, how fast it is moving, and in what direction. For example, the state of a vehicle can be defined by the x, y, and z coordinates. State estimation is a domain of dynamic systems that combines a system model with the sensor's measurements to estimate the system state.

KF has been widely used in many applications, including dynamic ships, navigation, vehicle control, and aircraft (Barrau & Bonnabel, 2018). Figure 4 shows the general structure of KF used in the state estimation problem.

Figure 4. Kalman filter that estimates an object's position and the corresponding steps for prediction and correction

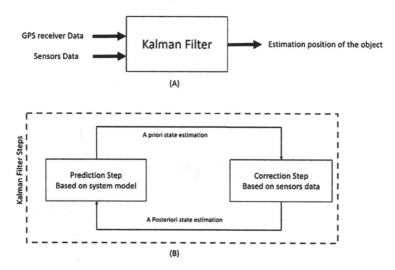

KF uses the GPS receiver and sensor data to estimate the object's position (see Figure 4(A)). Figure 4(B) illustrates the primary two steps of KF. First, using the system model and the previous state value, KF can compute a priori state estimation. Later, based on the sensor's measurement, a correction step is performed to calculate a posterior state estimation that is more accurate than the prior one (Zhao, Qiu, & Feng, 2016).

KF is used if the linear model can represent the object. For the non-linear model, many extensions of KF have been developed. In this chapter, three extensions of KF will be described briefly:

- The Extended Kalman Filter (EKF) is a non-linear system extension of the classic Kalman Filter that approximates nonlinearity using the first- or second-order derivative. Although EKF is simple, it suffers from instability due to linearization and incorrect parameters, costly Jacobean matrix calculation, and the biased nature of its estimates. Unlike KF, the EKF is usually not an optimal estimator. It is optimal only if the measurement and the state models are linear (e.g., KF) (Zhou, Hou, Liu, Sun, & Liu, 2017).
- When tracking with non-linear dynamics models and measurements that are non-linear functions of the target state, the unscented Kalman filter (UKF) is a valuable alternative to the extended Kalman filter (EKF). Compared to the Extended Kalman Filter, it performs better at non-linear estimation (EKF). It is widely used in Control systems, Signal Processing, and navigation systems (Yang, Shi, & W. Chen, 2017).
- Recent researchers have developed many extensions of KF based on fuzzy logic theory, such as the Fuzzy Kalman Filter proposed by Sasiadek and Wang (1999). In this filter, the EKF and the noise factor have been adjusted based on a fuzzy logic adaptive system. It gives better results (more accurate) than the EKF.

Digital Map

The existing digital map is created using Geographic Information System (GIS), a computer-based system used to capture, store, check, and show data associated with positions on Earth's surface. Therefore, GIS is a collection of tools that permit the spatial processing of data into information (see Figure 5). This collection is open-ended, but it includes data input, data, storage, data manipulation, and a reporting system. Table 1 shows the different types of data stored in GIS (Bolstad, 2016).

Figure 5. Example of Spatial Data: it illustrates only the x-y coordinates of spatial data. In (A), a part of the Google map is shown; in (B), the x-y coordinates of Palma Beach in Tripoli, Lebanon, are presented.

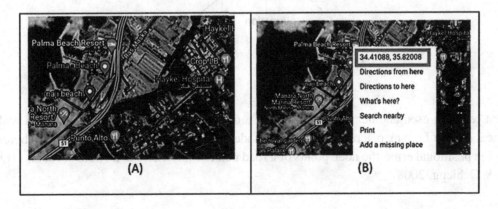

Table 1. Types of data stored in GIS

Data Type	Description
Spatial Data	Represents elements with a known location on Earth (see Figure 5)
Attribute Data	Illustrates the information of the geographic elements (spatial data)
Data Layer	Represents the result of integrating spatial and attribute data by adding the attribute database to the spatial location
Layer Types	Refers to the way spatial and attribute information are linked. There are two major layer types: vector and raster
Topology	Represents relationships between every two geographic attributes

Road Representation in GIS

Usually, in digital maps, roads are represented by a single-line road network. This map illustrates a road by a limited sequence of points. Therefore, each road is represented by a set of linked lines that express the centerlines of the road.

Figure 6 illustrates an example of a road representation in a digital map; two roads are represented (Quddus, 2006):

- **Road 1** is illustrated by one line and two endpoints (A_2 and A_3). Node A_3 also represents a junction (intersection between Roads 1 and 2).
- **Road 2** is modeled by two lines connecting three nodes (A_1, A_4, and A_5). Node A_4 represents the shape points. However, nodes A_1 and A_5 are the endpoints of Road 1.

Figure 6. Roads representation in digital map

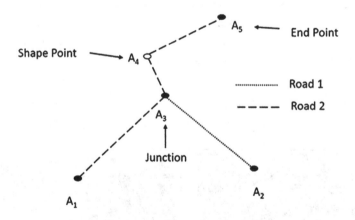

Recent research used another representation of a digital map. Indeed, to consider road width and geometrical errors of the map, a rectangular road model is used, as illustrated in Figure 7. Therefore, to consider the positional error, the node points of a road r can be anywhere in a circle of radius l (Quddus, Noland, & Ochieng, 2008).

Figure 7. Recent representation of road in a digital map that considers error shapes, road width, and geometrical errors
(Abdallah, Nassreddine, & Denoeux, 2011).

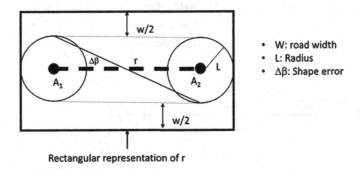

Error Sources in Digital Map

The quality of a digital map depends on point precision and the reliability of other map attributes. Usually, a digital map has two significant error types (Quddus, Ochieng, & Noland, 2007):

- **Geometrical errors** represent the imprecision of the nodes describing the roads (Endpoints and shape points).
- **Topological errors** are caused by the lack of reliability of attributes in the digital map—for example, lousy representation of road intersections.

Map Matching Technique

Map Matching (MM) represents a process that gives a location in a digital map to a geographical object. Typically, geographical objects are represented by point positions received from a positioning system, often a GPS receiver. Recently, the MM technique has played an essential function in the navigation system. It uses a digital map database to enhance the precision and reliability of the navigation system. Generally, MM algorithms can be categorized into three classes (Abdallah, Nassreddine, & Denoeux, 2011):

- **Class 1:** MM algorithms use only the geometric relationships between the available position of the object and a digital map (Quddus, Noland, & Ochieng, 2008).
- **Class 2:** Other than geometric information, MM techniques also use the topology of the road network and historical data regarding the object's position (Asghar, Garzón, Lussereau, & Laugier, 2020).
- **Class 3:** MM methods in this class referred to advanced techniques and the use of advanced tools such as the Kalman Filter (KF), Bayesian networks, Dempster-Shafer theory, or fuzzy logic (Kubicka, Cela, Mounier, & Niculescu, 2018).

The basic concepts of the map-matching algorithm are explained in the steps below (Xu, Lin, Zhou, & Huang, 2016), as illustrated in Figure 8.

Figure 8. The map-matching technique

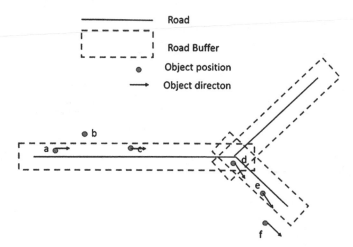

1. The object's position is collected from the processing unit or GPS receiver and considered the initial data source of the MM algorithm.
2. For each road, a segment creates a buffer with a width equal to the average positioning error of the navigation system.
3. If the object's position is out of all road segment buffers (see points b and f in Figure 2), it will be removed from the initial data source, and the remaining data is the actual data set for map matching.
4. If the object's position is out of all road segment buffers (see points b and f in Figure 2), it will be removed from the initial data source, and the remaining data is the actual data set for map matching.
5. Calculate the buffer number it locates for each object's position in the data set. If the number is equal to one (see points a, c, and e in Figure 8), it locates on the only road segment. Otherwise, if the number is above one (see point d in Figure 8), a process of comparison between the angle of the object's velocity direction and the direction of every road section in the object is located to choose the corresponding road segment that has the minimum angle.

Recently, some MM techniques used topological data of the digital map and historical data of navigation systems, as illustrated in Figure 9.

Figure 9. MM technique with topological data of the digital map together with historical data of navigation system

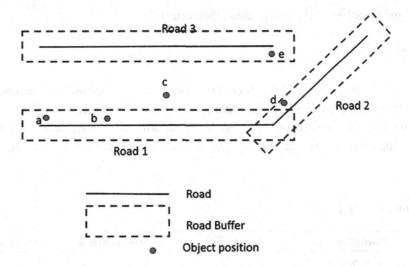

Figure 9 shows that the object was first located on Road 1 (points a and b). Point c is outside the road buffer. However, as the object was first on Road 1, the MM algorithm considers that object still on this road. Point e is on Road 3. However, the topological information on the map explains that there is no relation between Roads 2 and 3. Therefore, the object is considered on Road 2 (Abdallah, Nassreddine, & Denoeux, 2011).

ARTIFICIAL INTELLIGENCE SYSTEMS

An AI system is a machine-based system that gives appropriate predictions or decisions based on data collected from real or virtual environments. Based on specific inputs or data collected from sensors, it can perceive the real or virtual environment for taking the appropriate decisions or actions (OECD, 2019). Figure 10 shows the general function of AI systems.

AI system can collect specific data from real or virtual environment using sensors or other sources. These data can be manipulated and analyzed by the operation logic part of AI systems to take appropriate actions using actuators. The AI operation logic builds a model of the environment to be interpreted for decision making. In addition, AI systems may take the decision or predict outputs.

Generally, AI comprises several branches, illustrated as follows:

1. Machine learning that also comprises deep learning
2. Natural language processing that consists of text generation, context extraction, and machine translation
3. Expert systems
4. Vision that is categorized into machine vision and image recognition
5. Speech recognition that is composed into text-to-speech and speech-to-text
6. Planning

7.   Robotics

In this section, some branches of AI will be described briefly.

Machine Learning

Machine Learning (ML) is a branch of AI. It covers all systems that permit the machine to learn from historical data without being explicitly programmed. Using ML, machines can identify patterns, learn and make decisions with little human intervention. Many algorithms are used in ML, including decision trees, regression, rules systems, and ensemble approaches. Table 2 summarizes a comparison between these techniques.

Table 2. ML techniques comparison

	Description	Advantages	Disadvantages	Application Fields
Regression	-A technique to explore the association between independent variables (features) and one dependent variable (outcome), used for predicting continuous outcomes	-Include many variables -The output of this model is an equation that is effortless to understand	-Cannot work correctly if the input data contains errors -Reliability of the regression models decreases with the number of variables	-Financial forecasting -Trend analysis -Marketing -Drug response modeling
Clustering	-A method of grouping unlabeled data into different clusters that contain similar data points	-Clustering with high efficiency -Suitable for any data formats	-Resulting in low quality if the density of the data space is not uniform -It requires ample memory space if the volume of data is huge -Susceptible result to predefined parameters	-Market research, -Pattern recognition -Data analysis -Image processing
Neural Networks	-A method to process data in a way that imitates the human brain -A system learning process called deep learning that uses interconnected nodes (named neurons) in a layered structure that simulates the human brain	-Continuous Learning -Efficiency -Multitasking	-Hardware and data dependent -Complex Algorithms	-Facial Recognition -Stock Market -Prediction -Social Media
Ensemble Methods	A technique to combine several base models to produce one optimal predictive result	-Higher predictive accuracy -Very useful when there is both linear and non-linear type of data in the dataset	-Less interpretable -Hard to learn -Wrong selections lead to lower predictive accuracy -Expensive in terms of time and space	-Email Filtering -Healthcare -Banking -Retail

Deep learning, a subset of ML, allows systems to solve perceptual problems such as image and speech recognition. It is an effective system used in many financial and biological sciences applications. Usually, multiple processing layers are used in DL to discover patterns and structures from massive data sets. Generally, prior data processing is not used in DL. It automatically extracts properties from available data.

In ML techniques, a feature extraction stage is inquired before applying the model. This stage is very complex and typically needs the expert's intervention and may be handcrafting. However, DL does not necessarily need features. Hence, there is no need for an expert to define any features in the model (Ongsulee, 2017).

Natural Language Processing

Artificial Intelligence systems' main goal is imitating the human mind's capability. Language is the most critical capability of the human mind. It allows a person to communicate and understand the need of each other. For this reason, many researchers are recently interested in enhancing machines' and other systems' Natural Language Processing (NLP) (Hirschberg & Manning, 2015). NLP aims to help machines understand natural language and execute textual digit tasks. It is a combination of computer science, AI, and linguistic theories. NLP is generally a composite of three parts:

- **Text Generation** generates natural language text to satisfy systems' communication requirements. It combines computational linguistics and artificial intelligence (Liu & Özsu, 2009).
- **Context Extraction** requires breaking down sentences into n-grams (continuous sequences of words or symbols in a document) and noun phrases to extract the subject and features from a collection of unstructured text. Using this technique, data analysts and decision-makers can make better-informed decisions and recommendations based on their goals (Tixier, Hallowell, Rajagopalan, & Bowman, 2016).
- **Machine Translation** describes a computer-based activity that automatically converts an input text from one natural language into another. It produces a fluent text of the output language and preserves the text's meaning. Indeed, machine translation delivers an effectual output with speed and cost-effectiveness (Tan, Wahidin, Khalil, Tamaldin, & Rauterberg, 2016).

Expert Systems

Expert Systems (ES) aims to solve complex problems as it is computer-based software designed to provide decision-making ability like a human expert. Expert systems solve problems using reasoning and inference rules to extract knowledge from their knowledge base according to the user's existing queries. It is a branch of AI developed for the first time in 1970. The main structure of ES is shown in Figure 13 (Alshawwa, Elkahlout, El-Mashharawi, & Abu-Naser, 2019).

ES is composed of three main parts:

- **Knowledge Base:** It comprises problem-solving rules and procedures from the human expert. Usually, the knowledge base is structured as If/Then rules of the form:

$$IF \langle antecedent \rangle \, THEN \, \langle consequent \rangle$$

Where antecedent is the condition that must be satisfied, the consequence is the action performed when the rule fires. The rule is triggered if the condition in the antecedent is satisfied.

- **The rules engine** (Called inference engine) is the central processing unit of ES. It chooses the most appropriate rules to be fired from existing rules. In addition, it uses the knowledge base to get conclusions about situations. It is responsible for collecting the information from the user by asking a set of questions and applying it if necessary.
- **The user interface** allows users to interact with ES. It can be done through dialog boxes, command prompts, or other input tools. ES can interact with other applications or directly with human users.

Computer Vision

Vision or Computer Vision is a main branch of AI. It is a computer science field that trains computers and machines to replicate the human vision system. Vision techniques allow digital devices to process and identify objects in images or videos like humans (Xu, et al., 2021). Vision in AI can be classified into:

- **Machine vision** refers to the techniques and methods used to give imaging-based automatic inspection and examination for applications such as process control and robot guidance. The machine vision process is typically divided into three main steps: Image capturing, processing, and action. Vision sensors (digital or infrared) capture images through one or more instances. These images are transformed into digital data to be used later in the processing step. After that, digital data coming from the images are analyzed using image processing algorithms such as image processing. Finally, necessary actions are performed based on the information extracted in the previous step.
- **Image recognition** is the ability of software or machine to identify patterns such as objects, places, people, or writing in images. It is a subfield of AI vision. There are many tasks that image recognition can perform:
  - Image Classification is associating one or more labels to a given image.
  - Tagging involves recognizing the presence of different shapes or objects in the same image. It is a classification task. However, the accuracy degree of tagging is higher.
  - Detection consists of detecting the presence of one object within the image. Once the object is detected, a bounding box is placed around it to locate it.
  - Segmentation is a detection task that locates an element on an image to the nearest pixel.

Speech Recognition

Speech recognition is divided into two central parts: speech-to-text (STT) and text-to-speech (TTS) (Gaikwad, Gawali, & Yannawar, 2010). STT represents the ability of a system or machine to identify spoken words and convert them into readable text. On the other hand, TTS consists of converting the existing text into speech (Tihelka, Hanzlíček, Jůzová, Vít, Matoušek, & Grůber, 2018).

In STT systems, computer algorithms are usually used to operate and clarify spoken words to convert them into text (Shadiev, Hwang, Chen, & Huang, 2014). STT is used in many mobile applications for education, healthcare, disability assistance, and others. Recorded sounds using a microphone are converted into written text that computers and humans can understand through the following three steps:

1. Analyze the audio;

2. Break audio into parts; and
3. Convert it into a computer-readable format using an algorithm to choose the most suitable text representation.

In addition, TTS has been widely used in many applications, including education and disability assistance. In the education section, recent research shows that by using TTS software, students may focus on the content rather than on reading and help get a better understanding of the material (Moorman, Boon, Keller-Bell, Stagliano, & Jeffs, 2010). In disability assistance, TTS is used to create a voiceover for a video or to help people with visual problems "read" (SRMIST & Student, 2018).

Planning

AI Planning is a branch of AI exploring the process of using independent techniques to resolve scheduling and planning issues. Usually, in a planning problem, the desired goal state should get through the application of a set of actions from an initial starting state. Planning is an essential task for the industry area. It is used in many applications like robots, autonomous systems, cognitive assistants, cyber security, and service composition (Bozic, 2019).

Robotics

Robotics is a branch of AI that combines Computer Science, Electrical Engineering, and Mechanical Engineering. A robot can be considered a mechanical structure or shape designed to accomplish a particular task. It contains some electrical components used to control and survey the machinery. In addition, intelligent devices such as micro-processor are embedded in robots. These devices contain software applications that determine what, when, and how a robot does something (Cain, Thomas, & Alonso Jr, 2019).

NAVIGATION SYSTEMS: ARTIFICIAL INTELLIGENCE APPLICATION

The primary sensors used in such a system are INS and GPS. Several fusion methods are employed to integrate INS and GPS data. The main methods are Bayesian filtering approaches like Kalman Filters (KF), such as Extended Kalman Filter (EKF) and Unscented Kalman Filter (UKF). KF can give accurate geo-referencing solutions if the system model is correct, GPS and INS errors can be modeled using stochastic models KF can produce, and there is continuous access to GPS signals. If GPS outages arise, KF works only in the prediction model, and INS measurements are used to correct system errors. However, KF and its extensions have limitations. One of the main concerns of KF utilization in the navigation system is the need for an exact stochastic model for each sensor error. In addition, there are many significant problems with KF, including sensor dependency and observability (Tang, et al., 2008).

These limitations of KF and others have pushed researchers to find alternative methods of INS/GPS integration, mainly based on AI (Zhang & Lu, 2021). Due to the enormous development of technology and the computer hardware evolution, AI has been receiving more attention. It has been proven a successful and effective technique for providing solutions to many applications like healthcare, banking, Finance, and many others.

AI includes many recent technologies, such as artificial neural networks (ANNs), Neuro-Fuzzy systems, evolutionary computing, and expert systems, to deliver intelligence and robustness in complex and uncertain systems (Gupta, 2013). Table 3 compares KF and its extensions with AI algorithms (Al Bitar, Gavrilov, & Khalaf, 2020).

Table 3. Comparison between KF and AI

Property	Kalman Filter	Artificial Intelligence
Dependency to model	Mathematical model; deterministic model + stochastic model	Empirical and adaptive model
Prior Knowledge	Required measurements and state vector covariance matrices prior knowledge is an essential need	Prior training is required. However, no prior knowledge is needed.
Sensor dependency	Re-design or re-tuning parameters of KF is needed for different system	System independent algorithm
Linearity	Required for KF and EKF	Non-linear processing

Nowadays, many types of research have tried to explore AI techniques in navigation systems. The researchers have used different approaches for integrating the AI tools in the INS/GPS. These approaches can be decomposed into two main categories (Al Bitar, Gavrilov, & Khalaf, 2020):

1. **Category 1:** The AI module is just used to replace the INS/GPS integration technique.
2. **Category 2:** AI and KF are used in the INS/GPS integration part to improve the overall navigation accuracy.

These two categories are also split into subcategories based on AI modules or inputs/outputs (I/O).

Category 1 Techniques

In this section, the author will represent some existing techniques belonging to this category. For instance, Adusumilli, Bhatt, Wang, Bhattacharya, and Devabhaktuni (2013) presented a random forest regression algorithm to integrate INS and GPS to provide continuous, accurate, and reliable information navigation solutions. Random forest regression has proven that it is an effective model for a navigation system with non-linear INS error due to its improved generalization capability. This technique has been proved by bridging the period of GPS outages. Four simulated GPS outages are considered over actual field test data. The proposed method represents a significant decrease in the positional error by 24–56%.

Wang, Xu, Yao, and Tong (2019) represented a new fusion algorithm that uses a back propagation neural network (BPNN) has been proposed. This algorithm improves the performance of the GPS and INS/GPS integration system during GPS outages. The performance of the proposed method has been experimentally assessed in a land vehicle navigation test. The results demonstrate that the proposed model can efficiently predict position increment and compensate for INS errors during GPS outages. In addition, the positioning accuracy of the new model becomes more noticeable when the GPS observations are unavailable for a long time. Using the current and historical information as the input of the BPNN model can effectively offset the computation burden and accuracy.

In (Ebrahimi, Sadeghi, Nezhadshahbodaghi, Mosavi, & Abdolkarimi, 2021), the authors proposed an improvement of the INS/GPS navigation system based on Artificial Intelligence (AI) tools during GPS outages. In this study, the INS outputs at time t and t-1 are pushed as input to the AI module with the positioning and timing information. During the availability of the GPS signal, the AI module performs the training step, and its output is compared with the GPS output. Indeed, the role of the AI module in this study is to drive the INS output during the GPS outage. This approach has been evaluated and compared to some different intelligence systems. The Neural Networks (NNs) have been used as an AI module in five different NNs: multilayer perceptron (MLP), radial basis function (RBF), support vector regression (SVR), Wavelet, and adaptive neuro-fuzzy inference system (ANFIS). The used dataset to compare all five developed methods has been gathered from a natural environment by a mini-airplane. The results of all five methods illustrate that the proposed methods have superior performance compared to other traditional methods.

In (Hamidi, Abdolkarimi, & Mosavi, 2020), authors proposed an Interval Type-2 Fuzzy Logic System (IT2FLS) to predict the MEMS-based sensor errors in GPS blockage caused by the stochastic noise, bias, and drift of the low-cost MEMS-based inertial sensor outputs over time. The IT2FLS can represent input and training data's uncertainty and stochastic noise in complex, noisy environments such as our application. Therefore, the proposed approach was used to forecast the cumulative INS error during GPS outages to enhance the accuracy of the navigation system. The experimental tests have shown that the IT2FLS delivers acceptable real-time performance and accuracy in predicting the INS error during long-term GPS outages.

Category 2 Techniques

The integrated navigation system comprises an INS and GPS that provides endless high-accuracy positioning. However, the navigation accuracy during a GPS outage decreases because of INS error divergence. Thus, a gated recurrent unit (GRU) and adaptive Kalman filter (AKF)-based hybrid algorithm has been proposed to reduce such decrease (Tang, et al., 2022). The GRU network has been constructed to predict the position variations during GPS outages. Furthermore, in this study, the GRU-predicted error accumulation has been considered. Therefore, AKF has been introduced as a supplementary methodology to improve navigation performance. The proposed hybrid algorithm has been trained and tested by practical road datasets. It also has been compared with four algorithms, including the standard KF, Multi-Layer Perceptron (MLP)-aided KF, Long Short Time Memory (LSTM) aided KF, and GRU-aided KF. Periods of 180 and 120 s GNSS outages have been used to test the accuracy of the proposed algorithm in different time scales. The comparison result between the traditional KF and neural network-aided KF has proved that the neural network may be an effective methodology in case of GPS outages.

Moreover, a comparison between three kinds of neural networks has been made. This comparison has proved that both recurrent neural networks surpass the MLP in prediction position variation. In addition, the GRU transcends the LSTM in prediction accuracy and training efficiency. Furthermore, it has been concluded that the adaptive estimation theory effectively complements neural network-aided navigation, as the GRU-aided AKF reduced the horizontal error of GRU-aided KF by 31.71% and 16.12% after 180 and 120 s of GPS outage, respectively.

In (Wei, et al., 2021), the authors have proposed a navigation method consisting of a wavelet neural network based on random forest regression (RFR-WNN). This method helps adaptive Kalman filter (AKF) to enhance the navigation systems' performance by combining INS and GPS under complex environments, such as GPS outages. AKF has usually been used to correct INS errors. It is an improvement of KF by introducing an adaptive factor to remove the impact of the complex environment and random errors on the filtering accuracy. RFR-WNN has been used to build a high-precision prediction model during the period of good availability of GPS. In addition, it provided the required observations for AKF updates when GPS outages. In order to demonstrate the efficacy and improvement of the proposed method, vehicle navigation experiments were done. The results indicate that the proposed method performed better navigation accuracy and precision than the methods used during GPS outages.

In (Liu, Luo, & Zhou, 2022), a deep learning network architecture named GPS/INS neural network (GI-NN) has been proposed to assist the INS during bridge GPS outages and improve navigation performance. The GI-NN integrates a convolutional neural network and a gated recurrent unit neural network to extract spatial features from inertial measurement unit (IMU) signals and follow their temporal characteristics. The associations among the attitude, specific force, angular rate, and the GPS position increment have been modeled. In contrast, the current and previous IMU data have been utilized to estimate the vehicle's dynamics by GI-NN. In order to evaluate the proposed method, numerical simulations, actual field tests, and public data tests are performed. In addition, a comparison with the traditional machine learning algorithms has been made. The results show that the proposed method can provide more accurate and reliable navigation solutions in GPS-denied environments.

Kim, Petrunin, and Shin (2022) have reviewed 55 papers that suggested KF with AI techniques to enhance its performance. Based on this review, the authors grouped papers into four groups based on the role of AI as follows:

- Methods adjusting the parameters of KF
- Methods of balancing errors in KF
- Methods revising state vector or measurements of KF
- Methods that produce an estimation of pseudo-measurements of KF

In the end, the authors have pointed out the directions for future research. They suggested concentrating more on combining the categorized groups.

FUTURE RESEARCH DIRECTIONS

According to this paper study, existing approaches have been implemented in different versions and compared with each other. Thus, in the future, these approaches that integrate AI in navigation systems should be compared to provide their accuracy and performance. Moreover, different types of AI integration in navigation systems (AI for adjusting parameters, AI for balancing parameters, AI for revising state vectors) may be developed to check for better accurate results.

CONCLUSION

Artificial Intelligence (AI) has recently received massive attention from researchers due to its efficacy in resolving many complex problems in different areas such as banking, healthcare, smart cities, and others. The navigation system is a computing system that assists humans in navigation. It is an essential system in our daily life because it integrates data collected from sensors such as INS sensors and GPS receivers under a Bayesian filter to deliver an accurate real-time estimation of the current position. Bayesian Filters like the Kalman filter suffers from many drawbacks, especially when there is a GPS outage or the system model is not linear. For this reason, many researchers try to develop a more objective approach based on AI to improve the performance of navigation systems. This chapter reviews Artificial Intelligence and navigation systems; different parts of the navigation systems have been described briefly, followed by a review of AI and its different branches. In addition, a review of existing research on combining AI techniques in navigation systems is illustrated. The authors conclude that AI may be used in the navigation system to replace KF completely, and AI may be used for adjusting or balancing the parameters of KF. Moreover, AI may be utilized for revising state vectors or measurements of KF.

FUNDING

This research received no specific grant from any funding agency in the public, commercial, or not-for-profit sectors.

REFERENCES

Abdallah, F., Nassreddine, G., & Denoeux, T. (2011). A multiple-hypothesis map-matching method suitable for weighted and box-shaped state estimation for localization. *IEEE Transactions on Intelligent Transportation Systems*, *12*(4), 1495–1510. doi:10.1109/TITS.2011.2160856

Adusumilli, S., Bhatt, D., Wang, H., Bhattacharya, P., & Devabhaktuni, V. (2013). A low-cost INS/GPS integration methodology based on random forest regression. *Expert Systems with Applications*, *40*(11), 4653–4659. doi:10.1016/j.eswa.2013.02.002

Al Bitar, N., Gavrilov, A. I., & Khalaf, W. (2020). Artificial Intelligence Based Methods for Accuracy Improvement of Integrated Navigation Systems During GNSS Signal Outages: An Analytical Overview. *Gyroscopy and Navigation*, *11*(1), 41–58. doi:10.1134/S2075108720010022

Alshawwa, I. A., Elkahlout, M., El-Mashharawi, H. Q., & Abu-Naser, S. S. (2019). An Expert System for Depression Diagnosis. *International Journal of Academic Health and Medical Research*, *3*(4).

Asghar, R., Garzón, M., Lussereau, J., & Laugier, C. (2020). Vehicle localization based on visual lane marking and topological map matching. *IEEE International Conference on Robotics and Automation (ICRA)*, (pp. 258-264). IEEE. 10.1109/ICRA40945.2020.9197543

Ayhan, M. E., & Almuslmani, B. (2021). Positional accuracy and convergence time assessment of GPS precise point positioning in static mode. *Arabian Journal of Geosciences*, *14*(13), 1–12. doi:10.100712517-021-07428-1

Barrau, A., & Bonnabel, S. (2018). Invariant Kalman filtering. *Annual Review of Control, Robotics, and Autonomous Systems*, *1*(1), 237–257. doi:10.1146/annurev-control-060117-105010

Bolstad, P. (2016). *GIS fundamentals: A first text on geographic information systems.* Eider (PressMinnesota).

Bozic, J. T. (2019). Chatbot testing using AI planning. *2019 IEEE International Conference On Artificial Intelligence Testing (AITest)* (pp. 37-44). IEEE. 10.1109/AITest.2019.00-10

Britting, K. (2010). *Inertial navigation systems analysis.* Artech House.

Cain, L. N., Thomas, J. H., & Alonso, M. Jr. (2019). From sci-fi to sci-fact: The state of robotics and AI in the hospitality industry. *Journal of Hospitality and Tourism Technology*, *10*(4), 624–650. doi:10.1108/JHTT-07-2018-0066

Chung, J. Y. (2020). Implementation of a precise drone positioning system using differential global positioning system. *Journal of the Korea Academia-Industrial cooperation. Society*, *21*(1), 14–19.

Duffany, J. L. (2010). Artificial intelligence in GPS navigation systems. *2nd International Conference on Software Technology and Engineering* (pp. V1-382). IEEE.

Ebrahimi, A., Sadeghi, M., Nezhadshahbodaghi, M., Mosavi, M. R., & Abdolkarimi, E. S. (2021). Improving INS/GPS Integration with Artificial Intelligence during GPS Outage. *Electronic and Cyber Defense*, *9*(2), 143–157.

Gaikwad, S. K., Gawali, B. W., & Yannawar, P. (2010). A review on speech recognition technique. *International Journal of Computers and Applications*, *10*(3), 16–24. doi:10.5120/1462-1976

Grewal, M., Andrews, A., & Bartone, C. (2020). *Global navigation satellite systems, inertial navigation, and integration.* John Wiley & Sons. doi:10.1002/9781119547860

Gupta, N. (2013). Artificial neural network. *Network and Complex Systems*, *3*(1), 24–28.

Haid, M., Budaker, B., Geiger, M., Husfeldt, D., Hartmann, M., & Berezowski, N. (2019). Inertial-based gesture recognition for artificial intelligent cockpit control using hidden Markov models. *IEEE International Conference on Consumer Electronics (ICCE)*, (pp. 1-4). 10.1109/ICCE.2019.8662036

Hamidi, H., Abdolkarimi, E. S., & Mosavi, M. R. (2020). Prediction of MEMS-based INS error using interval type-2 fuzzy logic system in INS/GPS integration. *25th International Computer Conference, Computer Society of Iran*, 1-5. IEEE. 10.1109/CSICC49403.2020.9050081

Hasan, A. M., Samsudin, K., Ramli, A. R., Azmir, R. S., & Ismaeel, S. A. (2009). A review of navigation systems (integration and algorithms). *Australian Journal of Basic and Applied Sciences*, *3*(2), 943–959.

Hirschberg, J., & Manning, C. D. (2015). Advances in natural language processing. *Science*, *349*(6245), 261–266. doi:10.1126cience.aaa8685 PMID:26185244

Huang, J. Y., Tsai, C. H., & Huang, S. T. (2012). The next generation of GPS navigation systems. *Communications of the ACM*, *55*(3), 84–93. doi:10.1145/2093548.2093570

Jokanoviж, V. (2022). *Artificial Intelligence.* Taylor and Francis, Boca Raton.

Kim, S., Petrunin, I., & Shin, H. S. (2022). A Review of Kalman Filter with Artificial Intelligence Techniques. Integrated Communication, *Navigation and Surveillance Conference* (pp. 1-12). IEEE.

Kubicka, M., Cela, A., Mounier, H., & Niculescu, S. I. (2018). Comparative study and application-oriented classification of vehicular map-matching methods. *IEEE Intelligent Transportation Systems Magazine, 10*(2), 150–166. IEEE. doi:10.1109/MITS.2018.2806630

Lei, M., Liang, X., Tang, J., & Zhou, J. (2021). Multipath Error Correction Method for Slope Monitoring Based on BP Neural Network. *China Satellite Navigation Conference (CSNC 2021) Proceedings* (pp. 101-110). Springer. 10.1007/978-981-16-3138-2_11

Lihua, M., & Wang, M. (2013). Influence of Ephemeris Error on GPS Single Point Positioning Accuracy. *Artificial Satellites, 48*(3), 125–139. doi:10.2478/arsa-2013-0011

Liu, L., & Özsu, M. T. (2009). *Encyclopedia of database systems* M. T. Özsu, (ed.). (Vol. 6). Springer. doi:10.1007/978-0-387-39940-9

Liu, Y., Fan, X., Lv, C., Wu, J., Li, L., & Ding, D. (2018). An innovative information fusion method with adaptive Kalman filter for integrated INS/GPS navigation of autonomous vehicles. *Mechanical Systems and Signal Processing, 100*, 605–616. doi:10.1016/j.ymssp.2017.07.051

Liu, Y., Luo, Q., & Zhou, Y. (2022). Deep Learning-Enabled Fusion to Bridge GPS Outages for INS/GPS Integrated Navigation. *IEEE Sensors Journal, 22*(9), 8974–8985. doi:10.1109/JSEN.2022.3155166

McCarthy, J. (2019). *Artificial Intelligence tutorial - It's your time to innovate the future*. Data Flair. https://data-flair.training/blogs/artificial-intelligence-ai-tutorial

Moorman, A., Boon, R. T., Keller-Bell, Y., Stagliano, C., & Jeffs, T. (2010). Effects of text-to-speech software on the reading rate and comprehension skills of high school students with specific learning disabilities. *Learning Disabilities (Pittsburgh, Pa.), 16*(1), 41–49.

OECD. (2019, November 15). *Scoping the OECD AI principles*. OECD Library. https://www.oecd-ilibrary.org/science-and-technology/scoping-the-oecd-ai-principles_d62f618a-en

Ongsulee, P. (2017). Artificial intelligence, machine learning and deep learning. *15th International Conference on ICT and Knowledge Engineering (ICT&KE)*, (pp. 1-6). 10.1109/ICTKE.2017.8259629

Quddus, M., Ochieng, W., & Noland, R. (2007). Current map-matching algorithms for transport applications: State-of-the art and future research directions. *Transportation Research Part C, Emerging Technologies, 15*(5), 312–328. doi:10.1016/j.trc.2007.05.002

Quddus, M. A. (2006). *High integrity map matching algorithms for advanced transport telematics applications*. Imperial College London.

Quddus, M. A., Noland, R. B., & Ochieng, W. Y. (2008). A high accuracy fuzzy logic-based map-matching algorithm for road transport. *Journal of Intelligent Transportation Systems: Technology, Planning, and Operations*, 103-115.

Santerre, R., & Geiger, A. (2018). The geometry of GPS relative positioning. *GPS Solutions, 22*(2), 1–14. doi:10.100710291-018-0713-2

Shadiev, R., Hwang, W. Y., Chen, N. S., & Huang, Y. M. (2014). Review of speech-to-text recognition technology for enhancing learning. *Journal of Educational Technology & Society*, 65–84.

Tan, C. F., Wahidin, L. S., Khalil, S. N., Tamaldin, N. H., & Rauterberg, G. W. (2016). The application of expert system: A review of research and applications. *Journal of Engineering and Applied Sciences (Asian Research Publishing Network)*, *11*(4), 2448–2453.

Tang, Y., Jiang, J., Liu, J., Yan, P., Tao, Y., & Liu, J. (2022). A GRU and AKF-Based Hybrid Algorithm for Improving INS/GNSS Navigation Accuracy during GNSS Outage. *Remote Sensing*, *14*(3), 752. doi:10.3390/rs14030752

Tang, Y., Wu, Y., Wu, M., Wu, W., Hu, X., & Shen, L. (2008). INS/GNSS integration: Global observability analysis. *IEEE Transactions on Vehicular Technology*, *58*(3), 1129–1142. doi:10.1109/TVT.2008.926213

Edward, S. (2018). Text-to-speech device for visually impaired people. *International Journal of Pure and Applied Mathematics*, *119*(15), 1061–1067.

Tihelka, D., Hanzlниек, Z., Jшzovб, M., Vнt, J., Матоилек, J., & Grшber, M. (2018). Current state of text-to-speech system ARTIC: a decade of research on the field of speech technologies. *International Conference on Text, Speech, and Dialogue* (pp. 369-378). Springer. 10.1007/978-3-030-00794-2_40

Tixier, A. J., Hallowell, M. R., Rajagopalan, B., & Bowman, D. (2016). Automated content analysis for construction safety: A natural language processing system to extract precursors and outcomes from unstructured injury reports. *Automation in Construction*, *62*, 45–56. doi:10.1016/j.autcon.2015.11.001

Wang, G., Xu, X., Yao, Y., & Tong, J. (2019). A novel BPNN-based method to overcome the GPS outages for INS/GPS system. *IEEE Access: Practical Innovations, Open Solutions*, *7*, 82134–82143. doi:10.1109/ACCESS.2019.2922212

Wei, X., Li, J., Feng, K., Zhang, D., Li, P., Zhao, L., & Jiao, Y. (2021). A mixed optimization method based on adaptive Kalman filter and wavelet neural network for INS/GPS during GPS outages. *IEEE Access: Practical Innovations, Open Solutions*, *9*, 47875–47886. doi:10.1109/ACCESS.2021.3068744

Xu, S., Wang, J., Shou, W., Ngo, T., Sadick, A., & Wang, X. (2021). Computer vision techniques in construction: A critical review. *Archives of Computational Methods in Engineering*, *28*(5), 3383–3397. doi:10.100711831-020-09504-3

Xu, Z., Lin, Z., Zhou, C., & Huang, C. (2016). Detecting traffic hot spots using vehicle tracking data. *2nd ISPRS International Conference on Computer Vision in Remote Sensing. 9901*, pp. 218-224. SPIE.

Yang, C., Shi, W., & Chen, W. (2017). Comparison of unscented and extended Kalman filters with application in vehicle navigation. *Journal of Navigation*, *70*(2), 411–431. doi:10.1017/S0373463316000655

Zhang, C., & Lu, Y. (2021). Study on artificial intelligence: The state of the art and future prospects. *Journal of Industrial Information Integration*, *23*, 100224. doi:10.1016/j.jii.2021.100224

Zhang, T., & Xu, X. (2012). A new method of seamless land navigation for GPS/INS integrated system. *Measurement*, *15*(2), 691–701. doi:10.1016/j.measurement.2011.12.021

Zhao, L., Qiu, H., & Feng, Y. (2016). Analysis of a robust Kalman filter in loosely coupled GPS/INS navigation system. *Measurement*, *80*, 138–147. doi:10.1016/j.measurement.2015.11.008

Zhou, W., Hou, J., Liu, L., Sun, T., & Liu, J. (2017). Design and simulation of the integrated navigation system based on an extended Kalman filter. *Open Physics*, *15*(1), 182–187. doi:10.1515/phys-2017-0019

KEY TERMS AND DEFINITIONS

Differential Global Positioning System: It utilizes a network of fixed ground-based reference stations to compute and send the difference between the positions given by the GPS satellite system and known fixed positions.

Extended Kalman Filter: The non-linear version of the Kalman filter linearizes an estimate of the current mean and covariance. In the case of well-defined transition models, the EKF has been used.

Geographic Information System: It produces, manages, and analyzes all kinds of map data.

Inertial Measurement Unit: It contains gyroscopes to measure angular rate and accelerometers to measure specific force.

Inertial Navigation Unit: It contains an inertial measurement unit (IMU) and computational unit.

Kalman Filter: It is an algorithm usually used for state estimation problems. It delivers estimates of a system state based on inaccurate and uncertain measurements.

Map Matching: It matches recorded geographic coordinates to a logical model of real-world objects using a digital map.

Unscented Kalman Filter: It is a suboptimal non-linear filtration algorithm, however. It uses an unscented transformation (UT) instead of linearization of non-linear equations with the integration of Taylor series expansion.

Chapter 6
Artificial Intelligence Methods and Applications in Aviation

Tetiana Shmelova
https://orcid.org/0000-0002-9737-6906
National Aviation University, Ukraine

Maxim Yatsko
https://orcid.org/0000-0003-0375-7968
Bees Airline, Ukraine

Iurii Sierostanov
Bees Airline, USA

Volodymyr Kolotusha
National Aviation University, Ukraine

ABSTRACT

The authors make an analysis of the International Civil Aviation Organization documents on applications of new technology for minimizing risk and improving safety in the aviation system. ICAO defined new approaches for effectiveness in aviation – application of artificial intelligence (AI) models for the organization of collaborative decision making (CDM) by all aviation specialists (pilots, air traffic controllers, engineers, etc.) using CDM models based on general information on the flight. The AI is presented in models of decision making (DM) in air navigation system (ANS) as expert systems. The effectiveness of ANS operators' decisions depends on the rational use of intelligent automation at all stages of aircraft flight in the form of intelligent decision support systems (IDSS), with hybrid intelligence (natural intelligence), and AI in DM. Models may be used in the education of aviation specialists and in IDSSs in real flight, especially in emergencies. The chapter presents some examples of CDM models in an emergency "engine failure in flight."

DOI: 10.4018/978-1-6684-6937-8.ch006

INTRODUCTION

Aviation plays a major role in the world. To maintain a safe and efficient operation of aviation enterprises the maximum is using enhanced capabilities provided by new advances in technology. Nowadays one of the goals is applicant Artificial Intelligence in aviation for searching for effective solutions and support if have difficult situations. Artificial intelligence (AI) is a system that can perform inherent human intellectual activities associated with the perception and processing of knowledge, which is important in aviation, especially for decision-making in emergencies. The aviation system is a complex system that requires investigation of how human performance may be affected by its multiple and interrelated components such as technical, political, physical, social, economic, cultural, etc. The aviation systems such as Air Navigation systems (ANS) can be considered Sociotechnical systems (STS), which tend to have two principal features: high technologies and high-risk activities. Thus, the efficiency and safety of the operation of the systems depend to a high degree on the quality of a human operator's decisions that in its turn are guided by the factors of education, competence, experience, and versatility of application of modern-day information and data processing technologies and others.

The AI is presented in models of decision-making in the Air Navigation Sociotechnical systems (ANSTS) as expert systems, decision support systems (DSS)s, intelligent DSS for operators of ANSTS such as pilots, air traffic controllers, engineers, flight dispatch s, operators of unmanned aircraft, especially in emergencies.

BACKGROUND

To maintain the safe and efficient operation of aviation companies International Civil Aviation Organization (ICAO) in its recent documents extended the existing and defined new approaches to improve the practical and sustainable implementation of preventive aviation security measures based on modern advances in information technology (ICAO, 2018). One approach is using AI systems in aviation. The first AI research was aimed at creating computers with "intelligent" behavior, scientists sought to obtain new artificial systems with abilities to perform work better than the systems with the control of a human operator named Natural Intelligence (NI). Nowadays, the range of AI technologies has expanded considerably with successful applications in many areas (Kashyap, 2019a; Izonin, 2022; Salem, 2020).

For aviation to need the efficient operation of aviation enterprises and aviation services that allows maximum use to be made of enhanced capabilities provided by technical advances to maintain safety. The IATA (International Air Transport Association) also presents the advantages of the application of the modern technologies of AI such as Machine learning (ML), Natural Language Processing (NLP), Expert Systems, Vision, Speech, Planning, and Robotics (IATA, 2018). Developing AI Systems such as Expert Systems, DSS, Intelligent Decision Support Systems (IDSS) considering new concepts in aviation need with using modern information technologies, and modern courses such as Data Science, Big Data, Data Mining, Multi-Criteria Decision Analysis, are relevant now.

Support for the safe functioning of aviation and ANS too is one of the most important scientific and technical problems. Statistical data show that human errors account for up to 80% of all aviation accidents (ICAO, 2004; Leychenko, 2006; National Transportation Safety Board (NTSB), 2022).

Aviation systems cannot be wholly free from dangerous factors and connected with their risks, while the elimination of aviation events and serious incidents continues to be the final goal of human activity in the sphere of aviation safety. Neither human activity nor systems created by it guarantee a total absence of operating errors and their consequence (ICAO, 2013a; 2013b). In such a way, safety is a dynamic characteristic of aviation with the help of which risk factors for flight safety should steadily decrease. It is important to note that the adoption of efficiency indices for ensuring flight safety is frequently influenced by internal and international standards and by cultural features and principles of safety culture (ICAO, 2009; ICAO, 2013a; Shmelova, Sikirda & Kovalyov, 2018).

The global air traffic management (ATM) operational concept of the ICAO vision directs an integrated, harmonized, and globally interoperable ATM system. The planning horizon is up to and beyond 2025. A lot of automation or technology will be required for the solution; however, they must be considered at each evolutionary stage. Safety can never fall below minimum acceptable levels (ICAO, 2009; ICAO, 2017a; ICAO, 2013b; ICAO, 2014). While risk factors into flight safety and operating errors are under control, such open and dynamic systems as civil aviation systems may be controlled providing the necessary balance between flight performance and safety requirements (Figure 1).

Figure 1. Safety balance model
(ICAO;2005)

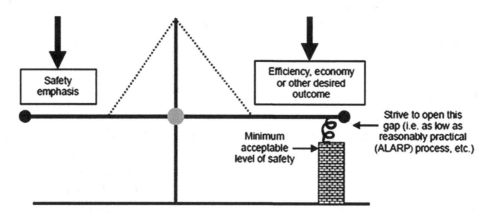

The latest demands of international aviation organizations are directed at the implementation of an integrated approach for the improvement of aviation safety. Many ICAO documents describe the problems in aviation and recommend the creation of support for a solution in each professional situation (ICAO, 2005; ICAO, 2012; ICAO, 2009). One of the ways to increase safety is the timely support of pilots in emergency situations (ICAO, 2012). A modern approach, founded on the characteristics (Performance-Based Approach – PBA) (ICAO, 2009) are basing on the next three principles:

1.   A strong focus on desired/required results.
2.   Informed decision making (DM) driven by those desired/required results.
3.   Reliance on facts and real data for DM.

Herein the principle "using facts and data while DM" admits that tasks shall comply with the widely known criteria SMART in management, which corresponds to the abbreviation of five words:

- Specific,
- Measurable,
- Achievable,
- Relevant,
- Time-bound.

So-called aeronautical DM is DM in a unique environment – aviation. It is a systematic approach to the mental process used by pilots to consistently determine the best course of action in response to a given set of circumstances. It is what a pilot intends to do, based on the latest information he has (Federal Aviation Administration [FAA], 2014).

As known, ICAO constantly develops and improves proactive, based on the evaluation of the risks, and methods, directed on the further decrease in the number of aviation events in the world (ICAO, 2021). Also, ICAO encourages aviation communities to recognize the importance of adherence to the single global approach for safety improvement and monitoring (ICAO, 2013b). Manual of ICAO "Global Air Traffic Management Operational Concept" (ICAO, 2005) presents basic methods and benefits of the support of aviation operators in their professional operations for effective organization of ATM systems:

Safety. The attainment of a safe system is the highest priority in ATM, and a comprehensive process for safety management is implemented.

Humans. Humans play an essential and, where necessary, central role in the global ATM system. Humans are responsible for managing the system, monitoring its performance, and intervening, when necessary, to ensure the desired system outcome.

Technology. The ATM operational concept addresses the functions needed for ATM without reference to any specific technology and is open to new technology. Communication, Navigation, and Surveillance (CNS) systems, and advanced information management technology are used to functionally combine the ground-based and airborne system elements into a fully integrated, interoperable, and robust ATM system.

Information. The ATM systems depend extensively on the provision of timely, relevant, accurate, accredited, and quality-assured information to collaborative DM and make informed decisions. Sharing information on a system-wide basis allows the ATM community to conduct its operations in a safe and efficient.

Collaboration. The ATM system is characterized by strategic and tactical collaboration in which the appropriate members of the ATM community participate in the definition of the types and levels of service. The ATM community collaborates to maximize system efficiency by sharing information, leading to dynamic and flexible decision-making (DM).

Continuity. The realization of the concept requires contingency effective measures to provide maximum continuity of service in emergencies (major outages, natural disasters, civil unrest, security threats or other unusual circumstances).

So, documents of ICAO have presented concepts about the Flight & Flow Information for a Collaborative Environment (FF-ICE), including support for a Performance-Based Approach (PBA), Collaborative Decision Making (CDM), System-Wide Information Sharing and Management (SWIM) by trajectory (ICAO, 2012b; ICAO, 2014; ICAO, 2015; EUROCONTROL, 2017). To ensure effective CDM, it is necessary to create a Collective Intelligent Decision Support System. Previously, the authors presented intelligent decision support systems for pilots and controllers (Shmelova, Sikirda, Yatsko & Kasatkin, 2022; Shmelova, Logachova & Yatsko, 2022). One of the progressive directions in the development of aviation systems is the use of AI systems in big control systems.

Artificial intelligence is the simulation of human intelligence processes through simulation, computer systems, and machines. These processes include learning (obtaining information and rules for using information); reasoning, evaluation, and modeling (the use of rules to obtain conclusions (approximate or definite results)); self-correction (evaluation of the obtained models). Specific applications of AI include Expert systems (ES); Decision support systems (DSS); automated systems; systems for pattern recognition, speech recognition, machine vision, etc. (ICAO, 2017a; ICAO, 2017b; IATA, 2018). AI (and DSS) is effective in minimizing risks and improving the quality of decisions in the aviation system.

Expected Benefits of this approach such as

1. From the airspace user (pilots) point of view - security systems have greater equity in access to airspace, greater access to timely and relevant information for decision support, and greater autonomy in DM, including conflict management, which will enable better performance business and individual results within an appropriate security framework.
2. On the part of the service provider (ATM) - security systems, including systems of airfield operators, can work in an information-rich environment, with real-time data, as well as system trends and forecast data, which will be promising for decision-making or DM tools will optimize the service to airspace users.
3. From a regulatory point of view, security systems will be reliable and open, which will not only make it easier to measure and control security, but also compare and integrate it at the global level, not for its own sake, but as a platform for continuous improvement.

Maximum effectiveness and efficiency of actions can be obtained by activities undertaken in the early phases of any system's life cycle (LC) since correcting problems during requirements definition and design is generally the most effective (Shmelova, Sterenharz & Dolgikh, 2020). The LC may include all components of AI for improving the effectiveness, safety, and activity of the aviation system and obtaining a synergetic effect (Figure 2). Usually, AI supports, DM in simple situations for data processing (Chialastri, 2019; Shmelova, Sikirda & Sterenharz, 2020). Hybrid Intelligence (HI) – effective aggregation of Natural Intelligence (NI) and Artificial Intelligence (AI) in DM. Intelligent Decision Support Systems with Hybrid Intelligence opportunity DM in an emergency – support of pilot in-flight.

Decision support systems contain common sets of components. These components include data-related components, algorithm-related components, user interface, and display-related components. Data-related components consist of modules that receive data, format data, store data, transmit data and archive data. Algorithm-related components use various methods such as decision models, rule-based algorithms, fuzzy logic algorithms, statistical algorithms, DM algorithms under uncertainty and risk, and data mining algorithms. A lot of research is being done to improve the operation of DSS - systems for supporting operators (Kashyap, 2019b; Subsorn & Singh, 2020; Shmelova & Sikirda, 2021). The problems of DSS information support were considered in the works of scientists (Tarasov, Gerasimov, 2007; Gerasimov, Lokazyuk, 2007; S Sirodzha, 2002). So, DSS can be defined as "an interactive computer system designed to support various types of decision-making activities, including semi-structured and unstructured tasks" (Tarasov, Gerasimov, 2007; Gerasimov, Lokazyuk, 2007; Zhang, 2011).

The development of *automated systems* in aviation, associated with an anthropocentric approach and the principles of human-oriented automation, required new approaches to solving problems of the human-machine interface (ICAO, 2002). One of the effective means of improving flight safety is the inclusion of AI systems in the automated air traffic control (ATC) systems of operators and pilots

(Kharchenko, Shmelova, Sikirda, 2012; 2016; Shmelova, Sikirda, Belyaev, 2014; Shmelova, Sikirda, Yatsko & Kasatkin, 2022), development of DSS for flight operators (Kharchenko, Shmelova, and Sikirda, 2012; 2016; Shmelova & Sikirda, 2021). Now, with the advent of Unmanned Aerial Vehicles (UAV)s, new systems are being considered, such as local DSS for operators of remotely piloted aircraft systems (RPAS) (Shmelova, Bondarev, 2019; Shmelova, Lazorenko & Burlaka, 2020; Shmelova, Sikirda, 2019).

Figure 2. The synergetic effect - LS of aviation technique with using AI capability
(Shmelova, Sterenharz, & Dolgikh, 2020)

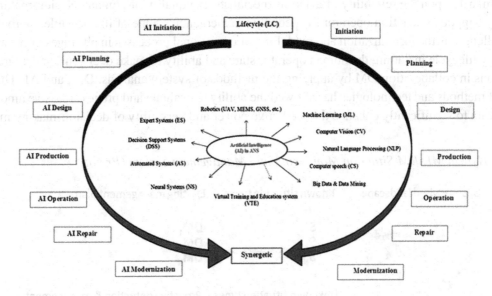

So, to simulate DM under conditions of an emergency, the next steps are proposed:

- deep analysis of an emergency
- intelligent data processing
- identification of the situation
- formalization of the situation using integrated models
- decomposition of the complex situation into subclasses
- synthesis of adapted deterministic models to AI-determined actions.

In cases of large and complex data, methods can be integrated into traditional and next-generation hybrid DM systems by processing unsupervised situation data in the deep landscape models (Figure 3), potentially at high data rates and in near real-time, producing a structured representation of input data with clusters that correspond to common situation types (Dolgikh, 2018). In Figure 3, a Deterministic action model is targeted to a specific situation type. Another benefit of these models is the potential ability of such systems to learn to identify relationships between different types of situations, again almost entirely in a self-supervised training regime with very limited requirements for ground truth data. Possible applications of such capabilities of machine intelligence models may extend to for example, learning to detect early signs or symptoms of developing situations via relationships between situation types, and the ability to raise notifications and early alerts that a human operator would be able to attend to proactively before the situation develops.

Nowadays a new approach to flight safety provision is forming in global practice. Building an effective safety management system (SMS) for aviation activity requires integrated research of the environment and conditions in which aviation enterprises and operators operate. The ICAO's term "Safety Management System" (SMS) integrates operations and technical systems with the management of financial and human resources to ensure aviation safety or the safety of the public (ICAO, 2009).

The effectiveness of aviation systems that manifests in the safe and efficient operation of flights depends primarily upon the reliability of aviation specialists, the quality of human decision-making, and the timely support of aviation operators, especially in emergencies. One of the possible approaches to these challenges is the formalization and modelling of operational processes in all stages of the aviation technology lifecycle including the human operator state and ability to make decisions, and aggregation of decisions in collaboration DM by applying the methods of system analysis, DM, and AI. The addition of AI methods and technologies has allowed the ability to evaluate and process massive amounts of relevant data to significantly enhance the predictive power and versatility of decision-making models.

Figure 3. Hybrid ML-DM Situation Monitoring and Management System (Prototype)

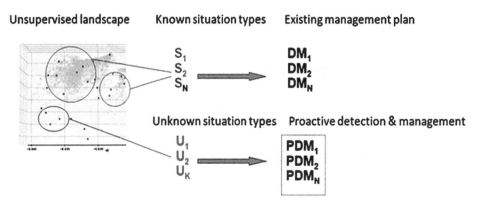

The Purposes of the work are

- The analysis and examples of the benefits of using AI models in aviation systems.
- The Intelligent Decision Support System for the Air Navigation System's human operators
- Models of CDM by ANS personnel (pilots, air traffic control operators (ATCO)s, engineers, etc.).

INTELLIGENT DECISION SUPPORT SYSTEMS IN AIR NAVIGATION SYSTEM

The effectiveness of ANS human operators' decisions depends on the rational use of intelligent automation at all stages of aircraft flight in the form of IDSS, with Hybrid Intelligence (NI or AI) in DM. Control of intellectualization processes and development of appropriate intelligent systems depends on the availability of initial data according to the quality of functioning of objects and subjects of subsystems in ANS. AI systems need to rationally support humans in their efforts essentially in difficult situations.

To design and develop an AI system, it is necessary to create an Expert system. An Expert system is an informal model of the system being created, with the help of an expert assessment, of small data it's possible to create a demo version of the AI system. The accumulation of data creates a real AI system. Ready-made AI systems have varying degrees of performance and DM. The degree of productivity changes from simple (simple actions) to complex (creative actions):

- Simple AI actions - repeating actions.
- Complicating AI actions - repeating actions and creating new actions according to existing rules.
- Complex AI actions - repeating actions, creating new actions, changing the rules for performing

So, steps for building an AI system:

1. Expert system - a data description information – using experts (according to statistics, experience, skills data too).
2. DM and CDM models – to improve and prepare data.
3. AI systems without training data and effective DM in difficult processes.
4. Big Data to create AI systems with training data and more effective DM /CDM.
5. Big Data to create an AI system with machine learning (ML) and intelligence DSS (IDSS)
6. Big Data to create an AI system with deep learning (DL) and IDSS, DM models, models of forecasting of development situations, and optimal solutions.
7. Intelligent systems of DM – combine natural and AI – Hybrid DSS.

The steps to create the IDSS for the ANS human operators in an emergency are presented in Table 1.

Table 1. The steps to create the IDSS for the ANS human-operators in an emergency

Step	System	Models	Input Data	Output Data
I	Expert System – a demo version of the Intelligent System	Expert estimates, statistics	Expert estimates	Expert estimates, statistics
II	DSS	Individual and CDM models	Expert estimates, statistics	Expert estimates, statistics, optimal solutions (individual and collaborative decision-making)
III	AI (without training)	Artificial Neural Network (ANN) of DM	Expert estimates, statistics, optimal solutions	The results of ANN solutions, Big Data
IV	AI with ML	ML ANN	Expert estimates, statistics, optimal solutions, Big Data	Big Data, DM, and forecasting the situation
V	AI with self-learning Deep Learning (DL)	Deep Learning (DL) Artificial Neural Network (ANN)	Big Data	Big Data, situation identification, DM, and forecasting the situation
VI	Intelligent systems, flexible systems with Hybrid Intelligence (HI) *IDSS*	Models of DM by the subjects of the situation (NI /AI)	Expert estimates, statistics, optimal solutions, Big Data, Analytical Data	Optimal/rational data, situation development control, data of DM by AI and NI

To simulate DM under conditions of an emergency, the next steps:

1. Deep analysis of an emergency and identification of the situation.
2. Decomposition of the complex situation into subsystems/subclasses.
3. Intelligent data processing.
4. Formalization of the situation using integrated models.
5. Synthesis of adapted deterministic models to AI-determined actions.

A scheme of the intelligent control module of IDSS for the ANS human operators in an emergency, which is based on Hybrid (combined) intelligence, is created (Figure 4). In its figure: AI – artificial intelligence; ANN – artificial neural network; ANS – air navigation system; BD – big data; CDM – collaborative decision-making; HI – hybrid intelligence; ML – machine learning. The intelligent control module of IDSS allows the ANS operators to control DM by AI in an emergency.

Figure 4. A scheme of the intelligent control module of IDSS for the ANS human-operators in an emergency

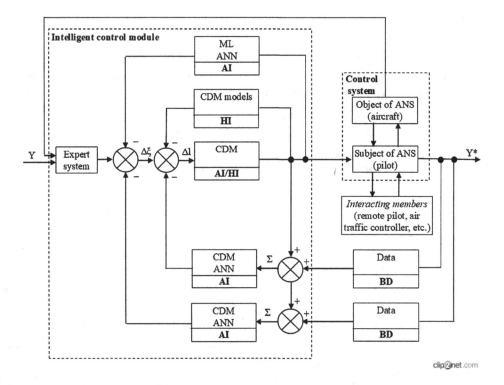

The input data required for the formation of decisions by the IDSS are divided into groups: expert, statistical, and experimental data. Expert data are stored in the knowledge base and constantly accumulated. Statistics and experimental data are gradually added to the results of the aviation experts' evaluation. The results of individual and collective DM by ANS human operators in an emergency are stored in the database of models and constantly accumulated too. The content of data and knowledge bases is adjusted based on information. The variety of data types for making decisions in an emergency requires a new approach to measuring potential subsequence. Machine Learning and, when enough data accumulates, Deep Learning (DL), based on ANN, is proposed. The ANN benefits are training ability on the examples, real-time operation, determinism, and robustness (Shmelova, Sikirda & Jafarzade, 2019; Sikirda, Kasatkin, & Tkachenko, 2019; Shmelova, Sikirda, Yatsko, Kasatkin, 2022) which determines the choice of the ANN for CDM by ANS operators in an emergency. The structure of the intelligent data processing for CDM by ANS operators in an emergency is given in Figure 5.

Figure 5. The structure of the intelligent data processing for CDM by ANS operators in the emergency based on ANN

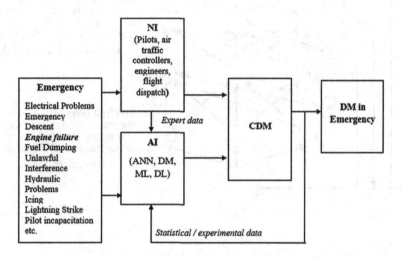

In the case of Machine Learning, normalization is a procedure for pre-processing of input data (training, testing, and validation samples, as well as real data), in which the values of the characteristics in the input vector are reduced to a certain range, for example, [0 … 1] or [-1 … 1] (Alharbi & Prince, 2020). The expert estimates are received based on the expert judgment method (EJM) (Salem & Shmelova, 2021).

Artificial Neural Networks for the IDSS by the ANS's Human-operators in an Emergency

For using CDMs (NI and AI) in IDSS in an emergency, a multilayer recurrent artificial neural network (ANN) with biases is developed (Figure 6). An ANN can approximate any functional dependence due to the hidden neuron layers and is capable of learning (Shmelova, Sikirda & Jafarzade, 2019; Sikirda, Shmelova, Kharchenko, & Kasatkin, 2021).

Figure 6. ANN model for CDM by the ANS human-operators in the emergency

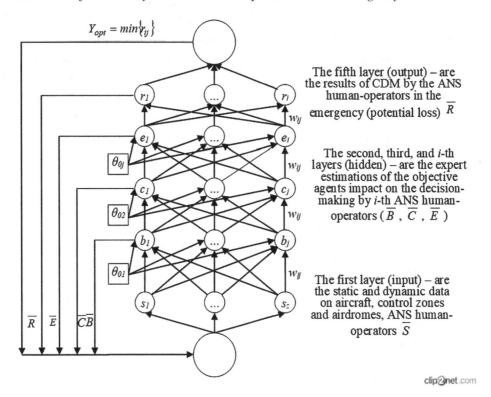

Consider the ANN model:

- The first layer (input) – corresponds to the losses in the emergency depending on the type of flight situation ($\bar{U}$).
- The second layer (hidden) – the standard time to perform technological procedures for emergency parrying ($\bar{T}$).
- The third layer (hidden) – the normative sequence of technological procedures for emergency parrying ($\bar{S}$).
- The fourth layer (output) – the risk assessment of emergency ($\bar{R}$). Additional input bias $\bar{\theta}$ characterizes the interaction of ANS operators.

Output vectors of the second, third, fourth layers:

$$\bar{T} = f\left(\bar{W}_1, \bar{U} - \bar{\theta}_j\right) \tag{1}$$

$$\bar{S} = f\left(\bar{W}_2, \bar{T} - \bar{\theta}_k\right) \tag{2}$$

$$\bar{R} = f\left(\bar{W}_3, \bar{S}\right) \tag{3}$$

where

$\bar{W}_1$ – are the weights that take into account the probability of violation of the standard time of technological procedures for emergency parrying, $\bar{W}_1 = \left\{w_{ij}\right\}$;

$\bar{W}_2$ – are the weights that take into account the probability of violation of the normative sequence of technological procedures for emergency parrying, $\overline{W}_2 = \left\{w_{jk}\right\}$;

$\bar{W}_3$ – are the weights that take into account the probability of complicating the flight situation (for example, engine failure can lead to a fire), $\bar{W}_3 = \left\{w_{kl}\right\}$;

$\bar{\theta}_j, \bar{\theta}_k$ – are the biases of indicators of timeliness and correctness of technological procedures for emergency parrying at joint concerted actions of ANS operators.

The following output signals of vectors of ANN layers are set $\bar{T}, \bar{S}, \bar{R}$:

$$T, S, R = \begin{cases} 1; \text{if } f\left(w_{ij}u_i - \theta_j\right), f\left(w_{jk}t_j - \theta_k\right), f\left(w_{kl}s_k\right) > 0 \\ 0; \text{if } f\left(w_{ij}u_i - \theta_j\right), f\left(w_{jk}t_j - \theta_k\right), f\left(w_{kl}s_k\right) \leq 0 \end{cases} \tag{4}$$

where f – is a nonlinear activation function.

Using Neuro Solutions version 7.1.1.1 (development of Neuro Dimension, Inc.) on the example of emergency "Failure and fire of the engine on the aircraft when climbing after take-off" (Sikirda & Shmelova, 2021) the multilayer feedforward perceptron with biases was built and trained with the teacher by the procedure of the error backpropagation (Figure 7). Input, intermediate, and output components of ANN are set according to statistics and expert evaluations by aviation experts (pilots, air traffic controllers, engineers, flight dispatch, etc.).

Figure 7. Example of ANN for FE "Failure and fire of the engine on the aircraft when climbing after take-off", which was built in the NeuroSolutions neuropackage

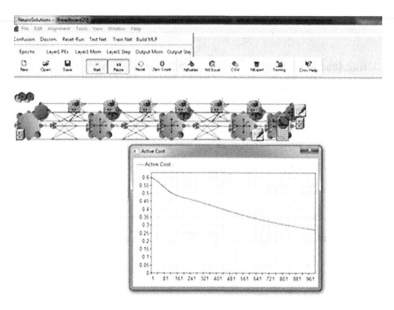

Input, intermediate, and output components of ANN are set according to statistics and expert evaluations by aviation experts (pilots, ATCOs, flight). Sometimes specialists from other fields, such as emergency and ground services, and medical staff may be involved in joint DM (Figure 8). For example, digital health and telemedicine in emergencies are applied, allowing to invite qualified medical personnel for consultation in case of incapacitation of one of the pilots or one of the passengers (Salem, 2020; Emergency telemedicine, 2022; Shmelova, Yatsko, Logachova, 2022).

Figure 8. The team of operators involved in Collaborative Decision-Making during the flight

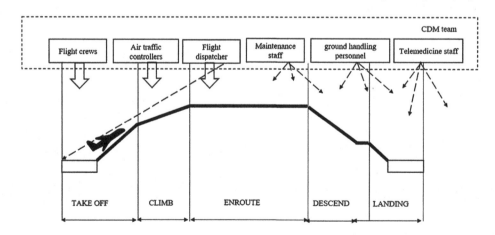

The learning ANN takes part as a partner in the SDM.

The basic models used in IDSS:

- DM's deterministic models ()
- DM's stochastic models (DM in risk and DM in uncertainty);
- CDM in Uncertainty
- Integrated DM models

Models of preferences obtained using the method of expert assessments (Salem & Shmelova,2018). The basic methods used in IDSS:

- Objective-subjective method for finding joint solutions to conflict management (Shmelova, Yatsko, Logachova, 2022)
- Neural networks - providing an easy way to model complex nonlinear functions for solving diagnostic and prognostic problems;
- Genetic algorithms - are able to approximate complex relationships in incomplete data sets, to find an optimal solution to complex problems;
- Fuzzy sets - can quantitatively encode qualitative information;
- Dynamic structural models - can simulate the basic functions of management, etc.

An ANN to evaluate the effectiveness of alternative options for completing the flight of the aircraft was developed (Figure 9). In ANN:

1. The aerodrome:
    a. Technical suitability of the airfield $\bar{B} = \{b_i\}$, $i = \overline{1,3}$
    b. Suitability of the airfield according to meteorological conditions $\bar{C} = \{c_j\}$, $j = \overline{1,3}$
2. Landing place (touchdown zone):
    a. Type of place $\bar{D} = \{d_k\}$, $k = \overline{1,1}$
    b. Type of underlying surface $\bar{E} = \{e_l\}$, $l = \overline{1,5}$
    c. Suitability of the site according to meteorological conditions $\bar{F} = \{f_m\}$, $m = \overline{1,3}$

The input parameters of the model in the form of ANN are the factors characterizing the potential alternative of flight completion. A binary vector is assigned to each input parameter, which reflects the presence (1) or absence (0) of a certain factor. The criterion for the effectiveness of alternative options for completing the flight Y_G is the potential loss resulting from the choice of a certain alternative decision (t_{cer}) with a limited flight time (t_{cr}):

$$t_{cer} \leq t_{cr}$$

$$Y_{Gaep} = f_G \left(\left[\bar{B} \cup \bar{C} \right] W_{BC,G} \right)$$

$$Y_{Gмайд} = f_G \left(\left[\bar{D} \cup \bar{E} \cup \bar{F} \right] W_{DEF,G} \right)$$

where

f_G - is the activation function, which is applied element-by-element to the components of the vector string placed in parentheses.

Figure 9. ANN model for evaluating the effectiveness of flight termination alternatives: a potential flight termination alternative – an aerodrome (a); a potential alternative to the end of the flight - the place (b)

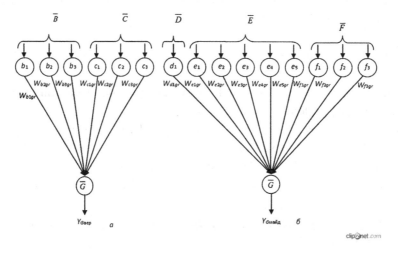

Effectiveness will depend on the type of potential landing place and what factors characterize it. The optimal option for completing the flight with minimal risk is chosen based on the minimization of potential damage:

$$Y_{Gopt} = \min f_G(\overline{G}).$$

Machine learning of ANN was done by modifying the weight coefficients of connections between neurons until the moment when the error reaches a minimum value and stops decreasing. A nonlinear sigmoid activation function was used for learning ($a > 0$):

$$f(x) = \frac{1}{1 + e^{-ax}}$$

The output fields for ML the network was estimated by the method of least squares with backlash, when the objective function of the ANN error to be minimized is the value:

$$\xi = \sum_j P(\frac{Y_j - Y_j'}{\varepsilon})$$

where

$$P(\Delta) = \begin{cases} (|\Delta| - 1)^2, if\ |\Delta| \geq 1, \\ 0, if\ |\Delta| < 1; \end{cases}$$

Y_j - the output according to the learning sample;

Y'_j - the output of the neural network;

ε - is a backlash that can vary from zero to the limit of the range of changes in the output field values.

The network is trained to predict the value of this field with an accuracy of +10% (- 10%) of the range of changes in the values of the potential loss, which fully satisfies the problem statement. A gradient descent algorithm with perturbation was used to train the ANN, which allows overcoming local irregularities of the error surface and not stopping at local minima. The backpropagation method, considering the perturbation, implements the following increase of weighting coefficients:

$$\delta W_{ij}(t) = \varphi \delta W_{ij}(t-1) + (1-\varphi)\eta g(t),$$

where

δ – increase in the weight vector;

φ – disturbance parameter;

η – learning rate factor, $0<\eta<1$;

$g(t)$ – gradient vector of the error function at the t-th iteration.

The developed neural network model based on a two-layer perceptron differs from the known ones in that it makes it possible to determine the amount of possible damage with a greater degree of accuracy in real time due to the comprehensive consideration of the influence of individual factors of different importance that characterize the potential place of forced landing. The proposed neural network model for assessing potential damage made it possible to increase the efficiency of choosing the optimal alternative to ending the flight due to considering the combined effect of individual factors characterizing the possible place of forced landing. It is advisable to include the developed model in the form of an intelligent module as part of the air traffic controller's decision-making support system in non-staff flight situations.

The Illustrative Example of the Collaborative Decision-Making by the Participants (Operators of the ANS and AI) in the Emergency "Engine Failure"

Data from the NTSB shows that over the past 10 years, there are about 25 incidents a year involving a jet engine failing either in flight or on the ground (NTSB, 2022). One of the reasons for aviation accidents during engine failure is considered improper and untimely decision-making by the aircrew (Kharchenko & Shmelova, 2012; Shmelova, 2019; Shmelova, Chialastri, Sikirda, Yatsko, 2021). There is presented an example of CDM by the ANS human-operators in the emergency "Engine failure" in flight. A similar problem was considered when a bird got into the engine.

Decision-making in this situation requires close interaction between the aircraft crew, air traffic controller's unit, and engineering service. A similar problem was considered when a bird got into the engine – DM in emergency "Engine failure during takeoff due to bird strike" (Shmelova, Yatsko, Sikirda, 2022), models of DM by the plot in emergency "Engine failure during take-off" (Shmelova, Chialastri, Sikirda, Yatsko, 2021). Joint DM in this situation requires close interaction between the aircraft crew, air traffic controller's unit, and engineering service. The authors propose to consider the problem of CDM, when, together with operators (NI), AI previously learned using ANN with the help of all specialists (pilots, air traffic controllers, and engineers) participates in DM.

Initial Data

1. Aircraft: Antonov An-148-100A, medium range aircraft (maximum landing mass 38550 kg).
2. Flight route (Figure 10): airdrome Kharkiv (UKHH) (A1) – airdrome Lviv (UKLL) (A2).
3. Participants:
   a. Pilot (on bord).
   b. Air traffic control operator (ATCO) (on ground) .
   c. Engineer (on bord).
   d. AI (DM using ANN)
4. Alternate airdromes:
   a. Boryspil (A_{r1});
   b. Hostomel (A_{r2}).
5. During the flight emergency "Engine failure". Commander decided to continue climbing flight level 200 which was slightly less than maximum level with one engine inoperative and proceed to the arrival airdrome Lviv. Distance to the destination was less than an hour with one engine inoperative.
6. While climbing, the weather conditions at the alternate airdrome Boryspil deteriorated.
7. An-148-100A is performing the flight in the segregated airspace, along the route there are UAV group flights.
8. Factors that impacting DM by the human-operators:
   a. $\{b\}$ – the factors that are analyzed by the human-operator H_1 (pilot);
   b. $\{c\}$ – the factors that are analyzed by the human-operator H_2 (controller);
   c. $\{e\}$ – the factors that are analyzed by the human-operator H_3 (engineer).
9. Factors that impacting DM by the AI - participant:
   a. $\{f\}$ – the factors that are analyzed by the H_4 (AI).

Figure 10. The flight route Lviv (A₁)–Kharkiv (A₂) at the navigation map

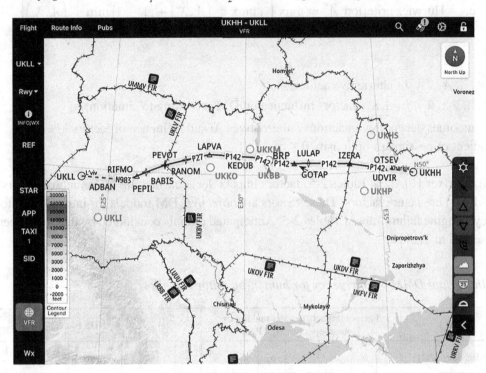

For the effective CDM, all human-operators have analyzed the actual situation. There are three human-operators in the CDM process: pilot (H_1), ATCO (H_2), engineer (H_3). Each human-operator has formed a DM matrix (DMM), where the possible decisions are the applicable airdromes for the route "Kharkiv–Lviv", and each human-operator has considered the identical factors in the actual situation, but with the varied benefits. When selecting the optimal airdrome, human-operators (H_1, H_2, H_3) is guided by the same factors (b_j, c_j, e_j) and AI (H_4) as ANN is guided by the same factors too:

i. b_1, c_1, e_1, f_1 – the weather conditions at the applicable airdromes/touchdown zone;
ii. b_2, c_2, $e_2 f_2$ – the distance to the applicable airdromes/ touchdown zone;
iii. b_3, c_3, $e_3 f_3$ – the technical characteristics of the runways;
iv. b_4, c_4, $e_4 f_4$ – the quantity of fuel onboard;
v. b_5, c_5, $e_5 f_5$ – the available navigation aids;
vi. b_6, c_6, $e_6 f_6$ – the sustainability of radio communication;
vii. b_7, c_7, $e_7 f_7$ – other factors (intensity of the air traffic, logistics, commercial questions, etc.).

10. Optimal solution A_{opt} chosen according to criteria Wald (minmax), Laplace, Hurwitz. The choice of criterion depends on the type of situation (for the first time, often occurs) and the degree of optimism:

   a. Minmax (Wald) criterion $A^* = \max_{A_i} \left\{ \min_{\lambda_j} u_{ij} \left(A_i, \lambda_j \right) \right\}$

   b. Laplace criterion $A^* = \max_{A_i} \left\{ \frac{1}{m} \sum_{j=1}^{n} u_{ij} \left(A_i, \lambda_j \right) \right\}$

c. Hurwicz criterion $A^* = \max\limits_{A_i} \left\{ \alpha \max\limits_{\lambda_j} u_{ij}\left(A_i, \lambda_j\right) + \left(1-\alpha\right) \min\limits_{\lambda_j} u_{ij}\left(A_i, \lambda_j\right) \right\}$

where

$A = \{A_1, A_2 \ldots A_i \ldots A_m\}$ - alternative actions;

$\lambda = \{\lambda_1, \lambda_2 \ldots \lambda_j \ldots \lambda_n\}$, $j = \underline{1, n}$ - factors influence on DM according to situation;

$u_{ij}(A_i, \lambda j_j$- outcomes depending on actions / alternatives Ai and influence of factors λj

α – coefficient of pessimism-optimism, $0 \leq \alpha \leq 1$

In DM matrixes $[U(A;\lambda)]$(Tables 2-5) factors impact decision-making by human-operators (H$_1$, H$_2$, H$_3$) and AI (H$_4$) are nature factors. These factors are *objective*. DM models for human-operators in the emergency "Engine failure" are in Tables 2-5. Anticipated outputs considered by the pilot (operator H_1) are represented in Table 2.

Table 2. Individual DMM in emergency for human-operator H_1 (pilot)

The Matrix 1		Factors Impact Decision-making by Human-operator H_1 – Pilot							Decisions				
Possible decisions {PD}		b_1	b_2	b_3	b_4	b_5	b_6	b_7	W	L	H, α=0.7	H, α=0.3	H, α=0.5
Departure airdrome	Kharkiv (A_1)	3	7	8	10	9	7	4	3	6,86	**7,9**	5,1	**6,5**
Arrival airdrome	Lviv (A_2)	9	4	8	6	9	8	9	**4**	**7,57**	7,5	**5,5**	**6,5**
Alternate airdromes	Boryspil (A_{r1})	5	5	9	8	10	9	3	3	7,00	**7,9**	5,1	**6,5**
	Hostomel (A_{r2})	5	5	7	7	7	7	3	3	5,86	5,8	4,2	5

The optimal airdrome for emergency landing on the route "Kharkiv–Lviv" according to the pilot's decision by the criteria of Wald and Laplace, optimal solution - is Lviv (A_2); by the criteria of Hurwitz (α=0.7) are Kharkiv (A_1) and Boryspil (A_{r1}), by the criteria of Hurwitz (α=0.3) is Lviv (A_2). The coefficient of optimism-pessimism indicates the degree of rationalism (1£α£1). For joint solutions, a solution with α=0,3 (rationalism with minimal risk). Anticipated outputs considered by the controller (operator H_2) are represented in Table 3.

Table 3. Individual DMM in emergency for human-operator H_2 (controller)

The Matrix 2		Factors Impact Decision-making by Human-operator H_2 – Controller							Decisions		
Possible decisions {PD}		c_1	c_2	c_3	c_4	c_5	c_6	c_7	W	L	$H, \alpha=0.5$
Departure airdrome	Kharkiv (A_1)	2	7	8	7	7	7	4	2	6.00	5.0
Arrival airdrome	Lviv (A_2)	9	4	8	6	9	8	9	**4**	**7.57**	**6.5**
Alternate airdromes	Boryspil (A_{r1})	5	6	9	8	9	9	2	2	6.86	5.5
	Hostomel (A_{r2})	5	6	7	7	9	7	2	2	6.14	5.5

The optimal airdrome for emergency landing on the route "Kharkiv–Lviv" according to the controller's decision by the criteria of Wald, Laplace, and Hurwitz is Lviv (A_2). The matrix of the anticipated outputs of decision-making by the engineer is represented in Table 4.

Table 4. Individual DMM in emergency for human-operator H_3 (engineer)

The Matrix 3		Factors Impact Decision-making by Human-operator H_3 – Engineer							Decisions		
Possible decisions {PD}		e_1	e_2	e_3	e_4	e_5	e_6	e_7	W	L	$H, \alpha=0.3$
Departure airdrome	Kharkiv (A_1)	3	7	8	7	7	7	4	3	6.14	4.5
Arrival airdrome	Lviv (A_2)	9	4	8	9	9	8	9	**4**	**8.00**	**5.5**
Alternate airdromes	Boryspil (A_{r1})	5	5	9	8	9	9	3	3	6.86	4.8
	Hostomel (A_{r2})	5	5	7	9	9	7	3	3	6.43	4.8

The optimal airdrome for emergency landing on the route "Kharkiv–Lviv" according to the human-operator H3 - engineer decision by the criteria of Wald, Laplace, and Hurwitz is Lviv (A_2). The matrix of the anticipated outputs of decision-making by the AI (participant - H_4) is represented in Table 5. Participant H4 - AI, in the creation of which the pilots, dispatchers, and engineers participated as experts. Considered a similar problem "Emergency situation on the An-148", considers the influence of factors on decision-making. The choice of the optimal alternative using the expert judgment method (EJM) was evaluated. An AI system has been created, with training, which helps to decision-making in an emergency (Figure 9).

Table 5. Individual DMM in emergency for participant H_4 (AI)

The Matrix 3		Factors Impact Decision-making by Participant H_4 – AI							Decisions		
Possible decisions {PD}		f_1	f_2	f_3	f_4	f_5	f_6	f_7	W	L	H, $\alpha=0.7$
Departure airdrome	Kharkiv (A_1)	3	8	9	8	7	7	4	3	6,57	7,2
Arrival airdrome	Lviv (A_2)	8	4	8	6	9	8	10	**4**	**7,57**	**8,2**
Alternate airdromes	Boryspil (A_{r1})	6	5	9	8	9	9	3	3	7,00	7,2
	Hostomel (A_{r2})	7	5	8	8	9	7	3	3	6,71	7,2

The optimal airdrome for the emergency landing on the route "Kharkiv–Lviv" according to the AI's decision by the criteria of Wald, Laplace, and Hurwitz ($\alpha=0.7$) is Lviv (A_2). To determine the consistency of participants, collective DMMs were formed, in which the factors in the individual DMM for the operators (pilot (H_1), controller (H_2), and engineer (H_3)) and DM of AI (H_4) are identical, the decisions of the participants are taken from the matrices, represented in Tables 6. In the collective matrices, the *subjective* factors – opinions of the participants are consumed. The optimal collective decisions by the criterion of Wald are presented in Table 6. In this case, the optimal airdrome for landing is determined by the objective factors (weather conditions at the applicable airdromes, distance to the applicable airdromes, technical characteristics of the runways, a quantity of fuel onboard, available navigation aids, sustainability of radio communication, etc.) and subjective factors (the features of the pilot, controller, engineer, AI).

Table 6. Collective DMM in emergency for all operators

{A}	Participants (Operators (Pilot (H_1), Controller (H_2), and Engineer (H_3)) and AI (H_4)														
	Criteria of Wald					Criteria of Laplace					Criteria of Horwitz				
	H_1	H_2	H_3	H_4	W	H_1	H_2	H_3	H_4	L	H_1 ($\alpha=0,3$)	H_2 ($\alpha=0,5$)	H_3 $\alpha=0,3$	H_4 ($\alpha=0,7$)	H, ($\alpha=0,5$)
Kharkiv (A_1)	3	2	3	3	2	6,86	6,00	6,14	6,57	6,39	5,10	5	4,5	7,2	5,85
Lviv (A_2)	4	4	4	4	4	7,57	7,57	8,00	7,57	7,68	5,50	6,5	5,5	8,2	6,85
Boryspil' (A_{c1})	3	2	3	3	2	7,00	6,86	6,86	7,00	6,93	5,10	5,5	4,8	7,2	6,00
Hostomel' (A_{c2})	3	2	3	3	2	5,86	6,14	6,43	6,71	6,29	4,20	5,5	4,8	7,2	5,70

The optimal airdrome for landing in the emergency "Engine failure", determined based on the objective and subjective factors, is the arrival airdrome Lviv (A_2) according to the criterion of Wald, Laplace, and Hurwitz. The optimal collective decision according to the Hurwitz criterion considers different degrees of optimism when decision-making (pilot - $\alpha=0,3$, dispatcher - $\alpha=0,5$, engineer - $\alpha=0,3$; AI - $\alpha=0,7$). Collaborative DM of all participants according to the Hurwitz criterion had degrees of optimism $\alpha=0,5$ (rationalism). The accounts demonstrated a balance between the flight safety and value of the flight (maximization of flight safety and minimization of loss).

Education of AI Methods of Aviation Operators, Collaborative DM in Education, Expert Judgment Method

To improve the efficiency of aviation systems, it is proposed to introduce AI methods for training aviation specialists. It is necessary to integrate training systems for various specialists (pilots, air traffic controllers, flight dispatchers, engineers) in solving joint tasks. In the operation of aviation systems, there is often a need for CDM (ICAO, 2014). CDM is a concept of rational interaction of specialists involved in DM. To determine the consistency of the opinions of experts and decision-making participants, the method of expert evaluation is used (Shmelova, Sikirda, Salem, Rizun, Kovalyov, 2018).

In AI, an ES is a computer system that simulates the DM ability of a human-operators (IATA, 2018). The ICAO documents recommend developing Intelligent ESs in aviation to support operators (ICAO, 2011, 2012a, 2018). There are many ESs needing and implicating in ANS by students at National aviation University (Shmelova, Kharchenko, Sikirda, 2016), such as: quantitative estimation of the complexity of the stages the aircraft flight; navigation parameters of flight; landing system GNSS, ILS, VOR, etc. Knowledge - characteristics of systems obtained because of practice and professional experience of experts. To build an emergency, the following Algorithm of the building of Expert Systems is used:

The Algorithm for the building of Expert Systems

1. Building main components of ES: Users interface; Database; Base Knowledge.
2. System analysis of complex system. Decomposition of complex systems on subsystems:
   a. Definition subsystems for expert estimation of their significance and description of the characteristics of subsystems.
   b. Definition of criteria estimation and description of criteria features.
   c. Estimation of subsystems using EJM by criterion and obtaining weight coefficients of subsystem significance by criterion.
3. Aggregation subsystems in systems.
   a. 3. a. Additive aggregation of subsystems:

$$W_j = \sum_{i=1}^{n} \omega_i F_{ij}, i = \overline{1,n}, j = \overline{1,m} \tag{5}$$

   b. 3. b. Multiplicative aggregation of subsystems:

$$W_j' = \prod_{i=1}^{n} F_{ij}^{\omega_i}, i = \overline{1,n}, j = \overline{1,m} \tag{6}$$

4. Graphical presentation of significance of subsystems in Expert System.

For student Training N1 "Expert Judgment Method (EJM) / Multi-criteria decision problems" was building, it includes:

Expert Judgment Method (EJM) / Multi-criteria decision problems" was building, it includes:

1. Lessons:
2. Theory. Basic of EJM for ANS (Classification of methods of DM. The algorithm of EJM. The matrix of individual and group preferences. Coordination of experts' opinion. Multi-criteria decision problems.
3. Practice. Tasks: Quantitative estimation of the complexity of the aircraft flight 2. 7 stages – definition of significance (complexity) of the phases of flight of the aircraft (Figure 11).

Figure 11. The process of applying solutions to many similar tasks in the quantitative estimation of the complexity of the aircraft's flight stages.

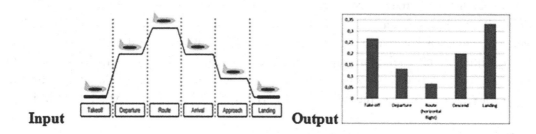

4. *Individual work.* DM in the Team. Lottery-choice of tasks for the team.
5. *Presentation* of results

To build an expert system, it is necessary to determine the significance of the subsystems (parameters, characteristics, values, etc.) in the system, which is investigated with the help of expert knowledge. The main method for building the Knowledge Base in the Expert System is the *Expert Judgment.* At the level of education "master" students study the course "Application of AI in the ANS" and study main methods of building AI systems (Machine Learning (ML); Expert Systems (ES); Neural Networks).

Therefore, it is necessary to present ANS as socio-technical system (STS) too and to applicate AI methods for development capacity of AN STS. ANS may be referred to as STS within which close cooperation between human and technological components occurs. The distinguishing feature of the STS is the availability of hazardous kinds of activity as well as usage of the high-level technologies in production. Since operations in STS generally involve high-risk / high-hazard activities, the consequences of safety breakdowns are often catastrophic in terms of loss of life and property (ICAO, 2004). The more an operator is trying to control a production process being aided by high-level technologies, especially in case of distant operation, the more non-transparent becomes the result of the operation of a system, which is accompanied by a high degree risk of catastrophe causing (ICAO, 2002).

So, the consequence of the interdependence between people and technology, complex and often overlooked changes in STS may occur over time. Accident prevention activities in STS recognize that major safety problems do not belong exclusively to either the human or the technical components; rather, they often emerge from poorly understood interactions between people and technology (ICAO, 2002). Therefore, it is necessary to analyze and classify all the factors in the ANS that have an impact on the H-O in the performance of professional activities guided by the requirements of ICAO documents. The authors analyzed the factors that affect the operator of ANS in the social environment and are represented by the ANS as an STS, which needs diagnostics and monitoring of all professional and non-professional factors that influence DM by the operators in STS. Non-professional factors (individually psychological, socio-psychological, and psychophysiological factors) influence on DM of operators too (Kharchenko, Shmelova & Sikirda, 2012).

Examples of Applied AI in education course "Informatics of Decision Making" and "Application of AI in the ANS" for aviation students and future personal of ANS in Table 7.

Table 7. Applied AI in education course "Informatics of DM".

Content	Pilot	ATCO	Engineer	UAV Operator
Aviation man-machine system (MMS)	Analysis and synthesis of aviation using theory of automatic control			
	MMS "pilot – aircraft" Analysis and synthesis of aviation using theory of automatic control	MMS "ATCO - aircraft"	MMS	MMS "operator UAV"
Aviation expert system of quantitative estimation	Expert Judgment Method / Multi-criteria decision problems			
	Significance (complexity) of the phases of flight of the aircraft	Controller's workload for aircraft service	Significance of the Landing System (GNSS, ILS, VOR, VOR/DME)	Significance of the UAVs, phases of flight of the UAVs
Decision Support system of H-O in ANS	Models of DSS: deterministic and stochastic models of DM			
	DM of pilot in emergency	DM of ATCO in emergency	DM of engineer in service/emergency	DM of unmanned pilot
DM in certainty	Network planning of action of H-O in service/ emergency			
	Graph of procedures of pilot in emergency	Graph of procedures of ATCO in emergency	Graph of procedures in service of equipment	Graph of procedures of unmanned pilot in emergency
DM in risk	Decision tree of forecasting of action of H-O in emergency			
	DM in emergency	DM in emergency	DM in service of equipment	DM in emergency
DM in uncertainty	Criteria optimal DM in uncertainty (Wald, Laplace, etc.)			
	Optimal landing aerodrome in emergency	Optimal landing aerodrome in emergency	Optimal action in emergency	Optimal landing aerodrome/place in emergency
Neural Networks	Forecasting of outcomes in emergencies			
Markov Networks	Neural network admission student to simulator training			
GERT-models	Development and forecasting the emergency /Preventing catastrophic situation			
Fuzzy logic	Quantitative estimation of the outcomes /risk in emergencies			
ANSTS	Analysis of ANS as STS and diagnostics, monitoring of the factors (professional and non-professional) that influence on DM by the H-O in STS (individual-psychological, socio-psychological, and psychophysiological factors)			

What distinguishes an AI system from a standard software system is its inherent ability to learn, improve, and predict. Through learning, an AI system can generate knowledge and apply it to new situations that have never been encountered before. But the first step that needs to be taken to build an AI system is to select experts. There are different specialties of experts, such as pilots, air traffic controllers, engineers, and flight dispatch, all have main goals - to provide safety and efficiency in aviation systems.

Training of Air Traffic Controllers, Minimization of Errors

An air traffic controller (ATC) is one of the main elements of the global air traffic service (ATS) system, whose duties are to maintain a safe, orderly, and accelerated flow of air traffic. There are strict requirements for the dispatcher in terms of skills, abilities, and level of knowledge as participants of ANS. The ANS faces a simple task "to ensure the availability of the right specialist for a certain ANC unite to serve the required air traffic flow". In error management, two main approaches can be distinguished:

1. *Organizational.* It consists of the management of errors on the part of the air navigation system: The specialist has a right to make a mistake, but the system should prevent him from doing this or minimize its effect.
2. *Individual.* Refers to the specialist's individual abilities to control his own psychophysiological state and error management. Characterized by the specialist's ability to warn, detect, and correct the error, thanks to the awareness of one's own psychophysiological state during work.

An organizational approach to minimize the probability of errors was considered based on error management of the ANS in which the specialist works. A block approach can be applied for detection and analysis of air traffic controller errors, depending on the scale of the review (Table 8). Considering the principles of a competence-oriented approach, the availability of a database regarding aviation accidents, incidents, risks, and factors influencing the ATC's performance at the level of the relevant workplace within the air traffic service authority, allows it to precisely detect those errors that are specific to this workplace. One of the advantages of AI is that it considers the rate of assimilation of educational material, needs, and preferences in the choice of means and methods of conveying information, adjusted by the individual study profile of each student. That allows adapting the training process to the training needs of each "student".

Table 8. Sources of information on air traffic controller error statistics

The Scope of Error Review	Sources of Information on Air Traffic Controller Errors
ICAO level	ICAO database of aviation accidents, incidents and dangerous factors affecting the air traffic controller's performance
EUROCONTROL level	EUROCONTROL Database of aviation accidents, incidents, and dangerous factors affecting on work capacity of air traffic controller (EUROCONTROL, 2018)
Air navigation service provider level	National database of aviation accidents, incidents and dangerous factors affecting the ATC's performance
Level of the regional structural unit as part of provider	The database of aviation accidents, incidents and dangerous factors affecting the ATC's performance
Level of the ATS unite	Air traffic service unites database of aviation accidents, incidents and dangerous factors affecting the performance of the air traffic controller
The level of the corresponding worker place as a part of ATS unites	Relevant workplace of air traffic service unites database of aviation accidents, incidents and dangerous factors affecting the ATCs work capacity

According to Gartner Forecasts (Gartner, 2021) applied AI and the introduction of ML are two of the most significant technological trends in the AI market. In a generalized form, the architecture of the AI system in the training of ATC specialists has the following view (Figure 12). In Figure 12 next definitions and values

- instructor is a person who carries out a certain stage of the student's training. It can be a teacher, theoretical training instructor, practical training instructor
- the marks Δt_B or I_B. Realization of training for a certain period or before passage certain topics, practical exercises, etc.
- Q_{ALC}. Demonstration by the trainee of the actual level of competence.
- Q_{RLC}. Required level of competence
- $Xi, Yi, Zi ...Ni$, markers of the actual level of the competences, that demonstrated by the trainee at the intermediate control.

Figure 12. Generalized architecture of AI system for the training of air traffic controllers.

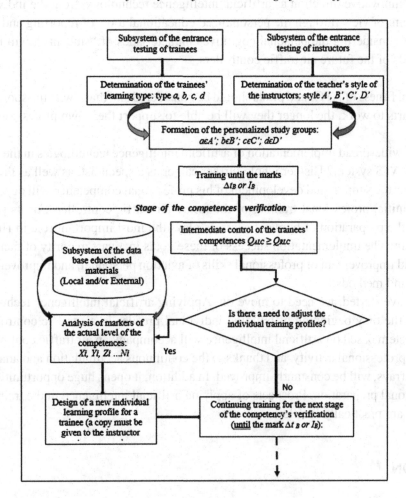

Some intermediate conclusions:

1.   Of course, this architecture is given in its most generalized form. Because, for example, the subsystem of the initial testing of trainees for determining the preferred type of training for each of them, or a subsystem of the educational materials database (local and/or external) will be constantly improving and developing and, will be a complex artificial intelligence system in their area of responsibility.
2.   One of the advantages of artificial intelligence is that it considers the rate of learning material, requirements, and preferences in the choice of means and methods of conveying information. It gives the opportunity to adapt the training process to the educational needs of each "student". The possibility of training anytime and anywhere is another huge advantage of artificial intelligence technology.
3.   Modern students (and future air traffic controllers are no exception) are quite pragmatic people and most of them pay for their education. Therefore, they do not want to spend money on abstract things. With their own money, they want to get (in a short period of time) a high-quality professional education, thanks to which they will be able to build a successful career. Implementation of such an innovative direction as artificial intelligence technology, from the individualization of training point of view through the personalized educational tools of reporting and assimilation of knowledge considering the personal cognitive characteristics of "students", will be able to meet the demands of the future air traffic controllers.

Note. Medical fitness of ATCs and pilots should be considered and that's why the sooner this category of specialists starts to work, the longer they will be able to support their own professional longevity.

4.   What does widespread implementation of artificial intelligence technologies in the training system give to the ATS system? His/her whole further career as a specialist, as well as the organization's expenses for the support and development of his professional competence will depend on the quality of the initial professional training of the future air traffic controller. For its part, ICAO also notes that the preparation of human resources plays the most important role in flight safety goal achievement. The implementation success of these goals in a vast majority of factors depends on training and improvement of professional skills of aviation personnel, and improvement of training programs and methods.
5.   Once we have started, we need to move on. Applying artificial intelligence technology in initial training is the only beginning of building individual profiles in air traffic controller training. A training system based on artificial intelligence will accompany an air traffic controller throughout all his\her professional activity, and thanks to the continuous accumulation and analysis of significant data arrays, will be constantly improved. In addition, it opens huge opportunities in the sphere of professional preparation. Prospects of applying artificial intelligence in the training of aviation specialists are practically limitless.

CONCLUSION

The effectiveness of aviation systems depends on the use of innovative technology in aviation nowadays such as AI. Education of aviation operators using modern information technologies and modern courses such as Expert systems, AI, Decision Making, Data Science, Big Data, Data Mining, Multi Criteria Decision Analysis, Collaboration DM, Blockchain, and Neural networks, are important nowadays.

The steps to create the IDSS for the ANS operators in an emergency are presented. A scheme of the intelligent control module of IDSS for the ANS operators in an emergency, which is based on the HI, is worked out. The statistical, experimental, and expert input data required by Intelligent Decision Support System for the ANS operators in an emergency are determined. ANN model for CDM by the ANS human operators (pilot, air traffic controller, and engineer) in the emergency is designed. The order of the CDM by the varied aviation collaborators for selecting the most appropriate landing airdrome in an emergency during the aircraft flight in the integrated airspace is developed. The examples of the individual and collective models of decision-making by the pilot, air traffic controller, and engineer in the emergency "Engine failure" in the conditions of segregated airspace based on the methods of decision-making under uncertainty are presented. The direction of further research is the development of individual and collective decision-making models by all aviation collaborators in emergencies to use as a part of IDSS for the cooperation of human and artificial intelligence. Models of CDM where participant operators (pilots, air traffic controllers, engineers) and AI participate together in decision-making in an "Engine failure" emergency were obtained. Intelligent Decision Support Systems with Hybrid Intelligence opportunity DM in an emergency – support of operating pilot were presented.

FUTURE RESEARCH DIRECTIONS

Next research is required to develop a methodology for effective interaction between AI systems and ANS subjects (pilot, remote pilot, air traffic controller, ground operator, flight dispatcher, engineer, etc.). This decision is made based on both the objective factors (weather conditions at the applicable airdromes, distance to the applicable airdromes, technical characteristics of the runways, a quantity of fuel onboard, available navigation aids, sustainability of radio communication, etc.) and subjective factors (the features of the pilot, controller, engineer). The calculation results demonstrated a balance between flight safety and the value of the flight (maximization of flight safety and minimization of loss). The authors have presented ANS as STS and AI systems. The evolution of HF's models is associated with the appearance of new system components such as culture, AI, CDM, safety culture, etc. These concepts must influence on safe and efficient operations of the aviation industry.

Further research should be also directed to the solution of the problem of emergency situations prerequisites and preventing catastrophic situations. Models of flight emergency development and of DM by an operator in-flight emergency will allow modeling of the operator's actions and CDM obtained of operator behavior in extreme situations. It is necessary to develop Hybrid systems in Air Navigation systems where participants such as operators (pilots, air traffic controllers, flight dispatchers, and UAV's operators too) and AI participate in joint decision making in in-flight emergencies and in other situations.

REFERENCES

AirCare Access Assistance. (2022). Emergency telemedicine and mission safety support (TM), (2022). Aircare. https://www.aircareinternational.com/inflight-emergency-tele medicine

Alharbi, B., & Prince, M. (2020). A hybrid artificial intelligence approach to predict flight delay. In *International Journal of Engineering Research and Technology. 13*(4), 814-822. http://www.irphouse.com/ijert20/ijertv13n4_29.pdf

Chialastri, A. (2019). AF 447 as a Paradigmatic Accident: The Role of Automation on a Modern Airplane. In T. Shmelova & Yu. Sikirda (Eds.), *Automated Systems in the Aviation and Aerospace Industries* (pp. 166–192). IGI Global. doi:10.4018/978-1-5225-7709-6.ch006

Dolgikh, S. (2018). Spontaneous Concept Learning with Deep Autoencoder. [Canada.]. *International Journal of Computational Intelligence Systems*, *12*(1), 1–12. doi:10.2991/ijcis.2018.25905178

EUROCONTROL. (2017). Airport CDM Implementation. *Manual*, Brussels, Belgium, Available from: Eurocontrol. https://www.eurocontrol.int/sites/default/files/publication/files/airport-cdm-manual-2017.PDF

EUROCONTROL. (2018). EUROCONTROL Voluntary ATM Incident Reporting (EVAIR) *Bulletin No 19*. Eurocontrol. https://www.eurocontrol.int/sites/default/files/publication/files/evair-bulletin-19.pdf

Federal Aviation Administration. (2014). *Pilot/Controller Glossary*. FAA.

Gartner. (2022) *Forecasts Worldwide Artificial Intelligence*. Gartner. https://www.gartner.com/en/newsroom/press-releases/2021-11-22-gartner-forecasts-worldwide-artificial-intelligence-software-market-to-reach-62-billion-in-2022

Gerasimov, B., & Lokazyuk, V. (2007). *Intelligent Decision Support Systems: monograph*. European University Press.

International Air Transport Association (IATA). (2018) Artificial intelligence (AI) in the aviation industry. https://hosteddocs.ittoolbox.com/AI-White-Paper.pdf

International Civil Aviation Organization. (2002). Human Factors Guidelines for Safety Audits Manual (1st ed.). Doc. ICAO 9806-AN/763.

International Civil Aviation Organization. (2004). *Cross-Cultural Factors in Aviation Safety: Human Factors Digest Nº 16. Circ. ICAO 302-AN/175.*

International Civil Aviation Organization. (2005). *Global Air Traffic Management Operational Concept. Doc. ICAO 9854.*

International Civil Aviation Organization. (2009). Manual on Global Performance of the Air Navigation System (PBA). Doc. 9883.

International Civil Aviation Organization. (2012a). Manual on the Approval of Training Organizations. Doc. ICAO 9841-AN/456.

International Civil Aviation Organization. (2012b). *Manual on Flight and Flow Information for a Collaborative Environment (FF-ICE). Doc. 9965.*

International Civil Aviation Organization. (2013a). Safety Management Manual (SMM) (3rd ed.). Doc. ICAO 9859-AN 474.

International Civil Aviation Organization. (2013b). *State of Global Aviation Safety*.

International Civil Aviation Organization. (2014). *Manual on Collaborative Decision-Making (CDM), Doc. 9971*.

International Civil Aviation Organization. (2015). *Manual on System Wide Information Management (SWIM) Concept*, Doc. 10039-AN/511.

International Civil Aviation Organization. (2017a). *Global Aviation Security Plan (GASP)*.

International Civil Aviation Organization. (2017b). *Global Air Navigation Plan (GANP), Doc 9750 Canada*.

International Civil Aviation Organization. (2018). Potential of Artificial Intelligence (AI) in Air Traffic Management (ATM). *In: Thirteenth Air Navigation Conference ICAO*, Montréal, Canada.

International Civil Aviation Organization. (2021). Handbook for CAAs on the Management of Aviation Safety Risks related to COVID-19. Doc 10144.

Izonin, I., Tkachenko, R., Shakhovska, N., Ilchyshyn, B., & Singh, K. K. (2022). A Two-Step Data Normalization Approach for Improving Classification Accuracy. In *Medical Diagnosis Domain. Mathematics, 10*(11), 1942. doi:10.3390/math10111942

Kashyap, R. (2019a). Artificial Intelligence Systems in Aviation. In T. Shmelova & Yu. Sikirda (Eds.), *Cases on Modern Computer Systems in Aviation* (pp. 1–26). IGI Global.

Kashyap, R. (2019b). Decision Support Systems in Aeronautics and Aerospace Industries. In T. Shmelova & Yu. Sikirda (Eds.), *Automated Systems in the Aviation and Aerospace Industries* (pp. 138–165). IGI Global. doi:10.4018/978-1-5225-7709-6.ch005

Kharchenko, V., Shmelova, T., & Sikirda, Y. (2012). *Decision-Making of Operator in Air Navigation System: monograph*. Kirovograd: KFA of NAU.

Kharchenko, V., Shmelova, T., & Sikirda, Y. (2016). *Decision-Making in Socio-Technical Systems: monograph*. NAU.

Leychenko, S., Malishevskiy, A., & Mikhalic, N. (2006). *Human Factors in Aviation: monograph in two books. Book 1st*. YMEKS.

National Transportation Safety Board. (2022). *Aviation Accident Statistics*. National Transportation Safety Board (NTSB). https://www.ntsb.gov/Pages/search.aspx#k=Aviation%20Accident%20Statistics

Salem, A.-B. (Ed.). (2020). *Innovative Smart Healthcare and Bio-Medical Systems: AI, Intelligent Computing and Connected Technologies*. CRC, Press.

Salem, A.-B., & Shmelova, T. (2021). Intelligent Expert Decision Support Systems: Methodologies, Applications, and Challenges. In *Research Anthology on Decision Support Systems and Decision Management in Healthcare, Business, and Engineering* (pp. 510–531). IGI Global. doi:10.4018/978-1-7998-9023-2.ch024

Shmelova, T. (2019). Integration deterministic, stochastic, and non-stochastic uncertainty models in conflict situations. In CEUR Vol 2805 Workshop Proceedings (Vol. 2588). CEUR-WS.

Shmelova, T., & Bondarev, D. (2019). Automated System of Controlling Unmanned Aerial Vehicles Group Flight: Application of Unmanned Aerial Vehicles Group. In T. Kille, P. R. Bates, & S. Y. Lee (Eds.), *Unmanned Aerial Vehicles in Civilian Logistics and Supply Chain Management* (pp. 208–242). IGI Global. doi:10.4018/978-1-5225-7900-7.ch008

Shmelova, T., Chialastri, A., Sikirda, Y., & Yatsko, M. (2021) Models of Decision-Making by the Pilot in Emergency "Engine Failure During Take-Off" In *CEUR*. https://ceur-ws.org/Vol-3101/Paper26.pdf

Shmelova, T., Lazorenko, V., & Burlaka, O. (2020). Unmanned Aerial Vehicles for Smart Cities: Estimations of Urban Locality for Optimization Flights. In José A.Tenedório, R.Estanqueiro & C. D. Henriques (Eds.) Methods and Applications of Geospatial Technology in Sustainable Urbanis (pp.444-477) IGI Global.

Shmelova, T., Lohachova, K., & Yatsko, M. (2022) Integration of Decision-Making Stochastic Models of Air Navigation System Operators in Emergency Situations: In *CEUR*. https://ceur-ws.org/Vol-3137/paper18.pdf

Shmelova, T., & Sikirda, Yu. (2019). Applications of Decision Support Systems in Socio-Technical Systems. In *Unmanned Aerial Vehicles: Breakthroughs in Research and Practice. Information Resources Management Association* (5th ed., pp. 182–214). IGI Global. doi:10.4018/978-1-5225-8365-3.ch008

Shmelova, T., & Sikirda, Yu. (2021). Applications of Decision Support Systems in Aviation. In *Encyclopedia of Information Science and Technology* (5th ed., pp. 658–674). IGI Global. doi:10.4018/978-1-7998-3479-3.ch046

Shmelova, T., Sikirda, Y., & Belyaev, Y. (2014). Informational Support of Air Navigation System's Human-Operator. *Scientific Works of the National University of Food Technologies*, 20(4), 7–18.

Shmelova, T., Sikirda, Yu., & Jafarzade, T. R. (2019). Artificial Neural Network for Pre-Simulation Training of Air Traffic Controller. In T. Shmelova, Yu. Sikirda, & D. Kucherov (Eds.), *Cases on Modern Computer Systems in Aviation* (pp. 27–51). IGI Global. doi:10.4018/978-1-5225-7588-7.ch002

Shmelova, T., Sikirda, Yu., Salem, B., Rizun, N., & Kovalyov, Yu. (Eds.). (2018). *Socio-Technical Decision Support in Air Navigation Systems: Emerging Research and Opportunities*. IGI Global. doi:10.4018/978-1-5225-3108-1

Shmelova, T., Sikirda, Yu., & Sterenharz, A. (Eds.). (2020). *Handbook of Research on Artificial Intelligence Applications in the Aviation and Aerospace Industries*. IGI Global. doi:10.4018/978-1-7998-1415-3

Shmelova, T., Sikirda, Y., Yatsko, M., & Kasatkin, M. (2022) Collective Models of the Aviation Human-Operators in Emergency for Intelligent Decision Support System. In *CEUR*. https://ceur-ws.org/Vol-3156/paper10.pdf

Shmelova, T., Sterenharz, A. Yu., & Dolgikh, S. (2020) Artificial Intelligence in Aviation Industries: Methodologies, Education, Applications, and Opportunities. In T.Shmelova, Yu.Sikirda., & A.Sterenharz (Eds.) Handbook of Research on Artificial Intelligence Applications in the Aviation and Aerospace Industries (pp. 1-35). IGI Global.

Sikirda, Yu., Kasatkin, M., & Tkachenko, D. (2019) Intelligent Automated System for Supporting the Collaborative Decision Making by Operators of the Air Navigation System During Flight Emergencies. In T.Shmelova, Yu.Sikirda., & A.Sterenharz (Eds.) Handbook of Research on Artificial Intelligence Applications in the Aviation and Aerospace Industries (pp. 66-90). IGI Global.

Sikirda, Yu., Shmelova, T., Kharchenko, V., & Kasatkin, M. (2021) *Intelligent System for Supporting Collaborative Decision Making by the Pilot/Air Traffic Controller in Flight Emergencies* In *CEUR*. https://ceur-ws.org/Vol-2853/paper12.pdf

Sirodzha, I. (2002). *Quantum Models and Methods of Artificial Intelligence for Decision Making and Management: monograph.* Naukova Dumka.

Subsorn, P., & Singh, K. (2020) *DSS Applications as a Business Enhancement Strategy.* Citeseerx. https://citeseerx.ist.psu.edu/viewdoc/download?doi=10.1.1.87.8235&rep=rep1&type=pdf

Tarasov, V., & Gerasimov, B. (2007). Intelligent Decision Support Systems: Theory, Synthesis, Efficiency: monograph. Kyiv: International Academy of Computer Science and Systems.

Zhang, P., Zhao, S. W., & Tan, B. (2011). Applications of Decision Support System in Aviation Maintenance. *In Tech Open.* https://www.intechopen.com/chapters/18807

KEY TERMS AND DEFINITIONS

AI (Artificial Intelligence): Is the simulation of human intelligence processes by modeling, computer systems, and machines.

Air Navigation System: A complex of organizations, personnel, infrastructure, technical equipment, procedures, rules, and information that is used to provide of airspace users of safe, regular and efficient air navigation service.

Air Navigation Socio-Technical System: A complex large-scale, high-tech man-machine system, which require complex interactions between their human and technological components; the operations in socio-technical systems generally involve high-risk/high-hazard activities; the consequences of safety breakdowns are often catastrophic in terms of loss of life and property.

Air Traffic Management (ATM): Is an aviation term encompassing all systems that assist aircraft to depart from an aerodrome, transit airspace, and land at a destination aerodrome.

Collaborative Decision Making (CDM): Collaborative DM by operators in ANS, is a joint government/industry initiative aimed at improving air traffic flow management through increased information exchange among aviation community stakeholders.

Decision Support System (DSS): Is the interactive computer system intended to support different types of activity during the decision making including poorly-structured and unstructured problems.

Expert Systems (ES): Is a computer system that emulates the decision-making ability of a human expert. Expert systems are designed to solve complex problems by reasoning through bodies of knowledge, represented mainly as if–then rules rather than through conventional procedural code.

Hybrid System: Effective aggregation of Natural Intelligence (NI) and Artificial Intelligence (AI) in DM and IDSS.

Intelligent Decision Support System (IDSS): Is the interactive computer system intended to support different types of activity during the decision-making including AI subsystem in the structure.

Natural Intelligence (NI): Decision-making by human-operators.

Socio-Technical Systems: A large-scale, high-technology systems, because they require complex interactions between their human and technological components; the operations in socio-technical systems generally involve high-risk/high-hazard activities; the consequences of safety breakdowns are often catastrophic in terms of loss of life and property.

Chapter 7
The Impact of Artificial Intelligence on Search Engine:
Super Intelligence in Artificial Intelligence (AI)

Jana Saab
Lebanese University, Lebanon

ABSTRACT

In an aim to improve search engine results, AI interferes to boost it. Thus, this chapter investigates the impact of artificial intelligence on search engine. It includes the most advanced techniques of artificial intelligence that improve search engine optimization (SEO) rankings. In order not to fall in the hassle of having no ranking for your website, artificial intelligence can uplift a website position in the search engine. It is important to state that the growth of SEO has an integral role in digital marketing through AI. Moreover, the obtained results in research studies approve that the integration of artificial intelligence is vital for the progress of search engines.

INTRODUCTION

In the era of technology, the rise of AI has gained an important position. Indeed, artificial intelligence is transforming the world into a more digital one. Furthermore, artificial intelligence is used in various domains in life (Mohapatra et al., 2018). In fact, search engines are powered by artificial intelligence. A question is raised here, are you running your business, and you want your brand to standout in the digital world? Then, artificial intelligence can do it all.

Whether your aim is to search for a product or to search for anything you need, the search engine can offer you everything with one click. Additionally, the advancement of search engine optimization (SEO) enables a website rank higher in search engine. To add more, the growth of AI has positively influenced search engine. The use of highly ranked keywords strengthens your content (Mohapatra et al., 2018). Besides, artificial intelligence has an integral role in increasing a content visibility. Thus, companies will get high conversions. To add more, users can find all their answers on the search engine.

DOI: 10.4018/978-1-6684-6937-8.ch007

Moreover, Artificial Intelligence helps you rank algorithms (Nick, 2021). Therefore, search engines can work better and in a more advanced way.

Furthermore, users' search has an important role in ranking algorithms. Therefore, this allows a website in the search engines. To add more, artificial intelligence is significant in enabling search engines understand languages (Nick, 2021). Additionally, artificial intelligence elevated search engines and grants them the chance to be the keys to get all answers for everything. Not only do users search for texts, but they also search for images. This is a stunning creation by AI!

The influence of artificial intelligence on search engines lies in the progress of businesses. For example, clickable Ads ranks can boost a business leads. Thus, in order to rank high at the top of the search, you have to implement the most convenient content (Nick, 2021). In this case, AI can uplift search engines and lets a website standout. All in all, the main aim is to embrace the main influences of Artificial Intelligence on Search Engine. Also, the way search engines can boost websites based on researches and studies. Highlighting the main issues that make a drastic change from the traditional ways into the modern ones will enhance SEO.

Therefore, the chapter is divided into several sections. To begin with, section 1 includes a background about artificial intelligence (AI) and Natural Language Processing (NLP). Section 2 investigates search engine and information retrieval. Indeed, section 3 involves artificial intelligence in contribution to SEO. Moreover, section 4 manifests crawling, indexing, and ranking in the search engine. Additionally, section 5 elaborates about the importance of evaluating search engine. Lastly, there is a conclusion that sums up the whole chapter and recommendations for further research.

BACKGROUND

1. What Is Artificial Intelligence (AI)?

The term "Artificial Intelligence" is mainly associated with the intelligent tasks that a computer does. Artificial intelligence (AI) is known as a machine that is able to understand the human language (Ertel, 2017). Additionally, it can solve many problems in computers. Specifically, it has solutions for many problems associated with human language. Artificial intelligence enables computers to work similar to the level of humans and even higher than that; in other words, it surpasses human beings. To add more, "autonomous robots" is an integral part of AI (Ertel, 2017).

Additionally, Rich indicates that the high intelligence of machine lies in its knowledge in the top linguistic level, mainly pragmatics. To specify more, it can excel in the understanding of a sentence beyond the literal meaning (Ertel, 2017). In addition, it is capable of controlling data of all types and solving any problem (Copeland, 2022). Through artificial intelligence, a computer can get big data in order to be analyzed and manipulated (Copeland, 2022). To add more, the escalating of World Wide Web paves the way for artificial intelligence to operate data (Tecuci, 2012).

It is said that "Much of the power of an intelligent agent derives from the knowledge in its knowledge base. A main goal of the knowledge acquisition and machine learning research is precisely to enable an agent to acquire or learn this knowledge from a user, from input data, or from agent's own problem-solving experience" (Tecuci, 2012, p. 8). It is noteworthy to say that Natural Language Processing is a part of Artificial Intelligence that has a great role in the progress of search engine (Copeland, 2022).

2. The Vitality of Text Processing

When texts are collected, they should be identified if they will be "modified" or no. Thus, they will undergo "text processing" in order to be indexed and present in the search results. It is confirmed that the included "indexed terms" that are mostly searched by many users can improve its indexing. After the text is being gathered, users may search for some terms; thus, the "word processor" scans the presented document and marks the searched word in it (Croft et al., 2015). Hence, the user can directly reach the required information.

There are some limitations while searching in a text. For instance, if someone is searching for the term "digital marketing" and the text includes "Digital marketing." As a result, the typed word in the search does not exactly match the same one in the text. As noticed here, the difference is in the capitalization of the first letter (Croft et al., 2015). However, text processors do not give this difference a great importance because search engines can facilitate the process by ignoring such things during the search. For instance, they can give no attention to punctuations that separate words or split words (Croft et al., 2015). Indeed, in an aim to facilitate query, some words not noticed at all; this known as "stopping" (Croft et al., 2015). In the English language, some words are derived from their stems. For example, the word "play" and "playing" are similar to each other. Thus, the search engine considers them the same when users search about them.

Moreover, other texts include several formats of titles, chapters and fonts (Croft et al., 2015). Likewise, linking in significant for ranking; for instance, it is the case of linking web pages to each other (Croft et al., 2015). All in all, word occurrence in a text is tackled here. On the other hand, there is more deep understanding of a text through linguistic levels such as syntax that is concerned with studying the structure of a word and semantics that is concerned with the meaning of a word. Therefore, delving deeply into the minute details of Natural Language Processing can clarify more details about its relation with search engine optimization. Also, "understanding of the statistical nature of text" is prerequisite for understanding the "retrieval models" and "ranking algorithms" (Croft et al., 2015, p. 74).

Languages have a variety of words that are included in several types of writing in different forms. Besides, upon writing a text there are some recurring words that are mentioned many times like 'the" or "and" to describe something or someone (Croft et al., 2015, p. 75). As a result, Luhn conducted a study to show the importance of the frequent words in a text that help in information retrieval, ranking and indexing (Croft et al., 2015). In this realm, a research study was conducted to ensure that some words in English like "the" and "of" are highly frequent in a text. The following results emphasize that the more the word is frequent in a text, the more it is significant in it. That's why it is worth mentioning that "the most frequent six words account for 20% of occurrences, and the most frequent 50 words are about 40% of all text! On the other hand, given a large sample of text, typically about one half of all the unique words in that sample occur only once" (Croft et al., 2015, p. 75).

3. Review of Literature on Natural Language Processing

The evolution of languages has impacted the Natural Language processing. For instance, there are different levels of language that suit each age. In other words, the way a teen receives language only suits their age; however, adults need a different language level. That's why search engines are always in progress to meet the needs of all users and suit their interests (Graham, 2022). To illustrate more, the language of social media is different from the professional language that is used in medicine and engineering. In this case, artificial intelligence manages to understand the languages of all and goes parallel with the progress of language.

To illustrate more, computer programming succeeded in analyzing the human language and has contributed to the progress of search engines. Indeed, NLP works on the basic language levels, like lexical, syntactic, and semantic levels (Graham, 2022). Besides, the increased use of search engines to search for keywords and get answers to all their questions elevated the browsing of many websites for several purposes. Thus, search engines become a basic building block of humans' everyday life (Jackson & Moulinier, n.d.).

It is important to note that the field of Linguistics is fundamental in NLP (Liddy et al., n.d.). In addition, it is proclaimed that there is a transformation in NLP from focusing on language and its grammar to more data processing of a text (Liddy, et al., n.d.). However, the transition from the theoretical techniques to more practical ones has been a controversial issue in NLP.

For further illustration, Liddy et al. contended that algorithms are not able to analyze the language of human beings. On the other hand, it is mentioned that algorithms can accomplish great performance with respect to humans' language (Ringger et al., 2004). Additionally, the lexical, morphological, and syntactic levels; that are known as the micro levels in Linguistics, are suitable for "statistical analysis" (Joseph, et al., 2016). On the other hand, the macro levels in linguistics work more in "computational linguistics" (Wiebe, 2003).

3.1. The Power of Natural Language Processing

Nowadays, artificial intelligence has a keen connection with understanding languages. Thus, Natural Language Processing aims to enhance the main uses of language. Additionally, the use of NLP has extended to reach various domains in language (Carlstedt, 2017). For instance, its use in understanding language, generation and evolution of language, speeches and voices, grammar, syntax, and semantics has enhanced its work (Carlstedt, 2017).

3.2. Determining the Part of Speech of Words

NLP has improved to the extent that it can determine the part of speech of a word (Carlstedt, 2017). However, due to the variety of parts of speech for a single word, this can stand as an obstacle in NLP to determine its correct part of speech (Carlstedt, 2017). For instance, the word "right" can be used as a noun or as an adjective depending on the context. Therefore, a new technique interferes to solve this ambiguity that is called "Part -Of -Speech –Tagging" (Carlstedt, 2017). It classifies the part of speech of each word so that the machine can understand the part of speech of a word ("A guide to a hidden Markov Model," 2021).

3.3. Knowledge of Parts of Speech of a Word Through Morphology

In the study of the parts of speech of a language, morphology comes at the top. When a word is entered into a computer, this linguistic level is analyzed at the beginning in NLP (Reshamwala et al., 2013). When words are divided in to several parts, this facilitates the understanding of the word in a sentence. After analyzing the word's fragmented structure, you can know its meaning through context in a sentence.

3.4. Applying Markov Model in NLP

Each word has several meanings and makes identifying its exact meaning not easy at all. For example, the word "Dessert" means a dry land; however, it also means to leave someone. Thus, it depends on the place of the word in a context (Croft et al., 2015). Additionally, the aim of Markov Models is to generate sentences and put entities in order (Croft, wt al., 2015). Upon determining the parts of speech of a word, Markov Model can successfully perform that. To be more specific, it depends on probability. While data analysis is performed, algorithms play a key role in calculating values and probabilities to come up with accurate results (Carlstedt, 2017). Not only does it determine the part of speech of a word; when applied, it can identify an audio, a video, and a text. See figure 1.

Figure 1. Probability Analysis for Words
(Adapted from A guide to hidden Markov model, 2021)

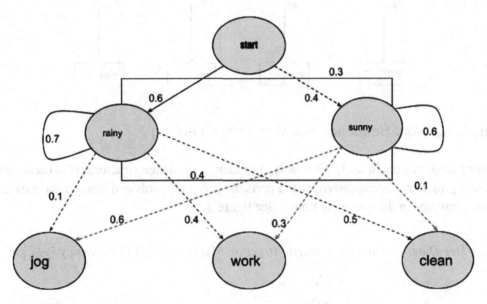

As a result, the above image clarifies the probabilities of Markov Model which is a good way to determine the part of speech of a word. Also, what is only visible is the outer form of the sentence.

In an attempt to recognize an entity, there should be training data. In this way, the machine learning model is trained to expect the upcoming entities to fulfill a purpose in any domain (Croft et al., 2015). Then, the probability of the investigated words will be clear. Generating training data that is made up of annotated text with the "correct entity tags" is done to know the quality of "transition and output probability" (Croft et al., 2015, p. 117). Therefore, "the probability of words associated with a given category and "the probability of transition between categories" are directly detected (Croft et al., 2015). To add more, this Model involves "features that are highly associated with named entities, such as capitalized words and words that are all digits" (Croft et al., 2015, p.117).

3.5. POS Tagging

The part of speech of a word can change the meaning of a whole sentence. For example, there are adjectives, nouns, verbs, adverbs, conjunction, and more. "In the below image, we can see that we have emission probabilities of the words in the sentence given in the vertical lines and the horizontal lines are representing all the transition probabilities" (A guide to hidden Markov model, 2021).

Figure 2. Probability of Markov Model
(Adapted from A guide to hidden Markov model, 2021).

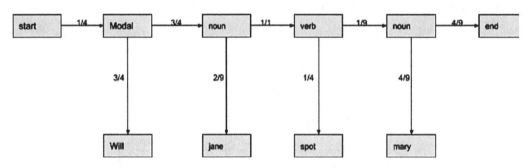

3.6. Identifying Word Sequence and Grammar Checking

The usage of modern techniques in NLP is vital to identify sentence structures (Carlstedt, 2017). For example, tree presentations can determine the parts of speech of words and identify the meaning of the sentence as presented in the following figure. See figure 3.

Figure 3. A Tree Diagram Showing Syntactic structure of a sentence in Dependency Relation

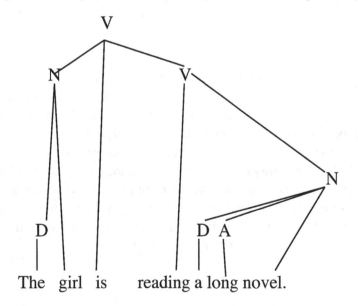

Therefore, NLP is able to determine the structure of a sentence with correct grammar. The division of the parts of a sentence that is presented above can determine correct sequence of the sentence. In addition, it is clear that the meaning of the sentence is identified; thus, the context will be clear. See figure 4.

Figure 4. Constituent Relation
(Adapted from Natural Language Processing, n.d.)

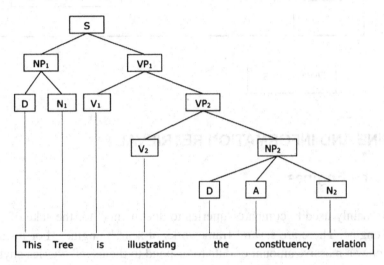

Additionally, in the above figure, the tree diagram shows the constituents of the sentence by the fragmentation in to noun clause, adverb clause, verb, and noun. Thus, this helps in sentence analysis in NLP.

3.7. Main Uses of NLP

Natural Language Processing is best applied to many cases nowadays. First, NLP can be used in detection of spam in emails. For example, it solves problems of writing names of companies in a wrong way and grammatical errors in an email. Second, the presence of the translation machine offered a great assistance in the translation from one language to another (Natural Language Processing, 2020). Hence, it provides users with the same meaning by deriving the same message with different language. Furthermore, NLP succeeded in business by providing analysis to social media language, posts, tone, and the way visitors respond to the products. Indeed, it boosts advertising campaigns in business. As a result, artificial intelligence tends to analyze texts in advertisements to increase business conversions. See figure 4 below:

Figure 5. The Implementation of NLP Search Engine
(Adapted from Carlstedt, 2017)

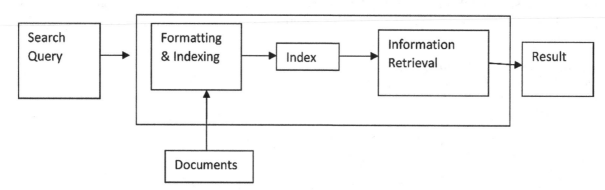

SEARCH ENGINE AND INFORMATION RETRIEVAL

1. Types of Search Engines

Search engines are mainly used to compare "queries to documents" for the sake of obtaining ranking lists in the search engine. There are several frameworks of search engines. For instance, Google and Yahoo are able to craw a massive amount of data to respond to the users' queries anytime (Croft et al., 2015). To clarify more, enterprise search engines, known as commercial search engines, allow indexing and crawling for an implemented content in a company. Moreover, this sort of search engines enables a company to have solutions for their business through data mining. Indeed, data mining paves the way for companies to explore upcoming trends to further make decisions for enhancing their business (Croft et al., 2015). Additionally, Microsoft Vista, a desktop search engine, integrates a variety of information such as web pages, documents, and email (Croft et al., 2015).

Furthermore, "open source" is another types of systems. There are links in Wikipedia for information retrieval (Croft et al., 2015). For more illustration, Lucen, Lemur, and Galago are the main systems. For example, Lucen is used for commercial purposes. Additionally, Lemur is basically used in information retrieval and it involves "Indri C++." Indeed, Galago is a "Java-based search engine" that mainly depends on Lemur and Indri (Croft et al., 2015). To add more, detecting the "performance" of search engines can be through the following ways. When users include a query in the search engine, their aim is to get information about what they need. In addition, there is a time between submitting the query and receiving results in the search engine. This depends on the speed of indexing of the document. The importance of indexing relies in enhancing the position of a website in the search engine (Croft et al., 2015). The speed of data integration in the indexes is important here as well. In other words, the faster the data implementation, then the faster it is stored in the search engine (Croft et al., 2015).

Search engines have many uses; for example, it is used with emails, documents, and websites. To illustrate more, "Scalability" is concerned with the design of search engine. When the quantity of data escalates and there are many users, these designs will not stop working. It is mentioned previously that search engines can do multitasks at the same time. In this realm, the customizability and adaptability of search engines have a great role in performing this part. Therefore, "the ranking algorithm, the interface, or the indexing strategy, must be able to be tuned and adapted to the requirements of the application"

(Croft et al., 2015). To further illustrate, there is the issue of spamming that can occur in the search engine which decreases the possibility of ranking in the search engine (Croft et al., 2015). The follwoin g figure summarizes the process.

1.1. Significance of Information Retrieval in Search Engines

When it comes to text documents, there are many attributes and structures that are included within them. For instance, all documents such as web site pages, email, books, and research papers involve the author's name, date of publication, titles, subtitles in addition to the main content. According to data base records, the information in this document is unorganized (Croft et al., 2015). For more illustration, in order to detect the glaring contrast here, the "account number and the balance number" are taken into consideration. Then upon comparing the "values of these attributes", the integration of algorithms can clarify the records (Croft et al., 2015, p. 2).

To illustrate more, "consider a news story about the merger of two banks. The story will have some attributes, such as the headline and source of the story, but the primary content is the story itself. In a database system, this critical piece of information would typically be stored as a single large attribute with no internal structure. Most of the queries submitted to a web search engine such as Google that relate to this story will be of the form "bank merger" or "bank takeover" (Croft et al., 2015). In this case, the role of algorithms is crucial in comparing the two texts to see if the results are achieved. Moreover, it is stated that text comparison is easier than figuring out the meaning of a sentence or a word. Indeed, the bulk of information retrieval is the comprehension of text comparison and computer algorithms (Croft et al., 2015). In fact, most social media posts include content such as posts, videos, audios. However, texts are still difficult to be compared. So, the usage of search engines is important in information retrieval (Croft et al. 2015).

1.2. Most Significant Issues in Information Retrieval

There are certain issues in information retrieval that researchers mainly focus on. For this reason, a re-search study was conducted on a "1.5 megabyte text" and the "relevance" issue (Croft et al., 2015). It is noteworthy to state that the information that someone is searching for are found in this relevant document (Croft et al., 2015). Indeed, upon integrating algorithms to check compared texts and ranked documents, some issues should be taken into consideration (Croft et al., 2015). Therefore, when comparing the two texts with each other, the obtained results are not good. This shows that vocabulary words do not match. Additionally, the included text should answer the questions in search. In other words, the relevance of the topic is significant for the user's search to find the sought information.

Moreover, researchers aim at examining "retrieval models." It is the way of showing how relevant the documents with the queries. Also, it is fundamental in ranking algorithm (Croft et al., 2015). As a result, the documents that matched the queries rank higher in the search. Furthermore, it is portrayed that the word counts mater more than the part of speech of a word for ranking algorithms (Croft et al., 2015). To add more, evaluation is considered as another important issue in information retrieval. Thus, evaluation is investigated for the comparison of ranking algorithms. In an aim to improve evaluation techniques, Cyril Cleverdon used "precision" and "recall." The former is concerned with the relevant documents and the latter is concerned with the retrieved documents (Croft et al., 2015).

It is mentioned that "when the recall measure is used, there is an assumption that all the relevant documents for a given query are known. Such an assumption is clearly problematic in a web search environment, but with smaller test collections of documents, this measure can be useful. A test collection for information retrieval experiments consists of a collection of text documents, a sample of typical queries, and a list of relevant documents for each query" (Croft et al., 2015, p. 5-6). Therefore, relevance between a topic and the user's search can enhance ranking in the search engine. Besides, the "click through data" is crucial in the evaluation of retrieved data for recording clicked documents during the search (Croft et al., 2015).

It is worth mentioning that meeting the needs of users in the search is important is evaluating the quality of the text. Therefore, researches emerged to study the users' feedback and interactions towards search engines. Additionally, through the evolution of technology in the field of artificial intelligence, people can express their needs in the search. To elaborate more, "a one-word query such as "cats" could be a request for information on where to buy cats or for a description of the Broadway musical" (Croft et al., 2015, p. 6). The word "Cat" is broad; in other words, the user here did not specify the type of cat or a shop of cats. Although it is an unspecified word, it is used in the search engine. See figure 5

Figure 6. Search engine design and the core information retrieval issues
(Adapted from Croft et al., 2015)

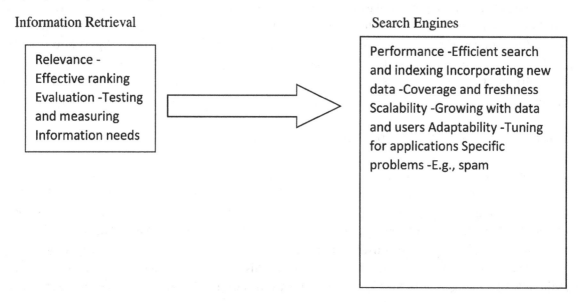

1.3. Machine Learning and Information Retrieval

It is clear that information retrieval has a great connection with machine learning. Users' feedback on a document is a great evaluation for the text that contributes to its ranking (Croft et al., 2015). One of the most forefront roles of machine learning is to determine whether the document is relevant or not based on "training data" (Croft et al., 2015). At the beginning, ranking algorithms were known through users' feedback. Moreover, with the development of technology throughout many years, there emerged research studies about machine learning approaches to classify texts (Croft et al., 2015).

On the other hand, the restricted amount of data training has influenced the implementation of machine learning in information retrieval (Croft et al., 2015). It is contended that "If the system is trying to build a separate classifier for every query, there is very little data about relevant documents available, whereas, other machine learning applications may have hundreds or even thousands of training examples" (Croft et al., 2015, p. 284). Also, many approaches used training data to learn ranking algorithms (Croft et al., 2015).

ARTIFICIAL INTELLIGENCE AND SEO

1. Artificial Intelligence in Contribution to SEO

Search engines enable websites to have traffic through outstanding search engine methods (Mohapatra et al., 2018). Indeed, when people search for a keyword in the search engine, this can increase rankings. Additionally, artificial intelligence is always in progress in the way of data collection, classification, and categorization (Mohapatra et al., 2018). Therefore, AI goes hand in hand with the progress of SEO including relevant content, optimization, and link building (Mohapatra et al., 2018).

1.2. A General Review on SEO

Search Engine Optimization (SEO) is the technique that has a key role in enhancing traffic in a website. Besides, it ensures your website visibility in search engines (Kaukoranta, 2015). For example, if your website is not getting high traffic, SEO can solve this problem and makes it easily accessible (Surati & Pajapati, 2018). Pohjanen (2019) contended that when your website is positioned in the first few pages in the SERP, this is important in driving more traffic. Iskandar and Komara (2018) stated "SEO can be seen as a process of creating a website that ranks effectively for chosen keywords within the organic search results and simultaneously through those keywords improving the quality and volume of traffic to the website."

Furthermore, including relevant content and well-organized Meta description with a focus key phrase paves the way for your website to rank higher (Sharma, & Verma, 2020). Thus, it depends on your content to be at the top of the search. For more illustration, On-page SEO and Off-page SEO are the main techniques of SEO. For example, in On-page SEO you can control everything is the website (Lopezosa et al., 2020). However, the Off-page SEO is mainly related to the creation of external links that lead users to other trusted pages (Faustine, et al., 2020). As a result, back links improve your ranking in the search engine.

Upon creating a website, the integration of SEO techniques is significant in order to confirm the visibility of your website (Wilson et al., 2006). They added that relevant keywords should be included in the context to achieve high ranking and increase traffic to your website. Additionally, SEO advancements should be taken into consideration (Wilson et al., 2006). Furthermore, Killoran (2013) conducted a study to show the importance of ranking in search engines for marketers. Indeed, he stressed that the implementation of links and keywords with high search and looking for competitors' work play an important role in ranking.

Besides, a study was conducted by Gudivada et al. (2015) to interpret the main ways of website ranking. They obtained that most users do organic search. This indicates that search engine optimization influences website traffic. To add more, there are other factors that affect the website ranking such as the page loading speed and the low bounce rate. In other words, when the pages of a website have high speed load, there will be more traffic.

1.2.1. Importance of Keyword Search in SEO

The choice of keywords mainly depends on the users' search in the search engine. To be more specific, SEO cares about the usage of relevant keywords in content. Additionally, when the average search of a keyword is high, this means that users tend to use it the most. Indeed, there are specific keywords used for each type of content (Wang et al., 2017). Also, they are classified by Google when any web page is crawled or indexed (Kaukoranta, 2015). Moreover, the type of chosen keywords depends on the company. To illustrate more, if the company is a digital marketing agency, the marketer should look for the words that are mostly searched by customers. For example, "Conversions" is a general keyword; instead, using a more specific keyword would be better to obtain high ranking in the search. As a result, when the keywords are used wisely and specified, this encourages users to visit your page.

It is important to note that short-tail keywords and long-tail keywords are the two kinds of keywords. First, users search for short-tail keywords on daily basis. This means that when they get high search, the competition on these words definitely increases (Choudhari & Bhalla, 2015). Therefore, using this type of keywords will be a hindrance for a website to rank high. On the other hand, long-tail keywords are more specified and include the exact information that users search for and have low competition (Wang et al., 2017). As a result, using long-tail keywords are of high quality, most searched by customers, and bring more conversions.

To illustrate more, the customer's needs are vital for choosing the most convenient words in content. In this realm, Google Ads manager, that includes Keyword Planner, is the ultimate place to search for keywords (Johansson, 2016). For example, it provides you with a detailed analysis about the keyword. To be more specific, it includes the keyword with the number of searches for it and the range of competition for it. Hence, it facilitates choosing the highly searched keywords with low competition. Also, those keywords should be included in the content such as in the headers, URL, title, meta description, and the whole text.

Proper keyword placement is crucial to achieve high ranking. For instance, keywords should be included in h1, h2, and h3. Indeed, these tags need to be optimized in order to be crawled ("Search Engine Optimization," 2021). Thus, if there is no optimization, then there is no website ranking. Upon including the relevant keywords, their frequency has an important role in affecting the text in a positive way. To specify more, over optimizing can decrease your website's presence on the search engine. Another significant point is the implementation of the keyword in the URL where users will click on. Better results are obtained when producing short URLs (Search Engine Optimization, 2021). To add more, users are more attracted to the meta description text that involves a brief description of your text. That's why it should include the targeted keywords to increase traffic. Indeed, unique and original content is a valuable in enhancing ranking. The website can be reached more when it includes a text that is long enough and includes the keywords.

CRAWLING, INDEXING, AND RANKING

1. Crawling and Indexing in SEO

In fact, search engines operate crawlers for the purpose of indexing. Then, when a website is indexed, it will be presented in the search results ("What is a web crawler," 2022). Crawling is the act of "accessing a website and obtaining data via a software program" ("What is a web crawler," 2022). Indeed, web crawlers store words that users mostly search for in order to get back to them later on.

After web crawlers collect data, the search engine offers the web pages that are browsed by users. In this way, the types of pages that the user has visited are known. Therefore, it emphasizes the interests of users in various domains. For example, "a web crawler bot is like someone who goes through all the books in a disorganized library and puts together a card catalog so that anyone who visits the library can quickly and easily find the information they need." ("What is a web crawler," 2022). Hence, it needs to be organized, but it is not easy to do so. This is a considered a hindrance for indexing. In an aim to ensure successful crawling, a web crawler follows specific strategy. For instance, it begins with well-known pages and then through some of its hyperlinks it can move to other pages" ("What is a web crawler," 2022).

The increase in the number of web pages on the Internet makes it difficult and even impossible to know their number ("What is a web crawler,'" 2022). So the URL that they receive, crawlers can crawl many other pages in the search engine and the process goes on. Most importantly to mention that they crawl the most important pages according to content and high number of visitors ("What is a web crawler," 2022). Besides, what is special about web crawlers is that they visit again the up dated web pages.

Additionally, Google has limits for crawling some pages. Besides, it has certain number of URLs that should be crawled. Moreover, the site loading speed influences crawling. For instance, when the web site loads faster, this increases the pages crawling. Indeed, when the web page is more popular and unique, there is a high possibility for Google to crawl a page in the search engine. On the other hand, "if a server responds to a lot of requests from Google with error codes, that will discourage Google from trying to crawl pages because that will look like a website with a lot of problems" ("The role of search engine crawlers," n.d.). This is called crawler budget.

The most significant role of web crawlers is indexing pages for search engines ("Web crawler 101," 2022). Additionally, they explore and discover links. Moreover, "crawlers store the pages in the index, so Google's algorithm can sort them for their contained words to later fetch and rank for users" (Web crawler 101, 2022).

There are several types of crawlers in the search engine. For instance, Googlebot is a Google's crawler. Besides, it's mainly known as the desktop and mobile crawler at the same time. Googlebot access the web page to enhance its presence in the search engine ("Google Search Central," n.d.). Thus, the web page can be visited by many users to achieve ranking. To illustrate more, its aim is to crawl large number pages of a website. To add more, Yahoo! Slurp for Yahoo is another crawler (Baker, 2004). In addition, crawling serves indexing. In other words, documents are collected from the web and indexed. Since there are pages that include related links to these documents, they are crawled (Baker, 2004).

1.1. Ranking in the Search Engine

One of the main factors to achieve ranking is the implementation of links; the backlinks. (Ziak et al., 2019). Google takes into account the number of the back links included in a website and their quality.

After that, Google algorithms make calculations to analyze these links (Ziak et al., 2019). This algorithm is called "Pagerank" and uses a 0 to 10 scale to determine a relative score of that page's importance and authority (Ziak et al., 2019, p. 7). In addition, this "Pagerank" is fundamental for a website ranking. As a result, the relevance and strength of back links is vital for getting high ranking.

Moreover, easy website navigation accelerates a website's ranking in the search engine. Likewise, the usage of the HTML links in the navigation bar facilitates browsing each page in the website. It is important to mention that when there is an inextricable connection between the website and social media platforms, ranking is achieved in high rates (Ziak et al., 2019). For example, the integration of social media platform, like Facebook, Instagram, LinkedIn, and TikTok, links in a website drives more traffic. Also, the role of the content creators cannot be ignored because they can affect a website ranking. Moreover, web 404 pages appear when a website page cannot be reached. Additionally, "The customization includes pointers to home page or other pages of the site and even references to other sites with relevant to the user's search content" (Ziak et al., 2019, p. 7).

Secure Socket Layer, that involves a link between the servers, also influences ranking. The website that uses the https protocol ranks higher than other websites that use http protocol. This is because the former provides more security and safety for a website (Ziak et al., 2019). Hence, it can rank in the search engine. Indeed, creating a sitemap paves the way for crawling. It provides "the search engines with any changes made to the website, the degree of significance of every page, the frequency of the website updates, and other information" (Ziak et al., 2019, p. 7). Besides, it helps search engine to index a website easily. All of this is crucial for website optimization to improve its ranking. (Ziak et al., 2019). It is more important to note that the ranking is affected by the domain age. In other words, older domains tend to rank higher in the search engine (Ziak et al., 2019). So, all of the mentioned factors elevate the ranking in search engine optimization.

Killoran (2013) conducted the study under the title "Mobile path to Purchase" about the most prominent used device during the search. Results have showed that half of the users searched about their needs through the mobile. However, some websites are not suitable to be opened by the mobile device ending up in no ranking. Therefore, a successful and well-planned website should suit all devices in order to achieve high ranking in the search engine. To further illustrate, keyword optimization in the content can really improve a website's position in the search. Additionally, the time spent on a website can impact its ranking (Ziak et al., 2019).To be more specific, when the content is valuable and meets the audience needs, then they will stay more time on the website. The knowledge of the percentage of a website visitors who just visit the website immediately leave has a key role in ranking (Ziak et al., 2019).This is called the bounce rate! In addition, the lower the bounce rate, the more your website is successful and is ranking in the search.

SEARCH ENGINE EVALUATION

1. Why Evaluate Search Engines?

In order to achieve great results, make sure to evaluate search engines. The examination of the efficiency of a search engine can enable you to know if it is correctly used in an application. It is important to know the difference between "efficiency" and "effectiveness" in search engine assessment. The former examines how search engine can recognize the correct information, while the latter is concerned with the speed of finding this (Croft et al., 2015). To be more specific, it has stated that "effectiveness is a measure of how well the ranking produced by the search engine corresponds to a ranking based on user relevance judgments" (Croft et al., 2015, p. 297). To add more, efficiency is more related to the specified time and place of the algorithm in ranking (Croft et al., 2015).

Besides, effectiveness and efficiency are affected by the different types of users. This is because they have different insights and interests. Thu, they have various searches about many topics. The main goal of information retrieval is enhancing the effectiveness of search (Croft et al., 2015). Hence, good information and high speed of ranking are inextricably connected with each other for obtaining successful results. To add more, certain cost is required in order to get good result of effectiveness and efficiency (Croft et al., 2015).

It is mentioned that whenever you decide to search for a text through "Grep", you will not get sufficient effectiveness and even sufficient efficiency. On the other hand, when the search is done through "staff analysts at the "Library of Congress," you will get perfect results because high effort is exerted here (Croft et al., 2015). So, using the most convenient technique can make a huge difference in the results of effectiveness and efficiency at the same time.

It is noteworthy to investigate the importance of optimization in this realm. Performance optimization is directly connected with the parameters of indexing and retrieval techniques (Croft et al., 2015). Training data and cost identify the importance of efficiency and effectiveness (Croft et al., 2015). To be more specific, "The training data could be samples of queries with relevance judgments, and the cost function for a ranking algorithm would be a particular effectiveness measure. The process of optimization uses the training data to learn parameter settings (Croft et al., 2015). This is done for the ranking algorithm in order to increase effectiveness. This shows how optimization here differs from that of search engine optimization.

The table 1 summarizes all the sources implemented in this chapter.

Table 1. All Resources Used in the Chapter

Referenced Articles/ Books	Brief Description
1. (Graham, 2022)	Includes language terms that suit all generations on social media and the way AI understands langauges
2. (Copeland, 2022)	The ability of a computer to receive big data and analyze languages (related to AI)
3. (What is a web crawler, 2022)	Crawling and indexing take place in the search engine
4. (Web crawler 101, 2022)	The way crawlers store pages in the search engines and how crawlers explore links
5. (Nick, 2021)	The influence of search engine on artificial intelligence
6. (A guide to hidden Markov Model, 2021)	Probability analysis of words and the way a sentence is divided to know it meaning
7. (Search engine optimization, 2021)	The significance of appropriate URLs, keywords, and meta description in driving traffic to a website
8. (Sharma, & Verma, 2020)	Including relevant content and meta description
9. (Lopezosa et al., 2020)	Importance of off page SEO and on page SEO
10. (Faustine, et al., 2020)	The focus on external links by using reliable searches
11. (Natural language processing 2020)	Presence of translation machine to facilitate translation from one language to another
12. (Ziak et al., 2019)	The presence of back links to confirm ranking
13. Pohjanen (2019)	When a website gets traffic, it directly appears in the SERP
14. (Ziak et al., 2019)	The presence of back links to confirm ranking
15. (Surati & Pajapati, 2018)	SEO makes your website always accessible.
16. (Mohapatra, et al., 2018)	The presence of AI in different domains and its significance in ranking
17. (Iskandar and Komara, 2018)	The quality of traffic is enhanced through search engine optimization.
18. (Ertel, 2017)	AI solved many problems in search engines and understands human languages
19. (Carlstedt, 2017)	Linguistics an important part in NLP and the application of Markov Model in NLP
20. (Wang et al., 2017)	Ranking depends on the most searched keywords in the search engine
21. (Joseph, et al., 2016)	The micro levels of language are suitable for statistical analysis
22. (Croft et al., 2015)	Investigates the way a text is processed, data training, issues, types, and information retrieval in search engine
23. (Kaukoranta, 2015)	The role of SEO in promoting the visibility of a website
24. (Gudivada et al., 2015)	Explanation about the ways of website ranking
25. (Choudhari & Bhalla, 2015)	Differences between short- tail and long- tail key words
26. (Kaukoranta, 2015)	Ensure website visibility through SEO
27. (Reshamwala et al., 2013)	The division of a word into several parts facilitates the understanding of its meaning.
28. (Killoran, 2013)	A study was conducted to show how ranking is vital in enhancing marketing
29. (Tecuci, 2012)	The Implementation of machine learning to analyze data

Continued on following page

Table 1. Continued

Referenced Articles/ Books	Brief Description
30. (Wilson et al., 2006)	Importance of implementing relevant keywords in driving traffic
31. (Ringger et al., 2004)	Algorithms are able to understand human language
32. (Baker, 2004).	Collecting documents from a website to get indexed
33. (Wiebe, 2003).	Macro levels are included in computational linguistics
34. (Jackson & Moulinier, n.d.)	The progress of search engine and its usage in our daily life
35. (Liddy et al., n.d.)	NLP transformed to focus on data processing
36. (Natural language processing, n.d.)	Sentence constituents in a tree model
37. ("The role of search engine crawlers", n.d.)	Pages with lots of errors are not crawled by Google
38. ("Google Search Central", n.d.).	Types of crawlers: Google, Yahoo! And the ways they crawl a website

CONCLUSION

To conclude, artificial intelligence will progress to achieve more successful results in the world of technology. Technologies have created recent pathways in digital marketing. The contribution of AI in search engine optimization has taken businesses to another level. Additionally, it saves a lot of time for marketers to launch their marketing campaigns and paves the way for them to reach their target audience.

Moreover, AI finds solutions for various types of problems in digital marketing and search engine. Besides, its influence on Natural Language Processing has developed modern methodologies in analyzing languages. Accepting the huge data enabled machines to understand languages and other things. All in all, artificial intelligence is the hopeful future of enhancement.

Additionally, machine learning has contributed to the progress in information retrieval in the search engine. Types of search engines and their roles in understanding data have affected information retrieval as well. Moreover, a users' feedback on a document in the search engine is important in ranking because they have to get the suitable responses for their queries.

Search Engine Optimization can thrive more with artificial intelligence. The knowledge of on page SEO and off page SEO techniques can facilitate the boosting of a website in the search engine. Indeed, the most significant thing is to asses search engine.

RECOMMENDATIONS FOR FUTURE RESEARCH DIRECTIONS

The progress of search engine nowadays is escalating to reach its peak in many fields. Digital marketing, as a trending domain in the 21st century, mainly depends on search engines and its types for the growth of business all over the world. Thus, including the approaches of artificial intelligence in search engine are important. Moreover, search engine optimization (SEO) enhances marketing strategies. Additionally, following content improvement can improve businesses presence in the digital world. Indeed, applying more a lot of experiments and case studies is important in studying the relationship between AI and search engine.

REFERENCES

A guide to hidden Markov model and its applications in NLP. (2021).

Baker, L. (2004). *Yahoo intros new search robot – Yahoo! Slurp*. Search Engine Journal.

Carlstdet, M. (2017). Using NLP and context for improved search result in specialized search engines.

Choudhari, K., & Bhalla, V. (2015). Video Search Engine Optimization Using Keyword and Feature Analysis. *Procedia Computer Science*, *58*, 691–697. doi:10.1016/j.procs.2015.08.089

Cloud Flare. (2021). *What is a web crawler*. Cloud Flare. https://www.cloudflare.com/en-gb/learning/bots/what-is-a-web-crawler/

Copeland, B. (2022). Artificial intelligence. *Encyclopedia Britannica*. https://www.britannica.com/technology/artificial-intelligence

Croft, W. B., Metzler, D., & Strohman, T. (2015). *Search Engines: Information Retrieval in Practice*. www.search-engines-book.com

Egri, G., & Bayrak, C. (2014). The role of search engine optimization on keeping the user on the site. *Procedia Computer Science*, *36*, 335–342. doi:10.1016/j.procs.2014.09.102

Ertel, W. (2017). *Introduction to Artificial Intelligence*. Upgraduate Topics in Computer Science. doi:10.1007/978-3-319-58487-4

Faustine, C., Dramilio, A., Sanjaya, S., & Soewito, B. (2020). The effect and technique in search engine optimization. *International Conference on Information Management and Technology*, 348-353.

Google. (n.d.). Googlebot. *Google search Central*. https://developers.google.com/search/docs/advanced/crawling/googlebot

Graham, M. (2022). Using Natural Language Processing to Search for Textual References. In D. Hamidović, C. Clivaz, & S.B. Savant (eds.), Ancient Manuscripts in Digital Culture. (pp.115-132). Brill.

Gudivada, V. N., Rao, D., & Paris, J. (2015). Understanding search-engine optimization. *Computer*, *48*(10), 43–45. doi:10.1109/MC.2015.297

Iskandar, M., & Komara, D. (2018). Application marketing strategy search engine optimization (SEO). *IOP Conference Series. Materials Science and Engineering*, *407*, 012011. doi:10.1088/1757-899X/407/1/012011

Jackson, P., & Moulinier, I. (2012). *Natural Language Processing for Online Applications*. Cambridge University press.

Joseph, S. (2016). Natural Language Processing: A Review. *International Journal of Research in Engineering and Applied Sciences*, *6*(3), 207–210. http://www.euroasiapub.org

Kaukoranta, M. (2015). How to reach more target customers by search engine optimization (SEO) and search engine advertising (SEA), 19-33. Seinäjoki University of Applied Sciences.

Killoran, J. B. (2013). How to use search engine optimization techniques to increase website visibility. *IEEE Transactions on Professional Communication*, *56*(1), 50–66. doi:10.1109/TPC.2012.2237255

Liddy, L., Hovy, E., Lin, J., Prager, J., Radev, D., Vanderwende, L., & Weischedel, R. (2016). Natural Language Processing. *Research Gate*.

Lopezosa, C., Codina, L., Díaz-Noci, J., & Ontalba, J. (2020). SEO and the digital news media: From the workplace to the classroom. *Media Education Research Journal, 28*(63), 65-75.

Mohapatra, M., Mohapatra, S., & Mohanti, J. (2018). Artificial Intelligence (AI)'s Role in Search Engine Optimization (SEO). *International Journal of Engineering Science Invention*, *7*(5), 76–79.

Nick, E. (2021). How Artificial Intelligence Is Powering Search Engines. *Data Science Central*.

Pohjalainen, R. (2019). The benefits of search engine optimization in Google for businesses. *Semantic Scholar*.

Reshamwala, A. (2013). Review on natural language processing. *Research Gate*.

Ringger, E. K., Moore, R. C., Charniak, E., Vanderwende, L., & Suzuki, H. (2004). Using the Penn Treebank to Evaluate Non-Treebank Parsers. In *Language Resources and Evaluation Conference (LREC)*, Lisbon, Portugal.

Sharma, S., & Verma, S. (2020). Optimizing website effectiveness using various SEO techniques, 918-922. IEEE.

Surati, S. B., & Prajapati, G. I. (2018). SEO-A Review. *International Journal of Research and Scientific Innovation*, *5*(2), 13–17. https://www.rsisinternational.org/

Tecuci, G. (2012). Artificial Intelligence. *Wiley Interdisciplinary Reviews: Computational Statistics*, *4*(2), 168–180. doi:10.1002/wics.200

Veglis, A., & Geomelakis, D. (Eds.). (2021). *Search engine optimization.*

Wang, Z., Hahn, K., Kim, Y., Song, S., & Seo, J. (2017). A news-topic recommender system based on keywords extraction. *Multimedia Tools and Applications*, *77*(4), 4339–4353. doi:10.100711042-017-5513-0

WebFX. (2022). Web crawlers 101: What is a web crawler and how do crawlers work? WebFX.

Wiebe, J., Breck, E., Buckley, E., & Cardie, C. (2003). *Davis, P. Fraser, P. Litman, D., Pierce, D., Riloff, E., Wilson, T., Day, D., & Maybury, M.* Recognizing and Organizing Opinions Expressed in the World Press.

Wilson, R. F., & Pettijohn, J. B. (2006). Search engine optimisation: A primer on keyword strategies. *Journal of Direct, Data and Digital Marketing Practice*, *8*(2), 121–133. doi:10.1057/palgrave.dddmp.4340563

Woorank. (n.d). *The role of search engine crawlers.* Woorank. https://www.woorank.com/en/edu/seo-guides/search-engine-crawlers

Ziakis, C., Vlachopoulou, M., Kyrkoudis, T., & Karagkiozido, M. (2019). Important factors for improving google search rank. *Future Internet. 11*(32). https://www.firstcry.ae/

KEY TERMS AND DEFINITIONS

Algorithms: An algorithm is a process used to carry out a computation or solve a problem.

Artificial Intelligence: The machines are the programmed to mimic human activities and their actions.

Crawling: It means that when search engines search for content that lead them to another web pages.

NLP: Natural language processing.

Search Engine Optimization: It is the process of obtaining high visibility of your website in the search engine.

Chapter 8
A Survey About the Application of Artificial Intelligence in Search Engines:
Opportunities and Challenges of Artificial Intelligence

Rajab Ssemwogerere

ⓘ https://orcid.org/0000-0002-9786-8898

University of Electronic Science and Technology of China, China

Assadig Abdelrhman Sajo

University of Electronic Science and Technology of China, China

Nambobi Mutwalibi

ⓘ https://orcid.org/0000-0001-6822-616X

Islamic University in Uganda, Uganda

Asha Khamis Mzee

University of Electronic Science and Technology of China, China

ABSTRACT

Artificial intelligence (AI) mimics or stimulates human behaviors or thinking to solve specific problems. It has been applied in the analysis of huge datasets and provides reliable outputs without human supervision in various online platforms, for example, information retrieval in search engines, digital assistants, voice assistants, digital marketing, personalized learning, social media, etc. This technology has provided many opportunities and challenges in line with strengthening the authenticity of the information provided via different search engines. This chapter reviews the current pieces of literature about the different AI algorithms used in the most popular metasearch engines and the application of artificial intelligence in these search engine contexts.

DOI: 10.4018/978-1-6684-6937-8.ch008

INTRODUCTION

Communication using social media and Information searching are the two most prevalent activities done on the Internet (Polak, 2017). A user may use any browser like Mozilla firefox, Google chrome, Microsoft edge, safari, or internet explorer when searching for a keyword. This process will be enhanced by a sophisticated program called a *search engine*. This program uses specific algorithms to find related information over the internet that appears to match the keyword defined by the user in the search query (Sharma et al., 2019). Web search engines allow internet users to find all important information from extensive big data. The web search business lives to offer an excellent search service to a user's search request, therefore it is very necessary to be improved frequently so that it can respond to the user in the most precise way, quickly, and with reliable information.

However, most unauthentic information owned by different individuals and businesses is highly ranked due to commercial interest of attracting customers making relevant valued information be hidden away from the top position results returned by the search engine. There are several different search engines, for example, e-commerce search engines (Amazon and eBay), and social media search engines like (FaceBook, and YouTube), most popular search engines include, Google, Bing, Baidu, and Yandex. These most popular search engines help a user when searching for information, maps, videos, images, products, or something local. Search engines like Google use several search algorithms all working together to mine useful information. Examples of Google search algorithms (GSA) include PageRank, Pigeon, Hummingbird, Mobilegeddon, Intrusive Interstitials Update, Panda, and Penguin, among others.

The primary aim of GSAs is to rank websites with the best factors such as the backlinks, content, keywords, user experience, and several others. These classified algorithms were limited due to the dramatic growth of the **internet, Big data,** and **massive information** circulating across the globe. This slows down the effectiveness of getting reliable search results (Neogy & Paruchuri, 2014). Hence a need for complex advanced navigation algorithms. Web search engines were also considered to be exhaustive and thoughtfully considered to respond to users' ambiguity when formulating search requests to search engines and their interest to reach a wider audience (Serrano, 2016b).

The new branch of computer science called *artificial intelligence* (AI) helps search engines listen to the user requests, understand the language and keywords provided in the search query, perform ranking, and provide improved search results to the user. AI advancements, implementation, and combination with other technologies like machine learning (ML) in search engines, promise ease, and improved search results. These AI and ML advancements are outperforming the traditional search tools that are based on keywords relevance or statistical algorithms (Sharma et al., 2019). The traditional search tools are ignorant of the meaning of the keywords searched for in context.

Furthermore, they are challenged with getting a sense of unstructured information which includes; text files, email, social media, mobile data, business applications, and other formats. Search engines deploy several AI algorithms to provide a good user experience. They only require to be trained on huge datasets to acquire embedded knowledge to work efficiently and effectively in a long run. Strategies to overcome the challenges. Any type of Search engine is computer software that needs to understand human language as well to successfully and precisely find the information users they're looking for. This acquires them with cognitive features of understanding the meaning of keywords written in human language in search engines and also enables them to extract meaningful information from any webpage. Hence, lays the foundation for the application of Natural Language Processing (NLP), a field of AI devoted to training computers to comprehend human written language.

WHAT IS EXACTLY A SEARCH ENGINE?

The search engine is generally classified based on the information they collect and retrieve. They are composed of four major components; search algorithm, search interface, crawler sometimes called a spider or a bot, and database The search engine has both the front engine composed of an interface where the user inputs the piece of information, a search query, and a backend composed of the database together with an algorithm that retrieves links to some pierce web content information that appears to match the term the user entered.

The increased use of both the internet as a source of information and smartphone devices has also greatly improved search engine algorithms. Over the internet, the major source of information retrieval is the use of Search engines. This factor has motivated the introduction of new and sophisticated technologies for example Artificial Intelligence which has also transformed search engines.

Brief History of Search Engines

The first search tool used on the internet called Archie was developed by Alan Emtage a student at McGill University in Montreal in 1990 (Escandell-Poveda et al., 2022; Sharma et al., 2019). This tool could download and index computer files in searchable databases of websites. Later on, rejoined Mark McCahill a student at the University of Minnesota, and created Veronica (Very Easy Rodent-Oriented Net-wide Index to computerized Achieves) and Jughead (Jonzy's University Gopher Hierarchy Excavation and Display) (Frana, 2004; Seymour et al., 2011). This innovation enabled users to search some indexed information with the keyword. To search for information on the web, the first real search engine was developed by Matthew Gray in 1993, it was called Wandex (Couvering, 2008; Ledford, 2015; Seymour et al., 2011).

The concept of a search engine is now approximately 28 years old. Examples of some famous search engines: are Google, Bing, Yahoo, Baidu, (America Online) Aol.com, Ask.com, DuckDuckGo, Wolfram Alpha, Yandex, Lycos, Chacha.com, Ecosia, Exalead, Excite, Mojeek, Searx, and among many others.

The most common search engines are; Google developed by Larry Page and Sergei Brin in 1996 and believed to be the biggest search engine in the whole world, Bing commonly known as Live Search, Windows Live Search, and MSN Search owned by Microsoft, Baidu mainly used by the Chinese, Yandex mainly used by Russophone countries and Russia, and DuckDuckGo that emphasis privacy of its users, and Yahoo which is now powered by Bing. However, there are other specialist search engines like YouTube, Amazon, Skyscanner, and Facebook.

The search engine searches different web pages looking for the required information filtering content from any pages (necessary and unnecessary) using advanced algorithms (Shaikh et al., 2010). All search engines' main purpose is to get accurate results in the smallest time possible to solve user queries. However, they do the opposite by either displaying inaccurate or accurate but unreliable results.

Common Components of a Web Search Engine

A web search engine commonly consists of three parts; a crawler or spider, a search indexer or algorithm, and a query search handler (Henzinger, 2004).

Web Crawler / Spider / Internet Bot

This is at times called an automatic indexer that analytically crawls the web. The internet bot simply downloads some selection of web content. It then crawls or searches repeatedly this downloaded data plus the links linked to other pages mentioned in this data. Then several pages are produced containing information with a high potential of answering a searched query. A search engine then indexes, and catalog this information in the Search Engine Results Pages (**SERPs**) and also rank these pages based on some factors like high-quality content, page speed, on-page optimization, and internal or external links among others (Lewandowski & Kammerer, 2021). This helps organize the web pages so that they appear to the user's search request by order of relevance (Agichtein et al., 2006). Through this mechanism, any search engine such as Bing, Yandex, and Google, among others swiftly responds to every user query with a precise response by applying its search algorithm to the web crawler data.

A search Indexer or Algorithm

This is a primary component of the performance of a search engine (Seymour et al., 2011). It's generally divided into three categories: on-page algorithms, whole-site algorithms, and off-site algorithms. A search algorithm's input for a search engine is a keyword or similar phrase being searched for throughout the entire database. The output or result, are related pages that contain a word or similar phrase of a word being searched for using a search engine (Ledford, 2015). The output of the search algorithm is based on the perceived quality of the page expressed in the quality score. Every search engine has a different form of search algorithm.

On-page Algorithms

These measure the on-page factors for example; elements of the page that inspire the user to browse the specific page. It determines this based on the proximity of related words, the number of times some specific keywords and phrases are used, and how other words are related on that webpage. From that this algorithm can identify the topic of that specific webpage.

Whole-site Algorithms

These inspect the relationship of pages on a website for example; "does the information of the index page correlate with the information of other web pages?" It also identifies whether all the pages of a specific website are interlinked together.

Off-site Algorithms

They filter good incoming links from users who have picked a good interest concerning the content of your site. This algorithm adds another feature of how the quality of your website is ranked. Most search engines have an automated script called a ***crawler*** sometimes called a ***spider*** or a ***bot*** that crawls billions of different sites to collect information about these sites and create their entries in a search engine index. The search engines need this information to know which pages to display in response to any search engine query. (Ledford, 2015), identified some criteria used by the search engine crawler to determine your site's ranking in a given set of results; Anchor text, Site popularity, Link context, Topical links, Title tags, Keywords, Site language, Content, and Site maturity.

A Query Search Handler

This component responds to the user queries using the indexed information by the indexer. A search engine responds to a user's search queries using an indexer that generates a result page containing top-ranked documents. As users interact with the search results, a search engine logs their browsing behavior and leverages this data to improve the search quality (Henzinger, 2004).

Search User Interface

The search user interface helps users understand and express their information needs, formulate queries, select among available information sources, understand search results, and keep track of the progress of their search (Hearst, 2011). This platform provides access to users to find the content of an index page. For any developer when designing the search user interface, some guiding principles should be followed. A good search user interface must consist of a textbox and a button next to it and position at the top right position of a web page. This component must be available on all web pages of a website and accessible via a hyperlink to a search page. This interface must be initially empty and be in a position to accommodate long search texts. Lastly, the designed search user interface should by default only search within the content of your website.

WHAT IS ARTIFICIAL INTELLIGENCE (AI)?

Originally, AI was defined as the modesty of how computer systems exhibit smart or intelligent human characteristics. Currently, AI is defined as a way in which computer systems exhibit complex behaviors similar proportionally to living things like an octopus, and neural systems among others (Van Zuylen, 2012; Yusuf et al., 2021). AI is a combination of deep learning and machine learning techniques that teach a computer to perform and solve a specific problem without human assistance. It has gone beyond helping human beings gather reliable information over the internet through the optimization of search engines (Yuniarthe, 2017).

The significance of artificial intelligence is almost attached to every sector (healthcare, education, communications, transportation, agriculture, among others). It is rapidly gaining popularity, and adoption, and is developing on a large scale because several IT corporations like Facebook, Amazon, Microsoft, Google, and others have incorporated AI, hence positively impacting their development. AI has successfully optimized traffic to these websites and other sites through search engine optimization from the search engines. For example, facial recognition systems on Facebook use AI, recommender systems and opinion mining use AI and ML algorithms on Youtube and Netflix (Akgun & Greenhow, 2021). Voice assistants such as Amazon Alexa, Google Assistant, Apple Siri, Microsoft Cortana, and Samsung Bixby among others assist people with information searches all use AI to perform their roles diligently (Zwakman et al., 2021). In the study conducted (Laricchia, 2017), they observed that approximately 52% of the people prefer using voice assistants over website search engines.

Algorithms are the core elements or fundamentals of AI. They are essentially mathematical instructions comprising hundreds and thousands of lines of code designed and followed by any computer system when solving a specific problem (Akgun & Greenhow, 2021).

Artificial Intelligence Algorithms in Search Engines

Among all search engines, Google is at the forefront and has deployed new AI technologies like Rank-Brain, Neural Matching, Bidirectional Encoder Representations from Transformers (BERT), and Multitask Unified Model (MUM) (Sun et al., 2019). AI and ML algorithms, understand language more like how a human would understand language, this is termed Natural Language Processing (NLP).

However, Google's AI and ML algorithms aren't the only ones used in other search engines worldwide. Other search engines like Yandex which is the most used search engine in Russia also utilize algorithms like Matrixnet (2009), Palekh (2016), Korolyov (2017), and CatBoost (2017) that learn from different datasets and provide predictions, recommendations, and decisions, hence providing better search results and experiences to users (Polak, 2017; Stankova et al., 2017).

In 2017, the Bing search engine also introduced the *"intelligent search"* model which uses deep neural networks (DNNs) to provide a faster response (Chung et al., 2018). This AI model can read and understand billions of web documents and provide more relevant answers faster and directly to users. In 2000, the Baidu search engine was established and ranked as the most popular and largest search engine in China capturing over 75% of China's search market according to the Wikipedia Website Rankings (Fang et al., 2019; Haiyan, 2010).

To improve search queries, (Serrano, 2016a) proposed an Intelligent Search Assistant (ISA) developed using Random Neural Networks (RNN) that performs as an intermediary between every search engine and user queries. ISA acquired a query from the user input and returned one result from each of the various web search engines (Google, Yahoo, Yandex, and Bing). This ISA provided good results than Google and other search engines, despite the biased returned results caused by the user's concentration on the first results returned that were already presented to the algorithm.

Integration of Artificial Intelligence and Search Engines

There are two kinds of artificial intelligence, (Physical AI and virtual AI). In search engines, virtual AI is the kind of artificial Intelligence. The user can neither feel nor touch the mechanism but just achieves wonders in the attained results or output from the search engines. An augmented number of websites providing information correspondingly requires an increased level of accuracy of the retrieved information from the search engines. Not only do companies or institutions provide both private and public online content, but also single users create websites and share weak views, and content. This raises concern about the integrity of retrieved content shared online because it is not reviewed, or controlled (Hay et al., 2008). Additionally, computers have inherited the bad habits of humans such as racism, ageism, and sexism, all of this is due to the application of AI in search engines (Yuniarthe, 2017).

In the survey done by (Jones & Fox, 2009), they observed that 74% of the united states adult population use the internet but 61% of the sample use it to find medical information. Most patients before their first appointment at hospitals or medical centers, search for medical information from websites unknowingly that they are controlled by only the authors and webmasters. Some physicians use the web as the first source of medical information (Google search and PubMed) to assist them to diagnose difficult medical cases (Dragusin et al., 2011; Svenstrup et al., 2015).

Additionally, as long as the patient discusses the searched information with the physician (Tan & Goonawardene, 2017), they both need the internet to seek health information. This builds a good relationship between them, however, they stand a higher risk of experiencing diagnostic errors, developing cyberchondria, decreased quality of life, difficulty to check the integrity of the information they obtained, harmful health practices, and false news in form of texts, video, audio, and images. The most common socially problematic impact of the internet is false information that is hard to detect and spreads just in a couple of minutes (Jwa et al., 2019).

AI was sought to be an excellent solution to overcome such risks. Some search engines have deployed AI algorithms in their search output results. A Scottish software engineer John Giannandrea led AI integration into Google (Bhushan, 2021). Integration of AI in search engines promised proper decision-making, cost-effectiveness, speed, and improved search engine optimization results (SEO) among others. Most importantly, retrieving precise and integrity results from search engines promised to improve patient engagement in the management of their diseases in interaction with their doctors (Negrini et al., 2021). Among all search engines, Google adopted and constantly increased the use of AI and deep learning DL to achieve continuous perfection in search results and ranking the results based on a cumulative number of variables.

Search engines are vulnerable in answering search queries, but the results displayed are unreliable with either inaccurate or accurate results from untrusted blogs. To try to solve this issue (Shaikh et al., 2010), introduced a Semantic Web-Based Intelligent Search Engine (SWISE) that includes domain knowledge in the web pages that helps to answer intelligent queries. This model achieved good results and could work on any platform, however, required the conversion of existing information into a machine-readable format.

Description of Google AI Systems

Google uses several metrics to rank web pages in its search engines. Among these metrics is the *"PageRank algorithm"* that is developed by Sergey Brin and Larry Page. PageRank focuses on both the quality and quantity of page links pointing to a specific web page. The backlinks, internal or inbound links, and external links influence Google PageRank. These factors are very important in the description of PageRank calculation as shown in the formula below.

$$PR(A) = (1-d) + d\left[\frac{PR(T1)}{C(T1)} + ... + \frac{PR(Tn)}{C(Tn)}\right] \tag{1}$$

Where

PR(A) represents the page ranking of a certain page **A,**
PR(T1...Tn) represents page rank of pages from **1** to **n**, which link to page A,
Parameter **d** represents a damping factor which can be set between **0** and **1,**
C(T1)... C(Tn) is the number of outbound links on page **A.**

When calculating the PageRank we can use the matrix representation, MapReduce, the iterative approach represented in ***equation I*** given above among others.

Diagram Illustrating Ten Connected Web Pages

See Figure 1.

Figure 1. Represents a mathematical PageRank of a simple network of websites (A, B, C, D, E, F, G, H, E, and F.
Source (Wikipedia, 2008))

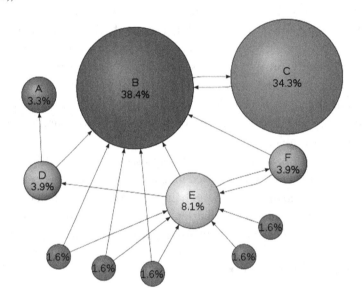

RankBrain AI Algorithm

Google was founded in 1998 by Lawrence Edward Page an American computer scientist and since then to date, it has been growing tremendously (Sullivan, 2012). RankBrain is a deep machine learning algorithm or a neural network that predicts the best query results given the historical data. It adjusts the ranking of web pages based on the similarity of user queries and works well for new queries that don't have passed data or historical information.

This sophisticated AI algorithm was launched in 2015. RankBrain algorithm combines machine learning and AI techniques. It deals with all languages and generates quick responses to user search queries by, first understanding the language of both the query and content, crawling billions of web pages, and then ranking webpages it believes to be the best. This implies that more content is used to determine the suitable search ranking. This algorithm helps Google rank its search results in both the search query and the language of the content. (Sajjadi et al., 2021) examined the content of the most frequently asked questions (FAQs), the quality plus information transparency of sources used by Google to answer the FAQs about COVID-19 vaccines using the RankBrain ML algorithm. Under their survey, they used Google's rich snippet feature called the "People Also Ask" feature to obtain the FAQs and the

"Rothwell Classification of Questions" to classify questions based on content. Their search generated 28 unique FAQs about COVID-19 vaccines, with the most FAQ being related to COVID-19 vaccine safety and effectiveness.

Neural Matching AI Algorithm

Neural matching (NM) is sometimes called a ranking algorithm. It was the second AI Google release after the innovation of RankBrain in 2015. It was released in 2018 and then expanded locally to the local search results in 2019 (Moreno & Redondo, 2016). This AI helps the Google search engine understand how searches relate to pages by looking at the whole content and understanding the whole content on the page. Currently, it is used in most queries for all languages and across all regions.

Bidirectional Encoder Representations From Transformers (BERT) AI Algorithm

BERT is a general-purpose deep neural network model based on transformer architecture that learns contextual relations between words or subwords. This model can be fine-tuned for many other specific tasks, hence consuming less time to train for the new task and achieving greater accuracy even on a smaller dataset (Mohammadi & Chapon, 2020). The pre-trained BERT model when layers are added to it and trained on data specific to the tasks at hand, it can perform other new tasks like sentiment analysis, classification, summarisation, and translation.

This AI new generation word embedding algorithm was innovated in 2019 (Alaparthi & Mishra, 2020). BERT is a powerful general-purpose NLP neural network that helps the Google search engine recognize how sequences of texts on a page express different meanings (Nogueira & Cho, 2019; Othan et al., 2019). This AI is a ranking algorithm used in all languages and plays an important role in every English query to help Google rank search results. This algorithm has achieved impressive results on various NLP tasks such as question-answering and natural language inference among others (Nogueira & Cho, 2019).

The study of (Jwa et al., 2019) looked at numerous methods of detecting false text news, they applied the BERT model and developed a model that detects and analyzes the false news anomaly by examining the association between the news headline and the text content. (Nogueira & Cho, 2019) reimplemented BERT for query-based passage re-ranking. The study (Achsas, 2022) examined aggregated search paradigms in the academic domain hence improving search performance by using the BERT model to help researchers easily find all the information needed about a specific topic.

Multitask Unified Model (MUM) AI Algorithm

Currently, MUM is used for naming the COVID vaccine (Romeo & Frontoni, 2022). It is the current innovation for Google introduced in 2021 (Bie & Yang, 2021).MUM helps Google generate languages and also to understand variations and new terms in those languages (Clark et al., 2019). Other AI systems like RankBrain, NM, and BERT can perform an additional purpose of ranking webpages except for MUM.

OPPORTUNITIES AND CHALLENGES OF AI IN SEARCH ENGINE CONTEXT

Improved Search Results and Greater Understanding of Search Queries

Enhanced quality of search results in terms of precision (excluding irrelevant information) and recall (ability to provide interesting results). In search engines such as Google, AI has played an important role in providing authentic information (search results) to its users. Hence this has promoted the ranking of google search engine amongst all other search engines used worldwide. This reliable access to authentic information reduces the rate of propagation of false information and content over the internet. Intelligent search saves most company employees time against the ineffective search of information that could have positively impacted the development of the organization and also help it to achieve success against its competitors. AI has made it possible for search engines to understand the meaning of the content of a site and its information, as well as the sentiment of the content using NLP that educates computers to comprehend human written language. Today, Google greatly understands human search using its pre-trained language model BERT. This model (BERT) fully understands the context of a search, not just the keywords in it (Ghadhab et al., 2021). Secondly, companies use AI-enabled multimedia spam detection systems to separate high-quality information from low-quality content (Rao et al., 2021).

Development of Online Business and Relationship Between Retailers and Customers

AI has greatly developed online eCommerce online business and Improved relationships between the customer and retailer (Nagy & Hajdú, 2021). This is achieved in several ways, for example, a user-friendly and interactive interface improves the user experience and strengthens online assistance using AI-enabled systems like the messaging-based chatbot developed by Google, Bing, Yandex, and Baidu that have a good interface and interactive search engine (Aqle et al., 2018).

AI-enabled Voice Search

The integration of AI in search engines has also favored those with sight problems in searching the web through the implementation of Natural Language Processing (NLP) in the **"search by voice"** mechanism found in search engines like Google (Yadav & Chakraborty, 2022). This branch of computer science, its major backbone is AI which enables computers to understand the text and spoken words in the same way as a human.

The NLP technology has got so advanced to the extent of actually understanding the human voice in real-time, for example, when you use a Google voice Assistant the AI-powered systems easily comprehend your words spoken in real-time, translate them, and return the search results.

Relationship Between Physicians and Patients

increased physicians' and patients' trust in online information (Ball & Lillis, 2001; Huang & Penson, 2008). Hence this saves cost and reduces time to diagnose and manage the state of a specific disease (Ellahham et al., 2020). All this is achieved through search engines outputted results effectiveness, efficiency, and accuracy.

Improvement in Content and Digital Marketing

Improved content can be achieved through the use of Predictive Intelligence for Creating Unique Experiences. The role of AI in content marketing may vary significantly. First, It can help digital marketers make better use of all online information available, proportionally increasing the process of content creation and building an effective content strategy among other benefits. Secondly, Predictive intelligence allows retailers to understand the needs of their customers better and create content that suits customer interests. NLP can help marketers work efficiently by automatically generating precise content, for example, Allen Institute for AI developed a model that captures the top headlines from aggregator sites and produces new articles (Chen et al., 2021). AI has also been ease monitoring the website performance, analysis, and discovering better insights. When doing online business, there is nothing special than understanding the behaviors of the audience. This helps you to prepare and deliver better and personalized services to your clients. All has been trended by the power of NLP which is a branch of AI.

Improved Curation of Engaging and Relevant Content

AI improves the creation and curation of engaging and relevant Content for e-commerce websites (Dias & Ferreira, 2017; Thandekkattu & Kalaiarasi, 2022). Creating curate content that is attractive to the world, and engaging and relevant daily is a time-consuming activity. However, AI algorithms can help to obtain popular keyword search and their meaning, and create content that is relevant and highly searched quickly. And another most difficult task is crawling through this obtained content manually, which may consume a lot of time and effort. AI can help do this automatically, making it possible to create content on relevant and highly searched topics quickly.

Reduction of Search Engine Spam

Search engine spam refers to the deliberate manipulation of various search engines by their authors to achieve a placement in the top ranking results returned by the search engines. The major goal of artificial intelligence in search engines is to read and understand the keywords or search queries. AI achieves this by using a neural network spam classifier that labels each webpage as either spam or nonspam (Henzinger et al., 2002).

Enabled Image Search to Understand Photos

Images are composed of vast hidden information (Subramanian et al., 2021). Image Analysis is one of the weaknesses of traditional search algorithms (they can't understand photos or find hidden content in images) (Zhang & Sun, 2021). Using a combination of AI and ML image analysis, users can search for their desired content by simply adding a photo. This is a common activity on social media platforms where every second, thousands of photos are uploaded to Twitter, Instagram, and Facebook among other social media. AI technologies in search engines can analyze what is being represented in an image, then deliver relevant search results around that image (Bastanta et al., 2021).

CONCERNS RELATED TO THE APPLICATION OF ARTIFICIAL INTELLIGENCE IN SEARCH ENGINES

Limited Support and Trust With AI Systems

This challenge is termed the "***AI Black box***" which describes AI's ability to provide invisible, choices and solutions to human problems. It is a common challenge affecting systems applying artificial intelligence in contemporary society (Zednik, 2021). This leaves many questions to humans about how AI algorithms precisely work out and provide such outstanding results. Finding ways to enable humans to understand the results provided by AI systems is now an active area of research using Explainable Artificial Intelligence (XAI) to solve this challenge (Szczepański et al., 2021). Up to date, there is limited trust in the precise results returned by AI-enabled search engines (Pires et al., 2018).

Bias Problems in Line With Race and Sex

Racism

Many cases and challenges have continuously ascended in most applications where Artificial intelligence is applied. A good and common challenge is proved in facial recognition that has been highlighted with significant risks of discrimination which was termed the "sea of dudes" problem (Makhortykh et al., 2021). In another scenario, A.I. in a Google online photo service organized photos of Black people into a folder called "gorillas." And Hewlett-Packard's web camera software had difficulty recognizing people with dark skin tones (Crawford, 2016). AI systems were egregiously biased against Black people's faces that couldn't be identified until they need to put on a white mask (Amershi et al., 2019). Another similar error emerged in Nikon's camera software that misjudged Asian images of people as blinking.

Sexism

The challenge is well explained by the majority of digital assistants, including chatbots, assigned names, voices, visual representations, and even "characters" that are stereotypically female and reflect male-controlled ideology (Brown, 2022). Computer scientists from Carnegie Mellon University discovered that women had fewer chances than men to be publicized on Google ads for highly paid jobs (Crawford, 2016).

CONCLUSION

In search engines and any everyday task, artificial intelligence promises better, precise, and reliable results. But one needs to know how to use it from the data collection process, to what problems can be solved with the collected data. Applications of AI in vast sectors plus its precise unnoticeable solution to complex problems has comforted human. It has proved its application in eCommerce, education, modern lifestyle, navigation, robotics, healthcare, agriculture, gaming, automobiles, social media platforms, marketing, chatbots, and banks. AI has increased efficiency, improved workflows, reduced human errors, performed deeper data analysis, performed precise decision making, and in simple terms, AI has tried to make human life easier. AI will never be perfect, but the more humans interact with it, the smarter it becomes. Therefore, in the future projection, humanity will be better off due to human's strong relationship with artificial intelligence and the development of explainable artificial intelligence which will make humans trust the precise unnoticeable results generated by search engines.

REFERENCES

Achsas, S. (2022). Academic Aggregated Search Approach Based on BERT Language Model. *2022 2nd International Conference on Innovative Research in Applied Science, Engineering and Technology (IRASET)*, 1–9.

Agichtein, E., Brill, E., & Dumais, S. (2006). Improving web search ranking by incorporating user behavior information. *Proceedings of the 29th Annual International ACM SIGIR Conference on Research and Development in Information Retrieval*, 19–26. ACM. 10.1145/1148170.1148177

Akgun, S., & Greenhow, C. (2021). Artificial intelligence in education: Addressing ethical challenges in K-12 settings. *AI and Ethics*, 1–10.

Alaparthi, S., & Mishra, M. (2020). Bidirectional Encoder Representations from Transformers (BERT): A sentiment analysis odyssey.

Amershi, S., Weld, D., Vorvoreanu, M., Fourney, A., Nushi, B., Collisson, P., Suh, J., Iqbal, S., Bennett, P. N., & Inkpen, K. (2019). Guidelines for human-AI interaction. *Proceedings of the 2019 Chi Conference on Human Factors in Computing Systems*, 1–13. Semantic Scholar.

Aqle, A., Al-Thani, D., & Jaoua, A. (2018). Conceptual interactive search engine interface for visually impaired Web users. *2018 IEEE/ACS 15th International Conference on Computer Systems and Applications (AICCSA)*, 1–6. IEEE.

Ball, M. J., & Lillis, J. (2001). E-health: Transforming the physician/patient relationship. *International Journal of Medical Informatics*, *61*(1), 1–10. doi:10.1016/S1386-5056(00)00130-1 PMID:11248599

Bastanta, A., Nuryansyah, R., Nugroho, C. A., & Budiharto, W. (2021). Image data encryption using DES method. *2021 1st International Conference on Computer Science and Artificial Intelligence (ICCSAI)*, *1*, 130–135.

Bhushan, S. (2021). The impact of artificial intelligence and machine learning on the global economy and its implications for the hospitality sector in India. *Worldwide Hospitality and Tourism Themes*, *13*(2), 252–259. doi:10.1108/WHATT-09-2020-0116

Bie, Y., & Yang, Y. (2021). A multitask multiview neural network for end-to-end aspect-based sentiment analysis. *Big Data Mining and Analytics*, *4*(3), 195–207. doi:10.26599/BDMA.2021.9020003

Brown, L. M. (2022). Gendered Artificial Intelligence in Libraries: Opportunities to Deconstruct Sexism and Gender Binarism. *Journal of Library Administration*, *62*(1), 19–30. doi:10.1080/01930826.2021.2006979

Chen, Q., Leaman, R., Allot, A., Luo, L., Wei, C.-H., Yan, S., & Lu, Z. (2021). Artificial intelligence in action: Addressing the COVID-19 pandemic with natural language processing. *Annual Review of Biomedical Data Science, 4*(1), 313–339. doi:10.1146/annurev-biodatasci-021821-061045 PMID:34465169

Chung, E., Fowers, J., Ovtcharov, K., Papamichael, M., Caulfield, A., Massengill, T., Liu, M., Lo, D., Alkalay, S., Haselman, M., Abeydeera, M., Adams, L., Angepat, H., Boehn, C., Chiou, D., Firestein, O., Forin, A., Gatlin, K. S., Ghandi, M.,, & Burger, D. (2018). Serving dnns in real time at datacenter scale with project brainwave. *IEEE Micro, 38*(2), 8–20. doi:10.1109/MM.2018.022071131

Clark, K., Luong, M.-T., Khandelwal, U., Manning, C. D., & Le, Q. V. (2019). Bam! born-again multi-task networks for natural language understanding. doi:10.18653/v1/P19-1595

Van Couvering, E. (2008). The history of the Internet search engine: Navigational media and the traffic commodity. In *Web search* (pp. 177–206). Springer. doi:10.1007/978-3-540-75829-7_11

Crawford, K. (2016). Artificial intelligence's white guy problem. *The New York Times, 25*(06).

Dias, J. P., & Ferreira, H. S. (2017). Automating the extraction of static content and dynamic behaviour from e-commerce websites. *Procedia Computer Science, 109*, 297–304. doi:10.1016/j.procs.2017.05.355

Dragusin, R., Petcu, P., Lioma, C., Larsen, B., Jørgensen, H., & Winther, O. (2011). Rare disease diagnosis as an information retrieval task. *Conference on the Theory of Information Retrieval*, 356–359. Springer. 10.1007/978-3-642-23318-0_38

Ellahham, S., Ellahham, N., & Simsekler, M. C. E. (2020). Application of artificial intelligence in the health care safety context: Opportunities and challenges. *American Journal of Medical Quality, 35*(4), 341–348. doi:10.1177/1062860619878515 PMID:31581790

Escandell-Poveda, R., Iglesias-García, M., & Papí-Gálvez, N. (2022). *From Memex to Google: The origin and evolution of search engines.* INDOCS.

Fang, J., Wu, W., Lu, Z., & Cho, E. (2019). Using baidu index to nowcast mobile phone sales in China. *The Singapore Economic Review, 64*(01), 83–96. doi:10.1142/S021759081743007X

Frana, P. L. (2004). Before the web there was Gopher. *IEEE Annals of the History of Computing, 26*(1), 20–41. doi:10.1109/MAHC.2004.1278848

Ghadhab, L., Jenhani, I., Mkaouer, M. W., & Ben Messaoud, M. (2021). Augmenting commit classification by using fine-grained source code changes and a pre-trained deep neural language model. *Information and Software Technology, 135*, 106566. doi:10.1016/j.infsof.2021.106566

Haiyan, C. (2010). An impact of social media on online travel information search in China. *2010 3rd International Conference on Information Management, Innovation Management and Industrial Engineering, 3*, 509–512.

Hay, M. C., Cadigan, R. J., Khanna, D., Strathmann, C., Lieber, E., Altman, R., Mcmahon, M., Kokhab, M., & Furst, D. E. (2008). Prepared patients: Internet information seeking by new rheumatology patients. *Arthritis Care and Research, 59*(4), 575–582. doi:10.1002/art.23533 PMID:18383399

Hearst, M. (2011). User interfaces for search, 21–55. *Modern Information Retrieval.*

Henzinger, M. R. (2004). Algorithmic challenges in web search engines. *Internet Mathematics, 1*(1), 115–123. doi:10.1080/15427951.2004.10129079

Henzinger, M. R., Motwani, R., & Silverstein, C. (2002). Challenges in web search engines. *ACM SIGIR Forum, 36*(2), 11–22.

Huang, G. J., & Penson, D. F. (2008). Internet health resources and the cancer patient. *Cancer Investigation, 26*(2), 202–207. doi:10.1080/07357900701566197 PMID:18259953

Jones, S., & Fox, S. (2009). *Generations online in 2009.* Pew Internet & American Life Project Washington.

Jwa, H., Oh, D., Park, K., Kang, J. M., & Lim, H. (2019). exbake: Automatic fake news detection model based on bidirectional encoder representations from transformers (bert). *Applied Sciences (Basel, Switzerland), 9*(19), 4062. doi:10.3390/app9194062

Laricchia, F. (2017). *Factors surrounding preference of voice assistants over websites and applications, worldwide, as of 2017.* Statista. https://www.statista.com/statistics/801980/worldwide-preference-voice-assistant-websites-app/

Ledford, J. L. (2015). *Search engine optimization bible* (Vol. 584). John Wiley & Sons.

Lewandowski, D., & Kammerer, Y. (2021). Factors influencing viewing behaviour on search engine results pages: A review of eye-tracking research. *Behaviour & Information Technology, 40*(14), 1485–1515. doi:10.1080/0144929X.2020.1761450

Makhortykh, M., Urman, A., & Ulloa, R. (2021). Detecting race and gender bias in visual representation of AI on web search engines. *International Workshop on Algorithmic Bias in Search and Recommendation,* (pp. 36–50). Springer. 10.1007/978-3-030-78818-6_5

Mohammadi, S., & Chapon, M. (2020). Investigating the Performance of Fine-tuned Text Classification Models Based-on Bert. *2020 IEEE 22nd International Conference on High Performance Computing and Communications; IEEE 18th International Conference on Smart City; IEEE 6th International Conference on Data Science and Systems (HPCC/SmartCity/DSS),* 1252–1257. IEEE.

Moreno, A., & Redondo, T. (2016). Text analytics: The convergence of big data and artificial intelligence. *IJIMAI, 3*(6), 57–64. doi:10.9781/ijimai.2016.369

Nagy, S., & Hajdú, N. (2021). Consumer acceptance of the use of artificial intelligence in online shopping: Evidence from Hungary. *Amfiteatru Economic, 23*(56), 155. doi:10.24818/EA/2021/56/155

Negrini, D., Padoan, A., & Plebani, M. (2021). Between Web search engines and artificial intelligence: What side is shown in laboratory tests? *Diagnosis (Berlin, Germany), 8*(2), 227–232. doi:10.1515/dx-2020-0022 PMID:32335539

Neogy, T. K., & Paruchuri, H. (2014). Machine Learning as a New Search Engine Interface: An Overview. *Engineering International, 2*(2), 103–112. doi:10.18034/ei.v2i2.539

Nogueira, R., & Cho, K. (2019). Passage Re-ranking with BERT.

Othan, D., Kilimci, Z. H., & Uysal, M. (2019). Financial sentiment analysis for predicting direction of stocks using bidirectional encoder representations from transformers (BERT) and deep learning models. *Proc. Int. Conf. Innov. Intell. Technol.*, *2019*, 30–35.

Pires, R., Goltzsche, D., Ben Mokhtar, S., Bouchenak, S., Boutet, A., Felber, P., Kapitza, R., Pasin, M., & Schiavoni, V. (2018). CYCLOSA: Decentralizing private web search through SGX-based browser extensions. *2018 IEEE 38th International Conference on Distributed Computing Systems (ICDCS)*, (pp. 467–477). IEEE.

Polak, Y. (2017). Yandex and Others: On 20 Years of Russian Search in Internet. *2017 Fourth International Conference on Computer Technology in Russia and in the Former Soviet Union (SORUCOM)*, (pp. 172–175). IEEE. 10.1109/SoRuCom.2017.00034

Rao, S., Verma, A. K., & Bhatia, T. (2021). A review on social spam detection: Challenges, open issues, and future directions. *Expert Systems with Applications*, *186*, 115742. doi:10.1016/j.eswa.2021.115742

Romeo, L., & Frontoni, E. (2022). A Unified Hierarchical XGBoost model for classifying priorities for COVID-19 vaccination campaign. *Pattern Recognition*, *121*, 108197. doi:10.1016/j.patcog.2021.108197 PMID:34312570

Sajjadi, N. B., Shepard, S., Ottwell, R., Murray, K., Chronister, J., Hartwell, M., & Vassar, M. (2021). Examining the Public's Most Frequently Asked Questions Regarding COVID-19 Vaccines Using Search Engine Analytics in the United States: Observational Study. *JMIR Infodemiology*, *1*(1), e28740. doi:10.2196/28740 PMID:34458683

Serrano, W. (2016a). A big data intelligent search assistant based on the random neural network. *INNS Conference on Big Data*, (pp. 254–261). Springer.

Serrano, W. (2016b). The random neural network applied to an intelligent search assistant. *International Symposium on Computer and Information Sciences*, (pp. 39–51). Springer. 10.1007/978-3-319-47217-1_5

Seymour, T., Frantsvog, D., & Kumar, S. (2011). History of search engines. *International Journal of Management & Information Systems*, *15*(4), 47–58.

Shaikh, F., Siddiqui, U. A., Shahzadi, I., Jami, S. I., & Shaikh, Z. A. (2010). SWISE: Semantic Web based intelligent search engine. *2010 International Conference on Information and Emerging Technologies*, 1–5. 10.1109/ICIET.2010.5625670

Sharma, D., Shukla, R., Giri, A. K., & Kumar, S. (2019). A brief review on search engine optimization. *2019 9th International Conference on Cloud Computing, Data Science & Engineering (Confluence)*,(pp. 687–692). Semantic Scholar.

Stankova, E. N., Grechko, I. A., Kachalkina, Y. N., & Khvatkov, E. V. (2017). Hybrid approach combining model-based method with the technology of machine learning for forecasting of dangerous weather phenomena. *International Conference on Computational Science and Its Applications*, (pp. 495–504). Springer. 10.1007/978-3-319-62404-4_37

Subramanian, N., Elharrouss, O., Al-Maadeed, S., & Bouridane, A. (2021). Image steganography: A review of the recent advances. *IEEE Access: Practical Innovations, Open Solutions*, *9*, 23409–23423. doi:10.1109/ACCESS.2021.3053998

Sullivan, D. (2012). *Google: 100 billion searches per month, search to integrate Gmail, launching enhanced search app for iOS*. Search Engine Land.

Sun, C., Qiu, X., Xu, Y., & Huang, X. (2019). How to fine-tune bert for text classification? *China National Conference on Chinese Computational Linguistics*, (pp. 194–206). Springer. 10.1007/978-3-030-32381-3_16

Svenstrup, D., Jørgensen, H. L., & Winther, O. (2015). Rare disease diagnosis: A review of web search, social media and large-scale data-mining approaches. *Rare Diseases*, *3*(1), e1083145. doi:10.1080/216 75511.2015.1083145 PMID:26442199

Szczepański, M., Choraś, M., Pawlicki, M., & Pawlicka, A. (2021). The methods and approaches of explainable artificial intelligence. *International Conference on Computational Science*, (pp. 3–17). Springer. 10.1007/978-3-030-77970-2_1

Tan, S. S.-L., & Goonawardene, N. (2017). Internet health information seeking and the patient-physician relationship: A systematic review. *Journal of Medical Internet Research*, *19*(1), e5729. doi:10.2196/jmir.5729 PMID:28104579

Thandekkattu, S. G., & Kalaiarasi, M. (2022). Customer-Centric E-commerce Implementing Artificial Intelligence for Better Sales and Service. *Proceedings of Second International Conference on Advances in Computer Engineering and Communication Systems*, (pp. 141–152). Springer. 10.1007/978-981-16-7389-4_14

Van Zuylen, H. (2012). Difference between artificial intelligence and traditional methods. *Artificial Intelligence Applications to Critical Transportation Issues*, *3*.

Wikipedia. (2008). *Mathematical PageRanks for a Simple Network Are Expressed as Percentages*. Wikipedia. https://en.wikipedia.org/wiki/PageRank#/media/File:PageRanks-Example.svg

Yadav, S., & Chakraborty, P. (2022). Using Google voice search to support informal learning in four to ten year old children. *Education and Information Technologies*, *27*(3), 4347–4363. doi:10.100710639-021-10789-5

Yuniarthe, Y. (2017). Application of Artificial Intelligence (AI) in Search Engine Optimization (SEO). *Proceedings - 2017 International Conference on Soft Computing, Intelligent System and Information Technology: Building Intelligence Through IOT and Big Data, ICSIIT 2017, 2018-January*, 96–101. 10.1109/ICSIIT.2017.15

Yusuf, F., Olayiwola, T., & Afagwu, C. (2021). Application of Artificial Intelligence-based predictive methods in Ionic liquid studies: A review. *Fluid Phase Equilibria*, *531*, 112898. doi:10.1016/j.fluid.2020.112898

Zednik, C. (2021). Solving the black box problem: A normative framework for explainable artificial intelligence. *Philosophy & Technology*, *34*(2), 265–288. doi:10.100713347-019-00382-7

Zhang, W., & Sun, W. (2021). Research on small moving target detection algorithm based on complex scene. *Journal of Physics: Conference Series*, *1738*(1), 12093. doi:10.1088/1742-6596/1738/1/012093

Zwakman, D. S., Pal, D., & Arpnikanondt, C. (2021). Usability evaluation of artificial intelligence-based voice assistants: The case of Amazon Alexa. *SN Computer Science*, *2*(1), 1–16. doi:10.100742979-020-00424-4 PMID:33458698

Chapter 9
Artificial Intelligence Applications in Cybersecurity

Tesfahiwet Abrham
Zayed University, UAE

Sanaa Kaddoura
ⓘ https://orcid.org/0000-0002-4384-4364
Zayed University, UAE

Hamda Al Breiki
Zayed University, UAE

ABSTRACT

For the past decades, cyber threats have been increasing significantly and are designed in a sophisticated way that is tough to detect using traditional protection tools. As a result, privacy and sensitive personal information such as credit card numbers are being continuously compromised. Therefore, it is time to find a solution that can stand against the spreading of such threats. Artificial intelligence, machine learning, and deep learning could be among the top methods of detecting cyber threats. These methods could help to improve the detection technologies and engines for computer network defense. This chapter mainly focuses on artificial intelligence in cybersecurity. The main goal of this chapter is to highlight the drawbacks of the traditional security protection tools and discuss the improvements that has been made so far by applying artificial intelligence to solve the current cybersecurity problems.

INTRODUCTION

Almost every week, an individual's or a company's data is compromised in today's world. Each incident serves as a reminder of the flaws in standard cybersecurity methods. Traditional network protection tools are currently used to protect enterprises from ransomware and complex malware. Those tools, however, are not guaranteed enough for the task as new sophisticated and interconnected cyberattacks are developed (Calderon, 2019). These attacks can adversely affect the information assets of the organization. The most sophisticated tools, including Intrusion Detection and Prevention Systems (IDPS),

DOI: 10.4018/978-1-6684-6937-8.ch009

have been evaded by skilled cybercriminals, making botnets almost impossible to detect. Cyber incidents are hazardous because of central network warfare (Gupta & Sheng, 2019). Reduced sales, operational disruption, additional hiring, and a loss of competitive edge are just a few examples of the harm that can result from theft or penalties. Threats are becoming viral worldwide, so computer network defense technologies cannot quickly adapt to next-generation cybersecurity threats due to their discovery and detection engine limitations.

To reduce the destructive effects of cyber threats, we need to find a solution designed to provide complete protection against a wide range of attacks. Security teams need to always think like a hacker to understand the techniques and goals of the actual attack. Currently, experts are using Artificial Intelligence (AI) to get ahead of cyber criminals so that they can counter new attacks (Jean-Philippe, 2018). Therefore, to have continuous protection against such attacks, the security systems need a steady adjacent to new threats.

According to Gupta and Sheng, researchers, governments, and public and private companies or organizations are all working hard to reach an ideal level of cybersecurity protection in which they can safeguard their information assets or systems with the most efficient and cutting-edge technologies (Gupta & Sheng, 2019). Consequently, artificial intelligence and machine learning have become crucial tools for cybersecurity systems to collaborate with humans in the face of cyber threats and other obstacles. AI and machine learning (ML) landscape prioritize threat detection, and businesses rely on AI and ML for faster responses, better outcomes, and increased productivity.

Many researchers suggest that AI and ML may be the future paradigms in cybersecurity automation. Using predictive analytics to form statistical inferences, AI and ML can help reduce cyber dangers while using fewer resources (LAZIĆ, 2019). In the subject of cybersecurity, AI and ML can help detect new attacks more quickly and provide an effective tool for drawing statistical inferences and pushing that information to endpoint security systems. Due to a significant number of attacks and a shortage of cybersecurity workers, AI and ML are becoming increasingly vital tools.

AI and ML are valuable and powerful tools in today's technology. AI and ML have demonstrated their worth by deciphering data from various sources and spotting crucial relationships that people would miss. On the other hand, hackers are skilled enough- they can develop tools to stand against AI and may use it for offensive reasons. Therefore, businesses and governments should consider incorporating AI into their systems. The rapid advancements and growth of AI technology, causes cybersecurity norms and standards to continuously expand and change not be tracked by the new tools. With the versatility of AI applications, hackers will use AI approaches to avoid detection. As a result, having another AI machine is an excellent way to deal with an AI threat from hackers (McAfee Labs 2019). The three critical issues explored in this chapter are the influence of AI and ML on cybersecurity, the benefits and drawbacks of employing AI tools for security, and whether AI and ML can assist the cybersecurity industry in reducing cyber risks.

CYBERSECURITY

In the present, the internet makes the world a small village in many ways, but it has also exposed us to influences that have never been so diverse and difficult. The realm of hacking expanded as quickly as security. Privacy and information protection are the primary security practices that each organization is concerned with (Rajasekharaiah et al., 2020). Due to the evolving nature of threats online, people are becoming targets of cyberattacks more regularly today (Chang & Hawamdeh, 2020). Pathways are built by malicious and offensive behaviors that provide predators (hackers and crackers) unauthorized access to computer systems or networks. These actions are known as cyber threats. To create these paths, predators work on the systems' and networks' defects and flaws (Bhatele et al., 2019).

By conducting some studies, cybersecurity is constantly growing in importance for the following reasons:

1. There is a greater chance that systems may be compromised or that information will leak as more gadgets (including security cameras, not just computers, and smartphones) connect to the Internet (Nurse, 2021).
2. More people are using sophisticated smartphones as portable personal computers to access work information at their places of employment.
3. Organizations are operating online more frequently, which increases their reliance on the Internet (Martínez Torres, 2019).
4. Hackers and other criminals who use computers are becoming more skilled, and they are improving on earlier cybercrime technologies.
5. Businesses are producing, capturing, and storing more data online.
6. Hackers are getting smarter: Hackers discover new data access techniques every day. Identifying security risks before hackers do is the job of an information security analyst. To guard against cyberattacks, they subsequently create and put into place new preventative security policies (Veale & Brown, 2020). An increasing number of cybersecurity experts are required to design and deploy cutting-edge security solutions as hackers' techniques become more sophisticated.
7. Everything is automated: As business operations are automated, technology is becoming more and more ingrained in a company's infrastructure. Every automated system is built using code that hackers can access when they intrude. Therefore, the more operations conducted digitally, the more opportunities hackers have to acquire personal data.

Additionally, cybersecurity can aid with risk management by preventing cyberattacks, data breaches, and identity theft. An organization is better able to stop serious of these attacks when it has a strong awareness of network security and an efficient incident response plan. For instance, end-user protection safeguards data, prevent loss or theft, and scans machines for harmful software (Seemma et al., 2018). Furthermore, information is the most precious resource in terms of an individual, business sector, state, and nation.

Cybersecurity Techniques

In some articles, the authors discussed some techniques that can be used to improve cybersecurity as follow:

1. **Access Control and Password Security**: The concept of a username and password serves as a necessary means of data assurance. It might be the most critical cybersecurity precaution (Kalakuntla, 2019).
2. **Anti-virus Software**: It is a computer application that categorizes, avoids, and attempts to destroy or remove harmful software programs, such as viruses and worms. The auto-update feature found

in most anti-virus products allows the software to download profiles of new viruses so that it may check for them when they are discovered (Kalakuntla, 2019).

3. **Malware Scanners**: These programs check all the files and archives currently stored in the system for malicious code or dangerous viruses (Rajasekharaiah et al., 2020). Trojan horses, worms, and viruses are examples of malicious software that are frequently assembled and referred to as malware.

4. **Firewall**: A software program or equipment that helps monitor hackers, infections, and all types of worms that endeavor to access PC over the Internet. Data transmitted over the web go through the firewall, which looks at every individual message and hinders those who do not meet the security requirements. They classify them as threats, try to block them from the system, and monitor their activities.

Challenges in Cybersecurity

Security challenges to computer network infrastructure are there every day, and they are increasing in number and complexity. Despite increased awareness of cyber threats, much money has been spent on combating cybercrime. Many parties are involved in cyberspace, including individuals, companies, non-state actors, and governments, all seeking to protect their cyber assets (Chang & Hawamdeh, 2020).

Although cyberspace is heterogeneous and dynamic, certain similarities in attacks and countermeasures can serve as foundations for a holistic security framework. Cyber-attacks typically follow a cyber kill chain comprised of several attack phases (Wirkuttis & Klein, 2017). This framework supposes that a sequence of every single attack begins with a reconnaissance phase-an attacker attempts to find gaps and weaknesses in a target system. Following that is the weaponization phase, in which the discovered flaws are utilized to create targeted malicious programs. The malware is then transported to the possible victim during the delivery phase. The exploit phase begins once the infection has been successfully transmitted, and it is at this step the malware initiates the installation of an intruder's code. After that, the compromised host system allows the attackers to establish a command-and-control channel, allowing them to carry out malicious acts. Countermeasures can be determined depending on where an adverse action appears in the cyber kill chain.

Additionally, some researchers suggested the main challenges of cybersecurity as follows:

Cybersecurity Is Always Evolving

The continual development of technology, which provides hackers with an ever-expanding range of potential opportunities to exploit, is perhaps the biggest problem facing cyber security (Opara & Dieli, 2021). Cybercriminals always create new strategies for carrying out cyberattacks, which makes this even more difficult. Because of this, developers of cyber security software and specialists consistently come up with new fixes to plug potential holes, but hackers just keep coming up with new ways to launch attacks. Cybersecurity, as a result, is constantly evolving. Opara & Dieli (2021) supposed that the continually changing nature of cyber security makes it extremely difficult and expensive for enterprises to keep up-to-date. It necessitates ongoing updates as well as persistent attention to the security sector.

The Amount of Data

Most firms' data volume is a significant obstacle to cyber security. A corporation becomes a desirable target as more data becomes available, especially when it involves sensitive data (Sarker et al., 2020). Such an amount of data puts the organization in danger of lawsuits if the information maintained by the organization is obtained negligently. Consequently, the organization where the people's data is stored is compromised, and their information is stolen.

The Need for Training and Education

Another possible difficulty is that user education is just as crucial for cyber security as software or other solutions. An organization's staff members must be aware of risky behaviors (Haderlie et al., 2021). For instance, they download viruses accidentally or click links in anonymous emails. Such necessitates taking time away from their regular duties for training, and the business must set aside funds for it (Crumpler & Lewis, 2019).

Not Enough Cybersecurity Professionals

In addition to all the difficulties mentioned above, the field of cyber security is now understaffed. According to some estimates, there are up to two million open cybersecurity positions worldwide (Logpoint Team, 2021). Besides, there are not enough numbers of professionals globally, and hence, emerging nations are more concerned about this issue (Mogoane & Kabanda, 2019). ML and other technological advancements have helped to some extent to overcome this issue, but it still exists.

An alternative term for cyber security is "Cyber intelligence." It is the gathering and analyzing of data to recognize, monitor, and anticipate cyber capabilities, intentions, and actions to provide solutions that improve decision-making. The ability to better comprehend an attacker depends on the fact that attackers leave trails when attempting to attack a possible target system. As a result, an Integrated Security Approach's (ISA) holistic perspective of an organization's security necessitates collecting and analyzing a wide range of data to gain cyber intelligence (Wirkuttis & Klein, 2017). However, there are difficulties in obtaining pertinent data and processing, evaluating, and utilizing it. As a result, security technologies that strive to automate supporting security activities are frequently used to successfully enhance associated efforts to prevent, detect, and respond to harmful intrusions.

BACKGROUND

Artificial Intelligence, Machine Learning, and Deep Learning

Ever since the technological revolution, considerable development in the field of technology has emerged. Such a development shows that new technologies have been replacing traditional manual work. Among these technologies are Artificial Intelligence, machine learning, and deep learning highly replace the manual work that is done in various fields.

Artificial Intelligence: An emerging branch of technology known as artificial intelligence researches and creates theories, methods, techniques, and software tools that mimic, enhance, and extend human intelligence (Smith & Eckroth, 2017). It is a branch of computer science that aims to comprehend the fundamentals of intelligence and develop a new breed of intelligent machine that behaves in a way comparable to human intelligence (Lidestri, 2018). AI analyzes natural language processing, computer vision, robotics, and expert systems (Xin, 2018). Moreover, it is possible to create intelligent software and systems by examining how the human brain works and how people learn, make decisions and collaborate when attempting to solve a problem. Commonly, people define intelligence as the capacity to acquire knowledge and use knowledge to reason about difficulties. Intelligent machines will soon take over many human functions in the future.

Machine Learning: Researchers suggested that machine learning is a branch of computer science that allows computers to learn without being explicitly programmed (Gupta & Sheng, 2019). It is also a branch of artificial intelligence that studies and builds algorithms to learn from and forecast data (Thomas, 2020). These algorithms avoid following rigidly static program instructions by making data-driven predictions or decisions by developing a model from sample inputs. ML teaches a computer how to predict responses, allowing it to respond to situations it has never faced before. Machine learning can be categorized as either supervised or unsupervised based on whether or not it requires labeled data (learning strategy):

- **Supervised**: Each sample has a label, so we can calculate the difference between the actual and anticipated values and change the model's parameters as necessary (Gupta & Sheng, 2019). Among the most popular supervised methods are decision trees, support vector machines (SVM), and multilayer perceptron (MLP)
- **Unsupervised**: Because there are no labels in the dataset in this situation, clustering algorithms are primarily used to solve the problem. The algorithms work by clustering data, meaning samples within each cluster are more similar to one another than samples inside the other cluster (Martínez Torres, 2019).

Deep learning: Additionally, the study of artificial neural networks and related machine learning techniques with more than one hidden layer is known as deep learning (Xin, 2018). Deep learning entails providing a massive dataset to a computer system, which then uses it to make decisions on other datasets (Jean-Philippe, 2018). Methods use techniques such as artificial neural networks (ANN) to achieve deep learning.

Due to its sophistication and capacity for self-learning, DL offers processing that is both faster and more accurate. The exploration of DL applications in security domains is necessary given the success of DL in many disciplines and the limitations of conventional approaches to cybersecurity (Imamverdiyev & Abdullayeva, 2020). DL approaches have a wide range of features for effective use in cybersecurity challenges, including the ability to detect DDoS attacks, behavioral anomalies, malware, and protocols, as well as botnets and voice recognition of individuals. Besides, to create a neural architecture with intricate interconnections, DL mimics the function of human neurons. The application of DL in various industrial contexts has become commonplace, and it is currently a hotbed of academic research (Li, 2018). Generally, Artificial intelligence has a component called machine learning, and deep learning is a subclass of machine learning (Salih et al., 2021), as shown in Figure 1.

Figure 1. The relationship among AI, ML & DL

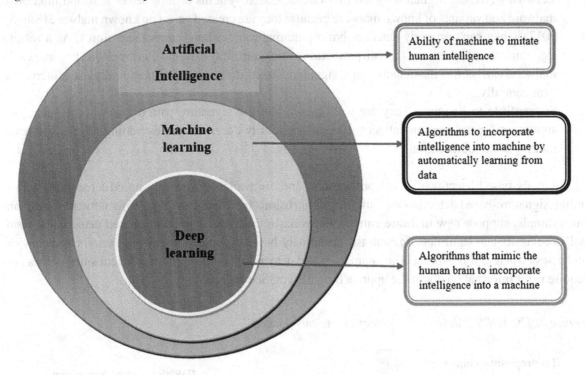

The corporate and public sectors are paying more attention to AI applications for cybersecurity needs. A survey estimates that the cybersecurity industry for AI will expand from $1 billion in 2016 to $34.8 billion in 2025 (Taddeo & McCutcheon, 2019). Several nations have included AI capabilities in their most recent national cybersecurity and defense agendas.

APPLICATIONS

Network Intrusion Detection

Intrusion Detection System (IDS) and Intrusion Prevention System (IPS) comprise the intrusion detection and prevention systems (IDPS). According to Priyadarshini & Sharma, IDS is a technique to detect anomalies or any ongoing attacks. It is a passive system that scans incoming traffics (Priyadarshini & Sharma, 2022, p. 43). Once it identifies dangerous or suspicious traffic, it can send alerts. IPS, on the other hand, can actively block or prevent intrusions. IDPSs rely on signature-based and anomaly-based systems (Calderon, 2019). Signature-based detection systems use databases of known threats to detect intrusions. They then look at incoming packets, extract signatures from network packets, and compare them to a database. The method assumes an incursion has been detected if there is a match. It's a good way to spot previously reported attacks, but one of the significant drawbacks is that it only works against threats it recognizes. The signature-based detection system has the following shortcomings:

1. **Zero-Day Attack**: Signature-based malware detection systems cannot detect new and unknown malware and variants of known malware because they are created based on known malware (Singh, 2017). They can't properly detect polymorphic malware without correct signatures. As a result, signature-based detection offers no protection against zero-day exploits. Furthermore, because each malware variant has its signature in a signature-based detector, the signature database increases exponentially.
2. **Susceptible to Evasion**: They are well-known because signature patterns are used to generate signatures for malware and attacks. Hackers can easily deceive them by adding no-ops and rearranging code (obfuscation).

Anomaly-based detection systems, on the other hand, are available. Anomaly-based detection systems, unlike signature-based detection systems, detect intrusions or attempts by analyzing network behavior. For example, suppose new malware enters a network. In that case, a signature-based detection system will not classify it as legitimate. In contrast, an anomaly-based detection system will examine its behavior and assess whether it is a threat. The anomaly-based detection method is more efficient since it does not require prior information about the approaching danger. See Figure 2.

Figure 2. The IDPS is designed to detect suspicious packets.

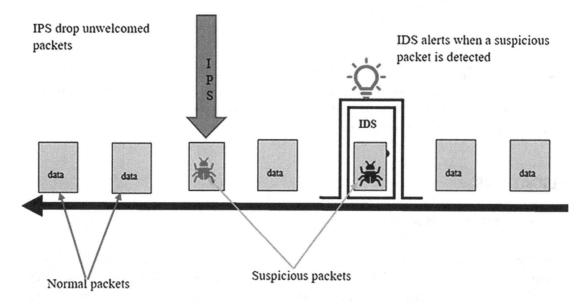

Cybersecurity professionals will require more advanced tools and tactics to safeguard their networks as fraudsters become more skilled. One approach for IDPS is machine learning. IDPS based on machine learning could improve defenses while lowering false positives. There are many types of machine learning methodologies, each with its traits and benefits that cybersecurity professionals can use. Every machine learning algorithm is not created equal; thus, researchers must provide the relevant data for the ML-based system to function correctly (Jean- Philippe, 2018).

Lambora et al. state that the Genetic Algorithm helps with machine learning optimization issues (Lambora et al., 2019). It is a crucial algorithm since it speeds up the process of solving complex problems that would otherwise take a long time (Halim et al., 2021). He also argues that it is designed to increase the classifiers' accuracy and identifies risks by gaining knowledge from prior anomalous behavior. Moreover, GA-based Feature Selection achieves a maximum accuracy of 99.80% (Halim et al., 2021). GA is significant for detecting threats that have recurring trends. As a result, GA makes decisions based on previous patterns when faced with new patterns that the system cannot detect. Researchers could improve detection rates for new abnormalities by applying this strategy to ML-based IDPS systems. For instance, if ransomware succeeds in getting past the firewall via email or another vector to spread and encrypt files, the ML-based IDPS with GA will identify it and prevent the encryption of a big cluster of devices across the network (Calderon, 2019). To sum up, the IDPS system, which is ML-based, may make judgments based on new patterns. Regular IDPSs lack these features since they rely on earlier configurations to keep networks safe.

An artificial Neural Network is another method. According to Jean-Phillipe, artificial neural networks (ANN) are capable of spotting patterns that humans find difficult to comprehend (Jean-Phillipe, 2018). ANNs can also recognize patterns that aren't perfectly defined. The use of ANN in IDPS improves network security - has demonstrated exemplary performance against DoS attacks (Priyadarshini & Sharma, 2022, p. 62). Cybercriminals have figured out how to get around security safeguards. They can launch attacks that do not generate system alerts, making detection more difficult for cybersecurity specialists (Kaddoura et al., 2021). Because of the connection patterns, ANN would be capable of determining when a connection is valid and when it should raise a security alert.

On the other hand, Sikos (2018) mentioned the main limitations of ANN-network intrusion detection systems: inferior detection precision for low-frequency attacks and weaker detection stability, which restricts their applicability. The unequal distribution of various attack kinds is the cause of these. For instance, there are far fewer low-frequency training data instances than prevalent attacks. As a result, training the ANN to recognize these low-frequency attacks' properties is difficult.

Another approach for IDPS is deep learning. Artificial Neural networks consist of three layers: inputs, hidden layers, and outputs. Deep learning neural networks are fed with data in the input layer. Several hidden layers then process the input data to produce possible outcomes (inputs) (Salih et al., 2021), as shown in Figure 3 below. For intrusion detection systems, many deep learning algorithms have been applied. Salih et al. supposed that extraction characteristics and classification tasks are the primary goals of deep learning in constructing intrusion systems.

Botnet Detection

A botnet comprises several internet-connected devices that may have been purposefully infected with software by cybercriminals. Botnets can be used to launch distributed denial-of-service (DDoS) attacks, steal information, or get access to equipment (Calderon, 2019). A botnet attack is a malicious attack employing many linked computers to attack or bring down a network, network device, website, or IT environment. It is committed to interfering with regular business activities or degrading the target system's overall level of service. As a result, successful botnet detection and prevention would be crucial for computer security (Alshamkhany et al., 2020).

The process of identifying and separating these botnet devices can be carried out using a variety of machine-learning approaches as more devices become candidates to be botnet devices. Researchers and security professionals use a variety of strategies and ways to address the issue as botnets grow more dangerous. The detection strategy, such as detection by behavior or signature, establishes how the solution works.

Main Methods for Botnet Detection

1. **Honeypot Analysis:** Honeypot trapping allows the capture of many malicious code samples, such as botnet binary files from existing botnets, for analysis and monitoring in a controlled environment and discovering the bots and their malicious behaviors (Li et al., 2016). Active detection is involved in this behavior.
2. **Communication Signature:** The technique based on communication signature detection is a frequently employed protection technique that identifies bot activity based on predetermined patterns and signatures recovered from well-known bots (Xing et al., 2021). Regular expressions, whitelists, and blacklists are often used techniques. The authors further presented that traditional intrusion detection systems, like Snort, have a vast signature database and can quickly and precisely identify botnet activity by creating feature-matching rules in advance. The communication signature-based approach is appropriate for botnets with specific traits, which contributes to a deeper understanding of botnets' communication mechanisms and potential weaknesses.
3. **Deep Learning:** Before the model can be established, researchers determine its characteristics through experience. A network flow can be measured by measuring the number of data packets, average data packet size, and the average interval between two adjacent streams, as well as by measuring behavior, for example, whether to access the same server. Experiments found that these models had low false-negative and false-positive rates (Xing et al., 2021).

Credit Card Fraud Detection Using Machine Learning

Credit card fraud refers to the physical loss of a credit card or the loss of sensitive credit card information. Credit card fraud is one of the most frequent scams since cashless transactions are becoming more widespread. When a fraudster uses a credit card for personal expenses without the cardholder's knowledge, this is referred to as credit card fraud (Varmedja et al., 2019). It is possible to withdraw a substantial amount of money without the owner's knowledge, within a short period, with no risks involved. Because fraudsters always attempt to pass off fraudulent transactions as legitimate, it is challenging to identify fraud (Dornadula & Geetha, 2019). To conceal the fraud, fraudsters always attempt to make fraudulent transactions seem legitimate.

According to Varmedja, credit card fraud can come in two different forms. One is physical card theft, while the other is taking private data from the card, like the card number, CVV code, kind of card, and others (Varmedja, 2019). Before the cardholder realizes it, a fraudster can steal a significant sum of money or make a substantial purchase using stolen credit card information. Companies use various machine-learning techniques to distinguish between legitimate and fraudulent transactions (Khan et al., 2022). Besides, Xuan supposed that fraudulent activities involving credit and debit cards had established themselves as one of the key reasons for monetary losses in the banking sector (Xuan, 2018). The development of technology poses a serious threat that could result in significant financial losses across the globe. Thus, to prevent financial losses, it is crucial to carry out credit card fraud detection.

A study conducted by FTC found 1,579 data breaches and 179 million records, with 133,015 reports of credit card fraud. Other fraud reports included 82,051 employment or tax fraud, 55,045 reports of phone fraud, and 50,517 bank fraud (Dornadula & Geetha, 2019). Furthermore, Nguyen et al. supposed that card scams have cost financial organizations millions of dollars in lost revenue and increased stress for people who use credit cards worldwide. In 2017, Nguyen found about 20.48 billion cards (including credit, debit, and all prepaid cards) were used globally (Nguyen et al., 2020).

Machine learning helps distinguish between valid and fraudulent transactions. Any banking organization or financial organization that issues debit and credit cards must implement a reliable system to identify any instances of fraudulent activity. According to Khan et al., ANN, SVM, k-nearest neighbors, and other techniques are remarkable ways to help detect credit card fraud. Let us briefly discuss the abovementioned approaches (Khan et al., 2022).

1. **Artificial Neural Network (ANN):** Supervised and unsupervised methods are the two types of methodologies on which ANN is built. Due to its 95% accuracy rate, the Unsupervised Neural Network is frequently employed to identify fraud instances (Bin Sultan et al., 2022). The unsupervised neural network looks for comparable patterns between the present credit cardholders and those from prior transactions.

2. **K-Nearest Neighbors (KNN):** According to Malini and Pushpa, Outlier identification algorithms can also detect fraud. They effectively reduce false alarm rates and raise the fraud detection rate (Malini & Pushpa, 2017).

3. **Support Vector Machine:** Researchers frequently look at consumers' credit card usage trends in this method. Datasets were gathered about the clients' payment habits. The support vector machine approach categorizes consumer patterns into fraudulent or non-fraudulent transactions. When fewer features from the dataset are employed, the SVM method is efficient and yields accurate results (Sasank et al., 2017). The main goal of SVM is to divide the data into several categories by creating a suitable split plane (Li, 2018). He also added that researchers achieved 96.95% accuracy with a low false-negative rate of 0.018 by using an SVM to assess the efficiency and performance of the derived features.

Additionally, Mohammed suggested that using algorithms based on anticipated user behaviors, an artificial intelligence-based fraud detection system called Decision Intelligence has been deployed by MasterCard to identify fraudulent transactions. To assess if a purchase is odd, it looks at the buyer's typical buying habits, the seller, the transaction's location, and many more intricate algorithms (Mohammed, 2020). Figure 4 shows the Benefits of Machine Learning in detecting credit card fraud and others.

Figure 3.

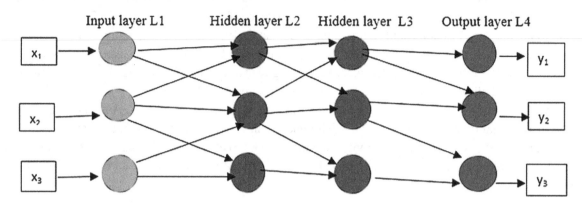

Figure 4. Benefits of Machine Learning

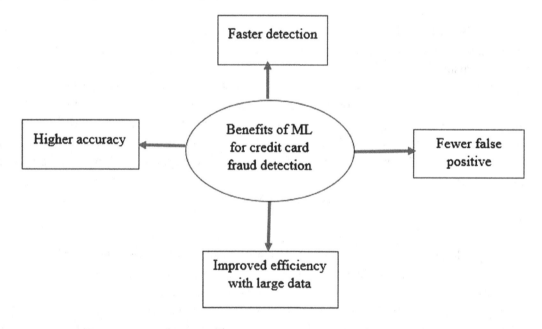

Major Challenges Involved in Credit Card Fraud Detection

1. Every day, significant amounts of data are collected, and the model development must be quick enough to detect scams in time.
2. Data imbalance, 99.8% of transactions are legitimate rather than fraudulent, making it very challenging to identify the fraudulent ones (Nguyen, 2020).
3. Data accessibility since most data is public and has many false alarms (Nguyen, 2020).
4. Misclassified data is another significant problem because not all fraudulent transactions are discovered and reported.

Thus, to tackle these challenges, researchers have been taking some steps:

1. The employed model must be rapid and easy to use to identify the abnormality and categorize the transaction as fraudulent as soon as possible (Lucas, 2020).
2. The dimensionality of the data might be decreased to safeguard the user's privacy.
3. At the very least, for model training, it is necessary to use a more reliable source that verifies the data.
4. We can make the model straightforward to understand so that, after the attacker figures it out, we can quickly release a new model by making a few minor adjustments.

Therefore, to convince banks and other financial institutions to use this technology, it is still necessary to work toward overcoming the limits that are currently in place (Bin Sulaiman, 2022).

Spam Email Detection and/or Phishing Detection

According to Yaseen, online communication has become an integral part of our everyday lives due to the increase in Internet and social network usage (Yaseen, 2021). Due to its open access, speed, and dependability, email is one of the most popular forms of official and corporate communication. Spam emails are one or more unsolicited messages that take the guise of advertisements or promotional materials, such as debt-reduction plans, get-rich-quick schemes, online dating, etc., which were fast expanding as email usage increased. Furthermore, Ahmed et al. stated that spam emails are becoming more prevalent in education, politics, chain messaging, stock market advice, and marketing (Ahmed et al., 2022). Anyone with Internet access and malicious motives can send spam from anywhere. Spams are unsolicited emails sent to those who do not need or want them. These spam emails are sent to several recipients and contain fake content, typically links to phishing scams and other risks (Jain et al., 2019). They are designed to steal users' personal information and utilize it against their will to benefit materialistically. Nowadays, many different types of spam are emerging, and researchers categorize them as shown in Figure 5 below.

Figure 5. Types of Spam attacks

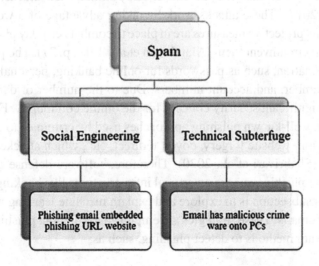

Phishing Life Cycle

Step 1: An attacker takes advantage of the vulnerabilities of the target organization. So they can exploit and monitor the traffic going in and out of the traffic of the targeted network. Then, they install a phishing website into the victim's webserver.

Step 2: The attacker will send out the phishing email to the victim as if it comes from a legitimate organization to convince them.

Step 3: When the victim clicks the fraud link, the access controls might be altered so that the attacker may gain privileged access to the victim's system. The system may also install malware, allowing the attacker to access and modify its settings.

Step 4: Now, the attacker collects essential data like bank accounts and other sensitive personal information or may be able to control the system remotely. See Figure 6.

Currently, numerous businesses create various methods and algorithms for effective spam detection and filtering. One of the most important methods of securing email networks is spam filtering. Although many research publications have been published utilizing different machine-learning techniques to recognize and handle spam emails, there are still certain knowledge gaps. One of the critical alluring research areas for bridging the gaps is junk mail (Pitchaimani et al., 2019). Due to this, numerous studies on the classification of spam have already been conducted using various techniques to increase the reliability and value of email communication for users. Work is being provided to create a condensed version of the many machine-learning models and techniques currently used for email spam detection (Kaddoura et al., 2020).

Similarly, phishing emails fool recipients into disclosing sensitive data, such as usernames, passwords, and credit card details. Researchers suggested that with the growing number of Internet and email users, criminal activity and email fraud are also growing (Jean-Philips, 2018). Consumers and businesses continue to be concerned about phishing attacks, which have increased in number and severity over the past few years. In short, phishing exploits vulnerabilities found in system processes by tricking the victim into deploying malicious code.

Unknown zero-day phishing emails are currently regarded as one of the commercial world's major hazards. Such phishing occurs because they are launched by unidentified attackers who get past security measures (Gupta et al., 2017). These attacks work by taking advantage of a weakness in the targeted system. Even though many protective measures are in place to combat zero-day phishing attacks, phishers constantly devise ways to circumvent them (Alauthman et al., 2019, p. 27). The purpose of online fraud is to steal sensitive information, such as passwords for online banking, personal identification number (PIN), social security number, and account numbers. Due to the number of daily online transactions, phishing has become a significant security concern for the online community. Furthermore, according to Shahrivari et al., some well-known phishing approaches used by criminals to deceive people are link manipulation, filter evasion, website forgery, covert redirect, etc., which attackers use to lure sensitive information from users (Shahrivari et al., 2020). Therefore, software defense mechanisms should be involved to defend against phishing attacks on critical infrastructures like banking and other businesses.

The main goal of this subsection is to explore and explain machine learning methods for preventing and identifying phishing emails. These strategies are employed to filter out phishing attempts. Researchers can use several software methods to detect phishing, such as:

1. **Visual Similarity-based Phishing Detection:** This detection method is used to spot phishing websites by examining how closely they resemble trustworthy websites (Gupta et al., 2017). These approaches leverage the view of the web page rather than the coding underlying it because we know that most phishing websites are almost identical to those of their target websites.

2. **List-based Approach:** Blacklist-based anti-phishing techniques that are built into web browsers are one of the extensively utilized techniques for phishing detection. Both the whitelist and the blacklist, which keep track of dangerous websites, are used in these techniques. The whitelist contains the names of legitimate websites (Shahrivari et al., 2020). Typically, the blacklist is compiled using user input or third-party reports produced using another phishing detection method.

3. **Heuristics and machine learning-based:** Machine learning techniques have effectively categorized malicious behaviors or artifacts, such as spam emails or phishing websites. Shahrivari et al. state that most of these techniques call for training data; thankfully, plenty of phishing websites are available to train a machine learning model (Shahrivari et al., 2020). Some machine learning systems employ vision techniques by examining a webpage snapshot; others use the website's features and content to identify phishing attempts. It is mainly used for email phishing detection, and its accuracy reached up to 94.8% (Gupta et a., 2017).

Spam Email and Phishing Detection Using Machine Learning Approaches

As phishing emails are significant issues, programmers have created many ways to identify these emails. In contrast, phishers have developed several strategies to get around these efforts and attack the weaknesses of the targeted system. One of the critical approaches for detecting phishing attacks is machine learning. The main benefit of machine learning is the capacity to design adaptable models for specific tasks, such as phishing detection. Figure 7 shows the general steps for spam detection. Machine learning models can be effective tools for phishing because it is a categorization problem (Shahrivari et al., 2020).

Figure 6.

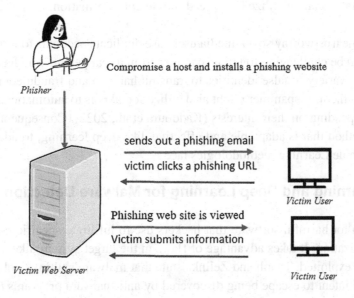

Compromise a host and installs a phishing website

Phisher

sends out a phishing email

victim clicks a phishing URL

Victim User

Phishing web site is viewed

Victim submits information

Victim Web Server

Victim User

Figure 7. Steps for Spam detection

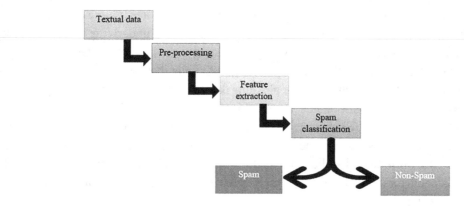

Challenges of Spam Detection

According to Pitchaimani et al., the following are some significant difficulties that spam filters face (Pitchaimani et al., 2019):

1. Adversarial machine learning threatens to reduce the effectiveness of many spam detection techniques. When ML models are being trained and tested, adversaries may launch various attacks. During testing, adversaries can produce undesirable samples to avoid detection, poison training data to cause a classifier to classify the data erroneously, and steal sensitive training data using a learning model.
2. Systems for detecting spam have a significant challenge from the expanding volume of data on the Internet and its numerous new features.
3. Another major problem spam detection systems are currently dealing with is deep fake. Images and videos can be produced, altered, and styled using neural network models and image creation models. Deep fakes can be utilized to spread fraudulent information.

Additionally, some trustworthy social media users use duplicate accounts to interact with a circle of known friends. It can be challenging to tell a spammer from a real person who has a duplicate profile. Spammers also use a variety of false identities to transmit harmful and fraudulent materials, making it more difficult to find them. A spammer might also utilize social bots to automatically send messages on the user's behalf, depending on their interests (Kaddoura et al., 2022). Consequently, there is a critical need to pursue a method that is adaptable and effective, like deep learning, to address the difficulties that traditional Machine Learning methodologies face.

AI, Machine Learning and Deep Learning for Malware Detection

Malware is the term for harmful software that hackers use to infiltrate specific machines or an entire network of an organization. It takes advantage of flaws in the target system, like a defect in legitimate software that can be exploited. Thanh and Zelinka state that malware's ultimate objective is to conceal its presence and evil intent to escape being discovered by anti-malware programs (Thanh and Zelinka,

2019). A malware intrusion can have catastrophic results, including data theft, extortion, or the crippling of network systems. Malware is a broad term with many classes, see Figure 8.

Figure 8.

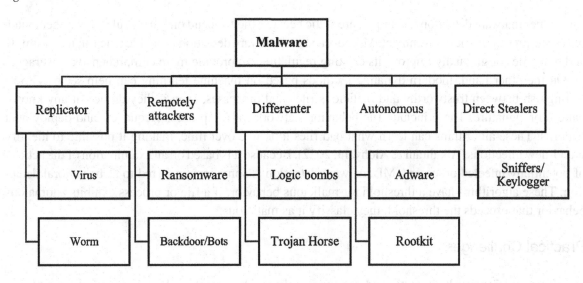

Important of Malware Detection?

According to Faruk et al., the most significant security risk on the Internet nowadays is malware. Malware is the root cause of most Internet issues, including spam emails and DoS attacks. Malware-infected computers are frequently networked to create botnets, and numerous attacks are made utilizing these nefarious, attacker-controlled networks (Faruk et al., 2021). Therefore, new strategies are needed to detect and stop any harm they may bring to deal with the latest malware created. Machine learning has become more effective in detecting malware by using multiple data types from the host, network, and cloud-based anti-malware components.

Utilizing methods and technologies to recognize, stop, notify, and react to malware threats is malware detection. Basic malware detection methods, including applications, allow listing, checksumming, and signature-based detection can assist in identifying and limiting known risks. Advanced malware detection systems use machine learning and artificial intelligence to proactively search for and identify new and undiscovered malware threats.

AI Approach

Malware detection aims to safeguard the system from various forms of malicious attacks by following the detection and prevention policy. Although many existing malware detection methods exist, with the development of malware technology, artificial intelligence adoption is essential for effective and reliable malware protection apps. Locating the malicious source code is the first step in detecting malware (Rokon et al., 2020). Faruk et al. suggested that artificial intelligence is rapidly developing, and its breakthroughs enable impressive outcomes in many application areas. As a result, creating effective anti-malware systems will be important in overcoming the limitations of current preventative technology (Faruk et al., 2021).

Machine Learning Approach

The earlier malware detection techniques are static because they depend on binary rules that either match or run the process in the environment. Moreover, static malware detection is unable to learn; it can simply add new rules or gradually improve its existing regulations to provide more comprehensive coverage.

On the other hand, modern dynamic methods based on machine learning can help security tools distinguish between trustworthy and malicious files and processes, even if they do not fit any known pattern or signature. These include file behavior, network traffic, process frequency, and deployment patterns. These algorithms can learn what bad files look like over time, making it possible to identify brand-new infections (Alkahtani & Aldhyani, 2022). Because it is based on an examination of the actions of potentially infected processes, ML malware detection is sometimes referred to as behavioral detection. These algorithms have a threshold for malicious behavior; if a file or process exhibits anomalous behavior that exceeds the threshold, they classify it as malicious.

Practical Challenges

Despite promising results in static and dynamic analysis when machine learning is used for malware detection, substantial obstacles prevent machine learning-based malware detectors from being widely adopted. According to Saad et al., one possible challenge is malware detector interpretability. Any malware detector will produce false positives, and malware analysts will not accept those black box malware detectors unless they can comprehend and analyze the circumstances around them a benign application's incorrect classification as malicious (Saad et al., 2019). So far, no research has examined how machine-learning models interpret malware detection. He also added another challenge which is adversarial malware-which can be used to circumvent a machine learning-based malware detection system. Furthermore, Saad et al. supposed that the accuracy of system detection with adversarial malware decreased from 94% to roughly 50%. To sum up, algorithms for machine learning are not intended to handle hostile cases (Saad et al., 2019).

FRAUD DETECTION

Nowadays, fraud prevention is challenging due to fraudsters' constant evolution and adaptation. As soon as you learn how to spot and avoid one scam, a new one pops up to take its place. The greatest technology to combat fraud must therefore be able to adapt and evolve just as quickly as the fraudster's methods. MasterCard deploys Decision Intelligence algorithms based on consumer expectations to detect fraudulent transactions to employ artificial intelligence. When determining whether a transaction is unusual, the program examines the customer's standard purchasing patterns, the seller, the location, and many other aspects (Welukar & Bajoria, n.d).

Organizations have typically used rules-based systems to identify fraud. Rules use if-then logic, which can be thorough in spotting recognized fraud trends. Furthermore, rules can only identify patterns you are already familiar with and can encode into the logic, even if they are still a crucial fraud-fighting tool, mainly when used in conjunction with more sophisticated techniques (Mhlanga, 2020). They are not good at adjusting to new fraud trends, finding hidden schemes, or recognizing more complex fraud strategies. Because of this, many sectors are using machine learning and artificial intelligence to detect fraud.

Challenges of Fraud Detection

Like other detection challenges, there are some problems with fraud detection and machine learning. Fraud involves conflict (adversarial). When patterns are consistent and crucial data is not purposefully withheld or, even worse, altered, machine learning algorithms perform at their best. In many machine learning applications, parties are either neutral toward the system or actively working with it to help it learn (such as in medical applications). Fraudsters aim to stop people from discovering when they commit fraud (Bao et al., 2022). Additionally, fraudsters are always coming up with new scams. There might not be a previous example of computers recognizing a new kind of fraud.

Practical Considerations in Model Building

It is difficult to protect data from being compromised by fraudsters in the modern world. Bao et al. (2022) suggested that data quality is essential for AI to be effective. The quantity and caliber of data that models require increase when systems go from rules to simple structural models, from structural models to machine learning, and finally from machine learning to deep learning. This flow poses several difficulties. The quantity of data is the first problem. As the cost of gathering and storing unstructured data in data lakes and structured data in data warehouses declines, this problem is gradually resolved. It can still be a problem for smaller businesses, sporadic events, or excessively intricate calculations. The data's quality, integrity, and completeness are a second problem. If the data is not correctly formatted, the torrential flood of information coming from many sources has no use; even just keeping up with data requires effort.

AI and Fraud Detection

Using artificial intelligence to detect fraud has helped businesses improve internal security and streamline corporate operations. Because of its increased efficiency, artificial intelligence has emerged as an effective tool for avoiding financial crimes.

The AI model can also provide cause codes for the transaction that has been flagged. These reason codes direct the investigator where they should look for flaws and help expedite the investigation. Fighting against fraud by using AI is more efficient for the below reasons:

1. **Respond Quickly:** fraud detection is one thing; fraud prevention is quite another (Gençer, 2021). Automating procedures with AI/ML model offer a 7/24 fast response, which is necessary for fraud prevention. Algorithms may automatically reject a transaction if the data shows it is fake after examining a sizable dataset (Bao et al., 2022).
2. **Effective Data Interpretation:** Because AI/ML models have greater processing power than humans, they are increasingly influential as datasets grow in size. Interpreting a large dataset is essential for fraud detection as larger datasets offer better insights into client preferences and behavior as well

as fraud patterns. As a result, AI/ML models assist businesses in differentiating between fraud and legitimate transactions (Gençer, 2021).

ADVANTAGES OF AI IN CYBERSECURITY

As we explored above AI has numerous benefits and applications in cybersecurity. With the rapid evolution of cyberattacks and device proliferation occurring today, AI and machine learning can assist in keeping up with cyber criminals, automating threat detection, and responding more efficiently than traditional software or human-driven methods. Some of the advantages and applications of using AI in cybersecurity are as follows:

1. **Detection and Response Times are Boosted:** Threat detection is the first step in protecting the network of any company. The ideal situation would be practical if you could see problems immediately, such as deceptive data. Integrating AI with cybersecurity is the best way to identify and react to attacks in real time. Your entire system is risk-analyzed using artificial intelligence. AI will improve your security operations by identifying risks earlier than humans can. LAZIĆ states that the time it takes to find threats and breaches is decreased overall by up to 12% with AI (LAZIĆ, 2019). Additionally, using AI takes 12 percent less time to patch up a vulnerability or respond to an attack. A few businesses could even decrease these time metrics by more than 15%.

2. **Battling Bots:** Bots may be dangerous and currently make up a large amount of Internet traffic. Bots could pose a real concern, from account takeovers using stolen passwords to establishing fake accounts and data theft (Mohammed, 2020). Automated threats cannot be defeated solely by manual responses. AI and machine learning support the development of a thorough understanding of website traffic and the distinction between beneficial bots (such as search engine crawlers) and people and malicious bots. AI makes processing enormous amounts of data easier by AI, which also helps cybersecurity teams adapt their strategy in response to a dynamic threat landscape.

3. **AI Lowers the Cost to Detect and Respond to Breaches**: Organizations can comprehend and utilize danger patterns to find new threats by utilizing AI for cybersecurity. As a result, locating occurrences, looking into them, and eliminating dangers take less time and effort overall. 64% of executives claim that the cost of detecting and responding to breaches is reduced due to artificial intelligence. Most firms experience expense reductions from 1% to 15%-with an average of 12% (LAZIĆ, 2019).

4. **Better Endpoint Protection:** AI can assist in securing all of the rapidly expanding remote-working gadgets. Virtual private networks (VPNs) and antivirus software can help defend against remote malware and virus attacks, although they typically rely on signatures. This indicates that to protect oneself from current risks, one must adhere to the definitions of signatures (Mohammed, 2020). If virus definitions are behind, it may be because the antivirus program was not updated or because the software makers were uninformed. As a result, signature protection might not be able to stop a novel type of malware attack from being found. Mohammed added that by building a foundation of endpoint behavior through a recurrent training process, AI-driven endpoint security adopts a novel approach.

Drawbacks of Using AI for Cybersecurity

Wirkuttis and Klein (2017) claimed that while AI has many positive aspects, there are also risks associated with its use in cybersecurity. The following are some drawbacks of AI in general:

1. **Lack of Regulation:** the lack of control over AI's autonomy is one of the major concerns. Existing legal frameworks may not apply to AI because of its unique and unpredictable nature.
2. **Inability to Maintain Cybersecurity Autonomously:** Security systems are not yet fully autonomous, despite huge advancements in adapting AI techniques to cybersecurity. Human decision-making is still necessary for some tasks since computers cannot replace them entirely.
3. **Data Privacy:** The advances in hardware have made AI techniques, such as ANNs and DNNs, more advanced, and new methods emerge regularly. However, the increasing need for big data can be negative regarding privacy. In some cases, both private and public organizations are unwilling to share their sensitive data due to the analysis of vast amounts of data.
4. **Machine Gaining Control Over Humans:** It's the earliest AI-related issue. This issue has previously been depicted in many films and pieces of literature. To avoid such a shortcoming, experts must take steps/actions.
5. **Loss of Job:** Artificial Intelligence is viewed as a threat since some studies anticipate that AI will replace a considerable portion of the workforce.
6. **Not Everyone is Familiar with AI:** Not everyone is eager to learn about and work with new technological technologies.

Additionally, organizations would require significantly more resources and financial investments to develop and maintain an artificial intelligence system (LAZIĆ, 2019). Furthermore, because AI systems learn from data sets, you will need to collect a large number of different sets of malware codes, non-malicious codes, and anomalies to train your system. Acquiring all of these data sets takes time and requires expenditures beyond most businesses' financial capabilities. If AI systems do not have access to large amounts of data and events, they may produce inaccurate results or false positives. Obtaining incorrect information from untrustworthy sources may also have negative consequences (Mohammed, 2020). Another significant drawback is that hackers can use artificial intelligence to evaluate their software and conduct increasingly sophisticated attacks, which leads us to the next point.

Risks of Using AI for Cybersecurity

On the other hand, trusting AI to do cybersecurity activities is a two-edged sword: it can improve cybersecurity procedures significantly, but it can also promote new types of attacks against AI applications, posing serious security risks (Taddeo et al., 2019). Users are frequently unaware of the security concerns they confront when utilizing a new technology. Security fixes for users' devices are commonly overlooked. They often utilize and execute unpatched apps. As a result, unpatched apps run in the background, where typical users rarely use them.

Since AI is widely used, information about AI has become readily available to the general public. Attempts to prevent malicious uses by restricting AI code proliferation will not fully succeed, both because compliance is low and because sufficiently motivated and well-resourced actors can acquire such code through espionage (Brundage et al., 2018, p.59). By making systems more secure, being more responsible about disclosing developments that could be misused, and increasing policymakers' awareness of AI risks, the risk from less capable actors is likely to be reduced. A growing number of cybercriminals are learning to exploit artificial intelligence maliciously as they become more resourceful (Calderon, 2019).

CONCLUSION

Effective cybersecurity strategies are essential in a world where bad intelligence and cyber threats are rising at a breakneck pace. In this chapter, artificial intelligence is analyzed in the context of cybersecurity issues. AI is required first and foremost to react to the web's attacks quickly. This chapter shows how artificial intelligence is increasingly used in information security to improve its effectiveness. Security professionals now require artificial intelligence to mitigate the risk of a breach and enhance the security posture of their organizations since humans can no longer adequately secure enterprise-level attack surfaces. The paper also discussed the roles of machine learning and deep learning in detecting some threats such as malware, botnet, fraud, etc. Despite AI having numerous roles in cybersecurity, it negatively impacts technology. Attackers may use it for malicious purposes to circumvent AI-based detection (adversarial); however, the positive side outweighs the adverse effects.

REFERENCES

Ahmed, N., Amin, R., Aldabbas, H., Koundal, D., Alouffi, B., & Shah, T. (2022). Machine learning techniques for spam detection in email and IoT platforms: Analysis and research challenges. *Security and Communication Networks, 2022*, 2022. doi:10.1155/2022/1862888

Alauthman, M., Almomani, A., Alweshah, M., Omoush, W., & Alieyan, K. (2019). Machine learning for phishing detection and mitigation. In *Machine Learning for Computer and Cyber Security* (pp. 48–74). CRC Press. doi:10.1201/9780429504044-2

Alkahtani, H., & Aldhyani, T. H. (2022). Artificial Intelligence Algorithms for Malware Detection in Android-Operated Mobile Devices. *Sensors (Basel), 22*(6), 2268. doi:10.339022062268 PMID:35336437

Alshamkhany, M., Alshamkhany, W., Mansour, M., Khan, M., Dhou, S., & Aloul, F. (2020, November). Botnet attack detection using machine learning. In *2020 14th International Conference on Innovations in Information Technology (IIT)* (pp. 203-208). IEEE. 10.1109/IIT50501.2020.9299061

Bao, Y., Hilary, G., & Ke, B. (2022). Artificial intelligence and fraud detection. In *Innovative technology at the interface of finance and operations* (pp. 223–247). Springer. doi:10.1007/978-3-030-75729-8_8

Barreno, M., Nelson, B., Joseph, A. D., & Tygar, J. D. (2010). The security of machine learning. *Machine Learning, 81*(2), 121–148. doi:10.100710994-010-5188-5

Bhatele, K. R., Shrivastava, H., & Kumari, N. (2019). The role of artificial intelligence in cyber security. In *Countering Cyber Attacks and Preserving the Integrity and Availability of Critical Systems* (pp. 170–192). IGI Global. doi:10.4018/978-1-5225-8241-0.ch009

Bin Sulaiman, R., Schetinin, V., & Sant, P. (2022). Review of Machine Learning Approach on Credit Card Fraud Detection. *Human-Centric Intelligent Systems*, 1-14.

Brundage, M., Avin, S., Clark, J., Toner, H., Eckersley, P., Garfinkel, B., & Amodei, D. (2018). The malicious use of artificial intelligence: Forecasting, prevention, and mitigation.

Calderon, R. (2019). *The benefits of artificial intelligence in cybersecurity*. Lasalle University.

Chang, H. C., & Hawamdeh, S. (Eds.). (2020). Cybersecurity for Information Professionals: Concepts and Applications. Auerbach Publications.

Crumpler, W., & Lewis, J. A. (2019). The cybersecurity workforce gap (p. 10). Center for Strategic and International Studies (CSIS).

Dornadula, V. N., & Geetha, S. (2019). Credit card fraud detection using machine learning algorithms. *Procedia Computer Science*, *165*, 631–641. doi:10.1016/j.procs.2020.01.057

Faruk, M. J. H., Shahriar, H., Valero, M., Barsha, F. L., Sobhan, S., Khan, M. A., & Wu, F. (2021, December). Malware detection and prevention using artificial intelligence techniques. In *2021 IEEE International Conference on Big Data (Big Data)* (pp. 5369-5377). IEEE. 10.1109/BigData52589.2021.9671434

Gençer, G. (2021, November 22). *How AI can improve Fraud Detection & Prevention in 2022?* AIMultiple.

Giles, M. (2018). AI for cybersecurity is a hot new thing—and a dangerous gamble. *Technology Review*. https://www. technologyreview. com/s/611860/ai-for-cybersecu rity-is-a-hot-new-thing-and-a-dangerous-gamble

Gupta, B. B., & Sheng, Q. Z. (Eds.). (2019). *Machine learning for computer and cyber security: principle, algorithms, and practices*. CRC Press. doi:10.1201/9780429504044

Gupta, B. B., Tewari, A., Jain, A. K., & Agrawal, D. P. (2017). Fighting against phishing attacks: State of the art and future challenges. *Neural Computing & Applications*, *28*(12), 3629–3654. doi:10.100700521-016-2275-y

Haderlie, D. M., Cornelius, A., Crouch, A., Macatuno, F., Jackson, M., & Johnson, W. (2021). Understanding How Organizations Handle Cybersecurity (No. INL/EXT-21-64319-Rev000). Idaho National Lab (INL).

Halim, Z., Yousaf, M. N., Waqas, M., Sulaiman, M., Abbas, G., Hussain, M., Ahmad, I., & Hanif, M. (2021). An effective genetic algorithm-based feature selection method for intrusion detection systems. *Computers & Security*, *110*, 102448. doi:10.1016/j.cose.2021.102448

Imamverdiyev, Y. N., & Abdullayeva, F. J. (2020). Deep learning in cybersecurity: Challenges and approaches. *International Journal of Cyber Warfare & Terrorism*, *10*(2), 82–105. doi:10.4018/IJCWT.2020040105

Jain, G., Sharma, M., & Agarwal, B. (2019). Optimizing semantic LSTM for spam detection. *International Journal of Information Technology*, *11*(2), 239–250. doi:10.100741870-018-0157-5

Jean-Philippe, R. (2018). *Enhancing Computer Network Defense Technologies with Machine Learning and Artificial Intelligence* [Doctoral dissertation, Utica College, USA].

Kaddoura, S., Alfandi, O., & Dahmani, N. (2020, September). A spam email detection mechanism for English language text emails using deep learning approach. In *2020 IEEE 29th International Conference on Enabling Technologies: Infrastructure for Collaborative Enterprises (WETICE)* (pp. 193-198). IEEE. 10.1109/WETICE49692.2020.00045

Kaddoura, S., Arid, A. E., & Moukhtar, M. (2021, November). Evaluation of Supervised Machine Learning Algorithms for Multi-class Intrusion Detection Systems. In *Proceedings of the Future Technologies Conference* (pp. 1-16). Springer.

Kaddoura, S., Chandrasekaran, G., Popescu, D. E., & Duraisamy, J. H. (2022). A systematic literature review on spam content detection and classification. *PeerJ. Computer Science*, *8*, e830. doi:10.7717/peerj-cs.830 PMID:35174265

Kalakuntla, R., Vanamala, A., & Kolipyaka, R. (2019). Cyber Security. *Holistica.*, *10*(2), 115–128. doi:10.2478/hjbpa-2019-0020

Khan, S., Alourani, A., Mishra, B., Ali, A., & Kamal, M. (2022). Developing a Credit Card Fraud Detection Model using Machine Learning Approaches. *International Journal of Advanced Computer Science and Applications*, *13*(3). doi:10.14569/IJACSA.2022.0130350

Kuzlu, M., Fair, C. & Guler, O. (2021). Role of artificial intelligence in the inter-net of things (iot) cybersecurity. *Discover Internet of things, 1*(1). doi:10.1007/s43926-020-00001-4

Lambora, A., Gupta, K., & Chopra, K. (2019, February). *Genetic algorithm-A literature review. In 2019 international conference on machine learning, big data, cloud and parallel computing (COMITCon).* IEEE.

Lazić. L. (2019, October). *Benefit from Ai in cybersecurity.* In The 11th International Conference on Business Information Security (BISEC-2019). *Belgrade, Serbia.*

Li, J. H. (2018). Cyber security meets artificial intelligence: A survey. *Frontiers of Information Technology & Electronic Engineering*, *19*(12), 1462–1474. doi:10.1631/FITEE.1800573

Li, K., Fang, B., Cui, X., & Liu, Q. (2016). Research on the development of botnets. *Jisuanji Yanjiu Yu Fazhan*, *53*(10), 2189–2206.

Logpoint Team. (2021, October 13). *Cyber security: Definition, importance and benefits of cyber security.* LogPoint.

Lucas, Y., & Jurgovsky, J. (2020). Credit card fraud detection using machine learning. *Survey (London, England).*

Malini, N., & Pushpa, M. (2017, February). Analysis on credit card fraud identification techniques based on KNN and outlier detection. In *2017 third international conference on advances in electrical, electronics, information, communication and bio-informatics (AEEICB)* (pp. 255-258). IEEE. 10.1109/AEEICB.2017.7972424

Martínez Torres, J., Iglesias Comesaña, C., & García-Nieto, P. J. (2019). Machine learning techniques applied to cybersecurity. *International Journal of Machine Learning and Cybernetics*, *10*(10), 2823–2836. doi:10.100713042-018-00906-1

Mhlanga, D. (2020). Industry 4.0 in finance: The impact of artificial intelligence (ai) on digital financial inclusion. *International Journal of Financial Studies, 8*(3), 45. doi:10.3390/ijfs8030045

Mogoane, S. N., & Kabanda, S. (2019, October). Challenges in Information and Cybersecurity program offering at Higher Education Institutions. In ICICIS (pp. 202-212).

Mohammed, I. A. (2020). Artificial intelligence for cybersecurity: a systematic mapping of literature. *International Journal of Innovations in Engineering RESEARCH and technology, 7*(9).

Nayyar, A. N. A. N. D., Rameshwar, R. U. D. R. A., & Solanki, A. R. U. N. (2020). Internet of Things (IoT) and the digital business environment: a standpoint inclusive cyber space, cyber crimes, and cybersecurity. In *The Evolution of Business in the Cyber Age* (pp. 111–152). Apple Academic Press. doi:10.1201/9780429276484-6

Nguyen, T. T., Tahir, H., Abdelrazek, M., & Babar, A. (2020). Deep learning methods for credit card fraud detection.

Nurse, J. R. (2021). Cybersecurity awareness. doi:10.1007/978-3-642-27739-9_1596-1

Ongsulee, P. (2017, November). Artificial intelligence, machine learning and deep learning. In *2017 15th International Conference on ICT and Knowledge Engineering (ICT&KE)* (pp. 1-6). IEEE. 10.1109/ICTKE.2017.8259629

Opara, E. U., & Dieli, O. J. (2021). Enterprise cyber security challenges to medium and large firms: An analysis. *International Journal of Electronics and Information Engineering, 13*(2), 77–85.

Pitchaimani, S., Kodaganallur, V. P., Newell, C., & Kalsi, V. (2019). *U.S. Patent No. 10,491,595*. U.S. Patent and Trademark Office.

Priyadarshini, I., & Sharma, R. (Eds.). (2022). *Artificial Intelligence and Cybersecurity: Advances and Innovations*. CRC Press.

Rajasekharaiah, K. M., Dule, C. S., & Sudarshan, E. (2020, December). Cyber security challenges and its emerging trends on latest technologies. *IOP Conference Series. Materials Science and Engineering, 981*(2), 022062. doi:10.1088/1757-899X/981/2/022062

Rokon, M. O. F., Islam, R., Darki, A., Papalexakis, E. E., & Faloutsos, M. (2020). {SourceFinder}: Finding Malware {Source-Code} from Publicly Available Repositories in {GitHub}. In *23rd International Symposium on Research in Attacks, Intrusions and Defenses (RAID 2020)* (pp. 149-163). USENIX Association.

Saad, S., Briguglio, W., & Elmiligi, H. (2019). The curious case of machine learning in malware detection. doi:10.5220/0007470705280535

Salih, A. A., Ameen, S. Y., Zeebaree, S. R., Sadeeq, M. A., Kak, S. F., Omar, N., & Ageed, Z. S. (2021). Deep learning approaches for intrusion detection. *Asian Journal of Research in Computer Science*, 50-64.

Sarker, I. H., Kayes, A. S. M., Badsha, S., Alqahtani, H., Watters, P., & Ng, A. (2020). Cybersecurity data science: An overview from machine learning perspective. *Journal of Big Data, 7*(1), 1–29. doi:10.118640537-020-00318-5

Sasank, J. S., Sahith, G. R., Abhinav, K., & Belwal, M. (2019, July). Credit Card Fraud Detection Using Various Classification and Sampling Techniques: A Comparative Study. In *2019 International Conference on Communication and Electronics Systems (ICCES)* (pp. 1713-1718). IEEE. 10.1109/IC-CES45898.2019.9002289

Seemma, P. S., Nandhini, S., & Sowmiya, M. (2018). Overview of cyber security. *International Journal of Advanced Research in Computer and Communication Engineering*, *7*(11), 125–128. doi:10.17148/IJARCCE.2018.71127

Shahrivari, V., Darabi, M. M., & Izadi, M. (2020). Phishing Detection Using Machine Learning Techniques. *arXiv preprint arXiv:2009.11116*.

Sikos, L. F. (Ed.). (2018). *AI in Cybersecurity* (Vol. 151). Springer.

Singh, A. P. (2017). A study on zero-day malware attack. *International Journal of Advanced Research in Computer and Communication Engineering*, *6*(1), 391–392. doi:10.17148/IJARCCE.2017.6179

Smith, R. G., & Eckroth, J. (2017). Building AI applications: Yesterday, today, and tomorrow. *AI Magazine*, *38*(1), 6–22. doi:10.1609/aimag.v38i1.2709

Taddeo, M., McCutcheon, T., & Floridi, L. (2019). Trusting artificial intelligence in cybersecurity is a double-edged sword. *Nature Machine Intelligence*, *1*(12), 557–560. doi:10.103842256-019-0109-1

Thanh, C. T., & Zelinka, I. (2019, December). A survey on artificial intelligence in malware as next-generation threats. In Mendel, 25(2), 27-34. doi:10.13164/mendel.2019.2.027

Thomas, T. P., Vijayaraghavan, A., & Emmanuel, S. (2020). Machine learning and cybersecurity. In *Machine Learning Approaches in Cyber Security Analytics* (pp. 37–47). Springer. doi:10.1007/978-981-15-1706-8_3

Varmedja, D., Karanovic, M., Sladojevic, S., Arsenovic, M., & Anderla, A. (2019, March). Credit card fraud detection-machine learning methods. In *2019 18th International Symposium INFOTEH-JAHORINA (INFOTEH)* (pp. 1-5). IEEE 10.1109/INFOTEH.2019.8717766

Veale, M., & Brown, I. (2020). Cybersecurity. *Internet Policy Review*, *9*(4), 1–22. doi:10.14763/2020.4.1533

Welukar, J. N., & Bajoria, G. P. (2020). *Artificial Intelligence in Cyber Security-A Review*. Northeastern Illinois University.

Wirkuttis, N., & Klein, H. (2017). Artificial intelligence in cybersecurity. *Cyber, Intelligence, and Security*, *1*(1), 103–119.

Xin, Y., Kong, L., Liu, Z., Chen, Y., Li, Y., Zhu, H., Gao, M., Hou, H., & Wang, C. (2018). Machine learning and deep learning methods for cybersecurity. *IEEE Access: Practical Innovations, Open Solutions*, *6*, 35365–35381. doi:10.1109/ACCESS.2018.2836950

Xing, Y., Shu, H., Zhao, H., Li, D., & Guo, L. (2021). Survey on botnet detection techniques: Classification, methods, and evaluation. *Mathematical Problems in Engineering*, *2021*, 2021. doi:10.1155/2021/6640499

Xuan, S., Liu, G., Li, Z., Zheng, L., Wang, S., & Jiang, C. (2018, March). Random forest for credit card fraud detection. In *2018 IEEE 15th international conference on networking, sensing and control (ICNSC)* (pp. 1-6). IEEE. 10.1109/ICNSC.2018.8361343

Yaseen, Q. (2021). Spam email detection using deep learning techniques. *Procedia Computer Science*, *184*, 853–858. doi:10.1016/j.procs.2021.03.107

KEY TERMS AND DEFINITIONS

Artificial Intelligence: This is the state where machines are able to perform like humans by coordinating human-like behaviors while accomplishing some tasks.

Cybersecurity: This is an area of security focused on securing cyberspace or computer networks from unauthorized access and related fraud.

Deep Learning: This is part of machine learning that uses many receptors to have a more layered procedure of machine learning.

Machine Learning: This is when machines or in most cases computers learn from exposure to different environments they have been subjected to.

Malware: A file or a network that is sent to target devices through a network to create a vulnerability or malfunctioning behavior that is designed by an attacker.

Network Intrusion Detection: This is a system that detects malicious activities on the network of a given device or a set of devices.

Phishing: This is a malicious activity where attackers send emails that look legitimate to lure individuals to give out their sensitive personal details.

Spam: This is unsolicited email or other messaging means that is sent to individuals in bulk.

Chapter 10
Text to Image Synthesis Using Multistage Stack GAN

V. Dinesh Reddy

SRM University, India

Yasaswini Desu

SRM University, India

Medarametla Sindhu

SRM University, India

Chilukuri Vamsee

SRM University, India

Neelissetti Girish

SRM University, India

ABSTRACT

Many recent studies on text-to-image synthesis decipher approximately 50% of the problem only. They failed to compute all the imperative details in it. This chapter presents a solution using stacked generative adversarial networks (GAN) to generate lifelike images based on the given text. The stage-I GAN creates a distorted images by depicting the rudimentary/basic colours and shape of a scene predicted on text illustration. Stage-II GAN ends up on generating high-resolution images with naturalistic features using Stage-I findings and the text description as inputs. The output generated by this technique is more credible than many other techniques which are already in use. More importantly, stack GAN produces 256 x 256 images based on the text descriptions, while the existing algorithms produces 128 x 128.

DOI: 10.4018/978-1-6684-6937-8.ch010

INTRODUCTION

Text-to-image synthesis describes that we are trying to convert the text descriptions into meaningful and appropriate images. It is one amongst the arduous problems in the computer vision (CV) sector and natural language processing (NLP) sector. We generally observe image captioning, where a caption will be given to an image after processing it. But, here we are trying to approach the problem in the reverse fashion i.e. caption to image mapping. A pictorial representation speaks a thousand words compared to oral or textual descriptions. Oral or textual descriptions can't provide comprehensive information. So, with the advancement of technology, this chapter is grueling towards converting human thoughts (textual descriptions) and ideas into visions. In a real-world scenario, text-to-image synthesis is a back-breaking issue due to the reason that there can be more than one scene that represent a single caption.

Nowadays, we have different neural network models like the Convolutional Neural Network (CNN), Recurrent Convolutional Neural network (RCNN), and many other models which uses the encoder-decoder mechanism. These architectures produce fact-based information. To our knowledge, we cannot generate captions with the help of limited or synthetic images. To address this issue, Generative Adversarial Networks (GANs) came into the picture, where we can generate synthetic images based on the given captions (Dosovitskiy et al. (2015)).

There are various Generative Adversarial Networks like Deep Convolutional GAN (DCGAN) that works on ConvNets. The ConvNets are using a stride without a pooling layer and the neurons in this model are not fully connected. The main drawback of using DCGAN is while converting the descriptions, the model parameters will never converge. Moreover, the generator of the GAN will translate only a few samples, and it is quite sensitive to hyperparameters. So, to overcome these disadvantages of DCGAN, the conditional GAN (CGAN) came into existence, where we can add some parameters for labeling the inputs in both generator and discriminator to classify the input-text correctly (T. Salimans et al.(2016)).

Generative Adversarial Networks are comprised of a generator(G) and discriminator(D), which work parallelly by a competitive goal (T. Salimans et al.(2016)). The generator is designed in such a way that it keeps on generating the sample tests towards the original data dispersal to bypass or dope the discriminator. Whereas the discriminator is designed in such a way that it always tries to identify real data samples over the generated fake samples. We are interested to work on translating the single-sentence text into its equivalent image pixels. For example: *"A white Bird with a black crown and a yellow peak"*. GANs have numerous applications in the real world like photo editing, image quality enhancement, computer-assisted design, etc. But they failed to spawn the high-resolution images using the text descriptions as shown in Figure 1.

Figure 1. Comparison of Stack GAN stages for the above text input
(S. Reed et.al (2016)).

This bird sits close to the ground with his short yellow tarsus and feet; his bill is long and is also yellow

The Bird is black with green and has a very short break

Stage-I images

Stage-II images

Recently, GANs have shown a positive outcome to this hurdle by generating 64 x 64 images based on given text inputs. However, the generated images were also lacking in detailing parts like many of the image's pixels failed to be synthesized with high-quality examples like 128 x 128 and 256 x 256. The Conditional Generative Adversarial Network cannot fulfill all the requirements, because of its robustness. To overcome this issue, researchers proposed Least Square GAN (LSGAN). The main idea behind LSGAN is minimizing the loss function of the discriminator. But it failed to minimize the penalties of outliers which lead to a low inception score. Stack GAN uses the Generator and discriminator together to work with the competency goal. So, to handle these circumstances, this chapter proposes to decompose the problem into two more subproblems where we can manage to produce highly synthesized images with the assistance of a **Stack Generative Adversarial Network (Stack GAN)**. Initially, a low-definition image will get produced with the assistance of Stage–1 GAN. Where, the generator will produce a rudimentary/basic appearance and primary colours of the object image according to the given text input and generate the framework area. The generated fake sample object images will have many defects, for example, the object's parts may not be formed properly, and the shape of the object can be experienced with distortions.

So, to enhance the image quality and rectify all the defects, we propose to use Stage-2 Stack GAN which produces a high-synthesized image as output (256 x 256). Stage-2 will only focus on delivering a high-quality image by adding more details and rectifying the defects of the existing image. This is an easy method to develop high-resolution images from scratch. The main aim of this work is to implement Stacked Generative Adversarial Network which can produce highly synthesized images. We perform extensive experiments to compare the existing works related to text-image generation with the proposed staked GAN and found that the proposed method generates more realistic images. There are numerous applications in the text-image synthesis field: For example, in interior designs for houses- we can use this method to convert human thoughts into pictorial views. Further, we can use this method to create a virtual crime scene with the help of text descriptions given by corroborative witnesses.

RELATED WORK

Image synthesis and image modeling are one of the important parts of computer vision. We know that, in recent times deep learning techniques emerged on a large scale and there was a tremendous development in image generation. Dosovitskiy et al. (2015) have developed a deconvolutional neural network that can generate a 3D view of various chairs, cars, and tables with the help of respective datasets. They implemented this neural network with standard backpropagation to handle Euclidian reconstruction error. They implemented this neural network with standard backpropagation to handle Euclidian reconstruction error. This convolutional neural network is developed in such a manner that it can handle the intermediate images which permit smooth morphing between intermediate stages. The architecture of this neural network is pretty simple but it is showcasing complex behaviour.

Generating a 3D object from a lone source image can be a very difficult task for both graphics and vision synthesizing of the 3D image. Yang et al. (2015) and some other groups came up with deterministic Neural networks for 3d view synthesis with a repetitive convolutional encoder-decoder network whose task is to provide the rotated objects starting from a solitary image. It permits to get long-term dependencies in addition to a series of transformations. In this study, the issue of forecasting an object's altered looks when it is rotated in three dimensions from a single photograph was taken into account. Creating new perspectives of a 3D object from a single picture is a significant challenge for both graphics and vision. Due to the ill-posedness of inferring object shape and pose and the intrinsic partial observability involved in projecting a 3D object onto the image space, this is especially difficult. However, if we focus on particular object categories for which we can amass a sufficient amount of training data, this can be done by training a neural network to tackle the issue. An innovative end-to-end trained recurrent convolutional encoder-decoder network for rendering rotated objects is proposed in this research.

Kingma et al. (2014) have come up with Auto-Encoding Variational Bayes which can compute the probabilistic graphical models to achieve the maximum lower bound of the likelihood. In continuation of the work done on VAE, u initiated a DRAW model which can be correlated to existing VAE for generating realistic images. Generative Adversarial Networks performed well in generating sharper object samples, but the main issue with GANs was their instability during training dynamics. A unique spatial attention mechanism that replicates the foveation of the human eye and a framework for sequential variational auto-encoding that enables the repeated creation of intricated visuals are combined in DRAW networks. When trained on the Street View House Numbers dataset, the system significantly outperforms the state-of-the-art for generative models on MNIST and creates images that are virtually impossible to tell apart from real data. Salimans et al.(2016) have proposed various techniques to improve GANs training and have shown promising results in generating room interiors and synthesizing human faces. The generative adversarial neural network was lacking stable data training and lack of evaluation metrics. So, to improve the training of GANs There are numerous techniques like Minibatch discrimination, Feature matching, historical averaging, and virtual batch normalization. And coming to the evaluation metrics we have the Inception score which provides a partial solution for the problems with GANs. Zhao et al.(2016) have proposed a new technique called Energy-based GAN for making the training part even more stable.

Denton et al. (2015) implemented deep generative neural network models with the aid of the Laplacian pyramid technique of Adversarial Networks. This technique has shown adequate results in generating high-quality image samples. To generate images in a course-to-fine manner they extended their model architecture by incorporating cascades of convolutional neural networks called convents with the Laplacian pyramid technique. They trained distinct generative convnet models at every level of the Laplacian pyramid with the help of Generative Adversarial Nets (GAN). Our model's samples are of much higher quality than those from alternative models. Their CIFAR10 samples were confounded for original images around 40% of the time in a quantitative assessment by human evaluators, compared to 10% for GAN samples. Gregor et al., 2015 introduce the Deep Recurrent Attentive Writer (DRAW) neural network architecture for the generation of pictures, it copies the foveation of the human eye, with a successional variational auto-encoding framework. This can be further edited using Zhang et al. (2016) neural photo editing approach with introspective adversarial networks, because it is one of the most feasible applications beyond image generation. It is an interface that holds the power of generative neural networks to make large changes to existing images. It works based on the hybridization of VAN and GAN.

Kaiming He et al.(2016) suggested a new framework called Residual learning, which assisted in the effortless training of deep neural networks when compared to previous models. Instead of using the unreferenced functions they explicitly redefined the input layers as learning residual functions. This can be showcased as comprehensive support for these residual networks that can be optimized easily and can obtain better accuracy by considerably increasing the depth. Carl Doersch et al.(2016) presented a tutorial on variational autoencoders, which come out to be one of the most concrete perspectives on unsupervised learning for intricate distributions. These are the most used VAEs constructed on top-grade functional approximations, and these can be trained using a gradient descent approach. By figuring out how to approximate alignment between text and producing canvas. Mansimov et al.(2016) created an Align DRAW model. This model describes a mechanism for creating images based on captions. In particular, captions are represented as a series of phrases that follow one another, and images are represented as a series of patches that are painted on a canvas. The model can be seen as a component of the framework for sequence-to-sequence analysis. To produce impressive picture synthesis results, Radford et al. (2016) employed a basic convolutional decoder but created a highly efficient and robust architecture that included batch normalization. Our model conditions on text descriptions in place of class labels, which is the prime difference between our model and the conditional GANs discussed above. To the best of our knowledge, it is the first architecture from end to end that forms character at the pixel level. Additionally, we present a GAN generator with a manifold interpolation regularizer. It notably raises the standard of generated samples, especially those for CUB's held-out zero-shot categories.

BACKGROUND

As we discussed earlier Generative Adversarial Networks are giving almost optimal results in approaching the language conversion problem. There are various methodologies and approaches for constructing the GAN models. But, irrespective of the methodologies. There are three foremost architectures, and every GAN model will try to adopt one of them. They are

1. Direct architecture
2. Iterative architecture

3.   Hierarchical architecture

These three architectures are also known as the prime pillars of every GAN model.

The Direct architecture consists of a single generator and discriminator. It is also known as simple architecture. In this method, we will try to pass the input text embeddings to the generator, and the generator will try to produce the output. subsequently, the output will be passed on to the discriminator as input, and the discriminator will try to differentiate between actual or fake images. If the discriminator fails to recognize the fake images, ultimately, it denotes our final goal has been achieved.

To overcome the drawbacks of the simple architecture. The hierarchical architecture was introduced. In this method, the GAN models consist of two generators and also two discriminators. Both of these generators and discriminators work as individual components to attain better-quality images. The main objective of dividing the components is to improve the quality of the image by separating them into two subdivisions. The first generator will focus on developing the texture of the image whereas the other will be trying to develop the background of the image. They both can work sequentially or in parallel to achieve the goal. When we try to pass the input to generator 1 the basic structure of the image will get generated and given as input to the discriminator. The discriminator will try to distinguish the image, if it fails to identify the fake images, then the output will be passed on to the second generator. The same process will be repeated and provides the enhanced quality of images. Generally, SGAN follows this type of architecture.

While using the hierarchical method, the image quality is not up to the mark. So, the iterative method came into the picture. In this architecture, there are multiple generators and discriminators which take the input from its predecessors and work on detailing part of the image. Stack GAN uses this methodology to produce enhanced-quality images. But it is quite expensive and more time taking to complete this entire process.

In this particular study, we have used Stacked Generative Adversarial Networks (Stack GAN) to perform text-to-image synthesis. StackGAN3 and STACKGAN++4 work on the combinations of multi-scale GANs to enhance the snapshot quality and boost image precision. AttnGAN5 embraces the detailing mentioned in the information provided and the snapshot characteristics as a result produces a correlative text-image characteristic matching deprivation as a supplemental entity. The method is very collaborative contrary to the reranking with CLIP, processed offline. The ability of GAN to vitalize data dispensation as the text, images, and videos has recently come into sharp focus.

Despite the macher, it is a very challenging task to train the architecture. The selection of hyper-parameters usually has an impact on how unbalanced and subtle the training procedure is. As per the results of the survey that is conducted as part of the research, the discontinuous supports of the data dispensation and the respective model dispensation are partly due to inconsistency.

During the process of training the architecture to produce the highly enhanced snapshot, this issue becomes critical. Since the opportunity is infrequent for the highly enhanced snapshot dispensation and the architecture dispensation to disperse supports in a high-dimensional area.

Additionally, mode collapse, where most of the generated samples share the same colour or texture pattern, is a frequent non-fulfillment phenomenon for GAN training.

STACKED GENERATIVE ADVERSARIAL NETWORKS (STACK GAN)

Intending to produce high-definition images with naturalistic details, we use stacked GAN. GAN is embraced of two fragments, a generator, and discriminator which works parallelly with a competitive goal.

- **Generator G**: It is optimized to produce pictures that are difficult for discriminator D to evolve from actual/real images.
- **Discriminator D**: It is optimized to differentiate actual images from artificial images generated by G.

It breaks the text-to-image generation into two divisions:

- **Stage-I GAN:** This stage gives the basic shape and colours of an object based on the text given; this stage depicts the background layout which yields a very low-resolution image. It also provides the structural information of the image. This stage usually generates 64 x 64 images.
- **Stage-II GAN:** It alters and rectifies the faults in the Stage-1 pictures and gives a complete detailed image of the object by analyzing the text, producing a high-quality realistic image. It uses the output of stage-1 as input, this stage samples 256 x 256.

Preliminaries

GAN is composed of G and D. G is augmented to duplicate the true data p_{data} by producing the pictures that are strenuous for D to transform from real images. D, alternatively it is tuned to categorize between actual and synthetic images which are produced by G.

Loss Functions are:

Scores from the Discriminator D:

$C_r \neg Di(x,h)$ {original image, correct text}

$C_w \neg Di(x, \hat{h})$ {original image, incorrect text}

$C_f \neg Di(\bigcirc,h)$ {fake image, correct text}

This entire training is identical to a min-max game with the function below,

$$\min_G \max_D V(D, G) = E_{X \sim Pdata}[\log D(x)] + E_{z \sim Pz}[\log(1 - D(G(z)))] \tag{1}$$

where, x = real image from true data distribution p_{data}.

z = noise vector samples from distribution p_z.

Stage-I GAN

As discussed above, the stage-1 GAN only focuses on developing the rough shape of the object image with primary colours. By the end of this stage 1, we can generate a low-definition image of resolution 64 x 64. However, before implementing stage-1 we have to perform conditioning argumentation on the text explanation. Previously Reed et.al (2016), the work done on GAN used non-linear text embeddings to generate latent variables for the generator which forms high dimensional data.

It is a difficult job to train our generator using the high-dimensional text of smaller-size data. So instead of using the non-linear transformation technique, we are going to use conditioning argumentation to train our generator. Initially, we will pass text description t to the encoder which gives ϕt text embeddings to the generator.

In stage-1, we going to select the random sample variables from the Gaussian distribution $N(\mu(\phi t), \Sigma(\phi t))$, where $\mu(\phi t)$ is the average of the data and the diagonal covariance matrix is $\Sigma(\phi t)$. In addition to these two functions, we are going to add some of the regulations to the existing notation. Which maintains robustness and avoids overfitting the model at the time of generator training.

$$D_{KL}(N(\mu(\phi_t), \Sigma(\phi_t)) \parallel N(0, I) \tag{2}$$

The above equation refers to Kullback-Leibler divergence (difference between conditioning gaussian distribution and standard gaussian distribution) So, the generator and discriminator will keep on trying to attain the minimum L_{Go} in Eq (3) and maximum L_{Do} *in Eq (4)* respectively.

$$L_{G0} = E_{z \sim pz,\ t \sim Pdata}[\log(1 - D_0(G_0(z, c_0), \phi t))] + \lambda D_{KL}(N(\mu(\phi_t), \Sigma(\phi_t)) \parallel N(0, I)) \tag{3}$$

$$L_{D0} = E(I_0, t) \sim p_{data}[\log D_0(I_0, \phi t)] + E_{z \sim pz,\ t \sim Pdata}[\log(1 - D_0(G_0(z, c_0), \phi t))] \tag{4}$$

Where t is the text description getting from the true distribution P_{data}. I_0 is a real image, Z is the noise vector which got from randomly sampled gaussian distribution data P_z. λ is the parameter that regularizes the balance in the Kullback-Leibler equation and gaussian distribution equation, we generally use $\lambda=1$. Φt is text embeddings and C_0 is the gaussian conditioning variable.

Model Architecture: Initially the text embeddings Φt are given as load/inputs via an attached layer, also called a connected layer, to the generator to generate μ_0 and σ_0 for the Gaussian distribution equation. Thereafter C0 will compute the Ng dimensional vector using the formulae $c_0 = \mu_0 + \sigma_0 \odot \varepsilon$ (Where $\odot$ represents the multiplication of every component and ε will be in the range of $0 - 1$). Then Ng dimensional vector is chained with N_z dimensional noise vector to compute $W_0 \times H_0$ of the image's samples.

Now for Discriminator, the existing text embeddings Φt are compressed into to Nd dimensional vector using a fully connected tensor layer to produce $M_d \times M_d \times N_d$ tensor. During this interval, the discriminator will keep on blocking the image sample which was given in the form of a series of downsampling blocks until the image sample has $M_d \times M_d$ dimensions. So, a new tensor will be created by adding an image filter map. 1 X 1 convolutional layer input will be given to the new tensor to compute the features of the image and text. In the end, a fully-connected layer with a single node will give us the decision score.

Stage-II GAN

Stage-II Gan is constructed on top of Stage-I GAN to develop naturalistic high-definition images. The fuzzy images that are produced by Phase-1 GAN. lack of vivid object components and in addition to it the generated images will be dis-oriented or distorted, within the Stage-II of the GAN methodology, we tend to contemplate these low-resolution images that are generated within the early stages.

The text embeddings to correct the mistakes and the distortions within the Stage-I results are associated to train the model to gather and collage the data of the unheeded text input to put forward with the more realistic high-resolution images which incorporate the complete information given as an input in the beginning.

Here the Generator (G) and Discriminator (D) of Stage -II GAN have trained with competency goal alternatively for achieving the Maximum LD and Minimum L¬G in Eq (6). S0 represents the sample space of low-definition images and the Gaussian latent variables are denoted by C.

$$L_D = E_{(I,t) \sim pdata} [\log(D_0(I,\phi t))] + E_{s0 \sim PG0, \, t \sim pdata}[\log(1-D(G(s0, c),\phi t)))] \tag{5}$$

$$L_G = E_{s0 \sim PG0, \, t \sim Pdata}[\log(1-D(G(s0, c),\phi t)))] + \lambda D_{KL}(N(\mu(\phi_t), \Sigma(\phi_t)) \, \| \, N(0, I)) \tag{6}$$

Where $s0 = G0(z, c_0)$ is produced in the previous stage i.e., by Stage- I GAN, at which we haven't considered the random noise factor z on assuming that the uncertainty has already preserved in s_0, which diverged it from the original GAN formulation. Gaussian conditioning variable C_0 which was used in Stage-I and C which currently we are using in Phase-II will inherit the identical premature text encoder. They both end up producing the same text-embeddings φt. Perhaps, they make use of separate 100% integrated layers for the production of various averages and standard deviations. Hence, Stage-II follows the above procedure to learn how to capture useful information in the text embeddings from the results of the Stage-I GAN.

Model Architecture: Initially the text embeddings Φt are employed to come up with the Gaussian conditioning vector c of dimension Ng similar to the Stage-I, that is dimensionally derived to model a M x M x N Tensor. The sample Space s0 which was created from Phase-I GAN will be updated into many down-samplings till it reaches the size of M x M size spatial. The tensor which contains text and the image filter will be combined on the channel dimension which results in the creation of various residual blocks [11,9]. The resultant will combinedly encrypt the image as well as the text attributes. By the end of these sequential operations, we will end up producing a W x H dimensional image by utilizing the up-sampling blocks.

The structure of the discriminator is a close design with a little difference of having extra down-sampling blocks of the discriminator used in the Stage-I GAN generation, as the image size is comparatively big in this stage. Instead of using the naive discriminator, we are going to use the different one which was proposed by Reed et al. (2016) for solving this complete problem. As a part of training the model, the discriminator will keep on collecting the real images along with their corresponding text as a sample pair. Whereas the negative samples are going to be divided into 2 groups and are given as inputs to the discriminator. During the initial stages, we are passing the real images along with the embeddings. Later on, during the second stage, the synthesized images along with their conditioning embedding will be given as input.

IMPLEMENTATION DETAILS

Before going to implement the Stack GAN we need to convert the user text input into embedding using pre-defined character embeddings. There are different types of text embeddings. In this paper we tried to implement two dissimilar types of text embeddings they are char CNN text embeddings and Bidirectional Encoder Representations from Transformers. We know the Stacked Generative Adversarial Neural Network is divided into two stages. Initially, we will convert the user text input into embeddings with the help of any pre-trained character embeddings. Then, we pass the existing text embeddings to conditional Augmentation (CA), and then the Augmented input will be again passed as input for the Stage-1 Generator, which produces 64 x 64 resolution images.

The up-sampling blocks contain nearest neighbours followed by 3 x 3 convolution. We apply different normalization techniques for every convolution excluding the final layer. The down-sampling consists of 4 x 4 convolutions and performs the normalization excluding the first layer. After completing the Stage-1 implementation we will store the stage-1 model weights and results we will start implementing Stage-2 which produces 256 x 256 resolution images.

By default, we initialize the $Ng = Nd = 128$, $Mg = 16$, $Md = 4$, $W0 = H0 = 64$, $W = H = 256$, and Learning rate $= 0.0002$. For training stage 1 and stage 2 we first iteratively train the discriminator (D0) and Generator (G0) for 800 epochs by fastening Stage-2 GAN. Thereafter we recursively train the Discriminator and the Generator of Stage-2 for 600 epochs by keeping stage-1 constant. All the neural networks were trained with the assistance of ADAM Solver (which optimizes the neural networks in terms of computation, memory, and large datasets) with a batch size of 64, and the learning rate will be decayed by half of its preceding values for each 100 epochs

Figure 2. The model architecture of Stack GAN. Initially, a low-definition image will get produced with the assistance of Stage – 1 GAN where the generator will produce a rudimentary/basic appearance and primary colours of the object image according to the given text input and generate the framework area. Based on images of Stage -I, Stage-II will try to generate the enhanced images with 256 x 256 resolution Zhang et al.(2016).

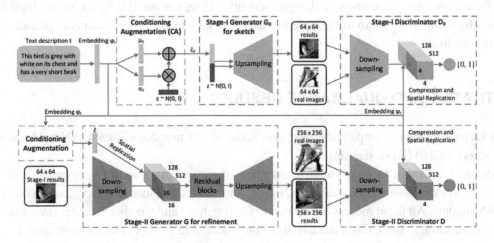

Experiments

For substantiating our methodology, we performed large-scale Quantitative and qualitative evaluations on the Birds dataset (Caltech – UCSD) that is broadly used in text-to-image synthesis. We have tried many existing base models to redesign our model architecture. We have implemented only stage 1 GAN for the first baseline to check whether the Stack structure performance is generating 64 x 64 resolution images. Then we tried to implement the existing GAN for generating 128 x 128 images but they were less optimal when compared to 64 x 64 images. We tried to give input of text at both stages but it was not shown a promising result.

CUB (Birds dataset) (Reed et.al (2016)) comprises 200 varieties of bird species with 11,788 sample pictures. The object image ratios are < 0.5 so as a part of recoding the data we crop all the images to make sure the boundary boxes are > 0.75. We diverged the CUB dataset into two segments, training (with 150 classes) and testing (50 test classes).

Evaluation Metrics

It is quite a laborious job to analyze the performance of Generative Adversarial Neural Networks. The best method to record the performance of GAN models is by asking Human volunteers to determine the image quality and other parameters. Recently, (Salimans et al.(2016)) a new type of score was introduced to evaluate the GANs called *the Inception Score* for quantitative Evaluation

$$I = \exp(\text{Ex DKL}(p(y \mid x) \parallel p(y))),$$

Here x refers to our generated sample and y refers to the predicted label by this model. The divination beyond using this metric is a perfect model that can produce better accuracy. So, the KL divergence between conditional and marginal distribution must be huge. In our experiments, we performed this process with different text inputs and recorded the average inception score of our model. To cross-validate our model with the existing GANs, we gathered multiple inception scores of various models which can perform the text-to-image synthesis. Although inception scores are not 100% precise, we tried to verify the outputs by showcasing them to multiple humans to correlate with their perspectives and they gave satisfactory feedback.

QUANTITATIVE AND QUALITATIVE RESULTS

We tried various inputs to compare the inception score of our proposed Stack GAN model with other GAN models on CUB (Birds dataset).

You can look a Table 1 to get a complete overview of our inception scores comparison with various GAN Models We can observe that Stack GAN gives a more optimal inception score when compared to other GAN models. All these models are related to CUB dataset and we also have the flower dataset for a better understanding. Some GAN models also implemented this process for flower dataset.

Table 1. Comparison of various models with their inception score.

Method	Inception Score
GAN – INT – CLS (S.Reed et. al (2016))	2.88 ± 0.4
Attn – GAN (T.Xu et al.(2018))	2.36 ± 0.21
Mirror GAN (T. Qiao et.al (2019))	2.64 ± 0.41
DM – GAN (M.Zhu et.al (2019))	3.23 ±0.23
OP – GAN (G.Yin et.al (2019))	2.78 ± 0.12
GAWW N (S. Reed et.al(2016))	3.62 ± 0.7
Our Stack GAN	3.70 ± 0.4

In comparison to Stack GAN, we considered some of the existing GANs. Our initial suggestion for improvement is CLS-GAN. By using (text, image) pairs as common observations and teaching the discriminator to distinguish between actual and fake pairs, it is easiest to train a conditional GAN. Whether actual training images match the context of the text embedding is not explicitly known to the discriminator. To account for this, GAN-CLS adds a third type of input consisting of actual photos with incompatible text, which the discriminator must adapt to grade as false, in addition to the real/fake inputs to the discriminator amidst training. The discriminator can give the generator an additional signal by learning to maximize picture/text matching besides image realism.

Similarly, for INT-GAN several studies have exhibited that deep neural networks develop representations with interpolations between embedding pairs that are typically close to the data manifold. By simply interpolating amongst the embeddings of the captions from the training set, the authors produced a significant number of extra text embeddings. The discriminator D does not have equivalent "actual" image and text pairs to train on because the interpolated embeddings are artificial. But D has the ability to foretell whether or not pairs of images and texts will correspond.

In the same way, Attn GAN allows attention-driven multi-stage refinement for fine-grained text-to-image synthesis. By focusing on the keywords in the natural language description, the AttnGAN, a new attentional generative network, can create fine-grained features in various image subregions. Additionally, a fine-grained image-text matching loss for training the generator is proposed to be computed using a deep attentional multimodal similarity model. Same as in our model, this Attn GAN has m generators that takes hidden states as the input which is used to generate images. It boosts the inception score compared to the previous models. And CUB dataset is comparatively easier than the COCO dataset. But the existing methods struggle a lot in producing high-quality images. The proposed attention mechanism in the AttnGAN is effective, which is essential for text-to-image creation for complicated scenarios, as shown by extensive experimental data.

To process a snapshot from the provided detailed description we have to achieve certain targets. Optical pragmatism and interpretation stability. Following the generative adversarial networks (GAN) algorithm we can generate an image through the given details, but still, the interpretation stability between the detailing and optical matter is difficult. To minimize this issue a new type of GAN was proposed called the Mirror GAN works on the idea of semantic-preserving text-to-image-to-text.

Mirror GAN is formed of 3 parts

1.   Linguistics (Semantic) text embedding module (STEM)

2. Global-local collaborative attention module for cascaded image generation (GLAM)
3. Linguistics (Semantic) text regeneration and alignment module (STREAM)

through which Mirror GAN learns the text-to-image production by multi-processed particularization. STEM produces embeddings at the term and syntax levels. Through the usage of both local term attention and global syntax attention, GLAM uses a streamed structure to breed the output snapshots from rough to full elaborate pictures sequentially improving their diversity and linguistic coherence. The created snap that's conceptually in line with the provided details is employed by STREAM to renew the text description.

Till now, we discussed different GANs that are capable of generating images for the given text input. As time progress we have various techniques to optimize the existing algorithms. Similarly, OP GAN came into existence by adding multiple object pathways to the ATTN GAN Architecture. For suppose there is a flower, bird or person, etc. called an object. While training the model the same object pathway is applied multiple times at different places to get proper output. We can produce high-resolution images with the help of this OP GAN. The other change in OP GAN Architecture is the evaluation metric.

There are few evaluation scores like caption generation etc. But they do not consider captions to evaluate the images. To tackle this drawback object accuracy metric was introduced to estimate the image quality. There will be a pre-trained objector in addition to the GAN architecture. The main aim of this object detector is to check whether the objects given as captions were present in the image or not. If they are not present then it will automatically reject the image so that the model accuracy can be improved. This is one of the greatest advantages of using OP Gan but every coin has its opposite side. Similarly, this method cannot produce high-resolution images.

Our Stack GAN achieves the best inception score on the CUB dataset than other methods. Our model produced better results it varied at about 26.96% when compared with GAN-INT-CLS in terms of inception score on the CUB dataset. In figure 3, 64 x 64 samples produced by GAN-INT-CLS can only mirror generate colour and the bird layout. But we observed that their results lack some parts of the birds like legs, feathers, etc and the plausible details are most of the images were looking in a non-realistic manner.

We have observed that GAWWAN (Reed et.al (2016)) obtained somewhat better results on the CUB dataset, which is slightly lesser than Stack GAN. But produced high-resolution images than GAN-INT-CLS. But the only problem with GAWWAN is that it failed to produce believable images when the text input is given. But the thing is, in our Stack GAN, stage-1 produced blurry images with low-resolution, it also includes missing details and various defects. And in Stage-2, it generates high resolution images and it brought about 4 x higher resolution images with more conclusive details to enhance and mirror the corresponding text details. Tier 2 architecture of the model pervades in the specifications provided, whereas the tier 1 architecture has generated realistic forms and colours. For example, in Figure 2, in the first column, a Tier 2 architecture is centralized to provide a better outcome inwards the quality and all the finest detailing provide in the text. as a suitable Tier-I outcome. Details for the tail and legs are also included. In any alternative case, Stage-II photos have various levels of detail added to them. In many other circumstances, by processing the text description, Tier-II GAN can address the flaws in Tier-I results again. In all other comparison studies, the results are not as good as Stack GAN. Importantly, the Stack GAN achieves good results by capturing the intricate underlying language-image interactions rather than just memorizing training data. We extract the actual optical attributes from our depictions and entire depictions are trained by tier 2 architecture's discriminator D. of our model. For all the output depictions, its accessible neighbours from the instruction set can be reclaimed. By analyzing the training depictions, we conclude that the produced depictions in the drive have some homogeneous properties with the retrieved instruction images but are different.

CONCLUSION

In this paper, we suggested Stacked Generative Adversarial Networks for text-to-image synthesis. This methodology is very helpful in synthesizing high-quality images. We divided this complex implementation part into two chunks. Where Stage-1 that completely focuses on developing the outline and primary colours of the image. Stage-2 of the GAN will completely focus on image quality enhancement like adding more photorealistic details by rectifying the defects. We have performed an extensive qualitative and quantitative analysis to illustrate the performance of our model. We computed the Inception Score as a part of the evaluation metrics. When compared with the other existing GAN models our stack GAN has shown promising results in generating higher-definition pictures (256 x 256) with more naturalistic details.

Figure 3. Example results generated by Stack GAN from CUB dataset.

REFERENCES

Brock, A., Lim, T., Ritchie, J. M., & Weston, N. (2016). *Neural photo editing with introspective adversarial networks*. Academic Press.

Denton, E. L., Chintala, S., Szlam, A., & Fergus, R. (2015). Deep generative image models using a laplacian pyramid of adversarial networks. In *Proceedings of the Conference on Neural Information Processing Systems*. Semantic Scholar.

Doersch, C. (2016). *Tutorial on variational autoencoders*. Academic Press.

Dosovitskiy, A., Springenberg, J. T., & Brox, T. (2015). Learning to generate chairs with convolutional neural networks. In *Proceedings of the Conference on Computer Vision and Pattern Recognition*. IEEE. 10.1109/CVPR.2015.7298761

Gregor, K., Danihelka, I., Graves, A., Rezende, D. J., & Wierstra, D. (2015). DRAW: A recurrent neural network for image generation. In *Proceedings of the International Conference on Machine Learning*. Semantic Scholar.

He, K., Zhang, X., Ren, S., & Sun, J. (2016). Deep residual learning for image recognition. In *Proceedings of the Conference on Computer Vision and Pattern Recognition*. Semantic Scholar.

Kingma, D. P., & Welling, M. (2014). Auto-encoding variational Bayes. In *Proceedings of the International Conference on Learning Representations*. Semantic Scholar.

Mansimov, Parisotto, Ba, & Salakhutdinov. (2016). Generating images from captions with attention. In *Proceedings of the international conference on learning representations*. Semantic Scholar.

Qiao, T., Zhang, J., Xu, D., & Tao, D. (2019). Mirrorgan: Learning text-to image generation by redescription. In *Proc. IEEE Conf. Comput. Vis. Pattern Recognit.* (pp. 1505–1514). IEEE. 10.1109/CVPR.2019.00160

Radford, A., Metz, L., & Chintala, S. (n.d.). *Unsupervised representation learning with deep convolutional generative adversarial networks*. Academic Press.

Reddy, V. D., Nilavan, K., Gangadharan, G. R., & Fiore, U. (2021). Forecasting Energy Consumption Using Deep Echo State Networks Optimized with Genetic Algorithm. In Artificial Intelligence, Machine Learning, and Data Science Technologies (pp. 205-217). CRC Press. doi:10.1201/9781003153405-11

Reed, S., Akata, Z., Mohan, S., Tenka, S., Schiele, B., & Lee, H. (2016). Learning what and where to draw. *Proceedings of the Conference on Neural Information Processing Systems*.

Reed, S., Akata, Z., Yan, X., Logeswaran, L., Schiele, B., & Lee, H. (2016). Generative adversarial text-to-image synthesis. *Proceedings of the International Conference on Machine Learning*.

Salimans, T., Goodfellow, I. J., Zaremba, W., Cheung, V., Radford, A., & Chen, X. (2016). Improved techniques for training GANs. In *proceedings of the Conference on Neural Information Processing Systems*. Semantic Scholar.

Wah, C., Branson, S., Welinder, P., Perona, P., & Belongie, S. (2011). *The Caltech-UCSD Birds-200-2011 Dataset*. Technical Report CNS-TR-2011-001, California Institute of Technology.

Xu, T., Zhang, P., Huang, Q., Zhang, H., Gan, Z., Huang, & He, X. (2018). Attngan: Fine-grained text to image generation with attentional generative adversarial networks. In *Proceedings of the IEEE conference on computer vision and pattern recognition* (pp. 1316–1324). IEEE.

Yang, J., Reed, S. E., Yang, M., & Lee, H. (2015). Weakly. supervised disentangling with recurrent transformations for 3d view synthesis. In *Proceedings of the Conference on Neural Information Processing Systems*. Semantic Scholar.

Yin, Liu, Sheng, Yu, Wang, & Shao. (2019). Semantics disentangling for text-to-image generation. In *Proceedings of the IEEE conference on computer vision and pattern recognition* (pp. 2327–2336). IEEE.

Zhang, H., Xu, T., Li, H., Zhang, S., Huang, X., & Wang, X. (2016). Dimitris Metaxas. StackGAN: Text to Photo-realistic Image Synthesis with Stacked Generative Adversarial Networks.

Zhao, J., Mathieu, M., & LeCun, Y. (2016). *Energy-based generative adversarial network*. Academic Press.

Zhu, M., Pan, P., Chen, W., & Yang, Y. (2019). Dm-gan: Dynamic memory generative adversarial networks for text-to-image synthesis. In *Proceedings of the IEEE conference on computer vision and pattern recognition* (pp. 5802–5810). IEEE.

KEY TERMS AND DEFINITIONS

Discriminator: The discriminator in a GAN is simply a classifier. It differentiates the original data from the data generated by the generator. It could use any network architecture appropriate to the type of data it's classifying.

Generative Adversarial Networks: GANs are like deep convolutional networks that are an approach to generative modeling.

Generator: The generator is part of a GAN, and it learns to create fake data by taking feedback from the discriminator. The portion of the GAN that trains the generator includes random input, generator network, discriminator network, discriminator output, and generator loss.

Image Augmentation: Is a technique that is used to alter the existing data to expand the dataset. This is done by using a combination of different techniques like random rotation, shift, brightness, zoom image, etc.

Inception Score: The Inception Score is an objective metric for evaluating the quality of generative image models. This metric was shown to correlate well with human scoring of the realism of generated images.

Stacked Generative Adversarial Networks: Stacked GANs composes of an encoder and a decoder. This is used to invert the hierarchical representations of a bottom-up discriminative network. It consists of a stack of GANs, each learned to generate lower-level representations conditioned on higher-level representations.

Text-to-Image Synthesis: Text-to-image synthesis is effective architecture for generating an image based on an input textual description automatically. This has been used in many applications like graphics, image editing, etc.

Chapter 11
The Application of Machine Learning for Predicting Global Seismicity

Viacheslav Shkuratskyy

ⓘ https://orcid.org/0000-0001-9142-1262

York St. John University, UK

Aminu Bello Usman

York St. John University, UK

Michael S. O'Dea

York St. John University, UK

ABSTRACT

An earthquake is one of the deadliest natural disasters. Forecasting an earthquake is a challenging task since natural causes such as rainfall or volcanic eruptions disrupt data. Earthquakes can also be caused by human beings, such as mining or dams. Solar activity has also been suggested as a possible cause of earthquakes. Solar activity and earthquakes occur in different parts of the solar system, separated by a huge distance. However, scientists have been trying to figure out if there are any links between these two seemingly unrelated occurrences since the 19th century. In this chapter, the authors explored the methods of how machine learning algorithms including k-nearest neighbour, support vector regression, random forest regression, and long short-term memory neural networks can be applied to predict earthquakes and to understand if there is a relationship between solar activity and earthquakes. The authors investigated three types of solar activity: sunspots number, solar wind, and solar flares, as well as worldwide earthquake frequencies that ranged in magnitude and depth.

DOI: 10.4018/978-1-6684-6937-8.ch011

INTRODUCTION

Since ancient times cataclysmic disasters such as droughts, floods, earthquakes, volcanic eruptions, storms, and many other types of natural catastrophes, have had a profound impact on humans, at the cost of countless lives. These disasters are classified as natural disasters (Wirasinghe et al., 2013). The most severe natural disaster in recent history was the flood of the Yangtze–Huai River in China, in summer 1931. Up to 25 million people were affected by the effects of this flood (National Flood Relief Commission, 1933), hence it is considered the deadliest natural disasters since 1900 excluding epidemics and famines.

The number of deaths from natural disasters may change depending on the type of disaster and the affected area. But, from the average point of view, around 40,000 people per year are killed by natural disasters. For example, Figure 1 shows the yearly average of global annual deaths from natural disasters between 1900 and 2010s. The graph was created based on data from (*OFDA/CRED International Disaster Data*, 2021).

Figure 1. Yearly average global of annual deaths from natural disasters, by decade.

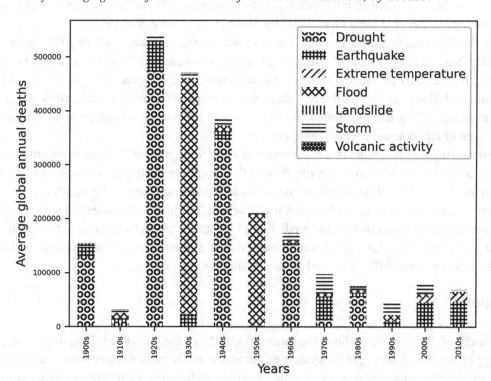

As seen in Figure 1 the three deadliest natural disasters are droughts, floods, and earthquakes. However, in the last decades, the most dangerous natural disasters for people are considered to be earthquakes, extreme temperature, and floods. Even though the average global death toll from natural disasters in the 21st century is less than in the previous century, the average death rate is still high.

Most of the Earth's meteorological processes are localised, and they make good weather forecasts only in a limited area. Space weather is always global on the planetary scale (Koskinen et al., 2001).

Further, the assumption that solar activities could have an influence on Earth's natural disasters is not new. Back in 1853 the astronomer Wolf (1853) suggested sunspots might influence earthquake events. Since then, several studies, using statistical methods, have showed the correlation between solar activity and earthquakes. Odintsov et al. (2006) reported that seismic activity is related to the sunspot maximum during the solar cycle. Marchitelli et al. (2020) showed a correlation between solar activity and earthquakes with a magnitude(M) M>5.6.

Modern solar activity data and natural disaster data, as well as worldwide data, which exponentially increase every year with improved or new technologies – they contain a plethora of different parameters for solar but also natural disaster events. Reinse et al. (2018) stated that the International Data Corporation predicts an increase of the global dataset from 33 ZB in 2018 to 175 ZB by 2025. To work with such a huge amount of data, computer processing power must be faster but also algorithms more intelligent. There is a part of computer science that tries to achieve this goal by employing artificial intelligence. Studies focussing on intelligence of animals (Thorndike, 2000) and plants (Calvo et al., 2020) proved that one of the most crucial requirements for intelligence is learning. High intelligence is based on comprehensive learning and artificial intelligence is not an exception. Therefore machine learning is one of the most important and vital parts of artificial intelligence (Dunjko & Briegel, 2018).

One of the first occasions that machine learning was mentioned, was back in 1959, in the Samuel (1959) study. Samuel (1959) created a checkers programme, where two "machine-learning procedures" were used, and the study provided a start for the development of learning methods that would exceed average human abilities and would solve real life problems. A quote from the original article best describes machine learning: *"Programming computers to learn from experience should eventually eliminate the need for much of this detailed programming effort."*

With increasing the processing power of computer systems in parallel to the growing amount of solar and climate data, together with implementing powerful data analyses techniques, will allow more accurate prediction levels of risks and threats of disasters, but also time and place of the disasters.

However, there are a lack of studies, that use Machine Learning techniques, which try to find the best and most appropriate method in the prediction of natural disasters using solar activity. This can be attributed to the fact that solar and natural disasters data are often raw and unstructured, which makes them due to their volume difficult to analyse and challenging to process.

Motivation

With a variety of different algorithms, the most difficult tasks can be solved. Despite the fact that the percentage of machine learning techniques used for space and natural disaster studies increases daily, there are only a few studies which use machine learning techniques for trying to predict earthquakes based on the solar activity events.

Although, it has not yet been conclusively established that solar activity events influence natural disasters. However, in accordance with findings of Love & Thomas (2013) the statement that solar activity events have an impact on natural disasters cannot be rejected, even though they did not find a strong correlation between solar activity and earthquakes.

Thus, there is a growing need to understand by using data and machine leaning algorithms – if solar activity can influence earthquake activity.

Problem Definition

Solar activity and earthquakes appear to be unrelated at first glance. However, some studies have consistently shown that there is a relationship between solar activity and earthquakes (Gribbin, 1971; Han, 2004; Odintsov et al., 2007; Novikov et al., 2020):

1. Earthquakes are influenced by the 11-year solar cycle.
2. Earthquakes are influenced by some solar activity.
3. Earthquakes are influenced by solar activity's electric current.
4. A correlation between solar activity and earthquakes can be established using statistical techniques.

However, it is still not clear of how and to what extent solar activity affects earthquakes. Moreover, all the above theories are not yet sufficiently developed to allow reliable predictions of the likelihood of future earthquakes.

Therefore, this study attempts to build a model that tests the relationship between solar activity and earthquakes using machine learning techniques.

Research Contribution

The connection between solar activity and earthquakes isn't a novel one. However, just a few research studies have used machine learning approaches to investigate this association.

- It is still unknown whether solar activity events have an impact on earthquakes.
- The statement that solar activity events have an impact on earthquakes, on the other hand, cannot be dismissed (Love & Thomas, 2013).
- The study based on seismology finding that were conducted and that would assist them in employing machine learning approaches to support their results.
- Using machine learning techniques, the authors attempted to uncover any probable links between these two events.
- It can serve as a foundation for future earthquake research.

The study given here is only a step toward earthquake prediction using machine learning techniques, but it has important long-term implication.

EARTHQUAKE

The word "disaster" is defined in the Oxford English Dictionary (2021) as *"An event or occurrence of a ruinous or very distressing nature; a calamity; esp. a sudden accident or natural catastrophe that causes great damage or loss of life."*

Based on the Wirasinghe et al., (2013) study, there are two main classifications for all disasters: they are classified as

1. Natural disasters – events that are natural

2. Human-made disasters – events that occurred as a result of human activity.

In the last decades, as can be seen from Figure 1, the most dangerous natural disaster for people are earthquakes. According to Kanamori & Brodsky (2004) the simple definition of an earthquake is an event shaking the Earth's surface. Worldwide earthquakes are one of the most severe natural disasters. According to Dong & Shan (2013), about 60% of all deaths that occurred due to natural disasters are caused by earthquakes.

An earthquake occurs as a result of global tectonic plate movement. There are several basic parameters that characterise an earthquake, such as depth of an earthquake, hypocentre, and magnitude:

*   Earthquake Depth: The depth indicates where an earthquake can occur between the Earth's surface and 700 kilometres below the surface. The depth is divided into three zones: shallow (0 – 70 km), intermediate (70 – 300 km), and deep (300 – 700 km).
*   The hypocentre is the point of initiation of an earthquake.
*   Earthquake Magnitude(M): The magnitude is the measure of the size of an earthquake source.

Earthquakes happen at conservative and collisional plate margins (Merle, 2011). In the conservative the tectonic plates are **sliding past** each other, while in the collision the continental tectonic plates are moving **towards** each other.

The significant earthquakes, which took place during 23rd solar cycle, are shown in Figure 2, together with the plate tectonics map in Figure 3 show, that earthquake events mainly take place at the plate tectonic boundary.

Figure 2. Earthquake events map during 23rd solar cycle, distributed by magnitude

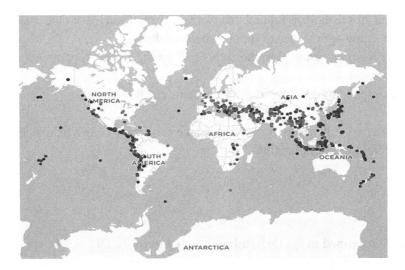

The earthquake data for Figure 2, were collected from the open-source National Geophysical Data Center / World Data Service (NGDC/WDS) (1972). The dataset consists of information about significant earthquakes which meet one of the criteria such as "caused deaths, caused moderate damage (approximately $1 million or more).

Figure 3. Plate Tectonics Map - Plate Boundary Map.
Source: *Plate Tectonics Map - Plate Boundary Map (2021)*

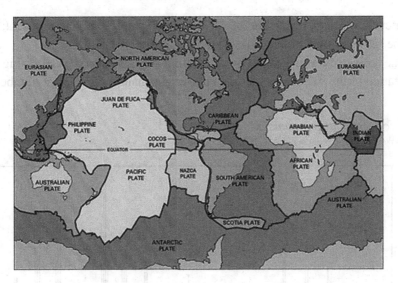

There are few ways to predict an earthquake. Animal behaviours: dogs started to bark before earthquakes (Fidani, 2010), behaviour of mice different before and after an earthquake (Li et al., 2009), cows produce less milk than usual (Yamauchi et al., 2017). Other studies focussed on analysing the change in Earth's water levels (Orihara et al., 2015; Singh et al., 2010) One of the natural triggers of earthquakes can be volcanic eruptions (McNutt & Roman, 2015), however, on the other hand earthquakes also can be a trigger for volcanos (Nishimura, 2017). The other examples of natural triggers of earthquakes are rainfall (Hainzl et al., 2006), tidal stress (Métivier et al., 2009), solar weather (Sytinskii, 1973). Furthermore, earthquakes may be caused by man's interference with nature: heavy water pressure in dams (Chander, 1999), mining (Redmayne, 1988), testing nuclear bombs (Tian et al., 2018). Arguably, the methods of using these signs to predict earthquakes are far from being perfect (Schorlemmer et al., 2018).

SOLAR ACTIVITY

Sunspots and Solar Cycles

A sunspot is a dark area which appears on the Sun's surface. The temperature within the dark area is cooler than the surrounding surface. Sunspots have various shapes and range in size showing different diameters. The lifetime of sunspots depends on their size. The smaller the area, the shorter the lifetime. A 10 Mm diameter sunspot may last for 2 – 3 days, a 60 Mm – up to 90 days (Priest, 2014).

Solar activities depend on a solar cycle. The sun is generating a magnetic field, which goes through a cycle. During this cycle, the magnetic field reverses and the north and south poles of the sun switch position. During the next solar cycle, the poles revert back. One solar cycle has a period of approximately 11 years (Figure 4). The length of the solar cycle may vary. The solar cycle has:

- solar minimum – at the beginning and end of each solar cycle, the minimum number of sunspots
- solar maximum – in the middle of the solar cycle, the maximum number of sunspots.

The first solar cycle was documented in the 18th century (Priest, 2014). The present, 25th solar cycle, began in December 2019 (Potter, 2020).

The state of the solar cycle is measured by calculating sunspots (Priest, 2014). Figure 4 provides a graphic representation of the solar cycles, based on average quantity of sunspot number per year.

Figure 4. Solar cycle and sunspot number
Data source: SILSO World Data Center website (2021)

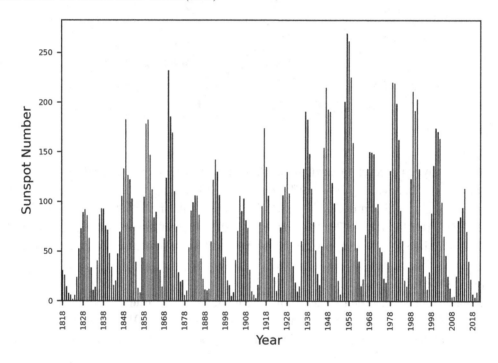

Solar Flares

A solar flare is an explosion of energy also accompanied by coronal mass ejection. This explosion of energy occurs because magnetic fields intersect and reorganise near sunspots. Based on the flare's strength, flares are classified as: A-class, B-class, C-class, M-class, and X-class. A-class is the smallest and X-class is the largest solar flare by size. In turn, each flare class has a scale from 1 to 9; – however, X-class flares can exceed the top scale of 9 (Priest, 2014).

Asaly et al. (2021) based on two datasets Ionospheric Total Electron Content data and solar flare data used Support Vector Machine for solar flare prediction. They found a high probability of predicting large-size solar flares of the M and X-class. However, the method they chose did not work for the prediction of small-sized solar flares.

Solar Wind

The solar wind, according to the description of the NASA/Marshall solar physics (2014), is a "not uniform" stream of charged participles, that flows from the Sun in all possible directions, with a speed of about 400 km/s.

The source of the solar wind is the Sun's outer atmosphere, which is called corona. The highest speed of around 800 km/s, occurred over regions where the corona is dark, and the lowest speed of around 300 km/s was observed over large cap-like coronal structures

According to Wood et al., 2009 the measurements of the solar wind are solar wind speed (velocity), proton density, and proton temperature.

The mean distance from the Sun to the Earth is 1.5×10^{11} m (Meyer-Vernet, 2012). So, the average time when the solar wind reaches the Earth is 4.3 days (1.5×10^8 km $\div$ 400 km/s = 375,000 sec). However, the real time between detection of the solar wind and its arrival on Earth may be shorter, because of the location of satellites, which detect the solar wind. For example, the location of ACE (Advanced Composition Explorer) satellite between the Earth and the Sun is about 1.5×10^6 km forward of the Earth (*ACE real-time solar wind | NOAA / NWS space weather prediction center*, 2021).

EARTHQUAKES AND SOLAR ACTIVITY

The two events, solar activity and earthquakes, take place at different location within the solar system, on the surface of the Sun and the Earth, separated by, approximately, 1.5×10^{11} m (Meyer-Vernet, 2012). However, starting from Wolf (1853), researchers have tried to find out if there are any connections between these two seemingly separate events.

However, there is an opposite opinion. Love & Thomas (2013), using χ^2 and Student's t tests, claimed that there is no statistically valid explanation proving that solar-terrestrial interaction favours earthquake incidence. For their study they used data from the *SPDF - OMNIWeb Service* (2021) and *Sunspot-numbers - monthly*, (2021). On the other hand, they acknowledged that they do not have proof that the notion that solar activity has no affect is correct.

There is an assumption, that earthquakes are influenced by several factors. Bijan et al. (2013) in their study classified earthquakes into two categories (Figure 5):

1. Earthquakes that have happened as a result of the Tectonic Effect or Internal Earth's Effects, for example rainfall, volcanic eruptions, landslides.
2. Earthquakes that have happened because of the Non-Tectonic Effect or External Earth's Effects, for example Sun and Moon gravitation, solar activity.

Figure 5. Classification of Triggers of Earthquakes
Source: Bijan, Saied and Somayeh (2013)

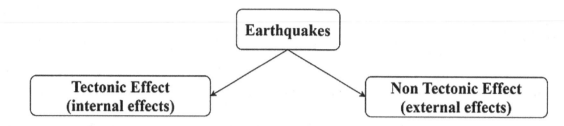

The study Novikov et al. (2020) showed the possibility that strong solar flares impact the triggering of earthquakes. In the first part of their study, they discussed the results of the laboratory experiments: electric current, generated by the artificial generator, injected into the Earth, what creates a telluric current, and copied the impact of ionizing radiation from solar flares on earthquake sources. They noticed an increase in the quantity of earthquakes with magnitude M<3, after injection of electric current into the Earth's crust. They mentioned that the current density in the Earth's crust depends on its electrical conductivity. It was shown, that if electrical conductivity in the depth of 10 km is higher than the electrical conductivity in the Earth surface, the current density will increase by an order. It has been found that geomagnetic pulsations caused by X-rays from X-class solar flares, as well as geomagnetic storms, can generate geomagnetically induced currents in earthquake sources.

Novikov et al. (2020) observed earthquakes between August and September 2017 (on September 6, an X-class solar flare occurred). They used a quantity of global earthquakes, with magnitude $M^3 4$, and a quantity of regional (Greece) earthquakes, with magnitude $M^3 3$. The result is based on the comparison the numbers of earthquakes before and after the solar flare. The number of earthquakes increased in both groups of earthquakes: global (increased by 68%) and regional (increased by 120%), after the solar flare.

Odintsov et al. (2006) and Odintsov et al. (2007) tried to confirm the hypothesis of Sytinskii, (1973) that earthquakes with magnitude M>6.5 matches with high-speed solar winds whose velocity is more than 500 km/s. For their study they used a 27-year period, daily number of earthquakes with magnitude $M^3 5.5$, and solar wind with velocity 500 km/s and above. They identified 307 cases of solar wind with this velocity.

Odintsov et al. (2006) and Odintsov et al. (2007) analysed the quantity of earthquakes on the day of solar wind arrival and a few days before and after solar wind arrivals. They found an increase of the quantity of earthquake on the day of high-speed solar wind arrival and the day after.

Also, Odintsov et al. (2007) observed nine full solar cycles to find out if there is a connection between earthquakes and solar activity. For this part they used quantity of earthquakes with magnitude $M^3 7$. They compare average yearly sunspot number and average yearly number of earthquakes and found that during the 11-year solar cycle number of earthquakes there are two maxima. The first maximum is the same as the maximum of sunspot number and the second maximum is during the descending phase of the 11-year solar cycle.

Besides, Sytinskii, (1973) claimed that the total seismicity of the Earth, expressed through the total energy of earthquakes and the number of catastrophic earthquakes per year, depends on the phase of the 11-year solar cycle. The time of occurrence of individual strong earthquakes with magnitude $M^3 6.5$ depends on the position of active regions on the Sun. Earthquakes occur mainly 2-3 days after the passage of the active region through the central solar meridian.

Furthermore, recent data-driven studies have discovered a link between global earthquakes and solar activity. Nishii et al. (2020) set out to determine whether solar activity is a source of earthquakes. They used data from *SPDF - OMNIWeb Service* (2021) for solar activity data and the *Usgs earthquake hazards program* (2021) catalogue for earthquake data. They discovered a link between solar activity and earthquakes using support vector regression, notably for earthquakes with a magnitude M<6.

Using statistical methods, Solar activity and earthquakes are linked, according to Marchitelli et al. (2020). They used two characteristics of solar wind for their research: proton density and velocity for solar activity data, and worldwide earthquakes with magnitude $M^3 5.6$ over a 20-year period. For the earthquake data they used Storchak et al. (2013) earthquake catalogue; solar activity data from the Solar and Heliospheric Observatory (SOHO) satellite.

According to previous research, it is still unclear whether solar activity events are the cause of natural disasters. On the other hand, the assertion that solar activity events have an impact on earthquakes, cannot be dismissed.

MACHINE LEARNING

There are a lot of ways to use machine learning in the earthquake sphere, from prediction of earthquake events to management of post-earthquake events. Mangalathu et al. (2020), as a part of post-earthquake management, classified earthquake-induced building damage. For their study, they had chosen four machine learning algorithms: linear discriminant analysis, k-nearest neighbour, decision trees, neighbour forest. All four algorithms showed accuracy prediction rates of around 60%, the highest accuracy of 66% was shown by using the random forest algorithm.

Asim et al. (2017) based on the earthquake data and the seismic parameters studied predicted earthquakes using pattern recognition neural network, recurrent neural network, random forest, and linear programming boost ensemble classifier. Every algorithm showed a different result when compared to each other.

The very first tasks of machine learning are to clarify a problem and explore data. Understanding the data is one of the most important parts of machine learning. A knowledge of the problem and data will help to choose the right machine learning technique. Without this understanding, the choice of the machine learning techniques would be random (Müller & Guido, 2016). The basic stages of machine learning process are presented graphically in the Figure 6.

Figure 6. Basic stages for machine learning process
Adapted from Kuncheva (2004).

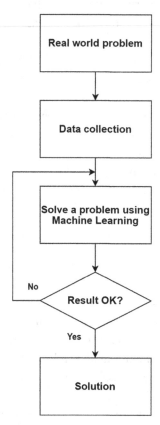

There are three main types of what is called the learning process: supervised learning, unsupervised learning, and reinforcement learning (Kaplan & Haenlein, 2019), (Figure 7):

- Supervised learning is based on the relationship between inputs and their outputs, based on the result and knowledge gained, which allows to make a future prediction. In supervised learning data is pre-categorized or numerical (Kotsiantis, 2007).
- Unsupervised learning is used to know more about data. In unsupervised learning input data points are not labelled and do not belong to categories. Unsupervised learning can be considered as finding patterns in data (Ghahramani, 2004).
- Reinforcement learning algorithm is also called the agent. The agent learns from an environment using feedbacks and compares actions based on feedbacks by trying to choose the best one (Sutton and Barto, 2018).

Figure 7. Taxonomy of machine learning algorithms.

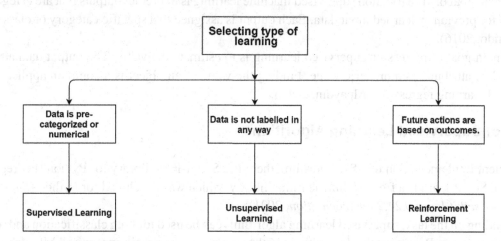

Supervised Learning (SL)

Solar activity data and earthquake data are labelled. As previously stated, supervised learning uses labelled data. Hence, supervised learning is the most appropriate option in this case.

SL methods are based on relationship between inputs and their outputs. For example, let the input variables be represented with a label "X" and an output variable "Y" and supervised learning algorithms are used to learn the mapping function from the input "X" to the output "Y" (Kotsiantis, 2007; Mohamed, 2017).

Since the inputs and outputs are known during the learning process, high accuracy of a prediction can be achieved. That is why supervised learning is highly used in the spheres of solar activity and natural disasters. Novianty et al. (2019) used SL to detect tsunamis, Nishii et al. (2020), used SL for finding if solar activity effects on earthquake events. Murwantara et al. (2020) and Mallouhy et al. (2019) used SL predict earthquakes.

There are two major types of SL, Figure 8. The first one is classification, and the other is regression (Mohamed, 2017; Müller & Guido, 2016). A classification problem predicts "a category", while a regression problem predicts "a number". (Kotsiantis, 2007).

Figure 8. Supervised learning.

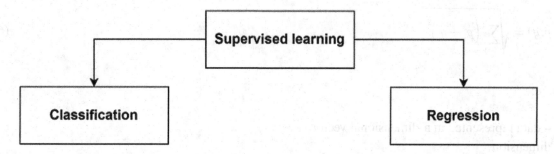

The main goal of classification supervised machine learning is to predict outputs that are categorised in nature for previously learned input data. Each output is assigned to a specific category or class (Müller & Guido, 2016).

The main goal of regression supervised learning is to estimate the value. The output data attribute of input data attributes is a numeric value. Finding the value of an object is a common application of supervised learning regression (Alpaydin, 2014).

Types of Supervised Learning Algorithms

For efficient implementation of a SL algorithm, there is a Scikit-learn library for Python (Pedregosa et al., 2011). Scikit-learn is a free machine learning library, which was developed for Python (*Supervised learning — scikit-learn 0.24.2 documentation*, 2021).

Depending on the task, supervised learning algorithms can be used for both classification and regression learning types. Below are the descriptions of the summary of the main supervised ML algorithms.

1. **K-Nearest Neighbours Algorithm (KNN)** is one of the easiest algorithms, it is easy to implement and has been used in natural disasters studies. However, with the increase in data size it becomes slower. For example, Novianty et al. (2019) measured the accuracy of the identification of tsunamis based on earthquake events using the KNN algorithm with an earthquake dataset and a tsunami dataset. They used three variations of the datasets and different "K" values and found that with increasing "K" value the accuracy of the identification tsunami is increasing; however, after a certain value of "K" there was no significant change in accuracy.

KNN implementation requires only two parameters: *"K"* value, what means the number of nearest datapoints to the new data point, and the distance function. The value for *"K"* depends on a dataset. However, the higher the *"K"* values the less noise influences the classification and the forecast becomes more accurate, although boundaries between classes are less clear. There is no need to build a model and new data can be easily added. KNN can be used for classification (mostly) and regression learning types (Alpaydin, 2014).

The measure between two data points is normally calculated using Euclidean distance, *equation* (6), as the square root of the sum of the squared differences between two points, new and existing. Manhattan Distance – distance between real vectors using the sum of their absolute differences – is an alternative variation.

$$D\left(p,q\right) = \sqrt{\sum_{i=1}^{n}\left(p_i - q_i\right)^2} \qquad (6)$$

Where:

p,q – data represented in n-dimensional vector
n – dimension

For the regression task, the closest "K" data points are chosen based on their distance from the new point, and the average of these data points is used to make the final forecast for the new point.

2. **Support Vector Machine Algorithm (SVM)** is one of the most popular algorithms used to solve data analytics problems. The main goal of SVM is to find a function $f(x)$ that separates classes (Smola & Schölkopf, 2004). SVM is to find the best line, which has maximum distance between datapoints. This line is called a hyperplane. The dimension of a hyperplane depends on the dimension(s) of a dataset. If a dataset has n features, a hyperplane will have (n-1) dimension. Also, there are data points, which are the closest to hyperplane, they are called support vectors (Figure 9). SVM can be used for classification (mostly) and regression learning types. For regression tasks, SVM is called Support vector regression (SVR).

Figure 9. SVM, two dimensions
Adapted from Smola & Schölkopf, 2004.

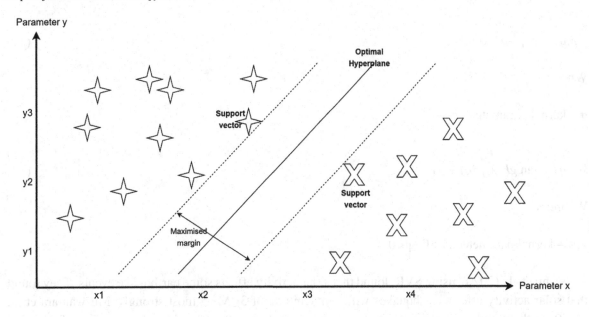

SVM is based on a collection of mathematical functions known as the kernel. The kernel's job is to take data and turn it into the needed format. Different types of kernel functions are used by different tasks solved using SVM. A kernel is described by form, *equation (8)*.

$$k(p,q) = (\Phi(p) * \Phi(q)) \tag{8}$$

Where:

k – kernel
p,q – vectors
$\Phi(p), \Phi(q)$ – feature space

The Kernel approach, which basically aids in solving the linearity and non-linearity of the equation in a very straightforward manner, is the most often utilised and useful feature of SVM. There are different types of kernels, such as linear, *equation (9)*, polynomial, *equation (10)*, radial basis function (RBF), *equation (11)*, and sigmoid, *equation (12)* (Ghaedi et al., 2016; Benkedjouh et al., 2015; Loutas et al., 2013; Jacobs, 2012).

$$k(p,q) = p * q \tag{9}$$

$$k(p,q) = ((p*q) + c)^a \tag{10}$$

Where:

c, a – kernel parameters, $c \geq 0$, $a \in N$

$$k(p,q) = \exp(-p - q^2/\sigma 2^) \tag{11}$$

Where:

σ – kernel parameters, $\sigma > 0$

$$k(p,q) = \tan gh(\lambda(p*q) + \psi) \tag{12}$$

Where:

λ, ψ – kernel parameters, $\lambda > 0$, $\psi < 0$

Nishii et al., (2020), using SVR, found that solar activity effects some earthquake events. They found that solar activity affects earthquakes with a magnitude of $3 \leq M < 5$ most strongly. Murwantara et al. (2020) in their study compared three algorithms to predict earthquakes in Indonesia. They found that the algorithm, which showed the best result in earthquake prediction, was SVM.

The following algorithms are tree-based algorithms. Tree-based algorithms can be used for both classification and regression learning types. Tree-based algorithms are the collection of nested "If-Else" conditions Figure 10. Tree-based algorithms start with a full population and split the data based on some condition. The splitting will continue until the stopping criteria is met (Verdhan & Kling, 2020).

3. **Random Forest Algorithm (RF)** is a tree-structured algorithm, based on ensemble learning conception. RF is a classifier that contains a number of tree-structured classifies – decision trees, which consist of independent vectors. A raw dataset is separated into randomly selected sub-features, and then particular subtrees are generated (Breiman, 2001; Alpaydin, 2014).

Figure 10. Tree-based algorithm, split by some conditions

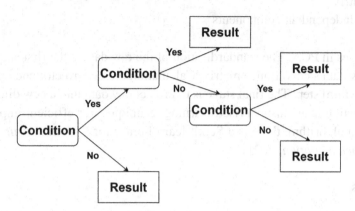

Each tree has one vote. If the problem is a classification problem, the class with the most votes is the final result. For regression problem – the average of all subtrees results is the final outcome. The greater number of trees the higher the accuracy of the prediction. RF does not have an overfitting problem, it uses a random subspace method (Breiman, 2001; Hothorn et al., 2006).

Mallouhy et al. (2019) compared in their study eight different algorithms for predicting earthquake events, based on earthquake data. They found that the best prediction percentage was RF. Very close to RF was KNN.

Dimension Reduction

When analysing data of moderate or high dimensions, it is frequently beneficial to look for ways to restructure the data and lower its dimensionality while retaining the most relevant information or preserving some trait of interest. Dimension reduction is the process of reducing the number of traits, variables, and characteristics (Alpaydin, 2014). Reddy et al. (2020) in their study used the supervised algorithm Linear Discriminant Analysis (LDA) and the unsupervised algorithm PCA to reduce the size of a dataset and their impact on the final outcome. To train the reduced dataset, they used four machine learning techniques, including Random Forest and SVM. They discovered that PCA outperformed LDA in terms of final results. They also noticed that the dimensionally reduced dataset showed better results than the original one. However, they also indicated that when the data size is too small, dimensionality reduction methodologies have a negative impact on the performance of machine learning algorithms.

One of the most popular unsupervised dimension reduction algorithms is **Principal Component Analysis** (PCA), *equation (15)*. An orthogonal transformation is used in PCA, which is a statistical process. A set of correlated variables is converted to a group of uncorrelated variables using PCA. For exploratory data analysis, PCA is utilised (Reddy et al., 2020).

$$x = W\chi \tag{15}$$

Where:

x – the observations

W – is the mixing matrix

χ – the source or the independent components

There are four stages in PCA. The standardisation of the raw data is the first stage. The second step is to calculate the raw data's co-variance matrix. Calculation the eigenvector and eigenvalue of the co-variance matrix is the third step. The final stage is to project raw data into a new dimensional subspace.

Dimensional reduction is an unsupervised learning technique. For efficient implementation of this unsupervised learning algorithm, there is a Scikit-learn library for Python (*Unsupervised learning — scikit-learn 0.24.2 documentation*, 2021).

Neural Networks

Neural networks (NN) can solve both supervised and unsupervised problems. Also, NN are great method for developing nonparametric and nonlinear classification/regression (Verdhan & Kling, 2020).

There are a lot of types of different NN, such as Recurrent Neural Network, Convolutional Neural Networks, Feed Forward Neural Networks, and Generative Adversarial Networks.

One of the most well-known neural networks is the Recurrent Neural Network (RNN). RNN is a neural network that has connections between passages related to sequences and lists and is dependent on previous states.

The standard RNN, on the other hand, has a weakness: the gradient vanishes as information is lost over time. The Long Short Term Memory network (LSTM) was created to avoid the long-term dependency problem. The structure of LSTM is similar to that of standard RNN, but the repeating module is different (Hochreiter & Schmidhuber, 1997).

According to Hochreiter & Schmidhuber (1997), there are few steps of LSTM. The first step in LSTM is deciding what information from the cell state will be removed, *equation (16)*.

$$f_t = \sigma\left(W_t x_t + U_f h_{t-1} + b_f\right) \tag{16}$$

The second step in LSTM is deciding what "new" information will be stored in the cell state, *equations (17)(18)*.

$$i_t = \sigma\left(W_i x_t + U_i h_{t-1} + b_i\right) \tag{17}$$

$$\tilde{c}_t = \sigma\left(W_c x_t + U_c h_{t-1} + b_c\right) \tag{18}$$

And finally, output, *equations (19)(20)(21)*:

$$c_t = f_t c_{t-1} + i_t \tilde{c}_t \tag{19}$$

$$o_t = \sigma\left(W_o x_t + U_o h_{t-1} + b_o\right) \qquad (20)$$

$$h_t = o_t \sigma_h\left(c_t\right) \qquad (21)$$

Where:

x_t – input vectors

h_t – hidden vectors

f_t – forget gate's activation vector, between 0 and 1

σ – sigmoid function

W, U – weights

b_t – bias vector

i_t – update gate's activation vector, between 0 and 1

$\tilde{c}_t$ – cell input activation vector, between -1 and 1

c_t – cell state activation vector

o_t – output gate's activation vector, between 0 and 1

The above steps, which included fitting the model and obtaining prediction values, can be completed using Python libraries. *Keras: the Python deep learning API* (2021) is a popular library that comes highly recommended (Verdhan & Kling, 2020).

One of the most important advantages of NN compared to traditional algorithms is that NN can work well with an increasing size of data. The bigger the training data size, the better the accuracy will get in the final result.

Zhang et al. (2017) applied an LSTM network to forecast sea surface temperature, based on the sea surface temperature dataset. Yuan et al. (2019) based on historical North Atlantic Oscillation index data created an LSTM network to predict North Atlantic Oscillation index.

Evaluation Metrics in Supervised Learning, Regression

Evaluation metrics determine how accurate a prediction is. Regression is a type of predictive modelling that entails forecasting a numerical value. Calculating an error score to summarise a model's prediction ability is one of the regression metrics. The regression metrics demonstrate how closely the predicted values match the actual ones (Draper & Smith, 1998). According to Draper & Smith (1998) the challenges that require estimating a numeric value are known as regression predictive modelling, like in this situation. As a result, the authors looked at the regression metrics in greater depth.

Error is used in regression metrics. Error is a metric that measures how close forecasts were to their predicted values on average. Witten & Frank (2017) have compiled a list of useful regression metrics. However, the R-squared error, mean absolute percentage error, mean absolute error, mean squared error, and root mean squared error are arguably the most extensively used metrics.

R-squared (R^2), *equation (1)* – is the fraction of the variance in the dependent variable that can be predicted by the independent variable. The closer R^2 to "1" the better the model fits data.

$$R^2 = 1 - \frac{\sum_{i=1}^{n}\left(p_i - p_i'\right)^2}{\sum_{i=1}^{n}\left(p_i - \bar{p}\right)^2} \tag{1}$$

Where:

n – the number of data points
$p_1', p_2', \ldots, p_n'$ – predicted values
$p_1, p_2, \ldots, p_n$ – actual values
$\bar{p}$ – mean of actual values

Mean absolute percentage error (MAPE), *equation (2)* – mean absolute percentage deviation. MAPE has a percentage value.

$$MAPE = \frac{1}{n}\sum_{i=1}^{n}\left|\frac{p_i - p_i'}{p_i}\right| \tag{2}$$

Where:

n – the number of data points
$p_1', p_2', \ldots, p_n'$ – predicted values
$p_1, p_2, \ldots, p_n$ – actual values

Mean absolute error (MAE), *equation (3)* – the average of the difference between the predicted and actual values. MAE has the same units as the original data. MAE shows how close the predicted values to the actual values.

$$MAE = \frac{1}{n}\sum_{i=1}^{n}\left|p_i - p_i'\right| \tag{3}$$

Where:

n – the number of data points
$p_1', p_2', \ldots, p_n'$ – predicted values
$p_1, p_2, \ldots, p_n$ – actual values

Mean squared error (MSE), *equation (4)* – the difference between estimated and actual values, expressed as an average squared difference. MSE has the squared units of the original data.

$$MSE = \frac{\sum_{i=1}^{n}\left(p_i' - p_i\right)^2}{n} \tag{4}$$

Where:

n – the number of data points

$p_1', p_2', \ldots, p_n'$ – predicted values

$p_1, p_2, \ldots, p_n$ – actual values

Root mean squared error (RMSE), *equation (5)* – square root of MSE. RMSE has the same units as the original data.

$$RMSE = \sqrt{\frac{\sum_{i=1}^{n}\left(p_i' - p_i\right)^2}{n}} \tag{5}$$

Where:

n – the number of data points

$p_1', p_2', \ldots, p_n'$ – predicted values

$p_1, p_2, \ldots, p_n$ – actual values

The same rule applies to MAPE, MAE, MSE, and RMSE: the lower the error, the better the model matches the data.

Data Splitting

Building computational models with good prediction and generalisation skills is one of the most important needs in machine learning (Alpaydin, 2014). To forecast the output, a model should first be trained, and then the model should be evaluated. A dataset should be divided into training and testing sets for this purpose. This causes two issues: with a smaller training data set, the data parameter estimations are more variable, and with a smaller test data set, the performance statistics are more variable. Therefore, the data should be separated such that none of the variances are very large (Kononenko & Kukar, 2007).

Regarding to the previous studies the most popular ratios for training/testing sets are 70/30 (Dao et al., 2020) and 80/20 (Pham et al., 2020; Das et al., 2011). Nguyen et al. (2021) in their study claimed, 70/30 is the best ratio, however they used rather small dataset of 538 samples. However, Rácz et al. (2021) suggested that 80/20 ratio is likely to be superior, especially for large datasets.

There are over 8000 records in the data used in this study. This indicate that, an 80/20 ratio would be the best option for the data.

Types of Normalising

Data normalising is the processes of converting the values of numeric columns in a dataset to a similar scale without distorting the ranges of values (Muhamedyev, 2015). Normalising helps to reduce data redundancy. Normalising helps to remove anomalies and minimisation null values, what the dataset contains null values. Data redundancy can be reduced by normalising. Normalization aids in the removal of anomalies and the reduction of null values, both of which are common in the data. Furthermore, Raju et al. (2020) demonstrated that when data was normalised, the findings were more accurate when compared to the original data.

To normalise data, there are a number different normalisation and standardisation methods that may be used (Raju et al., 2020). Different techniques are used by different methods; some change the range of values, while others change the distribution. The authors will use boxplots to compare the results of these methods in order to find the best method.

MinMaxScaler – For each component, the base guess is set to 0, the most extreme value is set to 1, and all other values are set to a decimal between 0 and 1, *equation (22).*

$$p_{scaled} = \frac{\left(p - p_{\min}\right)}{\left(p_{\max} - p_{\min}\right)} \tag{22}$$

Where:

p – data point
$p_{\min}$ – minimum value in a dataset
$p_{\max}$ – maximum value in a dataset

MaxAbsScaler – similar to MinMaxScaler, the range between 0 and 1, *equation (23).*

$$p_{scaled} = \frac{p}{\max\left(abs\left(p\right)\right)} \tag{23}$$

Where:

p – data point

StandardScaler – is usually used inside each component to scale it to the point where the distribution is currently centred around 0 with a standard deviation of 1, *equation (24).*

$$p_{scaled} = \frac{\left(p - \mu\right)}{\sigma} \tag{24}$$

Where:

p – data point

μ – mean of a dataset

σ – standard deviation of a dataset

RobustScaler – eliminates the centre and scales the data according to the Interquartile Range (IQR). The interval between the first quartile (25th quantile) and the third quartile is known as the IQR (75th quantile), *equation (25)*.

$$p_{scaled} = \frac{\left(p - median \right)}{IQR_{1,3}} \qquad (25)$$

Where:

p – data point

median – median of a dataset

$IQR_{1,3}$ – the range between the first and the third quartiles (25th and 75th quantiles)

QuantileTransformer – is changed to follow a uniform or ordinary dispersion using this approach. As a result, in general, this alteration will spread out the most continuous attributes for a specific example. It also reduces the impact of (minor) deviations, making this a good pre-planning strategy. The update is applied independently to each case. QuantileTransform produces non-linear standardisation modifications by contracting the distance between minimal exceptions and inliers. The range between 0 and 1.

Based on the comparison of all the methods, the *QuantileTransformer* showed the best result, which is why the authors chose this method.

EXPERIMENT METHOD

The experiment is based on the findings of previous seismological studies. Novikov et al. (2020) and Odintsov et al. (2007) showed the relationship between strong earthquakes (magnitude M>5.5) and solar activity. However, in their studies, they did not use earthquakes with magnitude M<5. They compare the number of earthquakes before and after solar activity events in their studies. They discovered that after solar activity events, the number of earthquakes increased. As for solar activity, Novikov et al. (2020) used solar flares, Odintsov et al. (2007) used solar wind velocity.

On the other hand, Nishii et al. (2020) using Support Vector Regression demonstrated that solar activity affects earthquakes with magnitude M<5, and that earthquakes with magnitude 3 and 4 the most strongly influenced by solar activity. For their study they used quantity of earthquakes with magnitude M^{3}3 and nine measurements of solar activity, including sunspot number, solar wind velocity, proton temperature. They also showed that not all nine measurements of solar activity affected earthquakes.

Therefore, the authors decided to use:

- Solar activity:
  - Sunspot Number

- ◦ Solar Wind (speed, proton density, and proton temperature)
- ◦ Solar Flares (A, B, C, M, X classes)
- Earthquake:
  - ◦ Earthquakes with magnitude M<5.5
  - ◦ Earthquakes with magnitude M≥5.5

Also, Novikov et al. (2020) noticed the increasing of earthquakes with magnitude M<3 after the influence of electric current on the Earth crust, what similar to solar exposure. The Earth crust has different electrical conductivity in different regions. According to Novikov et al. (2020) and Novikov et al. (2017) the higher electrical conductivity the higher current density in the lower Earth crust levels, what also leads to an earthquake. It can be assumed that, in different regions of the Earth, solar activity may have an influence on earthquakes depending on their depth. Since the authors are studying global earthquakes, the authors decided to use two earthquake options:

- Global earthquakes
- Global earthquakes divided by their depth:
  - ◦ Shallow zone earthquakes
  - ◦ Intermediate zone earthquakes
  - ◦ Deep zone earthquakes

For the experiment, the authors chose algorithms with a variety of backgrounds from both traditional machine learning and deep learning. Also, a non-linear relationship between the earthquakes and solar activity was taken into account:

- KNN – uses Euclidean distance
- SVR – kernel-based algorithm
- RFR – tree-based algorithm
- LSTM – neural networks.

For the evaluation method, it is suggested to use a variety of metrics (Chai & Draxler, 2014). Spiess & Neumeyer (2010) study used various simulation models and found that R-squared leads to false conclusions which nonlinear models are better. Also, MAPE, is not suitable here, as the earthquake dataset has a lot of zero value, would give a division by zero, *equation (2)*. Furthermore, Willmott & Matsuura (2005) indicated that RMSE is not a good measure of model performance, and it may be a deceptive indicator of average error. They suggested MAE is a preferable metric. On the other hand, Chai & Draxler (2014) stated that avoiding RMSE is not the best practice. Also, RMSE avoid using absolute values what is the benefit over MAE. Hence, for the evaluation, the authors decided to use:

- MAE
- RMSE

Based on the experiment results, the LSTM model had the best accuracy. However, the accuracy of the prediction of all algorithms is very close to each other. Moreover, the authors made a prediction that the LSTM model, compared to the other models, has more potential for increasing accuracy in further work as it has more changeable parameters than other algorithms.

CONCLUSION

In this chapter, the authors explored whether machine learning is effective in predicting earthquakes based on solar activity. To attempt this, the authors first tried to find characteristics and types of earthquakes and solar activity that should be used. Based on the seismological studies, the authors chose global earthquakes ranging in magnitude and depth. As for the solar activity, the authors chose sunspot number, solar wind, and solar flares. To evaluate the efficacy and effectiveness of the machine learning algorithms used in the study, the authors opted for normalised values of RMSE and MAE. During the experiment, it was found that the relationship between earthquakes and solar activity is nonlinear, which is one of the conditions for choosing algorithms. The experiment showed that the lowest accuracy had the KNN algorithm, while the highest accuracy had the LSTM algorithm. However, all algorithms' prediction accuracy was quite close to one another. Moreover, it can be assumed that there is a possible connection between solar activity and earthquakes. However, to be sure about this statement, there are some steps that need to be taken in future work.

Also, while it is noted that the neural network showed the most potential, it is far from perfect in predicting earthquakes based on solar activity. Besides improving neural network performance, one of the first steps, based on the finding of a non-linear relationship, is to research the non-linearity of the relationship. However, neural networks require more energy and more expensive resources; therefore, additional experiments with different neural networks and traditional machine learning algorithms are required.

Furthermore, another thing to pay attention to is data. The data that were used is a good starting point, but it is better to try to use data from different sources to supplement them to improve the accuracy. Also, increasing the quantity of characteristics of earthquakes, such as earthquake location, solar activity events, such as solar energetic particles, and additional events, such as distance from the Earth to the Sun, will lead to improved prediction using machine learning algorithms. Additionally, to improve the accuracy, besides the quantity of solar flares, it is worthwhile to try the images of solar flares.

The combination of all these factors, together with experiments using different algorithms and their settings, should help improve the quality of the prediction.

ORGANIZATION BACKGROUND

York St John University is a public university in York, United Kingdom, that has been educating people for 180 years. One of the founding goals of York St John University was to expand the transformative reach of education so that everyone might reap its advantages. Similarly, effective research is now one of the pillars of this modern and aspirational university. The research conducted at York St. John University attempts to positively impact the community by combating bias and unfairness and fostering a fairer and more just society.

REFERENCES

Alpaydin, E. (2014). *Introduction to machine learning* (3rd ed.). The MIT Press.

Asaly, S., Gottlieb, L.-A., & Reuveni, Y. (2021). Using support vector machine (SVM) and Ionospheric Total Electron Content (TEC) data for solar flare predictions. *IEEE Journal of Selected Topics in Applied Earth Observations and Remote Sensing, 14*, 1469–1481. https://doi.org/10.1109/JSTARS.2020.3044470

Asim, K. M., Martínez-Álvarez, F., Basit, A., & Iqbal, T. (2017). Earthquake magnitude prediction in Hindukush region using machine learning techniques. *Natural Hazards, 85*(1), 471–486. https://doi.org/10.1007/s11069-016-2579-3

Benkedjouh, T., Medjaher, K., Zerhouni, N., & Rechak, S. (2015). Health assessment and life prediction of cutting tools based on support vector regression. *Journal of Intelligent Manufacturing, 26*(2), 213–223. https://doi.org/10.1007/s10845-013-0774-6

Bijan, N., Saied, P., & Somayeh, M. (2013). The effect of solar cycle's activities on earthquake: A conceptual idea for forecasting. *Disaster Advances, 6*, 8.

Breiman, L. (2001). Random forests. *Machine Learning, 45*(1), 5–32. https://doi.org/10.1023/A:1010933404324

Calvo, P., Gagliano, M., Souza, G. M., & Trewavas, A. (2020). Plants are intelligent, here's how. *Annals of Botany, 125*(1), 11–28. https://doi.org/10.1093/aob/mcz155

Chai, T., & Draxler, R. R. (2014). Root mean square error (RMSE) or mean absolute error (MAE)? – Arguments against avoiding RMSE in the literature. *Geoscientific Model Development, 7*(3), 1247–1250. https://doi.org/10.5194/gmd-7-1247-2014

Chander, R. (1999). Can dams and reservoirs cause earthquakes? *Resonance, 4*(11), 4–13. doi:10.1007/BF02837323

Dao, D. V., Adeli, H., Ly, H.-B., Le, L. M., Le, V. M., Le, T.-T., & Pham, B. T. (2020). A sensitivity and robustness analysis of GPR and ANN for high-performance concrete compressive strength prediction using a monte carlo simulation. *Sustainability, 12*(3), 830. https://doi.org/10.3390/su12030830

Das, S., Samui, P., Khan, S., & Sivakugan, N. (2011). Machine learning techniques applied to prediction of residual strength of clay. *Open Geosciences, 3*(4). doi:10.2478/s13533-011-0043-1

Dong, L., & Shan, J. (2013). A comprehensive review of earthquake-induced building damage detection with remote sensing techniques. *ISPRS Journal of Photogrammetry and Remote Sensing, 84*, 85–99. https://doi.org/10.1016/j.isprsjprs.2013.06.011

Draper, N. R., & Smith, H. (1998). *Applied regression analysis* (3rd ed.). Wiley.

Dunjko, V., & Briegel, H. J. (2018). Machine learning & artificial intelligence in the quantum domain: A review of recent progress. *Reports on Progress in Physics, 81*(7), 074001. https://doi.org/10.1088/1361-6633/aab406

Fidani, C. (2010). The earthquake lights (EQL) of the 6 April 2009 Aquila earthquake, in Central Italy. *Natural Hazards and Earth System Sciences, 10*(5), 967–978. https://doi.org/10.5194/nhess-10-967-2010

Geoscience News and Information. (2021). *Plate Tectonics Map—Plate Boundary Map*. Geology.com. https://geology.com/plate-tectonics.shtml

Ghaedi, M., & Rahimi, M. reza, Ghaedi, A. M., Tyagi, I., Agarwal, S., & Gupta, V. K. (2016). Application of least squares support vector regression and linear multiple regression for modeling removal of methyl orange onto tin oxide nanoparticles loaded on activated carbon and activated carbon prepared from Pistacia atlantica wood. *Journal of Colloid and Interface Science, 461*, 425–434. doi:10.1016/j.jcis.2015.09.024

Ghahramani, Z. (2004). Unsupervised learning. In O. Bousquet, U. von Luxburg, & G. Rätsch (Eds.), *Advanced Lectures on Machine Learning: ML Summer Schools 2003*, (pp. 72–112). Springer. doi:10.1007/978-3-540-28650-9_5

Gribbin, J. (1971). Relation of sunspot and earthquake activity. *Science, 173*(3996), 558–558. https://doi.org/10.1126/science.173.3996.558.b

Hainzl, S., Kraft, T., Wassermann, J., Igel, H., & Schmedes, E. (2006). Evidence for rainfall-triggered earthquake activity. *Geophysical Research Letters, 33*(19), L19303. https://doi.org/10.1029/2006GL027642

Han, Y. (2004). Possible triggering of solar activity to big earthquakes (Ms>8) in faults with near west-east strike in China. *Science in China Series G, 47*(2), 173. doi:10.1360/03yw0103

Hochreiter, S., & Schmidhuber, J. (1997). Long short-term memory. *Neural Computation, 9*(8), 1735–1780. https://doi.org/10.1162/neco.1997.9.8.1735

Hothorn, T., Hornik, K., & Zeileis, A. (2006). Unbiased recursive partitioning: A conditional inference framework. *Journal of Computational and Graphical Statistics, 15*(3), 651–674. https://doi.org/10.1198/106186006X133933

Jacobs, J. P. (2012). Bayesian support vector regression with automatic relevance determination kernel for modeling of antenna input characteristics. *IEEE Transactions on Antennas and Propagation, 60*(4), 2114–2118. https://doi.org/10.1109/TAP.2012.2186252

Kanamori, H., & Brodsky, E. E. (2004). The physics of earthquakes. *Reports on Progress in Physics, 67*(8), 1429–1496. https://doi.org/10.1088/0034-4885/67/8/R03

Kaplan, A., & Haenlein, M. (2019). Siri, Siri, in my hand: Who's the fairest in the land? On the interpretations, illustrations, and implications of artificial intelligence. *Business Horizons, 62*(1), 15–25. https://doi.org/10.1016/j.bushor.2018.08.004

Keras. (2021). *Keras: The Python deep learning API*. Keras.https://keras.io/

Kononenko, I., & Kukar, M. (2007). *Machine learning and data mining: Introduction to principles and algorithms*. Horwood Publishing.

Koskinen, H., Tanskanen, E., Pirjola, R., Pulkkinen, A., Dyer, C., Rodgers, D., Cannon, P., Mandeville, J.-C., & Boscher, D. (2001). Space weather effects catalogue. *ESA Space Weather Study, 2*, 11–21.

Kotsiantis, S. B. (2007). Supervised machine learning: A review of classification techniques. In I. G. Maglogiannis (Ed.), *Emerging artificial intelligence applications in computer engineering: Real word AI systems with applications in eHealth, HCI, information retrieval and pervasive technologies* (pp. 3–24). IOS Press.

Li, Y., Liu, Y., Jiang, Z., Guan, J., Yi, G., Cheng, S., Yang, B., Fu, T., & Wang, Z. (2009). Behavioral change related to Wenchuan devastating earthquake in mice. *Bioelectromagnetics*, *30*(8), 613–620. https://doi.org/10.1002/bem.20520

Loutas, T. H., Roulias, D., & Georgoulas, G. (2013). Remaining useful life estimation in rolling bearings utilizing data-driven probabilistic e-support vectors regression. *IEEE Transactions on Reliability*, *62*(4), 821–832. https://doi.org/10.1109/TR.2013.2285318

Love, J. J., & Thomas, J. N. (2013). Insignificant solar-terrestrial triggering of earthquakes: INSIGNIFI-CANT TRIGGERING. *Geophysical Research Letters*, *40*(6), 1165–1170. https://doi.org/10.1002/grl.50211

Mallouhy, R., Jaoude, C. A., Guyeux, C., & Makhoul, A. (2019). Major earthquake event prediction using various machine learning algorithms. *2019 International Conference on Information and Communication Technologies for Disaster Management (ICT-DM)*, 1–7. doi:10.1109/ICT-DM47966.2019.9032983

Mangalathu, S., Sun, H., Nweke, C. C., Yi, Z., & Burton, H. V. (2020). Classifying earthquake damage to buildings using machine learning. *Earthquake Spectra*, *36*(1), 183–208. https://doi.org/10.1177/8755293019878137

Marchitelli, V., Harabaglia, P., Troise, C., & De Natale, G. (2020). On the correlation between solar activity and large earthquakes worldwide. *Scientific Reports*, *10*(1), 11495. https://doi.org/10.1038/s41598-020-67860-3

McNutt, S. R., & Roman, D. C. (2015). Volcanic seismicity. In The Encyclopedia of Volcanoes (pp. 1011–1034). Elsevier. https://doi.org/10.1016/B978-0-12-385938-9.00059-6.

Métivier, L., de Viron, O., Conrad, C. P., Renault, S., Diament, M., & Patau, G. (2009). Evidence of earthquake triggering by the solid earth tides. *Earth and Planetary Science Letters*, *278*(3), 370–375. https://doi.org/10.1016/j.epsl.2008.12.024

Meyer-Vernet, N. (2012). *Basics of the solar wind*. Cambridge University Press. https://www.vlebooks.com/vleweb/product/openreader?id=none&isbn=9780511535765

Mohamed, A. E. (2017).. . *Comparative Study of Four Supervised Machine Learning Techniques for Classification.*, *7*(2), 14.

Muhamedyev, R. (2015). Machine learning methods: An overview. *CMNT*, *19*, 14–29.

Müller, A. C., & Guido, S. (2016). *Introduction to machine learning with Python: A guide for data scientists* (1st ed.). O'Reilly Media, Inc.

Murwantara, I. M., Yugopuspito, P., & Hermawan, R. (2020). Comparison of machine learning performance for earthquake prediction in Indonesia using 30 years historical data. *TELKOMNIKA (Telecommunication Computing Electronics and Control)*, *18*(3), 1331. doi:10.12928/telkomnika.v18i3.14756

NASA. (2014). *NASA/Marshall solar physics*. NASA. https://solarscience.msfc.nasa.gov/

NASA. (2021). *SPDF - OMNIWeb Service*. NASA. https://omniweb.gsfc.nasa.gov/

National Flood Relief Commission. (1933). *Report Of The National Flood Relief Commission 1931 1932*. The Comacrib Press. https://archive.org/details/reportofthenatio032042mbp

National Geophysical Data Center / World Data Service (NGDC/WDS). (1972). *NCEI/WDS Global Significant Earthquake Database* [Data set]. NOAA National Centers for Environmental Information. doi:10.7289/V5TD9V7K

NGDC. (2021). *Sunspot-numbers—Monthly*. NOAA. https://www.ngdc.noaa.gov/stp/space-weather/solar-data/solar -indices/sunspot-numbers/american/lists/list_aavso-arssn_mon thly.txt

Nguyen, Q. H., Ly, H.-B., Ho, L. S., Al-Ansari, N., Le, H. V., Tran, V. Q., Prakash, I., & Pham, B. T. (2021). Influence of data splitting on performance of machine learning models in prediction of shear strength of soil. *Mathematical Problems in Engineering, 2021*, 1–15. https://doi.org/10.1155/2021/4832864

Nishii, R., Qin, P., & Kikuyama, R. (2020). Solar activity is one of triggers of earthquakes with magnitudes less than 6. *IGARSS 2020 - 2020 IEEE International Geoscience and Remote Sensing Symposium*, (pp. 377–380). IEEE. https://doi.org/10.1109/IGARSS39084.2020.9323381

Nishimura, T. (2017). Triggering of volcanic eruptions by large earthquakes: Triggering of Volcanic Eruptions. *Geophysical Research Letters, 44*(15), 7750–7756. https://doi.org/10.1002/2017GL074579

Novianty, A., Machbub, C., Widiyantoro, S., Meilano, I., & Irawan, H. (2019). Tsunami potential identification based on seismic features using knn algorithm. *2019 IEEE 7th Conference on Systems, Process and Control (ICSPC)*, (pp. 155–160). IEEE. doi:10.1109/ICSPC47137.2019.9068095

Novikov, V., Ruzhin, Y., Sorokin, V., & Yaschenko, A. (2020). Space weather and earthquakes: Possible triggering of seismic activity by strong solar flares. *Annals of Geophysics, 63*(5), 13. https://doi.org/10.4401/ag-7975

Novikov, V. A., Okunev, V. I., Klyuchkin, V. N., Liu, J., Ruzhin, Y. Ya., & Shen, X. (2017). Electrical triggering of earthquakes: Results of laboratory experiments at spring-block models. *Earthquake Science, 30*(4), 167–172. doi:10.1007/s11589-017-0181-8

Odintsov, S., Boyarchuk, K., Georgieva, K., Kirov, B., & Atanasov, D. (2006). Long-period trends in global seismic and geomagnetic activity and their relation to solar activity. *Physics and Chemistry of the Earth Parts A/B/C, 31*(1–3), 88–93. https://doi.org/10.1016/j.pce.2005.03.004

Odintsov, S. D., Ivanov-Kholodnyi, G. S., & Georgieva, K. (2007). Solar activity and global seismicity of the earth. *Bulletin of the Russian Academy of Sciences. Physics, 71*(4), 593–595. https://doi.org/10.3103/S1062873807040466

OFDA/CRED (2021). *International Disaster Data*. Our World in Data. https://ourworldindata.org/ofdacred-international-disaster-d ata

Orihara, Y., Kamogawa, M., & Nagao, T. (2015). Preseismic Changes of the Level and Temperature of Confined Groundwater related to the 2011 Tohoku Earthquake. *Scientific Reports*, *4*(1), 6907. https://doi.org/10.1038/srep06907

Pedregosa, F., Varoquaux, G., Gramfort, A., Michel, V., Thirion, B., Grisel, O., Blondel, M., Prettenhofer, P., Weiss, R., Dubourg, V., Vanderplas, J., Passos, A., & Cournapeau, D. (2011). Scikit-learn: Machine Learning in Python. *MACHINE LEARNING IN PYTHON*, *6*.

Pham, B. T., Qi, C., Ho, L. S., Nguyen-Thoi, T., Al-Ansari, N., Nguyen, M. D., Nguyen, H. D., Ly, H.-B., Le, H. V., & Prakash, I. (2020). A novel hybrid soft computing model using Random Forest and particle swarm optimization for estimation of undrained shear strength of soil. *Sustainability*, *12*(6), 2218. https://doi.org/10.3390/su12062218

Potter, S. (2020, September 15). *Solar Cycle 25 Is Here. NASA, NOAA Scientists Explain What That Means* [Text]. NASA. https://www.nasa.gov/press-release/solar-cycle-25-is-here-nasa-noaa-scientists-explain-what-that-means

Priest, E. (2014). Magnetohydrodynamics of the sun. Cambridge University Press. https://doi.org/10.1017/CBO9781139020732.

Rácz, A., Bajusz, D., & Héberger, K. (2021). Effect of dataset size and train/test split ratios in qsar/qspr multiclass classification. *Molecules (Basel, Switzerland)*, *26*(4), 1111. https://doi.org/10.3390/molecules26041111

Raju, V. N. G., Lakshmi, K. P., Jain, V. M., Kalidindi, A., & Padma, V. (2020). Study the influence of normalization/transformation process on the accuracy of supervised classification. *2020 Third International Conference on Smart Systems and Inventive Technology (ICSSIT)*, (pp. 729–735). IEEE. doi:10.1109/ICSSIT48917.2020.9214160

Reddy, G. T., Reddy, M. P. K., Lakshmanna, K., Kaluri, R., Rajput, D. S., Srivastava, G., & Baker, T. (2020). Analysis of dimensionality reduction techniques on big data. *IEEE Access: Practical Innovations, Open Solutions*, *8*, 54776–54788. https://doi.org/10.1109/ACCESS.2020.2980942

Redmayne, D. W. (1988). Mining induced seismicity in UK coalfields identified on the BGS National Seismograph Network. *Geological Society, London, Engineering Geology Special Publications*, *5*(1), 405–413. doi:10.1144/GSL.ENG.1988.005.01.45

Reinse, D., Gantz, J., & Rydning, J. (2018). *The Digitization of the World From Edge to Core* (#US44413318). Seagate IDC. https://www.seagate.com/files/www-content/our-story/trends/files/idc-seagate-dataage-whitepaper.pdf

Samuel, A. L. (1959). Some studies in machine learning using the game of checkers. *IBM Journal of Research and Development*, *3*(3), 210–229. https://doi.org/10.1147/rd.33.0210

Schorlemmer, D., Werner, M. J., Marzocchi, W., Jordan, T. H., Ogata, Y., Jackson, D. D., Mak, S., Rhoades, D. A., Gerstenberger, M. C., Hirata, N., Liukis, M., Maechling, P. J., Strader, A., Taroni, M., Wiemer, S., Zechar, J. D., & Zhuang, J. (2018). The collaboratory for the study of earthquake predictability: Achievements and priorities. *Seismological Research Letters*, *89*(4), 1305–1313. https://doi.org/10.1785/0220180053

SciKit. (2021). *Supervised learning—Scikit-learn 0.24.2 documentation*. SciKit Learn. https://scikit-learn.org/stable/supervised_learning.html

SciKit. (2021). *Unsupervised learning—Scikit-learn 0.24.2 documentation*. SciKit Learn. https://scikit-learn.org/stable/unsupervised_learning.html

SILSO. (2021). World Data Center for the production, preservation and dissemination of the international sunspot number. https://wwwbis.sidc.be/silso/home

Singh, S., Kumar, A., Bajwa, B. S., Mahajan, S., Kumar, V., & Dhar, S. (2010). Radon monitoring in soil gas and ground water for earthquake prediction studies in north west himalayas, india. *Diqiu Kexue Jikan*, *21*(4), 685. https://doi.org/10.3319/TAO.2009.07.17.01(TT)

Smola, A. J., & Schölkopf, B. (2004). A tutorial on support vector regression. *Statistics and Computing*, *14*(3), 199–222. https://doi.org/10.1023/B:STCO.0000035301.49549.88

Space Weather Prediction Center. (2021). *ACE real-time solar wind | NOAA / NWS space weather prediction center*. Space Weather Prediction Center. https://www.swpc.noaa.gov/products/ace-real-time-solar-wind

Spiess, A.-N., & Neumeyer, N. (2010). An evaluation of R2 as an inadequate measure for nonlinear models in pharmacological and biochemical research: A Monte Carlo approach. *BMC Pharmacology*, *10*(1), 6. https://doi.org/10.1186/1471-2210-10-6

Storchak, D. A., Di Giacomo, D., Bondar, I., Engdahl, E. R., Harris, J., Lee, W. H. K., Villasenor, A., & Bormann, P. (2013). Public release of the isc-gem global instrumental earthquake catalogue(1900-2009). *Seismological Research Letters*, *84*(5), 810–815. https://doi.org/10.1785/0220130034

Sutton, R. S., & Barto, A. G. (2018). *Reinforcement learning: An introduction* (2nd ed.). The MIT Press.

Sytinskii, A. D. (1973). Relation between seismic activity of the earth and solar activity. *Uspekhi Fizicheskih Nauk*, *111*(10), 367. doi:10.3367/UFNr.0111.197310i.0367

Thorndike, E. L. (2000). *Animal intelligence: Experimental studies*. Transaction Publishers.

Tian, D., Yao, J., & Wen, L. (2018). Collapse and earthquake swarm after North Korea's 3 September 2017 nuclear test. *Geophysical Research Letters*, *45*(9), 3976–3983. https://doi.org/10.1029/2018GL077649

USGS. (2021). *Usgs earthquake hazards program*. USGS. https://earthquake.usgs.gov/

Verdhan, V., & Kling, E. Y. (2020). *Supervised learning with Python: Concepts and practical implementation using Python*. Apress.

Willmott, C., & Matsuura, K. (2005). Advantages of the mean absolute error (MAE) over the root mean square error (RMSE) in assessing average model performance. *Climate Research*, *30*, 79–82. https://doi.org/10.3354/cr030079

Wirasinghe, S. C., Caldera, H. J., Durage, S. W., & Ruwanpura, J. (2013). *Preliminary Analysis and Classification of Natural Disasters*. doi:10.13140/RG.2.1.4283.5041

Witten, I. H., & Frank, E. (2017). *Data mining practical machine learning tools and techniques*. Elsevier Science & Technology Books.

Wolf, R. (1853). On the periodic return of the minimum of sun-sport; the agreement between those periods and the variations of magnetic declination. *The London, Edinburgh and Dublin Philosophical Magazine and Journal of Science, 5*(29), 67–67. https://doi.org/10.1080/14786445308646906

Wood, B., Howard, R., Thernisien, A., & Socker, D. (2009). The three-dimensional morphology of a corotating interaction region in the inner heliosphere. *The Astrophysical Journal. Letters, 708*, L89. https://doi.org/10.1088/2041-8205/708/2/L89

Yamauchi, H., Hayakawa, M., Asano, T., Ohtani, N., & Ohta, M. (2017). Statistical Evaluations of Variations in Dairy Cows' Milk Yields as a Precursor of Earthquakes. *Animals (Basel), 7*(12), 19. https://doi.org/10.3390/ani7030019

Yuan, S., Luo, X., Mu, B., Li, J., & Dai, G. (2019). Prediction of north atlantic oscillation index with convolutional LSTM based on ensemble empirical mode decomposition. *Atmosphere, 10*(5), 252. https://doi.org/10.3390/atmos10050252

Zhang, Q., Wang, H., Dong, J., Zhong, G., & Sun, X. (2017). Prediction of sea surface temperature using long short-term memory. *IEEE Geoscience and Remote Sensing Letters, 14*(10), 1745–1749. https://doi.org/10.1109/LGRS.2017.2733548

KEY TERMS AND DEFINITIONS

Algorithm: A step-by-step procedure for solving a problem.

Dimension Reduction: The process of reducing the number of traits, variables, and characteristics.

Earthquake: Event shaking the Earth's surface.

Earthquake Depth: Indicates where an earthquake can occur between the Earth's surface and 700 kilometres below the surface.

Earthquake Magnitude: The measure of the size of an earthquake source.

Evaluation Metrics: Determine how accurate a prediction is.

Machine Learning: A system that can learn from the data.

Neural Networks: Network of neurons to solve problems.

Solar Activity: Sunspot, solar flares, and solar wind the example of solar activity.

Solar Cycles: The magnetic field, generated by the sun, reverses and the north and south poles of the sun switch position.

Solar Flare: An explosion of energy also accompanied by coronal mass ejection.

Solar Wind: "Not uniform" stream of charged participles, that flows from the Sun in all possible directions.

Sunspot Number: Calculation of sunspots to measure the state of the solar cycle.

Sunspots: A dark area which appears on the Sun's surface.

Supervised Learning: The relationship between inputs and their outputs that allows to make a future prediction, uses labelled data.

Chapter 12
Convergence of Blockchain to Artificial Intelligence Applications

Suja A. Alex

ⓘD https://orcid.org/0000-0003-4429-6715

St. Xavier's Catholic College of Engineering, India

B. Gerald Briyolan

St. Xavier's Catholic College of Engineering, India

ABSTRACT

In the era of modern technology, blockchain is out of harm's way in making proceedings ample of its reliability trademark, and chiefly for its immutability, and it doesn't hang on any mediator network while any transaction happens. The use of this technology helped solve many problems in society by detecting the problem which happens in the industry sphere, similarly trust, unambiguously, security, and reliability of statistics processing. The objective of the article is to review the blockchain technologies with the focus of reviewing blockchain in artificial intelligence (AI) applications. With the exception of cryptocurrency, blockchain technology can also avail oneself of financial and social services and healthcare facilities, which is risk-free.

INTRODUCTION

Blockchain is a system in which a curriculum vitae of proceedings that are made in Bitcoin, Ethereum, or other cryptocurrencies are maintained across multitudinous computers that are bracketed in a peer-to-peer network. Blockchain technology is the fastest-growing network in the field of digitalizing sector, due to its purveying of secure data and sharing services with detectability, non-repudiation, and well established than other platforms. The blockchain method has undergone various changes in operational management, identifying impuissant codes, poor ascendable, and the detection of evil-intentioned be-

DOI: 10.4018/978-1-6684-6937-8.ch012

havior in the system of blockchain data. Blockchain is earning ample attention due to its reliability and dispersed resource-sharing manner.

The modern development of Artificial Intelligence has played a major role in the burgeoning of blockchain technology (Dinh & Thai, 2018). Now, these technologies are used for business, banking, and so on. Blockchain and AI tend to adequately through which affiliates both the innovative systems (Panarello et al., 2018; Marwala & Xing, 2018). Blockchain technology is one of the secure methods for protecting data, in which there is no single point of failure. Hacking into one part of the system won't affect the other parts of the system, because one of the particular data is stored in many systems. As a result, proactive and autonomic actions can be made to prevent blockchain from disruptive or illicit actions. Blockchain is entirely a chain-like data structure, in which proceedings are verified by a majority of vertex throughout the entire network (Landa, 1994).

Blockchain works with the peer-to-peer transfer of digital assets without intermediates (Aste et al., 2017). The focus of this blockchain technology is to safeguard and prop up the cryptocurrency (Bitcoin). Bitcoin was organized in the year 2008. Then in January 2009, Satoshi Nakamoto implemented the bitcoin software as open-source code. On 3rd January 2002, the bitcoin network was created when Satoshi Nakamoto mined the starting block of the chain, known as the genesis block (Wolff-Mann, 2018). In recent times the world is only looking around the global businesses, the finance sectors, and many sectors are trying to implement their business in their start-ups without depending on other third parties for their privacy contents. As Alcazar (2017) perceived, "Blockchain as a technology continues to evolve, yielding new types and potential uses" (Alcazar 2017), and now the refinement in the technology is not long ago leading the construction sector too (Ramage, 2018). A blockchain is a chain of blocks that stores all the transactions that are made, using a public ledger (Salah et al., 2019). These chains grow rapidly when new blocks conjoin them. Blockchain works in a decentralized environment that is enabled by legion core technologies, such as cryptographic hash, digital signatures, encrypted documents, and distributed consensus algorithms. Every transaction is monitored in a decentralized manner that demands the requirements for any intermediates to validate and verify the transactions if the transaction arises any queries (Litke et al., 2019).

Blockchain has smattering key characteristics, to the same degree as decentralization, unambiguously, immutability, and audibility (Kouhizadeh & Sarkis, 2018). Blockchain is mostly pre-owned in the application of bitcoin. There is some other software that uses this technology to protect their data and the data that are provided by the individuals. Afterward, it sanctions payments to be finalized without any interrupts from the bank or any intermediates, blockchain technology can be utilized in various financial sectors, such as online payments, proceedings, and digital assets (Peters et al.,2015). Blockchain is a praised innovative technology in which a large number of data can be maintained privately. This reputation is attributed to its worldly goods of accessing mutually mistrusting entities to exchange financial statistics and interact without relying on any trusted third parties or other unauthorized third parties. A blockchain provides integrity-protected data storage and allows it to provide processes unambiguously without any involvement of other sites and securities (Wood, 2014). Due to these properties blockchain technology is adopted by many other countries all over the world to maintain their transactions privacy and the data are maintained in cloud storage, smart property, Internet of Things (IoT), supply chain management, healthcare, ownership, and royalty distribution, and decentralized autonomous organizations just to name a few among them (Brown, 2016).

At this moment in time, blockchain has been universally perturbed, but there is no ensign definition for it. Howbeit there are certain theories and indagating that are prospering rapidly. Melanie Swan pointed out that the "blockchain: is the blueprint for a new economy". Blockchain is an open, unambiguous, and decentralized database (Swan, 2015). Harald then advertises that blockchain is a technical solution for overall maintaining a reliable database by decentralizing and distrusting (Vranken, 2017). "China Blockchain Technology and its Application Development White paper (2016)" by the Ministry of Industry and Statistics Technology of China narrates the conceptualization of blockchain. Blockchain technology is the new application model of computer technology such as distributed data storage, point-to-point proceedings, consensus mechanisms, and encryption algorithms (Ping et al., 2016). Yan et al., Yuan, and Wang proposed a definition: "Blockchain technology is a new trademark of infrastructure and computing paradigm" (Yan et al., 2017; Wang et al., 2018). Relying upon the time-stamped "block and chain" data structure, this technology is used to allocate node consensus algorithms to add and renovate the data, there is a method that is used to secure data transference and access, and smart contracts made up of automated script code to program and manipulates the date is the cryptographic method (Yan et al., 2017).

A Blockchain is a type of invoice of digital guidance like events, proceedings, and curriculum vitae data that chiefly required a type of security in which this statistic is maintained privately in the digital security and is certified and nourished by the entrant using a cluster of consensus convention all over the decentralized network that tends to be involved in the treaty (Sorrell, 2016). The name of blockchain is derived from its string of statistics, where at the interval schedules, each piece of statistics of any proceeding will be stored or documentation as a 'block' and it is annexed as a 'chain' that builds up an unbribable ledger of 'blockchain' in the digitalized world. Blockchain was the finance sector's first decentralized proceeding and data management technology (Ramage, 2018).

Cybersecurity is a traditional technology to Blockchain technology because the data is stored in a centralized fashion rather than decentralized fashion (Demirkan et al., 2020). Cybersecurity is necessary to any organization such as Banking, Hospital, Education Department, Space Research because the data needs to be protected from the attackers. Internet of Things (IoT) is another evolving technology that works with blockchain technology to promote promising solutions (Daim et al., 2020).

BACKGROUND

The block is an assembly of data containing kindred statistics and curriculum vitae, and it is the rudiment factor of the blockchain (Zhang et al., 2016). The data structure of the blockchain is chiefly tranquil of a block header and a block body (Wu et al., 2018). The block header chiefly contains the hash value of the erstwhile block, which is used to fetter the erstwhile block to ensure the integrity of the blockchain, the block of the body accommodates many important statistics about the block such as proceedings done by the user. These statistics all together with the hash value of the preceding block and the random number together incarnations a hashed hash value of the block which is obtained now. The data transfer embraces the sender and recipient pinpointing, the proceeding amount, time, and other supplementary data accumulated from the user to permit a safe proceeding. In the computation of these data, each data contains a block ID, timestamp, interlinked between the blocks, and so on. Then the blocks are interconnected into a chain that holds all the historical data of the proceeding throughout the entire network. When the user once authenticates and added to the chain, they cannot be replicated or disavowal, and it is hard to be tampered with, thus it ensures the unambiguously and reliability of the entire database throughout the blockchain technology (Yang, 2017). The composition of the blockchain is shown in Fig. 1.

Figure 1. Composition of Blockchain

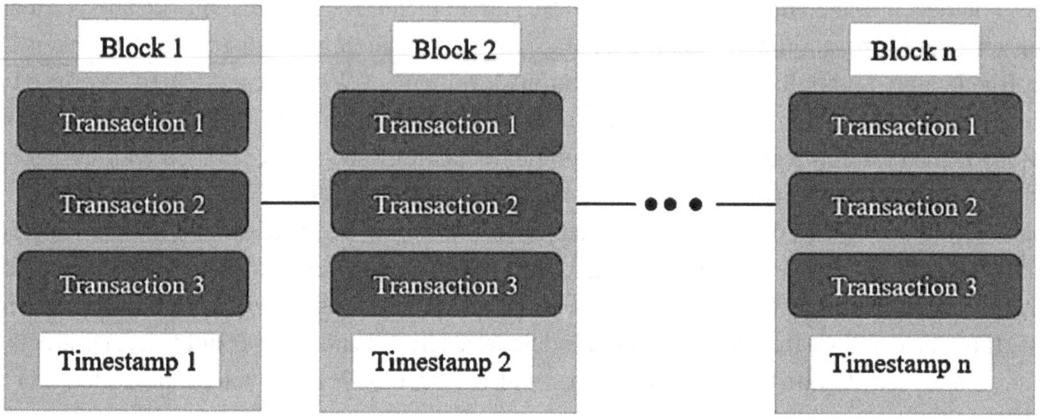

ARCHITECTURE OF BLOCKCHAIN

The Technology architecture of blockchain is made up of a data layer, a network layer, a consensus layer, a contract layer, an incentive layer, and an application layer (Yan et al., 2017). The underlying data blocks, timestamps, and every single one of the proceeding data and statistics curriculum vitae are stored in the data layer in the incarnation of a blockchain. The network layer included the practicality of peer-to-peer network topology also known as point-to-point transmission topology, verification mechanisms, and propagation mechanisms. It finalizes the consensus algorithm, data storage, encrypted signatures, and a lot more to substantiate. The consensus layer chiefly suppresses the consensus mechanism, which permits the nodes to stick out with the consensus on the blocks of data which is efficient in the decentralized system where the determination power is highly decentralized within the layer. Next, there is an Incentive layer that integrates economic factors within blockchain technology, which comprises chiefly the issuance mechanisms and the distribution mechanism of economic incentives. The premier occasion of these incentives is to captivate partakers to bestow computing power. Then the contact layer precis innumerable script codes, algorithmic mechanisms, and smart exposure. Its exposition synchronizes and auditable contract specifications (Aggarwal & Kumar, 2021). Table 1 shows the properties of different consensus Algorithms.

Table 1. Comparison among Different Consensus Algorithms

Property	PoW	PoS	PFBT	DPoS	Tendermint
Identity Management of Node	Open	Open	Permissioned	Open	Permissioned
Energy Consumption	High	Low	Very Low	Very Low	Very Low
Adversary Tolerance	£ 25%	< 51%	£ 33.3%	< 51%	£ 33.3%
Performance (Transaction per second)	< 20	< 20	< 1000	< 500	< 10000
Forking	While two nodes identify the suitable nonce at the same time	Very Difficult	Probability	Consistent if less than one-third of nodes are byzantine	Highly unlikely
Consensus confirmation time	High	High	Low	Medium	Low
Scalability	Strong	Strong	Weak	Strong	Strong
Block creation Speed	Fast	Fast	Fast	Depends on variant	Fast
Example	Bitcoin (BTC), Ethereum (ETH)	Peercoin (PPC), Nextcoin (NXT)	Hyperledger Fabric	Bitshares	Tendermint

Advantages of Blockchain Technology

Blockchain technology uses a decentralized system and there are many benefits to a particular company after implementing this technology in their sectors. Without any interruption of the mediator organization or any central administrator, it is not requisite that a company needs these when they are transferring a payment. This implements that a system can implement without any intermediary and all the partakers of this Blockchain can make the decision. There are many systems, each system has a particular database to store data, and one piece of data is stored in all the systems which are immutable and can't be encrypted by an anonymous user. If not, there is protection needed for the database, because when the system works with any unbiased observer organizations there might be a chance of hackers encrypting the database or the data might be misused when it gets into the wrong hands. It can be avoided by using blockchain technology since it has its proof of validity and authorization to enforce the constraints (Bahga & Madisetti, 2016; Fauvel, 2017). The two popular proofs are Proof of Work (PoW) for Ethereum Blockchain and Proof of Stake (PoS) for the Bitcoin network. The convenience of using blockchain is every action that is done is documentation and the data of documentation are available to all the participants of the blockchain process and that can't be edited or expunged. The unambiguously of the blockchain is achieved by the documentation and immutability and it is trusted completely (Bahga & Madisetti, 2016; Bahga & Madisetti, 2014).

There are two or more participants, who don't even know each other, in which the trust in the blockchain is at the top level of the technology. There are more split processes and documentation of the proceeding between unknown participants. In the future, the trust bond between the participants might increase (Fauvel, 2017; Songara & Chouhan, 2017) The proceedings are agreed upon and done under the blockchain technology at a place the immutable is achieved. That also depends on the system's kind if the system is centralized, such as the blockchain. This benefit makes the technology of blockchain unalterable and indestructible. All the users of the blockchain have empowers to have control of all the proceedings and access the particular statistics. To change or delete the statistics into the blockchain is possible when the intruder has the fantastic computing power to be able to overwrite or delete the statistics on all the computers. This also includes the blockchain before the next block which is documentation there. Blockchain consists of a small number of computers, in which the technology is more exposed to being attacked by anonymous users. If there are a lot of computers in the blockchain then the system becomes safer and safer and it becomes more unambiguous to the user (Bahga & Madisetti, 2016; Fauvel, 2017; Bahga & Madisetti, 2014; Songara & Chouhan, 2017). The research on diabetic prediction using deep learning helps the diabetic patients to know the impact of disease earlier (Alex et al., 2022). However, the security to this diabetic data storage is a great concern to the organization Blockchain is currently prevalent in cloud-based diabetic data storage (Liu et al., 2021).

Types of Blockchain

The development in blockchain technology can be split up into three categories:

- Blockchain 1.0 - This is characterized by the digital currency system in which Bitcoin is in its initial state.
- Blockchain 2.0 - It maintains the main financial sector system as the main feature. Which contain smart contacts which are emerged during Blockchain 2.0, and the other type of assets were converted through smart contacts, which prop up with the blockchain application which is beyond the currency sector.
- Blockchain 3.0 - It is mostly characterized by a programmable society. This is based on the existing infrastructures such as the Internet and mobile communication, this utilization of blockchain is gradually extended to all aspects of society and for the life of an individual, such as in science, education, culture, and other sectors (Peters & Panayi, 2016; Swan 2015).

All over the world, all countries are paying more consciousness to the development of blockchain technology. The blockchain market size is awaited to rise from USD 241.9 Million in 2016 to USD 7683.7 Million by 2022, at a compound annual growth rate of 79.6%. The business of this type of supplier includes payments, documentation, exchanges, and other programs designed to increase the efficiency of business operations. The world is being developed day by day and countries have begun to explore industrial applications in many areas, such as digital currency, trading securities, cross-border payment, identification, academic certification, a donation to society, etc. in a global scale, there is no new mature blockchain application have emerged except the Bitcoin. China is at the same level as the world in the usage of bitcoin. Next, the US Nasdaq took the lead in instigating the blockchain technology-based securities trading platform Linq in the year 2019 December, which has become a supreme milestone in the decentralization trend of financial and securities markets. Is based on the Blockchain as a service which is launched by a company Azure which is a Microsoft cloud service platform, and startup R3 CEV which has signed a blockchain cooperation outline with over 40 major major banking institutions including HSBC, Goldman Sachs, and Citibank, and it is dedicated to the developing of the banking industry which has standards and certain protocols which are applicable for everyone. The Canadian ATB Financial Banking has successfully used blockchain technology to send 1000 Canadian dollars to Germany in the '20s, In the traditional payment methods which generally take more than two working days to finish the job (Wu & Tran, 2018). Alipay cooperated with the Charity Foundation that is to set up the first blockchain-based public welfare project on its love donation platform, which can technically protect the authenticity of public interest data and save on the cost of statistics disclosure.

According to the research done by Lei and Gang, they provided a conceptualization that the block-chain falls into the category of three (Aggarwal & Kumar, 2021):

- Public blockchain
- Consortium blockchain or Federated blockchain
- Private blockchain

In recent times, Bitcoin (BT) and Ethereum (ETH) fall under the category of the public blockchain. In the consortium blockchain, Blockchain Alliance R3 and Hyperledger fall under it. Next, the while Coin Science and Eris Industries come under the category of a private blockchain, which servicer the company that depends upon blockchain technology (Sun et al., 2017; Zheng et al., 2017). Table 2 shows the comparative study on different types of blockchain in terms of openness, writability, readability, anonymity, transaction speed, and decentralization (Yang et al., 2017; Cai et al., 2017; OuYang et al., 2017).

Table 2. Comparison of Types of Blockchain

Items	Public Blockchain	Consortium Blockchain	Private Blockchain
Openness	Completely open	Open to specific organizations and groups	Open to an individual or an entity
Writability	Anybody	Specified multiple nodes	Completely internal control
Readability	Anybody	Anybody	Open to the public / be restricted by any degree
Anonymity	High	Low	Low
Transaction speed	Low	Fast	Extremely fast
Decentralized	Fully distributed	Partial decentralization	Partial decentralization

Blockchain Applications

Blockchain technology can be used in manifold sets of applications. It is important to recognize that bitcoin is not the one that depends on blockchain technology, instead, it is one of the most successful applications of blockchain technology. Some other sectors use this type of technology to protect the data from unauthorized factors (Crosby, 2016). Bitcoin is a type of cryptographic digital currency. Bitcoin is a proceeding that uses an open, public, and anonymous blockchain network. Despite that, the virtuoso claim that this technology can be accomplished for finding solutions for different domains, such as healthcare, identify management, voting, governance, supply chain, energy, resources, and so on. Some predictions might fall under this technology depending on the future development in the domain, that might influence the digital realm similar to the internet. Now, we are currently in the early stage of the blockchain and there is much more to be unlocked, and that might be used in all sectors, thus there might be secure transactions (Twesige, 2015).

Healthcare

Blockchain technology also serves in the field of health services to ensure medical data verification (McGhin, 2019). This technology can influence the traceability of drug content and the patient's data management. Some types of drugs can be counterfeited and that is a major trouble in the pharmaceutical industry. There is an organization named Health Research Funding Organization that revealed that there are 10% to 30% of the drugs sold in developing countries are counterfeited (Glass, 2014). 16% of counterfeit drug contains wrong ingredients which are very harmful to human health, while the other 17% contain an imprecise level of essential ingredients, as estimated by the World Health Organization (WHO). When the patient intake these drugs, that might lead to the patient's life in danger as these drugs won't have to ability to cure a certain disease, rather it triggers secondary effects on the body which might lead to death. In the view of the economy of drugs, counterfeiting is responsible for an annual fall of about 10.2 billion euros for European pharmaceutical organizations. So, this problem is analyzed with the help of blockchain technology, which provides a better solution because all the transactions are included in the distributed ledger which is immutable and digitally timestamped, which makes it attainable to detect the product and also gather statistics from tamper-proof to verify the exact amount.

In healthcare domain, the database maintains the patient's personal details with identity information. The risk arises when the attackers penetrate the healthcare database to steal patient information. Cybersecurity provides several solutions to treat different attacks on patient databases (Kaddoura et al., 2021). The data integrity of a particular patient is one of the major concerns for the healthcare industry (Azaria et al., 2016). Every patient has unique data, their treatment also is varied from one person to other if they are affected by the same disease too. So, it is very necessary to access every patient a complete medical history for their disease. There is a lack of privacy in the auditing of medical documentation. Right now, blockchain can offer a framework for the integration of medical documentation among miscellaneous healthcare facilities as well as data integrity features through its unyielding ledger technology.

Blockchain technology ensures data management ability to an organization for storing patient data for period of time and provides access rights on the data (Kaddoura & Grati 2021). MedChain is a permissioned blockchain-based framework, which is built upon Hyperledger Fabric that provides all the documentation of the patients on their medical documentation (Shen et al., 2019). The rights are provided to the patients to access their health statistics to doctors or health care centers (Pilkington, 2017). Brain-Computer Interface technology also is popular in healthcare applications. Recent researches focus on integrating Brain Computer Interface (BCI) with IoT in order to develop smart healthcare products (Alex et al., 2021). Machine learning is an essential component of smart healthcare applications. It helps the patients to use wearable devices by providing risk prediction of diseases like Brain Stroke (Alex et al., 2022).

Energy Industry

In energy-related applications blockchain technology is used in the application of Microgrids. Which is a localized set of electric power sources and loads integrated and managed with the objective that enhancing energy production and consumption (Lasseter & Paigi, 2004). The energy power sources are distributed power generators, renewable energy stations, and energy storage components in facilities created and owned by different organizations as a share of the energy produced. The main superiority of microgrid technology is that it doesn't allow residents and other electric power patrons. They also set off and get rid of the excess energy from the grid. Blockchain is used to ease, document, and validate the power of buying and selling transactions in microgrids (Cohn et al., 2016).

Correspondingly, blockchain is used at a large scale to enable energy trading in smart grids to avoid any unwanted problems. Blockchain props up with security and maintains privacy about consumption monitoring and energy trading without any need for a central intermediary (Aitzhan & Svetinovic, 2016). Smart contracts can be used to ensure the programmatic descriptions of anticipated power flexibility degrees, the validation and traceability of the demand response agreements, and the balance between power needs and generation. In the trade of energy, the technology of blockchain gets involved, in the Industrial Internet of Things (IIOT) (Li et al., 2017).

Stock Market

For a fragmented market system, blockchain props up a lot to solve the issues in the system of the data encrypted. Which includes trust, interoperability, and unambiguously which are more important in the system of markets (Lee, 2015). Anticipate the role of the intermediates in the managerial process and operational trade clearance, which consumes more than 72 hours to warm up the transactions. At the stock market participants traders, regulators, brokers, and the stock exchange are undergoing the process of cumbersome. Blockchain might provide a solution in the stock exchange and other exchanges like decentralization and automation (Tapscott & Tapscott, 2017). This is possible by eliminating the intermediates and speeding up the transaction settlements while easing the monotonous paperwork of the trade and legal ownership transfer along with the secured post-trade process.

Voting

Blockchain can avail oneself in various fields as a quick fix to the problems that a habitual database might have. Voting comes under this problem which can be solved by blockchain technology. There is a gossip that the majority of the U.S. voting machine manufacturer had consecrated remote access software on some of the voting machines. Using this type of software allows the alternation of votes when casting up the total of the vote. Specifically, that turns out a deficiency of assurance in the voting system of America. Blockchain technology would be a better solution for this issue by providing a distributed ledger that would ensure votes are counted since the ledger a voter owns is the same as the one counting the total.

Insurance

Blockchain will also support the markets of insurance which is the market in which the policy is taken by the clients, policyholders, and insurance companies. Blockchain can be implemented to haggle, buy, and register insurance policies, submit and process claims, also to support reinsurance policies that apply to the clients. Various insurance policies can be self-regulating using smart contracts, which will significantly bring down the supervisory cost associated with it (Gatteschi et al., 2018). Since there is a high administration cost associated with processing insurance claims. In many situations, the claims of the administration are a very formidable process due to differences of opinion and misinterpretations of the terms and conditions. Some smart contracts can evade these problems by structuring insurance policies. These policies assure the Self-acting of accomplishing the terms by the digital protocols that precisely implement the agreed-upon costs of execution. Insurance companies can also reduce the cost of their insurance products and be more competitive to attract more customers. At the same time, it also allows insurance companies to launch new automated insurance products for their clients without worrying too much about their administrative overhead and costs. In the bargain, blockchain sanctions insurance companies to be thickened globally.

Identity Management

In the world of reality and fantasy, personal identity can be verified by using identity documents such as a National ID card, Passport, and driver's license. Blockchain would withhold the approach to take on this serenity. This technology can be used to develop a platform to safeguard an individual's identity from pilfering or reduce fraudulent activities. Blockchain may allow individuals to develop an enciphered discerning. By using this technology, the user doesn't need any username or password while providing more reliable features and control over accessing their data. By comprising identity verification with that decentralized blockchain principle, a digital data ID can be generated. This ID will get ingress permission for every online transaction to identify and also avoid the possibility of chicanery by verifying the identity on real-time transactions. Blockchain technology can also be developed in apps for authentication for online payment access and can be verified by usernames, passwords, or biometric methods (Jacobovitz, 2016). There is a scheme which is proposed by Paul Dunphy et al. that identity management, unambiguously, and used control by leveraging distributed ledger technology (Dunphy & Petitcolas, 2018).

Trade Finance

Banks facilitate the trade finance process by letting a letter of credit as a payment settlement method, which has been not effective and also enables a lot of risks if mitigation (Harfield, 1982). That causes high complexity, very high cost, and delays in contracts, which doesn't account for less than one-fifth of international trade. With the increase in the cost and time for issuing a Letter of Credit (LC), it becomes less attractive to the trading parties which results in low-value transactions. This incident might disintermediate banks as well as there is a risk of open trade. Automating the LC with the potential of blockchain technology will provide reduced transaction costs and operational complexity. The model of blockchain technology can be placed in compliance with all specified conditions mentioned in LC which is between the client and the supplier, by which the buyers guarantee the payment once the trade merchandise is delivered. This might be the solution for mitigating the contractual ambiguities and discrepancies of the statistics that leads to reducing the time and cost of LC amendments in trading (Fridgen et al., 2018). Another survey provides an approximation of 80% of the respondents expressed concern regarding traditional trade finance. That might not see any growth or decline shortly.

Platforms for Blockchain

The blockchain based distributed applications (DApps) are developed using various platforms. After the requests, we can get ETH from these test networks. Metamask is one of the ways to enter any Blockchain. Ethereum blockchain network helps to develop DApps and evaluated using Hyperledger Caliper (Choi & Hong, 2021). Ropsten is one of the test networks that is similar to main network and it uses Proof-of-Work as a consensus protocol. The Ropsten takes time approximately from 8.25 seconds to 19.16 seconds to generate 12 blocks (Zhang et al., 2019). Kovan is another test network that consumes approximately 143 seconds to produce the same 12 blocks (Zhang et al., 2019). The consensus protocol Proof of Authority (PoA) is used in Kovan network. The geographic data is very important in the present situation, hence it is managed and stored using Internet of Things (IoT) (Tapas et al., 2020). It is implemented and tested in Ganache, which is a local test network and Rinkeby which is a public test network.

Blockchain With AI Applications

The information or the date to learn, get together, and settle on the official alternatives depends on the computer-based AI system. The calculations which have been done by the use of AI, which is more reliable when a piece of information is converged from information and stored which is dependable, secured, more valid, and it is trusted. Blockchain has broadcasting of records at which the information will be tomb and it is executed in such a manner where it is cryptographically marked, accepted, and conceded by all the mining hubs. The information which is gathered by blockchain technology is highly respectable and strong, and it cannot be modified. They make use of the luminous agreements for the establishment of the AI calculations and also to settle on the way out and also to mount an examination, and thus the results are obtained of these alternatives which are undisputed and have confidence in. Thus, the union between Blockchain and AI will provide a secure, changeless, decentralized framework for the profoundly elegant data that AI-driven frameworks collect, store, and use (Marwala & Xing, 2018). This concept brought up the significant upgrades and also to make sure about the information, which is gathered and data in various areas, which includes clinical, individual, banking, exchanges, legitimate information, and pecuniary. The accessibility of the numerous blockchain stages provides a profit in the use of the AI which leads to the execution of the calculations and the information that is put away on the decentralized P2P stock-piling frameworks. An assortment of sources is incorporated which are regularly started by the brilliant associated items to the information provided. The highlights and administrations of the cloud can be likewise bridled for off-chain AI examination and expert dynamic, and information representations (Strobel et al., 2018). The importance of utilizing blockchain for AI is summarized and denoted in the points below.

- **Aggregate Decision-Making:** In the system of mechanical, all the specialists anticipate working in coordination to accomplish multiple objectives (Strobel et al., 2018). Without the requirements for focal positions, decentralized and appropriated dynamic calculations have been received in numerous automated applications. Robots take alternatives by casting a ballot and the results are controlled by larger parts that run the show. Every robot can make its alternative as an exchange, where the blockchain is open-source for all the robots that are used for the confirmation of the casting ballot results. Thus, this procedure is rehashed by the total robots until the multitude arrives at an equivalent resolution.
- **Upgraded Data Security:** Data which are held inside the blockchain is exceptionally secure. The individual information in diskless situations for putting away delicate are very notable by the use of blockchain. The data in the blockchain data houses holds the information that is marked carefully, which implies that the private keys are also to be secured (Marr, 2018). This entitles the AI calculations that deal with securing the information, and along with these lines guarantee more trust and sounds alternative results.
- **Enhanced Efficiency:** For the multiuser business forms, which include numerous partners, the data set of singular clients, business firms, and legislative associations are innately wasteful be-

cause of the multi-parties of business exchanges. The union of the two advancements empowers Intelligent Decentralized Autonomous Agents to the program and the quick approval of the data/information/esteem/resource which moves among the various partners (Magazzeni et al., 2017).

- **Decentralized Intelligence:** The regard to taking shrewd significant levels of an alternative that also includes numerous operators that to perform diverse subtask that approach the regular preparing information, distinctive users which uses the cybersecurity AI specialists that will be consolidated to provide completely organized security over the basic systems and also to settle the booking issues (Janson et al., 2008; Brambilla et al., 2013).

- **Enhances Trust:** Alternatives that are done by AI operators become useless when it is hard for the clients to comprehend and trust the shoppers. This is notable for taking down exchanges in the decentralized records on a premise of point-to-point by the blockchain, and also making it simpler to acknowledge and believe the alternatives which are selected, with certainty that they are no alterations of records while examining the human process. While documenting the dynamic procedure of an AI framework. The mechanical alternatives of the blockchain are built up in straightforwardness and would increase open trust among the users that wipe out a multitude of mechanical systems (Campbell, 2018; Castelló Ferrer, 2018).

CONCLUSION

The blockchain is a new type of database which is involved in solving some of the problems in a centralized system, in which all the proceedings have occurred without the interference of an unbiased observer organization, and the time spent on each proceeding is unilateral or special detection or modification of data in the blockchain. There are various advantages to this technology, none of the chain technology produces unambiguously, multi-copying of the proceedings, is completely trustable, and the decentralized digital ledger, the blockchain technology is reliable and not destructible, and all the mentioned attacks could disrupt the system work, not the technology. Blockchain technology is widely used and versatile all over the world because it can clear the way for most of the systems in different industries, but it is new, and its accomplishment is little analyzed issue on practice. Blockchain technology promises us a well-developed and bright future without any swindling and deception due to the benefits of blockchain technology. Some developers are trying to develop this technology for the real-time practical application and implementation of the blockchain which is already in the existing systems of the industrial directions, blockchain can bring up the honest and trusty business, government, and logistic systems. There are some difficulties in the blockchain but the outcome of the have a greater predominance than a stumbling block. In the near future, it is important to continue exploring Blockchain development and its applications in different AI areas since this new technology can help to solve many problems, which disturb and prevent the systems from working appropriately. The communication overhead is more in blockchain based applications because it uses verification mechanism. Cyber-physical contingency due to decentralized network system. The private key can be hacked by the attackers that leads to security risk.

This research received no specific grant from any funding agency in the public, commercial, or not-for-profit sectors.

REFERENCES

Aggarwal, S., & Kumar, N. (2021). Blockchain 2.0: Smart contracts. *Advances in Computers*, *121*, 301–322. doi:10.1016/bs.adcom.2020.08.015

Aitzhan, N. Z., & Svetinovic, D. (2016). Security and privacy in decentralized energy trading through multi-signatures, blockchain, and anonymous messaging streams. *IEEE Transactions on Dependable and Secure Computing*, *15*(5), 840–852. doi:10.1109/TDSC.2016.2616861

Alcazar, C. V. (2017). Data you can trust. *Air and Space Power Journal*, *31*(2), 91–101.

Alex, S. A., Kumaran. U, & Santhana Mikhail Antony. S (2021) Novel Applications of Neuralink in HealthCare-An Exploratory Study, In *Proceedings of ACM/CSI/IEEE-CS Research & Industry Symposium on IoT Cloud For Societal Applications* (pp. 27-31). ACM.

Alex, S. A., Nayahi, J., Shine, H., & Gopirekha, V. (2022). Deep convolutional neural network for diabetes mellitus prediction. *Neural Computing & Applications*, *34*(2), 1319–1327. doi:10.100700521-021-06431-7

Alex, S. A., Ponkamali, S., Andrew, T. R., Jhanjhi, N. Z., & Tayyab, M. (2022). Machine Learning-Based Wearable Devices for Smart Healthcare Application With Risk Factor Monitoring. In *Empowering Sustainable Industrial 4.0 Systems With Machine Intelligence* (pp. 174–185). IGI Global. doi:10.4018/978-1-7998-9201-4.ch009

Aste, T., Tasca, P., & Di Matteo, T. (2017). Blockchain technologies: The foreseeable impact on society and industry. *Computer*, *50*(9), 18–28. doi:10.1109/MC.2017.3571064

Azaria, A., Ekblaw, A., Vieira, T., & Lippman, A. (2016). Medrec: Using blockchain for medical data access and permission management. In *Proceedings of 2nd international conference on open and big data* (pp. 25-30). IEEE. 10.1109/OBD.2016.11

Bahga, A., & Madisetti, V. (2014). Internet of Things: A hands-on approach. *Pvt.*

Bahga, A., & Madisetti, V. K. (2016). Blockchain platform for the industrial internet of things. *Journal of Software Engineering and Applications*, *9*(10), 533–546. doi:10.4236/jsea.2016.910036

Brambilla, M., Ferrante, E., Birattari, M., & Dorigo, M. (2013). Swarm robotics: A review from the swarm engineering perspective. *Swarm Intelligence*, *7*(1), 1–41. doi:10.100711721-012-0075-2

Brown, R. G., Carlyle, J., Grigg, I., & Hearn, M. (2016). Corda: an introduction. *R3 CEV, 1(15)*, 14.

Cai, W. D., Yu, L., Wang, R., Liu, N., & Deng, E. Y. (2017). Research on blockchain-based application system development method. *Journal of Software*, *28*(6), 1474–1487.

Campbell, D. (2018). Combining ai and blockchain to push frontiers in healthcare. Macadamian. http://www. macadamian. com/2018/03/16/combining-ai-and blockchain-in-healthcare/.

Castelló Ferrer, E. (2018). The blockchain: a new framework for robotic swarm systems. In *Proceedings of the future technologies conference* (pp. 1037-1058). Springer.

Choi, W., & Hong, J. W. K. (2021). Performance Evaluation of Ethereum Private and Testnet Networks Using Hyperledger Caliper. *In Proceedings of 22nd Asia-Pacific Network Operations and Management Symposium* (pp. 325-329). IEEE. 10.23919/APNOMS52696.2021.9562684

Cohn, A., West, T., & Parker, C. (2016). Smart after all: Blockchain, smart contracts, parametric insurance, and smart energy grids. *Geo. L. Tech. Rev.*, *1*, 273.

Crosby, M., Pattanayak, P., Verma, S., & Kalyanaraman, V. (2016). Blockchain technology: Beyond bitcoin. *Applied Innovation*, *2*(6-10), 71.

Daim, T., Lai, K. K., Yalcin, H., Alsoubie, F., & Kumar, V. (2020). Forecasting technological positioning through technology knowledge redundancy: Patent citation analysis of IoT, cybersecurity, and Blockchain. *Technological Forecasting and Social Change*, *161*, 120329. doi:10.1016/j.techfore.2020.120329

Demirkan, S., Demirkan, I., & McKee, A. (2020). Blockchain technology in the future of business cyber security and accounting. *Journal of Management Analytics*, *7*(2), 189–208. doi:10.1080/23270012.2020.1731721

Dinh, T. N., & Thai, M. T. (2018). AI and blockchain: A disruptive integration. *Computer*, *51*(9), 48–53. doi:10.1109/MC.2018.3620971

Dunphy, P., & Petitcolas, F. A. (2018). A first look at identity management schemes on the blockchain. *IEEE Security and Privacy*, *16*(4), 20–29. doi:10.1109/MSP.2018.3111247

Fauvel, W. (2017) Blockchain Advantages and Disadvantages. *Medium.* https://medium.com/nudjed/blockchain-advantage-and-disadvantagese76dfde3bbc0

Fridgen, G., Radszuwill, S., Urbach, N., & Utz, L. (2018). Cross-organizational workflow management using blockchain technology: towards applicability, auditability, and automation. In *Proceedings of 51st Annual Hawaii International Conference on System Sciences*. Scholar Space. 10.24251/HICSS.2018.444

Gatteschi, V., Lamberti, F., Demartini, C., Pranteda, C., & Santamaría, V. (2018). Blockchain and smart contracts for insurance: Is the technology mature enough?. *Future internet, 10*(2), 20.

Glass, B. D. (2014). Counterfeit drugs and medical devices in developing countries. *Research and Reports in Tropical Medicine*, *5*, 11. doi:10.2147/RRTM.S39354 PMID:32669888

Harfield, H. (1982). Identity crises in letter of credit law. *Arizona Law Review*, *24*, 239.

Jacobovitz, O. (2016). Blockchain for identity management. *The Lynne and William Frankel Center for Computer Science Department of Computer Science. Ben-Gurion University, Beer Sheva, 1*, 9.

Janson, S., Merkle, D., & Middendorf, M. (2008). A decentralization approach for swarm intelligence algorithms in networks applied to multi-swarm PSO. *International Journal of intelligent computing and cybernetics*.

Kaddoura, S., & Grati, R. (2021). Blockchain for Healthcare and Medical Systems. In *Enabling Blockchain Technology for Secure Networking and Communications* (pp. 249–270). IGI Global. doi:10.4018/978-1-7998-5839-3.ch011

Kaddoura, S., Haraty, R. A., Al Kontar, K., & Alfandi, O. (2021). A parallelized database damage assessment approach after cyberattack for healthcare systems. *Future Internet*, *13*(4), 90. doi:10.3390/fi13040090

Kouhizadeh, M., & Sarkis, J. (2018). Blockchain practices, potentials, and perspectives in greening supply chains. *Sustainability*, *10*(10), 3652. doi:10.3390u10103652

Landa, J. T. (1994). *Trust, Ethnicity, and Identity: beyond the new institutional economics of ethnic trading networks, contract law, and gift-exchange*. University of Michigan Press.

Lasseter, R. H., & Paigi, P. (2004). Microgrid: A conceptual solution. *In Proceedings of 35th annual power electronics specialists conference* (vol. 6, pp. 4285-4290). IEEE.

Lee, L. (2015). New kids on the blockchain: How bitcoin's technology could reinvent the stock market. *Hastings Bus. LJ*, *12*, 81. doi:10.2139srn.2656501

Li, Z., Kang, J., Yu, R., Ye, D., Deng, Q., & Zhang, Y. (2017). Consortium blockchain for secure energy trading in industrial internet of things. *IEEE Transactions on Industrial Informatics*, *14*(8), 3690–3700. doi:10.1109/TII.2017.2786307

Litke, A., Anagnostopoulos, D., & Varvarigou, T. (2019). Blockchains for supply chain management: Architectural elements and challenges towards a global scale deployment. *Logistics*, *3*(1), 5. doi:10.3390/logistics3010005

Liu, Y., Yu, Z., & Sun, H. (2021). Treatment effect of type 2 diabetes patients in outpatient department based on blockchain electronic mobile medical app. *Journal of Healthcare Engineering*, *2021*, 1–12. doi:10.1155/2021/6693810 PMID:33728034

Magazzeni, D., McBurney, P., & Nash, W. (2017). Validation and verification of smart contracts: A research agenda. *Computer*, *50*(9), 50–57. doi:10.1109/MC.2017.3571045

Marr, B. (2018*)*. Artificial intelligence and Blockchain: 3 major benefits of combining these two mega-trends. *Forbes*. https:// www.forbes. com/sites/Barnard Marr/2018/03/02/artif icial-intelligence and-blockchain-3-major-benefits-of combin ing-these-two-mega-trends/

Marwala, T., & Xing, B. (2018). Blockchain and artificial intelligence. arXiv.

McGhin, T., Choo, K. K. R., Liu, C. Z., & He, D. (2019). Blockchain in healthcare applications: Research challenges and opportunities. *Journal of Network and Computer Applications*, *135*, 62–75. doi:10.1016/j.jnca.2019.02.027

OuYang, X., Zhu, X., Ye, L., & Yao, J. (2017). Preliminary applications of blockchain technique in large consumers direct power trading. *Zhongguo Dianji Gongcheng Xuebao*, *37*, 3672–3681.

Panarello, A., Tapas, N., Merlino, G., Longo, F., & Puliafito, A. (2018). Blockchain and iot integration: A systematic survey. *Sensors (Basel)*, *18*(8), 2575. doi:10.339018082575 PMID:30082633

Peters, G. W., & Panayi, E. (2016). Understanding modern banking ledgers through blockchain technologies: Future of transaction processing and smart contracts on the internet of money. In *Proceedings of Banking beyond banks and money* (pp. 239–278). Springer. doi:10.1007/978-3-319-42448-4_13

Peters, G. W., Panayi, E., & Chapelle, A. (2015). *Trends in cryptocurrencies and blockchain technologies: A monetary theory and regulation perspective.* arXiv:1508.04364.

Pilkington, M. (2017). Can blockchain improve healthcare management? Consumer medical electronics and the IoT. *Consumer Medical Electronics and the IoMT.*

Ping, Z., Yu, D., & Bin, L. (2016). White paper on China's blockchain technology and application development. *Ministry of Industry and Information Technology of People's Republic of China.*

Ramage, M. (2018). *From BIM to blockchain in construction: What you need to know.* Trimble Inc.

Salah, K., Rehman, M. H. U., Nizamuddin, N., & Al-Fuqaha, A. (2019). Blockchain for AI: Review and open research challenges. *IEEE Access: Practical Innovations, Open Solutions, 7,* 10127–10149. doi:10.1109/ACCESS.2018.2890507

Shen, B., Guo, J., & Yang, Y. (2019). MedChain: Efficient healthcare data sharing via blockchain. *Applied Sciences (Basel, Switzerland), 9*(6), 1207. doi:10.3390/app9061207

Songara, A., & Chouhan, L. (2017). Blockchain: a decentralized technique for securing Internet of Things. In *Proceedings of Conference on Emerging Trends in Engineering Innovations & Technology Management.* Research Gate.

Sorrell, W. H. (2016). Blockchain Technology: Opportunities and Risks. Vermont Office of the Attorney General.

Strobel, V., Castelló Ferrer, E., & Dorigo, M. (2018). Managing byzantine robots via blockchain technology in a swarm robotics collective decision-making scenario.

Sun, H., Mao, H., Bai, X., Chen, Z., Hu, K., & Yu, W. (2017). Multi-blockchain model for central bank digital currency. In *Proceedings of 18th International conference on parallel and distributed computing, applications and technologies* (pp. 360-367). IEEE. 10.1109/PDCAT.2017.00066

Swan, M. (2015). Blockchain thinking: The brain as a decentralized autonomous corporation [commentary]. *IEEE Technology and Society Magazine, 34*(4), 41–52. doi:10.1109/MTS.2015.2494358

Swan, M. (2015). *Blockchain: Blueprint for a new economy.* O'Reilly Media, Inc.

Tapas, N., Longo, F., Merlino, G., & Puliafito, A. (2020). Experimenting with smart contracts for access control and delegation in IoT. *Future Generation Computer Systems, 111,* 324–338. doi:10.1016/j.future.2020.04.020

Tapscott, D., & Tapscott, A. (2017). How blockchain will change organizations. *MIT Sloan Management Review, 58*(2), 10.

Twesige, R. L. (2015). A simple explanation of Bitcoin and Blockchain technology.

Vranken, H. (2017). Sustainability of bitcoin and blockchains. *Current Opinion in Environmental Sustainability, 28*, 1–9. doi:10.1016/j.cosust.2017.04.011

Wang, F. Y., Yuan, Y., Zhang, J., Qin, R., & Smith, M. H. (2018). Blockchainized Internet of minds: A new opportunity for cyber–physical–social systems. *IEEE Transactions on Computational Social Systems, 5*(4), 897–906. doi:10.1109/TCSS.2018.2881344

Wolff-Mann, E. (2018). *Only good for drug dealers': More Nobel prize winners snub bitcoin.* Yahoo Finance.

Wood, G. (2014). Ethereum: A secure decentralised generalised transaction ledger. *Ethereum project yellow paper, 151*, 1-32.

Wu, J., & Tran, N. K. (2018). Application of blockchain technology in sustainable energy systems: An overview. *Sustainability, 10*(9), 3067. doi:10.3390u10093067

Yan, Y., Zhao, J., Wen, F., & Chen, X. Y. (2017). Blockchain in energy systems: Concept, application and prospect. *Electric Power Construction, 38*(2), 12–20.

Yang, D., Zhao, X., Xu, Z., Li, Y., & Li, Q. (2017). Developing status and prospect analysis of blockchain in energy Internet. *Zhongguo Dianji Gongcheng Xuebao, 37*, 3664–3671.

Yang, T., Guo, Q., Tai, X., Sun, H., Zhang, B., Zhao, W., & Lin, C. (2017). Applying blockchain technology to decentralized operation in future energy internet. In *Proceedings of IEEE Conference on Energy Internet and Energy System Integration* (pp. 1-5). IEEE. 10.1109/EI2.2017.8244418

Zhang, L., Lee, B., Ye, Y., & Qiao, Y. (2019). Ethereum transaction performance evaluation using testnets. *In Proceedings of European Conference on Parallel Processing* (pp. 179-190). Springer.

Zhang, N., Wang, Y., Kang, C., Cheng, J., & He, D. (2016). Blockchain technique in the energy internet: preliminary research framework and typical applications. In *Zhongguo Dianji Gongcheng Xuebao/ Proceedings of the Chinese Society of Electrical Engineering.* IEEE.

Zheng, Z., Xie, S., Dai, H., Chen, X., & Wang, H. (2017). An Overview of Blockchain Technology: Architecture, Consensus, and Future Trends. In *proceedings of IEEE International Congress on Big Data* (pp. 557-564). IEEE. 10.1109/BigDataCongress.2017.85

KEY TERMS AND DEFINITION

Artificial Intelligence (AI): Extensive scientific discipline that uses computer programs to handle problems by imitating the biological concepts including learning and reasoning.

Bitcoin (BTC): Virtual Currency which is a kind of cryptocurrency released in 2009.

Brain Computer Interface (BCI): A communication paradigm that measures neural activity.

Ethereum (ETH): A cryptocurrency that is suitable for decentralized platforms preferably Ethereum blockchain networks.

Industrial Internet of Things (IIOT): Consumer IoT designed for economic purpose.

Internet of Things (IoT): The devices connected to Internet that enables communication between the devices to make smart solutions.

Nextcoin (NXT): A second generation digital coin that uses Proof of Stake.

Peercoin (PPC): A cryptocurrency that is released in 2012. Both Proof of Work and Proof of Stake are involved in block generation.

Proof of Stake (PoS): A consensus protocol in which some nodes involved in computation on a peer-to-peer electronic communication.

Proof of Work (PoW): The miners apply some computing rules to produce a hash value in which the average time between two hash values generation is predefined.

Chapter 13
Machine Learning Approach in Human Resources Department

Ishraq Abdulmajeed
Jinan University, Lebanon

Ghalia Nassreddine
iD https://orcid.org/0000-0001-9434-2914
Jinan University, Lebanon

Amal A. El Arid
iD https://orcid.org/0000-0001-5712-2138
Rafik Hariri University, Lebanon

Joumana Younis
CNAM, Lebanon

ABSTRACT

Artificial intelligence is one of the essential innovations made by scientists to simplify people's life. It allows intelligent computers to imitate human behaviors to accomplish specific tasks. Machine learning is a branch of artificial intelligence in which devices can learn from existing data to predict new output values. Machine learning is used in different domains, including human resources management. This chapter presents an application of machine learning in the human resources department. Machine-learning techniques help select the most suitable candidate for a job vacancy during recruitment stages based on different factors. Factors could include educational level, age, and previous experience. Based on these factors, a decision system is built using the binary classification method. The results show the effectiveness of this method in selecting the best candidate for a job vacancy, revealing the flexibility of the approach in making appropriate decisions. In addition, obtained results are accurate and independent of the dataset imprecision.

DOI: 10.4018/978-1-6684-6937-8.ch013

INTRODUCTION

Machine learning (ML) is an artificial intelligence type that allows an intelligent machine to learn from experience without being explicitly programmed (Haenlein & Kaplan, 2019). ML allows systems to learn from previous data, identify patterns, and make decisions with minimal human intervention. Many algorithms are used in ML, including decision trees, Regression, Support vector machines, and ensemble approaches (Bzdok, Krzywinski, & Altman, 2018).

Moreover, ML is widely used in business because it helps enterprises understand customer and employee behavior trends from one side and business processes from the other. In addition, it supports the decision of whether new products are worth being developed. Consequently, ML has become a significant competitor for many companies (Garg, Sinha, Kar, & Mani, 2021).

Hence, ML is often classified by tools that allow an artificial intelligence application to have more accuracy in its predictions. There are four main approaches in machine learning: supervised learning, unsupervised learning, semi-supervised learning, and reinforcement learning. Based on the type of the predicted date, an approach of machine learning can be selected (Bzdok, Krzywinski, & Altman, 2018).

In this chapter, supervised machine learning are investigated. This technique runs the developed application with sample data considered a training data set. Then, the accuracy of the supervised algorithm is tested with another sample of data, called testing data. The training and testing datasets should be entirely independent to achieve precise results. Supervised learning algorithms are usually composed of the following main techniques (Bzdok, Krzywinski, & Altman, 2018):

- Binary classification allows an application to choose one of two possible solutions.
- Multi-class classification helps the application in selecting one of many answers.
- Regression modeling predicts continuous values from historical data.

Therefore, one of the supervised machine learning techniques' goals is to build a consistent model that assigns class labels to the testing instances when the values of the predictor features are known. However, it is crucial to note that the value of the class label is unknown.

In developing countries, most companies suffer from enormous non-digitalization data that becomes difficult to manage with the company's scalability. For this reason, many organizations are using new technology tools and moving toward digital transformation to strengthen their business processes. Thus, decision-making problem is a necessary process that helps organizations solve their problems by choosing appropriate actions. However, the effort in this domain in these countries is still weak. Decision-making problems can significantly change the organizations' management by implementing advanced technological administration based on machine learning techniques.

For instance, selecting the proper candidate process is essential during the recruitment phases. However, the selection is very complex due to the massive number of applicants applying for a job. Thus, if the method used in the selection process is unsuitable, the result may be confused and irrelevant. For this reason, a clear description of the job should be available. Moreover, the criteria for selecting the best candidate must be convenient.

The human resources department in any company may request new employees for many reasons, including one of the below suggestions:

1. One or more of its employees resigned. Therefore, detailed descriptions of available jobs are posted on different platforms (official company website, LinkedIn, Instagram, etc.) Moreover, the necessary skills are posted to attract the appropriate candidates.
2. New departments or new posts have been recently added to an organization. Hence, good descriptions of these posts are developed to create a list of needed skills for the appropriate candidates.

Selecting the most suitable employee through an intelligent system will be more apparent using an accurate and precise job description. As the number of applicants may be enormous, an automated decision system is beneficial and time-saving. Moreover, this system may perform well based on specific criteria and entirely away from bias selection or human feelings.

This chapter will explore the use of ML techniques in selecting the most suitable employee from a set of candidates. First, the HR department and recruitment process are described. Later, ML techniques are presented. Decision making problem is illustrated. Moreover, classification techniques are listed. The use of ML techniques in the HR department will be reviewed in section VI. This chapter concludes on the importance of using ML tools in the HR department.

HUMAN RESOURCES DEPARTMENT AND RECRUITMENT PROCESS

The HR department is a group of individuals who make up an organization's or business sector's workforce to emphasize that employees are an essential part of the business and should be viewed as an asset to the companies for which they work that must be managed effectively to achieve success. The term encompasses all people working in the organization, including managers and employees, who have been hired under specific conditions. The one establishes plans, policies, and all procedures that organize work to achieve its goals in implementing the organization's strategy and ensuring its future success (Beaumont, 1993).

The human element (Zayed, 2006) has been the focus of attention of researchers in the field of management and focused on research in achieving human well-being by maximizing the way to benefit from human resources throughout the ages.

When the organization obtains human resources that have the skill and knowledge, here it can be said that the organization possesses a stock of human resources, so it must maintain the following (Hassan, 2011):

- The presence of individuals willing to develop skills appropriately ensures the development of their competencies.
- Through skills, individuals become ready to achieve their personal goals and self-realization by contributing effectively to the institution's goals.

Therefore, the goal of the HR department is to achieve excellent efficiency in the performance of the organization's employees through their good management and through the procedures performed to raise the productivity and commitment of employees and increase competition among them to reach the best possible result. In addition, HR employees work to attract Competencies and appoint the best of them, in addition to motivating employees for their performance and achievements through rewards, which contributes to raising productivity and improving performance (Jones, 1997).

Human Resources Primary Responsibilities

Human resources activities differ from one institution to another. The human resources function is linked to the institution. It has many activities that it undertakes alone or jointly with other departments in the same institution, such as conducting personal interviews, preparing development programs, planning, performance evaluation, and decision-making. These functions refer to tasks implemented within the organization in coordination with human resources, which affect many areas. The primary responsibilities of the HR department can be summarized in Figure 1 (Edgley-Pyshorn & Huisman, 2011):

Figure 1. Human Resources' primary responsibilities adapted in most organizations, including planning, analyzing the workforce, recruiting, resolving problems, and making discussions

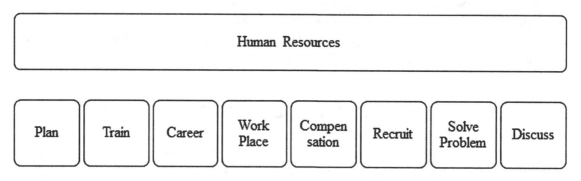

- Planning is a critical function in the HR department. It is a process aimed at translating the goals and business plans of the organization into quantitative or qualitative needs of the human element and requires the prediction of the size of human resources.
- Analysis of the current workforce includes preparing detailed lists of each task in all institution's departments, showing the number of current employees, job types, and their relationships. This process may clarify the availability of conditions in each job to help the administration give a clear idea of the current workforce in terms of number, type, and specialization (Carlson & Kavanagh, 2011).
- Training is vital to raise employees' skill levels, positively affecting their job behavior (Ballout, 2002).
- Career Path: Through his career, the employee can achieve a set of promotions and transfers, whether vertically or horizontally. This process is called a career path. It represents the compatibility between the individual's capabilities and the institution's needs. The goal of planning career paths is to increase the institution's efficiency. It remains within the successful institutions, distinguishes individuals between appropriate and raises their competencies or inappropriate, and takes measures for them, thus affecting the decision-making process (Hölzle, 2010).
- Compensation and returns include all wages received by human resources. Compensation aims to create an incentive for individuals and an incentive to increase production. The more the incentive is good, the more it will affect the individual's attraction and employment in the service of the institution's goals (Ballout, 2002).

- Recruitment: The HR department works to search for suitable qualifications for jobs to improve the work of the organization by providing the organization with the best possible cadres to work in it.
- The HR department is working on developing products and improving the quality and quantity of production.
- The HR department works to provide tools and means to improve the work of employees and to pay wages and incentives that contribute to increasing the effectiveness and productivity of employees through the provision of a set of training programs.
- The HR department conducts the relevant discussions with the executive management through coordination and organization between all administrative units and the particular tasks of employees.
- The HR department contributes through its work to identify the main problems of employees, which in one way or another negatively affect the productivity of the organization. It provides necessary assistance to managers to implement policies and helps them solve problems or issues related to employees.

Human Resources Types

Only nine of the twelve essential HR types will be discussed in this chapter (Hadadi, 2014).

Type 1: Employment Specialists

They are also known as "job placement specialists," who use their knowledge and experience to match people with specific jobs. They frequently work in human resources or for an employment agency. Employment specialists understand a company's job descriptions, hiring processes, salaries, and benefits packages inside and out. To find candidates, they may go to job fairs, schools, and professional organizations, and they usually advertise services in print publications and online.

Type 2: HR Assistants

The HR Assistant provides administrative support to directors and managers. HR assistants record employee absences, terminations, performance reports, grievances, and compensation information. They frequently assist with recruitment by writing job descriptions, contacting references, and communicating with candidates.

Type 3: HR Coordinators

Human resources coordinators assist the HR director or manager in facilitating HR programs and functions. Their responsibilities include scheduling orientations, addressing employee concerns, and coordinating employee training and development—coordinators research industry trends and best practices to improve employee satisfaction and HR processes and policies.

Type 4: Recruiters

They work for specific companies to find candidates for internal positions or for recruitment agencies that vet candidates for other companies. They frequently hire the best candidates for specific roles in specific industries. They spend significant time posting job listings online, reviewing applications, and contacting potential hires for interviews to find the most qualified candidates. They negotiate salaries and assign candidates to related jobs.

Type 5: Recruitment Managers

Recruitment managers must have a strong background in recruiting to supervise other recruiters. Moreover, they help manage a company's sourcing and interviewing for a better employment process. These managers should understand labor legislation. They should also meet with other department managers to project future hiring needs to ensure efficient recruiting practices.

Type 6: HR Managers

HR managers supervise the entire department and ensure employees carry out their responsibilities effectively. They meet with executive-level employees to plan the hiring process and work to ensure that their team members complete tasks that achieve the desired results. HR managers frequently handle exit interviews and sensitive employee issues. They keep tracking department records and organizational charts.

Type 7: Labor Relations Specialists

Labor relations specialists know economics, labor laws, wage data, and union collective bargaining trends. Their specialized role entails preparing information for executive managers during collective bargaining. They also manage grievance procedures, advise human resources staff, and compile statistical data to assist businesses in making employee contract decisions.

Type 8: Employee Experience Directors

Employee experience directors are knowledgeable about business strategy, including how to solve problems to make teams more efficient. These directors collaborate with other executives to make recommendations for career planning, team-building exercises, and other employee-satisfaction programs. Above all, their leadership abilities contribute to the positive shaping of company culture.

Type 9: HR Directors

HR directors have extensive experience in human resources, particularly in team management. Their primary responsibility is overseeing the company's human resources department to ensure efficiency and profitability. Consequently, an HR director reports to the company's CEO on all aspects of human resources, including implementing policies and procedures. They oversee database management procedures, direct employee orientation, and training programs, and ensure compliance with federal, state, and local laws. HR directors may also be in charge of the department's budget.

Recruitment

Employee constitutes the most critical resource for any organization. Accordingly, the recruitment process is one of the essential functions within the company. The success of this process has a significant effect on the overall company's success. The HR department must do this process.

Recruitment is the activity that advertises vacancies and entices qualified individuals to work in an organization. Afterward, the recruitment process continues by selecting and appointing the best applicants to achieve the goals (Alayan, 2007).

Each country has its law to achieve and match employment conditions. Through research, most countries have agreed on the availability of the following employment conditions:

- The employee should have the nationality that represents his country.
- The employee should receive their civil rights.
- The employee's judicial history certificate does not carry a note that contradicts the practice of the job he wants to join.
- The employee should be in a legal position for national service.
- The employee should meet the conditions of age, physical and mental ability, and the qualifications required to join the job he wants.

Recruitment Principles

Employment is based on many principles, including:

- The principle of permanence: that is, employment is a continuous administrative process, starting from its selection to the last stages of life, according to the specific law.
- The principle of equality or equal opportunities: that is, giving an equal opportunity to all applicants.
- Efficiency principle: It is the selection of the best-advanced elements for the advertised jobs and the most capable of performing them.

Recruitment Process

Three essential stages for the recruitment process are explained (see Figure 2) (Yakubovich, 2006):

Stage 1: Define Job Requirements
It consists of defining the job requirements. This stage can be decomposed into two main steps:

- Writing the jobs description
- Fixing main specifications, including employee's skills

Stage Two: Attract Potential Employees

This stage can be performed by job advertising using media and social media tools.

Stage Three: Select Right People

The selection process includes the differentiation between individuals applying for a particular job according to their skills (Abdel Baki, 2001).

Executive managers entrust them with the task of this process within the small enterprises as for the large ones. The selection decision is shared by more than one party at the final selection stage (Maher, 2018).

Figure 2. The three stages of the recruitment process, including job requirements definition, potential employees attraction, and selection of the suitable candidates

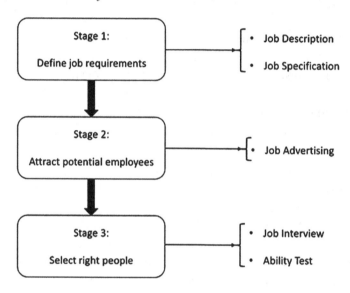

According to criteria and specifications included in job requirements, a job analysis is derived to obtain high-performance levels based on a set of conditions that must be met by job applicants (Hamdawi, 2004):

- Education level includes academic qualification, specialization, degree, and graduation authority.
- Experience is considered an indicator of the individual's possibility of success in his work. It is used in most organizations because previous experience makes working easy for the job seeker.
- Personal characteristics consist of marital status, age, gender, etc.

Selecting the right candidate is the essential stage of the recruitment process. It may be decomposed into two steps:

- A job interview is a differentiation between applicants for vacant positions by verifying the accuracy of the submitted data, obtaining the approval of the General Administration for the selected candidates, and issuing the final decision for an appointment.
- Ability test is mandatory after verifying the accuracy of the information provided and through various interviews. Based on the ability test results, a list of eligible candidates is prepared for the appointment. Accordingly, their files are presented to the higher management to issue appoint-

ment decisions. The final appointment usually depends on the candidates passing the medical examination, which achieves the extent of their safety and their ability to perform duties.

Modern Recruitment Approaches in Personal Selection

According to many studies (Kraev & Tikhonov, 2020), candidates' personal information can be obtained from their pages on social networks. It is possible to create a unique profile for the applicant, but it is far from the files presented in the questionnaire and the interview. Then his candidacy can be rejected immediately after analysis. The company thus saves significant money in selecting and rejecting candidates at an early stage of the study. To formalize and develop a methodology that allows assessing the level of the applicant's psychological qualities, focusing on some points to determine personality traits through the following information:

- Honesty: correspondence of the birth date and place, educational level and institution, information on foreign language skills, profile photo, and phone number.
- Opening: the public view profile defines the candidate's personality, quotes on the home page, the number of friends, the number of profile pictures, and the indicated phone number.
- Restraint: noticeable by communication in the comments, a few smiles during communication
- Etiquette: measuring the extent to which strangers are formally addressed on social networks, knowledge of candidate ethics in posting and sending non-standard videos, posting and sending unethical and impolite posts, photos and videos.
- Religious Tolerance: Focuses on the lack of statements, images, and videos calling for one's religion or humiliation of another religion
- Hobbies: participating in thematic groups, active discussion, and disseminating results and achievements
- Updated profile: it is essential to check whether the profile information is recent (text, photo, video, etc.) through posted dates. Old dates correspond to irrelevant one's information.

In the development process, it is necessary not only to fill out the staffing table but also to establish rules that make the selected candidate suitable for the team and work more efficiently for the organization. It is possible only through an objective assessment of the psychological aspect, the candidate's level, and qualifications to determine their characteristics. The most crucial factor is the efficiency of personnel service, which consists of inexpensive and effective personnel selection methods.

MACHINE LEARNING

Because of the massive development in information technology, it has become necessary to develop new technologies to manage and analyze the vast available information (Smola & Vishwanathan, 2008). ML is an advancing branch of computational algorithms invented to imitate human intelligence by learning from the available information and local environment. ML Techniques have been successfully used in applications such as recognition, computer vision, spacecraft engineering, finance, entertainment, and computational biology to biomedical and medical applications (Baştanlar & Özuysal, 2014; El Naqa & Murphy, 2015). Accordingly, many experts are interested today in developing and improving the work of ML techniques. Most of these experts are machine learning researchers and business professionals. Most experts aim to build advancing ML techniques to improve their companies' workflow (Braiek, Khomh, & Adams, 2018).

ML is a subset of artificial intelligence concerned with designing and developing algorithms and techniques that allow computers to possess the "learning" feature using specific Software and tools (Smola & Vishwanathan, 2008). Nowadays, specialists can perform their application goals in an advanced way using simple and small code (Braiek, Khomh, & Adams, 2018). ML algorithms are developed based on programming languages such as R, Python, C++, Java, etc. Figure 3 shows a simple comparison between some programming languages used in ML. Python is superior, with 83% of users preferring it to other programming languages. It is an elegant language and simple to use. Data used in this static are from the Kaggle Machine Learning and Data Science Survey in 2018; there were 18,827 respondents to the question (Kaggle, 2018).

Figure 3. Programming languages used in ML are compared, showing that nowadays, the Python programming language is the most helpful tool to be used

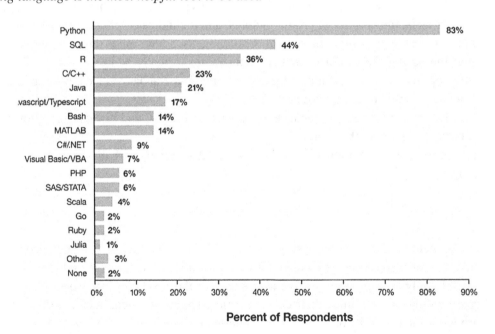

ML techniques play a significant role in healthcare, industry, physical science, etc. These techniques prove their efficiency in many human daily tasks. Recently, ML techniques have been widely used in hospitals to detect breast cancer, heart arrhythmia, thyroid di, and many other diagnostic applications (Shailaja, Seetharamulu, & Jabbar, 2018). Many researchers continue to improve machine-learning algorithms to enhance prediction accuracy in medical applications (Williams, Idowu, Balogun, & Oluwaranti, 2015).

In addition, ML techniques have been widely applied in industry, primarily in technical industries (Candanedo, Nieves, González, Martín, & Briones, 2018) and the physical sciences (Carleo, et al., 2019). Machine learning in physics is used in different fields such as cosmology, high energy, and statistical and quantitative physics (Karniadakis, Kevrekidis, Lu, Perdikaris, Wang, & Yang, 2021). The algorithms for machine learning can be used according to the data type and determine the appropriate algorithm to take advantage of it in solving the problem (Carleo, et al., 2019).

Advantages and Disadvantages of Machine Learning

Each coin has two faces, and each face has its characteristics and features. In addition, ML, a potent tool that can build a system that learns and acts without human intervention, has advantages and disadvantages. Table 1 summarizes some advantages and disadvantages of using ML techniques (Khanzode & Sarode, 2020).

Table 1. List of advantages and disadvantages of using machine learning techniques

Advantages	Disadvantages
• Automation • Scope of improvement • Efficient handling data • Wide range of application	• Selection of the correct algorithm • Time complexity • Space • High possibility of errors • Collection of a tremendous amount of data

Machine Learning Steps

Seven steps are required to perform the goal of ML. These steps (See Figure 4) should work sequentially (Swamynathan, 2019; Alam & Yao, 2019).

- Data collection: gathering and storing information from different sources to be used later for developing practical machine learning solutions
- Data preparation: The process of modifying raw data that should be run through machine learning algorithms to uncover insights or make predictions
- Choosing a model: The process of selecting one machine learning model from a set of candidate models for a specific problem
- Training: The process of using a training set to train the chosen model
- Evaluation: The process of using different evaluation techniques to understand the performance of the ML model, its robustness, and limitations
- Parameter tuning: The process of choosing a set of optimal parameters for an ML model
- Prediction: The output of an ML model after training with the dataset and applying it to new data

Figure 4. The seven steps of machine learning techniques, starting with data collection and ending with prediction and classification

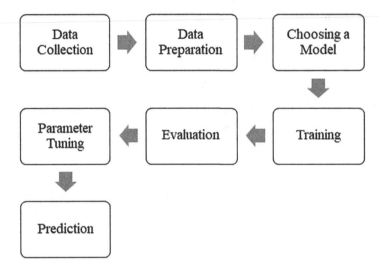

Machine Learning Types

ML techniques can be classified into several types based on the demanded outcome (Ayodele, 2010). The most familiar types are:

- Supervised Learning (Supervised ML) is a subcategory of machine learning that uses labeled datasets to train algorithms to classify data or accurately predict outcomes.
- Semi-supervised learning consists of a trained algorithm based on labeled and unlabeled data. Usually, this combination includes a minimal amount of labeled data and a considerable amount of unlabeled data. First, the programmer will cluster similar data using an unsupervised learning algorithm. After that, the existing labeled data is used to label the rest of the unlabeled data.
- Unsupervised learning is a type of ML that deals with unlabeled data. The users do not need to supervise the model using a technique of this type. Instead, it permits the model to work independently to determine the pattern and detect available information.
- Reinforcement learning: In this type, a training method is adopted based on enriching preference behaviors or punishing unflavored ones. Generally, an agent of this type can perceive and interpret its environment to take appropriate actions and learn through trial and error.

Table 2 shows some applications in which the four machine learning techniques are applied.

Table 2. Machine-learning applications according to technique types: supervised, semi-supervised, unsupervised, and reinforcement

Supervised Learning	Semi-supervised Learning	Unsupervised Learning	Reinforcement Learning
-Text categorization -Face detection -Signature recognition -Bio-Informatics -Spam detection	-Text document classifier -Audio and video manipulation	-Anomaly detection -Dimension reduction -Clustering -Similarity detection	-Trajectory optimization -Motion planning -Controller optimization

Machine Learning Algorithms

Machine learning consists of various algorithms, each dealing with a specific problem. ML algorithms are grouped into four categories, as shown in Table 3. This section briefly represents regression, decision tree, and random forest algorithms.

Table 3. ML algorithms groups: continuous unsupervised, continuous supervised, categorical unsupervised, and categorical supervised

	Unsupervised	Supervised
Continuous	o Clustering o Singular Value Decomposition o Principal Component Analysis o K-means	● Regression o Liner o Polynomial ● Decision tree ● Random forests
Categorical	● Association analysis o Apriori o FP-growth ● Hidden Markov model	● Classification o KNN o Trees o Logistic Regression o Naïve-Bayes o Super Vector Machine

Regression

Regression is generally used for two problems: prediction and determining causal relations between the independent and dependent variables (Maulud & Abdulazeez, 2020). Regression can be divided into simple linear and multiple Regression (Kavitha, Varuna, & Ramya, 2016).

- Linear Regression is one of the most well-known and understood statistics and machine learning algorithms. Linear Regression is a model that takes a linear form. For example, it assumes a linear relationship between each input variable (x) and the output variable (y). Therefore, (y) can be calculated easily using the linear relationship. The equation is called simple linear regression when there is one input variable (x). However, the equation is called multiple-linear regression when there are many input variables. For example, the equation of the line is as follows:

$$y = \beta 0 + \beta 1 \text{x}$$

Where x is an input variable, y is the output variable, and $\beta 0 + \beta 1$ are the coefficients

- Multiple-Linear regression is a method used to predict the dependent variable with the help of two or more independent variables. The primary purpose of these methods is to determine the relationship between the dependent and independent variables. Multiple independent variables are chosen to predict the dependent variable, which can help predict the dependent variable. It is used when linear regression cannot serve the purpose. Regression analysis helps validate whether the predictor variables are good enough to help predict the dependent variable. The basic model for multiple-linear regression is:

$$y = \beta 0 + \beta 1 \text{x}1 + ... + \beta \text{mxm} + \varepsilon$$

Where y is the dependent variable, $\beta 0$ is the intercept, and βi is the slope for Xi, a_nd Xi ar_e the independent variables

Decision Tree

Decision tree algorithms are tree-like flowcharts considered supervised learning algorithms. Each tree branch represents the test result, and each leaf node bears the class mark. A regular tree consists of a root, branches, and leaves. The same distribution is followed in the decision tree. Decision trees simulate the levels of thinking in humans, so they are easy to use through which regression and classification problems can be solved. The primary purpose of creating decision trees is to create a training model, and its purpose is used in prediction (Nasserddine & Arid, 2022).

Random Forest

Random forest is a collective learning technique built from decision trees. It involves the creation of multiple decision trees using preliminary datasets from the original data. Because of classification tasks, the random forest chooses the class most trees select. However, for regression tasks, the mean or average prediction of the individual trees is calculated (See Figure 5) (Feng, Sui, Tu, Huang, & Sun, 2018).

Figure 5. The random forest technique starts with testing a sample input to generate multiple predictions, averaging them together to come up with a single random forest prediction

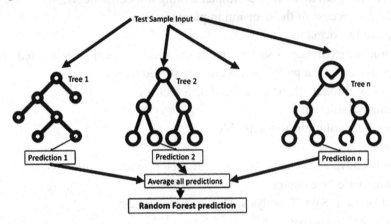

DECISION MAKING PROBLEM

Decision-making is one of the most critical problems in the business sector. A wrong decision may lead to an enormous problem for the company's status. Therefore, the persons responsible for making decisions should have a good knowledge of the problem. When using a decision-maker system, all essential elements should be considered. In addition, the objective complexity should be considered due to the massive number of variables that enter the system (Derakhti, Zavadskas, & Varzandeh, 2013, Smith, 2003; Zolfani, Aghdaie).

Decision Concept

A decision concept is a mental, objective, and intellectual activity seeking the best alternative solution among a set of possible choices (Nasserddine & Arid, 2022). The alternative solution generally represents the most appropriate solution to the problem. This decision should be based on the decision maker's sequential practical steps to reach the most appropriate decision (Guillemette, Laroche, & Cadieux, 2014).

The decision-making process always strives to get a correct conclusion to the problem. It means that it studies all the alternatives, and the correct choice should be made according to specific criteria. Decision-making differs from making the decision:

- Decision-making is a preparation for the stage of making a decision.
- Making the decision means the final decision formulation with its adoption and approval. It includes selecting a specific alternative, announcing it to those concerned, and documenting it officially and transparently.

Decision-Making Process

The general structure of the decision-making process consists of six steps (Lunenburg, 2010):

1. Identify the decision to be made
   a. Determine the goal to achieve by implementing a specific decision
   b. Measure the success of the decision implementation
2. Gather significant information
   a. Determine the existence of sufficient current and historical issue-related data
   b. Check whether such a problem was already solved before
   c. Check for additional information from different sources
3. Identify alternative solutions
   a. Look for other solutions to the problem
4. Weight the evidence
   a. Identify the advantages and limitations of each possible solution
   b. Eliminate ineffective choices
   c. Tools to be used: SWOT analysis, Decision matrix, etc.
5. Choose among the alternatives
   a. Make a final decision
6. Implement the decision
   a. Take action on the chosen decision
   b. Create the implementation plan
   c. Monitor progress
7. Review the decision and its corresponding impact
   a. Monitor the success metric: was the problem solved? Did the decision have a good or bad impact? Is the decision beneficial?
   b. If the success metric was not satisfied, find an iterative form to manage the problem and its solution

Decision Types

There are several types of decisions (Gibler & Lindholm, 2012; Hassanien, Langer, & Abdolrazaghi, 2018; Schoemaker, 1993) (see Table 4):

• Strategic Decisions and Routine Decisions (SD-RD): These types do not require much evaluation and analysis. Lower levels can delegate powers to make these decisions within the organization's policy structure. When a strategic decision is taken, it is unlikely to be changed in the long term.

• Programmed Decisions and Non-Programmed Decisions (PD-NPD): Programmed decisions are pre-existing and iterative over time to develop an existing set of rules to guide the process. These decisions can be simple or complex. However, non-programmed decisions are new decisions, previously not existing, that require thought and attention to become a decision.

• Policy and Operating Decisions (POD) are decisions that exist but are modified and changed from time to time. It frequently changes in line with the modification in current external and internal conditions and their impact for no more than a year or even one day.

• Organizational Decisions and Personal Decisions (OD-PD) are the processes by which one or more organizational units decide on behalf of the entire organization. Sometimes the decision-making unit is as small as an individual, for example, a manager, or as large as an entire organizational member. A personal decision is one's decision without referring to anyone, and it may be related to something that belongs to one's self, such as. personal belongings

- Individual Decisions and Group Decisions (ID-GD): Individual decision refers to the singular decision-making process in which an individual chooses the course of action that he will follow from among many alternatives. In contrast, group decision refers to the decision of the whole group that occurs by the collective and mutual agreement of the group.

Table 4. Examples of different decision types

Decision Type			Example
SD-RD			What to eat in the morning
			Where to sit on the bus
			What shampoo to purchase from the supermarket
PD-NPD	PD		Periodic reorders of inventory
			Merit system for the promotion of state employees
	NPD		Diversification into new products and marked
			Reorganization
POD	Policy		Budget
			Allocation of resources
	Operating		Determining the company's cash need
			Personnel scheduling
OD-PD			Relating to organizational matters of the company
ID-GD			The inboard of directors is a group decision

CLASSIFICATION

Classification is the process of classifying according to predefined classes or categories. It usually needs machine learning algorithms to assign a class for the available data. Classification of emails as "spam" or "not spam" is a simple example of a classification problem. In addition, it is used to predict the appropriate dataset associated with the input. Therefore, classification assigns a class to each input X based on a classification model (Neelamegam & Ramaraj, 2013).

Both classification and regression can be used for prediction. The target attribute of classification (dependent variable) is discrete (name type), and the target attribute of regression (dependent variable) is continuous (numerical type). Classification and clustering are considered different because classification requires that the training set be given class labels, and the generated classifier can be used simultaneously to make predictions. In contrast, clustering is used to train samples of unknown classes and find similar sets manually based on the characteristics of the set, Set Category Label.

Hence, there are two main types of classifications.

- Binary classification (Bellinger, Sharma, & Japkowicz, 2012) is where data is divided into two predefined categories. This type of classification is used in many real applications such as:

- Diagnosing diabetes type II using a soft intelligent binary classification model (Khashei, Eftekhari, & Parvizian, 2012)
- In bankruptcy prediction (Min & Jeong, 2009)
- In predicting the developmental toxicity of industrial chemicals in zebrafish (Ghorbanzadeh, Zhang, & Andersson, 2016)
- In quantum detection theory (Buccio, Li, Melucci, & Tiwari, 2018)

- Multi-category classification in which data can be categorized in several classes. Unlike binary, it does not restrict itself to any number of classes.

In this chapter, only binary classification will be studied.

Example of Binary Classification

In this paragraph, a binary classifier example is presented, showing two classes (Yordanov, 2021):

- Dog with label 1
- Not a dog with label 0

These classes are called Positive and Negative. Suppose that ten new photos have been passed to this binary classifier. Each photo receives a prediction that includes the label (0 or 1) representing the two classes (dog or not a dog). Given this information, a confusion matrix for these ten photos can be generated (see Figure 6).

Figure 6. Confusion matrix showing the actual negative and positive vs. predicted negative and positive resulting in four different classes.

	Predicted Negative	Predicted Positive
Actual Negative	True negative	False Positive
Actual Positive	False negative	True Positive

Each row in the matrix represents the instances in the actual class, while each column shows the instances of the predicted class:

- A cell on row one, column one: Contains the number of True Negatives (the number of correctly predicted photos of not a dog).
- A cell on row one, column two: Represents the number of False Positives (the number of predicted dogs photos, but the photos do not contain a dog).
- A cell on row two, column one: contains the number of False Negatives (the number of predicted as not dogs, but the photos contains a dog).

- A cell on row two, column two: contains the number of True Positives (the number of correctly predicted photos that contain a dog).

MACHINE LEARNING IN HR DEPARTMENT

Recently, the use of intelligent applications in business data has increased. Therefore, researchers and companies focus on developing new machine learning tools for business applications. Recently, many companies have used new strategies focusing on Business Analytics and Optimization as Key technologies to improve their routine operations and strategic decisions. They got away from the traditional "descriptive" analytics methods and focused more on predictive analytics, where the meta-analytic of the data allows the user to obtain a file Integrated retrospectively on business and answer questions such as "what happened," "how often," and" Where did he happen?". Thus, predictive analytics allows the user to get a file of a futuristic view of business and answers to questions such as "what could happen" and "what will happen next...". However, meta-analytic allows the user to get helpful commands to solve and answer questions through a particular set of expectations and action restrictions (Apte, 2010). Only the application of ML tools in the HR department will be represented in this chapter.

The human Resource (HR) department is the main component of modern companies. One of the central roles of HR is to recruit employees for the open vacancies within the companies. Indeed, HR staff works to provide the requirements and skills needed for the open vacancies. Recent studies have clarified the potential supporting role of new technologies, such as machine learning (ML), for human resource recruitment tasks (Laumer, Maier, & Weitzel, 2022).

Nowadays, ML techniques are integrated into all parts of HR. They are used in recruitment, performance management, and text mining classification. ML applications are still in an early stage. HR and machine learning professionals start working together to enhance the integration of ML techniques in HR jobs.

Based on ML techniques, candidates will be dealt with equally, and submitted documents will not be ignored due to personal decisions. In addition, the selection process through ML can obtain the best qualifications for the CVs depending on the fundamental determinants required in each vacancy (Rąb-Kettler & Lehnervp, 2019).

ML tools can also assist in identifying the opportunities for individual development without bias. They link the candidate's education and skills to choose the best appropriate positions for each candidate. The process becomes more accurate, efficient, and faster than most manual tasks (Ahmad, 2018). Adopting human resources management with modern methods, such as machine learning, is the key to success, as human resources are the main base for any institution. Therefore its use of technology will help it develop all human and practical aspects in the future. Thus this development will help reduce their working hours; it helps them carry out their duties intelligently, considering all aspects.

A machine learning-based semi-supervised job title classification system has been developed with a proposed system known as Carotene (Javed, Luo, McNair, Jacob, Zhao, & Kang, 2015). It holds a set of classification and clustering tools and techniques to design a scalable classification system for an extensive taxonomy of job categories. It enclosed all these techniques in cascade classifier architecture.

In (Awujoola, Odion, Irhebhude, & Aminu, 2021), a modern and accurate machine-learning classification model is proposed to predict and assess job applicants' attributes based on their academic performance datasets in other to select the most appropriate candidate. In this model, both supervised and unsupervised machine learning classifiers were used.

In (Liu, Allen, L., Blickstein, Okidi, & Shi, 2021), data from thousands of historical clinical trials are used to explore a new machine learning that predicts the number of patients enrolled per month at a clinical trial site throughout a trial's enrollment duration. The developed method can reduce the error and propose opportunities for further improvement.

In (Choi & Choi, 2020), Machine learning techniques predict employees' job involvement. Therefore, human resource (HR) management leaders can take proactive measures or introduce a plan of succession for preservation. Indeed, job involvement has a significant impact on work outcomes.

The employee turnover rate can highly affect the organization's performance. For this reason, predicting employee turnover has recently become an invaluable tool for any organization seeking to retain employees and predict their future behavior. Alaskar, Crane, and Alduailij (2019) used machine learning (ML) algorithms to predict whether employees would leave a company. It is based on a comparative performance combination of five ML algorithms and three Feature Selection techniques. This study identifies the best predictors using the SelectKBest, Recursive Feature Elimination (RFE), and Random Forest (RF) model. Different ML algorithms were trained, which included logistic regression, decision tree (DT), naïve Bayes, support vector machine (SVM), and AdaBoost with optimal hyperparameters. The predictive models' performance was evaluated using several critical metrics. The empirical results have demonstrated that two predictive models performed better: DT with SelectKBest and the SVM-polynomial kernel using RF.

In (Lechner, Strittmatter, & Knaus, 2020), the heterogeneity effects of job search programs for unemployed workers have been studied. The authors combined non-experimental causal empirical models with Lasso-type estimators to investigate possibly heterogeneous employment effects. The empirical analyses are based on rich administrative data from Swiss social security records. As a result, the authors found considerable heterogeneities only during the first six months after training. Consistent with previous literature results, unemployed persons with fewer employment opportunities profit more from participating in these programs. Furthermore, the authors document heterogeneous employment effects by residence status. Moreover, they show the potential of easy-to-implement program participation rules for improving the average employment effects of these active labor market programs.

In (Fallucchi, Coladangelo, Giuliano, & Luca, 2020), the authors analyze how objective factors influence employee attrition in order to identify the leading causes that contribute to a worker's decision to leave a company and to be able to predict whether a particular employee will leave the company. After the training, the obtained model for the prediction of employees' attrition is tested on a real dataset provided by IBM analytics, which includes 35 features and about 1500 samples. Results show that the algorithm that produced the best results for the available dataset is the Gaussian Naïve Bayes classifier. It reveals the best recall rate (0.54) since it measures the ability of a classifier to find all the positive instances and achieves an overall false negative rate equal to 4.5% of the total observations.

In (Jain & Nayyar, 2018), a novel model for predicting Employee Attrition using Machine Learning based approach is proposed. This model is highly robust. The data set is acquired via an online database and fetched to the system to validate the accuracy of the system proposed for Employee Attrition. Highly stunning, and the system regarding Employee turnover behavior shows precision results.

In (Kakulapati, Chaitanya, Chaitanya, & Akshay, 2020), the authors applied ML techniques to analyze the employee information to improve their position in the organization. Compensation and job performance information from revenue rates and personnel characteristics to payroll and service history, never before have HR executives had such liberated right to use individual details. In this research, the authors applied random forest classification, which facilitates employee classification based on their monthly income and is an informal way to execute analytics on data. Further, they use clustering techniques based on the performance metrics similarity to analyze employee performance.

CONCLUSION

As a branch of artificial intelligence, machine learning allows applications to enhance accuracy and predict output without being programmed. Usually, ML algorithms use historical data as input to predict the new output values. Nowadays, ML techniques are widely used in many applications such as healthcare areas, navigation systems, business fields, and power systems. In this chapter, the use of ML tools in the Human resources department has been presented. Indeed, many companies in developing countries suffer from enormous non-digitalization data that becomes heavy to manage with the company's scalability. For this reason, the use of new technology tools such as ML and artificial intelligence becomes an essential need.

Human resource (HR) is the central department of any company. It covers many responsibilities such as analyzing the workforce, resolving employees' problems, and recruitment. Thus, recruitment is one of the most critical processes of the HR department. It performs the selection of the right candidate for any new position. However, the selection is very complex due to the massive number of applicants applying for a job. Thus, if the method used in the selection process is unsuitable, the result may be confused and irrelevant. For this reason, using ML techniques in this process is critical.

In this chapter, ML has been presented. The authors focused on classification and decision-making problems. In addition, recent research on using ML techniques in the recruitment step has been presented. In future work, a discussion about the efficiency of using new ML techniques in the HR department should be done.

REFERENCES

Abdel Baki, S. (2001). *Scientific and applied aspects of human resource management in organizations*. University house.

Ahmad, O. (2018). Artificial intelligence in HR. *International journal of research and analytical reviews*, 971-978.

Alaskar, L., Crane, M., & Alduailij, M. (2019). Employee turnover prediction using machine learning. *In International conference on computing* (pp. 301-316). Springer.

Alayan, R. M. (2007). Foundations of contemporary management (1 ed.). Dar Safaa for printing, publishing and distribution.

Apte, C. (2010). *The role of machine learning in business optimization*. Semantic Scholar.

Awujoola, O., Odion, P., Irhebhude, M., & Aminu, H. (2021). Performance evaluation of machine learning predictive analytical model for determining the job applicants employment status. *Malaysian Journal of Applied Sciences*, 67-79.

Ayodele, T. O. (2010). Types of machine learning algorithms. *New Advances in Machine Learning*, *3*, 19–48.

Ballout, H. I. (2002). *Human resource management from a strategic perspective* (1st ed.). Arab Renaissance House for Printing, Publishing and Distribution.

Beaumont, P. B. (1993). Human resource management: Key concepts and skills. Sage.

Bellinger, C., Sharma, S., & Japkowicz, N. (2012). One-class versus binary classification: Which and when? *In 2012 11th international conference on machine learning and applications*, (pp. 102-106). IEEE.

Braiek, H. B., Khomh, F., & Adams, B. (2018). The open-closed principle of modern machine learning frameworks. *IEEE/ACM 15th International Conference on Mining Software Repositories* (pp. 353-363). IEEE.

Buccio, E. D., Li, Q., Melucci, M., & Tiwari, P. (2018). Binary classification model inspired from quantum detection theory. *In Proceedings of the 2018 ACM SIGIR International Conference on Theory of Information Retrieval*, (pp. 187-190). ACM. 10.1145/3234944.3234979

Bzdok, D., Krzywinski, M., & Altman, N. (2018). Machine learning: Supervised methods. *Nature Methods*, *15*(1), 5–6. doi:10.1038/nmeth.4551 PMID:30100821

Candanedo, I. S., Nieves, E. H., González, S. R., Martín, M., & Briones, A. G. (2018). Machine learning predictive model for industry 4.0. *International Conference on Knowledge Management in Organizations* (pp. 501-510). Springer. 10.1007/978-3-319-95204-8_42

Carleo, G., Cirac, I., Cranmer, K., Daudet, L., Schuld, M., Tishby, N., Vogt-Maranto, L., & Zdeborová, L. (2019). Machine learning and the physical sciences. *Machine learning and the physical sciences. Reviews of Modern Physics*, *91*(4), 045002. doi:10.1103/RevModPhys.91.045002

Carlson, K. D., & Kavanagh, M. J. (2011). HR metrics and workforce analytics. *Human resource information systems: Basics, applications, and future directions*, 150.

Choi, Y., & Choi, J. (2020). A study of job involvement prediction using machine learning technique. *The International Journal of Organizational Analysis*.

Edgley-Pyshorn, C., & Huisman, J. (2011). The role of the HR department in organisational change in a British university. *Journal of Organizational Change Management*, *24*(5), 610–625. doi:10.1108/09534811111158886

Fallucchi, F., Coladangelo, M., Giuliano, R., & Luca, E. W. (2020). Predicting employee attrition using machine learning techniques. *Computers*, *9*(4), 86. doi:10.3390/computers9040086

Feng, W., Sui, H., Tu, J., Huang, W., & Sun, K. (2018). A novel change detection approach based on visual saliency and random forest from multi-temporal high-resolution remote-sensing images. *International Journal of Remote Sensing*, *39*(22), 7998–8021. doi:10.1080/01431161.2018.1479794

Garg, S., Sinha, S., Kar, A. K., & Mani, M. (2021). A review of machine learning applications in human resource management. *International Journal of Productivity and Performance Management*.

Ghorbanzadeh, M., Zhang, J., & Andersson, P. (2016). Binary classification model to predict developmental toxicity of industrial chemicals in zebrafish. *Journal of Chemometrics, 30*(6), 298–307. doi:10.1002/cem.2791

Guillemette, M. G., Laroche, M., & Cadieux, J. (2014). Defining decision making process performance: Conceptualization and validation of an index. *Information & Management, 51*(6), 618–626. doi:10.1016/j.im.2014.05.012

Hadadi, S. A. (2014). *HR Management.* University of Biskra Repository.

Haenlein, M., & Kaplan, A. (2019). A Brief History of artificial intelligence: On the past, present, and future of artificial intelligence. *California Management Review, 61*(4), 5–14. doi:10.1177/0008125619864925

Haenlein, M., & Kaplan, A. (2019). A Brief History of Artificial Intelligence: On the Past, Present, and Future of Artificial Intelligence. *California Management Review, 61*(4), 61. doi:10.1177/0008125619864925

Hamdawi, W. (2004). *HR Management.* Université 8 mai 1945 - GUELMA.

Hassan, R. (2011). A strategic approach to planning and developing human resources (1 ed.). University house for printing, publishing and distribution.

Hölzle, K. (2010). Designing and implementing a career path for project managers. *International Journal of Project Management, 28*(8), 779–786. doi:10.1016/j.ijproman.2010.05.004

Jain, R., & Nayyar, A. (2018). Predicting employee attrition using xgboost machine learning approach. IEEE international conference on system modeling & advancement in research trends (smart), (pp. 113-120). IEEE.

Javed, F., Luo, Q., McNair, M., Jacob, F., Zhao, M., & Kang, T. (2015). Carotene: A job title classification system for the online recruitment domain. *IEEE First International Conference on Big Data Computing Service and Applications.* IEEE. 10.1109/BigDataService.2015.61

Jones, B. (1997). HR: Fated to a supporting role? *Management Review, 86*(3), 7–8.

Kaggle. (2018). *2018 Kaggle Machine Learning & Data Science Survey.* Kaggle: https://www.kaggle.com/datasets/kaggle/kaggle-survey-2018

Kakulapati, V., Chaitanya, K., Chaitanya, K., & Akshay, P. (2020). Predictive analytics of HR-A machine learning approach. *Journal of Statistics and Management Systems, 23*(6), 959–969. doi:10.1080/09720510.2020.1799497

Karniadakis, G. E., Kevrekidis, I. G., Lu, L., Perdikaris, P., Wang, S., & Yang, L. (2021). Physics-informed machine learning. *Physics-informed machine learning. Nature Reviews Physics, 3*(6), 422–440. doi:10.103842254-021-00314-5

Kavitha, S., Varuna, S., & Ramya, R. (2016). A comparative analysis on linear regression and support vector regression. Online international conference on green engineering and technologies. IEEE.

Khanzode, K. C., & Sarode, R. D. (2020). Advantages and Disadvantages of Artificial Intelligence and Machine Learning: A Literature Review. *International Journal of Library and Information Science, 9*(1), 3.

Khashei, M., Eftekhari, S., & Parvizian, J. (2012). Diagnosing diabetes type II using a soft intelligent binary classification model. *Review of Bioinformatics and Biometrics,* 9-23.

Kraev, V. M., & Tikhonov, A. I. (2020). Modern recruitment approaches in personnel selection. *Revista ESPACIOS, 41*(12).

Laumer, S., Maier, C., & Weitzel, T. (2022). HR machine learning in recruiting. In *Handbook of Research on Artificial Intelligence in Human Resource Management*. Edward Elgar Publishing.

Lechner, M., Strittmatter, A., & Knaus, M. (2020). Heterogeneous employment effects of job search programmes: A machine learning approach. *The Journal of Human Resources*.

Liu, J., Allen, P., L., B., Blickstein, D., Okidi, E., & Shi, X. (2021). A Machine Learning Approach for Recruitment Prediction. *Clinical Trial Design. arXiv*.

Lunenburg, F. C. (2010). The decision making process. *National Forum of Educational Administration & Supervision Journal, 27*(4).

Maher, A. (2018). HR Management (7 ed.). University house for printing, publishing and distribution.

Maulud, D., & Abdulazeez, A. M. (2020). A review on linear regression comprehensive in machine learning. *Journal of Applied Science and Technology Trends, 1*(4), 140–147. doi:10.38094/jastt1457

Min, J., & Jeong, C. (2009). A binary classification method for bankruptcy prediction. *Expert Systems with Applications, 36*(3), 5256–5263. doi:10.1016/j.eswa.2008.06.073

Nasserddine, G., & Arid, A. E. (2022). Decision Making Systems. In J. Wang (Ed.), *Encyclopedia of Data Science and Machine Learning* (Vols. 1–3). IGI Global.

Neelamegam, S., & Ramaraj, E. (2013). Classification algorithm in data mining: An overview. *International Journal of P2P Network Trends and Technology (IJPTT)*, 369-374.

Rąb-Kettler, K., & Lehnervp, B. (2019). *Recruitment in the times of machine learning*. Management Systems in Production Engineering. doi:10.1515/mspe-2019-0018

Shailaja, K., Seetharamulu, B., & Jabbar, M. A. (2018). Machine Learning in Healthcare: A Review. *Second international conference on electronics, communication and aerospace technology* (pp. 910-914). IEEE.

Smola, A., & Vishwanathan, S. V. (2008). Introduction to machine learning. Cambridge University, 32(24), 2008.

Williams, K., Idowu, P. A., Balogun, J. A., & Oluwaranti, A. I. (2015). Breast cancer risk prediction using data mining classification techniques. *Transactions on Networks and Communications, 3*(2), 01.

Yakubovich, V., & Lup, D. (2006). Stages of the recruitment process and the referrer's performance effect. *Organization Science, 17*(6), 710–723. doi:10.1287/orsc.1060.0214

Yordanov, V. (2021). *Classification Metrics — Confusion Matrix Explained*. Retrieved from Towardsdatascience: https://towardsdatascience.com/classification-metrics-confusion-matrix-explained-7c7abe4e9543

Zayed, A. (2006). Outstanding organizational performance. In *The way to the future organization* (2nd ed.). Arab Organization for Administrative Development.

Chapter 14
Artificial Intelligence in Higher Education:
A New Horizon

Fatima Al Husseiny

https://orcid.org/0000-0001-8547-6929

Lebanese International University, Lebanon

ABSTRACT

Artificial intelligence (AI) can address some of the most significant issues facing education today, innovate teaching and learning methods, and eventually quicken the fulfillment of SDG 4. However, these quick technological advancements carry with them several challenges that have thus far surpassed regulatory structures and policy discussions. The Education 2030 Agenda can be achieved with the help of AI technologies. AI has already been used in education, especially in various tools and assessment platforms that aid skill development. The goal is that as AI educational solutions continue to develop, they will help close gaps in learning and teaching and free up schools and teachers to accomplish more than before. To provide teachers the time and freedom to teach understanding and adaptability—uniquely human talents where computers would struggle— while AI can promote efficiency, personalization, and streamline administrative procedures. This chapter presents challenges and opportunities related to AI use in education and ends with recommendations.

INTRODUCTION

Artificial intelligence (AI) applications in education are expanding and have drawn much interest in recent years. The 2018 Horizon study (Educause, 2018) highlights AI and adaptive learning technologies as significant educational technology advancements, with two to three years of adoption. Horizon Report 2019 Higher Education Edition (Educause, 2019) predicts that AI applications related to teaching are expected to increase even more significantly. Still, experts anticipate AI in Education to grow by 43% between 2018 and 2022. There is little question that AI technology is inextricably related to the future of higher education, according to Contact North, an influential Canadian non-profit online learning group

DOI: 10.4018/978-1-6684-6937-8.ch014

(Contact North,2018). The German Research Centre for Artificial Intelligence1 (DFKI) and other non-profit public-private partnerships have made significant investments. Likely, this wave of interest will soon substantially impact higher education institutions (Popenici & Kerr, 2017). Google, for example, recently acquired European AI startup Deep Mind for $400 million.

Additionally, the Netherlands' Technical University of Eindhoven recently announced that it would establish an Artificial Intelligence Systems Institute with 50 new professorships for AI instruction and study. The 20th annual AIEd conference is being organized this year by the International AIEd Society (IAIED), founded in 1997 and published in the International Journal of AI in Education (IJAIED). On a larger scale, educators have only recently begun investigating the potential educational opportunities that AI applications provide for assisting students across the student life cycle. The development of AI applications in higher education introduces new ethical considerations and risks despite the enormous benefits that AI may provide to help teaching and learning. Though the field of artificial intelligence (AI) has its roots in computer science and engineering, it has also been heavily influenced by other academic fields like philosophy, cognitive science, neurology, and economics. There is limited consensus among AI researchers on a single definition and understanding of AI and intelligence in general due to the interdisciplinary nature of the discipline (Tegmark,2018).

This chapter discusses the recent trends in AI and education and challenges facing teachers and learners and ends with a recommendation section and a conclusion.

BACKGROUND

When John McCarthy organized a two-month workshop at Dartmouth College in the United States in the 1950s, artificial intelligence (AI) was born. McCarthy used the term "artificial intelligence" for the first time in the workshop proposal in 1956 (Russel & Norvig, 2010): The hypothesis that every facet of learning or any other characteristic of intelligence can, in theory, be so succinctly stated that a computer could be created to replicate. It is the foundation upon which the study [of artificial intelligence] is to proceed. The broad definition of artificial intelligence offered by Baker and Smith (2019) is: "Computers that do cognitive functions, often associated with human minds, particularly learning and problem-solving." They clarify that "AI" does not refer to a specific technology. It serves as a general phrase to describe various tools and techniques, including algorithms, neural networks, data mining, and machine learning. AI and machine learning are frequently used interchangeably. Machine learning is an artificial intelligence (AI) technique for supervised and unsupervised categorization and profiling. Machine learning is a branch of artificial intelligence, according to Popenici and Kerr (2017), that entails "software capable of recognizing patterns, making predictions, and applying newly discovered patterns to circumstances that were not included or covered by their initial design". AI is based on rational agents, which may be defined as anything that can perceive its environment through sensors and act on it through actuators (Russel & Norvig,2010).

Experts in the field distinguish between limited and general AI or weak and strong AI (Russel & Norvig, 2010).The philosophical dilemma of whether machines will ever be able to genuinely think or even develop consciousness, as opposed to just imitating thought and behaving rationally, continues. Such powerful or all-encompassing AI is unlikely to exist anytime soon. As a result, a critical question arises, what potential uses for AI in Education, specifically higher education, are there given this grasp of technology?

There are three kinds of AI software applications in Education a) personal tutors, b) intelligent support for collaborative learning, and c) intelligent virtual reality. Intelligent tutoring systems (ITS) can replicate one-on-one, individualized tutoring. Based on learner models, algorithms, and neural networks, they may decide on a student's learning route and the content to choose, offer cognitive scaffolding and assistance, and engage the student in conversation. ITS have immense potential, especially in large-scale institutions that offer distance education and run modules with thousands of students, where one-on-one coaching by humans is not viable. Numerous studies demonstrate that learning is a social activity; interaction and cooperation are at the core of the learning process (Jonassen, Davidson, Collins, Campbell, & Haag,1995). Online collaboration must, however, be promoted and moderated (Salmon,2000). AIEd can aid with the construction of adaptive groups based on learner models, promote online group interaction, or summarize discussions that can be utilized by a human tutor to direct students toward the course's goals and objectives. Last but not least, using ITS as well, intelligent virtual reality (IVR) is employed to involve and direct students in genuine virtual settings and game-based learning environments. For instance, in virtual or remote labs, virtual agents can take on the roles of teachers, facilitators, or peers for students (Perez et al.,2017).

AI can deliver real-time evaluation and feedback. AIEd can be integrated into learning activities to examine student achievement in place of stop-and-testing continually. High levels of accuracy have been achieved when using algorithms to forecast the likelihood that a student will fail an assignment or withdraw from a course.

In their latest report, Baker and Smith (2019) approach educational AI technologies from three angles: learner-facing, teacher-facing, and system-facing. Learner-facing Software, such as adaptive or personalized learning management systems or ITS, is what students utilize as AI tools to learn a subject. Through the automation of duties like administration, evaluation, feedback, and plagiarism detection, teacher-facing systems help teachers and lighten their workloads. AIEd systems also give teachers visibility into their students' learning progress, enabling them to provide proactive support and direction when necessary. System-facing AIEd is the technology that offers administrators and managers information at the institutional level, for instance, to track attrition patterns among faculties or colleges.

A Digital Shift

A considerable shift in the direction of the new realities in this digital age is necessary and urges everyone to take advantage of the chances offered by the increase in technological advancements and the increasing use of artificial intelligence. So, it should be no surprise that artificial intelligence will fundamentally alter how higher education is conducted. The technological advancement that will significantly improve human lives is artificial intelligence. It is a burgeoning technical field that has the power to change every facet of human interpersonal interactions (Bostrom, 2017). In the area of Education, AI has been observed to have already started implementing novel teaching and learning strategies that are now being tested and restructured in many situations (Bostrom, 2017). AI needs sophisticated infrastructures and a dynamic innovation ecosystem. As a result, the learning age is about to enter a new phase. In this era of big data and digitization, each leaves behind a trail of personal information that eventually generates a wealth of data that makes it possible to objectively quantify and measure social and human behavior, making it simple to track, model, and, some extent, predict it. There have been many discussions on how artificial intelligence development has the most significant potential to alter higher education of any technological breakthrough. Bates (2018), for instance, some of AI's benefits in higher education are but are not limited to: improving outcomes, broadening access, fostering retention, cutting costs, and shortening time completion.

Since the 2020s, How Has the Situation Changed?

The potential and restrictions of AI in Education have received very little attention to date, especially in light of the severe issues faced by least developed nations. It's crucial to comprehend how these changes will affect instruction and learning. In some societies, artificial intelligence has already found extensive applications. The list of applications of AI in higher education provided by Zuboff (2019) is comprehensive and shows the areas that researchers have tended to concentrate on. He lists the following four significant uses of AI in Education: profiling and prediction, intelligent tutoring systems, assessment and evaluation, and adaptive systems and personalization. In recent years, machine intelligence, deep learning, and cognitive architectures have seen a comeback, and many observers believe that AI will have a bright future in all spheres of society (Kaku, 2012; Kelly, 2017). For instance, Tegmark (2018) contends that we have not yet reached the state of "Artificial General Intelligence," in which machines' processing power matches humans' cognitive abilities. Bostrom (2017) also contends that we have already gone through an "AI Winter," during which time those who support AI have lost some credibility. These days, students are at the vanguard of a dizzying array of opportunities and challenging for teaching and learning in higher education.

Artificial intelligence (AI) holds the potential of significant educational advantages, including customized learning tailored to the preferences of each student, allowing them to learn at their speed and manage iterations to increase their understanding of the subject. According to university administrators, a future benefit of AI will be its capacity to "evaluate pupils, provide feedback, and originate and test scientific hypotheses at least as effectively as humans can" (Alexander et al., 2019).

AI's opportunities and challenges Particularly in expert systems, the complexity of human intellect has long been underrated. Technological constraints and managerial challenging still hamper the creation of expert systems. Despite inevitable hiccups, expert systems' future is bright with cutting-edge technologies' help. Benefits of the smart Campus The university experience can be intimidating, especially for first-year and overseas students who must negotiate a vast array of inquiries and resources. Chatbots that interact with the Microsoft bot platform make it easier for students to get answers to their queries. Students can find their needed data with Griffith University's "Sam." The "not" at the University of Sydney facilitates quick responses from the finance department to inquiries about POs and other relevant matters. To answer questions from students, the University of Canberra created Lucy, a student chatbot. If the offered response is unsatisfactory, the user can always flag the query to be answered by a human (Sharma, 2021).

Teachers and Robots for Learner's Welfare

The ideal scenario for AI in Education is one in which robots and teachers collaborate to benefit the learners by utilizing their most outstanding qualities. Educational institutions should actively exploit the available technology and expose students to AI's potential as they will work in the future where it is a reality. Educators have prioritized adapting instruction to meet the unique needs of each student through individualized and differentiated instruction. Still, AI will enable a level of differentiation that is currently hard for instructors to achieve with thirty learners in each class. Many businesses, including Carnegie

Learning and Content Technologies, are creating digital platforms with intelligent instruction design that use AI to deliver learning, testing, and feedback to students from pre-K to college level, identifying knowledge gaps and guiding them to new challenges when necessary (UNICEF, 2019).

As AI develops, it may be conceivable for a machine to analyze a student's facial expression to determine their difficulty understanding a concept and adjust a lesson accordingly. Currently, it is not practical to tailor the curriculum to each student's needs, but AI-powered machines will be able to do so (UNESCO, 2019). All pupils have access to everything. All students, including those who speak different languages or may have visual or auditory impairments, should be able to participate in global classrooms with the aid of artificial intelligence tools. A free PowerPoint add-in, Presentation Translator, generates real-time subtitles for the teacher's speech. This opens new opportunities for students who might be unable to attend class due to illness or who need instruction at a different level or in a subject not offered at their local institution. AI can assist in removing barriers between traditional grade levels and schools (Williamson, 2015). automate office procedures A teacher spends a lot of time marking assignments and exams. This is where artificial intelligence (AI) can help by quickly completing these jobs and providing suggestions to fill in any knowledge gaps. Machines are near to being able to evaluate written responses, even though they can already grade multiple-choice exams. Teachers now have more time to spend with each pupil as AI takes over the administrative responsibilities that used to be done manually.

Additionally, AI significantly promises to improve enrollment and admissions procedures (Williamson, 2015). Of course, issues with AI's adverse results are associated with the employment of artificial intelligence in higher education. The risk of unfavorable effects is the first. There will be undesirable unintended repercussions or even blowback despite the best efforts of individuals who build and use these systems. Consideration should be given to several different elements to avoid these negative results. The data these technologies use should be one of the first things considered. This information may be of varying quality, be out of date or come from a population subset that may not be representative of the students who are the target audience. For instance, AI learning algorithms tested on students in a specific type of California college or university could not produce the same results or reflect the same accuracy for students in another region. For natural digital learners, an AI system built on Generation X students would not be as effective.

How AI systems provide, insights are taught and interpreted depends on developer choices. Some give thorough details on many aspects of student learning or behavior so that teachers and administrators can take appropriate action. Other observations don't help interventions as much. For instance, in an organic chemistry class, one predictive analytics program predicted that 80% of the students wouldn't finish the term. The academics were aware of this but were unsure of what to do. Knowing in advance what you intend to do with the data these technologies provide is crucial (Sharma, 2021).

LEARNING ANALYTICS, COMPUTER-BASED INSTRUCTION, EDUCATIONAL DATA MINING, AND ARTIFICIAL INTELLIGENCE IN EDUCATION

Computer science, statistics, and education are all critical subjects combined to form artificial intelligence in Education (AIEd). AIEd is a fourth discipline that includes, but is not limited to, these three, such as cognitive psychology and neuroscience. Other sub-fields that are closely related to AIEd are also produced by the intersection of the three core fields, such as Educational Data Mining (EDM), Learning Analytics (LA), and Computer-Based Education (CBE). Learning analytics education encompasses collecting, analyzing, and reporting data on learners and their contexts to comprehend and improve the learning environment. (Baepler & Murdoch, 2010). The characteristics, passions, and objectives of Learning Analytics (LA) and EDM are comparable. However, some significant distinctions exist, particularly in methodology and emphasis (Siemens & Baker,2012). Statistic, visualization, discourse analysis, social network analysis, and sense-making models are LA's most often used approaches. However, clustering, classification, Bayesian modeling, association mining, and model-based discovery are some of the most often used techniques in EDMin. Another difference is that LA places greater emphasis on explaining data and results, whereas EDM places more emphasis on discussing and contrasting DM technology education using computers. The term "computer-based education" (CBE) refers to using computers to train students in educational settings. At first, CBE systems were standalone applications that ran on a local computer and had any AI-based capabilities to solve concerns like student modeling, adaptation, and personalization. With the widespread use of the Internet, new e-learning systems and other web-driven educational systems have evolved.

Additionally, new types of adaptive and intelligent systems for educational purposes have been driven by the growing usage of AI techniques. As a result, there are some overlaps between CBE and AIEd. For example, ITS (Mostow & Beck, 2006), learning management system (Romero, Ventura, & Garca, 2008), adaptive hypermedia and multimedia system, test and quiz system (Romero, Zafra, Luna, &Ventura, 2013), and ubiquitous learning environment are all significant types of CBE systems that are currently being used in higher education.

Modern cultures are characterized partly by the value assigned to education. (Marshall, 2016) A significant change in the educational landscape is necessary to facilitate participation in the digital society and allow countries to benefit from the 4IR. But "wicked challenging" can arise in the field of education. Problems typically involve mutually dependent, linked challenges and require several explanations for their significant components (Marshall, 2016). A fresh approach to considering ICT in Education is essential to solving some of the issues raised by the 4IR. Building on the 3IR's development of in-person instruction and diverse asynchronous educational materials is a requirement for any education plan for the 4IR.

A complicated, dialectical, and thrilling opportunity, education in the 4IR (HE 4.0) can improve society. For numerous other spheres of life, the 4IR has varied ramifications. As a result, it presents chances for education as well as challenges. The education sector could be revolutionized to provide solutions to new challenges using several 4IR components, such as IoT, 3D printing, quantum computing, and AI. Butler-Adam (2018) asserts that one of the 4IR's consequences for the education sector has more to do with curricula, teaching, and learning than robotic tutors. In other words, teaching and learning must occur across industries. The numerous elements necessary for the 4IR's successful implementation must be taught to students and educators from various backgrounds. Students studying the humanities and social sciences must comprehend at least the principles upon which AI is based and how it functions, according to Butler-Adam (2018). In turn, students studying the basic and applied sciences must comprehend the political and social nature of the world in which they live. Given the assertion above, the 4IR promotes the concept of a multidisciplinary field in which humanities and social sciences collaborate with technologies to solve problems. The 4IR and the advancement of biotechnology and AI fundamentally contradict preconceived notions about people and their interactions with nature.

The 4IR curriculum, in general, should respond to political and social tensions brought on by the rapid speed of technological innovation (Penprase,2018), and 4IR liberal arts curricula should be established to account for the social dislocations from the 4IR. Online instruction and the growing usage of AI require new principles to give a theoretical foundation for digital pedagogy in teaching and learning (Penprase,2018). For pupils to develop the adaptive skills necessary to engage in the global digital society, profit from the digital economy, and take advantage of new opportunities for employment, innovation, creative expression, and social inclusion, digital literacy is a fundamental precondition (Brown-Martin,2017). Any digital education strategy should consider the effect of change on the educational system. This poses a serious issue. If students are ill-prepared and not enough resources are invested, changes may impact the quality of graduates (Marshall, 2016). Regarding quality metrics, education is especially vulnerable to wicked challenges (Marshall, 2016). In a contested educational transformation and strategy area, conceptualizing and operationalizing quality measurements, performance indicators, and academic outcomes becomes increasingly challenging.

New technological developments are frequently cited as the primary impetus for research and development (R&D) (Xing & Marwala, 2017). Technology-assisted research has produced several beneficial results. According to Xing & Marwala (2017), technology-driven R&D can take many forms. For example, it may involve using mobile capabilities to increase the accuracy of data acquisition, advanced big data analytics to find hidden statistical patterns, and AI to retool information search, collection, organization, and knowledge discovery, to name a few. Additionally, the right abilities will be needed for the 4IR to implement in education successfully. Implementing, managing, and collaborating with others while using new technology requires specific skills (Butler-Adam,2018). The necessary set of skills is crucial to get the best benefits from new technology. According to Gray (2016), in the not-too-distant future, about 35% of the abilities that are vital in the job today will change. As a result, new skill sets will be needed for the new revolution and the application of new technology.

For example, workers in the sales and manufacturing industries will require technological literacy abilities (Gray, 2016). The latest technology will create new jobs, like those for social media specialists, and eliminate old jobs, like those for toll booth operators (Nordin & Norman,2018). Additionally, the 4IR may impact morale and ethical judgments that need to be considered. The effect of technology on people's life is diverse. Numerous dynamic changes occur due to the widespread adoption of new technology in business, government, and other areas of life. According to Hooker and Kim (2019), recent technology developments like the AI revolution could have a more drastic effect by displacing workers on a scale that has never been witnessed. This can result in a significant portion of the population losing employment possibilities. However, the above argument is not universally agreed upon by authors, researchers, academics, and politicians.

On the one hand, others contend that the new revolution will create more jobs. On the other hand, the argument is that the widespread use of technology will lead to the abolition of present or future careers. In some industries, the rise of machines is plainly and visibly demonstrated. It is unclear who will be held accountable for the decrease in labor and employment caused by adopting new technology like robotics—the government or business. One of the issues is the human cost associated with the work of new technologies. In terms of education, ethics is significant in the academic world. Ethical boundaries should be underlined to ensure that ethical ideals are fostered in education as more educational goods become accessible and available (Nordin & Norman, 2018).

It is currently unclear how the 4IR will affect society specifically. One thing is for sure: Education must act quickly to keep up with the development of technological innovation (Penprase, 2018). With the creation and application of new technologies come their own set of risks for the 4IR. To reduce these hazards, careful planning is required. New risk management systems and procedures will also need to be implemented. This suggests a chance for a good life change due to the latest technologies. However, the risks and unfavorable effects of these new technical developments should not be disregarded by society.

Inequality is the first danger of the 4IR for education. Income disparity and inequality are socio-economic problems in South Africa. Social issues like a high crime rate, gender violence, and unemployment, among others, are more prevalent in unequal societies. Inequality is a hotly contested issue in South Africa's education system, which new technological advancements could further reinforce.

There is a chance that new technologies for education will only be accessible to the wealthier segment of the population, leaving the poor behind. The implementation of the last three industrial revolutions has made this clear. Many still lack Internet access, transportation, or safe drinking water. As a result, more inequality between the "haves" and "have nots" will increase societal unrest, distrust, and alienation. Social justice and the human situation need to be firmly considered. Consideration should be given to the effects of changing economic power and technological innovation on society at various socioeconomic levels. Understanding the dangers that lurk in a world becoming more interconnected is essential, as is promoting multicultural understanding and steadfast respect for freedom and human rights. Consequently, intercultural, and social skills should be strengthened (Penprase,2018)

Fourth Industrial Revolution and Education

Fundamentally, the development of novel technologies and the incredible processing power of intelligent machines are advancing higher education. Therefore, as artificial intelligence advances, teaching and learning in higher education face new opportunities and challenges. Artificial intelligence can also significantly alter the fundamental structure of higher education institutions. Since Aristotle has had no definitive definition of "artificial intelligence." Scientists began looking at artificial intelligence remedies in the 1950s. Turing offered the first solution to the quandary of what constitutes an "intelligent" system (Russel & Norvig, 2010). He proposed using a simulation to evaluate a listener's ability to recognize the difference between a conversation with a machine and one with a human; if the system cannot do so, we will admit to using artificial intelligence (AI). John McCarthy provided the most thorough definition of artificial intelligence later that year: "AI is the basis of the assumption that every aspect of learning or any other feature of intelligence can be precisely described as the property of machine or program; the intelligence that the system demonstrates." (Kerr, 2017).

Most approaches to the definition and use of artificial intelligence primarily emphasize cognition and ignore other political, philosophical, and psychological factors. Based on a previous review, the fundamental purpose of artificial intelligence was developed and is still being developed by scholars(Pool & Qualter, 2012). Artificial intelligence is currently developing more quickly, and this has already had a significant impact on the services provided by higher education. As an example of an emerging application of artificial intelligence, Deakin University in Australia has already used IBM's supercomputer Watson to give students recommendations (Moles & Wishart, 2016). This invention has a significant, positive impact on the university's staff, busy time, and service quality. As a result, it is essential to note that "machine learning" is a rapidly expanding research area in the science of artificial intelligence. While some artificial intelligence solutions are heavily dependent on programming, others have a built-in ability to forecast the future and recognize patterns. This study referred to machine learning as a subcategory of artificial intelligence (Schölkopf, 2015). Machine learning software may predict outcomes, spot trends, and then apply those just-discovered patterns to situations that weren't initially anticipated.

When discussing AI tools or equipment in Higher Educational settings, it is widely used on campuses or nowadays. They have many technologies like smartphones, the Internet, various apps, search engines, and home appliances. A typical example of artificial intelligence is the complex combination of software that powers Siri on iPhones (Shulman & Bostrom, 2012). MIT researchers predict that technology used in education will shift, particularly with the release of the first iPhone model in 2007. However, 'crossbreeds' or cyborgs of humans and machines, could emerge in the field of education shortly if the emphasis on "cyborgs" switches from science fiction to computer application for both instructors and students. The impact of artificial intelligence on the economy, which has caught the attention of many observers, is something that can be seen. Google made the most outstanding investment ($400 million) in acquiring Deep Mind technology in the European Union in 2014.

There are good reasons to look for AI solutions adoption in education, given college students' financial challenges. The combination of a machine and a human brain is possible. This challenges the teachers to find new dimensions, functions, and pedagogies in various contexts for learning and teaching. For instance, researchers from all over the world are interested in the brain-computer interface. The experts in the field of computers have presented various solutions to manage the software with a brain-computer interface by combining some approaches in modern computing systems with analysis methods and brain signals (Kena et al., 2015). The brain activity can be captured and decoded via a brain-computer interface.

Additionally, it facilitates communication between people with motor function challenges (Pandarinath et al., 2017). The technology's rapid advancement and employment of AI functions improve human skills and capacities. According to Schleicher, "Innovation in education is not just about adding more technology to more classrooms; it is about changing ways of teaching so that students have the skills they need to thrive in competitive global markets" (Schleicher, 2012). Artificial intelligence (AI) approaches can emulate and develop human decision-making processes.

Adaptive educational systems have been used in a variety of AI approaches. Fuzzy logic, neural networks, decision trees, Bayesian networks, hidden Markov models, and genetic algorithms are some names for these methods. To determine which strategy has the best learning theory of AI to apply to a specific learning environment, there is currently no agreement on the construction of a standard approach. Additionally, scientists are constantly developing software tools to make it easier to identify the learning type from students' learning behaviors. A device that is simply adjustable and available in various learning situations, such as traditional or online learning, is necessary for learning and teaching. Artificial intelligence can be used in the educational system to attain and manage educational goals (AI). Using AI, instructors can evaluate each student in a class and identify those struggling to grasp the concepts. If an AI study reveals that a student is weak in a few areas or struggles to understand a few concepts, the lecturer or parents will be informed, and the proper steps will be taken to scaffold learning.

Furthermore, since lecturers might not always be aware of gaps in their instructional materials that can cause students perplexity, Artificial Intelligence has the potential to highlight which course topics need to be improved. Students' interests can be piqued by introducing them to various information and courses, and classes can be customized based on each student's profile. Additionally, AI can help professors with homework. For instance, Coursera, a sizable open online course provider, rates students' solutions to a challenge. Because Coursera discovered that many students submitted the wrong answer to a homework assignment, the system notifies the instructor. It sends a message to potential students with hints for the correct response.

This AI technology helps explain courses and ensure that every student develops the same conceptual foundation. As a result, professors using technology in their instruction can benefit from the automatic data generated by student interaction because modern digital information systems can quickly process and store vast volumes of data. In addition to these specialized algorithms, these systems could determine the degree of student participation and decipher the behavioral patterns that emerge in a teacher's class. They could communicate these findings to the teacher. This technology allows professors to organize their classrooms better, spend less time on administrative tasks, and get more information from AI technologies to produce higher-quality, research-informed instruction. Although AI may not wholly replace human grading, it is on the verge of doing so. Nearly all multiple choice and fill-in-the-blank tests can be graded using AI automated grading. Software for grading essays is still in its infancy but will advance over the coming years.

AI tutors may provide extra assistance to students. However, kids will be tutored by artificial intelligence machines. Human tutors can teach some things that computers cannot. There are currently some artificial intelligence-based tutoring applications available to assist students with writing, fundamental mathematics, and other disciplines. These AI programs can only teach pupils the fundamentals; nevertheless, these robots fail when teaching students higher-order thinking and creativity.

AI and Teachers' Roles

The rapid development of technology makes advanced teaching systems less of a pipe dream. AI programs can provide constructive feedback to lecturers and students. AI has the potential to give professors and students feedback on how well the course is going. Some colleges use AI systems to measure and monitor students' development and alert professors if there is a problem with their performance. Additionally, these AI systems offer students the proper assistance and give educators feedback to enhance the teaching of the relevant subject area.

AI may change teachers' roles. It can handle various jobs, including grading and providing helpful comments on students' performance. They may even serve as a substitute for instruction. They might be programmed to answer queries, impart knowledge, and gather data for the most elementary course materials. However, in a few instances where AI has been used in education, the teacher's position has been replaced by a facilitator. Teachers can include AI teachings as supplemental materials to help struggling students and give pupils practical experiences through human connection. AI reduces the challenge of trial-and-error learning. AI systems have been created to aid students in education; in this setting, learners find the trial-and-error process considerably less scary. Since AI systems give students a learning environment that is essentially free from criticism, AI tutors can also make recommendations to improve students' performance. Because AI usually learns by making mistakes, it is considered the ideal learning system. Finally, AI systems may alter learners' learning and help them acquire fundamental abilities.

AI and Learning

Current developments in artificial intelligence are poised to alter how people learn in educational settings dramatically. AI programs are replacing specific classroom instruction by enabling students to learn from anywhere globally at any time. Additionally, AI systems may take the position of lecturers in several subjects in the future. Developing a collaborative and active class throughout course delivery fosters an environment of active involvement in an online setting. The first steps are setting learning objectives, engaging students in instruction and learning activities, providing feedback and assessing progress, and, most importantly, creating an environment that encourages active learning (Kaddoura & Al Husseiny, 2021).

Currently, some educational programs include AI to help pupils master fundamental abilities. However, as AI programmers progress, AI will probably offer students a wide range of services. AI systems provide this level of knowledge to save time and give teachers access to additional information that may not be immediately apparent or easy for teachers to detect. AI systems used in classrooms can analyze data from a variety of sources and compare it to patterns that have been observed. They can identify issues and direct lecturers to provide consistent results across various classes.

Restricting the potential possibilities and choosing the best implementation strategy is challenging because there are many technology options. The use of AI in educational systems has shown to be a very alluring approach. Additional factors, such as the enormous student population and more significant financial constraints, contribute to the deployment of AI. As a result, these elements transform colleges into markets that may draw a sizable student body and raise enrollment levels. (Fahimirad, & Kotamjani, 2018).

The question of how to assist students in increasing their learning activities to achieve desired outcomes, conduct assessments, and provide helpful feedback has persisted. Sian Bayne noted in Teacherbot that interventions in automated teaching "are motivated by a production-oriented solutionism" rather than educational considerations (Ferguson et al., 2015). MOOC is one lesson that demands attention. When MOOCs were used for the first time in 2008, we started hearing about changes in higher education. The findings of this research demonstrated that MOOCs did not fulfill the promises made to participants. A significant concern, however, relates to some irrational and unrestrained beliefs that accompany MOOCs when the decision-makers neglect to consider fundamental principles like evidence-based argumentation or scholarly skepticism.

Additionally, they had little interest in learning and just cared about the money gains (Popenici, 2013). Online education can successfully aid higher education in achieving several crucial teaching, learning, and research goals. Unfortunately, MOOCs focus primarily on a technology solution without considering the debates, which can cause some distractions in the classroom. The educational system is utilizing AI for teaching and learning. In light of this, recent advances in non-invasive brain-computer interfaces have caused us to reevaluate the instructors' function, or they have attempted to replace them with teacher robots or virtual "teacher bots instead of actual teachers" (Hayes, 2015). This provides some suggestions for using brain-computer interface (BCI) tools so that students can concentrate on the learning tasks and content (Beam & Kohane, 2016).

The presence of teachers over the entire semester may be automatically checked thanks to supercomputers like IBM's Watson. The ability to communicate and command through the more general applications of AI in the learning and teaching domains points to a significant technological revolution that has the potential to alter the structure of the educational system fundamentally. Utilizing teacher bots and individualized learning, completely online classes can be run. Teacher bots' computer solutions are mainly used to handle content delivery, essential feedback, and monitoring of the administrative element of teaching, which can be problematic for traditional teaching assistants (Kena et al., 2015). Artificial intelligence has several uses, including managing student learning and acting as a tutor. It is concerning that an automated AI solution is being employed in place of instruction, which is a quick but effective answer. We are currently searching for a new pedagogical philosophy that will help students acquire some vital social skills.

Along with being exposed to a wide range of technological applications, it appears indispensable to reconsider how technology is used in education. While it is true that AI solutions are cutting-edge, it is inconceivable that they could ever take the place of the human mind. Despite some positive opinions, it seems doubtful that the current technological advancements will continue in the future. Its capabilities are relatively limited. It is intended to inspire decision-makers to reexamine educational paradigms and prioritize civic involvement and innovation. It is possible to provide information and materials based on the needs of the students by taking into account the function of AI in directing the students' learning and monitoring their engagement.

Additionally, it might offer them support and feedback. However, the teachers prepare the children for hyper-complexity by utilizing this technology. Therefore, in the future, employability will not be the primary goal of technology use (Ratliff et al., 2006). Knowing how to use teacher bots seems necessary for the pupils' benefit, despite being disruptive to regular teaching personnel (Mason, 2010). The public was mostly unaware of the teacher bot's potential in 2017. But shortly, AI technology will intrude into our lives and direct educational systems (Ferguson et al., 2015). AI tools can keep track of our actions, decisions, flaws, and strengths and give us feedback, comparative statistics, motivation, and predictive text. A teacher bot can use artificial intelligence to provide individualized instruction and is generally thought of as a complicated algorithmic interface. A teacher bot can also deliver the curriculum; in addition, it will act as the student's supervisor or guide.

Thus, it may benefit the lecturers. Teacherbots are any type of machine-based hardware or software that can arrange lesson plans and offer prompt answers to various inquiries in the capacity of a teacher.

Teachers who use outdated methods to deliver material to obedient pupils in a classroom or in front of a computer face an accessible and highly customized alternative in developing AI programs like "Jill Watson" (Bayne, 2008). Intelligent robots are more likely to meet students' learning demands even if personal assistance and contact time with faculty members are viewed as advantages in higher education to give quality education.

The Future of Human Machines in Education: Digital Humanism

The development of "human" values in students, the teacher's comprehension of the students, the teacher's consideration of the students' feelings and emotions, and student participation in the learning process are all aspects of the humanistic tendency in education. The realization of the humanistic direction in education is most vividly felt in the context of digital education. These concern how students should develop their personalities in the modern electronic educational environment, the positive and negative effects of the electronic environment on students' personalities, and the character traits that students should develop in digital education. The humanistic trend in education emphasizes, first and foremost, students' mutual assistance, co-creation between themselves and the teacher, the formation of students' so-called "soft skills," or skills to build human relationships, the ability to engage in a dialogue, interact, work in a team and create collective projects - "images of the future," and the development of creative abilities. Second, the humanistic trend in education promotes the development of students' universal competencies, including teamwork and leadership, communication, intercultural interaction, self-organization, and self-development (Voronin, 2016). This trend implies establishing conditions for the students' active participation while considering their interests. The student's personality is positioned at the center of the instructional process.

Students can display their activity in online classes and virtual exhibitions thanks to the modern electronic informative and educational environment. There is a virtual exhibition available on the university website. The display features abstracts, scientific publications, projects, technical innovation, etc. Additionally, this process is ongoing (Bodnar et al., 2018). The active use of information and communication technologies (ICT) for equitable quality education and lifelong learning, as well as ICT's contribution to knowledge generation and distribution, is the general trend of modernization of the world's educational systems (Bodnar et al., 2018) According to the current UK-6 standard for universal competence, the students will need to learn how to manage their time effectively and, more importantly, plan and carry out their development trajectory (Voronin, 2016). To do this, they must be familiar with and committed to the principles of lifelong learning. The motto of contemporary education is "Lifelong Learning." Avoiding losing the student's individuality in the flow of information and current technology is crucial in the setting of the electronic informational and educational environment. A modern student must have the skills necessary to function in the academic and informational digital arena while remaining a "person." He should also have a value-based perspective on the world and people, as people are the standard by which all other things are measured. A modern specialist should be knowledgeable about professional activity and the digital economy.

Focusing the pedagogical process on the individual student's personality also encourages student cooperation and collaboration between the teacher and the pupils. However, digitalization is only required as a tool. The attitude toward a human is the fundamental distinction between technocracy and humanism: A technocrat (of whatever professional affiliation) views her as a means, but a humanist sees her as the end. This became especially clear for education when it was classified as a service industry. In the 20th century, society's and schools' technocratic endeavors proved unworkable. Historically, "abstract humanism" has always been exemplified by humanistic undertakings. The self-actualization of an individual is the foundation of humanistic educational conceptions.

In contrast, technocratic ones (from the second half of the 20th century) are based on Skinner's ideas, which are still widely accepted by real-world individuals. Their resilience can be attributed to their ease of use, accessibility, and the success of information technology, which helped to usher in a new wave of technocracy. Though not immediately apparent, humanistic ideas have no substitute.

Sound judgment and social awareness are elusive personal qualities that have always been important. However, the emphasis on new capabilities that consider the changing demands of the globe is growing among pundits. The organizational dynamics of the industry, government, and society are changing due to automation brought on by artificial intelligence, big data, ever-increasing computing power, advanced robots, and the proliferation of low-cost advanced technology.

Many professions, from bus drivers and construction workers to doctors and lawyers, are replacing their physical and mental jobs with technology. Jobs requiring physical labor, memorization of procedures, computation of solutions, and even synthesizing various pieces of information into new forms are quickly being replaced by computers. While this is happening, the focus of human work is shifting to include more social and cultural considerations, creativity and innovative problem-solving, digital literacy and technological integration, and quick adaptability. In place of fact-based knowledge or procedural skills, modern core competencies frequently emphasize higher-order, more complex, and sophisticated capabilities. Similarly, today's savants are often "excellent generalists," able to synthesize across fields, quickly pick up new concepts and contexts, and adapt to changing circumstances. In the recent past, highly talented professionals typically advanced by focusing on specialized subjects. Compared to previous decades, there is a higher expectation that people will continuously learn and build new skills throughout their lives.

This is primarily prompted by how quickly the world is changing. The term "Age of Acceleration" was coined by Pulitzer Prize-winning author Thomas Friedman to describe this period in light of the unrestrained global revolution and exponential rise of technology. To succeed in this era, we must develop the ability to flourish amid uncertainty and complexity. We require in-depth knowledge across various cognitive, affective, interpersonal, and physical capacities, and we need to hone those skills as circumstances change continually. We must adopt a system dynamics perspective and use a strategic understanding of complex systems and the wide-ranging implications of decisions made within them. Organizations must learn to adapt to changing needs, quickly capture and integrate lessons gained, and make it possible for new ideas to spread rapidly throughout their respective businesses. In other words, to develop and maintain 21st-century competencies, people need a greater breadth of interdependent knowledge and skills, a greater range of interdependent expertise and skills, at a greater depth, i.e., more advanced levels of nuanced capabilities, and these competencies must be acquired at a more incredible speed. To satisfy these expectations, we must adopt a culture of continuous learning, identify more effective ways to develop and keep the necessary information and abilities and create dependable feedback loops to guarantee that our systems continue to function effectively in a constantly changing environment. Put another way.

We must completely restructure the integrated official and informal education, training, and experience continuum (Walcutt & Schatz, 2019).

RECOMMENDATIONS

Driving AI Innovation for the Benefit of All

The structural problems of previous years not only persist as a concern but have been made worse by COVID-related disruptions across the education pipeline as the higher education industry struggles with the "new normal" of the post-pandemic. Students have traditionally had a challenging time navigating the complexity of higher education, especially in underfunded schools where there aren't enough advisors to offer help and direction. Transfer and financial assistance are two notoriously challenging "black boxes," Students with limited funds and "college expertise" are frequently forced to make decisions on their own that could end up being expensive and detrimental.

Even though overburdened institutions have fewer resources to provide advising and other essential student services, the educational disruptions that many students have experienced during the pandemic are likely to deepen this complexity by causing more significant variations in individual students' levels of preparation and academic histories when these issues are considered holistically, resolving the equity gaps that the industry needs to close will be much more challenging.

The complexity that students and higher education institutions encounter can be somewhat reduced by current developments in artificial intelligence approaches, such as machine learning, even though they are not a cure-all. To ensure that these technologies are developed and applied ethically and equitably, researchers and decision-makers should approach them with care and a healthy dose of skepticism. This is not a simple endeavor and will call for long-term, meticulous research in addition to the field's rapid technological advancements. Technology for AI-assisted Education holds a lot of promise, but it also runs the risk of merely reproducing historical biases. The summary section below provides a small example from current research findings highlighting the challenges and possibilities of fair and ethical AI research.

One of the early uses of AI in higher education was grade prediction based on machine learning. When students are expected to be in danger of failing a course, it is most frequently utilized in early-warning detection systems to signal them for help. It is now beginning to be part of degree pathway counseling initiatives. These interventions are intended to benefit the underprivileged pupils; how fair are these models to them? These issues are being addressed by a rapidly developing field of AI research, with education providing particularly complex problems and trade-offs regarding equality and fairness.

Machine learning algorithms typically anticipate things most accurately when they have seen those things most frequently in the past. As a result, they will be better at predicting the student groupings that produce the most common grades using grade prediction. The lower students will receive the worst treatment from the algorithms designed to help them, while the most common rate is high, which will perpetuate inequality. A recent study from the University of California, Berkeley that evaluated the forecasts of millions of course grades at the major public university found this to be the case. Even while it reduces overall accuracy, having the model pay equal attention to all grades improved outcomes for underserved groups and increased performance equity.

While it's crucial to consider prejudice and race in a prediction model, doing so carelessly can worsen inequality. The same study found that adding race as a variable to the model without making any other changes resulted in the least equitable performance across groups. Researchers discovered that an approach known as adversarial learning, which teaches the model not to detect race and adds a machine learning penalty when the model successfully guesses race based on a student's input data, produced the most equitable result (e.g., course history). To increase accuracy, researchers also tried to train separate models for each group; nevertheless, data from all students consistently improved prediction for every group instead of solely using that group's data

FUTURE RESEARCH DIRECTIONS

The incredible rate of technological advancement in recent years (machine learning, artificial intelligence, the Internet of things, big data, 3- and 4-D impressions, among others) provides a framework to rethink the relationship with higher education while taking into account the fact that changes in teaching are gradual and not always obvious. The idea of "augmented humanity" starts to consider human-artificial hybridizations. Concerning social control mechanisms and our levels of decision-making autonomy, changes in body postures concerning technology, the progressive generalization of an interface body, and the advancements in datafication, digitalization, artificial intelligence, and robotics present challenging challenges. We live through a technological evolution enabled by the automation of economic-political processes, which creates a false impression of progress and has long-lasting, profound repercussions on our existence. When technology is used to mediate instruction, understanding the boundaries of autonomy in decision-making becomes extremely important. In this light, it is possible to ask questions like: Are there distinctions between manual and automated tutoring? What benefits do universities currently beginning to use self-study courses gain from higher-level teaching? What influence may AI breakthroughs have on how higher education is changing? We think AI is how we simulate the human brain's intelligence. Computer science is responsible for designing intelligent systems—systems that exhibit the traits we identify with intelligence in human behavior—and is a subfield of artificial intelligence.

From a different angle, AI might be viewed in words provided by Herrera and Muoz, who conceptualize it as a science devoted to the pursuit of a profound knowledge of intelligence, taking into consideration its limitations and potential and characterizing it as a highly complex task. But to understand AI's backdrop better, we must go back to its inception. Alan Turing was one of the forerunners in this field when he created the well-known Turing machine, which could perform any calculation under the conditions of a binary data processing system. He contemplated making the Turing machine test in the final years of his life. On the premise that the observer cannot clearly distinguish their behavior from a human being, this hypothetical scenario allowed the machine to be given the attribute of thought. In other words, something akin to mimetic independence; establishes an implicit paradigm as the origin of the foremost pioneers of this field of knowledge, including McCulloch, Turing, von Neumann, Wiener and Pitts, and Gardner, among others. The current AI breakthroughs are a part of a civilization heavily influenced by technology. The breadth of education technology as a field and the justifications for incorporating technologies into education must be examined within the context provided by the network society.

On the one hand, information and communication technology are developing and are integrated into critical societal activities like business, science, and social movements. On the other hand, they are beginning to support the development of a cognitive ecology that challenges the literate culture, including the types of specialized knowledge and the social and cultural movements that feature young people and necessitate a reexamination of educational procedures. To be precise, today's society is not primarily a disciplinary society; instead, it is a society that prioritizes performance, excludes what is unusual, and presents itself as a society of freedom when every move is being watched by the digital panopticon. We contribute to hyperactivity, extreme performance, low tolerance for monotony and boredom, and the disappearance of otherness because, in our desire to stand out, differences are blurred; because excessive communication makes us more solitary; and because connections, rather than relationships, have taken the form of bonds. These are some essential characteristics that are relevant to comprehending the setting of modern university life.

The learning opportunities provided by information and communication technologies in higher education have been explicitly stated in numerous papers published over the past few years that looked at trends in practices in educational settings that were affected by technology. These papers highlight the increased chances for active, personalized, continuous, and rhizomatic learning, game-based learning, the doing culture, story- and event-based learning, dynamic learning, and incidental learning. By supporting constructivist strategies for fostering an active learning environment, interactive technology in education has boosted student engagement. Integrating technology into the classroom increases students' passion for learning while enhancing their understanding and recall of the lessons. (Itani et al. 2022). The digital change that has characterized the 21st century affects the learner's personal and academic lives. Each student uses technology regularly and owns at least one smart gadget.

Consequently, it is difficult to envision a classroom that does not use technology. For students to achieve the competencies for the digital era, they must be actively involved in their learning. (Kaddoura & Al Husseiny, 2021).

Due to the pandemic's effects on the world, technology, particularly distance learning, have gained more attention. According to the UNESCO IESALC, the temporary closure will affect roughly 23.4 million students in higher education and 1.4 million teachers in Latin America and the Caribbean; this amounts to approximately more than 98 percent of the region's population of higher education students and teachers. According to an OECD survey on e-learning in Higher Education in Latin America, face-to-face instruction was still widespread before the COVID-19 pandemic, being the dominant model in 65 percent of the universities, as opposed to 16 percent with a predominant hybrid model and 19 percent focused on e-learning. Despite the epidemic and the shift to virtual classrooms, there hasn't necessarily been a significant transformation in university instruction because the explanation-application-verification didactic model is well-established. We have seen that this didactic framework has been retained in online lessons without substantial alterations. The AI discussion highlights the potential to challenge even the most established educational paradigms. How much does the use of AI undermine the teaching and learning process in light of the development of platforms that stake a bet on affective computing and hyper-personalization? With the development of AI, how will graduates be able to develop their critical thinking abilities? Before the development of extreme datafication and digitalization, were there any margins of autonomy in decision-making? How can we forge critical digital citizenship that responds to the intricate problems we'll face in the years ahead? (Green et al. 2020).

CONCLUSION

AI is still a sleeping giant in education. It is unlikely that "breakthrough" AI applications for teaching and learning will come from traditional higher education. The AI model above brings to light the crucial question of whether technology should try to automate the replacement of educators or whether it should be used to empower both educators and students. What will it cost us, humans, if AI is incredibly successful in lowering the costs of teaching and learning? Some nations are making use of the wealth of educational data that the Information Age brought with it. To deliver more individualized learning experiences, these nations and their separate educational institutions have started collecting insights from massive data sets. Of course, the problems with data accuracy and the use of AI are the proverbial "elephant in the room" and demand attention. Education systems have also actively engaged in change to ensure students learn the skills needed for an AI-enabled future workplace. This emphasis on lifelong learning is, of course, sensible given how quickly AI technologies are developing. As a result, it may be necessary to make this process of rethinking and updating educational programs in response to AI into something that happens frequently and continuously. AI is unavoidably a sector that encourages innovation and, as a result, raises nations' competitiveness. Countries will keep competing in such a diverse and quickly changing environment. However, there is also an opportunity for cooperation, the cornerstone of which is knowledge sharing, at least in education. More data regarding how nations are growing in this unpredictable and constantly changing territory is required to advance the conversation and the importance of embracing complete perspectives of AI in Education.

REFERENCES

Alexander, B., Ashford-Rowe, K., Barajas-Murph, N., Dobbin, G., Knott, J., McCormack, M., & Weber, N. (2019). *Horizon report 2019 higher education edition.* Horizon. https://library.educause.edu/resources/2019/4/2019-horizon-report

Baepler, P., & Murdoch, C. J. (2010). Academic analytics and data mining in higher education. *International Journal for the Scholarship of Teaching and Learning, 4*(2), 1–9. doi:10.20429/ijsotl.2010.040217

Bagnell, J., Chestnutt, J., Bradley, D., & Ratliff, N. (2006). Boosting structured prediction for imitation learning. *Advances in Neural Information Processing Systems,* 19.

Baker, T., & Smith, L. (2019). *Educ-AI-tion rebooted? Exploring the future of artificial intelligence in schools and colleges.* NESTA. https://www.nesta.org.uk/report/education-rebooted/

Bates, T. (2018, December 3). *Another perspective on AI in higher education.* Online Learning and Distance Education Resources. https://www.tonybates.ca/2018/12/02/another-perspective-on-ai-in-higher-education/

Bayne, S. (2008). Higher education as a visual practice: Seeing through the virtual learning environment. *Teaching in Higher Education, 13*(4), 395–410. doi:10.1080/13562510802169665

Bayne, S., & Ross, J. (2016). Manifesto Redux: making a teaching philosophy from networked learning research. In *Proceedings of the 10th international conference on networked learning. Sustainable Development Education and Research, 2*(1), 1–7.

Beam, A. L., & Kohane, I. S. (2016). Translating artificial intelligence into clinical care. *Journal of the American Medical Association, 316*(22), 2368–2369. doi:10.1001/jama.2016.17217 PMID:27898974

Bodnar, A., Bodnar, E., & Makerova, V. (2018). Technocratic and Humanistic Trends in Education: New Tunes. *KnE Life Sciences*, 172-181.

Bostrom, N. (2017). *Superintelligence: Paths, dangers, strategies.* Oxford University Press.

Brown-Martin, G. (2017). Education and the Fourth Industrial Revolution. *Scientific Research.* https://www.scirp.org/(S(351jmbntvnsjt1aadkozje))/reference/referencespapers.aspx?referenceid=2641203

Butler-Adam, J. (2018). The Fourth Industrial Revolution and education. *South African Journal of Science, 114*(5/6), 1–2. doi:10.17159ajs.2018/a0271

Contact North. (2018). *Ten facts about artificial intelligence in teaching and learning.* TeachOnline. https://teachonline.ca/fr/node/101327

EDUCAUSE. (2018). *Horizon report: 2018 higher education edition Learning Initiative and The New Media Consortium.* Educause. https://library.educause.edu/

EDUCAUSE. (2019). *Horizon report: 2019 higher education edition.* Learning Initiative and The New Media Consortium, Educause. https://library.educause.edu/

Fahimirad, M., & Kotamjani, S. S. (2018). A review on the application of artificial intelligence in teaching and learning in educational contexts. *International Journal of Learning and Development, 8*(4), 106–118. doi:10.5296/ijld.v8i4.14057

Ferguson, R., Clow, D., Beale, R., Cooper, A. J., Morris, N., Bayne, S., & Woodgate, A. (2015) Moving through MOOCS: Pedagogy, learning design and patterns of engagement. In *European Conference on Technology Enhanced Learning.* (pp. 70-84). Springer. 10.1007/978-3-319-24258-3_6

Gray, A. (2016). The 10 Skills You Need to Thrive in the Fourth Industrial Revolution. *WeForum.* https://www.weforum.org/agenda/2016/01/the-10-skills-you-need-to-thrive-in-the-fourth-industrial-revolution/

Green, E., Singh, D., & Chia, R. (2022). *AI Ethics and Higher Education: Good Practice and Guidance for Educators, Learners, and Institutions.* Globethics.

Hayes, S. (2015). *MOOCs and Quality: A Review of the Recent Literature.* QAA MOOCs.

Hooker, J., & Kim, T. W. (2019). *Ethical implications of the 4th Industrial Revolution for business and society*. Emerald Publishing Limited.

Itani, M., Itani, M. A., Kaddoura, S., & Al Husseiny, F. (2022). The impact of the Covid-19 pandemic on online examination: Challenges and opportunities. *Global Journal of Engineering Education.*, *24*(2), 1–16.

Jonassen, D., Davidson, M., Collins, M., Campbell, J., & Haag, B. B. (1995). Constructivism and computer-mediated communication in distance education. *American Journal of Distance Education*, *9*(2), 7–26. doi:10.1080/08923649509526885

Kaddoura, S., & Al Husseiny, F. (2021). Online learning on information security based on critical thinking andragogy. *World Transactions on Engineering and Technology Education*, *19*(2), 157–162.

Kaddoura, S., & Al Husseiny, F. (2021). An approach to reinforce active learning in higher education for IT students. *Global Journal of Engineering Education*, *23*(1), 43–48.

Kaku, M. (2012). *Physics of the future: the inventions that will transform our lives*. Penguin.

Kelly, K. (2017). *The inevitable: understanding the 12 technological forces that will shape our future*. Penguin Books.

Kena, G., Musu-Gillette, L., Robinson, J., Wang, X., Rathbun, A., Zhang, J., & Dunlop Velez, E. (2015). *The Condition of Education 2015 (NCES 2015-144)*. US Department of Education, National Center for Education Statistics.

Luckin, R., Holmes, W., Griffiths, M., & Forcier, L. B. (2016). *Intelligence unleashed: An argument for AI in education*. Pearson.

Marshall, S. (2016). Technological innovation of higher education in New Zealand: A wicked problem? *Studies in Higher Education*, *41*(2), 288–301. doi:10.1080/03075079.2014.927849

Mason, M. (2010, August). Sample size and saturation in Ph.D. studies using qualitative interviews. In Forum Qualitative Sozialforschung/Forum: qualitative social research, 11(3).

Moles, J., & Wishart, L. (2016). Reading the map: Locating and navigating the academic skills development of pre-service teachers. *Journal of University Teaching & Learning Practice*, *13*(3), 4. doi:10.53761/1.13.3.4

Mostow, J., & Beck, J. (2006). Some useful tactics to modify, map, and mine data from intelligent tutors. *Natural Language Engineering*, *12*(2), 195–208. doi:10.1017/S1351324906004153

Nordin, N., & Norman, H. (2018). Mapping the Fourth Industrial Revolution global transformations on 21st-century education in the context of sustainable development. *Journal of Sustainable Development Education and Research*, *2*(1), 1–7. doi:10.17509/jsder.v2i1.12265

Pandarinath, C., Nuyujukian, P., Blabe, C. H., Sorice, B. L., Saab, J., Willett, F. R., Hochberg, L. R., Shenoy, K. V., & Henderson, J. M. (2017). High-performance communication by people with paralysis using an intracortical brain-computer interface. *eLife*, *6*, 6. doi:10.7554/eLife.18554 PMID:28220753

Pearson. (2021). *Artificial intelligence in Higher Education.* Pearson. https://www.pearson.com/uk/educators/higher-education-educators.html

Penprase, B. E. (2018). The fourth industrial revolution and higher education. *Higher education in the era of the fourth industrial revolution, 10*, 978-981.

Perez, S., Massey-Allard, J., Butler, D., Ives, J., Bonn, D., Yee, N., & Roll, I. (2017). Identifying productive inquiry in virtual labs using sequence mining. In *International conference on artificial intelligence in education.* Springer. 10.1007/978-3-319-61425-0_24

Pool, L. D., & Qualter, P. (2012). Improving emotional intelligence and emotional self-efficacy through a teaching intervention for university students. *Learning and Individual Differences, 22*(3), 306–312. doi:10.1016/j.lindif.2012.01.010

Popenici, S. (2013). *Higher Education and Affluenza.* Popenici.

Popenici, S. A., & Kerr, S. (2017). Exploring the impact of artificial intelligence on teaching and learning in higher education. *Research and Practice in Technology Enhanced Learning, 12*(1), 1–13. doi:10.118641039-017-0062-8 PMID:30595727

Romero, C., Ventura, S., & García, E. (2008). Data mining in course management systems: Moodle case study and tutorial. *Computers & Education, 51*(1), 368–384. doi:10.1016/j.compedu.2007.05.016

Romero, C., Zafra, A., Luna, J. M., & Ventura, S. (2013). Association rule mining uses genetic programming to provide feedback to instructors from multiple-choice quiz data. *Expert Systems: International Journal of Knowledge Engineering and Neural Networks, 30*(2), 162–172. doi:10.1111/j.1468-0394.2012.00627.x

Russel, S., & Norvig, P. (2010). *Artificial intelligence - a modern approach.* Pearson Education.

Salmon, G. (2000). *E-moderating - the key to teaching and learning online* (1st ed.). Routledge.

Schleicher, A. (2012). *Preparing teachers and developing school leaders for the 21st century: Lessons from around the world.* OECD Publishing.

Schölkopf, B. (2015). Learning to see and act. *Nature, 518*(7540), 486–487. doi:10.1038/518486a PMID:25719660

Sharma, Y. (2011). *Boost university-industry AI research collaboration.* University.

Shulman, C., & Bostrom, N. (2012). How hard is artificial intelligence? Evolutionary arguments and selection effects. *Journal of Consciousness Studies.*

Siemens, G., & Baker, R. S. D. (2012). Learning analytics and educational data mining: towards communication and collaboration. In *Proceedings of the 2nd international conference on learning analytics and knowledge,* (pp. 252-254). ACM. 10.1145/2330601.2330661

Tegmark, M. (2018). *Life 3.0: Being Human in the age of artificial intelligence.* Penguin Books.

UNESCO. (2019). *Artificial Intelligence in Education: Challenges and Opportunities for Sustainable Development.* United Nations Educational, Scientific and Cultural Organization.

Voronin, V. (2016). The present conditions and perspectives of the humanitarianization of modern engineering education. In *INTED2017 11th International Technology Education and Development Conference*, (pp. 6323–6329). IEEE.

Walcutt, J. J., & Schatz, S. (2019). *Modernizing Learning: Building the Future Learning Ecosystem*. Advanced Distributed Learning Initiative.

Williamson, B. (2015). Governing software: Networks, databases and algorithmic power in the digital governance of public education. *Learning, Media and Technology*, *40*(1), 83–105. doi:10.1080/17439 884.2014.924527

Xing, B., & Marwala, T. (2017). Implications of the Fourth Industrial Age for higher education. *Think (London, England)*, *73*, 10–15.

Zuboff, S. (2019). *The Age of Surveillance Capitalism: The Fight for a Human Future at the New Frontier of Power*. Public Affairs.

KEY TERMS AND DEFINITIONS

4IR: Fourth Industrial Revolution.

Artificial Intelligence: The replication of human intelligence functions by machines, particularly computer systems, is known as artificial intelligence. Expert systems, natural language processing, speech recognition, and machine vision are some examples of specific ai applications.

CBE: Computer-based education.

Deep Learning: Artificial neural networks, a class of algorithms inspired by the structure and operation of the brain, are the focus of the machine learning discipline known as deep learning.

Digital Humanism: The movement toward people-literate technology and away from computer-literate people is known as digital humanism.

ICT: Information communication technology.

Machine Learning: With machine learning (ml), a form of artificial intelligence (ai), software programs can predict outcomes more accurately without having to be explicitly instructed to do so. To forecast new output values, machine learning algorithms use historical data as input.

Teacher Bots: The most recent innovation in education technology is ai teaching robots. These devices are used in many schools' programs to carry out all of the teachers' monotonous duties. These bots can keep tabs on pupils' academic achievement in the classroom.

Chapter 15
Smart Farming:
Automatic Detection and Classification of Olive Leaf Diseases

Imen Fourati Kallel
Ecole Nationale d'Electronique et des Télécommunications de Sfax (ENET'Com), Tunisia

Mohamed Kallel
Ecole Nationale d'Electronique et des Télécommunications de Sfax (ENET'Com), Tunisia

Mahmoud Ghorbel
Centre de Recherche en Numérique de Sfax (CRNS), Tunisia

Mohamed Ali Triki
The Olive Tree Institute of Tunisia, Tunisia

ABSTRACT

Olive trees diseases harm the quality and the quantity of the harvest seriously, which causes considerable economic losses for farmers, and more importantly affects the national economy in its entirety. The aim of this investigation is to work out a recognizing pattern method, based on the analysis of the texture and supervised classification. It essentially detects and classifies olive tree diseases in order to provide the farmers with tools helping them not only to get informed of their trees' diseases, but also to know how to treat them effectively.

INTRODUCTION

Presumably, agriculture is a perpetually significant and critical sector, which deeply motivates income-raising, poverty reduction and food security. However, the harvests depend essentially on the meteorological circumstances and the technical procedures. Agricultural scholars are able to intervene and act on the technicality of agriculture rather than on the weather unsettlement. In this respect, smart agriculture becomes more and more a necessity as it benefits from the technological and the scientific continuous

DOI: 10.4018/978-1-6684-6937-8.ch015

progress. Specifically, artificial intelligence and pattern recognition are volatile. They are proven to be effective in medical, military, industrial fields, and notably agricultural. Smart farming (Walter, 2017) is a newly growing agricultural system of dealing with plants as living organisms.

In Tunisia, the cultivation of the olive tree is one of the vital sectors of the agricultural policy, covering 1.68 million hectares. It is equivalent to 30% of its agricultural land. Furthermore, it is financially a significant source of currency for the Tunisian state, being classified as the second largest exporter of olive oil just after the European Union (Jakson, 2015). In searching for the equation of guaranteeing a profitable harvest and quantity loss minimization, the farmers have a current recourse to the massive use of pesticides in an often preventive but not curative way; which is full of risk not only for human health but also for the environment and the biological balance of the existing microsystems in farms and forests. In this respect, a careful reduction of the use of chemicals is practical for considering both human health and natural balance, and notably for controlling the expenses of the purchase and the extensive uses of pesticides.

In this chapter, the authors come up with an intelligent agricultural application, based on pattern recognition and artificial intelligence techniques or more precisely, a machine learning, which offers the farmers an automatic detection and classification of leaf diseases in the olive tree, namely the olive tree moth, the peacock's eye and the sooty mold.

In the second section, a description of the investigated leaf diseases is given meticulously. The third section is about a range of pattern recognition techniques for leaf diseases existing in the literature. The developed approach is presented in section 4. Analyzes and interpretations of the findings are demonstrated and compared to others, which basically rely on different methods. The current project ends up with a conclusive section.

BACKGROUND

Olive Leaves Diseases

As it is commonly known olive leaves are vulnerable to numerous diseases. In this section, the authors give an idea of the most widespread diseases, mainly peacock eye disease, sooty mold and the olive tree moth, giving the causes of their cropping up and the means of how to deal with them.

The olive tree moth (Ghoneim, 2015), is a whitish butterfly. Once adult, it does not represent any danger because it no longer feeds. However, at the very beginning of its life, this insect is perilous. The eggs are laid in March on the underside of the leaves, giving rise to green caterpillars with yellow heads and feeding on the young leaves present mainly in trees less than four years old. Accordingly, the attacked leaves will have their ends curled up and cut as shown in Figure 1.

Figure 1. Olive leaf attacked by olive tree moth caterpillars

The most appropriate and least harmful treatment to remedy this problem is the use of the bacterium "Bacillus thuringiensis ".

Peacock eye, also called Cyclonium, is caused by a Fusicladium oleagincum fungus, which proliferates on the leaves. It is common in spring, particularly in humid areas and at mild temperatures. It is recognizable by the shape of the spots it causes on the leaves. As shown in Figure 2, these spots are a succession of concentric circles whose color varies from brown to light yellow. This disease causes the tree leaves to fall, which considerably reduces the chlorophyll synthesis and subsequently leads to significant losses in the harvest (Viruega 1997).

Figure 2. Olive leaf attacked by Peacock's Eye

To avoid the development of the peacock eye disease on the olive trees' leaves, it is recommended to use a preventive and curative treatment based on copper, which is renewed after each rain.

Known as black olive, sooty mold is a cryptogamic disease, which is caused by several fungi. It forms a black mold covering the upper surface of the olive tree leaf, as shown in figure 3. (Chomnunti, 2014) . This disease is common in humid areas and at room temperature, especially in spring and autumn. For its development, it needs honeydew, identified as a sweet substrate and secreted by biting insects, feeding on the sap of the tree. This mold does not directly attack the tree. Initially, it causes some burns on the leaves, which are manifested in black color. Lastly, it affects the process of the photosynthesis to the point that the harvest loss is felt significantly.

Figure 3. Olive leaf affected by sooty mold

A copper-based treatment against sooty mold is recommended not only as a preventive but also as a curative measure. Aeration with and a significant reduction in the number of bronchi can also be useful against this disease.

LITERATURE REVIEW

After the demonstration of the olive tree leaf diseases, this section sets out to examine the impact of machine learning on the detection and the classification of foliar diseases. In addition to the most efficient pattern recognition system steps in each article, some results will also be presented.

Han et al (2013) propose two approaches for the detection of vine leaf diseases. The test images are taken by photographic sensors. This approach starts by changing the color space of the images from red, green, and blue (RGB) to a luma and chroma (YUV). Then, some pieces of information are extracted from these images. The act of combining color and texture, segmentation is done using the Mahalanobis distance. However, the type of the used classifier is not mentioned. The second approach uses thermal imaging and the "Signature Spectral" method to detect the disease before it becomes visible to the naked eye. This method is expensive, requiring highly specific equipment.

El Massi et al (2014) present another method for recognizing agricultural epidemics caused by the leaf miner. It is based on the k-means function and color moments. During the preprocessing stage, the image is firstly seized up to the size of 200x250 pixels. Consecutively, a median filter is used to remove noise. For the image segmentation, a change of the color space is performed from RGB to gray levels. Next, the image is binarized using Otsu thresholding. Subsequently, the color space is again modified from RGB to a lightness component L, and two color components a and b (Lab), enabling to subsume the pixels under five classes in accordance with the K-means function. The primitives which were chosen during the extraction of the characteristics are the moments of colors in addition to the level of gravity (Ng), which is calculated by the following function:

$$N_g = \left(\frac{P_d}{P_f}\right) * 100 \tag{1}$$

With: P_d the diseased area and P_f the total area of the leaf.

The proposed classifier is based on the neural network; the accuracy of this approach is 93.33%.

Mainkar et al (2015) suggest a detection approach, depending on the k-means functions, the co-occurrence matrix and the neural networks. The images are acquired by a high-resolution RGB digital camera. Each image is first filtered to remove noise. After that, the K-means function is used to divide the image into K distinct areas. The feature extraction phase is specifically localizing the diseased parts of the leaf. Indeed, a thresholding approach is proposed to mask all the pixels forming the healthy parts by assigning them the value zero (R=0, G=0, B=0). The co-occurrence matrix is mainly used to extract the information necessary for the classification provided by a neural network. The accuracy of this approach is 94%.

Rastogi et al (Rastogi, 2015) introduce a method similar to the two previous ones. However, it simply adds a process of calculation just following the classificatory step of the leaves, which is in accordance with the type of disease. They propose to calculate the total leaf area (S_t) and the diseased spots (S_m). Later, they calculate the percentage (P) indicating the risk of the disease as follows:

$$P = \left(\frac{S_m}{S_t}\right) * 100 \tag{2}$$

Afterwards, they use a fuzzy classifier to scale the risk percentages within a five category continuum of very low risk, low risk, medium risk, high risk, and very high risk.

Prajapati et al. (2017) use digital camera images of RGB infected rice plants. During the pre-processing phase, they capitalize on several background removal techniques. For segmentation, the image is divided into K zones. Practically, the K means function groups the pixels having the closest values into K Clusters. Concerning the feature extraction, three criteria are taken into consideration, namely the texture, color and shape. These features are leveraged for multiclass support vector machine (SVM) classification. The accuracy of this approach is 73.33% on the test dataset.

Halder et al (2019) showed that 10 leaf disease detection approaches with a comparison of the different methods whose accuracy varies from 80.45 to 95%.

Harakannanavar et al. (2022) display an automatic model for the detection of tomato leaf diseases. During the preprocessing, the authors applied an RGB to grayscale conversion, which is followed by K-mean clustering segmentation and ending with an edge detection to specify leaf edges. PCA Principal Component Analysis and GLCM co-occurrence matrix are used to extract informative features from leaf samples. Machine learning approaches such as Support Vector Machine, *K-Nearest Neighbors* and Convolutional Neural Network are exploited as tools for distinguishing between diseased and non-diseased leaves with an accuracy of 99%.

SUGGESTED METHOD

Patterns recognition approach is an identification of patterns in input data, which are subsequently used to make the necessary decisions (Bishop, 2006).

Machine learning-based pattern recognition approach includes the following steps:

- **Image acquisition:** The first step is to collect as large as possible amounts of data (images) from the real world.
- **Pre-processing:** At this step, the collected data are pre-processed to prepare the sets for feature extraction and classification steps.
- **Feature extraction:** The system searches and determines the distinguishing traits of the pre-processed sets of data. The extracted features will contain information about grey shade, texture, shape, or context of the image.
- **Classification:** Based on the extracted features in the previous step, data is assigned a class. In this step, the system assigns labels to data based on the predefined features. It is the case of the supervised learning.

Figure 4. Diagram of the developed patterns recognition approach

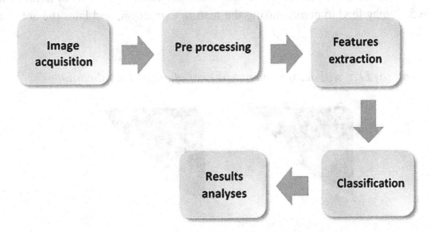

In this section, the different steps of the developed patterns recognition approach as illustrated in Figure 4 will be detailed.

Image Acquisition

The suggested approach begins with the basic image preparation step of sampling 240 olive leaves. The samples are obtained from the Institute of Olive Oil of Sfax. In fact, the image acquisition step is aimed to guarantee that all the sampled olive leaves are taken under the same conditions (Priya, 2015) and that light-related noise is considerably reduced. Added to that, it increases the certainty of keeping the scale of the images constantly the same, which is of a paramount importance for the feature extraction step.

Pre-processing

In the pre-processing step, the images are first resized into matrices of size 400x400 in order to facilitate the calculation and save the processing time. Then, a modified high-pass filter is used in order to increase the contrast.

$$I'\left(x,y\right) = \left(I * H\right)\left(x,y\right) = \sum_{i=-w}^{w}\sum_{j=-w}^{w}I\left(x - i, y - j\right).H\left(i,j\right) \tag{3}$$

With: I: the image matrix; H: the convolution filter

By applying the suggested approach, the high-pass filter is not only used to highlight the boundaries but also to facilitate the edge detection during segmentation.

$$H = \begin{vmatrix} -1 & -1 & -1 \\ -1 & 9 & -1 \\ -1 & -1 & -1 \end{vmatrix} \tag{4}$$

The use of the modified high-pass filter causes noise, and normally a loss of data, inside the leaf as shown in figure 5. It may lead to errors during the feature extraction, and later the act of classification itself.

Figure 5. Olive leaf: (a) Leaf without treatment, (b) Leaf after filter application

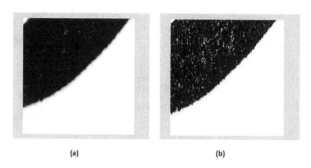

In order to avoid the expected potential errors of the modified high-pass filter, the image is converted into a binary one. This process is followed by a dilation function (Shih, 2017) to refine the edge of the sheet as shown in figure 6-b. A smoothing function is also applied to correct the noise caused by the high pass filter.

For segmentation, the binary image is used just after the smoothing process by filling each black pixel with its value in the input image. Actually, it gives a segmented image, which is ready for the feature extraction. The whole operation leads to getting a segmented image in the RGB color space on a single white font without amber and high contrast, as shown in Figure 6-c.

Figure 6. Pre-processing steps: (a) Filtered image, (b) Binarized and dilated image, (c) Final result of pre-processing steps

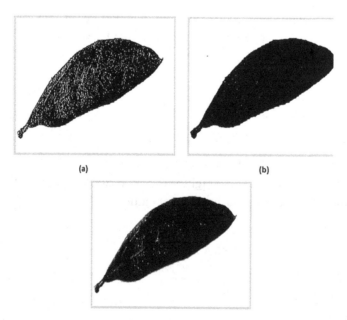

Features Extraction

Feature extraction is an essential step in the recognition system (Patil, 2011). Generally, it is possible to subsume its characteristics under three essential families: color, texture, and shape. In the present investigation, the treated samples are solely the leaves of the olive tree, belonging to the same species. Deductively, they all have the same morphological shape, which proves that the choice of the characteristics related to the shape is not decisive. With reference to the experts of the institute of olive oil of Sfax, color is not as an interesting criterion as it may be expected. Normal leaves are found with different colors, varying from yellow to dark green. There may be other intervening variables to take into account; they are the age leaf, access to light and even nutritional deficiency in some cases.

In this respect, the use of features related to texture is potentially promising. The co-occurrence matrix GLCM (Gray-Level-Co-Occurrence-Matrix) (Ou, 2014), (Al-Amin, 2015) is used to estimate the texture properties of the image relating to second-order statistics.

The GLCM matrix discloses the probability of the appearance of pairs of pixel values separated by a distance "d" in a direction "θ". It is assumed that d=1 and θ= (0°, 45°, 90°, 135°... multiples of 45°) within the same image. This matrix is used as a means to calculate the number of times on which a pixel of color level "u" appears at the distance "d" and according to the orientation "θ" of another pixel of color level "v" of the image. The co-occurrence matrix is of the size of NxN where N represents the number of gray levels of the image. For each couple (d, θ), the matrix φ(d, θ) is constructed. Accordingly, an average matrix is calculated, making its rotation invariant.

The figure 7 below represents an example of the calculation the Gray Level Co-Occurrence Matrix (c) of an image, having the size of 4x4 pixels (a) with 3 levels of gray (b), regarding that d=1 and θ = 0°.

Figure 7. Example of the construction of the GLCM matrix with d = 1 and θ =0° (Larroza, 2016)

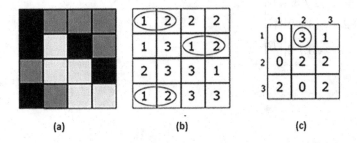

(a) (b) (c)

From the GLCM *matrix*, four characteristics are extracted (Singh, 2017). Namely, they are contrast, homogeneity, energy and correlation as it shown below:

$$Contrast = i.j \left(i - j\right)^2 \sum_{i=1}^{n}\sum_{j=1}^{n} C\left(i, j\right) \qquad (5)$$

$$Homogeneity = \sum_{i=1}^{n}\sum_{j=1}^{n} \frac{C_{(i,j)}}{\left(1+\left|i-j\right|\right)} \tag{6}$$

$$Energy = \sum_{i=1}^{n}\sum_{j=1}^{n} C_{(i,j)}^{2} \tag{7}$$

$$Correlation = \sum_{i=1}^{n}\sum_{j=1}^{n} \frac{\left(i-\mu_{i}\right).\left(j-\mu_{j}\right)}{\sqrt{\tilde{A}_{i}^{2}\tilde{A}_{j}^{2}}} .C_{(i,j)} \tag{8}$$

Where μ_i and μj represent the mean of the rows and columns of the GLCM matrix respectively; σi and σj the standard deviations of rows and columns of the GLCM matrix respectively and C (i,j) coefficient of the co-occurrence matrix.

Before creating the co-occurrence matrix from the sample image, a color space changes from red, green, and blue (RGB) space to hue, saturation and intensity (HSI). It is carried out just for getting any information, which is highly in agreement with the human perception of colors; and subsequently approaching the operation of the currently practical system of recognition of forms to the human reasoning. The color change from RGB space to the HSI one is essentially achieved by applying the following mathematical formulas (Zhang, 2000):

$$\begin{bmatrix} Y \\ C_1 \\ C_2 \end{bmatrix} = \begin{bmatrix} 1/3 & 1/3 & 1/3 \\ 1 & -1/2 & -1/2 \\ 0 & -\sqrt{3}/2 & \sqrt{3}/2 \end{bmatrix} \begin{bmatrix} R \\ V \\ B \end{bmatrix} \tag{9}$$

$$I = Y, S = \sqrt{C_1^2 + C_2^2} \tag{10}$$

$$H = \begin{cases} Arccos\left(\dfrac{C_2}{S}\right), C_1 \geq 0 \\ 2\pi - Arccos\left(\dfrac{C_2}{S}\right), C_1 < 0 \end{cases} \tag{11}$$

Once the color space change is made, a GLCM co-occurrence matrix will be established for each plane hue (H), saturation (S) and intensity (I), as shown in figure 8, in order to extract the four characteristics as follows: contrast, correlation, energy and homogeneity.

Figure 8. Creation of co-occurrence matrices.

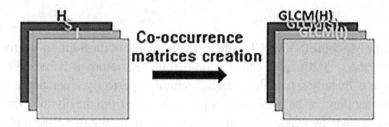

Accordingly, 12 parameters are obtained for each image. They are grouped together in a vector called the image descriptor vector. It forms forming a database, which will be used during the classification step with the columns representing the 12 extracted features and the rows of the various olive leaves samples.

The created database is subject to a normalization process before the classification step. Z-scores normalization (Cheadle, 2003) is the technique applied to modify the values of the numerical columns of the created data set to use a common scale, without altering differences in value ranges or losing information. Z-scores normalization is also necessary in order to model the data correctly. Each value in the dataset is transformed using the following formula to perform z-score normalization:

$$z_i = \frac{x_i - \mu}{\sigma} \qquad (12)$$

$$\mu = \frac{1}{m}\sum_{i=1}^{m} x_i \qquad (13)$$

$$\sigma = \sqrt{\frac{1}{m}\sum_{i=1}^{m}\left[x_i - \mu\right]^2} \qquad (14)$$

Where x_i is the input feature, z_i is the z-score value of the input feature, μ is the mean of the dataset from each data point, σ is the data set's standard deviation.

The interest in the z-score normalization is understood through the clear outlier in the dataset, which has been converted into a non-massive outlier. The normalized outlier will no longer have a considerable influence on the classification approach fit.

Classification

The classification is at the heart of the pattern recognition system. It is useful for classifying, the images in accordance with their descriptor vectors. The authors use supervised classifiers (Muhammad, 2015) since the image database provided by the agricultural engineers of the institute of olive oil of Sfax is subdivided into four classes in line with the state of the leaves: healthy, sooty mold, peacock eye and olive tree moth.

- **Support Vector Machine (SVM) Classifier:** The principle of the Support Vector Machine (SVM) algorithm(Cervantes, 2020) , also called wide-margin separators, is based on the idea that if the training sample is linearly separable, it seems natural to perfectly separate the elements from the two classes so that they can be positioned as far as possible from the dividing line (or hyperplane). This technique is done by maximizing the margin separating the two closest elements, which are effectively of different classes. (Tzotsos, 2008)

A wide margin separator SVM is a linear discriminator of the form below:

$$F(x) = signe(w^Tx+b) \tag{15}$$

where $w \in \mathbb{R}^p$ and $b \in \mathbb{R}$ w and b are given by solving the following problem:

$$\text{Minimize } \varphi\left(w\right) = \frac{1}{2}w \tag{16}$$

With

$$y_i(w^Tx_i+b)\geq1; \ i=1,n \tag{17}$$

Such that $\{(x_i,y_i); i=1,n\}$ a set of shape vectors labeled with $x_i \in \mathbb{R}^p$ and $y_i \in \{1,-1\}$

- **K-Nearest Neighbors (KNN) classifier:** The principle of the KNN (K-Nearest Neighbors) algorithm (Taunk,2019) is based on the comparison between the test sample and the elements used during learning in order to see the majority class in the k elements closest to the sample for classification. The comparative process between the classified sample and the learning elements is done using distances (Mathieu-Dupas, 2010). In this chapter, the Euclidean distance is used to indicate the dissimilarity between two individuals characterized by p characteristics.

The Euclidean distance is defined as follows:

$$d\left((x_1,x_2,\ldots,x_p),(u_1,u_2,\ldots,u_p)\right) = \sqrt{\left(x_1 - u_1\right)^2 + \left(x_2 - u_2\right)^2 +\ldots+\left(x_p - u_p\right)^2} \tag{18}$$

The nearest neighbor (xN,yN) for a new observation (x,y) is the one with the lowest Euclidean distance in the training sample:
instead of

$$d(x,x_n) = \min(d(x,x_i)) \tag{19}$$

The choice of the K value is essential in the classifying process by KNN. For this reason, the cross-validation approach is chosen in order to find the optimal value of K for ensuring a congruent compromise between overlearning (for K high) and noisy prediction (for K too low). The cross-validation method (Bergmeir, 2018) showed that for K less than 3 and K greater than 5 the error rate is more important. Hence, K=5 is selected for the rest of this work.

Firstly, a binary classification is carried out as it detects the diseased leaves. This classification is ensured by the two classifiers Support Vector Machine and K-Nearest Neighbors. However, the objective of this work is to classify the leaves of the olive tree in accordance with the class of disease. The second classification of the leaves in four classes (healthy, sooty mold, peacock eye and olive tree moth) is ensured by the classifier K-Nearest Neighbors.

ANALYSIS OF THE RESULTS

The experiments were realised on Intel Core i5-7500 7th generation processo, Matlab R2017a. These experiments have been performed on 240 olive leaves sampling into four classes: healthy, sooty mold, peacock eye and olive tree moth. The samples are obtained from the institute of olive oil of Sfax.

In order to evaluate the performance of the currently used approach, an analysis of the results is carried out, consisting of making a statistical study by calculating the accuracy of the classification and comparing the predictions made by the system to the actual classes of each test element.

The analysis includes three parts:

- An analysis of the binary results (healthy leaf / diseased leaf) of the SVM classifier and the KNN classifier.
- An analysis of the KNN classifier results of the classification of samples into four classes (healthy, sooty mold, peacock eye and olive tree moth).
- A statistical verification of the efficiency of descriptor vectors by the neural network test tool predefined on Matlab.

To train and test the proposed machine learning-based pattern recognition approach, the collected dataset is subdivided into three independent data sets: training set, testing set, and validation set (Lee, 2019). The training set plays an important role in building the approach model. It is the set of data, which is used to train and make the proposed model learn the hidden features (patterns in the input data). The used classification algorithms (machine learning algorithms) provide relevant information on how to associate the input data with the output decision. The validation set is a set of data used to validate the performance of the proposed model during training. This validation process allows an adjustment of the hyper-parameters and configurations of the model. It also helps to check whether the training is going in the right direction or not. The testing data is used to test the proposed model. It is the set of data, which verifies if the model is really producing the correct output after being trained or does the opposite. The testing data is used to quantify the accuracy of the proposed approach. The distribution of data is made as follows: 60% of the images database for training, 20% for the validation model, and finally, 20% for the testing model.

Binary Classification Analysis

As mentioned before, at first, the authors implement a binary classification (healthy leaf / diseased leaf) in order to detect the diseased leaves. This classification is ensured by the classifier K Nearest Neighbors (KNN) and later, the classifier Support Vector Machine (SVM). In applying both approaches, the authors use the same samples and equally the same number of images for the training phase.

The metrics used to evaluate the obtained classifications are error rate, accuracy, sensitivity, specificity and precision. They are delineated by the equation numbered 20, 21, 22, 23 and 24 respectively (Setiawan, 2020).

$$\text{Error rate} = \frac{FP + FN}{\left(TP + TN + FP + FN\right)} * 100 \tag{20}$$

$$\text{Accuracy} = \frac{TP + TN}{\left(TP + TN + FP + FN\right)} * 100 \tag{21}$$

$$\text{Sensitivity} = \frac{TP}{\left(TP + FN\right)} * 100 \tag{22}$$

$$\text{Specificity} = \frac{TN}{\left(TN + FP\right)} * 100 \tag{23}$$

$$\text{Precision} = \frac{TP}{\left(TP + FP\right)} * 100 \tag{24}$$

TP (True Positive): the image represents a sick leaf and that the prediction gives sick.
TN (True Negative): the image stands for a healthy leaf and that the prediction gives healthy.
FN (False Negative): the image signifies a diseased leaf that the prediction gives as healthy.
FP (False positive): the image means a healthy leaf while the prediction is sick.
The SVM classifier leads to the results in Table 1.

Table 1. Results of the SVM classifier

	Accuracy	Sensitivity	Specificity	Precision
SVM	92.7%	96.5%	80%	93%

With reference to table 1, it is noted that the accuracy is of 92.7% while the sensitivity is 96.5%, which is higher than the specificity 80%, indicating a convenient point for the proposed approach. Indeed, for olive farmers, it is obviously acceptable to believe that some of the olive trees are diseased and to apply a set of treatments fighting against the disease, as preventive measures in their eyes. Actually, it is much preferable than staying with their hands folded with no immediate reaction to save their crops from potential risks. Equally, by using the SVM classifier, it is worth noting that the two classifiers give comparable results.

The diagnostic procedures for knowing whether the leaf is diseased or not is not sufficient. Detecting the type of disease is a necessary stage before selecting the appropriate treatment for the olive oil leaf disease. To prove the case, in the second part of this work, a classification of leaves into four classes (healthy, sooty mold, peacock eye and olive tree moth) is ensured by using the KNN classifier only.

ANALYSIS OF THE CLASSIFICATION INTO FOUR CLASSES BY THE KNN METHOD

For the class of healthy leaves, an error rate of 9.8% (false positives) has been noted. The healthy leaves which are declared affected by the sooty mold, as a non-serious disease, a copper-based treatment is the most effective preventive measure against it. Practically, its estimation error will have no real impact on the harvest. However, an error rate of 5.7% (false negatives), which presents the diseased leaves affected by the moth declared healthy by mistake may possibly have negative repercussions on the harvest.

Figure 9. Percentage of correct estimates and false estimates according to classes.

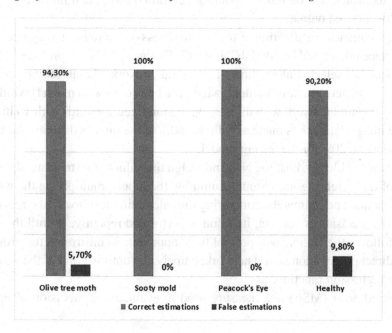

With reference to Figure 9, it is noted that the introduced approach gives promising results using the classification by the KNN method. The performance of the study itself does not only validate the pursued choices but also prove its different taken steps.

VERIFICATION OF THE STATISTICAL VALIDITY BY THE NEURAL NETWORK

The neural network is a machine learning models whose architecture is largely inspired by the functioning of the human brain. The artificial neural network (ANN) structure (Punitha, 2021) consists of three different layers: the input, the hidden and the output layer. Each layer contains a number of neurons connected to the other via link weights W_i (i = 1, 2, 3 ...n) and associated communication ones. The artificial neural network takes the inputs X_i (i = 1, 2, 3 ...n), calculates the weighed sum of the inputs, and includes a bias b. The weighed total is passed as input to an activation function, producing an output. The activation functions(Lexuan, 2020) specify whether a node should fire or not. Only those who are laid off make it to the output layer. The mathematical expression model is presented in Equation (25).

$$Y_i = f\left(\sum_{i=1}^{n} W_i X_i + b\right) \tag{25}$$

Where X_i (i = 1,2,3 ....n): inputs; Y_i (i = 1,2,3 ....n): output ; W_i (i = 1,2,3 ....n): weights; n : number of elements in input vector; b: Biais and f: activation function.

The Artificial neural network start by allocating random values to the weights of the connections between the neurons, which will be sets of updating iteration during the training process to get a more approximation to the desired output.

In this chapter, a statistical verification of the effectiveness of the suggested approach is provided by the graphical interface predefined by Matlab "nnstart" (Ocampo, 2021). It provides an interactive tool to easily loaded data and selected algorithms. The neural network Matlab toolbox offers a variety of parameters for the neural network development, which can be chosen with much flexibility. The adopted model is a multilayer neural network with direct propagation (feed-forward) with 10 hidden layers. The distribution of the image database is made as follows: 60% of the images database for training, 20% for the validation model and 20% for the testing model.

The training phase is able to adjust the bias and weigh the values. The training algorithm starts with the initialization of the weights, going through summing the inputs, multiplying the weights, passing it to the activation function and ultimately, comparing the calculation result with the real output via MSE. In case the expected precision is not met, iteration is performed repetitively until the best precision is reached. In what follows, the authors will present three approaches confirming the proposed classification method by a direct propagation neural network, namely, the optimization of the validation, the error histogram and the regression function.

The mean squared error (MSE) is a measure used to evaluate the precision of an estimator. It is defined as follows:

$$MSE = \left(\frac{1}{N}\right) \sum_{i=1}^{N} (Y_i - \hat{Y}_i)^2 \tag{26}$$

With N: the total number of samples, Y: the actual value of the sample $\hat{Y}$: the estimated value of the sample.

Figure 10 shows the evolution of the mean square error in relation to the number of Epochs performed during training, validation and testing.

Figure 10. Best validation performance in ANN

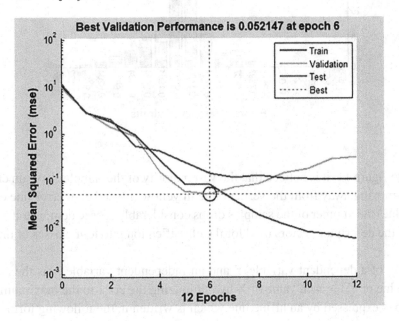

It is noted that the Mean Squared Error value of the lowest validation is obtained in the sixth Epochs with MSE = 0.052, and that from the following iteration the MSE value becomes higher, which causes an overfitting. Hence, the learning phase must stop at the sixth Epoch.

The same work is redone several times. In each time, an acceptable results are obtained (MSE = 0.15, MSE=0.2, ...) even by changing the percentages of the distributions of the images of the database and by changing the number of the hidden layers. The main issue is not to have a high MSE value (MSE » 0.6) (Tarik, 2008).

The error histogram is useful for visualizing the number of samples having the same error rates. It is precisely located between the target values and the predicted ones just after training a feedforward neural network. These error values illustrate how the predicted ones differ from the other target ones.

Bins are the number of vertical bars as it is shown in figure 10. The total error range is divided into 20 smaller bins here. The vertical axis indicates the number of samples from the dataset while the horizontal one axis points out the value relative to the error.

Figure 11. Error histogram

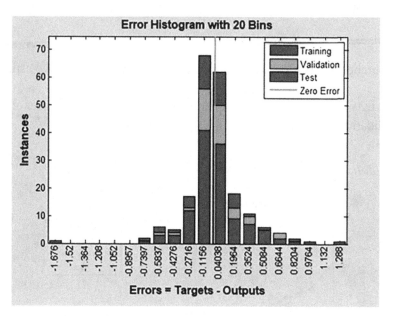

With regard to figure 11, it is noticed that the vast majority of the samples have an error rate close to zero and that by moving away from the vertical line in yellow (named zero error line corresponding to the zero error value) the number of the samples drops considerably. These demonstrated results confirm the efficiency of the descriptor vectors used for the classification into four classes of the system studied in this chapter.

The regression of a dependent variable Y and an independent variable X is the calculation of the most probable value of Y for each value of X by minimizing the error to the maximum (Specht, 1991). This relationship is expressed by an affine line which is written in the following form:

$$Y = \alpha + X\beta \tag{27}$$

With: Y the outputs (Output) and X the inputs (Input)

This line passes as close as possible to the mean of the points of the cloud representing the samples of the database. Most of the time, the linear regression model is estimated by the method of least squares. The distance which separates a point from the estimation line is the distance between the ordinate of the observed point (x_i, y_i) and the ordinate of the point $\left(x_i, \hat{y}_i\right)$, corresponding to it on the line of estimate.

$$d = y_i - \hat{y}_i \tag{28}$$

Since the value of the distance d can be either positive or negative, the method of least squares (Abdi, 2006) is often used.

Therefore, the regression line is defined as the one which minimizes the sum of the least squares:

$$R^2 = \frac{\sum_i \left(y_i - \hat{y}_i\right)^2}{\sum_i \left(y_i - y_{moy}\right)^2} \qquad (29)$$

Figure 12 shows four regression functions, which evaluate the performance of the neural network-based recognition system.

Figure 12. Provided regression lines

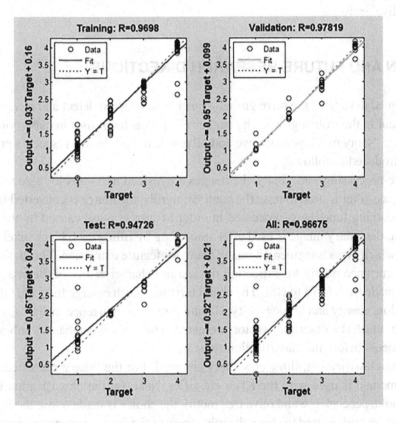

The regression function is claimed to be perfect when R=1, and random when R=0 .As it is seen in table 2, the obtained results converge towards 1 (R»1).

Table 2. Regression values

	Training Phase	**Validation Phase**	**Testing Phase**	**For the Overall System**
Regression: R	0.969	0.978	0.947	0.966

Accordingly, it is possibly to consider that the linear regression of this system gives remarkable results.

After the three validation approaches of the forward propagation (The optimization of the validation, the error histogram and the regression function), it can be concluded that the chosen descriptor vectors by the presented approach are statistically valid.

It is noteworthy that the accuracy of this approach is comparable to the one of the automatic leaf disease recognition approaches presented in the literature review section.

All the findings of the current work prove the effectiveness of this suggested machine learning-based pattern recognition approach, designed to help the farmers working in the field of olive growing to detect and recognize potential diseases such as sooty mold, peacock eye and olive tree moth, which may attack the olive grove.

CONCLUSION AND FUTURE RESEARCH DIRECTIONS

This project is aimed to support the olive growing farmers in order to detect and recognize the diseases that may be present in their olive grove. The suggested approach consists in classifying three types of olive tree diseases: "sooty mold, peacock eye and olive tree moth". In this respect, a proposed recognition system is introduced as follows:

During the pre-processing step, firstly, the images are resized into 400x400 size matrices; secondly a modified high-pass filter is used to raise the contrast; thirdly, the image is converted into a binary one, and finally, a smoothing function is processed in order to correct noise caused by the high pass filter. For segmentation, the binary image is used after smoothing by filling each black pixel with its value in the input image, which gives a segmented image ready for feature extraction. The choice is made to use the GLCM co-occurrence matrix for extracting the textural characteristics of the image. A color space change has been made from RGB to HSI. The characteristics which emerge from the GLCM matrix are: contrast, correlation, energy and homogeneity. Having three co-occurrence matrices, 12 characteristics are obtained with which the descriptor vector is created. The created database is subject to the z-score normalization process before the classification step.

Finally, for the classification, three classifiers are used. For the binary classification, the support vector machine method is used with the KNN classifier. Next, for the classification into four classes (healthy, sooty mold, peacock eye and olive tree moth), the choice is made to use the KNN classifier. In the end, the neural network is used to check the robustness of the descriptor vectors employed to classify the samples into four classes by increasing the number of Epochs.

For future work, other types of diseases affecting olive oil trees may be investigated. Other plant species may also be affected by the developed recognition system, such as the almond tree and citrus fruits, which are widely grown in Tunisia, proving to be of a considerable impact on the Tunisian economy and society.

ACKNOWLEDGMENT

The authors would like to thank all those who contributed to the conduct of this study. They thank all the people of the institute of olive oil of Sfax involved in the collection, the preparation of the leaves.

REFERENCES

Abdi, H. (2007). The method of least squares. Encyclopedia of measurement and statistics, 1, 530-532.

Al-Amin, M., Alam, M. B., & Mia, M. R. (2015). Detection of cancerous and non-cancerous skin by using GLCM matrix and neural network classifier. *International Journal of Computers and Applications*, *132*(8), 44–49. doi:10.5120/ijca2015907513

Bergmeir, C., Hyndman, R. J., & Koo, B. (2018). A note on the validity of cross-validation for evaluating autoregressive time series prediction. *Computational Statistics & Data Analysis*, *120*, 70–83. doi:10.1016/j.csda.2017.11.003

Bishop, C. M., & Nasrabadi, N. M. (2006). *Pattern recognition and machine learning* (*Vol. 4*, p. 738). Springer.

Cervantes, J., Garcia-Lamont, F., Rodríguez-Mazahua, L., & Lopez, A. (2020). A comprehensive survey on support vector machine classification: Applications, challenges and trends. *Neurocomputing*, *408*, 189–215. doi:10.1016/j.neucom.2019.10.118

Cheadle, C., Vawter, M. P., Freed, W. J., & Becker, K. G. (2003). Analysis of microarray data using Z score transformation. *The Journal of Molecular Diagnostics*, *5*(2), 73–81. doi:10.1016/S1525-1578(10)60455-2 PMID:12707371

Chomnunti, P., Hongsanan, S., Aguirre-Hudson, B., Tian, Q., Peršoh, D., Dhami, M. K., & Hyde, K. D. (2014). The sooty moulds. *Fungal Diversity*, *66*(1), 1–36. doi:10.100713225-014-0278-5 PMID:27284275

El Massi, I., Es-Saady, Y., & El Yassa, M. (2014). Reconnaissance des épidémies agricoles causées par la mouche mineuse à base de k-means clustering et de color moments. *Research Gate*. . doi:10.13140/RG.2.1.2407.4721

Ghoneim, K. (2015). The olive leaf moth Palpita unionalis (Hübner) (Lepidoptera: Pyralidae) as a serious pest in the world: a review. *International Journal of Research Studies in Zoology*, *1*(2), 1–20.

Halder, M., Sarkar, A., & Bahar, H. (2019). Plant disease detection by image pro-cessing: A literature review. *Image*, *1*, 3.

Han, S., & Cointault, F. (2013, June). Détection précoce de maladies sur feuilles par traitement d'images. In Orasis, Congrès des jeunes chercheurs en vision par ordinateur.

Harakannanavar, S. S., Rudagi, J. M., Puranikmath, V. I., Siddiqua, A., & Pramodhini, R. (2022). *Plant Leaf Disease Detection using Computer Vision and Machine Learning Algorithms*. Global Transitions Proceedings. doi:10.1016/j.gltp.2022.03.016

Jakson, D., Paglietti, L., & Ribeiro, M. (2015). Analyse de la filière oléicole, Tunisie. *Food and Agriculture Organization of the United Nations, Report No. 17*.

Larroza, A., Bodí, V., & Moratal, D. (2016). Texture analysis in magnetic resonance imaging: review and considerations for future applications. *Assessment of cellular and organ function and dysfunction using direct and derived MRI methodologies*, 75-106.

Lee, S. B., Gui, X., Manquen, M., & Hamilton, E. R. (2019, October). Use of training, validation, and test sets for developing automated classifiers in quantitative ethnography. In *International Conference on Quantitative Ethnography* (pp. 117-127). Springer. 10.1007/978-3-030-33232-7_10

Lexuan, Y. (2020). Improvements on Activation Functions in ANN: An Overview. *Management Science and Engineering*, *14*(1), 53–58.

Mainkar, P.M., Ghorpade, S., & Adawadkar, M.P. (2015). Plant Leaf Disease Detection and Classification Using Image Processing Techniques. *International Journal of Innovative and Emerging Research in Engineering*.

Mathieu-Dupas, E. (2010). *Algorithme des k plus proches voisins pondérés et application en diagnostic. In 42èmes Journées de Statistique*.

Muhammad, I., & Yan, Z. (2015). Supervised Machine Learning Approaches: A Survey. *ICTACT Journal on Soft Computing*, *5*(3).

Ocampo, I., López, R. R., Camacho-León, S., Nerguizian, V., & Stiharu, I. (2021). Comparative evaluation of artificial neural networks and data analysis in predicting liposome size in a periodic disturbance micromixer. *Micromachines*, *12*(10), 1164. doi:10.3390/mi12101164 PMID:34683215

Ou, X., Pan, W., & Xiao, P. (2014). In vivo skin capacitive imaging analysis by using grey level co-occurrence matrix (GLCM). *International Journal of Pharmaceutics*, *460*(1-2), 28–32. doi:10.1016/j.ijpharm.2013.10.024 PMID:24188984

Patil, J. K., & Kumar, R. (2011). Advances in image processing for detection of plant diseases. *Journal of Advanced Bioinformatics Applications and Research*, *2*(2), 135–141.

Prajapati, H. B., Shah, J. P., & Dabhi, V. K. (2017). Detection and classification of rice plant diseases. *Intelligent Decision Technologies*, *11*(3), 357–373. doi:10.3233/IDT-170301

Priya, P., & D'souza, D. A. (2015). Study of feature extraction techniques for the detection of diseases of agricultural products. *International Journal of Innovative Research in Electrical, Electronics, Instrumentation and Control Engineering*, *3*(2).

Punitha, S., Al-Turjman, F., & Stephan, T. (2021). An automated breast cancer diagnosis using feature selection and parameter optimization in ANN. *Computers & Electrical Engineering*, *90*, 106958. doi:10.1016/j.compeleceng.2020.106958

Rastogi, A., Arora, R., & Sharma, S. (2015, February). Leaf disease detection and grading using computer vision technology & fuzzy logic. In *2015 2nd international conference on signal processing and integrated networks (SPIN)* (pp. 500-505). IEEE 10.1109/SPIN.2015.7095350

Setiawan, A. W. (2020, November). Image segmentation metrics in skin lesion: accuracy, sensitivity, specificity, dice coefficient, Jaccard index, and Matthews correlation coefficient. In *2020 International Conference on Computer Engineering, Network, and Intelligent Multimedia (CENIM)* (pp. 97-102). IEEE. 10.1109/CENIM51130.2020.9297970

Shih, F. Y. (2017). *Image processing and mathematical morphology: fundamentals and applications*. CRC press. doi:10.1201/9781420089448

Singh, S., Srivastava, D., & Agarwal, S. (2017, August). GLCM and its application in pattern recognition. In *2017 5th International Symposium on Computational and Business Intelligence (ISCBI)* (pp. 20-25). IEEE. 10.1109/ISCBI.2017.8053537

Specht, D. F. (1991). A general regression neural network. *IEEE Transactions on Neural Networks*, 2(6), 568–576. doi:10.1109/72.97934 PMID:18282872

Tarik Al Ani. (2008). *Réseaux de neurones avec Matlab*. Laboratoire d'Ingénierie des Systèmes de Versailles Paris.

Taunk, K., De, S., Verma, S., & Swetapadma, A. (2019, May). A brief review of nearest neighbor algorithm for learning and classification. In *2019 International Conference on Intelligent Computing and Control Systems (ICCS)* (pp. 1255-1260). IEEE. 10.1109/ICCS45141.2019.9065747

Tzotsos, A., & Argialas, D. (2008). Support vector machine classification for object-based image analysis. In *Object-based image analysis* (pp. 663–677). Springer. doi:10.1007/978-3-540-77058-9_36

Viruega, J. R., & Trapero, A. (1997, September). Epidemiology of leaf spot of olive tree caused by Spilocaea oleagina in southern Spain. In *III International Symposium on Olive Growing 474* (pp. 531-534). ISHS.

Walter, A., Finger, R., Huber, R., & Buchmann, N. (2017). Smart farming is key to developing sustainable agriculture. *Proceedings of the National Academy of Sciences of the United States of America*, 114(24), 6148–6150. doi:10.1073/pnas.1707462114 PMID:28611194

Zhang, C., & Wang, P. (2000, September). A new method of color image segmentation based on intensity and hue clustering. In *Proceedings 15th International Conference on Pattern Recognition. ICPR-2000* (Vol. 3, pp. 613-616). IEEE. 10.1109/ICPR.2000.903620

KEY TERMS AND DEFINITIONS

Accuracy: Is a metric used to estimate the performance of a classification system .Accuracy is defined as the number of correct predictions divided by the total number of input samples.

Artificial Intelligence (AI): Is a branch of computer science that tries to reproduce and simulate human intelligence in a machine, so that machines can perform functions that ordinarily require human intelligence.

Co-Occurrence Matrix: It is a matrix that represents the distance and angular spatial relationship over an image sub region it is used as a texture analysis approach.

Cross-Validation Technique: It is a resampling procedure used to evaluate machine learning models by training several models on subsets of the available input data to determine the most suitable model.

HSI Color Space: It represents color similarly how the human eye senses colors. This color space represents every color with three components: Hue (H) represents the feeling of human sense to different colors, saturation (S) indicates the purity of the color that means the greater saturation is equivalent to the brighter color and intensity (I) is the brightness of the color.

Pattern Recognition: Is a data analysis method that uses machine learning algorithms to automatically recognize patterns and regularities in data.

Smart Farming: It represent the using of the new technologies like Internet of Things (IoT), artificial intelligence techniques, sensors, robotics and drones to increase the quantity and quality of agricultural products.

Chapter 16
A Comprehensive Overview of Artificial Intelligence in Healthcare

Farhan Sabir Ujager

https://orcid.org/0000-0002-7080-5141

De Montfort University, UAE

Souheyr Rim Hamacha

De Montfort University, UAE

Binish Benjamin

Allama Iqbal Open University, Pakistan

ABSTRACT

Artificial intelligence's (AI) learning, reasoning, problem-solving, and perception features have given a new horizon to the modern healthcare infrastructure. AI is demonstrating best practices in different domains of healthcare, such as efficient drug discovery processes, accuracy in disease diagnosis, assisted surgeries, efficient utilization of human resources, and many more. This chapter provides a comprehensive overview of AI in healthcare, its applications, and recent research studies with respect to disease prediction and information-processing healthcare applications. Associated technologies of AI healthcare applications have been discussed as the realization of concepts is not possible without considering these technologies. Furthermore, it is essential to present the ethical aspect of AI in healthcare, and discuss the ethical boundaries the ethical boundaries of the applications. AI is becoming inevitable for modern and future healthcare; however, certain challenges are associated with the realization of smart and intelligent healthcare infrastructure.

DOI: 10.4018/978-1-6684-6937-8.ch016

INTRODUCTION

Modern healthcare systems are heavily relying on technology. It is a continuous and ongoing advancement in the field of healthcare from the from a technological perspective, whether it is drug discovery or robotic surgeries, technology is transforming healthcare and opening several new avenues in healthcare with greater efficacy. The modern healthcare system is also referred to as, "Digital Healthcare." Digital technology is revolutionizing the healthcare sector by incorporating software applications, modern hardware, and a variety of services. Computer-aided systems became a part of the healthcare infrastructure for more than 50 years as decision support systems (Tohka & Van Gils, 2021). These healthcare computer-aided systems have not only optimized and transformed health consultations, surgeries, and related human resource services, but effectively contributed to the broader healthcare industry which includes pharmacy, logistics, insurance, medical instruments, and pathology to name a few.

One of the integral components of digital technology is data, without data digital technology will not exist. Data has hidden knowledge that is apparently invisible, this invisible knowledge needs to be extracted and can be used for a variety of applications, such as, to make machines learn and imitates intelligence. In the 1950s, John McCarthy proposed the term "Artificial Intelligence (AI)" (Andresen, 2002) and defined it as

"The science and engineering of making intelligent machines"

There are essential components of AI that includes data, algorithm, processing power, and scenarios. Data is the component that serves as the relevant experience for the machines to learn for the specific application, without data machines cannot be intelligent. With the help of an algorithm machine process the data and train (learn) itself over the processing power (i.e., hardware and software capabilities), and finally machine applies the learned knowledge to a situation (scenario). Massive health-related data is being generated and accumulated by healthcare organizations and institutes in the form of datasets, lab reports, electronic health records (EHR), medical imageries, drug data, clinical trials, insurance claims, and healthcare devices [12]. This significant or considerable amount of data can serve as learning knowledge by analyzing data and extracting the hidden patterns for diagnosis, prediction, treatment planning, drug discovery, and decision-making to make an intelligent and comprehensive healthcare system of the future (Johnson et al., 2021). The significance of AI in healthcare has been portrayed in Figure 1.

Figure 1. AI in Healthcare

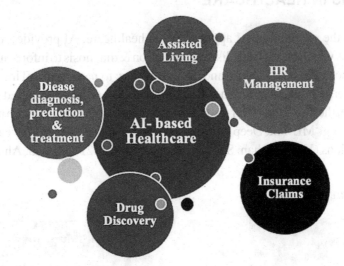

AI is now becoming a vital fragment of modern computer-aided digital healthcare infrastructure to achieve high accuracy in diagnosis/prognosis, prevalence/incidence, and improvement in the healthcare management systems in general. It is pertinent to mention that there are several best practices of AI in healthcare such as imaging analysis (Hardin Memorial Health) (IBM, 2019), a decrease in the cost of manufacturing drugs (Ebola outbreak Africa) (Mesko, 2017), oncology analysis (Watson on oncology) (Jie, Zhiying, & Li, 2021), Pharmbot (SafedrugBot) (Minutolo, Damiano, De Pietro, Fujita, & Esposito, 2022) and COVID-19 prevalence (Arık et al., 2021). AI has already stepped in the modern healthcare infrastructure, as these best practices suggest. However, it is important to understand the reason why healthcare is inclining toward AI-based services and procedures. The simplest and brief answer would be unifying the capabilities of the human brain with the accuracy and precision of machines. So far, the majority of AI-based healthcare systems have not achieved complete autonomy however, autonomous AI based health care systems may soon become common practice.

One of the important considerations of any healthcare-related application is the ethical aspect. While AI is revolutionizing healthcare, it is pertinent to consider the ethical, legal, and social aspects of these applications and processes. These aspects can be further trimmed down to the safety and transparency of the procedures and decisions. These are some important aspects that need to be considered while healthcare is adopting AI at a rapid pace.

The transformation of the conventional healthcare system to a modern artificial intelligence-based healthcare system is a challenging task, as several known and unknown challenges are associated with this transformation. These enormous challenges vary from ethical, legal, and social aspects as well as lack of regulatory standards, integration of technology, information security, the privacy of the patient's data, training and knowledge transfer, and bias in the training data to name a few. In this chapter, we will discuss AI in healthcare from several point of view; applications, best practices, associated technologies, ethical/ social aspects and challenges. This discussion will provide a comprehensive overview to the readers.

AI APPLICATIONS IN HEALTHCARE

This section explores the potential of AI applications in healthcare. AI provides a broader spectrum of healthcare applications which varies from disease prediction & diagnosis to information processing-based healthcare services such as assisted living, and drug discovery to name a few. This section discusses applications of AI in disease prediction/ diagnosis and information processing-based services, as shown in Figure.2. Furthermore, the latest and novel research studies have been explored with respect to subdomains of AI (Machine Learning 'ML' and Deep learning 'DL'). These subdomains have tremendous potential in healthcare applications (Viswanathan, Saranya, & Inbamani, 2021)(Hamad, Ahmed, & Saeed, 2022).

Figure 2. AI Healthcare applications

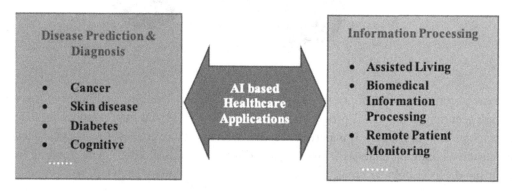

Disease Prediction and Diagnosis

In this subsection, AI applications in disease prediction and diagnosis have been discussed. Novel and out-of-the-box existing proposed models and concepts have been explored to understand the aids of AI in disease prediction and diagnosis.

Cancer

In recent times, several research studies based on AI have been conducted on cancer prediction and diagnosis. A good number of studies have been conducted at the genetic level from the point of view of cancerous cell proliferation, regeneration, and fatality. Most of the literature is mainly based on machine learning, deep learning, and meta-heuristic techniques for the diagnosis and prognosis of cancer. Literature shows that a wide range of research studies have been conducted on breast, prostate, glioblastoma, bladder, nasopharyngeal carcinoma, colorectal, oral, lungs, ovarian, glioma, spinal chordoma, pancreatic neuroendocrine cancers to name few. It is difficult to detect cancer at the early stages as well as its relapse, similarly, the prognosis of cancer is also difficult to predict. However, rich medical databases are beneficial when combined with AI domains such as ML and DL techniques for cancer diagnosis. Existing techniques and models have either utilized medical imagery data or gene expressions data for cancer prediction, diagnosis, and prognosis

Medical imaging has played a vital role in the detection of cancerous cells. MRI images are a painless process for taking detailed images of the human body, especially for brain tumors (Tahir et al., 2019). In image processing for disease detection, feature segmentation is crucial for anomaly detection. The most popular techniques that have been employed in literature for feature segmentation are the Otsu threshold, CNN, Fuzzy C-means, and clustering (Saba, 2020). Several other research studies have utilized SVM and self-organizing Map (SOM) (Vaishnavee & Amshakala, 2015), Long Short-Term (LSTM) along with Coevolutionary Neural Network (ConvNet) (Iqbal et al., 2019), 3DCNN (Ramzan, Khan, Iqbal, Saba, & Rehman, 2020) to name a few for brain tumor segmentation.

Researchers have explored other domains along medical imagery for the prediction, diagnosis, and prognosis of cancer, such as gene expressions. Gene study helps to understand genetic information from generation to generation. It becomes significant to detect gene deformity to predict cancerous genes. Several studies have been conducted which are based on ML and DL, (Kim, Haseong & Gelenbe, 2012) has utilized reverse engineering concept based on the Bayesian Model Average to the relevant gene interaction models, it has been observed that the proposed approach is significant in traditional methods. Another relevant research study ranks the established key cancerous genes based on the correlation evaluation of a large group of pan-cancer survivals of different cancer types (Nagy, Munkácsy, & Győrffy, 2021). In (Katzman et al., 2018), another survival analysis concerning gene expression is presented, the proposed technique is named as DeepSurv. DeepSurv follows a feed-forward Neural Network to process patient data and consider several hyperparameters for optimization.

Skin Disease

Skin diseases are ranked as the fourth main cause of nonfatal disease burden globally (Liu et al., 2020). Skin disease can also grow into malignant tissue such as skin cancer. One of the important reason is that dermatologists are low in number which leads to the low diagnostic accuracy of the disease 24-70% (Moreno, Tran, Chia, Lim, & Shumack, 2007) by non-specialists, which results in delayed and improper treatment.

Several studies suggest that AI can play a vital role in the diagnosis and bridging of the demand/supply gap. High-resolution images can be useful for the diagnosis of skin disorders. AI-based algorithms can be useful for the analysis of these images by using ML and DL techniques. Recent research studies from ML and DL have shown promising results in diagnosis and classification with high accuracy. In (Srinivasu et al., 2021) the proposed technique utilized state-of-the-art deep learning techniques MobileNet V2 with LSTM to classify these skin diseases; Melanocytic nevi, Benign keratosis-like lesions, Dermatofibroma, Vascular lesions, Actinic keratoses, Intraepithelial carcinoma, Basal cell carcinoma, and Melanoma with 85.34% accuracy, which is promising and better as compared to 24-70% non-specialist diagnostic accuracy. In another study, Multi Class Multi Label (MCML) technique is proposed, to diagnose early skin lesions assessment, the proposed technique has achieved 96.47% based on a deep learning approach (Hameed, Shabut, Ghosh, & Hossain, 2020). A deep learning-based approach is proposed by (Wu, H. et al., 2020), by utilizing EfficientNet-b4 Convolution Neural Network to diagnose inflammatory skin diseases. The proposed Artificial Intelligence Dermatology Diagnosis Assistant (AIDDA) shows overall accuracy of 95.80% and a specificity of 97.20% for the diagnosis of inflammatory skin diseases which are often misdiagnosed.

Diabetes

Diabetes is characterized by an elevated level of blood sugar in the human body. Diabetes may lead to other complicated diseases such as cardiovascular, chronic renal disease, and stroke. In 2021, 537 million people were living with diabetes, and it is predicted that this number will rise to 783 million by 2045 according to International Diabetes Foundation (IDF) (Diabetes facts & figures.2021). Diabetes is also responsible for 6.7 million deaths around the globe in 2021 as reported by IDF.

AI is contributing to the treatment and diagnosis of diabetes mainly in four areas, these are, self-management tools, diagnosis, risk categorization, and retinal screening (Dankwa-Mullan et al., 2019) (Nomura, Noguchi, Kometani, Furukawa, & Yoneda, 2021). In one of the interesting studies, the fatigue phases of diabetic and healthy patients are analyzed with high accuracy by using a wearable sensor (accelerometer) to evaluate the hand tremor data (Aljihmani et al., 2020). Along with higher prediction accuracy, the proposed model is not using any sensor that measures the blood glucose level, which is invasive in nature. Another noninvasive study is conducted by (Tsai, Li, Lam, Li, & Ho, 2019), this proposed model uses photoplethysmogram optical signals by using a vision wearable device for eye scanning, the proposed model is based on random forest and Adaboost regression that shows promising results in glucose prediction. A research study is conducted that relates the physiological parameters of a diabetic patient by using different sensors (smartphone, smartwatch, etc.) from the perceptive of remote monitoring as well as prediction of future blood glucose levels by using ML techniques (Rghioui, Lloret, Harane, & Oumnad, 2020).

Cognitive

Dementia is one of the cognitive impairments, that leads to loss of cognitive functionalities such as reasoning, remembering, and thinking with high prevalence in the elderly. According to the Alzheimer's society, UK, currently, 57.4 million people are living around the globe with dementia, the prediction is that in 2050 the number of dementia patients will increase to 152.8 million, and the percentage change increase will be 166.202% (Facts for the media about dementia.2022) which is quite significant. According to World Health Organization (WHO), there is a lack of specialized human resources for dementia patients, the specialized human resource includes neurologists, psychiatrists, psychologists, and geriatric and qualified caregivers (World Health Organization, 2018) and this is a widening gap. The diagnosis and prognosis of dementia are very challenging as there is no direct treatment, however, slowing down of decline and ensuring stabilized living is the best effort.

AI is showing promising results in early diagnosis by analyzing patient histories and behavior in a variety of different ways. The data which is being used for the training of the AI-based algorithm are clinical/ cognitive assessments, medical history, family history, neuropathology, genetic, demographic, and neuroimaging (Bellio et al., 2020) (Kumar, Sayantan et al., 2021). Several recent research studies have suggested that sensors data can also be used for behavior analysis for the prediction of cognitive impairments (Kim, Jungyoon, Cheon, & Lim, 2022) (Juneja, Dhiman, Kautish, Viriyasitavat, & Yadav, 2021). One of the promising research studies identifies the risk of dementia through the vocal features of telephonic conversation by analyzing ML techniques (Shimoda, Li, Hayashi, & Kondo, 2021). A deep Neural Network based prediction model is proposed for dementia by using an imaging dataset, the proposed model MCapNet follows a hierarchal approach to analyze image data points (Basheer, Bhatia, & Sakri, 2021). The proposed techniques demonstrate an accuracy of 92.39%. In another article (So,

Hooshyar, Park, & Lim, 2017), Mini-Mental State Examination in the Korean version (MMSE-KC) data along with demographic data is considered to classify normal and abnormal patients in the initial phase, the final phase Consortium to Establish a Registry for Alzheimer's Disease (CERAD-K) data is utilized to classify mild cognitive impairment and demented patients. ML-based techniques are utilized for classification in both phases.

AI is making substantial contributions to the prediction, diagnosis, and prognosis of diseases with promising accuracy. This contribution is mainly considered a decision support system for medical practitioners and experts. These proposed AI-based systems, models, techniques and frameworks are not autonomous yet and need the medical experts' opinions and overviews. These proposed existing techniques are optimizing healthcare practices, helping in better understanding of the novel and existing diseases, making procedures less time-consuming, cost-effective, personalized care, enhancing practitioner's knowledge, and automation several procedures to name a few benefits. The researchers and scientists are further optimizing the existing techniques and proposing novel methods for disease prediction, diagnosis, and prognosis by using AI techniques.

Information Processing

AI is facilitating existing healthcare in a broader perspective by using medical-related data for several healthcare applications besides disease prediction. These healthcare applications vary from assisted living to drug discovery processes, from biomedical information processing to human resource management. This section discusses the AI-based healthcare applications which use sensors/ IoT devices, Electronic Health Records (EHRs), drugs chemical features, and a variety of other data to improve, automate and propose smarter systems to the relevant application domain of the modern healthcare sector.

Assisted Living

The concept of independent living is prevailing in modern society for choice, control, equality, and freedom. However, the concept of independent living needs further elaboration when it comes to people of determination and the elderly, as they need assistance while living independently to perform their activities of daily living. There are several societal and economic aspects where human assistance is not available in most scenarios for people of determination and elderlies. Technology is playing an important role in the substantializing concept of assisted living and along with AI the true concept of independent living can be achieved.

IoT and sensor technology are vital for Ambient Assisted Living (AAL). An interesting study was conducted to determine the wellness of elderly people in a smart home environment, which is equipped with IoT devices and sensors to monitor the daily behavior of the elderly through these devices, the proposed model determines wellness in a non-intrusive manner by observing the daily activities by using Spatio-temporal correlation techniques (Ujager, Mahmood, & Khatoon, 2019). Similarly, the wellness of elderly people is determined (Ujager & Mahmood, 2019a), by monitoring their daily behavior along with the context of change in behavior in a smart ambiance by utilizing Lazy Associative Classification (LAC) in a non-intrusive manner. Several research studies have been conducted that aid out of the smart ambiance as well, (Mauldin, Canby, Metsis, Ngu, & Rivera, 2018) a smartphone application named SmartFall was developed to detect falls. A DL-based model utilizes smart watch and phone data for real-time fall detection. Another fall detection system is proposed by (Espinosa et al., 2019), this proposed system is based on image procession using the 2D-CNN inference method with promising results. Another imaging processing-based system is proposed by using ML techniques for the detection of stumbling, slipping, fainting, and other types of falls in a living environment (Shu & Shu, 2021).

Biomedical Information Processing

Biomedical information processing deals with medical data storage, analysis, and retrieval of data. This data can be Electronic Health Records (EHR), drug prescriptions, pathology reports, etc. This data is useful for the mentioned reasons. Additionally, this data can be processed for the extraction of some useful knowledge, which can be beneficial for the patients and as well for future medical practices.

One of the subdomains of AI is Natural Language Processing (NLP), which is a range of computational techniques to provide a human-like capability of analyzing and processing language for a variety of applications (Chowdhary, 2020). In (Acevedo et al., 2019), a model is proposed to identify the rate of breast lesions and cancer among women by analyzing the pathology reports of the patients by using an NLP algorithm with promising results. In another study, the proposed model predicts postoperative complications and readmission after ovarian cancer surgeries based on NLP and ML techniques (Barber, Garg, Persenaire, & Simon, 2021). A model is proposed for dementia detection based on speech data by using Average stochastic gradient descent Weight-Dropped Long Short-Term Memory (AWD-LSTM) models, and attention-based models (Zheng, Bouazizi, & Ohtsuki, 2022). In an interesting study, an NLP-based chatbot is developed based on fuzzy logic and fuzzy interference for assessing tropical diseases in Nigeria (Omoregbe et al., 2020). In this proposed study, the patient interacts with the chatbot by exchanging text messages, these text messages are analyzed by the proposed model for the prediction of disease.

Drug Development

Drug development is a lengthy and expensive process and especially for a novel disease, the process is lengthier and even more expensive. There are five steps for the drug development process according to FDA, these are, discovery and development, preclinical research, clinical research, FDA review, and FDA post-market safety monitoring (The drug development process.2018).

AI is playing an important role in adding efficiency to the overall process. Quantitative Structure-Activity Relationships (QSARs) are used for the correlation of chemical structure with activity and prediction of activities on untested chemicals. In a recent study, the DL-based QSAR method is proposed for feature extractions from the 3D-image structures of the chemical, the study claims to decrease the computational cost (Matsuzaka & Uesawa, 2022). Virtual screening in the drug discovery process helps to identify a molecule's structure that will bind to a drug target. NIMA-related kinase7 (NEK7) is a promising target for cancer-related drug discovery. In a recent study, a DL-based technique predicts the binding infinity of NEK-7 along with other important drug profiles which support the finding of virtual screening (Aziz et al., 2022).

Remote Patient Monitoring

The recent ongoing pandemic (COVID-19) has been eye-opening for researchers and scientists from the perceptive of remote patient monitoring. At the same time, remote monitoring is becoming crucial because of the widening gap between qualified medical human resources and the provision of medical services to patients, especially in underdeveloped countries and emergency-hit regions. With remote monitoring, medical experts and supporting staff can monitor several patients at the same time. IoT and medical sensor-based devices provide real-time information about each patient, however, the provided information needs to be accurately monitored and analyzed for each patient for providing timely medical service.

AI-based remote patient monitoring systems can be helpful in monitoring and analyzing patients intelligently. In a recent study, an embedded system is proposed for the remote monitoring of cardiovascular disease patients (Ashfaq et al., 2022), by using IoT devices to receive the required data and process it by utilizing the ML technique K Nearest Neighbor (KNN) to sense the emergency. In another study, a three-layer framework is proposed for COVID-19 diagnosis through wearable sensors, these three layers are the patient, cloud, and hospital. The patient layer is responsible for collecting vital data via sensors and transmit to the cloud for storage and transmission and the hospital layer uses the CNN algorithm for COVID-19 diagnosis for the suspected cases with promising results (El-Rashidy, El-Sappagh, Islam, El-Bakry, & Abdelrazek, 2020). A remote breast cancer auxiliary diagnosis scheme is proposed for remote areas where there is an unavailability of the required specialist (Yu et al., 2021). In this proposed scheme breast pathology images are being transmitted via a 5G network for the DL Inception-v3 for diagnostics with high accuracy of 98.19%.

There are several other applications of AI in healthcare besides the above-mentioned, and all these applications are contributing to making a smarter and more reliable modern healthcare infrastructure. These contributions in AI will further improve the overall healthcare processes with efficiency, ease, economy, accuracy, and value addition to healthy living.

AI BEST PRACTICES IN HEALTHCARE

This section aims to briefly explain best AI practices in the different areas of healthcare. Furthermore, this section provides the latest technological advancements in the current state of healthcare through AI.

AI is complementing and adding value to the existing healthcare systems in different ways. The majority of radiologists find it difficult to access additional relevant patient information while reading a medical image and going through EHR is time-consuming. Hardin Memorial Health has deployed an AI-powered system (Watson Imaging Patient Synopsis solution) for the radiologist to find the relevant information about the patients from EHR (IBM, 2019). In 2015, an Ebola outbreak was witnessed. To cater to this epidemic, there was an urgent need for drug treatments. A program was designed to combat this epidemic; Atomwise extended the relevant AI technology, Toronto University researchers provided the biological details of the virus and IBM facilitated supercomputing. This study helped to identify the reasons for viral entry, as a result, drugs for Ebola were made in a shorter period (Kumar, Akshara, Gadag, & Nayak, 2021). SafedrugBot is an AI-based chatbot, which is designed to assist health practitioners who would like to get drug related data for breastfeeding mothers. This chat service is available on the Telegram platform (Minutolo et al., 2022). An AI-based virtual health coaching app 'Noom Couch' teaches customers about healthy living that is not only limited to dietary and physical information but also psychological motivation. This app maintains a sustainable relationship with the customer by learning all the required information to offer customized services (Noom.2022). Furthermore, several best practices bring new AI opportunities in healthcare, such as autonomous actions in surgery (Gumbs et al., 2021), automated drug synthesis and discovery (Quazi, Jangi, Gavas, & Karpinski, 2022), NLP in future health decision making processes (Wen et al., 2019) to mention few.

This section provides insight into the existing AI applications in the current healthcare system. The above discussion is important to understand the conceptualization and the journey of the concept into working reality.

ASSOCIATED TECHNOLOGIES

The realization of a smart and intelligent healthcare system cannot be achieved only by excelling in the AI field, advancements in associated technologies are vital. This section of the chapter discusses associated technologies in connection with AI-based healthcare applications. These technologies are utilized with AI techniques for a specific application to provide input of data (learning purposes and test cases), perform an output operation (a response after a decision made by an AI technique), and secure the information (to make healthcare facilities more reliable). There are several associated technologies, however, this subsection will focus or focuses on those associated technologies with major AI based healthcare applications.

- Imagery
- Sensors and actuators
- Information Security
- Internet of Things (IoT)

Imagery

The past decade has witnessed amazing progress in the field of imagery, and especially when it comes to the high volume of details and information that is embedded in an image. Healthcare systems have been using this information for a number of years mainly related to diagnostics, monitoring, and treatment of medical conditions. The common imaging techniques that are being used in medicines are X-rays, Computed Tomography (CT), Ultrasound, Magnetic Resonance Imagining (MRI), and Nuclear medicine imaging (Positron Emission Tomography 'PET') images (Imaging explained.2019).

AI-based techniques utilize these images for learning and as input for the decision-making process for a variety of health-related applications. AI-based techniques are making a remarkable diagnosis of retinal diseases from fundus images (Ting et al., 2017), cardiovascular disease risk factors from retinal images (Poplin et al., 2018), and tuberculosis and COVID-19 diagnoses from chest radiology (Lakhani & Sundaram, 2017) (Ilyas, Rehman, & Naït-Ali, 2020) respectively.

Medical image analysis is facing the challenge of selecting optimal features and analyzing these visual features (Panayides et al., 2020). ML and DL-based image processing techniques have shown amazing accuracies in the segmentation and analysis of visual features (Iglesias & Sabuncu, 2015). Companies like Viz.AI, MaxQ AI, and Aidoc are doing remarkably well in medical imagery healthcare applications and have received clearance from FDA (Driver, Bowles, Bartholmai, & Greenberg-Worisek, 2020). Viz. AI has received FDA clearance for the identification of stroke in angiogram with an emergency alert to the on-call practitioner, this application is based on an AI algorithm. Similarly, Aidoc and MaxQ AI have the approval from FDA for assessing intracranial hemorrhage based on CT scan deep pathology.

Furthermore, in recent years, Aidoc received FDA approvals for assessing and raising flags for spine fractures and pulmonary embolisms.

Sensors and Actuators

Sensing technology is revolutionizing modern healthcare, recent advancement in microelectronics has provided accurate, easy-to-use, low-cost, smaller, and integrable sensors. These features of sensing technology have the potential to move modern healthcare to tele and remote medicine (Ujager & Mahmood, 2019b). For a smart healthcare application, medical sensors read human body data (depending on the application), and that data is sent for further processing for decision-making by an AI-based algorithm, however, to provide a physical response (based on the decision made by an algorithm) actuator technology is required and that physical response will be made by an actuator system. The simplest definition of the actuator can be *"actuator converts electrical energy to mechanical energy"*(Pons, 2005). Similar to sensing technology, advancements in the field of mechatronics have made amazing progress in actuator technology.

Sensors provide data to AI algorithms; this data is used for learning purposes as well as for actual analysis. Retrospective and instantaneous health-related data of a patient can be an ideal situation for the exact diagnosis of diseases as each patient has different medical history and sensors can provide a detailed description. AI-enabled health marker sensors include electrolytes, metabolites, heart rate, SpO_2, proteins, temperature, etc. These AI-enabled sensors are used for early diagnosis of a disease, such as early lung cancer prediction (Shin et al., 2020) and prostate cancer (Kim, Hojun et al., 2020) with promising accuracies. It is worth mentioning that advancements in sensing technology are promising not only from the point of view of accuracy and smaller in size but also non-intrusiveness such as graphene-hybrid electrochemical-based sensing devices for glucose monitoring through human perspiration (Lee et al., 2016). Sensing technology has proved to be instrumental in the behavioral analysis of induvial and based on the behavior wellness can be determined especially for elderly people who are living independently (Ujager & Mahmood, 2019). Furthermore, this technology along with the AI cloud concept is boosting the concept of personalized health such as companies like VirtueSense which allows fall prevention by tracking patient movement (Strubhar, Tan, Storage, & Peterson, 2018).

Robotic surgery is making its way into smart digital healthcare; robotic surgery machines use actuators for fine and precise surgeries. Robotic surgery machines have been categorized into two, haptic (surgeon guided) and active (without surgeon-guided) (Beyaz, 2020). ROBODOC (THINK Surgical Inc., Fremont, California, USA) is an example of active robotic surgery (Kayani et al., 2019). This robotic surgery machine is used for orthopedic surgeries.

Internet of Medical Things (IoMT)

IoMT is a concept where medical devices are connected over the network (public/ private/ personal) to provide comprehensive healthcare (Razdan & Sharma, 2021). IoMT is a subset of the Internet of Things (IoT) and covers wearable healthcare gadgets (e.g. Smartwatch), in-house medical monitoring (e.g. glucometer), and point of care (POC) medical devices (e.g. ECG machines).

IoMT serves as a comprehensive platform for learning individual patient medical history, as with this technology constant remote monitoring is easy, reliable, and cost-effective (Manickam et al., 2022). Furthermore, it provides effective drug management, 24/7 remote medical assistance, patient-centric care, better adherence to recommended medication, and lifestyle. Several AI-IoMT-based remote healthcare solutions have been proposed (Selvaraj & Sundaravaradhan, 2020), these solutions are behavioral analysis based for wellness determination (Ujager & Mahmood, 2019), cognitive impairment prediction (Wu, X. & Li, 2022), public health emergencies (Lu, S., Christie, Nguyen, Freeman, & Hsu, 2022), and other advance disease diagnosis (such as Venous thromboembolism (VTE)) (Lu, Z. et al., 2021).

Several companies and startups are providing healthcare services using IoMT technology, Neurotech company (www.neurotecheeg.com) is providing remote real-time EEG (Electro Encephalo Gram) monitoring to identify seizures and baseline changes for physician intervention if required to provide medical assistance. AliveCor is another company that uses IoT devices (such as iECG) to remotely monitor the heart rhythm of the patient (Halcox et al., 2017).

Information Security

As data and data-based services are becoming part of our lives, there is a dire requirement to protect data. Data related to health is different from other data as this data is not only vital but can be lifesaving. Information security is not only about encrypting the data, but also ensuring the timely availability of information and authenticating the information as well. Information security becomes crucial when the above discussion is contextualized from the perceptive of AI-based healthcare. Data is vital for AI learning and for healthcare applications it is significant that it should be free from any bias or misinformation (Cui & Lee, 2020).

Modern societies are inclining more towards IoT-based AI healthcare services especially because of the current pandemic (COVID-19) situation and the likelihood of a similar situation in the future. The main communication platform for IoT devices is a public network, where it becomes extremely difficult to protect and secure the data. According to the "Critical Insight" study that there is an increase of 84% in cyber-attacks from 2018 to 2021 and the number of victims increased from 14 million to 44.9 million from the year 2018 to 2021 respectively (Peyton Doyle, 2022). These attacks not only include stealing patients' health-related records but also Denial of Service (DoS) attacks on healthcare infrastructures, masquerading attacks, false insurance claims, and many others. Blockchain is emerging as a popular and potential candidate to deal with healthcare privacy and protection issues, especially with AI-based healthcare systems (Jabarulla & Lee, 2021). Blockchain can play a vital role in securing the data as well as in adding reliability to the source of data. The application areas of blockchain in modern healthcare are supply chain transparency, smart contracts, patient-centric electronic health records, medical staff credential verification, IoT-based remote monitoring applications, and pharma and clinical trial tracking (Tagde et al., 2021).

Advancements and improvements in associated technologies are important for the realization of AI-based healthcare applications. However, these technologies have their limitations. For instance, the lack of quality in images which is crucial in feature extraction and its effect in determining diseases in early stages (Lakhani et al., 2018), limited battery life of sensors or frequent charging of wearable devices (Park et al., 2020), precise movement of actuators (Santoso & Onal, 2021), and variety of novel cyber-attacks (Kumar, Ajitesh et al., 2022).

ETHICAL ASPECTS OF AI IN HEALTHCARE

Although the use of AI is rising in different industries, including healthcare, ethical barriers are one of the significant issues faced. In many instances, these are contextualized. In other words, the meaning differs according to stakeholders, and the inability to discern the meaning may lead to delay adoption of the technology and any benefits that derive from it. Therefore, the approach to using AI in healthcare should review the ethical language put together while deciding to implement AI (Bartoletti, 2019a).

This section aims to analyze the ethical and legal framework for artificial intelligence. The European Union General Data Protection Regulation (GDPR) provides a solid framework that hosts provisions which covers AI's ethical and legal implications, including for the healthcare industry. The legislation uses indicators that comprise traceability, accessibility, and interpretability to seek a framework that aims to protect against AI damages such as civil liability, data protection, confidentiality breach, and crimes. A normative perspective reviews the ethical understanding of using AI in healthcare. It is noted that the scope of this research excludes analyzing how data protection overlaps with other areas of the law to protect.

Defining Ethics

The definition of ethics has been debated among scholars. It is defined as a 'set of moral principles which informs judgments of rights or wrong for a particular group or activity. As previously mentioned, this research explores the normative aspect, which aims to offer structures and guidelines for behaviors that comprise rights. An evolving area of ethics that encompasses consideration to guide behaviors is applied ethics which forms part of the interaction of AI and healthcare. For example, Dafoe claims that 'the design of technological solutions can deliver intended outcomes and unintentional outcomes, especially in the event of unforeseen selective pressures'. These unintentional outcomes can then shape societal norms and expectations (Bartoletti, 2019).

Some core principles of ethics in healthcare include justice, beneficence, autonomy, and informed consent. Examples of ethical frameworks for AI include a person's documents that identify AI's opportunities and corresponding risks and improve human agency without removing human responsibility. In other words, human autonomy should be respected, and humans must keep self-determination and prevent harm. AI systems and the environments in which they operate must be safe and secure. They should neither cause nor create damage or otherwise adversely affect human beings (Calvo, Peters, Vold, & Ryan, 2020).

Furthermore, the legal framework includes substantive and procedural dimensions. The former aims to ensure fair and just treatment and prevent discrimination and stigmatization, whereas the latter implies the search for practical solutions through AI systems and humans. Moreover, some of the criteria that define the implementation of AI systems include the following:

- Explicability: Takes the form of algorithmic processes that must be transparent, the capabilities and purpose of AI systems must be openly asserted, and decisions explainable to those affected directly and indirectly. For example, informed consent in the healthcare industry.
- Human agency and oversight: comprise fundamental rights, such as the right to live, dignity, and privacy.
- Technical robustness and safety, including resilience to attack and security,

- Fallback plan and general safety, accuracy, reliability, and reproducibility.
- Privacy and data governance, including respect for privacy, quality and integrity of data, and access to data.
- Transparency, including traceability.
- Explainability and communication; - Diversity, non-discrimination, and fairness, including the avoidance of unfair bias,
- Accessibility and universal design, and stakeholder participation; - Societal and environmental well-being, including sustainability and environmental friendliness,
- Social impact, society, and democracy; - Accountability, including audibility, minimization, and reporting of negative implications, trade-offs, and redress.

Nonetheless, when it comes to the intersection of law and AI, data protection is at the heart of it. Other areas include consumer protection and competition laws, to name a few. The broader legal framework comprises a human right angle that includes the EU charter of Human rights, freedom of expression and information, the right to education, equality before the law, the right to a fair trial, and the right to healthcare is covered under article 35. It is perceived that automated decision-making and predictions offer more predictability and balanced decisions (McHale, 2010).

Although not explicitly mentioned in the GDPR, many provisions are relevant to AI. Some scholars argue that there are concerns over the impact of traditional data protection rules and principles, for example, big data, which involves data regarding individuals, and their social relations, a method of improving data protection principles consistent with AI means reviewing the conceptual framework surrounding subject rights (Mitrou, 2018).

CHALLENGES

AI is becoming inevitable for modern and future healthcare; however, certain challenges are associated with the realization of smart and intelligent healthcare infrastructure. As often, for a layman, AI technology is considered a black box and this black box receives input and provides the output, even the practitioner, does not know the mechanism which is being performed. Several ethical, legal, and societal aspects need to be considered while dealing with such process (Čartolovni, Tomičić, & Mosler, 2022). Furthermore, as AI-based applications are based on provided data and algorithms, if the disparities and social inequalities lie in the provided data and the designed algorithm then serious consequences may arise. The lack of regulatory and legal framework is another challenge while creating and assembling AI-based healthcare systems (Carter et al., 2020). Ethical, legal, and social aspects need to be considered and discussed from the perspective of safety, privacy, transparency (decision-making bias), accountability, and responsibility (Bartoletti, 2019b)(Safavi & Kalis, 2019). The psychological aspect of the patient is also important to consider such as the placebo effect on the patient concerning healthcare (Vetter, 2021). However, challenges in this chapter are considered from the perceptive of technology.

Data Integration

One of the major technology challenges is data integration from different sources, such as health data gathering from different devices (Shaheen, 2021), these devices present data in different structures. Even for the same type of information, it is difficult to integrate data, for instance, there are different standards for electronic health records (EHR), which is an important source of health data. Currently, the majority of AI-based healthcare applications are using data from a limited number of similar sources as these are experimental studies. For making these applications smart, other source data must be included as contextual information for validation and a realistic decision-making process. For example, EHR data can be used in the diagnosis of a particular disease, but this diagnostic system must be capable of accepting data from different EHRs otherwise the system would not be able to perform as per the requirements.

Data Quality

Furthermore, data quality is another issue where most health-related data is unstructured, noisy, and unreliable (Létinier et al., 2021). If the data is missing integrity, the outcome of the system will be unreliable and misguiding. There are several techniques to handle unstructured and noisy data, however, removing the noise of data and structuring the data by these techniques may result in losing valuable knowledge from the data. AI systems built on such data may result in unreliable outcomes.

AI Chasm

Theoretical performance metrics of the AI models cannot always be generalized and mapped to clinical applications. AI Chasm is the gap where the experimental AI model accuracy is not related to the clinical efficacy of a particular application (Shah, Milstein, & Bagley, 2019). There might be several reasons associated, however, one of the reasons could be that the AI model has not taken all the required features such as the relevant contextual features for the validation or taken additional features which have been affected in another way.

Data Bias

An important challenge that needs to be considered is the bias in the data, which means that certain points of the data are over presented, for example, a specific health solution can only be applied to a particular population only as the system has learned from the data of this population (World Health Organization, 2021). This results in biased outcomes and makes the model unreliable as the models are trained over such data. Data have several types of biases such as systematic, overfitting and underfitting, automation bias, selection bias, overgeneralization, and many others as well.

Other Challenges

Technology integration is one of the issues in realizing several AI healthcare applications from concept to reality due to a lack of technology integration such as nano communication in robotic surgery (Verma, Chowdary, Gupta, & Mondal, 2018). Similarly, data privacy and security issues are also among the top challenges in healthcare (Al Omar et al., 2021).

CONCLUSION

Artificial intelligence is opening several opportunities on the horizon of healthcare. These opportunities promise better diagnosis/prognosis, treatment, HR management, drug discovery, optimization of resources, assistance, and smart decision-making with precision and higher accuracy in healthcare. This chapter provides a comprehensive overview of AI in healthcare concerning the latest research findings, best practices, associated technologies, and ethical aspects. However, several challenges are associated with the realization of a smart and intelligent healthcare system. These challenges are not only technical but ethical, legal, and societal as well. Moreover, technical challenges and practicalities are also taken into consideration at the standardization, protocols, and framework levels.

REFERENCES

Acevedo, F., Armengol, V., Deng, Z., Tang, R., Coopey, S. B., Braun, D., & Colwell, A. (2019). Pathologic findings in reduction mammoplasty specimens: A surrogate for the population prevalence of breast cancer and high-risk lesions. *Breast Cancer Research and Treatment*, *173*(1), 201–207. doi:10.100710549-018-4962-0 PMID:30238276

Al Omar, A., Jamil, A. K., Khandakar, A., Uzzal, A. R., Bosri, R., Mansoor, N., & Rahman, M. S. (2021). A transparent and privacy-preserving healthcare platform with a ovel smart contract for smart cities. *IEEE Access: Practical Innovations, Open Solutions*, *9*, 90738–90749. doi:10.1109/ACCESS.2021.3089601

Aljihmani, L., Kerdjidj, O., Zhu, Y., Mehta, R. K., Erraguntla, M., Sasangohar, F., & Qaraqe, K. (2020). Classification of fatigue phases in healthy and diabetic adults using wearable sensor. *Sensors (Basel)*, *20*(23), 6897. doi:10.339020236897 PMID:33287112

Alzheimer's Society. (2022). *Facts for the media about dementia*. Alzheimer's Society. https://www.alzheimers.org.uk/about-us/news-and-media/facts-media#:~:text=How%20many%20people%20in%20the%20world%20have%20dementia%3F,to%20152.8%20million%20by%202050

Andresen, S. L. (2002). John McCarthy: Father of AI. *IEEE Intelligent Systems*, *17*(5), 84–85. doi:10.1109/MIS.2002.1039837

Arık, S. Ö., Shor, J., Sinha, R., Yoon, J., Ledsam, J. R., Le, L. T., & Epshteyn, A. (2021). A prospective evaluation of AI-augmented epidemiology to forecast COVID-19 in the USA and japan. *NPJ Digital Medicine*, *4*(1), 1–18. doi:10.103841746-021-00511-7 PMID:34625656

Ashfaq, Z., Mumtaz, R., Rafay, A., Zaidi, S. M. H., Saleem, H., Mumtaz, S., Shahid, A., Poorter, E. D., & Moerman, I. (2022). Embedded AI-based digi-healthcare. *Applied Sciences (Basel, Switzerland)*, *12*(1), 519. doi:10.3390/app12010519

Aziz, M., Ejaz, S. A., Zargar, S., Akhtar, N., Aborode, A. T., & Wani, A., T., & Akintola, A. A. (2022). Deep learning and structure-based virtual screening for drug discovery against NEK7: A novel target for the treatment of cancer. *Molecules (Basel, Switzerland)*, *27*(13), 4098. doi:10.3390/molecules27134098 PMID:35807344

Barber, E. L., Garg, R., Persenaire, C., & Simon, M. (2021). Natural language processing with machine learning to predict outcomes after ovarian cancer surgery. *Gynecologic Oncology, 160*(1), 182–186. doi:10.1016/j.ygyno.2020.10.004 PMID:33069375

Bartoletti, I. (2019a). AI in healthcare: Ethical and privacy challenges. Paper presented at the *Conference on Artificial Intelligence in Medicine in Europe*, (pp. 7-10). Springer. 10.1007/978-3-030-21642-9_2

Basheer, S., Bhatia, S., & Sakri, S. B. (2021). Computational modeling of dementia prediction using deep neural network: Analysis on OASIS dataset. *IEEE Access: Practical Innovations, Open Solutions, 9*, 42449–42462. doi:10.1109/ACCESS.2021.3066213

Bellio, M., Oxtoby, N. P., Walker, Z., Henley, S., Ribbens, A., Blandford, A., Alexander, D. C., & Yong, K. X. (2020). Analyzing large alzheimer's disease cognitive datasets: Considerations and challenges. *Alzheimer's & Dementia: Diagnosis, Assessment & Disease Monitoring, 12*(1), e12135. doi:10.1002/dad2.12135 PMID:33313379

Beyaz, S. (2020). A brief history of artificial intelligence and robotic surgery in orthopedics & traumatology and future expectations. *Eklem Hastaliklari ve Cerrahisi, 31*(3), 653–655. doi:10.5606/ehc.2020.75300 PMID:32962606

Calvo, R. A., Peters, D., Vold, K., & Ryan, R. M. (2020). *Supporting human autonomy in AI systems: A framework for ethical enquiry. Ethics of digital well-being.* Springer.

Carter, S. M., Rogers, W., Win, K. T., Frazer, H., Richards, B., & Houssami, N. (2020). The ethical, legal and social implications of using artificial intelligence systems in breast cancer care. *The Breast, 49*, 25–32. doi:10.1016/j.breast.2019.10.001 PMID:31677530

Čartolovni, A., Tomičić, A., & Mosler, E. L. (2022). Ethical, legal, and social considerations of AI-based medical decision-support tools: A scoping review. *International Journal of Medical Informatics, 161*, 104738. doi:10.1016/j.ijmedinf.2022.104738 PMID:35299098

Chowdhary, K. (2020). Natural language processing. *Fundamentals of Artificial Intelligence,*, 603-649.

Cui, L., & Lee, D. (2020). Coaid: Covid-19 healthcare misinformation dataset. *arXiv:2006.00885.*

Dankwa-Mullan, I., Rivo, M., Sepulveda, M., Park, Y., Snowdon, J., & Rhee, K. (2019). Transforming diabetes care through artificial intelligence: The future is here. *Population Health Management, 22*(3), 229–242.

Driver, C. N., Bowles, B. S., Bartholmai, B. J., & Greenberg-Worisek, A. J. (2020). Artificial intelligence in radiology: A call for thoughtful application. *Clinical and Translational Science, 13*(2), 216.

El-Rashidy, N., El-Sappagh, S., Islam, S. R., El-Bakry, H. M., & Abdelrazek, S. (2020). End-to-end deep learning framework for coronavirus (COVID-19) detection and monitoring. *Electronics (Basel), 9*(9), 1439. doi:10.3390/electronics9091439

Espinosa, R., Ponce, H., Gutiérrez, S., Martínez-Villaseñor, L., Brieva, J., & Moya-Albor, E. (2019). A vision-based approach for fall detection using multiple cameras and convolutional neural networks: A case study using the UP-fall detection dataset. *Computers in Biology and Medicine, 115*, 103520. doi:10.1016/j.compbiomed.2019.103520 PMID:31698242

FDA. (2018). *The drug development process.* FDA. https://www.fda.gov/patients/learn-about-drug-and-device-app rovals/drug-development-process

Gumbs, A. A., Frigerio, I., Spolverato, G., Croner, R., Illanes, A., Chouillard, E., & Elyan, E. (2021). Artificial intelligence surgery: How do we get to autonomous actions in surgery? *Sensors (Basel), 21*(16), 5526. doi:10.339021165526 PMID:34450976

Halcox, J. P., Wareham, K., Cardew, A., Gilmore, M., Barry, J. P., Phillips, C., & Gravenor, M. B. (2017). Assessment of remote heart rhythm sampling using the AliveCor heart monitor to screen for atrial fibrillation: The REHEARSE-AF study. *Circulation, 136*(19), 1784–1794. doi:10.1161/CIRCU-LATIONAHA.117.030583 PMID:28851729

Hamad, L. I., Ahmed, E. S. A., & Saeed, R. A. (2022). *Machine learning in healthcare: Theory, applications, and future trends. AI applications for disease diagnosis and treatment.* IGI Global.

Hameed, N., Shabut, A. M., Ghosh, M. K., & Hossain, M. A. (2020). Multi-class multi-level classification algorithm for skin lesions classification using machine learning techniques. *Expert Systems with Applications, 141*, 112961. doi:10.1016/j.eswa.2019.112961

IBM. (2019). *Hardin memorial health; AI solution informs radiologists with deep patient insights.* IBM. https://www.ibm.com/case-studies/hardin-memorial-health-watson-health

IDF. (2021). *Diabetes facts & figures.* IDF. https://idf.org/aboutdiabetes/what-is-diabetes/facts-figures.html#:~:text=Almost%201%20in%202%20(240,living%20with%20type%201%20diabetes .

Iglesias, J. E., & Sabuncu, M. R. (2015). Multi-atlas segmentation of biomedical images: A survey. *Medical Image Analysis, 24*(1), 205–219. doi:10.1016/j.media.2015.06.012 PMID:26201875

Ilyas, M., Rehman, H., & Naït-Ali, A. (2020). Detection of covid-19 from chest x-ray images using artificial intelligence: An early review. Imaging explained. https://www.nps.org.au/consumers/imaging-explained

Iqbal, S., Ghani Khan, M. U., Saba, T., Mehmood, Z., Javaid, N., Rehman, A., & Abbasi, R. (2019). Deep learning model integrating features and novel classifiers fusion for brain tumor segmentation. *Microscopy Research and Technique, 82*(8), 1302–1315. doi:10.1002/jemt.23281 PMID:31032544

Jabarulla, M. Y., & Lee, H. (2021). A blockchain and artificial intelligence-based, patient-centric healthcare system for combating the COVID-19 pandemic: Opportunities and applications. *Healthcare, 9*(8) 1019.

Jie, Z., Zhiying, Z., & Li, L. (2021). A meta-analysis of watson for oncology in clinical application. *Scientific Reports, 11*(1), 1–13. doi:10.103841598-021-84973-5 PMID:33707577

Johnson, K. B., Wei, W., Weeraratne, D., Frisse, M. E., Misulis, K., Rhee, K., Zhao, J., & Snowdon, J. L. (2021). Precision medicine, AI, and the future of personalized health care. *Clinical and Translational Science, 14*(1), 86–93. doi:10.1111/cts.12884 PMID:32961010

Juneja, S., Dhiman, G., Kautish, S., Viriyasitavat, W., & Yadav, K. (2021). A perspective roadmap for IoMT-based early detection and care of the neural disorder, dementia. *Journal of Healthcare Engineering, 2021*, 2021. doi:10.1155/2021/6712424 PMID:34880977

Katzman, J. L., Shaham, U., Cloninger, A., Bates, J., Jiang, T., & Kluger, Y. (2018). DeepSurv: Personalized treatment recommender system using a cox proportional hazards deep neural network. *BMC Medical Research Methodology, 18*(1), 1–12. doi:10.118612874-018-0482-1 PMID:29482517

Kayani, B., Konan, S., Ayuob, A., Onochie, E., Al-Jabri, T., & Haddad, F. S. (2019). Robotic technology in total knee arthroplasty: A systematic review. *EFORT Open Reviews, 4*(10), 611–617. doi:10.1302/2058-5241.4.190022 PMID:31754467

Kim, H., & Gelenbe, E. (2012). Reconstruction of large-scale gene regulatory networks using bayesian model averaging. *IEEE Transactions on Nanobioscience, 11*(3), 259–265. doi:10.1109/TNB.2012.2214233 PMID:22987132

Kim, H., Park, S., Jeong, I. G., Song, S. H., Jeong, Y., Kim, C., & Lee, K. H. (2020). Noninvasive precision screening of prostate cancer by urinary multimarker sensor and artificial intelligence analysis. *ACS Nano, 15*(3), 4054–4065. doi:10.1021/acsnano.0c06946 PMID:33296173

Kim, J., Cheon, S., & Lim, J. (2022). IoT-based unobtrusive physical activity monitoring system for predicting dementia. *IEEE Access: Practical Innovations, Open Solutions, 10*, 26078–26089. doi:10.1109/ACCESS.2022.3156607

Kumar, A., Gadag, S., & Nayak, U. Y. (2021). The beginning of a new era: Artificial intelligence in healthcare. *Advanced Pharmaceutical Bulletin, 11*(3), 414–425. doi:10.34172/apb.2021.049 PMID:34513616

Kumar, A., Singh, A. K., Ahmad, I., Kumar Singh, P., Verma, P. K., Alissa, K. A., & Tag-Eldin, E. (2022). A novel decentralized blockchain architecture for the preservation of privacy and data security against cyberattacks in healthcare. *Sensors (Basel), 22*(15), 5921. doi:10.339022155921 PMID:35957478

Kumar, S., Oh, I., Schindler, S., Lai, A. M., Payne, P. R., & Gupta, A. (2021). Machine learning for modeling the progression of alzheimer disease dementia using clinical data: A systematic literature review. *JAMIA Open, 4*(3), ooab052.

Lakhani, P., Prater, A. B., Hutson, R. K., Andriole, K. P., Dreyer, K. J., Morey, J., ... Itri, J. N. (2018). Machine learning in radiology: Applications beyond image interpretation. *Journal of the American College of Radiology, 15*(2), 350–359. doi:10.1016/j.jacr.2017.09.044 PMID:29158061

Lakhani, P., & Sundaram, B. (2017). Deep learning at chest radiography: Automated classification of pulmonary tuberculosis by using convolutional neural networks. *Radiology, 284*(2), 574–582. doi:10.1148/radiol.2017162326 PMID:28436741

Lee, H., Choi, T. K., Lee, Y. B., Cho, H. R., Ghaffari, R., Wang, L., & Hyeon, T. (2016). A graphene-based electrochemical device with thermoresponsive microneedles for diabetes monitoring and therapy. *Nature Nanotechnology, 11*(6), 566–572. doi:10.1038/nnano.2016.38 PMID:26999482

Létinier, L., Jouganous, J., Benkebil, M., Bel-Létoile, A., Goehrs, C., Singier, A., ... Micallef, J. (2021). Artificial intelligence for unstructured healthcare data: Application to coding of patient reporting of adverse drug reactions. *Clinical Pharmacology and Therapeutics, 110*(2), 392–400. doi:10.1002/cpt.2266 PMID:33866552

Liu, Y., Jain, A., Eng, C., Way, D. H., Lee, K., Bui, P., & Gabriele, S. (2020). A deep learning system for differential diagnosis of skin diseases. *Nature Medicine*, *26*(6), 900–908. doi:10.103841591-020-0842-3 PMID:32424212

Lu, S., Christie, G. A., Nguyen, T. T., Freeman, J. D., & Hsu, E. B. (2022). Applications of artificial intelligence and machine learning in disasters and public health emergencies. *Disaster Medicine and Public Health Preparedness*, *16*(4), 1674–1681. doi:10.1017/dmp.2021.125 PMID:34134815

Lu, Z., Qian, P., Bi, D., Ye, Z., He, X., Zhao, Y., Su, L., Li, S., & Zhu, Z. (2021). Application of AI and IoT in clinical medicine: Summary and challenges. *Current Medical Science*, *41*(6), 1134–1150. doi:10.100711596-021-2486-z PMID:34939144

Manickam, P., Mariappan, S. A., Murugesan, S. M., Hansda, S., Kaushik, A., Shinde, R., & Thipperudraswamy, S. P. (2022). Artificial intelligence (AI) and internet of medical things (IoMT) assisted biomedical systems for intelligent healthcare. *Biosensors (Basel)*, *12*(8), 562. doi:10.3390/bios12080562 PMID:35892459

Matsuzaka, Y., & Uesawa, Y. (2022). A deep learning-based quantitative Structure–Activity relationship system construct prediction model of agonist and antagonist with high performance. *International Journal of Molecular Sciences*, *23*(4), 2141. doi:10.3390/ijms23042141 PMID:35216254

Mauldin, T. R., Canby, M. E., Metsis, V., Ngu, A. H., & Rivera, C. C. (2018). SmartFall: A smartwatch-based fall detection system using deep learning. *Sensors (Basel)*, *18*(10), 3363. doi:10.339018103363 PMID:30304768

McHale, J. (2010). *Fundamental rights and health care* Health Rights..

Mesko, B. (2017). The role of artificial intelligence in precision medicine. *Expert Review of Precision Medicine and Drug Development*, *2*(5), 239–241. doi:10.1080/23808993.2017.1380516

Minutolo, A., Damiano, E., De Pietro, G., Fujita, H., & Esposito, M. (2022). A conversational agent for querying italian patient information leaflets and improving health literacy. *Computers in Biology and Medicine*, *141*, 105004. doi:10.1016/j.compbiomed.2021.105004 PMID:34774337

Mitrou, L. (2018). *Data protection, artificial intelligence and cognitive services: Is the general data protection regulation (GDPR) 'artificial intelligence-proof*. Artificial Intelligence and Cognitive Services.

Moreno, G., Tran, H., Chia, A. L., Lim, A., & Shumack, S. (2007). Prospective study to assess general practitioners' dermatological diagnostic skills in a referral setting. *Australasian Journal of Dermatology*, *48*(2), 77–82.

Nagy, Á., Munkácsy, G., & Győrffy, B. (2021). Pancancer survival analysis of cancer hallmark genes. *Scientific Reports*, *11*(1), 1–10. doi:10.103841598-021-84787-5 PMID:33723286

Nomura, A., Noguchi, M., Kometani, M., Furukawa, K., & Yoneda, T. (2021). Artificial intelligence in current diabetes management and prediction. *Current Diabetes Reports*, *21*(12), 1–6. doi:10.100711892-021-01423-2 PMID:34902070

Noom. (2022). Retrieved from https://www.noom.com

Omoregbe, N. A., Ndaman, I. O., Misra, S., Abayomi-Alli, O. O., Damaševičius, R., & Dogra, A. (2020). Text messaging-based medical diagnosis using natural language processing and fuzzy logic. *Journal of Healthcare Engineering*, *2020*, 1–14. doi:10.1155/2020/8839524

Panayides, A. S., Amini, A., Filipovic, N. D., Sharma, A., Tsaftaris, S. A., Young, A., ... Kurc, T. (2020). AI in medical imaging informatics: Current challenges and future directions. *IEEE Journal of Biomedical and Health Informatics*, *24*(7), 1837–1857. doi:10.1109/JBHI.2020.2991043 PMID:32609615

Park, J., Bhat, G., Nk, A., Geyik, C. S., Ogras, U. Y., & Lee, H. G. (2020). Energy per operation optimization for energy-harvesting wearable IoT devices. *Sensors (Basel)*, *20*(3), 764. doi:10.339020030764 PMID:32019219

Peyton Doyle. (2022). Healthcare breaches on the rise in 2022. *Tech Target*. https://www.techtarget.com/searchsecurity/news/252521771/Healthcare-breaches-on-the-rise

Pons, J. L. (2005). *Emerging actuator technologies: A micromechatronic approach*. John Wiley & Sons. doi:10.1002/0470091991

Poplin, R., Varadarajan, A. V., Blumer, K., Liu, Y., McConnell, M. V., Corrado, G. S., Peng, L., & Webster, D. R. (2018). Prediction of cardiovascular risk factors from retinal fundus photographs via deep learning. *Nature Biomedical Engineering*, *2*(3), 158–164. doi:10.103841551-018-0195-0 PMID:31015713

Quazi, S., Jangi, R., Gavas, S., & Karpinski, T. M. (2022). Artificial intelligence and machine learning in medicinal chemistry and validation of emerging drug targets. *Advancements in Controlled Drug Delivery Systems*, 27-43.

Ramzan, F., Khan, M. U. G., Iqbal, S., Saba, T., & Rehman, A. (2020). Volumetric segmentation of brain regions from MRI scans using 3D convolutional neural networks. *IEEE Access: Practical Innovations, Open Solutions*, *8*, 103697–103709. doi:10.1109/ACCESS.2020.2998901

Razdan, S., & Sharma, S. (2021). Internet of medical things (IoMT): Overview, emerging technologies, and case studies. *IETE Technical Review*, 1–14.

Rghioui, A., Lloret, J., Harane, M., & Oumnad, A. (2020). A smart glucose monitoring system for diabetic patient. *Electronics (Basel)*, *9*(4), 678. doi:10.3390/electronics9040678

Saba, T. (2020). Recent advancement in cancer detection using machine learning: Systematic survey of decades, comparisons and challenges. *Journal of Infection and Public Health*, *13*(9), 1274–1289. doi:10.1016/j.jiph.2020.06.033 PMID:32758393

Safavi, K., & Kalis, B. (2019). How AI can change the future of health care. *HBR*. https://hbr.org/webinar/2019/02/how-ai-can-change-the-future-of-health-care

Santoso, J., & Onal, C. D. (2021). An origami continuum robot capable of precise motion through torsionally stiff body and smooth inverse kinematics. *Soft Robotics*, *8*(4), 371–386. doi:10.1089oro.2020.0026 PMID:32721270

Selvaraj, S., & Sundaravaradhan, S. (2020). Challenges and opportunities in IoT healthcare systems: A systematic review. *SN Applied Sciences*, *2*(1), 1–8. doi:10.100742452-019-1925-y

Shah, N. H., Milstein, A., & Bagley, S. C. (2019). Making machine learning models clinically useful. *Journal of the American Medical Association*, *322*(14), 1351–1352. doi:10.1001/jama.2019.10306 PMID:31393527

Shaheen, M. Y. (2021). AI in healthcare: Medical and socio-economic benefits and challenges. *ScienceOpen Preprints,* Shimoda, A., Li, Y., Hayashi, H., & Kondo, N. (2021). Dementia risks identified by vocal features via telephone conversations: A novel machine learning prediction model. *PLoS One*, *16*(7), e0253988. doi:10.1371/journal.pone.0253988 PMID:34260593

Shin, H., Oh, S., Hong, S., Kang, M., Kang, D., Ji, Y., & Park, Y. (2020). Early-stage lung cancer diagnosis by deep learning-based spectroscopic analysis of circulating exosomes. *ACS Nano*, *14*(5), 5435–5444. doi:10.1021/acsnano.9b09119 PMID:32286793

Shu, F., & Shu, J. (2021). An eight-camera fall detection system using human fall pattern recognition via machine learning by a low-cost android box. *Scientific Reports*, *11*(1), 1–17. doi:10.103841598-021-81115-9 PMID:33510202

So, A., Hooshyar, D., Park, K. W., & Lim, H. S. (2017). Early diagnosis of dementia from clinical data by machine learning techniques. *Applied Sciences (Basel, Switzerland)*, *7*(7), 651. doi:10.3390/app7070651

Srinivasu, P. N., SivaSai, J. G., Ijaz, M. F., Bhoi, A. K., Kim, W., & Kang, J. J. (2021). Classification of skin disease using deep learning neural networks with MobileNet V2 and LSTM. *Sensors (Basel)*, *21*(8), 2852. doi:10.339021082852 PMID:33919583

Strubhar, A. J., Tan, P., Storage, L., & Peterson, M. (2018). Concurrent validity of the VirtuSense® gait analysis system for the quantification of spatial and temporal parameters of gait. *International Journal of Exercise Science*, *11*(1), 934–940.

Tagde, P., Tagde, S., Bhattacharya, T., Tagde, P., Chopra, H., Akter, R., Kaushik, D., & Rahman, M. (2021). Blockchain and artificial intelligence technology in e-health. *Environmental Science and Pollution Research International*, *28*(38), 52810–52831. doi:10.100711356-021-16223-0 PMID:34476701

Tahir, B., Iqbal, S., Usman Ghani Khan, M., Saba, T., Mehmood, Z., Anjum, A., & Mahmood, T. (2019). Feature enhancement framework for brain tumor segmentation and classification. *Microscopy Research and Technique*, *82*(6), 803–811. doi:10.1002/jemt.23224 PMID:30768835

Ting, D. S. W., Cheung, C. Y., Lim, G., Tan, G. S. W., Quang, N. D., Gan, A., & Lee, S. Y. (2017). Development and validation of a deep learning system for diabetic retinopathy and related eye diseases using retinal images from multiethnic populations with diabetes. *Journal of the American Medical Association*, *318*(22), 2211–2223. doi:10.1001/jama.2017.18152 PMID:29234807

Tohka, J., & Van Gils, M. (2021). Evaluation of machine learning algorithms for health and wellness applications: A tutorial. *Computers in Biology and Medicine*, *132*, 104324. doi:10.1016/j.compbiomed.2021.104324 PMID:33774270

Tsai, C., Li, C., Lam, R. W., Li, C., & Ho, S. (2019). Diabetes care in motion: Blood glucose estimation using wearable devices. *IEEE Consumer Electronics Magazine*, *9*(1), 30–34. doi:10.1109/MCE.2019.2941461

Ujager, F. S., & Mahmood, A. (2019a). A context-aware accurate wellness determination (CAAWD) model for elderly people using lazy associative classification. *Sensors (Basel)*, *19*(7), 1613. doi:10.339019071613 PMID:30987246

Ujager, F. S., Mahmood, A., & Khatoon, S. (2019). Wellness determination of the elderly using spatio-temporal correlation analysis of daily activities. *Journal of Ambient Intelligence and Smart Environments*, *11*(6), 515–526. doi:10.3233/AIS-190538

Vaishnavee, K. B., & Amshakala, K. (2015). An automated MRI brain image segmentation and tumor detection using SOM-clustering and proximal support vector machine classifier. Paper presented at the *2015 IEEE International Conference on Engineering and Technology (ICETECH)*, (pp. 1-6). IEEE. 10.1109/ICETECH.2015.7275030

Verma, V., Chowdary, V., Gupta, M. K., & Mondal, A. K. (2018). *IoT and robotics in healthcare. Medical big data and internet of medical things*. CRC Press.

Vetter, N. (2021). The promise of artificial intelligence: A review of the opportunities and challenges of artificial intelligence in healthcare and clinical trials in skeletal dysplasia: A paradigm for treating rare diseases. *British Medical Bulletin*, *139*(1), 1–3. doi:10.1093/bmb/ldab022

Viswanathan, J., Saranya, N., & Inbamani, A. (2021). *Deep learning applications in medical imaging: Introduction to deep learning-based intelligent systems for medical applications. Deep learning applications in medical imaging*. IGI Global. doi:10.4018/978-1-7998-5071-7.ch007

Wen, A., Fu, S., Moon, S., El Wazir, M., Rosenbaum, A., Kaggal, V. C., Liu, S., Sohn, S., Liu, H., & Fan, J. (2019). Desiderata for delivering NLP to accelerate healthcare AI advancement and a mayo clinic NLP-as-a-service implementation. *NPJ Digital Medicine*, *2*(1), 1–7. doi:10.103841746-019-0208-8 PMID:31872069

World Health Organization. (2018). *Towards a dementia plan: A WHO guide*. WHO.

World Health Organization. (2021). *Ethics and governance of artificial intelligence for health: WHO guidance*. WHO.

Wu, H., Yin, H., Chen, H., Sun, M., Liu, X., Yu, Y., & Zhang, J. (2020). A deep learning, image based approach for automated diagnosis for inflammatory skin diseases. *Annals of Translational Medicine*, *8*(9), 581. doi:10.21037/atm.2020.04.39 PMID:32566608

Wu, X., & Li, J. (2022). An AIoT-enabled autonomous dementia monitoring system. *arXiv:2207.00804*.

Yu, K., Tan, L., Lin, L., Cheng, X., Yi, Z., & Sato, T. (2021). Deep-learning-empowered breast cancer auxiliary diagnosis for 5GB remote E-health. *IEEE Wireless Communications*, *28*(3), 54–61.

Zheng, C., Bouazizi, M., & Ohtsuki, T. (2022). An evaluation on information composition in dementia detection based on speech. *IEEE Access*

KEY TERMS AND DEFINITIONS

Associated Technologies: Other sub-technological domains which complete the system.

Best Practices: Practices or procedures that are accepted to be correct.

Diagnosis: An identification of the subjection of interest.

Healthcare System: It is a system that provides health-related services to the targeted population.

Pattern Learning: Repeated features that are being used by the AI (ML/DL) techniques to train the algorithm.

Prediction: A subject of interest that has been forecasted.

Prognosis: The most likely course of a medical condition.

Chapter 17

Potential Integration of Artificial Intelligence and Biomedical Research Applications:
Inevitable Disruptive Technologies for Prospective Healthcare

S. Uma

Hindusthan College of Engineering and Technology, Coimbatore, India

ABSTRACT

Hospitals are experiencing an increase in patients due to the prevalence of chronic diseases and the growing elderly population. As a result, every day, a large volume of patient health data is generated, which must be stored and managed effectively. Artificial Intelligence (AI) has played a pivotal role in preventing, diagnosing, treating diseases and rehabilitating patients in the past few decades. Innovations and scientific breakthroughs have improved patient outcomes and population health as the healthcare industry has embraced the digital age. Hence, digital transformation is no longer an option, but rather an industry standard. Though, Biomedical engineering (BE) contributes to improving patient care quality, future healthcare applications will rely on AI enabled BE to solve complex healthcare issues. This book chapter uncovers the potential of AI and BE as a powerful tool for solving some of the most challenging issues of our age and brings comparable changes in scale to the renaissance, the Industrial Revolution in the healthcare sector.

1.0 INTRODUCTION

Business, society, and healthcare are increasingly integrating artificial intelligence (AI) and related technologies. Healthcare solutions have increasingly integrated artificial intelligence, machine learning (ML), biomedical engineering and natural language processing (NLP) into clinical development. From remote patient care to hospital administration, technology plays a crucial role today. The field of

DOI: 10.4018/978-1-6684-6937-8.ch017

biomedical engineering applies engineering principles and design concepts to medicine and biology to benefit health care. These technologies are capable of transforming many aspects of patient care as well as administrative processes within providers, payers, and pharmaceutical companies. The requirements of healthcare are vast and complex. The COVID-19 outbreak afforded AI the opportunity to demonstrate its abilities and sophistication with regard to quality of service in the healthcare field. Especially during pandemic period like COVID-19 outbreak, the need for more number of medical practitioners is felt. The safety of the medical practitioners should be ensured first, to foster lifesaving treatments for the massive public. Under such circumstances, clinical decision making becomes difficult/error prone due to the excess number of cases the medical practitioners have to attend, due to the increasing COVID-19 spread and the insufficient number of medical practitioners. Clinical diagnosis, decision making, treatments and remote patient care should be accurate, fast, cost effective, available 24x7 and should be scaled at large to address and enhance patient care with respect to the increase in population (Taylor 2015). Personalized medicine and the need for digital health records are driving artificial intelligence in the healthcare market.

Advances in biomedical engineering improve human health and health care at all levels. Biomedical engineering encompasses many sub disciplines, including active and passive medical devices, orthopaedic implants, medical imaging, tissue and stem cell engineering, clinical engineering and biomedical signal processing (Michigan Tech 2019). The integration of artificial intelligence with biomedical engineering enhances the accuracy of decision making, which is vital to identifying the right treatment at the earliest. Furthermore, biomedical engineering is involved in the development of artificial organs, the development of diagnostic machines, the training of clinicians in the use of machines, and the study of biological systems (Roberson 2017).

Currently, algorithms outperform radiologists in detecting malignant tumors and guiding researchers in how to construct cohorts for costly clinical trials. However, AI will not be able to replace humans for a wide range of medical processes for a variety of reasons. We explore both the potential of AI for automating aspects of healthcare and the barriers to rapid implementation of AI.

2.0 LITERATURE SURVEY

AI seems more feasible than ever due to advancements in computing and processing power, coupled with hardware modernizations. The most significant AI breakthroughs of recent years can be attributed to machine learning. Instead of giving AI a fixed set of directions, AI models for healthcare applications is trained using large data sets to overcome the bias in outcomes. Increasing data generation from healthcare has led to potential improvements in accountability, quality, efficiency, and innovation. A great deal of research and innovation is conducted within the healthcare industry and hospital workflows. This is done with the goal of improving patient safety, reducing physician stress levels, and increasing the overall state of healthcare.

Gene technology, based on bioinformatics, offers enormous benefits for disease prevention and health care. The field of medical informatics today includes the concept of linking information sources through information and communication technology, enabling medical personnel to access information from a distance regardless of whether it comes from a patient's body or from an electronic archive (Snyder et al. 2011).

With the integration of many data-driven AI solutions, the conventional ways of doing things in healthcare and clinical workflows are beginning to change. With digital innovations, healthcare professionals can spend more time listening to their patients, which increases patient satisfaction. However, there are limitations and concerns about the security of Protected Health Information that must be addressed in order to integrate artificial intelligence across the healthcare industry.

By using artificial intelligence techniques, clinicians are able to extract clinically relevant information from large data sets, creating a more efficient decision making process (Murdoch & Detsky 2013). Further, AI can be used to help researchers analyse huge clinical datasets quickly, resulting in a more successful healthcare facility (Kolker et al. 2016). Artificial Intelligence also assists physicians by providing them with updated information about clinical practice from journals, websites, and e-books. It is impossible to avoid all diagnostic and therapeutic errors, but the artificial intelligence can minimize them. As technology advances, Artificial Intelligence filters key data from gigantic population data to produce health risk alerts and therapeutic outcome predictions (Dilsizian & Siegel 2014). Using biosensors connected to smartphones, patients can monitor their vital functions with biosensors and adhere to therapeutic guidelines, thus filling in the gap as a means of distributing an electronic health record (Abdulnabi et al. 2017).

AI is now used in a wide variety of healthcare applications. There have been many applications of it, including the processing of signals and images, and the prediction of function changes such as urinary bladder control, epilepsy, and stroke. (Tantin et al. 2020). Blind people can work in specialized fields such as informatics and electronics with an "ambient intelligent system" called RUDO (Hudec and Smutny 2017).

In order to recognize human facial expressions as commands, NNs can be trained with specific image-processing steps. In addition, facial expression analysis-based human-machine interfaces (HMIs) enable people with disabilities to operate wheelchairs and robot assistance vehicles without using a joystick or sensors (Rabhi et al. 2018). A growing number of clinical researchers are utilizing artificial intelligence (AI), especially machine learning methods (a subset of AI), to combine complex information, for example genomic and clinical information. (Vamathevan et al. 2019) Smart robotic systems and AI applications are improving life quality for elderly and disabled people living in assisted living facilities. Recently, new research was published on smart home functions and tools for people with loss of autonomy (PLA) and intelligent solution models based on wireless sensor networks, data mining, and artificial intelligence (Dahmani el al. 2016).

The advancements in edge and cloud computing, deep learning, artificial intelligence (AI), machine learning (ML), and next-generation wireless communications are used in smart healthcare. In smart healthcare, numerous pathology detection systems have been integrated (Amin et al., 2019). Because they make our lives more comfortable and convenient, smart healthcare frameworks are growing in popularity. A person can receive medical advice from numerous doctors across the world while still at home, receive a diagnosis of their illness, and save the inconvenience of making an appointment at the hospital. Integrating edge and cloud computing, 5G networks, and the Internet of Things (IoT) enables smart healthcare's precision and decreased latency. The accuracy of healthcare systems has also grown because of powerful ML algorithms like deep learning algorithms (Hossain & Muhammad, 2018).

Healthcare organisations are currently using AI to predict mortality rates for patients with acute heart failure, perform robotic surgery that reduces blood loss and hospital stay, reduce false-positive results in breast cancer screening, and improve physician workflow while relieving and preventing burnout.

The Internet of Medical Things (IoMT) or the Internet of Health Things (IoHT) has the potential to change the way that healthcare is provided ((Amin et al., 2019), (Hossain & Muhammad, 2018)). The approach taken in research and practice can be broken down into different categories. First, wearable technology and smartphone applications are integrated with smart sensors in the IoMT environment to continuously monitor health vitals ((Islam, Rahaman, & Islam 2020), (John Dian, Vahidnia, & Rahmati 2020), (Tabei et al. 2020)). Machine learning algorithms analyze and display predictive analytics, such as forecasting illnesses, after the data is collected using smart sensors (Le et al. 2021). Other algorithms are additionally utilized to track persistent disorders like diabetes and cardiac problems and find irregularities in the patient's health.

Various interconnected gadgets that can share and manage data to improve patient health make up the Internet of Health Things. With multiple investments related to the creation and application of IoT, it has quickly expanded. According to data from the McKinsey report, by 2025, IoHT will have a $ 11.1 trillion annual financial impact ("By 2025, Internet of Things Applications Could Have $11 Trillion Impact" 2015). In the arsenal of artificial intelligence tools used in healthcare, machine learning has emerged as a key weapon. It gives Internet of Things (IoT) devices exceptional information inference, data analytics, and intelligence capabilities. For a variety of IoHT technology situations, including big data cloud computing and smart sensors, machine learning has emerged as a potent and successful solution.

3.0 AI APPLICATIONS IN HEALTHCARE

Diagnostic speed and accuracy of AI-driven medical image analysis surpass those of human experts. AI and biomedical engineering will impact the clinical practice of medicine by enabling researchers to extract information from scientific literature and collate diverse electronic medical records using natural language processing. Clinical errors due to human cognitive biases could be avoided with machine learning directly from medical data, improving patient care. Cognitive medical practice will remain important due to the fact that AI is neither proficient nor intuitive.

AI is already improving convenience and efficiency in the realm of health care, reducing costs and errors, and making health care more accessible for more patients through self-service, chat bots, computer-aided detection systems for diagnosis, and image data analysis for drug discovery (Kidwai & RK 2020). Chronic Disease Management, Cognitive Diagnostics and Electronic Medical Record Applications are some of important areas of applications of AI.

The AI technologies that are widely used for the healthcare applications are listed below (Davenport & Kalakota 2019).

- Machine learning – neural networks and deep learning
- Natural language processing
- Robotic process automation
- Rule-based expert systems
- Physical robots
- Clinical Diagnosis and treatment applications
- Patient engagement and adherence applications
- Healthcare Administrative applications

Due to the increased adoption of AI technologies in healthcare applications during the pandemic, key market players focused on product innovation and technology partnerships to expand their product portfolios. MIT-IBM Watson AI Lab, for instance, supported research projects exploring the health and financial effects of the pandemic in May 2020 (Martineau 2020). Similarly, Qventus has introduced AI-based patient flow automation tools for its healthcare facilities that manage essential resources, optimize hospitalization durations, plan Covid-19 scenarios, and increase ICU capacity (CDT 2022). During the COVID-19 pandemic period, hospitals across the globe used artificial intelligence-based virtual assistants and AI-assisted surgery robots to handle the continuous influx of patients, which would have otherwise operationally overburdened hospitals. Increasing computational power, declining hardware costs, extensive growth in digital health, quality of service and mobile health technologies, are the major drivers for the adoption of AI in healthcare applications. Persuasion and empathy are considered as human skills that cannot be replaced by AI which leads to misconception and reluctance for using AI based medical solutions by medical practitioners. Personalized medicine that applies data-driven science to enrich and guide clinically actionable knowledge is essential in the present scenario. As a result, it has stimulated the development of human-aware AI systems while posing several research challenges, such as interpretation, automation, intelligent control, crowd sourcing, and presentation.

Several countries protect patient health information under federal laws, so breaches and failures to maintain its integrity can result in legal and financial penalties. Since AI-based tools use multiple health datasets in order to deliver patient care, they have to adhere to all data security protocols implemented by government and regulatory authorities. The large volumes of personal healthcare records acquired from various data sources for use in AI platforms need to be stored in third party data centers and also requires high computational power and cloud storage for increasing the processing speed.

4.0 BIOMEDICAL ENGINEERING APPLICATIONS IN HEALTHCARE

The number of variables and patient characteristics—both known and unknown—may easily exceed the amount of data that can be analysed when dealing with the human body and diseases. Additionally, the accessible data is usually tainted with abnormalities, outliers, incorrect measurements, and mislabelling, particularly in biological applications. The Entropic Outlier Sparsification (EOS) method, developed by Prof. Horenko, seeks to improve prediction accuracy by eliminating anomalies and outliers (Università della Svizzera italiana 2022).

The fields of bioscience and healthcare have a great deal of promise for using this kind of approach. For instance, these techniques have a significant but untapped potential for improving the diagnosis of cardiovascular diseases (CVDs), which, according to the World Health Organization, account for around one third of all fatalities worldwide each year, or over 18 million deaths worldwide (and over 21,000 yearly deaths in Switzerland alone) (Università della Svizzera italiana 2022).

When predicting a patient's mortality from heart failure, for instance, Prof. Horenko claims that EOS can help to achieve a statistically-significant accuracy improvement compared to the conventional learning approaches now used for this purpose. For a large number of people in Switzerland and around the world, this advancement may mean more prompt and accurate diagnoses and better clinical care (Universita della Svizzera italiana 2022).

The use of platinum and its alloys in a variety of medical devices, including defibrillators, pacemakers, and coronary and peripheral catheters, dates back more than forty years. In more contemporary technologies, such as neuromodulation devices and stents, vital components in a variety of shapes are made possible by platinum's biocompatibility, durability, conductivity, and radiopacity. To meet the demand for cutting-edge medical treatments in the industrialised world as well as, increasingly, the developing world, medical device makers continue to invest in innovative technology. A significant role in these advances will unavoidably be played by platinum, the other Platinum Group Metals (PGMs), and their alloys (Woodward and Cowley 2011).

A researcher from City University of Hong Kong has successfully built a nanofiber-based biodegradable millirobot named Fibot (City University of Hong Kong 2022). Fibot can move and disintegrate in the intestines in reaction to the pH of its surroundings, releasing various medications from various anchoring sites. The study has provided insight into the creation of microrobots and their possible use in the controlled release of medications in specific areas of the intestines. The research has also aided in the creation of biodegradable and flexible technology with biomedical uses (City University of Hong Kong 2022).

Tendons, which are bands of fibrous connective tissue, join bones and muscles. Since they are soft tissues attached to rigid bones, a complicated interface with a very distinct structure is produced. This structure is damaged after injury, and the connective tissue transforms from a linear to a kinked configuration. Additionally, excessive scarring can happen, altering the tendon's mechanical characteristics and its capacity to support stresses (Terasaki Institute for Biomedical Innovation 2022).

Anybody would shudder at the mere mention of a ruptured Achilles tendon. The lengthy, challenging, and frequently unsuccessful healing procedures associated with tendon injuries are widely documented. Thirty percent of persons will encounter a tendon injury, with the risk being higher in women. Sudden or repetitive motion, such as that experienced by athletes or industrial workers, increases the risk of tendon rips or ruptures. Silk fibroin and GelMA (SG) were combined in various ratios to create thin nanofiber sheets (Terasaki Institute for Biomedical Innovation 2022).

Compared to those on silk fibroin (SF) sheets without Gelatin Methacryloyl (GelMA), the Mesenchymal Stem Cells (MSCs) on the Silk fibroin with GelMA (SG) sheets shown higher cell viability and proliferation. Genetic testing revealed that the relevant gene activity in SG MSCs was substantially higher than that on SF sheets, in contrast (Terasaki Institute for Biomedical Innovation 2022).

The bioactive properties of conventional implants comprised of metal, ceramic, or polymer are limited. The healing process can take a while and is more likely to be rejected. "Shrimp shells, according to Professor Rosei, are antibacterial, making them essential for the development of new implant materials (INRS 2021). The organic component of bone, collagen, promotes cell development and migration. Additionally, copper-doped phosphate glass promotes bone regrowth and blood vessel creation (INRS 2021).

"Implants with specific biological features may be made possible by the capacity to install such coatings. As these coatings can improve implant-host interactions, it shows potential for biological applications "said doctoral candidate Imran Deen (INRS 2021).

Using an antimicrobial coating that can be placed to orthopaedic implants minutes before surgery, biomedical engineers and surgeons at Duke University and University of California, Los Angeles have showed how to prevent an infection from developing around the device (Kingery 2021).

When the body temperature drops at night as part of the 24-hour rhythm, sleep is possible. With the new mattress, people can fall asleep more quickly and have better-quality sleep since it stimulates the body to make them feel drowsy. The ebb and flow of a 24-hour rhythm of a person's body temperature affects how awake or drowsy they feel in part. The A unique mattress and pillow system that uses cooling and heating to tell the body when it's time to sleep was developed by bioengineers at the University of Texas at Austin.

In the Journal of Sleep Research, the researchers released a proof-of-concept study regarding the novel cooling-warming, dual-zone mattress system and warming pillow combination (Austin 2022). The study compared two mattress models: one that uses water to regulate body temperature and the other that uses air. They used 11 people to test the mattresses, asking them to go to bed two hours earlier than usual on some nights and not on others, depending on whether they wanted to use the cooling-warming features of the beds (Austin 2022).

Even in the tough environment of an earlier bedtime, the study discovered that the warming and cooling-warming mattress assisted them in falling asleep more quickly—roughly 58 percent more quickly in comparison to nights when they did not use the cooling-warming function. In addition to greatly reducing the time needed to fall asleep, lowering internal body temperature also led to significantly better sleep (Austin 2022).

The team's leader, Wenfeng Xia, from the King's College London School of Biomedical Engineering & Imaging Sciences, explained that traditional light-based endoscopes frequently have vast footprints and can only distinguish tissue anatomical information on the surface. "Our innovative thin endoscope can resolve subcellular-scale tissue structure and molecular information in 3D in real-time and is small enough to be incorporated with interventional medical devices, allowing doctors to assess tissue during a surgery" (Optica 2022).

5.0 BENEFITS OF AI AND BIOMEDICAL ENGINEERING IN HEALTHCARE

Reduced storage costs and the acquisition of large volumes of data have made it feasible to analyse data in order to gain deeper insights and aid decision-making. AI and BE applications primarily involve diagnosis and treatment recommendations, patient engagement and adherence, and administrative activities AI systems are drastically improving their accuracy by using machine learning, wireless medical data transmission, and digitized data acquisition. AI and biomedical engineering could revolutionize the way medical practitioners diagnose and treat diseases. The use of artificial intelligence has made some significant inroads in the early diagnosis of several chronic diseases, well as capturing and organizing messy medical images, doctor's notes, and other unstructured data sources. Clinical diagnosis and decision making is inevitable in choosing the right kind of treatment. To err is human and since it cannot be avoided in the clinical services rendered by human doctors. Machine Learning algorithms play a major role in identifying existing patterns and explore new patterns in clinical diagnosis and decision making. The structure of NNs is usually layered, with a variety of configurations. Supervised learning, unsupervised learning and reinforced learning are the learning algorithms commonly used for pattern recognition in artificial enhanced, biomedical engineering research in healthcare. In the future, NLP and ML can become increasingly important in health care because they can (Mehta 2020):

- Enhance the productivity and quality of care for providers and clinicians
- Improve patient engagement and streamline patient access to care
- Increase the speed and reduce the costs of developing new pharmaceuticals
- Utilize analytics to mine previously untapped stores of non-codified clinical data to personalize medical treatment

Biomedical engineers contribute to the advancement of knowledge just as much as medical professionals in modern biomedical research and health care. The Recent trends and advances in computational techniques, artificial intelligence (AI), machine learning, the Internet of Things (IoT), big data and several other technologies have accelerated the deployment of biomedical engineering (BE) in healthcare.

Many health-related apps use artificial intelligence, such as Google Assistant, but there are also some apps like Ada Health Companion that use AI to predict diseases based on symptoms and help people maintain health. In expert systems, AI mimics the decision-making abilities of human experts in a computer system. For the detection of bacterial diseases and cancer, expert systems like MYCIN and CaDET are widely used (Prasad et al. 2020). When it comes to healthcare, image processing is crucial because we have to detect diseases using images from X-rays, MRIs (Magnetic Resonance Imaging (MRI)), and CT (Computed Tomography) scans, so an AI system that detects those minute tumor cells is extremely useful in detecting diseases earlier. The most fascinating and revolutionary invention is the surgical robot, which can change surgery forever.

Medical diagnosing systems designed with AI have the ability to perform 10^{25} operations per second. Artificial intelligence will be of great help in providing much unconditional help that takes humans long hours per day to perform. By automating much of the manual work, the processing will become faster. With digital systems, users would be able to accomplish tasks in a flash.

As part of the development of applications in biotechnology, biophysics, bioinformatics, genomics, and other areas, AI enhanced not only medical diagnosis but also groomed the relevant areas. There has been a steady increase in the value of AI-based medical imaging systems since there has been an increase in the requirements that are satisfied. In order to improve patient outcomes, AI will help doctors, surgeons, and physicians see and do more at an earlier stage. Applications and systems of artificial intelligence in medical science will certainly lead to a revolution.

6.0 AI ENHANCED HEALTHCARE WITH BIOMEDICAL ENGINEERING

AI's benefits for biomedicine have been envisioned for decades. Several reviews have been published on AI's role in biomedical engineering. In recent years, advances have been made in AI and its applications in biomedicine ("Four Ways Biomedical Engineering Has Enhanced Healthcare," n.d.).

Technology has enabled clinical leaders to successfully cut costs while accelerating research and development stages over the years. Creating the right healthcare tools, devices, and software has made it possible for billions of people to access life-changing solutions, which have improved the safety, productivity, and quality of their lives (Lotsch, Kringel, and Ultsch 2021). Biomedical engineering has transformed and enhanced healthcare services in four ways.

6.1 Inventions

In recent years, Biomedical Engineers have developed prosthetic limbs, artificial hearts, livers, bionic contacts lenses, and the camera pill, which contains a colour camera, battery, light, and transmitter to be able to capture internal processes.

6.2 Medicine

In addition to improving our health and treating diseases, the study of bodily functions can also lead to the development of new medicines and drugs. In addition to new medicine, bioengineers have also made advances in solving long-term health problems, such as laser surgery.

6.3 Tools and Devices

To solve health issues that benefit all healthcare professionals, bioengineers work with doctors, nurses, surgeons, and technicians. MRI machines, dialysis machines, diagnostic equipment, and ultrasounds have been developed as a result of this.

6.4 Biological Processes

The goal of biomedical engineers is to understand how biological systems work and why the body moves and sends signals. This has led to the development of new technology, such as wearable sensors and pacemakers, which offer patients comfort while monitoring their health condition remotely.

Head Mounted Displays (HMD) and Virtual Reality (VR) applications are used for 3D visualization in biomedical applications. Unity is one of many computation platforms that can be used to develop VR software for visualizing 3D datasets in virtual reality. Using ConfocalVR, Immersive Science helps visualize confocal microscopy images. By using immersive 3D visualization, users can gain an understanding of cellular architecture and protein distribution (Venkatesan et al. 2021).

7.0 RISKS OF AI IN HEALTHCARE

. Even though artificial intelligence can perform healthcare tasks as well or better than humans, implementation factors will prevent healthcare professionals from being fully automated for some time. Furthermore, artificial intelligence has its own limitations, as it may incorrectly forecast or predict the outcome of therapeutics when dealing with novel viral infections. For instance, during the outbreak of the Corona virus infection or COVID -19, limited information about the behaviour of this virus and definitive treatment options were available. In the absence of prior or historical knowledge of therapeutics, diagnosis, prognosis, and outcomes, AI models will have unknown reactions to new side effects or resistant cases, newly reported side effects, rare diseases, and novel treatment modalities. In the absence of information, AI cannot replace human knowledge and reasoning power. As a bridge between multispecialty hospitals and primary health care units, Telemedicine allows surgeons and super specialists to provide relevant suggestions and diagnoses online, but not surgical treatment. In spite of several potential benefits that artificial intelligence has brought to the healthcare industry, the associated risks should be taken care of in certain cases. A brief discussion on the risks in using AI in medicine and healthcare and possible solutions for overcoming these risks are listed in the following section.

7.1 Harm to Patients Caused by AI Errors

Researchers explain three main causes of AI errors: noise and artefacts in clinical inputs, data shift between AI training and real-world data, and unexpected variations in clinical contexts and environments. As a result of such errors, life-threatening conditions may not be diagnosed or may be misdiagnosed or may be incorrectly scheduled or prioritized (Hanks, Austin, and Lopez 2022).

7.2 Misuse of Biomedical AI Tools

Even accurate and robust AI tools depend on how they are used in practice and how their results are used; in healthcare, these human actors include patients, clinicians, and healthcare professionals. When AI tools are misused, they can lead to inaccurate medical assessments and decisions, which could result in harm to the patient. The proliferation of easily accessible online and mobile AI solutions without adequate explanation and information could contribute to AI misuse, including limited involvement of clinicians and citizens in AI development, inadequate AI training among healthcare professionals, and a lack of awareness among patients and the general public.

7.3 Bias in AI

Large scale data is needed for training the AI models meant for healthcare. If the training data does not reflect the target population, or when incomplete or insufficient data is used to train the AI models, the end results will not be correct. Various systemic human biases are often incorporated into AI models, including biases based on gender, race, ethnicity, age, socioeconomic status, geography, and urban or rural settings. Biased and imbalanced datasets are one of the main causes of AI biases in healthcare, which are often caused by structural bias and discrimination, disparities in access to quality equipment and digital technologies, and lack of diversity and interdisciplinarity in technological, scientific, clinical, and policymaking teams.

7.4 Inadequate Transparency

In the design, development, evaluation, and deployment of AI tools, there is a significant risk of lack of transparency. In order for AI to be transparent, it must be traceable and explainable, which correspond to two distinct levels of transparency: 1) transparency in the development and use of AI, and 2) transparency in the decision making processes using artificial intelligence. A lack of transparency in biomedical AI may lead to a lack of understanding and trust in predictions and decisions generated by the system, difficulty reproducing and evaluating AI algorithms independently, difficulty identifying the sources of AI errors and defining who or what is responsible, and a limited use of AI tools in clinical practice.

7.5 Privacy and Security

Preserving the privacy of patient health care data is a vital ethical principal, since privacy is bound by patient autonomy, personal identity, well-being and self-governance. Ensuring confidentiality of patient healthcare data and processes for getting consent from patient are important functionalities in healthcare. Recent developments in AI and technology in healthcare, particularly during the Covid-19 pandemic, have highlighted the potential risks of data privacy, confidentiality, and protection for patients and citizens. Privacy and security risks in AI for healthcare include sharing personal data without informed consent, repurposing data without consent, data breaches that may expose sensitive or personal information, and harmful cyberattacks on AI solutions, both at the individual and system level.

7.6 Accountability Gaps

In healthcare, algorithmic accountability is crucial to making AI trustworthy and effective. The current national and international regulations, especially in the area of medical AI, are still ambiguous as to who is responsible for errors or failures of AI systems. Multiple actors (e.g. healthcare professionals, AI developers) are involved in the medical AI process, making it difficult to define roles and responsibilities. Healthcare professionals who use AI in healthcare often find themselves in a vulnerable position due to this lack of definition, especially if the AI model they use is not completely transparent.

7.7 Real-World Healthcare Implementation Issues

Several medical AI tools have been developed in recent years; however, implementing, integrating, and using these tools in real-world clinical settings is still challenging. In addition to limited data quality, structure, and interoperability across heterogeneous clinical centers and electronic health records, AI medical tools could alter the physician-patient relationship; access to patient data may become unregulated; and AI tools may not integrate and interoperate with existing clinical processes.

7.8 The Principle of Ethical Double Effects

The innovations introduced for the well-being of the mankind may sometimes have opposite effects. Hence, while applying AI for healthcare applications, it must be carefully used, taking the principle of double effect into consideration.

7.9 Ethical Problem in Research and Biomedical Medicine

The biomedical ethical principles must be adhered to by AI in healthcare applications, as with any new scientific technology. In order to achieve these goals, we must consider autonomy, benefit, non-crime, and justice. Implementations for healthcare should consider and practice a number of factors such as privacy, safety, consent, decision making and voluntary participation, to name a few.

8.0 HEALTHCARE TRANSFORMATIONS WITH AI

AI requires large-scale health-related or supplemental data input for its functions. Unrepresentative, insufficient, or incomplete data may affect an algorithm's performance, and a lack of useable data may prevent an AI technology from being made available for a particular community ("Draft Global Strategy on Digital Health 2020- 2025 GLOBAL STRATEGY on DIGITAL HEALTH _ 1 GLOBAL STRATEGY on DIGITAL HEALTH _ 1 GLOBAL STRATEGY on DIGITAL HEALTH _ GLOBAL STRATEGY on DIGITAL HEALTH" 2021). Additionally, the World Health Organization (WHO) cautions against inflating the benefits of digital healthcare technology and emphasizes the necessity of contextualizing them. Therefore, the WHO suggests that the governance and control of AI be founded on the following principles ("Ethics and Governance of Artificial Intelligence for Health" 2021):

- Preserve human autonomy
- safeguard public interest
- Ensure transparency, clarity and intelligibility
- advance responsibility and accountability
- confirm inclusivity and equity and
- advance responsive and sustainable AI

These technological developments necessitate the implementation of suitable controls, data-driven interoperability and liquidity, and clear guidelines for the access, copying, and transfer of digital data. They also enhance the danger of data misuse, particularly with regard to highly sensitive personal information (Aggarwal 2021).

Additionally, data governance structures can be coordinated and put into place based on ethical oversight and processes for informed consent (empowerment), encouraging stricter accountability at all levels of the health system, securing data through data access controls (accountability), interoperable structures (trust), and enforcing pertinent legislation (ethical framework).

8.1 Wearable Devices Enabling Healthy Well-Being

Wearable technology is becoming more and more popular among consumers, giving doctors the ability to more properly check patients' health in real time. AI-enabled wearables assist people in tracking their vital signs and maintaining their health. People are already using artificial intelligence (AI) and the Internet of Medical Things (IoMT) to improve their health. Healthcare practitioners can use the ECGs in wearables and smartphones as a potent diagnostic tool to improve patient outcomes and enhance medicine (Archuleta 2022). Manufacturers of consumer wearables are also creating medical-grade functionality for their products; the most recent example is the Apple Series 4 Watch, which has US Food & Drug Administration certification for ECG monitoring (Das, Behera, and Shah 2020).Modern smart watches can track vitals, dietary habits, water consumption, exercise routines, and stress levels (Sharma 2022). The wearables may be designed to make fitness recommendations to users depending on their regular routines.

People are finding it simpler to comprehend and make decisions about their own health thanks to AI-enabled workout equipment. For instance, wearable fitness trackers let you compare your everyday activities to your wellness objectives. On the basis of specific daily milestones, some gadgets can even offer advice. The gadget can warn the user or offer immediate diagnostic and treatment recommendations if the wearer experiences a health emergency (as applicable).

A person is encouraged to be more proactive about maintaining a healthy lifestyle through wearable health technologies. Over time, good health management may lower that person's risk of contracting a chronic condition like diabetes or heart disease (Markowski 2018). AI techniques may forecast the future phases or potential manifestations of chronic ailments such chronic kidney disease, obstructive lung disorders/asthma, cancer, and allergies based on the data from wearables, implanted devices, or organ-specific monitors.

8.2 Improved Experience

Numerous hospitals and healthcare organizations place a high focus on patient happiness. Patient data may become priceless with machine learning and artificial intelligence (AI), offering insights into areas where the patient journey needs to be improved. Since patient happiness is closely correlated with better compliance and treatment adherence, machine learning systems provide hospitals the chance to enhance overall health outcomes.

Additionally, AI can offer more convenient and personalized healthcare. Patient happiness may be increased by healthcare organizations using chatbots. A Pegasystems survey of 2,000 healthcare consumers in 2019 found that more over half (42 percent) of respondents said they were comfortable with their doctors using AI to make healthcare decisions. It seems like many people are happy to see AI being used (Gray 2022).

Additionally, AI can deliver more convenient and customized healthcare experiences. Patient satisfaction can also increase when chatbots are utilized by healthcare organizations. Based on a Pegasystems survey of 2,000 healthcare consumers conducted in 2019, more than half (42 percent) feel comfortable with the use of artificial intelligence by their doctors for the purpose of making healthcare decisions. This suggests that many individuals are delighted to see AI being used (Gray 2022).

8.3 AI Driven Innovative Care Delivery

Hospitals can more quickly and accurately diagnose a variety of health issues by improving the use of AI for clinical surveillance. AI-enabled clinical monitoring for diseases that have previously shown resistance to prevention can save lives and cut expenses. In order to identify patients who are at risk for healthcare-associated infections, AI can analyze millions of data points. This allows physicians to act more rapidly to treat patients before their infections worsen and to stop the spread of diseases among hospitalized patients (Gray 2022).

According to the World Health Organization, healthcare systems will be able to recognize when a person is at risk of developing a chronic disease, for example, and offer preventive measures before the condition worsens, by 2030.Rates of diabetes, congestive heart failure, and COPD (chronic obstructive pulmonary disease) have decreased as a result of this advancement (Gray 2022).

8.4 Real-Time Observation and Home Diagnosis

In addition to wearing wearables, users use various connected, high-tech diagnostic medical devices to enable at-home telehealth services. One example is the TytoCare at-home physical examination equipment for ears, throat, heart, lungs, belly, skin, heart rate, and temperature (Das, Behera, & Shah 2020). Another example is Inui Health, which offers in-home urine testing utilising a smartphone app for colorimetric analysis, evaluating kidney and general health, and testing for urinary tract infections (Das, Behera, & Shah 2020). Together with smart home systems, all of these gadgets and sensors can improve resident monitoring and care, especially for the community of people who are ageing in place.

With AI, radiologists can distinguish between healthy tissues and abnormal situations like malignant tumours, allowing for the early discovery of deadly illnesses and the creation of more effective treatment regimens. More than 3,000 businesses and startups are creating AI-based products to take advantage of the benefits of the technology and detect catastrophic events like cardiac or renal failures by continually monitoring patient vitals and metabolites (Sharma 2022).

AI makes it possible for less qualified caregivers to diagnose the medical problems of patients at home in addition to improving the sensitivity and specificity (accuracy) of laboratory-based diagnostic tools used by professional technicians. In the next few years, more than 300 intelligent AI-enabled at-home diagnosis tools for home care are now on the market in the US and are anticipated to be accessible.

Smart implants, point-of-care devices, portable devices (ultrasound systems, stethoscopes, otoscopes, etc.), and smart tattoos are examples of linked and smart diagnosis tools (Sharma 2022). Smart implants include sensor-based cerebrospinal shunts, orthopaedic plates, and dental screws. A transition in treatment from hospitals, pathology labs, and radiology centres to homes is anticipated to occur soon due to their capacity to continually monitor health (Sharma 2022).

8.5 Smart Hospitals

Digital stethoscopes and other smart, digitised clinical tools are being used by primary care clinicians. In an effort to improve patient experience, hospitals are implementing indoor GPS, RFID, and beacon technology for wayfinding inside their buildings. Smart hospital rooms also enable patients to electronically engage with care professionals from their bedsides. IoMT technologies help hospitals by supplying data that may be analysed to offer a useful service or insight that was not previously conceivable or available.

8.6 Decision Making

Predictive analytics can support clinical decision-making and actions and help prioritise administrative activities. Improving treatment involves the alignment of massive health data with suitable and timely judgments.

Another area where AI is starting to take root in healthcare is the use of pattern recognition to identify people at risk of getting a condition or seeing it worsen owing to lifestyle, environmental, genomic, or other variables.

8.7 In-Community Leading to Smart Cities

Smart automobiles can monitor a passenger's health while they are travelling, and drones can be used to respond to any emergencies outside of homes and hospitals. The MIT Underworlds Project investigates sewers as a source of data to track the spread of diseases using sensors from a public health standpoint, although smart city projects are probably not tailored towards healthcare at the moment; we anticipate them to become a reality in the next 10–20 years (Das, Behera, & Shah 2020).

8.8 Treatment Plan and Outcomes

With the help of AI, doctors may thoroughly examine a patient's physical symptoms, emotional condition, and medical background before recommending the most appropriate course of action. Thus, it aids in the development and implementation of lengthy treatment plans for chronic diseases while enabling patients to predict the results of the treatment even before it has started. For instance, artificial intelligence (AI)-designed oncology models can assist physicians in determining the dosage of medications needed in chemotherapy and radiation therapy (Sharma 2022). AI assists dentists and smile designers in the aesthetic field by enabling them to show patients the results of the recommended treatment up front, helping to manage patient expectations.

AI provides practitioners with clean data rapidly, enabling more precise diagnosis. That unmistakably solves a major problem in the healthcare industry. According to estimates, misdiagnosis accounts for up to 80,000 hospital fatalities annually and billions of dollars' worth of unnecessary medical expenses (Mehra 2020). Terabytes of data would traditionally need to be processed in order to diagnose a patient. Businesses may now use AI to crunch numbers, with human review of the outcomes.

For more than 30 years, medical robots have been in use ("No Longer Science Fiction, AI and Robotics Are Transforming Healthcare," n.d.). They range from basic laboratory robots to extremely sophisticated surgical robots that can work alongside a human surgeon or carry out procedures on their own ("No Longer Science Fiction, AI and Robotics Are Transforming Healthcare," n.d.). They are used in hospitals and labs for repetitive jobs, rehabilitation, physical therapy, and support for people with long-term problems in addition to surgery.

Robots have the potential to completely transform end-of-life care by enabling patients to maintain their independence for longer and decreasing the need for inpatient care and nursing facilities. AI is making it possible for robots to go even further and interact socially with humans to keep ageing minds sharp through "conversations" and other social interactions.

8.9 AI-driven Drug Discovery, Clinical Trials and Research

One of the more recent applications of AI in healthcare is drug discovery. With the goal of cutting the time it takes for a new treatment to reach the patient, AI has the potential to speed up and make drug discovery procedures more affordable. Additionally, AI is quickening the dissemination of fresh results from medicinal research. This will make it possible for the pharmaceutical sector to offer doctors and patients better therapies more quickly.

In 2018, the pharmaceutical sector generated $1.2 trillion in global revenue, and between 2017 and 2030, it is expected to rise by 160% (Mehra 2020). However, reports suggest that the pipeline for developing new drugs is stagnate and that success rates are dropping (Mehra 2020). AI might accelerate progress on these fronts.

It takes a long time and money to get from the research lab to the patient. A medicine must travel from a research lab to a patient for an average of 12 years, according to the California Biomedical Research Association. Of the 5,000 medications that start preclinical testing, only five reach human testing, and only one of these five is ever authorized for use in humans. Additionally, from the research lab to the patient, developing a new treatment will run a corporation an average of US $359 million ("Fact Sheet New Drug Development Process," n.d.). It may be possible to dramatically reduce the time to market for new pharmaceuticals as well as their prices by applying the most recent developments in AI to automate the drug discovery and drug repurposing processes ("No Longer Science Fiction, AI and Robotics Are Transforming Healthcare," n.d.).

AI is capable of sifting through vast amounts of data and information from tissue or blood samples taken from individuals with the condition and those without it. This could facilitate development into novel drugs that might target certain proteins. AI was effectively employed during the coronavirus pandemic to find prospective medications that may be used to treat Covid-19.

The path to new medication creation and medical research is arduous and expensive. It takes a new medicine 12–15 years to reach the consumer, and the procedure is expensive overall (Sharma 2022). AI can expedite this process and cheaper. By utilizing predictive analytics, genetic code analysis, and data mining approaches, researchers can quickly discover novel chemicals and develop patient-specific treatments. They can speed up the entire trial procedure by using AI to evaluate the data and choose the best participants for clinical trials.

A solution to how proteins fold into their 3D structure was discovered by Google's Deepmind AI system AlphaFold last year, which may open up new possibilities for structure-based medicine creation (Gray 2022).

8.10 Personalized/Precision Medicine

Precision medicine, also known as personalized medicine, refers to the ability to customize a patient's care to meet their unique needs rather than using a common treatment strategy. Although customised health data is the "Holy Grail" for the practice of precision medicine, it is not the only issue with regard to interoperability, privacy, ownership, and security of health data (Das, Behera, and Shah 2020). Additionally, the current frameworks for legal and ethical health data exchange were created with a very different generation of medical and research practises in mind, which creates some significant barriers to the seamless exchange of personalized data to population-based genomic studies and research.

Businesses may now see tiny patterns and trends in massive volumes of patient data thanks to AI. Scientists can utilize that data to guide research and development for new treatments, improving patient outcomes, as opposed to relying on results from a small patient pool (Markowski 2018).

Precision medicine presented an opportunity, according to 92 percent of leaders in the global pharmaceutical industry surveyed recently, and 84 percent said it was on their corporate agenda ("Capitalizing on Precision Medicine: How Pharmaceutical Firms Can Shape the Future of Healthcare" n.d.). Furthermore, blockchain technology promises to foster previously unheard of collaboration between participants and researchers around innovation in medical research in areas like population health management and precision medicine thanks to its pervasive security infrastructure for seamless health data exchange.

8.11 Early Detection and Proactive Diagnosis

Modern healthcare is built around the idea of preventing disease and illness from occurring, and AI is essential to this endeavor. Artificial intelligence-powered predictive analytics reduce manual data processing (Archuleta 2022). By doing this, doctors may address medical concerns more quickly and prevent patients from developing more serious problems. To improve cancer detection and support doctors in prescribing better treatments, current radiological scanners, for instance, contain various AI features. By using AI, medical personnel can have a thorough understanding of a patient's medical history and decide on more individualized therapy that is more effective. AI is already being used to more precisely and early diagnose diseases like cancer. The American Cancer Society claims that a large percentage of mammograms provide misleading results, telling one in two healthy women they have cancer. Mammogram reviews and translations using AI are now 30 times faster and 99 percent accurate, which eliminates the necessity for pointless biopsies ("Fact Sheet New Drug Development Process," n.d.).

Healthcare businesses are using IBM's Watson for Health to deploy cognitive technology to unlock massive volumes of health data and enable diagnostics. Watson can review and store exponentially more medical data than any human, including every medical publication, symptom, and case study of a treatment's effectiveness worldwide ("No Longer Science Fiction, AI and Robotics Are Transforming Healthcare," n.d.).

To address pressing healthcare issues, Google's DeepMind Health collaborates with doctors, scientists, and patients. The technique combines systems neuroscience and machine learning to create neural networks that closely resemble the human brain and contain potent general-purpose learning algorithms ("No Longer Science Fiction, AI and Robotics Are Transforming Healthcare," n.d.).

Additionally, AI is advancing medical imaging technology and facilitating the early detection of diseases like cancer. Think about this According to the American Cancer Society, more than 12 million mammograms are conducted annually throughout the country. A false positive test result is obtained in about 50% of examined women; this could result in an incorrect diagnosis (Markowski 2018). However, a PwC analysis claims that AI is already 30 times faster and has 99 percent accuracy than humans, minimizing the need for pointless biopsies and the stress brought on by misdiagnosis (Markowski 2018).

8.12 Electronic Health Record (EHR) Management

Since the advent of electronic health records (EHR) and the development of online tools and resources for health management, the electronic sharing of patient health data has grown to a great extent. An organization's reputation could suffer long-term consequences from a breach in the security of patient healthcare data (Markowski 2018).

That requires healthcare organizations to make investments in technology that can protect patient data. AI-powered security systems can speed up response times and help firms detect security breaches more quickly (Markowski 2018). Growing demand for experts who can code and digitize patient records, as well as health information professionals to oversee the entire process and check for correctness and security, has been attributed to the spread of electronic patient data (Markowski 2018).

8.13 Protection Against Cyber Crimes

When it comes to adopting new technologies, healthcare businesses historically lag other industries by around 2 years (Archuleta 2022). Healthcare is one of the most endangered industries as a result of this gap, which has exposed numerous enterprises to cyber assaults. We may anticipate cyberattacks by implementing AI into our cyber security profile. Predictive analytics can be used to examine anomalies in our network and assess the level of danger each one carries.

NetApp is at the forefront of several fascinating developments in AI that are enhancing patient care (Archuleta 2022). Healthcare businesses must put technology at the heart of their organizational strategy if they are to keep up with the rate of change (Archuleta 2022).

8.14. Patient Risk Identification With AI

Predictive analytics can analyze vast volumes of historical and current data in the healthcare industry to produce insightful forecasts, projections, and recommendations on everything from individual patient treatment to broader public health (Gray 2022). Predictive analytics can forecast a variety of things by analyzing tens of thousands of data points, from a person's risk of contracting diseases to their chance of returning to a hospital with an infection.

Predictive analytics can assist medical practitioners in this by enabling them to be more proactive in their treatment strategies, perhaps resulting in a decrease in the need for costly and time-consuming operations or treatments.

8.15 Radiology Transformation With AI

Computer-aided cancer detection already makes use of AI-powered systems, which can categorize brain tumors and cut the time it takes to classify a tumor in half to three minutes. The technique may also be used to identify breast cancer, find hidden fractures, and find neurological disorders (Gray 2022). Additionally, AI can lighten radiologists' workloads by doing more boring jobs and provide doctors more time to focus on problems that require human interpretation.

8.16 Insurance and Governments

AI is assisting insurance companies and government-run insurance programmes to individualize the policy terms based on patients' current and anticipated health conditions and speed up the claim settlement process, providing cost efficiency, reducing the burden on state healthcare budgets, and improving patients' satisfaction (Sharma 2022). AI can be used by the insurance industry to enhance and automate its processes. Additionally, AI-based platforms can scan papers and find any irregularities; this aids in identifying and stopping fraud. AI may also be utilized to streamline underwriting. Despite its difficulties and limits, AI's full potential hasn't yet been realized. The capabilities of AI are constantly being increased, and new applications are being created. AI-enabled technologies and procedures are assisting doctors in making knowledgeable judgments, minimizing the loss of time on unimportant tasks, and improving the effectiveness and patient-friendliness of healthcare.

8.17 Education

AI makes it possible for trainees to experience realistic simulations in a way that is not possible with straightforward computer-driven algorithms. A trainee's answer to a question, choice, or piece of advice can be challenging in a manner that a person cannot because of the development of natural speech and an AI computer's ability to draw instantaneously from a massive database of scenarios. Additionally, the training programme can take into account the trainee's prior responses, allowing it to continuously modify the tasks to fit their learning requirements ("No Longer Science Fiction, AI and Robotics Are Transforming Healthcare," n.d.).

Additionally, training can be done anywhere thanks to the power of AI integrated in smartphones, making it possible to do brief catch-up sessions following challenging cases in a clinic or while travelling ("No Longer Science Fiction, AI and Robotics Are Transforming Healthcare," n.d.).

9.0 FUTURE PROSPECTS

Active implants, medical imaging, and mobile health services are the fastest-growing industries in healthcare sector. The field of neural engineering has opened up new opportunities and areas where new technologies are being developed, such as interfacing devices with tissue, changing cells and building artificial organs, and organizing large datasets from biology (Ereifej et al. 2019).

In future, it will be more common to have patients with more than one implantable electronic device either to improve or monitor health. Communication between the implanted electronic devices and adjusting the performance without hindering the functionality of other devices is essential for promoting wellness.

Functional tissue engineering will probably be the next improvement in biomedical engineering. It will be possible to grow tissue from biological material - cells - by placing them into the body. As soon as the newly implanted tissue is positioned correctly in the body, the newly implanted tissue will be able to perform its function (Ikada 2006). There is still much to learn about producing biomaterials with properties similar to or equal to human living tissue and which can withstand the same forces and strains. By using image guidance, the implant can be positioned exactly where it should be, and access to the area of interest will be precise. Due to the increased number of sensors for measuring or monitoring physiological and biomechanical quantities, from the surface and/or from the inside, data transfer and information processing in medical applications will become more demanding.

Research in biomedical engineering is continuously changing. With the rapid increase in knowledge on AI and biomedical engineering, latest equipments and resources are continuously needed to satisfy the research demands.

Healthcare service delivered via telemedicine depends fully on the speed of the underlying network, as do the video and data transmission quality and speed. Key remote medical procedures like remote surgery or even a straightforward remote video doctor consultation are complicated by the 4G networks. With 3G and 4G networks, dealing with massive amounts of patient data will be impossible. While 5G networks provide near-instantaneous data transfer of records like prescriptions, diagnostic test results, medical imaging, and other medical reports, as well as high-quality video interactions. 5G networks revolutionise the healthcare industry by enabling remote surgery, faster report transmission, patient monitoring, emergency response care, geriatric medical care, and healthcare equality.

Thanks to 5G and IoT, a new healthcare ecosystem may develop. The growing adoption of electronic medical records (EMRs), which produce large volumes of patient data, rising venture capital funding, rising healthcare costs, and an ageing population are the main factors driving the healthcare market. Other important factors include favourable government initiatives to promote technological advancements in the fields of AI and robotics (MarketsandMarkets 2022)

Artificial intelligence in healthcare is expected to grow from USD 6.9 billion in 2021 to USD 67.4 billion by 2027, growing at a CAGR of 46.2% from 2021 to 2027 (Mehra, n.d.). The global artificial intelligence based healthcare market is expected to grow at a CAGR of 40.51 by 2029 valued at USD 69.2 Billions as predicted by Maximize Market Research (Newsmantraa 2022). This growth rate can be attributed to the rapid advancement of IT infrastructure and the increased use of AI-based technologies in business endeavors. Increasing investments made by private investors, venture capitalists, and non-profits are driving adoption rates as they seek to improve therapeutic results, data analysis, and security.

10.0 CONCLUSION

It is necessary to use AI in health care administration, particularly to make medical decisions, especially when analysing predictive data, to diagnose and treat patients. There are several challenges to early adoption, sustainable implementation in the health system, and a lack of consideration for the user perspective. The public health sector must adopt AI, even though technology is not optimally used. AI clinical applications face a number of ethical issues, including safety, efficacy, privacy, information and consent, the right to decide, "the right to try," and costs (Sunarti et al. 2021). It is the responsibility of the hospitals and other medical institutions to take care of all types of high technology devices, including the hospital's information systems and networks, as well as their safety and security. As technology is increasingly used in health services, trained clinical engineers are needed. By leveraging AI and ML, we will be able to improve this relationship through better accuracy, productivity, and workflow, thereby developing a health system that goes beyond simply curing diseases, and preventing diseases before they occur, thus reforming the patient-doctor bond.

REFERENCES

Abdulnabi, M., Al-Haiqi, A., Kiah, M. L. M., Zaidan, A. A., Zaidan, B. B., & Hussain, M. (2017). A distributed framework for healthinformation exchange using smartphone technologies. *Journal of Biomedical Informatics*, *69*, 230–250. doi:10.1016/j.jbi.2017.04.013 PMID:28433825

Aggarwal, A. (2021). Beware Hype over AI-Based Healthcare in Lower-Income Countries. *FinancialTimes*. https://www.ft.com/content/f4dd834c-4835-4ee0-8737-ff98626fa010

Amin, S. U., Hossain, M. S., Muhammad, G., Alhussein, M., & Rahman, M. (2019). Cognitive Smart Healthcare for Pathology Detection and Monitoring. *IEEE Access: Practical Innovations, Open Solutions*, *7*, 10745–10753. doi:10.1109/ACCESS.2019.2891390

Archuleta, M. (2022). How Artificial Intelligence Is Transforming Healthcare. *Healthcare IT -CHIME*. https://chimecentral.org/mediaposts/how-artificial-intelligence-is-transforming-healthcare/

Austin, University of Texas. (2022). Engineered Mattress Tricks Your Body to Fall Asleep Faster. *Medicalxpress.com*. https://medicalxpress.com/news/2022-07-mattress-body-fall-asleep-faster.html

BCU. (2022). *Four Ways Biomedical Engineering Has Enhanced Healthcare*. Birmingham City University. https://www.bcu.ac.uk/health-sciences/about-us/school-blog/how-biomedical-engineering-enhanced-healthcare

CBRA. (2022). *Fact Sheet New Drug Development Process*. CA Biomed. https://www.ca-biomed.org/pdf/media-kit/fact-sheets/CBRADrug Develop.pdf

CDT. (2022). *Artificial Intelligence in Healthcare Market to Witness an Explosive CAGR of 38.4% till 2030, Driven by Rising Datasets of Patient Health-Related Digital Information*. Grand View Research, Inc. https://www.thecowboychannel.com/story/46467382/artificial-intelligence-in-healthcare-market-to-witness-an-explosive-cagr-of-384-till-2030-driven-by-rising-datasets-of-patient-health-related

City University of Hong Kong. (2022). Nanofiber-Based Biodegradable Millirobot That Can Release Drugs in Targeted Positions in the Intestines. Medicalxpress.com. https://medicalxpress.com/news/2022-04-nanofiber-based-biodegradable-millirobot-drugs-positions.html

Dahmani, K., Tahiri, A., Habert, O., & Elmeftouhi, Y. (2016,April). An intelligent model of home support for people with loss of autonomy:a novel approach. In *2016 International Conference on Control, Decisionand Information Technologies (CoDIT)* (pp. 182-185). IEEE.

Das, R., Behera, K., & Shah, S. (2020). *Challenges and Role of Digital Transformation.* Omnia Health, Informa Markets. https://insights.omnia-health.com/technology/innovations-healthcare-challenges-and-role-digital-transformation?utm_sourc e=AdWords&utm_medium=Paid+Search&utm_campaign=AEL22OMA-RK-Insights-Dynamic&utm_term=%7Bkeyword%7D&utm_content=Healthcare +technology&gclid=EAIaIQobChMIjJjtrf2n-QIVyg0rCh0ELQa6EAAYAy AAEgK3FfD_BwE

Davenport, T., & Kalakota, R. (2019). The Potential for ArtificialIntelligence in Healthcare. *Future Healthcare Journal, 6* (2), 94–98. doi:10.7861/futurehosp.6-2-94

Dian, J. F., Vahidnia, R., & Rahmati, A. (2020). Wearables and the Internet of Things (IoT), Applications, Opportunities, and Challenges: A Survey. *IEEE Access, 8,* 69200–69211. doi:10.1109/access.2020.2986329

Dilsizian, S. E., & Siegel, E. L. (2014). Artificialintelligence in medicine and cardiac imaging: Harnessing big data and advancedcomputing to provide personalized medical diagnosis and treatment. *Current Cardiology Reports, 16*(1), 1–8.

DraftGlobal Strategy (2021). Digital Health 2020- 2025. *Global strategy on digital health.* https://www.who.int/docs/default-source/documents/gs4dhdaa2a 9f352b0445bafbc79ca799dce4d.pdf.
</div>

Ereifej, E. S., Shell, C., Schofield, J., Charkhkar, H., Cuberovic, I., Dorval, A. & Graczyk, E. (2019). Neural Engineering: The Process, Applications, and Its Role in the Future ofMedicine. *Journal of Neural Engineering, 16* (6), 063002. doi:10.1088/1741-2552/ab4869

Gray, C. 2022. Transforming Healthcare with Artificial Intelligence. *Technologymagazine.com.* https://technologymagazine.com/ai-and-machine-learning/transforming-healthcare-with-artificial-intelligence

Hanks, H., Austin, A., & Lopez, V. (2022). *EU study into medical AI highlights they re risks and sortcoming of legal frameworks.* Freshfields Bruckhaus Deringer. .https://www.lexology.com/library/detail.aspx?g=74477d47-da0e -4cb7-b272-0134f58537de

Hossain, M. S., & Muhammad, G. (2018). Emotion-Aware Connected Healthcare Big DataTowards 5G. *IEEE Internet of Things Journal, 5*(4), 2399–2406. doi:10.1109/jiot.2017.2772959

Hudec, M., & Smutny, Z. (2017). RUDO: A home ambientintelligence system for blind people. *Sensors (Basel), 17*(8), 1926.

Ikada, Y. (2006). Challenges in Tissue Engineering. *Journal of the Royal Society, Interface, 3*(10), 589–601. https://doi.org/10.1098/rsif.2006.0124

Institut national de la recherche scientifique (INRS). (2021). Developing Bioactive Coatings for Better Orthopaedic Implants. https://medicalxpress.com/news/2021-12-bioactive-coatings-orthopaedic-implants.html

Islam, Md. Milon, Ashikur Rahaman, and Md. Rashedul Islam. 2020. "Development of SmartHealthcare Monitoring System in IoT Environment." *SN Computer Science* 1(3). doi:10.1007/s42979-020-00195-y

Kidwai, B. & Nadesh, R.K. (2020). Design and Development of Diagnostic Chabot for Supporting Primary Health Care Systems. *Procedia Computer Science 167*, 75–84. doi:10.1016/j.procs.2020.03.184

Kingery, K. (2021). *Antimicrobial Coating for Orthopedic Implants Prevents Dangerous Infections.* Medicalxpress.com. https://medicalxpress.com/news/2021-09-antimicrobial-coating-orthopedic-implants-dangerous.html

Kolker, E., Özdemir, V., & Kolker, E. (2016). How healthcarecan refocus on its super-customers (patients, n= 1) and customers (doctors andnurses) by leveraging lessons from Amazon, Uber, and Watson. *Omics: ajournal of integrative biology, 20*(6), 329-333.

Le, D.-N., Parvathy, V. S., Gupta, D., Khanna, A., Rodrigues, J., & Shankar, K. (2021). IoT Enabled Depth wise Separable Convolution Neural Network with Deep Support Vector Machine for COVID-19 Diagnosis and Classification. *International Journal of Machine Learning and Cybernetics.* https://doi.org/10.1007/s13042-020-01248-7

Lotsch, J., Kringel, D., & Ultsch, A. (2021). Explainable Artificial Intelligence (XAI) in Biomedicine: Making AI Decisions Trustworthy for Physicians and Patients. *BioMedInformatics, 2*(1), 1–17. doi:10.3390/biomedinformatics2010001

MarketsandMarkets. (2022). *Artificial Intelligence in Healthcare Market Worth $67.4 Billion by 2027.* MarketsandMarketsTM. https://www.prnewswire.co.uk/news-releases/artificial-intelligence-in-healthcare-market-worth-67-4-billion-by-2027-exclusive-report-by-marketsandmarkets-tm--878720500.html

Markowski, M. (2018). *4 Ways AI Is Transforming the Healthcare Industry.* Herzing University. https://www.herzing.edu/blog/4-ways-ai-transforming-healthcare-industry

Martineau, K. (2020). *Marshaling Artificial Intelligence in the Fight against Covid-19.* MIT News. https://news.mit.edu/2020/mit-marshaling-artificial-intelligence-fight-against-covid-19-0519

McKinsey. (2015). *By 2025, Internet of Things Applications Could Have $11 Trillion Impact.* McKinsey &Company. https://www.mckinsey.com/mgi/overview/in-the-news/by-2025-internet-of-things-applications-could-have-11-trillion-impact

Mehra, A. (n.d.) *Artificial Intelligence in Healthcare MarketWorth $45.2 Billion by 2026.* MarketsandMarkets. https://www.marketsandmarkets.com/PressReleases/artificial-intelligence-healthcare.asp

Mehta, S. (2020). *The Future of Artificial Intelligence (AI) in Healthcare.* Blockchain Technology, Mobility, AI and IoT Development Company. https://www.solulab.com/future-of-ai-in-healthcare/

Murdoch, T. B., & Detsky, A. S. (2013). The Inevitable Application of Big Data to Health Care. *Journal of the American Medical Association, 309*(13), 1351. https://doi.org/10.1001/jama.2013.393

Newsmantraa. (2022). Global Artificial Intelligence (AI) Healthcare Market Is Expected to Grow by USD 69.2 Billion during 2022-2029, Progressing at a CAGR of 40.51% during the Forecast Period. *Digital Journal.* https://www.digitaljournal.com/pr/global-artificial-intellig ence-ai-healthcare-market-is-expected-to-grow-by-usd-69-2-bi llion-during-2022-2029-progressing-at-a-cagr-of-40-51-during -the-forecast-period

Optica. (2022). *NewPhotoacoustic Endoscope Fits inside a Needle.* Medicalx-press.com. https://medicalxpress.com/news/2022-07-photoacoustic-endosco pe-needle.html

Prasad, P. S., Gunjan, V. K., & Pathak, R., & Mukherjee, S. (2020). *Applications of Artificial Intelligence in BiomedicalEngineering.* Taylor and Francis Group. . doi:10.1201/9781003045564-6

PwC. (2022). Capitalizingon Precision Medicine: How Pharmaceutical Firms Can Shape the Future ofHealthcare. PwC. https://www.strategyand.pwc.com/de/en/industries/health/capi talizing-precision-medicine.html

PwC. (2022). *No Longer ScienceFiction, AI and Robotics Are Transforming Healthcare.* https://www.pwc.com/gx/en/industries/healthcare/publications /ai-robotics-new-health/transforming-healthcare.html#:~:text =It%20puts%20consumers%20in%20control.

Rabhi, Y., Mrabet, M., & Fnaiech, F. (2018). A facialexpression controlled wheelchair for people with disabilities. *Computer Methods and Programs in Biomedicine, 165*, 89–105.

Roberson, J. (2017). *A Biomedical Engineer's Role in aHealthcare Facility.* Healthcare Facilities Today. https://www.healthcarefacilitiestoday.com/posts/A-biomedical -engineers-role-in-a-healthcare-facility--14740

Sharma, A. (2022). How the Health Sector Has Widely Implemented Artificial Intelligence. *Times of India Blog.* https://timesofindia.indiatimes.com/blogs/voices/how-the-hea lth-sector-has-widely-implemented-artificial-intelligence/

Snyder, C. F., Wu, A. W., Miller, R. S., Jensen, R. E., Bantug, E. T., & Wolff, A. C. (2011). The Role of Informaticsin Promoting Patient-Centered Care. *Cancer Journal (Sudbury, Mass.), 17*(4), 211–218. https://doi.org/10.1097/ppo.0b013e318225ff89

Sunarti, S., Rahman, F. F., & Naufal, M., Risky, M., Febriyanto, K., & Masnina, R. (2021). Artificial Intelligence inHealthcare: Opportunities and Risk for Future. *Gaceta Sanitaria, 35*(1), S67–70. doi:10.1016/j.gaceta.2020.12.019

Tabei, F., Gresham, J., Askarian, Behnam, Jung, K., & WoonChong, J. (2020). Cuff-Less Blood Pressure Monitoring System Using Smartphones. *IEEEAccess, 8*, 11534–45. doi:10.1109/access.2020.2965082

Tantin, A., Assi, E. B., van Asselt, E., Hached, S., & Sawan, M. (2020). Predicting urinary bladder voiding by means of a linear discriminantanalysis: Validation in rats. *Biomedical Signal Processing and Control, 55*, 101667.

Taylor, K. (2015). *The Deloitte Centre for Health Solutions*. Deloitte. https://www2.deloitte.com/content/dam/Deloitte/uk/Documents/life-sciences-health-care/deloitte-uk-connected-health.pdf

Tech, M. (2019). *What Is Biomedical Engineering?* Michigan Technological University. https://www.mtu.edu/biomedical/department/what-is/

Terasaki Institute for Biomedical Innovation. (2022). *Repairing Tendons with Silk Proteins*. Medicalxpress.com. https://medicalxpress.com/news/2022-05-tendons-silk-proteins.html

Università della Svizzera italiana. (2022). *Mathematics Helps AI in Biomedicine*. Medicalxpress.com. https://medicalxpress.com/news/2022-02-mathematics-ai-biomedicine.html

Vamathevan, J., Clark, D., Czodrowski, P., Dunham, I., Ferran, E., Lee, G., & Zhao, S. (2019). Applications of machine learning in drugdiscovery and development. *Nature Reviews. Drug Discovery, 18*(6), 463–477.

Venkatesan, M., Mohan, H., Ryan, J. R., Schürch, C. M., Nolan, G. P., Frakes, D. H., & Coskun, A. F. (2021). Virtualand Augmented Reality for Biomedical Applications. *Cell ReportsMedicine, 2* (7): 100348. doi:10.1016/j.xcrm.2021.100348

WHO. (2022). *Ethics and Governance of Artificial Intelligence for Health*. WHO. https://www.who.int/publications/i/item/9789240029200

Woodward, B., & Cowley, A. (2011). *The Sustainable Importance of Platinum in Biomedical Applications*. Mddionline.com. https://www.mddionline.com/ivd/sustainable-importance-platinum-biomedical-applications

Chapter 18
Using Graph Neural Network to Enhance Quality of Service Prediction

Lubana Isaoglu
 https://orcid.org/0000-0001-5193-1380
Istanbul University-Cerrahpaşa, Turkey

Derya Yiltas-Kaplan
 https://orcid.org/0000-0001-8370-8941
Istanbul University-Cerrahpaşa, Turkey

ABSTRACT

Quality of service (QoS) prediction has great importance in today's web services computing. Several researchers proposed methods to enhance the quality of service prediction. The most used one is collaborative filtering (CF), which can be categorized into three main categories: memory-based algorithms, model-based algorithms, and context-based CF algorithms. This paper proposes a model-based algorithm using the graph neural network (GNN) to predict the QoS values. To evaluate the performance of the proposed method, an experiment was conducted. The WS-dream dataset used in the experiment and the proposed method performance were compared with three baseline methods (User item-based Pearson correlation coefficient for QoS prediction-UIPCC, reputation-aware network embedding-based QoS Prediction-RANEP, and trust-aware approach TAP for personalized QoS prediction). The experiment results show that the proposed method, the GNN-based QoS prediction algorithm, performs better than memory-based and other model-based methods in terms of RMSE and MAE in most cases.

INTRODUCTION

With the development of technology, the use of web services increased. In addition, the volume of data transmitted over networks is rising, making studying technologies that facilitate the transmission of this data a necessity. In the next few decades, it is expected that many web services will offer the same

DOI: 10.4018/978-1-6684-6937-8.ch018

services. Clients will demand more value-added and informative services than those provided by single, isolated web services. As a result, the problem of synthesizing high-quality web services has been raised as a significant problem, and clients face the problem of choosing or creating a configuration plan from among the many possible projects that meet their quality of service (QoS) requirements. That is why QoS prediction for web services has been a hot research topic in services computing in recent years.

QoS is the description or measurement of the overall performance of a service. In other definition, QoS can be defined as a set of non-functional attributes that may impact the QoS offered by a web service (Kritikos & Plexousakis, 2009). QoS has many different features, such as accuracy, capacity, availability, reputation, and cost. Also, the response time and throughput are QoS attributes that can be considered essential. Several researchers proposed methods for QoS prediction. However, the most used one is collaborative filtering (CF). CF is technique recommender systems use that learns the user's previous behaviors, provides personalized service support and predicts their current preferences for particular products. Moreover, this is used to improve the accuracy of recommendations. In the general sense of CF, CF is the process of filtering information or patterns using methods involving collaboration between multiple agents, viewpoints, data sources, etc. In a narrower one, CF is a method of automatically predicting (filtering) a user's interests by collecting information about the preferences or tastes of many users (collaboration).

The advancement of neural networks encouraged researchers to investigate their ability to enhance QoS predictions. Neural Network is a subset of machine learning which, in turn, is a subset of artificial intelligence. Neural Network name and structure are inspired by the human brain, mimicking how biological neurons signal each other. One of these neural networks is the graph neural network (GNN). Best of our knowledge, two recently published works proposed using GNN for QoS prediction. The first is using a Two-Level Heterogeneous Graph Attention Network for QoS Prediction (Lv et al., 2022). The second combines multi-component graph convolutional CF and a DeepFM for QoS prediction (MGCCF-DFM) (Ding et al., 2021). Although these two methods achieved good performance, there is still some space for improvement. Hence, our main contribution is to propose another method that fills in the gap and improves the performance of QoS prediction.

This paper proposes a GNN-based QoS prediction method. The paper starts with a background description of some QoS methods and a background of the GNNs. Then the proposed method and the experiment description will be discussed. After that, the experiment results are presented. Finally, some conclusions are drawn, and future research direction is described.

BACKGROUND

Quality of Service

As mentioned before, the response time and throughput are QoS attributes that can be considered essential. Response time is the time to complete a web service request from a client's perspective. In contrast, throughput is the number of web service requests served at a given period. Many researchers have used QoS prediction methods to get accurate and feasible QoS values. One of the most important approaches for predicting the QoS is CF. CF-based methods can be classified into three main categories: memory-based algorithms, model-based algorithms, and context-based CF algorithms (Ghafouri et al., 2021).

The memory-based algorithms use simple statistical equations. First, the similarity is calculated then the unknown QoS values are predicted by the weight of similar users or services. Memory-based approaches include user-based, item-based, and hybrid algorithms. In user-based algorithms, the QoS for the active users can be predicted by finding similar users to their active users. While in the item-based algorithms, the similarities between different items are calculated, and then the user rating of an item will be predicted by the rating values of similar things. In the hybrid algorithm, both the similarities between services and the similarities between users are computed then a hybrid algorithm uses these similarities to predict the QoS values. These algorithms have better results than previous algorithms. These methods have been used in almost all studies requiring similarity to predict the QoS values.

One of those studies was proposed in 2016 by the article *'Transactions on Services Computing'* (Ma et al., 2016). In this study, the authors presented a highly accurate prediction algorithm (HAPA). HAPA is a CF-based algorithm from a memory-based category. It concretely consists of user-based and item-based HAPAs. They use the combination of the two HAPAs to make predictions more accurate. They first determined some crucial characteristics of Pearson Correlation Coefficient (PCC) similarity. Then based on these characteristics, they proposed the HAPA. The proposed HAPA predicts QoS values directly by the known rate of service values.

Additionally, the TAP algorithm was proposed (Su et al., 2017). TAP is a trust-aware approach to reliable personalized QoS prediction. In this algorithm, the authors first grouped the users and used a beta reputation system to calculate the user's reputations. Second, a list of similar trustworthy users is determined based on their reputation and similarity. Finally, a set of similar services is clustered and predicted to have active users based on their QoS data. Another hybrid memory-based algorithm was proposed by (Chen et al., 2017). This method is proposed for predicting QoS values first by identifying the user's trust. The geographic information of the users and services is collected. Using an improved PCC, the calculation of similarity between users and services is computed, and the QoS value is predicted.

Although these approaches have a high perceptual capability and acceptable accuracy, they have data sparsity, cold-start issues, scalability, and trust. Memory-based algorithms suffer from the data sparsity problem because the high number of web services users have only used very few of these services, which causes many users not to have shared services used and thus reduces the accuracy of their neighbor's detection. The cold start problem is another problem in memory-based algorithms because when a new service or a new user is introduced into the system, there are no neighbors as the user has not used any service yet or any user has not used the service; therefore, it is not possible to predict the QoS values. Suppose the number of services and users is very high. In that case, the cost of calculating the neighbors of services will also be higher, and the scalability problem in memory-based algorithms causes that. Moreover, since the CF method used the QoS values published by other users to make the prediction, the trust problem occurred.

To solve memory-based methods' drawbacks, the model-based algorithms were presented. In these methods, a dataset is used to design a pattern, and then the model is trained using the training data; then, it can predict the unknown QoS values. Clustering, matrix factorization, time series, and machine learning are used for learning the models. In the clustering algorithm, region KNN and LoRec are two methods for predicting the QoS and service recommender systems. They combine model-based and memory-based methods by clustering users and services by geographic location. It can be seen that in almost all clustering methods, clustering is only for data analysis before the original method is predicted. In addition, the clustering criterion in nearly all methods is the geographic similarity of users or services. As an example of clustering-based algorithms, the services are clustered based on their physical environment in (Chen et al., 2015). The QoS values are calculated based on the service values of the cluster center for the active user and the service deviation from its cluster center. In this way, the authors could reduce the computation time than the other CF-based methods. Another study that used the K-means clustering algorithm was proposed by several researchers (He et al., 2014). This work used the K-means clustering algorithm to cluster services and users according to their physical location. Then, the matrix factorization method, which is a model-based method, was used to predict the QoS values.

It can be adopted that matrix factorization is the most critical model-based approach used for QoS prediction. In this method, the user-service matrix is constructed, and the QoS values are predicted by a model built from historical importance and the learning process. These methods have an essential advantage: they can handle data sparsity and cold start problems. Different researchers proposed methods based on matrix factorization. One of these methods was proposed by (Xu et al., 2016). First, it calculates each user's reputation based on their QoS values to quantify user trust and then considers the users' reputation for making a more accurate QoS prediction. A factor model must be fitted to the user-item matrix to predict the QoS values for a given user-item pair. This factor model can then predict specific QoS values.

Zheng et al. (2013) have developed a model called NIMF that is able to provide an acceptable improvement in predicting QoS values by combining the MF method for global information and neighborhoods for local information. In this method, first, the similarity between the users is calculated by PCC, and top-k similar users are identified, and then the FM method is used for prediction. This method has also been proposed using the similarity of users in the modified MF equation. Another method has been developed by Yu et al. (2014). This method is based on SVD to overcome the data sparsity problem, which is also an MF method. They have been able to improve prediction by adding the service provider information and the country where the service was provided. Another method was proposed by Tang et al. (2016). The authors integrated the MF method with the network map in this paper. They have provided a network-aware MF method. They called it NAMF. This method first processes the network map to measure the distance of users on the network, then the neighbors calculate each user in terms of their distance in the network and add the similarity weight between them as a regularization term to the base MF relationship. By doing that, they had an acceptable improvement.

Another model-based technique is time series. This method predicts the QoS attribute values by that attribute's previous values. As an example of a time series technique, Zadeh and Seyyedi proposed a method for collecting response time and using a three-layer neural network for prediction (Zadeh & Seyyedi, 2010). Response time prediction based on the past behavior of the services is called Time Series Forecasting. Many different studies proposed using the time series technique. One of these studies was presented in 2012 by (Amin, Colman, et al., 2012). Their study combined two models (the ARIMA and GRACH) to increase prediction accuracy. ARIMA model is the AutoRegressive Integrated Moving Average, model. This model was proposed to model time series data and forecast their future values. However, this model has a major drawback since it depends on assumptions such as invertibility, normality, and serial dependency. Providing these assumptions to be supported by data is a very complicated task, which may lead to incorrect time series forecasts. To overcome this problem, ARIMA was combined with the generalization of the autoregressive conditional heteroscedastic model (GARCH), which designs the high volatility by describing the dynamic changes in time-varying variance as a deterministic function of past errors. This combined version performs capturing the QoS volatility and forecasts their future values and violations properly.

Another work (Amin, Grunske, et al., 2012) combined ARIMA with Self Exciting Threshold ARMA models (SETARMA). SETARMA starts with a linear model and then supports the parameters changing based on the past values of the time series process. With this combination, it was possible to capture and model the dynamic QoS behavior accurately and improve forecasting accuracy.

Overall, it can be stated that time series techniques have decent performance when there is a history of using a service in the past and can perform a fair prediction with a relatively simple model in a short time.

Machine learning techniques are also another category of model-based methods that have been used for QoS prediction. Many researchers have proposed prediction methods based on machine learning techniques. One of these methods was proposed by Anithadevi & Sundarambal (2019). The author introduced an intelligent web service recommender that uses CF methods combined with Nero fuzzy. This method first classifies the web services by geographical location information and enhances this classification by term frequency (TF) and inverse document frequency (IDF) algorithms.

Another machine learning technique is SVMCF4SR, proposed by Ren & Wang (2018). This method uses a support vector machine (SVM) to provide a service recommender that ranks web services based on user quality. This method, without requiring accurate prediction of QoS values, divides the services into positive and negative clusters with the active user ratings of the used services. The negative services are undesirable to the user, and the positive category services are the ones the user might like. Then using SVM and training it by the services used, the services not used are categorized and divided into one. Thus, by removing negative services, k desirable services are recommended to the users. This method does not suffer from data sparsity, and the amount of computation is less.

The stacked autoencoder is another machine-learning method used to predict the QoS. The traditional autoencoder is a type of neural network which compress the data from the input layer to the hidden layer. After that, the autoencoder decodes the hidden layer to match the original data as much as possible. The stacked autoencoder extended this model with additional hidden layers stacked together to enhance the model's performance. White et al. (2019) used a stacked autoencoder in their work to reduce training and request time compared to traditional matrix factorization algorithms. The stacked autoencoder considers the dynamic property of QoS attributes and uses a time-aware method for accurate prediction.

To improve the QoS prediction accuracy, a hybrid approach is provided by some methods which combine memory-based or model-based techniques with context-based strategies. These methods employ two critical contexts: the service or user geographical data and the service invocation time. Furthermore, to increase prediction accuracy, location, time, and trust are the three critical contextual factors used (Ghafouri et al., 2021).

Many studies focused on location-aware methods show that the users in the same location have similar QoS attribute values for the same services. In contrast, users with different locations observed different QoS values for the same services. Thus, the location-aware methods were combined with CF to increase the QoS prediction accuracy. One of these studies is a memory-based CF method presented by Tang et al. (2012). In this study, they extracted the geographic information of the services or the users, such as IP and the country's name to improve the QoS prediction.

The time-aware method was interesting to study for many researchers because features of the QoS, such as response time, throughput, and availability, can have different values for the users at different times of invocation. WSPred was the first time-aware method proposed by (Zhang et al., 2011). They used a tensor that included user, service, and time. Moreover, by the tensor factorization method, they were able to predict the response time and throughput values.

The contextual trust factors are significant because new QoS values will be predicted based on values published by other users in the CF-based prediction methods. Thus, the accuracy and precision of these values will depend on the accuracy and precision of the values posted by the users. One of the examples of the trust-aware method is proposed in the article (Kalaï et al., 2018). Other users have gained the user's trust, and each user's experience has been identified in the service domain. A service recommender is presented by combining these two factors with the CF method.

The deep learning technique is the most trend and attractive method for modeling the web service quality prediction problem of those three categories. In this work, a neural network technique is used for QoS prediction.

Graph Neural Network

Data can be easily represented in graphs in various applications, including image analysis, scene description, software engineering, and natural language processing. The simplest types of graph structures include single nodes and sequences. However, several applications organize the information in graph structures that are too complex such as acyclic graphs, cyclic graphs, or trees. This way, a graph can be defined as a data structure including two components: vertices and edges. Graph G can be defined by the set of vertices V and edges E as in equation (1).

$$G = (V, E) \tag{1}$$

Graphs are all around us; real-world objects are often defined in terms of their connections to other things. GNN is a type of Neural Network which directly works on the Graph structure. Researchers have developed it for over a decade (Scarselli et al., 2009). Recent developments have increased GNNs capabilities and expressive power. GNNs have been used in many different applications since it was presented by researchers. Some of the practical applications are in areas such as antibacterial discovery (Stokes et al., 2020), physics simulations (Sanchez-Gonzalez et al., 2020), fake news detection (Monti et al., 2019), traffic prediction (Jiang & Luo, 2021), and recommendation systems (Gao et al., 2021).

Using GNNs in any application improves the performance of the systems. For example, using GNNs in the recommender system has high success. A recommender system is a filtering system designed to provide personalized information to users to improve their experience and promote business profits (Gao et al., 2021). The earliest recommendation models capture the CF effect by calculating the similarity of interactions. Then model-based CF methods, such as matrix factorization (MF) or factorization machine, were proposed to approach recommendation as a representation learning problem. Yet critical challenges face these methods, such as complex user behaviors or data input. However, despite these challenges, these methods are effective in certain situations. To solve these problems, models based on neural networks have been proposed. Neural CF (NCF) was developed to improve the capacity of multi-layer perceptron (MLP). The deep factorization machine (DeepFM) combines the shallow model factorization machine (FM) with MLP. However, the methods used to predict and train models ignore the high-level structural information in observed data. That encouraged the researchers to use GNNs to create recommender systems.

The success of GNN-based recommenders can be explained as follows (Gao et al., 2021). By expressing all the data as nodes and edges on a graph, GNN provides a unified way to utilize available data. Also, GNN shows strong power in learning representations, and thus, high-quality embeddings for users, items, and other features can be obtained, which is critical to the recommendation performance. GNN-based models can effectively capture high-order connectivity. Specifically, the CF effect can be naturally expressed as multi-hop neighbors on the graph and incorporated into the learned representations through embedding propagation and aggregation. Also, GNN-based models can effectively incorporate multiple non-target behaviors, such as search and add to cart, by encoding semi-supervised signals over the graph, which can significantly improve recommendation performance.

The successes of using GNN in recommender systems motivated us to use it in QoS prediction systems. As far as we know, two recently published works proposed using GNN for QoS prediction. The first is using a Two-Level Heterogeneous Graph Attention Network for QoS Prediction (Lv et al., 2022). This method first unitizes the user's location information to construct an attributed user-service network. Then, the authors model a heterogeneous GNN based on a hierarchical attention machine (HGN2HIA) that includes node- and semantic-level attention. Specifically, node-level attention aims to learn the importance between a node and its meta-path-based neighbors, while semantic-level attention understands the importance of different meta-paths. Finally, user embedding generated by aggregating features from meta-path-based neighbors in a hierarchical manner is used for QoS prediction.

The second combines multi-component graph convolutional CF and a DeepFM for QoS prediction (MGCCF-DFM) (Ding et al., 2021). The main idea of this work is to capture the latent environment preference feature according to the history of QoS. Firstly, MGCCF-DFM decomposes the edges of the bipartite graph and extracts latent environment preference features. At the same time, MGCCF-DFM uses a neural network with node-level attention to optimize services' weight and aggregates them to obtain user and service feature components. Then, MGCCF-DFM uses the neural network with component-level attention to learn the weight of the feature components and then combines them to obtain the final embedding of user and service, which are put into the DeepFM model to get QoS prediction.

Although the proposed methods achieved good performance, there is still some space for improvement. Hence, in this paper, a GNN-based QoS prediction will be proposed.

EXPERIMENT DESCRIPTION

In this paper, the GNN-based QoS prediction method is proposed. We perform experiments to validate our GNN-based QoS prediction method and compare the results with those from other CF methods. This section discusses the model, dataset, competitor methods, and results.

Model Description

The GNN-based QoS prediction method is a CF method, and it is a model-based algorithm. To increase the model's performance, the GNN-based QoS prediction is proposed as a hybrid of three model-based algorithms. First, clustering is used to prepare user and service data to use in a training phase. Also, a (user-service) matrix is constructed. And the QoS is predicted using the Matrix factorization method. Next, a machine learning algorithm is used where a GNN is built from the users and services as the nodes, and they are connected with edges to describe the relationship between each user and service.

The data after clustering is used to train this model, and then the model can predict the unknown QoS values. The prediction is made at two different levels to increase the prediction accuracy. First, the prediction was predicted as a node-level prediction. Then the prediction was predicted as an edge-level prediction. The experiment was run several times with different matrix densities to test the model's performance compared with other state-of-the-art models. All the methods are implemented in Python. Notably, all methods are built and trained based on TensorFlow.

Data Set

In order to get good and accurate results this project uses a widely used dataset for QoS prediction called the WS-Dream dataset (WS-DREAM: Towards Open Datasets and Source Code for Web Service Research, n.d.). To our knowledge, this is the largest dataset in service computing. It was developed by The Chinese University of Hong Kong as an open dataset for web services research. WS-DREAM is a Distributed Reliability Assessment Mechanism for Web services. And it is a collection of QoS datasets for web service recommendation.

This dataset describes the real-world QoS evaluation results from 339 users on 5,825 Web services, which can be transformed into a user-service matrix. Each item of the user-service matrix is a pair of values: Round-Trip Time (RTT) and throughput (TP) (Zheng et al., 2014).

Evaluation Metrics

For QoS prediction, the essential criterion for evaluation is prediction accuracy. The Mean Absolute Error (MAE) and Root Mean Square Error (RMSE) are two typical evaluation indexes measuring the QoS prediction accuracy (Ghafouri et al., 2021). MAE, presented in equation (2), indicates the average absolute errors between predicted and observed values, and RMSE, presented in equation (3), indicates the sample standard deviation representing the difference between predicted and observed values.

These two values are extracted from equations (2) and (3) as follows:

$$MAE = \frac{\sum_{u,s} |q_{u,s} - \hat{q}_{u,s}|}{N} \tag{2}$$

$$RMSE = \sqrt{\frac{\sum_{u,s} |q_{u,s} - \hat{q}_{u,s}|^2}{N}} \tag{3}$$

Where N refers to the number of all predicted values, $q_{u,s}$ are the actual values for QoS, and $\hat{q}_{u,s}$ are the predicted values for QoS. When the value of RMSE and MAE gets smaller, the accuracy of QoS prediction gets higher, and the result becomes better.

Competitor Baseline Methods

To evaluate the performance of the model, we compared it with three other baseline models. We chose to compare our model with different model types to get a more accurate evaluation of our model. One of the models that we compared our model with is a model-based model while the other two are memory-based models. The following are the three baseline models:

- IPCC: A hybrid CF method that combines data of similar users and services for QoS prediction (Zheng et al., 2011). This model is a memory-based model.
- RANEP: A Web service QoS prediction method based on reputation-aware network embedding. This scheme considers the user's reputation, employs reputation-aware network embedding to learn the user nodes' vector representation, and finally adopts user-based CF for prediction (Wang et al., 2020). This model is a model-based model.
- TAP: A personalized reputation-aware QoS prediction method that employs k-means clustering and Beta distribution to calculate a user's reputation. Service clustering is exploited to identify similar services, while the data contributed by reliable and comparable users and services are utilized for QoS prediction (Su et al., 2017). This model is a memory-based model.

Experiment Results

The QoS dataset (a matrix) was randomly split into a training set and a test set based on a specific ratio to observe the model's performance. For instance, Matrix Density = 5% means that 5 percent of the QoS entries were randomly selected to predict the remaining 95 percent of QoS entries.

GNN-based QoS method and other comparison methods are run on the WS- DREAM dataset with {4%, 5%, 6%, 7%, 8%, 9%, 10%, 11%, 12%, 13%, and 14%} of the training dataset respectively. These matrix densities were chosen in such a way that they are different and give multiple results within a logical range so that the percentage is not too large. Ten different ratios were chosen, which increases the reliability of the results. Figure 1 compares all methods' prediction results (for response time and throughput) under various matrix densities.

Figure 1. The prediction results of all methods under various matrix densities

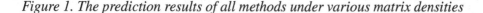
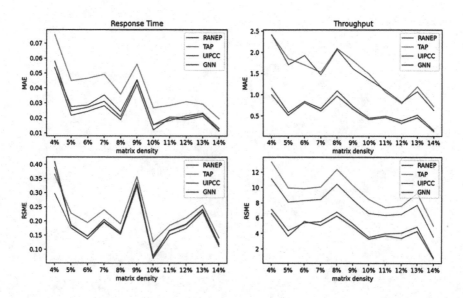

Table 1 shows all the MAE and RMSE values that present the QoS prediction accuracy based on the response time dataset with different matrix densities, and Table 2 shows all the MAE and RMSE values that present the QoS prediction accuracy based on the throughput dataset with different matrix densities.

Table 1. Performance comparison for response time prediction

Methods		IPCC	RANEP	TAP	GNN
Density = 4%	MAE	0.0534	0.0538	0.0758	0.0579
	RMSE	0.2974	0.3889	0.3647	0.4090
Density = 5%	MAE	0.0274	0.0216	0.0449	0.0248
	RMSE	0.1751	0.1860	0.2277	0.1836
Density = 6%	MAE	0.0286	0.0243	0.0464	0.0271
	RMSE	0.1361	0.1461	0.1938	0.1458
Density = 7%	MAE	0.0353	0.0281	0.0490	0.0310
	RMSE	0.1948	0.2048	0.2386	0.1974
Density = 8%	MAE	0.0242	0.0187	0.0358	0.0208
	RMSE	0.1533	0.1588	0.1901	0.1544
Density = 9%	MAE	0.0454	0.0423	0.0560	0.0451
	RMSE	0.3220	0.3376	0.3572	0.3285
Density = 10%	MAE	0.0154	0.0120	0.0267	0.0153
	RMSE	0.0683	0.0706	0.1272	0.0779
Density = 11%	MAE	0.0182	0.0196	0.0283	0.0205
	RMSE	0.1515	0.1664	0.1846	0.1649
Density = 12%	MAE	0.0214	0.0189	0.0307	0.0200
	RMSE	0.1740	0.1891	0.2113	0.1870
Density = 13%	MAE	0.0231	0.0211	0.0292	0.0226
	RMSE	0.2313	0.2421	0.2567	0.2385
Density = 14%	MAE	0.0130	0.0112	0.0194	0.0117
	RMSE	0.1111	0.1200	0.1407	0.1174

Table 2. Performance comparison for throughput prediction

Methods		IPCC	RANEP	TAP	GNN
Density = 4%	MAE	2.4159	1.1534	2.4054	0.9995
	RMSE	11.1249	7.1479	13.3251	6.5850
Density = 5%	MAE	1.7075	0.5797	1.8542	0.5159
	RMSE	8.1045	4.3625	9.9431	3.6481
Density = 6%	MAE	1.9265	0.8423	1.7025	0.8126
	RMSE	8.2963	5.3851	9.8449	5.5594
Density = 7%	MAE	1.4697	0.6757	1.5317	0.6169
	RMSE	8.4500	5.5331	10.0701	5.0679
Density = 8%	MAE	2.0639	1.0916	2.0896	0.9683
	RMSE	10.4247	6.7809	12.3521	6.2577
Density = 9%	MAE	1.6174	0.7264	1.8057	0.6593
	RMSE	8.4107	5.2765	10.2859	4.8779
Density = 10%	MAE	1.3577	0.4495	1.4888	0.4210
	RMSE	6.6042	3.4964	8.4635	3.2737
Density = 11%	MAE	1.1072	0.4964	1.0598	0.4680
	RMSE	6.3626	3.9568	7.3832	3.6964
Density = 12%	MAE	0.8208	0.3895	0.8000	0.3313
	RMSE	6.5075	4.0589	7.5980	3.3803
Density = 13%	MAE	1.0748	0.5222	1.1898	0.4607
	RMSE	7.7094	4.8408	9.2522	4.2664
Density = 14%	MAE	0.6347	0.1687	0.7233	0.1427
	RMSE	3.5543	0.8709	4.9762	0.7423

According to Table 1 and Table 2, the following observations can be drawn; the performance of the model-based method (e.g., RANEP) is better than memory-based methods (TAP, UIPCC) on both RMSE and MAE for all densities, which confirms the effectiveness of these methods in alleviating data sparsity. On the other hand, in most cases, our proposed method, the (GNN-based method) performs better than memory-based methods and other model-based methods in terms of RMSE and MAE. These results confirm that using deep neural networks provides a robust modeling ability for QoS prediction. Also, it is clear that the proposed method's performance outperformed other methods. Hence the proposed method improved the QoS prediction.

Our proposed method best performs in the response time prediction when matrix density equals 10% since the results show that the MAE is 0.0153 and RMSE is 0.0779. While in the throughput prediction, the GNN-based QoS prediction method best performs when matrix density is 14% since the MAE is 0.1427 and RMSE is 0.7423.

FUTURE RESEARCH DIRECTIONS

Although the proposed method achieves good performance, there is still some space for improvement. Future work shall consider testing the performance of the proposed method for different QoS attributes such as accuracy and availability. In addition to the benchmark method employed in this paper, newer comparative methods are available. Also, more information, such as user or service attributes, can be integrated into the model to enhance learning.

CONCLUSION

As mentioned above, there are different methods used for QoS prediction. One of these methods is CF which is categorized into three main methods. The memory-based methods, the model-based methods, and the context-based CF method. The memory-based methods were the first methods used for QoS prediction. They are simple and understandable and have good accuracy, but it suffers from data sparsity, cold start, and scalability problems. To overcome these problems, the model-based approaches were presented and studied. The model-based approaches do not suffer from these problems since the prediction depends on the models, which were built based on the previous behaviors of the users and the services. One of the model-based approaches that is getting more attention recently is neural networks. The neural network is considered one of the most promising models in this field.

This paper developed a new model-based web service quality prediction method based on a Graph neural network. It can be considered a hybrid of three model-based algorithms since clustering and matrix factorization was used to increase the accuracy of the performance. The experimental results highlight that the GNN-QoS method of this paper achieves a higher QoS prediction accuracy (on response time and throughput) than the competitor methods (User item-based PCC for QoS prediction (UIPCC), Reputation-Aware Network Embedding-based QoS Prediction (RANEP), and Trust-aware approach TAP for personalized QoS prediction). Furthermore, the results confirm that the deep neural networks provide powerful modeling ability.

REFERENCES

Amin, A., Colman, A., & Grunske, L. (2012). An approach to forecasting QoS attributes of web services based on ARIMA and GARCH models. *Proceedings - 2012 IEEE 19th International Conference on Web Services, ICWS 2012*, 74–81. IEEE. 10.1109/ICWS.2012.37

Amin, A., Grunske, L., & Colman, A. (2012). An automated approach to forecasting QoS attributes based on linear and non-linear time series modeling. *2012 27th IEEE/ACM International Conference on Automated Software Engineering, ASE 2012 - Proceedings*, 130–139. IEEE. 10.1145/2351676.2351695

Anithadevi, N., & Sundarambal, M. (2019). A design of intelligent QoS aware web service recommendation system. *Cluster Computing*, 22(6), 14231–14240. doi:10.100710586-018-2279-8

Chen, F., Yuan, S., & Mu, B. (2015). User-QoS-Based Web Service Clustering for QoS Prediction. *Proceedings – 2015 IEEE International Conference on Web Services, ICWS 2015*, 583–590. IEEE. 10.1109/ICWS.2015.83

Chen, K., Mao, H., Shi, X., Xu, Y., & Liu, A. (2017). Trust-Aware and Location-Based Collaborative Filtering for Web Service QoS Prediction. *Proceedings - International Computer Software and Applications Conference*, 2, 143–148. IEEE. 10.1109/COMPSAC.2017.8

Ding, L., Kang, G., Liu, J., Xiao, Y., & Cao, B. (2021). QoS Prediction for Web Services via Combining Multi-component Graph Convolutional Collaborative Filtering and Deep Factorization Machine. *Proceedings - 2021 IEEE International Conference on Web Services, ICWS 2021*, 551–559. IEEE. 10.1109/ICWS53863.2021.00076

Gao, C., Zheng, Y. U., Li, N., Li, Y., Qin, Y., Piao, J., Quan, Y., Chang, J., Depeng, J., He, X., Li, Y., Zheng, Y., & Jin, D. (2021). Graph Neural Networks for Recommender Systems: Challenges, Methods, and Directions. *ACM Transactions on Information Systems*, *1*(1), 46. doi:10.48550/arxiv.2109.12843

Ghafouri, H., Hashemi, M., & Hung, P. C. K. (2021). A survey on web service QoS prediction methods. In *IEEE Transactions on Services Computing*. Institute of Electrical and Electronics Engineers Inc., doi:10.1109/TSC.2020.2980793

Ghazal, T. M., Hussain, M. Z., Said, R. A., Nadeem, A., Hasan, M. K., Ahmad, M., Khan, M. A., & Naseem, M. T. (2021). Performances of k-means clustering algorithm with different distance metrics. *Intelligent Automation and Soft Computing*, *30*(2), 735–742. doi:10.32604/iasc.2021.019067

He, P., Zhu, J., Xu, J., & Lyu, M. R. (2014). A hierarchical matrix factorization approach for location-based web service QoS prediction. *Proceedings - IEEE 8th International Symposium on Service Oriented System Engineering, SOSE 2014*, 290–295. IEEE. 10.1109/SOSE.2014.41

Janiesch, C., Zschech, P., & Heinrich, K. (2021). Machine learning and deep learning. *Electronic Markets*, *31*(3), 685–695. doi:10.100712525-021-00475-2

Jiang, W., & Luo, J. (2021). Graph Neural Network for Traffic Forecasting. *Survey (London, England)*. doi:10.48550/arxiv.2101.11174

Kalaï, A., Zayani, C. A., Amous, I., Abdelghani, W., & Sèdes, F. (2018). Social collaborative service recommendation approach based on user's trust and domain-specific expertise. *Future Generation Computer Systems*, *80*, 355–367. doi:10.1016/j.future.2017.05.036

Koren, Y., Rendle, S., & Bell, R. (2022). Advances in Collaborative Filtering. *Recommender Systems Handbook*, 91–142. doi:10.1007/978-1-0716-2197-4_3

Kritikos, K., & Plexousakis, D. (2009). Requirements for QoS-Based Web Service Description and Discovery. *IEEE Transactions on Services Computing*, *2*(4), 320–337. doi:10.1109/TSC.2009.26

Lv, S., Yi, F., He, P., & Zeng, C. (2022). QoS Prediction of Web Services Based on a Two-Level Heterogeneous Graph Attention Network. *IEEE Access: Practical Innovations, Open Solutions*, *10*, 1871–1880. IEEE. doi:10.1109/ACCESS.2021.3138127

Ma, Y., Wang, S., Hung, P. C. K., Hsu, C. H., Sun, Q., & Yang, F. (2016). A highly accurate prediction algorithm for unknown web service QoS values. *IEEE Transactions on Services Computing*, *9*(4), 511–523. IEEE. doi:10.1109/TSC.2015.2407877

Monti, F., Frasca, F., Eynard, D., Mannion, D., Bronstein, M. M., Ai, F., & Lugano, U. (2019). *Fake News Detection on Social Media using Geometric Deep Learning*. arXiv. doi:10.48550/arxiv.1902.06673

Ren, L., & Wang, W. (2018). An SVM-based collaborative filtering approach for Top-N web services recommendation. *Future Generation Computer Systems*, *78*, 531–543. doi:10.1016/j.future.2017.07.027

Sanchez-Gonzalez, A., Godwin, J., Pfaff, T., Ying, R., Leskovec, J., & Battaglia, P. W. (2020). Learning to Simulate Complex Physics with Graph Networks. *37th International Conference on Machine Learning, ICML 2020, PartF168147-11*, (pp. 8428–8437). 10.48550/arxiv.2002.09405

Scarselli, F., Gori, M., Tsoi, A. C., Hagenbuchner, M., & Monfardini, G. (2009). The graph neural network model. *IEEE Transactions on Neural Networks*, *20*(1), 61–80. doi:10.1109/TNN.2008.2005605 PMID:19068426

Stokes, J. M., Yang, K., Swanson, K., Jin, W., Cubillos-Ruiz, A., Donghia, N. M., MacNair, C. R., French, S., Carfrae, L. A., Bloom-Ackerman, Z., Tran, V. M., Chiappino-Pepe, A., Badran, A. H., Andrews, I. W., Chory, E. J., Church, G. M., Brown, E. D., Jaakkola, T. S., Barzilay, R., & Collins, J. J. (2020). A Deep Learning Approach to Antibiotic Discovery. *Cell*, *180*(4), 688–702.e13. doi:10.1016/j.cell.2020.01.021 PMID:32084340

Su, K., Xiao, B., Liu, B., Zhang, H., & Zhang, Z. (2017). TAP: A personalized trust-aware QoS prediction approach for web service recommendation. *Knowledge-Based Systems*, *115*, 55–65. doi:10.1016/j.knosys.2016.09.033

Tang, M., Jiang, Y., Liu, J., & Liu, X. (2012). Location-aware collaborative filtering for QoS-based service recommendation. *Proceedings - 2012 IEEE 19th International Conference on Web Services, ICWS 2012*, 202–209.IEEE. 10.1109/ICWS.2012.61

Tang, M., Zheng, Z., Kang, G., Liu, J., Yang, Y., & Zhang, T. (2016). Collaborative Web Service Quality Prediction via Exploiting Matrix Factorization and Network Map. *IEEE eTransactions on Network and Service Management*, *13*(1), 126–137. doi:10.1109/TNSM.2016.2517097

Wang, X., He, P., Zhang, J., & Wang, Z. (2020). QoS Prediction of Web Services Based on Reputation-Aware Network Embedding. *IEEE Access: Practical Innovations, Open Solutions*, *8*, 161498–161508. doi:10.1109/ACCESS.2020.3020825

White, G., Palade, A., Cabrera, C., & Clarke, S. (2019). Autoencoders for QoS prediction at the Edge. IEEE International Conference on Pervasive Computing and Communications (PerCom), 1-9. https://doi.org/10.1109/PERCOM.2019.8767397

WS-DREAM. (2022). *Towards Open Datasets and Source Code for Web Service Research*. WS-Dream. https://wsdream.github.io/

Xu, J., Zheng, Z., & Lyu, M. R. (2016). Web Service Personalized Quality of Service Prediction via Reputation-Based Matrix Factorization. *IEEE Transactions on Reliability*, *65*(1), 28–37. doi:10.1109/TR.2015.2464075

Yi, B., Shen, X., Liu, H., Zhang, Z., Zhang, W., Liu, S., & Xiong, N. (2019). Deep Matrix Factorization With Implicit Feedback Embedding for Recommendation System. *IEEE Transactions on Industrial Informatics*, *15*(8), 4591–4601. doi:10.1109/TII.2019.2893714

Ying, R., He, R., Chen, K., Eksombatchai, P., Hamilton, W. L., & Leskovec, J. (2018). Graph convolutional neural networks for web-scale recommender systems. *Proceedings of the ACM SIGKDD International Conference on Knowledge Discovery and Data Mining*, 974–983. 10.1145/3219819.3219890

Yu, D., Liu, Y., Xu, Y., & Yin, Y. (2014). Personalized QoS prediction for web services using latent factor models. *Proceedings - 2014 IEEE International Conference on Services Computing, SCC 2014*, 107–114. 10.1109/SCC.2014.23

Zadeh, M. H., & Seyyedi, M. A. (2010). Qos monitoring for web services by Time Series Forecasting. *Proceedings - 2010 3rd IEEE International Conference on Computer Science and Information Technology, ICCSIT 2010, 5*, 659–663. 10.1109/ICCSIT.2010.5563998

Zhang, Y., Zheng, Z., & Lyu, M. R. (2011). WSPred: A time-aware personalized QoS prediction framework for Web services. *Proceedings - International Symposium on Software Reliability Engineering, ISSRE*, 210–219. IEEE. 10.1109/ISSRE.2011.17

Zheng, Z., Ma, H., Lyu, M. R., & King, I. (2011). QoS-Aware Web Service Recommendation by Collaborative Filtering. *IEEE Transactions on Services Computing, 4*(2), 140–152. doi:10.1109/TSC.2010.52

Zheng, Z., Ma, H., Lyu, M. R., & King, I. (2013). Collaborative web service qos prediction via neighborhood integrated matrix factorization. *IEEE Transactions on Services Computing, 6*(3), 289–299. doi:10.1109/TSC.2011.59

Zheng, Z., Zhang, Y., & Lyu, M. R. (2014). Investigating QoS of Real-World Web Services. *IEEE Transactions on Services Computing, 7*(1), 32–39. doi:10.1109/TSC.2012.34

KEY TERMS AND DEFINITIONS

Clustering: Is the process of grouping the data based on their similar properties. Meanwhile, it is the categorization of a set of data into similar groups (clusters), and the elements in each cluster share similarities, where the similarity between elements in the same cluster must be more minor enough to the similarity between elements of different clusters. Hence, this similarity can be considered as a distance measure. One of the most popular clustering algorithms is K-means, where distance is measured between every point of the dataset and centroids of clusters to find similar data objects and assign them to the nearest cluster (Ghazal et al., 2021).

Collaborative Filtering: Is a technique used by recommender systems that learn the user's previous behaviors, then provides personalized service support and predicts their current preferences for particular products. Moreover, this is used to improve the accuracy of recommendations. In the general sense of CF, CF is the process of filtering information or patterns using methods involving collaboration between multiple agents, viewpoints, data sources, etc. In a narrower one, CF is a method of automatically predicting (filtering) a user's interests by collecting information about the preferences or tastes of many users (collaboration) (Koren et al., 2022).

Graph: A data structure including two components: vertices and edges.

Machine Learning: Is a branch of artificial intelligence and computer science that focuses on using data and algorithms to imitate how humans learn and improve their accuracy (Janiesch et al., 2021).

Matrix Factorization: Is a class of collaborative filtering algorithms used in recommender systems to find the relationship between items' and users' entities (Yi et al., 2019).

Model-Based Algorithm: An approach to machine learning where all the assumptions about the problem domain are made explicit in the form of a model (Janiesch et al., 2021).

Neural Network: It is a subset of machine learning and is at the heart of deep learning algorithms. Its name and structure are inspired by the human brain, mimicking how biological neurons signal each other. Artificial Neural Networks consist of a node layer containing an input layer, one or more hidden layers, and an output layer. Each node, or artificial neuron, connects to another and has an associated weight and threshold. If the output of any individual node is higher than the specified threshold value, that node is activated, sending data to the next layer of the network. Otherwise, no data will be passed to the next layer of the network (Janiesch et al., 2021).

QoS Features: Are attributes used to optimize network performance, such as accuracy, capacity, availability, reputation, cost, time, and throughput.

Quality of Service: QoS Is the description or measurement of the overall performance of a service.

Recommender Systems: Are algorithms aimed at suggesting relevant items to users. Also, it can be considered as s a subclass of information filtering systems that provide suggestions for items that are most pertinent to a particular user (Ying et al., 2018).

Chapter 19
Rifle Detection and Performance Evaluation Using Deep Learning Frameworks

Adeyemi Abel Ajibesin

iD https://orcid.org/0000-0001-6518-0231

American University of Nigeria, Nigeria

Doken Edgar

American University of Nigeria, Nigeria

ABSTRACT

Deep learning models being used to improve human life has been an ongoing domain of research. Violence, especially with the proliferation of arms, has been on the increase worldwide. Many tragedies have occurred right across the globe, leading to people losing their lives as a result of being shot at with guns. This research sought to use deep learning frameworks to detect rifles in images and assess their performance based on the metrics of accuracy and F1 score. The study used a combination of images from Google open images and other sources to form a dataset of 2105 images; 1857 of those was used to train YOLOv3 and RetinaNet models to detect rifles, using Darknet-53 and ResNet50 respectively as the backbone networks. The models were evaluated after training using a test dataset containing 248 images, both the training and evaluation of the models were carried out using scripts written in Python. The results obtained showed that YOLOv3 had better output in terms of accuracy, precision, recall, and, consequently, the F1 scored better than RetinaNet

INTRODUCTION

Overview

Computer vision is a subarea of artificial intelligence that is focused on the study and automation of visual perception tasks (Rodriguez, 2020). For humans, it is quite a simple and straightforward task to

DOI: 10.4018/978-1-6684-6937-8.ch019

identify and recognize familiar objects, even in scenarios that may be unfriendly due to variations in light or distortions due to movements (Sharma & Thakur, 2017). However, these simple tasks of recognizing objects are very difficult for computers (Sharma & Thakur, 2017). As advances are being made in the field of artificial intelligence, being able to have computers recognize objects in videos and images is quite important. This process is known as object recognition (Zhao et al., 2017). Though sometimes used interchangeably, detecting, and classifying objects from an image are not the same. Classification is the ability to say what object is present in an image, that is, labeling the content of an image. Detection goes a little beyond that: it is not enough to say what object is in an image, but where the said object is located within the image (Rodriguez, 2020). For example, an algorithm can determine that an image contains a car, but with detection, it would take it further and provide a bounded box of where the car is situated within the image. Hence a combination of object classification and detection provides a more complete understanding of an image (Zhao et al., 2017).

Traditionally in machine learning, image classification was based on feature extraction of specific features from the training set. This makes it unable to extract other types of features from the training data (Krishna et al., 2018). This shortfall is addressed via the use of deep learning (Lee et al., 2009). With a deep learning model, the model isn't given a specific set of features, but it's allowed to learn through its method of computing. The deep learning model mimics the structure of the human brain and utilizes several algorithms expressed as Artificial Neural Networks (Krishna et al., 2018).

In the field of computer vision, object classification and detection have been studied and applied in many fields like autonomous vehicles, facial recognition (Bashbaghi et al., 2019), agriculture (Geffen et al., 2020), medicine and health and so many others. Object detection is one of the important features needed in the navigation of autonomous vehicles, without which it will be almost impossible to have a vehicle that is safe for passengers in the vehicle as well as other road users (Lewis, 2016). In virtually all of the fields that computer vision is applied, one important attribute to have is accuracy (Lewis, 2016).

Another important application of object detection is surveillance and security (Kanehisa & Neto, 2019). Due to a lot of areas making use of closed-circuit television and drones for surveillance, manning the output can be overwhelming and tedious for the operators. This is where object detection models can be used to assist security agencies to anticipate dangerous situations before they occur. The models can be used to detect firearms (Kanehisa & Neto, 2019) and other dangerous items from an image or video input, and then alert security agencies to respond before the situation escalates. Having such a system in place can sometimes be the difference between life and death situations, because, although human visual perception is usually quick and precise, it is prone to error if someone keeps watching the same thing for a long period (Narejo et al., 2021). To curb this limitation, the availability of huge datasets, faster processing, and computing capabilities using GPUs and machine learning algorithms are being considered to effectively develop surveillance systems that will function for long periods with high accuracy. Advances in machine learning and also image processing algorithms such as the usage of convolutional neural networks (CNNs) have made it possible to develop smart and effective surveillance systems. Convolutional neural networks can automatically extract features from data (An et al., 2012), unlike traditional means of extraction where the features are manually selected (Searle et al., 1997).

The state-of-the-art models used in object detection can be divided into two categories: one-stage and two-stage detectors. The two-stage detectors generally have higher accuracy than the one-stage detectors, but they use more computational power and take more time to execute than the one-stage detectors. But this does depend on what convolutional network is used as the backbone network as well as other configurations (Garcia et al., 2021). Two-stage detectors are so-called because the frameworks' detection processes are broadly divided into two parts: the region proposal and the classification stage. Examples of two-stage detectors include R-CNN, Faster R-CNN, and Cascade R-CNN, among others. In these frameworks, the models first create a region proposal of the objects, that is, many object candidates are proposed, known as regions of interest (ROI) using reference anchors, while in the second step, the proposals are classified, and the localization refined. One-stage detectors on the other hand use a single fully convolutional network that gives the bounding boxes and object classification. YOLO (Redmond & Farhadi, 2017) and SSD (Liu et al., 2016) were among the first algorithms to use a single architecture that does not require prior region proposals. Subsequently, RetinaNet was developed to build on and improve the performance of the architecture used in SSD (Lin et al., 2020)

Challenges, Motivation, and Structure

Object detection in computer vision plays a vital role in many applications that are important in everyday life. Being able to determine which algorithms are efficient is an important component in achieving object detection tasks. Even though there have been considerable advances in deep learning architectures and convolutional neural networks, there is still a need to explore the performance of existing object detection models (Garcia et al., 2021). Several object detection models were successfully tested for accuracy on general-purpose benchmark datasets, such as the COCO dataset (Lin et al., 2014), but this does not represent the actual performance when applied in a real-time environment, using a custom dataset containing classes that were not in the general-purpose benchmark dataset (Garcia et al., 2021). Being able to identify high-performing models is one part of the equation, applying them successfully to a problem domain is another task.

Apart from the popular application of object detection in autonomous vehicles, public safety, and video surveillance are other domains that can greatly benefit from the usage of object detection algorithms (Carrobles et al., 2019). Crowded places are easily susceptible to gun attacks, and mass shootings have become common occurrences in many parts of the world (Zhang et al., 2017). Even though most crowded places have CCTV that are being manned by operators, (Valestin et. al, 2006) noted that usually after 20 minutes of CCTV monitoring, most operators fail to detect objects in a video scene. This was corroborated by Ainsworth (2002), who reported that after continuous monitoring of CCTV footage for 12 minutes, an operator could miss up to 45% of screen activity, while after 22 minutes, this increases significantly to about 95% of activity missed out or overlooked. This implies that there's a need to determine if deep learning models can be used to augment human monitoring of digital input to detect the presence of weapons, which can be the difference between averting a disaster where many lives could be lost, and that disaster happening.

Thus, this research aims to evaluate the performance of selected deep learning models used in object detection, in an end-to-end pipeline, from training to evaluation and analyzing their performance on a test dataset. The main aim of this study is to find the performance level of the following deep learning algorithms in object detection: YOLOv3 and RetinaNet. To achieve this, the problem can be broken down into the following sub-tasks: Study the architecture of the two algorithms, Train models based on the two algorithms using a custom dataset, perform object detection tasks using a test dataset, and measure the performance of the models based on accuracy and F1 score.

As stated earlier, there are two types of object detection algorithms and frameworks, that is stage and two-stage detectors. In this study, two one-stage algorithms are considered: YOLO and RetinaNet. This research evaluates the two one-stage detectors after being trained on a dataset. The object of interest in the dataset is a rifle. Therefore, for this study, an analysis of the performance of one-stage algorithms on a test dataset to detect rifles in images is presented and discussed.

This chapter is structured into five sections, with each chapter comprising multiple subsections. The introduction has been presented in section one, Section two provides a review of related works and contributions to research. Section three discusses the research methodology adopted in carrying out the research. Section four analyses and discusses the results. Section five provides a conclusion on the findings obtained and possible future research recommendations are given.

BACKGROUND

Artificial Intelligence/Machine Learning

Artificial intelligence (AI) can simply be defined as the intelligence displayed by machines (Ongsulee, 2017). AI research is defined as the study of intelligent agents whereby a device can understand its environment and take decisions and actions that will improve its chances of completing a particular goal (Kohavi & Provost, 1998). AI seeks to have a machine that can mimic cognitive functions similar to humans, such as speech (Russell & Norvig, 2010), self-driving vehicles, intelligent routing, competing in games such as chess and go (Silver et al., 2017), and many others. This implies that general intelligence or the ability to have machines that reason, plan, learn, process natural language, and perceive is the overall goal of AI research (Goodfellow et al., 2016). Similarly, computer vision is a field of computer science that tries to mimic human vision using computers and AI (Brownlee, 2019), (Huang, 1996). Machine learning is a branch of computer science that gives computers the ability to learn by themselves and perform tasks without any human interaction (Marco, 2017). There are 3 types of machine learning: Supervised Learning, Unsupervised Learning, and Reinforcement Learning (Kang & Jameson, 2018), (Bushkovskyi, 2018; Chadalawada, 2020).

Artificial Neural Network (ANN)

Artificial neural networks are computational models that take inspiration from the brain (Kumar & Sharma, 2014). They are a popular type of supervised learning algorithm. As the name Artificial Neural Network implies, this type of model or network imitates the neural function of the human brain (Chadalawada, 2020). Just like the brain, an ANN is made up of interconnected nodes (neurons) in multiple layers (Bishop, 2006). And each node acts like a perceptron - it receives multiple signals (inputs) and provides the signal to an activation function, the activation function then produces the output of that node and passes it forward to the next node as an input (Agostinelli et al., 2015). Similar to how the connections between neurons in the human brain are known as synapses, the connections between the neurons in an artificial neural network are also known as synapses (Aaron, 2015). These are illustrated in figures 1 and 2.

Figure 1. A neuron
(Source: Maltarollo et al., 2013)

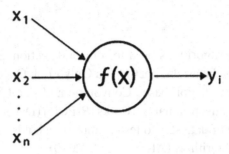

Figure 2. Simple Artificial Neural Network (ANN)
(Source: Maltarollo et al., 2013)

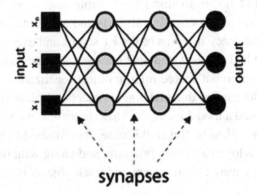

To simulate the synapses that connect the neurons in the brain, weighted values are used in ANNs. So, each neuron that is connected to n preceding neurons will have x_1 --- x_n connections, and each connection weights w_1 --- w_n. Therefore, the value that will be provided to the activation function to get the output of that neuron is the summation of the product of the weights wi against the inputs xi, plus the bias. This is represented below:

$$Y = \sum_{i=1}^{n} \left(w_n * x_n \right) + b \qquad (2.1)$$

Where x is the input value of the neuron, w is the weight associated with the input, n is the number of neurons, b is the bias and y is the output.

When the final output of the network is provided, it is compared against the expected output or ground truth, and the error is calculated. Consequently, the network works backward through the neurons and updates the weights using the error value obtained. This is done through a process called backpropagation and is among the features that make ANN reduce its error rate throughout training (Rumelhart et al., 1986).

LITERATURE REVIEW AND GAPS

Related Works

There are a lot of deep learning algorithms used for object detection and classification, such as Convolutional Neural Networks (Chadalawada, 2020), You Only Look Once (Redmon et al., 2016), Single Shot Detection (Liu et al., 2016), Region-based Convolutional Neural Network (R-CNN) (Girshick et al., 2014), Region-based Fully Convolutional Networks (R-FCN) (Dai et al., 2016). A lot of research has been carried out using a variety of data sets to test various thresholds of convolutional neural network (CNN) based object detection algorithms (Alganci et al., 2020).

In their research, Alganci et al., (2020) used very high-resolution satellite images from the Pleiades satellite to train and perform an evaluation on the Faster R-CNN, Single Shot Multibox Detection (SSD) and You Only Look Once (YOLO) neural network detection models. The task was to detect airplanes from the retrieved satellite images. Data augmentation was used to artificially increase the number of training set data and a non-maximum suppression algorithm was applied to the SSD (with InceptionV2 as the base network) and YOLO models to eliminate multiple detections. The models were applied to a test set, which consisted of five images covering airports and adjoining areas. The results showed that Faster R-CNN gave the best accuracy in terms of the F1 scores and average precision metrics. YOLO-v3 performed second best but had a decent trade-off between accuracy and speed. The SSD performed lowest in terms of object detection but scored high in object localization. The results also showed the algorithms performed best with images that had bigger objects (airplanes).

Chandan et al., (2018) trained a model using the SSD algorithm (with Google's VGG 16 as the base architecture) to detect 21 object classes. But in this case, they wanted to use the model on video data, not still images. They also developed a python program, and along with the SSD model, OpenCV, and video input from cameras, they were able to detect and track objects in the video feed with up to 99% confidence level in some classes.

Chadalawada (2020) similarly performed experiments at a scaled construction site to detect three types of vehicles - hauler, excavator, and wheeled loader - in real-time using Faster R-CNN, YOLOv3, and Tiny-YOLOv3, for an autonomous driving system. The differences between YOLOv3 and Tiny-YOLOv3 are that Tiny-YOLOv3 consists of 13 convolutional layers and 8 max-pool layers, while YOLOv3 has 75 convolutional layers plus 31 other layers making it have an overall count of 106 layers (Redmond & Farhadi, 2018). These experiments by Chadalawada (2020) showed that YOLOv3 was most accurate at 89.51%, Faster R-CNN at 84.07%, and Tiny-YOLOv3 at 74.05%. The reason given for YOLOv3's high accuracy score is because of its architecture, where detections are done at three different image scales, making it suitable for detecting small or partly visible objects.

Qiang et al., (2020) experimented with the performance of the existing object detection algorithms and identified some shortcomings, amongst which include: false detection may occur due to overlap and occlusion, interference due to the complex background can make detection difficult, some algorithms having slow speed, hence making them unsuitable for object detection using video streams as input. With these drawbacks in mind, they proposed a new object detection algorithm by jointing semantic segmentation. Subsequently, they tested the accuracy of their algorithm against Faster R-CNN, SSD, and Mask R-CNN using the PASCAL VOC 2012 dataset and obtained a mean accuracy precision value of 79.4%, which was higher than the other three traditional algorithms, because Faster R-CNN got 70.4%, SSD 72%, and Mask R-CNN 74.9%. The detection speed of their new algorithm was 24 frames per second;

lower only than SSD which is at 46fps, with the other two algorithms having only 5 fps. When the four algorithms were tested using the Microsoft COCO dataset, a similar trend was observed with the new algorithm having better readings than the existing ones.

Weapon Detection Using Artificial Neural Networks

Gonzalez et al. (2020) trained a Faster R-CNN model using an image dataset obtained from a real CCTV installed on a university campus for weapon detection in real-time. The model was able to achieve a 90 ms inference time, which was an improvement on the state-of-the-art two-stage weapon detection models. They observed that their proposal improved what was obtained by Olmos et al. (2018), by 3.91% in precision and 2.25% in F1, although having the same recall. They also noted that adding synthetic images to the dataset in addition to the real images improved the average precision by 0.8 points and also increased the average precision of small objects. Even though the model showed improvements in average precision, it is still considered low for small and medium objects. This was due to the poor visibility as a result of the movement, distance, and occlusion of the weapons. They noted that one of the major challenges in weapon detection using CCTV is the distance of the object from the camera because the detection improves only when the object is closer to the camera.

Another issue regarding the usage of CNNs for weapons detection is the detection of small objects (Gonzalez et al., 2020). Salido et al. (2021) tried addressing this by introducing pose information that is associated with how handguns that belong to the training set are being held. They trained a YOLOv3 model and a RetinaNet model with ResNet-50 as the backbone. The results obtained showed that RetinaNet had average precision of 96.36% and recall of 97.23% while YOLOv3 had 96.23% precision and an F1 score of 93.36%. They noted that YOLOv3 had the best improvements when pose information was added to the training dataset. They suggested using LSTM (long-term short memory) to add a variation of the pose in time, to see if that will further improve the accuracy of the models.

Carrobles et al. (2019) used the Faster R-CNN framework to develop a system for gun and knife detection. They used two approaches by having the base networks be GoogleNet and SqueezeNet to train the models on 15,000 images (originally 3,000 images were in the dataset, but augmentation techniques were applied to increase the number to 15,000). The results they observed showed that SqueezeNet backbone performed better for gun detection, having an average precision of 85.45% while GoogleNet performed better for knife detection, achieving an average precision of 46.68%. Kayalvizhi et al., (2020) used X-ray images to train the YOLOv3 algorithm using two backbone networks, InceptionV3 and ResNet-50 to detect sharp objects: Knives, Trenches, Pliers, and Scissors. The YOLOv3 with InceptionV3 backend was able to achieve a mean accuracy of 59.95% while the YOLOv3 with ResNet-50 backend achieved 63.35%. This showed that YOLOv3 with ResNet-50 backend had a roughly 2% increase in average precision compared to YOLOv3 with InceptionV3 as the backend.

Narejo et al., (2021) developed a smart surveillance system by training the YOLOv3 object detection algorithm on a custom dataset to detect guns and rifles. They showed that YOLOv3 outperforms YOLOv2 and the other traditional convolutional neural networks used in object detection. Ashraf et al., (2022) Proposed a framework based on You only look once (YOLO) and Area of Interest (AOI) with the aim to minimize the rate of false negatives and false positives in weapon detection, the research also showed that YOLO made it possible for high recall rate and speed of detection to be achieved, with speed reaching 0.010 s per frame.

Fatty and Saleh., (2022) investigated how to enable delay-sensitive applications in IoT contexts by integrating deep learning techniques with Software-Defined Network (SDN) architecture. They used the deployment of weapon detection in real-time video surveillance systems as the case study, and trained and assess different deep learning-based models for detection using precision, recall, and mean absolute precision. Aiming to improve Performance which will be achieved in terms of delay, by dynamically configuring the network to deliver varying QoS based on the type of supplied traffic, the present traffic load, and the destination of the traffic, it is possible to meet throughput and bandwidth requirements. Using the Mininet emulator to assess the suggested model's performance, it was shown that average throughput, mean jitter, and packet loss could all be improved by up to 75.0%, 14.7%, and 32.5%, respectively.

Ahmed et al., (2022) In contrast to previously suggested systems in the literature, the real-time weapon identification system they proposed and described in this work claim to exhibit a higher mean average precision (mAP) score and superior inference time performance. They constructed a cutting-edge Scaled-YOLOv4 model with a custom weaponry dataset, yielding 85.7 frames per second (FPS) on a powerful GPU and a 92.1 mAP score (RTX 2080TI). Additionally, using the TensorRT network optimizer, they adapted the model for use on the popular Jetson Nano GPU to benefit from lower latency, faster throughput and improved privacy.

Research Gap and Contribution to the Knowledge

Object detection algorithms can be classified into one-stage and two-stage detection algorithms (Erabati et al., 2020). One-stage algorithms include YOLO, SSD, etc. while two-stage algorithms include Faster-RCNN, RPN, RFCN, etc. Though a lot of research has been carried out to compare the performance of various object detection algorithms, they mostly comprise comparing algorithms that perform one-stage and two-stage detections. Therefore, from the reviewed literature, it was observed that most research was focused on the comparison of one-stage against two-stage algorithms. This leaves out exclusively comparing one-stage algorithms against each other. The review of the literature also showed that there was little research that was done to detect rifles, using only YOLOv3 and RetinaNet, the models chosen for this project. Therefore, it is necessary to carry out research in order to evaluate the existing state-of-the-art one-stage deep learning models to identify the best model for object detection. One-stage algorithms are mainly concerned with speed as well as the accuracy of prediction, some one-stage algorithms can have a processing speed of as much as 155 frames per second (Redmon et al., 2016), which implies that they can be used in real-time scenarios. Hence, this research is focused on finding the performance levels of two, one-stage deep learning algorithms used for object detection.

As a consequence of carrying out this research, the following are some of the contributions to knowledge that have been highlighted: In trying to determine what one-stage algorithm to use in object detection, this study can be used to support the claim that YOLOv3 can perform better than RetinaNet in detecting objects, to be more precise rifles. This study also shows that there are tasks such as monitoring a CCTV for specific objects or situations, that can be automated or a certain level of automation can be introduced.

RESEARCH METHODOLOGY AND APPROACH

The research methodology is presented in this section. The artificial neural network frameworks, as well as the tools and environments that were used to train and test the object detection models, are considered. The performance metrics used in evaluating the models are also explained.

Theoretical Background

Convolutional Neural Network (CNN)

Convolutional Neural Networks are one out of many existing types of artificial neural networks, others include Radial basis function neural networks, Feed-forward neural networks, Recurrent neural networks, etc. (Chadalawada, 2020). Out of these many networks, convolutional neural networks are more adept at applications such as image recognition, natural language processing, etc. A CNN is a deep neural network that has many layers, usually divided into 3 important categories - convolution layer, pooling layer, and fully connected layer. Before convolutional neural networks gained popularity, various techniques have been used by experts to design feature extractors used in machine learning (Kim, 2017). These feature extractors were usually manually designed, independent of machine learning, take a significant amount of time and cost, and still give inconsistent results. With CNN however, the feature extractor is automated, consisting of neural networks connected with weights, and is included as part of the whole training process. This automation is one of the most advantageous features that CNN has when it comes to image recognition.

It was observed that the deeper the neural network used in feature extraction, the better that CNN performs object detection (Kim, 2017), albeit with more complexities when performing training. In a simple overview, the architecture of a CNN consists of a neural network for feature extraction and another one for classification, as shown in Figure 3.

Figure 3. Architecture of CNN
(Source: Kim, 2017)

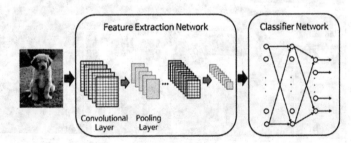

As seen in the Figure 3, the feature extraction network consists of many convolutional layers and pooling layer pairs. The convolutional layer, also known as filters, performs some convolution operations on the image while the pooling layer reduces the dimension of the image by combining adjacent pixels.

You Only Look Once (YOLO)

YOLO is an approach to object detection that has speed at its core, making it suitable for real-time detection. Originally developed by Redmon et al. (2016), the base model can process images at 45 frames per second while a smaller variant of it, Fast YOLO can go as high as 155 fps. The YOLO system works by first resizing the input image to 448 x 448, then it runs a single CNN on the image, and finally, it applies a non-max suppression algorithm to the resulting output (detections). YOLO is a very good algorithm for object detection because it is fast, has high accuracy, and has excellent learning capabilities. YOLOv3 has relatively speedy inference times with it taking roughly 30ms per inference. It takes around 270 megabytes to store the approximately 65 million parameter model. While it is fast, it still has an accuracy deficiency compared to other models (Redmon et al., 2016).

The YOLO algorithm was designed to work using the following processes:

1. Residual blocks
2. Bounding box regression
3. Intersection Over Union (IOU)

Residual Blocks

Here, the image gets divided into grids. Each grid is square-shaped having a dimension of S× S as shown in Figure 4.

Figure 4. Grids on an image
(Karimi, 2021)

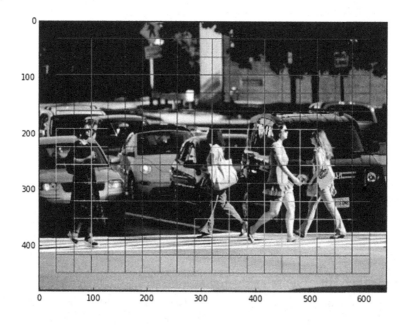

Each cell is tasked with detecting objects that appear in them. This means that if an object's center appears in a particular cell, the cell is then tasked with detecting the whole object.

Bounding Box Regression

A bounding box is usually a rectangular or square-shaped box or outline that depicts where an object is in an image. A bounding box is usually represented by:

y = (pc, bx, by, bh, bw, c)

where p_c is the probability of the object being class c,

b_x and by are the bounding box center
b_w and b_h are the width and height of the bounding box
c is the class being detected.

Figure 5. Bounding box
(Karimi, 2021)

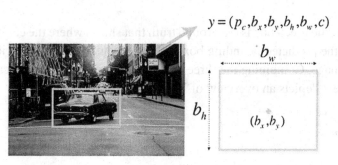

Figure 5 shows an image with a yellow bounding box. This shows the probability of an object being within the bounding box.

Intersection Over Union (IOU)

YOLO uses the IOU value to determine which bounding box to draw over an object that is being detected. IOU is a means of determining how a predicted or candidate box overlaps with the ground truth. Each grid cell predicts bounding boxes and confidence values for objects. An IOU value of 1 means that the predicted bounding box is the same as the ground truth, while an IOU of zero means that the bounding box does not even intersect the ground truth. The concept of bounding boxes is important because it helps to eliminate bounding boxes that are not the same or close to the ground truth.

Figure 6. IOU.
(Karimi, 2021)

As seen in Figure 6, the green box is the ground truth that shows where the cat is located in the image, while the blue box is the predicted bounding box with an acceptable IOU that tries to detect where the cat is located in the image. Combining the three outlined steps, YOLO can effectively detect an object from an image, Figure 7 depicts an overview of YOLO.

Figure 7. YOLO summary
(Source: Redmond, 2016)

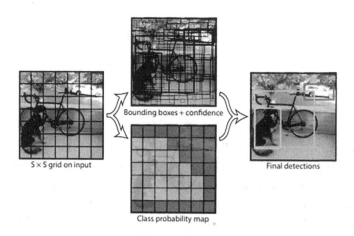

YOLOv3 Architecture

YOLOv2, which was the predecessor of YOLOv3 (Figure 8) used a feature extractor that consisted of 19 convolutional layers, known as Darknet-19, YOLOv3 on the other hand uses Darknet-53 as the feature extractor, which uses 53 convolutional layers (Almog, 2020; Mantripragada, 2020). The algorithm uses a further 53 layers for detection, making it have a total of 106 fully convolutional layer architectures.

The YOLOv3 algorithm performs detection at three different scales, where detection kernels are applied to feature maps at three places in the network; these are at the 82nd, 94th, and 106th layers (Chadalawada, 2020). Taking an input image 416 x 416 for example, up until the 82nd layer, the image will continually be downsampled. The 82nd layer uses a feature map of size 13 x 13 to perform the first detection at scale 3, resulting in a feature map that is of size 13 x 13 x 255 since the kernel size is 1 x 1 (Mantripragada, 2020). Subsequently, the second detection at scale 2 occurs at the 94th layer. For this, the feature map from the 79th layer is subjected to some convolution layers and up-sampled, which results in a dimension of 26 x 26. This feature map is then joined with the feature map from the 61st layer with 1 x 1 convolution layers resulting in a feature map at the 94th layer of size 26 x 26 x 255. Similarly, for the third detection, the feature map from the 91st layer is up-sampled 2x and convoluted to result in a feature map of dimensions 52 x 52. This is further joined with the feature map from the 36th layer and subjected to a 1 x 1 convolutional layer. The result is a feature map of 52 x 52 x 255 at the 106th layer which is used to detect objects at scale 1.

Figure 8. YOLOv3 architecture
(Wu et al., 2019)

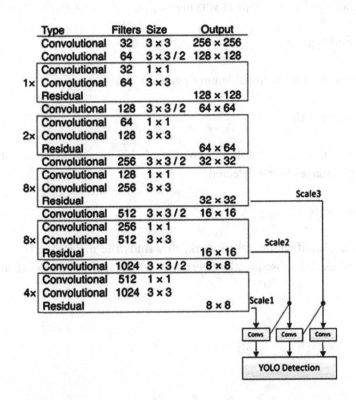

RetinaNet

RetinaNet is also a single-stage network that has a backbone network and two-task-specific subnetworks (Lin et al., 2017). A convolutional feature map is computed from the backbone network. This feature map serves as the input to the first subnet, and it is where object classification takes place. The second subnet is used for bounding box regression. RetinaNet achieves its high accuracy by introducing the concept of feature pyramid networks (FPN) (Lin et al., 2017) and focal loss (Lin et al., 2020).

A fundamental challenge in computer vision is being able to identify objects at varying scales (Lin et al., 2017). Adelson et al. (1984) proposed a solution that became a standard, called featurized image pyramids. These were used a lot in the early days of computer vision when hand-engineered features were prominent (Dalal & Triggs, 2005). However, these hand-engineered features have been replaced with features that were computed by convolutional networks (Krizhevsky et al., 2012). This allowed for representing higher-level semantics as well as features at varying scales (He et al., 2015). The main advantage of having FPN is that it allows strong multi-scale feature representation for all levels (Lin et al., 2017).

RetinaNet Architecture

The RetinaNet network architecture (Figure 9) comprises of

- A Backbone network

This is used to calculate the feature maps at varying scales, regardless of the input image size.

- A Feature Pyramid Network

This generates a multiscale convolutional feature pyramid

- Classification subnetwork

This classifies or predicts the probability of an object being present in a particular position by drawing anchor boxes of the images being detected

- Regression subnetwork

In parallel with the classification subnetwork, this finds the difference between anchor boxes to ground-truth object boxes and subsequently determines which anchor box to use as the output.

Figure 9. RetinaNet Architecture
(Lin et al., 2020)

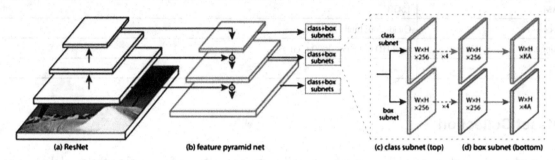

Proposed Solution

There are quite a several one-stage algorithms used by researchers in object detection including SSD, YOLO, RetinaNet, etc. For this work, the one-stage algorithms chosen are YOLO and RetinaNet. These algorithms were trained on an image dataset on Google Colab. Although the underlying architectures of the algorithms differ, the processes involved in training and testing the models are similar and are outlined below. The reason for choosing deep learning models is that they are adept at working with large data.

Experimental Setup

Even though machine learning models can be trained on computers running only a CPU, it will be slow and training will take a very long time. For that reason, it is advisable to run the training on a computer running a GPU to aid processing. Consequently, Google's Co-laboratory environment was used to set up and execute the project, both training, and detection. For this project, two Google Co-laboratory notebooks were created, one for YOLOv3 and RetinaNet, and the appropriate code was written for each. The Co-laboratory environment configurations used are summarized in Table 1.

Table 1. Google Co-laboratory Environment

GPU	NVIDIA Tesla K80 (12GB)
RAM	12GB
Disk	78GB
Tensorflow	2.6.0
Cudnn	7.6.5
Cuda	10.1
Python	3.7.12

The Google Co-lab notebooks were accessed via a Google Chrome browser running on a Mac Mini macOS Catalina computer having the following specifications as shown in Table 2.

Table 2. Hardware Environment

RAM	16GB
Processor	Quad-Core Intel Core i7
Graphics	Intel HD Graphics 4000 (2GB)
Disk	500GB

Dataset Collection

This involves the collection of the images that will serve as the basis for training the model. As a rule of thumb in deep learning, it is ideal to have at least 1000 images per class in the dataset (Chadalawada, 2020). To achieve this, and also avoid problems such as overfitting, data augmentation methods were applied to the dataset. Data augmentation involves zooming, flipping, panning, etc. of the images to create more variations of the images. Since the object of interest in this project is a rifle, there is only one class. Therefore, a total of 2105 images, comprising various rifles were collated to form the whole dataset for this project. 1857 of those images formed the training dataset. 1746 of those images were obtained from the Google Open Images Dataset Rifles collection, while 111 were downloaded from a Google Image search using the term 'Rifle'. For the testing and validation, it is advisable to feed the trained models images that had not been seen during training. Therefore, 248 images from 2105 were used to make up the test and validation dataset. Some video clips were used for testing and evaluation as well.

Data Pre-processing

This involves ensuring that the sizes and dimensions of the images being fed into the model are in a format that the model can use. Some models may want an image to be in the dimension 608 x 608, while some may need it to be 416 x 416. Having the images in an undesired dimension may lead to results that are inaccurate and execution speed will also be affected. If the environment in which the model is to be trained has sufficient memory resources, not having fixed image sizes may be a good idea as it helps avoid overfitting the model on a particular image size. For this experiment, the images weren't manually resized to a specific size, although during training the models adjusted the images to a format suitable to use.

Dataset Labelling

Also referred to as image annotation, this involves drawing bounding boxes on the particular object of interest in an image and giving it a class so that the model can learn from it. The collated images were labeled using a software called 'LabelImg'. These annotated images are what will comprise the training set for the algorithms. The test data set was also annotated because the annotation is what will be used to calculate the performance metrics during testing. Figure 10 shows an interface of LabelImg with an image that has been annotated. When the bounding box has been drawn on an object, LabelImg outputs an annotation file that contains the details of such annotations including the image name and path, the class name of the selected object(s) as well as the coordinates of the bounding box(es). The format of the annotation file depends on the algorithm it's intended for. Since the experiment involved using two different algorithms, the YOLOv3 algorithm required the annotation to be in a .txt file while RetinNet uses the PASCAL VOC format, which is a .xml file.

Figure 10. Bounding Box on LabelImg Interface

Framework

TensorFlow's Object Detection API, OpenCV, and Python were used to build and train the models. The TensorFlow API is a leading industry tool when performing object detection tasks, and was utilized for training and testing the YOLOv3 and RetinaNet algorithms.

Configuration

To effectively train and test the two models for this project, various changes were made to the default configuration files. These involve specifying things like what classes the models will act on, what the batch sizes are, how many epochs to train on, where to save snapshots of the model during training, etc.

Training

The experiment involves training two models that use the YOLOv3 and RetinaNet implementations. The models used were: for YOLOv3, the training was started using darknet (Redmond, 2016) which had weights trained on the COCO dataset, while for RetinaNet, Fizyr's RetinaNet implementation using ResNet50 backbone was used to kickstart the training. This means that transfer learning was used to train and adapt the weights to be able to detect the new class, that is a rifle. In both instances, the training keeps a 'step' or 'epoch' count, that is how many iterations of the training the model should do. When the training starts, the step count and classification loss are usually displayed on the screen. The loss value usually begins at a high value but as the training iteration goes on, it will be noticed that the loss value generally decreases. This is shown in Figure 11. After each iteration, the model calculates the loss values and keeps optimizing until an acceptable level of loss is reached, generally under 2.0.

Figure 11. Starting YOLOv3 Training

Performance Metrics

The performance of the models was evaluated using the following metrics:

Accuracy

This is defined as the number of correct predictions overall predictions made by the model. This can be represented as:

$$\text{Correct Predictions} = \text{True Positives} + \text{True Negatives} \tag{3.1}$$

$$\text{Total predictions} = CP + \text{False Positives} + \text{False Negatives} \tag{3.2}$$

$$\text{Accuracy} = \frac{CP}{TP} \tag{3.3}$$

F1 Score

This is also referred to as the harmonic mean of Precision and Recall:

$$\text{F1 Score} = \frac{2 * Precision * Recall}{\left(Precision + Recall\right)} \tag{3.4}$$

Where:

Precision: number of true positives over total positives predicted.

$$Precision = \frac{TruePositives}{\left(TruePositives + FalsePositives\right)} \tag{3.5}$$

Recall: the number of true positives over the sum of true positives and false negatives.

$$Recall = \frac{TruePositives}{\left(TruePositives + FalseNegatives\right)} \tag{3.6}$$

RESULT, ANALYSIS, AND DISCUSSION

Overview

The methods and steps outlined in Section 3 were followed and two models using the YOLOv3 and RetinaNet algorithms were trained on Google Co-lab. After the training, the models were subjected to perform detection tasks on the test dataset containing 248 images. Figure 12, Figure 13, Figure 14 and Figure 15 show some of the predictions done by the trained YOLOv3 and RetinaNet models. It can be seen that the models were able to correctly predict some objects, with very high confidence levels. However, on some images, one algorithm will correctly detect the object of interest in that image, but the other algorithm may completely miss it, as seen in Figures 14 and 15. A summary of the results obtained is shown in Table 3, and the values were used to calculate the performance metrics: Accuracy, F1 score, and the map.

Note that for the YOLOv3 predictions, predicted bounding boxes by the model, the confidence level, and the object class are what is shown, but for the RetinaNet output, it shows the ground truth box in red, the predicted bounding box in blue, and then the class and confidence level.

Figure 12. YOLO prediction

Figure 13. RetinaNet prediction

Figure 14. YOLO prediction

Figure 15. RetinaNet failed prediction (no blue box)

Discussion of Result

Table 4.1 shows a representation of the results obtained by the algorithms after performing evaluations on a test dataset containing 248 images with an intersection over a union threshold of 0.5.

Accuracy

This refers to how well a model can correctly predict a bounding box on an object if the object is present in an image, or not draw a bounding box if that object is not present in an image. The higher the accuracy of a model, the better its performance. The true positives, false positives, and false negative readings of the two models are shown in Table 3.

Table 3. Calculated Values

Algorithm	YOLOv3	RetinaNet
True Positives	220	215
False Positives	41	45
False Negatives	95	100

From the values obtained in Table 4.1, the accuracy of YOLOv3 has been calculated to be 61.80% and that of RetinaNet has been calculated to be 59.72% and it is visualized in Figure 16. This means that the YOLOv3 model is expected to perform slightly better than the RetinaNet model. This possibly explains why in the image in Figure 13, the YOLOv3 model was able to detect and print bounding boxes for the objects but the RetinaNet model (Figure 15) was unable to detect the presence of the rifles (objects).

Figure 16. Accuracy

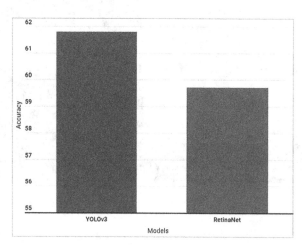

F1 Score

Another metric used to measure the accuracy of a model is the F1 score. It is defined as the harmonic mean of precision and recall. Therefore, to calculate the F1 score, the precision and recall of the model have to be calculated first.

Precision

The precision of a model is a fraction of the true positives against the total number of positive predictions made by the model, both true positives and false positives.

From Table 3, the precision was obtained as follows: for YOLOv3, the true positives were 220 and the false positives were 41. This gives a precision value of 0.8429. On the other hand, RetinaNet had 215 true positives and 45 false positives, this gives it a precision of 0.8269. This shows that YOLOv3 has a higher precision than RetinaNet allowing it to detect smaller objects better because it does its detections at three different scales.

Recall

Sometimes called the sensitivity of a model, recall is a fraction of true positive readings against all possible occurrences of an object, that is true positives and false negatives.

From Table 3, YOLOv3 had true positives to be 220 and false negatives to be 95. This gives YOLOv3 a recall of 0.6984. RetinaNet had true positives to be equal to 215 and false negatives to be 100. Its recall is then equal to 0.6825.

Using the Precision and Recall values obtained from the previous calculations, the F1 score for YOLOv3 and RetinaNet can then be calculated thus:

$$F_1 = \frac{2 X Precision * Recall}{Precision + Recall}$$

$$F_{1\ YOLOv3} = \frac{2 X 0.8429 * 0.6984}{0.8429 + 0.6984} = 0.7639$$

$$F_{1\ RetinaNet} = \frac{2 X 0.8269 * 0.6825}{0.8269 + 0.6825} = 0.7478$$

A graphical representation of the F1 score for YOLOv3 and RetinaNet is shown in Figure 17.

Figure 17. Graphical F1

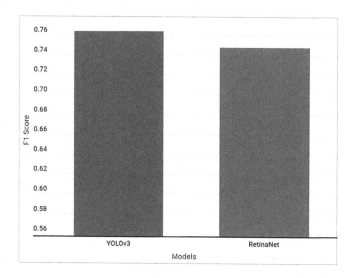

F1 Score

The results obtained for the F1 score depicted in Figure 17 are in line with what has been obtained by other researchers when evaluating deep learning models for object detection. Olmos et al. (2018), in creating an alarm system that detects small weapons performed various experiments on different datasets and got F1 scores ranging from 0.20 to the highest of 0.9143. Similarly, Warsi et al. (2019) and Mehta et al. (2020) used YOLOv3 for training object detection models and obtained an F1 score of 0.75 and 0.8548 respectively. These validate the results obtained in this research since it's in line with what has been observed by other researchers, even though on different datasets.

However, this study further showed that it is possible to apply machine learning and more specifically deep learning frameworks to help solve problems around security. It showed that it is possible to build and deploy a system that, in collaboration with a human supervisor, can be of great help in achieving better security whether in residential or official environments. The outcome of this research also implies that deep learning has a lot of potential application areas, which when appropriately implemented can help achieve more significant successes than what is currently being obtained. Research such as those in medicine, agriculture, and many others are possible areas in which deep learning models can be used, and by so doing further drive efficiency in those areas.

CONCLUSION

Computer vision is an increasingly popular field, with lots of applications that directly affect humans. It is therefore important to have models that give good performance and results. In this chapter, a study on the performance evaluation of two deep learning algorithms was carried out. The experiments carried out in this research focused on two deep learning algorithms YOLOv3 and RetinaNet. The models were trained and evaluated using a custom dataset consisting of 2105 images of different sizes and different orientations of the object of interest. 1857 of the images formed the training dataset, while 248 images were used for the testing and evaluation of the trained models. The objective was to check the performance of the models using these criteria: accuracy, precision, recall, and the F1 score. These will give an idea of how well the models are performing when undertaking prediction tasks on previously unseen datasets. The results obtained were presented in the preceding chapter.

An analysis of Figures 12 to 15 showed that the models perform differently on the same test data even though they had been trained on the same training set. This difference in performance can be attributed to the backbone architecture which each algorithm uses. The analysis of the result showed that YOLOv3 had better accuracy than RetinaNet. This consequently implied that YOLOv3 had better results in terms of precision, recall, and the F1 score. It was observed that YOLOv3 was able to pick up detections for objects that RetinaNet had missed, but the reverse was rarely seen. Although the YOLOv3 model was adjudged to perform better than RetinaNet, it also did miss out on some detections, and coupled with its accuracy value, it implies that there is room for improvement and that the model can be made to perform even better.

Future work may consider the evaluation of algorithm performance by using a much larger training dataset and employing augmentation techniques on the dataset. These will help in raising the performance levels of the models after training. Also, various configuration settings can be tried or experimented with, e.g. batch sizes, when performing training to see whether certain batch sizes can positively impact the accuracy of the final model after training. Trying out different application areas or problem domains can also be explored.

REFERENCES

Aaron, J. (2015). Everything You Need to Know About Artificial Neural Networks. *The Medium*. https://medium.com/technology-invention-and-more/everything-you-need-to-know-about-artificial-neural-networks-57fac18245 a1

Adelson, E. H., Anderson, C. H., Bergen, J. R., Burt, P. J., & Ogden, J. M. (1984). Pyramid methods in image processing. *RCA Engineer*, *29*(6), 33–41.

Agostinelli, F., Hoffman, M., Sadowski, P., & Baldi, P. (2015). Learning Activation Functions to Improve Deep Neural Networks. *International Conference on Learning (ICLR)*. arXiv.

Ahmed, S., Bhatti, M. T., Khan, M. G., Lövström, B., & Shahid, M. (2022). Development and Optimization of Deep Learning Models for Weapon Detection in Surveillance Videos. *Applied Sciences, 12*(12), 5772. doi:10.3390/app12125772

Ainsworth, T. (2002). *Buyer beware*. Security Oz.

Alganci, U., Soydas, M., & Sertel, E. (2020). Comparative Research on Deep Learning Approaches for Airplane Detection from Very High-Resolution Satellite Images. *Remote Sensing, 12*(3), 458. doi:10.3390/rs12030458

Almog, U. (2020). YOLO V3 Explained. *Towards Data Science*. https://towardsdatascience.com/yolo-v3-explained-ff5b850390f

An, Y.-K., Kim, M. K., & Sohn, H. (2012). 03 30). Airplane hot spot monitoring using integrated impedance and guided wave measurements. *Structural Control and Health Monitoring*, *19*(7), 592–604. doi:10.1002tc.1493

Ashraf, A. H., Imran, M., Qahtani, A. M., Alsufyani, A., Almutiry, O., Mahmood, A., & Habib, M. (2022). Weapons detection for security and video surveillance using cnn and YOLO-v5s. CMC-Computers. *Materials & Continua*, *70*(2), 2761–2775. doi:10.32604/cmc.2022.018785

Banupriya, N., Saranya, S., Swaminathan, S., Harikumar, S., & Palanisamy, S. (2020). Animal Detection Using Deep Learning Algorithm. *Journal of Critical Reviews*, *7*(1), 434–439.

Bashbaghi, S., Granger, E., Sabourin, R., & Parchami, M. (2019). Deep learning architectures for face recognition in video surveillance. In Deep Learning in Object Detection and Recognition, 133 - 154.

Bishop, C. M. (2006). *Pattern Recognition and Machine Learning*. Springer.

Boden, M. A. (2006). *Mind As Machine: A History of Cognitive Science*. Oxford University Press.

Brownlee, J. (2019). A Gentle Introduction to Computer Vision. *Machine Learning Mastery*. https://machinelearningmastery.com/what-is-computer-vision/

Bushkovskyi, O. (2018). 4 Types of Machine Learning Algorithms. *The App Solutions*. https://theappsolutions.com/blog/development/machine-learning-algorithm-types/

Campbell, M., Hoane, J. A. Jr, & Hsu, F.-H. (2002). Deep Blue. *Artificial Intelligence*, *134*(1-2), 57–83. doi:10.1016/S0004-3702(01)00129-1

Carrobles, M. F., Deniz, O., & Maroto, F. (2019). Gun and knife detection based on Faster R-CNN for video surveillance. *Iberian Conference on Pattern Recognition and Image Analysis*, (pp. 441–452). ACM.

Chadalawada, S. K. (2020). *Real-Time Detection and Recognition of Construction Vehicles: Using Deep Learning Methods* [Master's Thesis, Blekinge Institute of Technology, Sweden]. https://www.diva-portal.org/smash/get/diva2:1414033/FULLTEXT02

Chandan, G., & Jain, A., & Mohana. (2018). Real Time Object Detection and Tracking Using Deep Learning and OpenCV. *In Proceedings of the International Conference on Inventive Research in Computing Applications (ICIRCA 2018)*, (pp. 1305 – 1308). IEEE. 10.1109/ICIRCA.2018.8597266

Dai, J., Li, Y., He, K., & Sun, J. (2016). R-FCN: Object Detection via Region-based Fully Convolutional Networks. *Advances in Neural Information Processing Systems*, *29*, 379–387.

Dalal, N., & Triggs, B. (2005). Histograms of oriented gradients for human detection. *In 2005 IEEE computer society conference on computer vision and pattern recognition (CVPR'05)*, *1*, 886 - 893. IEEE.

Erabati, G. K., Goncalves, N., & Araujo, H. (2020, 07). Object Detection in Traffic Scenarios - A Comparison of Traditional and Deep Learning Approaches. *In CS & IT Conference Proceedings, 10*(9).

Fathy, C., & Saleh, S. N. (2022). Integrating deep learning-based iot and fog computing with software-defined networking for detecting weapons in video surveillance systems. *Sensors (Basel)*, *22*(14), 5075. doi:10.339022145075 PMID:35890755

Garcia, M. C., Mateo, J. T., Benitez, P. L., & Gutierrez, J. G. (2021). On the Performance of One-Stage and Two-Stage Object Detectors in Autonomous Vehicles Using Camera Data. *Remote Sensing*, *13*(1).

Geffen, O., Yitzhaky, Y., Barchilon, N., Druyan, S., & Halachmi, I. (2020). A machine vision system to detect and count laying hens in battery cages. *Animal*, *14*(12), 2628-2634.

Girshick, R., Donahue, J., Darrell, T., & Malik, J. (2014). Rich feature hierarchies for accurate object detection and semantic segmentation. *In Proceedings of the IEEE conference on computer vision and pattern recognition*, (pp. 580 – 587). IEEE. . 10.1109/CVPR.2014.81

Gonzalez, J. L., Zaccaro, C., Alvarez-Garcia, J. A., Morillo, L. M., & Caparrini, F. S. (2020). Real-time gun detection in CCTV: An open problem. *Neural Networks*, *132*, 297–308. doi:10.1016/j.neunet.2020.09.013 PMID:32977275

Goodfellow, I., Bengio, Y., & Courville, A. (2016). *Deep Learning*. MIT Press. https://www.deeplearningbook.org/

Groener, A., Chern, G., & Pritt, M. (2019, 10). A Comparison of Deep Learning Object Detection Models for Satellite Imagery. *In 2019 IEEE Applied Imagery Pattern Recognition Workshop (AIPR)*, (pp. 1 – 10). IEEE.

Gupta, A., Puri, R., Verma, M., Gunjyal, S., & Kumar, A. (2019). Performance comparison of object detection algorithms with different feature extractors. *In 2019 6th International Conference on Signal Processing and Integrated Networks (SPIN)*, (pp. 472 – 477). Semantic Scholar.

Haenlein, M., & Kaplan, A. (2019). A Brief History of Artificial Intelligence: On the Past, Present, and Future of Artificial Intelligence. *California Management Review*, *61*(4), 5–14. doi:10.1177/0008125619864925

He, K., Zhang, X., Ren, S., & Sun, J. (2015). Spatial pyramid pooling in deep convolutional networks for visual recognition. *IEEE Transactions on Pattern Analysis and Machine Intelligence*, *37*(9), 1904–1916. doi:10.1109/TPAMI.2015.2389824 PMID:26353135

Heidenreich, H. (2018, 12 4). *What are the types of machine learning?* Towards Data Science. https://towardsdatascience.com/what-are-the-types-of-machine-learning-e2b9e5d1756f

Huang, T. S. (1996). Computer Vision: Evolution and Promise. *CERN European Organization for Nuclear Research-Reports-CERN*, 21 - 24.

Hutson, M. (2018). *How Researchers Are Teaching AI to Learn Like a Child*. Science. https://www.sciencemag.org/news/2018/05/how-researchers-are-teaching-ai-learn-child

Kanehisa, R. F., & Neto, A. d. (2019). Firearm Detection using Convolutional Neural Networks. *Proceedings of the 11th International Conference on Agents and Artificial Intelligence (ICAART 2019)*, (pp. 707-714). Scitepress.

Kang, M., & Jameson, N. J. (2018). Machine Learning: Fundamentals. In Prognostics and Health Management of Electronics: Fundamentals, Machine Learning, and the Internet of Things, (First ed., pp. 85 - 109). John Wiley & Sons Ltd.

Kaplan, A., & Haenlein, M. (2019). Siri, Siri, in my hand: Who's the fairest in the land? On the interpretations, illustrations, and implications of artificial intelligence. *Business Horizons*, *62*(1), 15–25. doi:10.1016/j.bushor.2018.08.004

Karimi, G. (2021, 04 15). *Introduction to YOLO Algorithm for Object Detection*. Section. https://www.section.io/engineering-education/introduction-to-yolo-algorithm-for-object-detection/

Kayalvizhi, R., Malarvizhi, S., Topkar, A., Vijayakumar, P., & Choudhury, S. D. (2020). Detection of sharp objects using deep neural network-based object detection algorithm. *In 2020 4th International Conference on Computer, Communication and Signal Processing (ICCCSP)*, (pp. 1 – 5). Semantic Scholar.

Kim, P. (2017). *MATLAB Deep Learning: with Machine Learning, Neural Networks and Artificial Intelligence*. Apress. doi:10.1007/978-1-4842-2845-6

Kohavi, R., & Provost, F. (1998). Glossary of terms. *Machine Learning*, *2*(2/3), 271–274.

Krishna, M. M., Neelima, M., Harshali, M., & Rao, M. V. (2018). Image classification using Deep learning. *IACSIT International Journal of Engineering and Technology*, *7*.

Krizhevsky, A., Sutskever, I., & Hinton, G. (2012). ImageNet classification with deep convolutional neural networks. *Advances in Neural Information Processing Systems*, *25*, 1097–1105.

Kumar, P., & Sharma, P. (2014). 05). Artificial Neural Networks-A Study. *International Journal of Emerging Engineering Research and Technology*, *2*(2), 143–148.

Kusetogullari, H., Demirel, H., Celik, T., & Bayindir, S. (2007). Real time detection and tracking of vehicles for speed measurement and licence plate detection. In *The Seventh IASTED International Conference on Visualization, Imaging and Image Processing*, (pp. 53 – 58). Research Gate.

Lee, H., Grosse, R., Ranganath, R., & Ng, A. Y. (2009). Convolutional deep belief networks for scalable unsupervised learning of hierarchical representations. In *Proceedings of the 26th annual international conference on machine learning*, (pp. 609 – 616). ACM.

Lewis, G. (2016). *Object Detection for Autonomous Vehicles*. Stanford University. https://web.stanford.edu/class/cs231a/prev_projects_2016/object-detection-autonomous.pdf

Li, Y., Han, Z., Xu, H., Liu, L., Li, X., & Zhang, K. (2019). YOLOv3-Lite: A Lightweight Crack Detection Network for Aircraft Structure Based on Depthwise Separable Convolutions. *Applied Sciences (Basel, Switzerland)*, *9*(18), 3781. doi:10.3390/app9183781

Liebowitz, J. (1988). *Introduction to Expert Systems*. Mitchell Publishing/McGraw Hill.

Liebowitz, J. (1995). Expert Systems: A Short Introduction. *Engineering Fracture Mechanics*, *50*(5), 601–607. doi:10.1016/0013-7944(94)E0047-K

Lin, T.-Y., Dollar, P., Girshick, R., He, K., Hariharan, B., & Belongie, S. (2017). Feature Pyramid Networks for Object Detection. *Feature pyramid networks for object detection. In Proceedings of the IEEE conference on computer vision and pattern recognition*, (pp. 2117 – 2125). IEEE.

Lin, T.-Y., Goyal, P., Girshick, R., He, K., & Dollar, P. (2020). Focal Loss for Dense Object Detection. *IEEE Transactions on Pattern Analysis and Machine Intelligence, 42*(2), 318–327. doi:10.1109/TPAMI.2018.2858826 PMID:30040631

Lin, T.-Y., Maire, M., Belongie, S., Hays, J., Perona, P., Ramanan, D., & Zitnick, L. (2014). Microsoft COCO: Common Objects in Context. *European Conference on Computer Vision*, (pp. 740-755). Springer.

Liu, W., Anguelov, D., Erhan, D., Szegedy, C., Reed, S., Fu, C. Y., & Berg, A. (2016, 10). SSD: Single shot multibox detector. In *European conference on computer vision*, (pp. 21 – 37). Springer.

Lowe, D. G. (2004). Distinctive image features from scale-invariant keypoints. *International Journal of Computer Vision, 60*(2), 91–110. doi:10.1023/B:VISI.0000029664.99615.94

Maltarollo, V. G., Honório, K. M., & da Silva, A. B. (2013). Applications of artificial neural networks in chemical problems. *Artificial neural networks-architectures and applications*, (pp. 203 – 233). Semantic Scholar..

Mantripragada, M. (2020). Digging deep into YOLO V3 - A hands-on guide Part 1. *Towards Data Science*. https://towardsdatascience.com/digging-deep-into-yolo-v3-a-hands-on-guide-part-1-78681f2c7e29

Marco, V. (2017). What is Machine Learning? A Deinition. *Expert System*. www.expertsystem.com/machine-learning-definition/

Mehta, P., Kumar, A., & Bhattacharjee, S. (2020). Fire and Gun Violence based Anomaly Detection System Using Deep Neural Networks. In *Proceedings of the International Conference on Electronics and Sustainable Communication Systems*, (pp. 199 – 204). IEEE. 10.1109/ICESC48915.2020.9155625

Narejo, S., Panday, B., Vargas, D. E., Rodriguez, C., & Anjum, R. M. (2021). Weapon Detection Using YOLO V3 for Smart Surveillance System. *Mathematical Problems in Engineering, 2021*, 9. doi:10.1155/2021/9975700

Olmos, R., Tabik, S., & Herrera, F. (2018). Automatic handgun detection alarm in videos using deep learning. *Neurocomputing, 275*, 66–72. doi:10.1016/j.neucom.2017.05.012

Ongsulee, P. (2017). Artificial Intelligence, Machine Learning and Deep Learning. *In: Fifteenth International Conference on ICT and Knowledge Engineering*. ACM.

Qiang, B., Chen, R., Zhou, M., Pang, Y., Zhai, Y., & Yang, M. (2020). Convolutional Neural Networks Based Object Detection Algorithm by Jointing Semantic Segmentation for Images. *Sensors (Basel), 20*(18), 5080. doi:10.339020185080 PMID:32906755

Redmond, J. (2016). Darknet: Open Source. *Neural Networks*. https://pjreddie.com/darknet/

Redmond, J., Divvala, S., Girshick, R., & Farhadi, A. (n.d.). You Only Look Once: Unified, Real-Time Object Detection. *In Proceedings of the IEEE conference on computer vision and pattern recognition*, (pp. 779 – 788). IEEE.

Redmond, J., & Farhadi, A. (2017). YOLO9000: Better, Faster, Stronger. *2017 IEEE Conference on Computer Vision and Pattern Recognition (CVPR)*, (pp. 6517-6525). IEEE. 10.1109/CVPR.2017.690

Redmond, J., & Farhadi, A. (2018). Yolov3: An incremental improvement. In Computer Vision and Pattern Recognition, 1804 - 2767.

Rodriguez, R. V. (2020). The Reality About Object Detection As A Computer Vision Task. *Analytics India Magazine*. https://analyticsindiamag.com/the-reality-about-object-detec tion-as-a-computer-vision-task/

Rumelhart, D. E., Hinton, G. E., & Williams, R. J. (1986). Learning representation by back-propagating errors. *Nature, 323*(6088), 533 - 536.

Russell, S., & Norvig, P. (2010). *Artificial Intelligence A Modern Approach* (3rd ed.). Prentice Hall.

Salido, J., Lomas, V., Santaquiteria, J. R., & Deniz, O. (2021, 06). Automatic Handgun Detection with Deep Learning in Video Surveillance Images. *Applied Sciences, 11*, 6085.

Searle, I. R., Ziola, S. M., & Seidel, B. (1997). Crack detection on a full-scale aircraft fatigue test. *In Smart Structures and Materials 1997. Smart Sensing, Processing, and Instrumentation, 3042*, 267–277.

Sharma, K. U., & Thakur, N. V. (2017). A review and approach for object detection in images. *International Journal of Computational Vision and Robotics, 7*(1 - 2), 196 - 237.

Silver, D., Schrittweiser, J., Simonyan, K., Antonoglou, I., Huang, A., Guez, A., & Hassabis, D. (2017). Mastering the game of Go without human knowledge. *Nature, 550*(7676), 354–359. doi:10.1038/nature24270 PMID:29052630

Szeliski, R. (2010). *Computer Vision: Algorithms and Applications*. Springer.

Velastin, S. A., Boghossian, B. A., & Vincencio-Silva, M. A. (2006). A motion-based image processing system for detecting potentially dangerous situations in underground railway stations. *Transportation Research Part C, Emerging Technologies, 14*(2), 96–113. doi:10.1016/j.trc.2006.05.006

Warsi, A., Abdullah, M., Husen, M. N., Yahya, M., Khan, S., & Jawaid, N. (2019). Gun detection system using YOLOv3. *In Proc. of the 2019 IEEE 6th International Conference on Smart Instrumentation, Measurement and Applications*. IEEE.

Weizenbaum, J. (1966). ELIZA—A computer program for the study of natural language communication between man and machine. *Communications of the ACM, 9*(1), 36–45. doi:10.1145/365153.365168

Wu, F., Jin, G., Gao, M., He, Z., & Yang, Y. (2019). Helmet Detection Based on Improved YOLOv3 Deep Model. *2019 IEEE 16th International Conference on Networking, Sensing and Control (ICNSC)*, (pp. 363-368). IEEE.

Yadav, N., & Binay, U. (2017). Comparative Study of Object Detection Algorithms. *International Research Journal of Engineering and Technology, 4*(11), 586–591.

Zhang, Y., Wang, Y., Foley, J., Suk, J., & Conathan, D. (2017). Tweeting Mass Shootings: The Dynamics of Issue Attention on Social Media. *Proceedings of the 8th International Conference on Social Media & Society*, (pp. 1 – 5). ACM. 10.1145/3097286.3097345

Zhao, Z. Q., Zheng, P., Xu, S. T., & Wu, X. (2019). Object Detection with Deep Learning: A Review. *IEEE Transactions on Neural Networks and Learning Systems*, 30(11), 3212–3232. doi:10.1109/TNNLS.2018.2876865 PMID:30703038

Chapter 20
A Transfer Learning Approach for Smart Home Application Based on Evolutionary Algorithms

Mouna Afif
University of Monastir, Tunisia

Riadh Ayachi
University of Monastir, Tunisia

Yahia Said
Electrical Engineering Department, Northern Border University, Arar, Saudi Arabia

Mohamed Atri
College of Computer Science, King Khalid University, Abha, Saudi Arabia

ABSTRACT

Building new systems used for indoor sign recognition and indoor wayfinding assistance navigation, especially for blind and visually impaired persons, presents a very important task. Deep learning-based algorithms have revolutionized the computer vision and the artificial intelligence fields. Deep convolutional neural networks (DCNNs) are on the top of state-of-the-art algorithms which makes them very suitable to build new assistive technologies based on these architectures. Especially, the authors will develop a new indoor wayfinding assistance system using aging evolutionary algorithms AmoebaNet-A. The proposed system will be able to recognize a set of landmark signs highly recommended to assist blind and sighted persons to explore their surrounding environments. The experimental results have shown the high recognition performance results obtained by the developed work. The authors obtained a mean recognition rate for the four classes coming up to 93.46%.

DOI: 10.4018/978-1-6684-6937-8.ch020

1. INTRODUCTION

Indoor sign recognition and indoor wayfinding assistance present a very crucial assistance task especially for blind and visually impaired persons (VIP) to reach their destinations in a safer way. Blind persons have troubles when navigating in strange environments. They are unable to use the information posted on notice boards and indoor signs. Persons with vision impairments frequently need more help with daily tasks than people with other disabilities. A visual impairment restricts one's capacity for learning, social interaction, and object recognition. By developing new assistive systems, we can widely contribute to help persons presenting visual deficiencies to navigate safely in new unfamiliar indoor environments. Indoor sign identification and detection serve as a fundamental building block for numerous fields. It seeks to determine whether or not an indoor sign is present in the image.

Recently, deep learning architecture and deep convolutional neural networks (DCNNs) have demonstrated huge performances to perform new assistive technologies. DCNN architectures can be applied for different types of artificial intelligence and computer vision tasks. Deep learning-based models have made an outstanding success in computer vision and artificial intelligence areas.

Indoor sign recognition presents one of the most common problems that can affect the blind and the visually impaired (BVI) security. In order to ensure better life conditions for the BVI persons, new innovative and adaptive technologies and new navigational systems are increasingly needed. These new assistive technologies are generally used to ensure better inclusion of this category of persons in the social life.

Indoor wayfinding presents a crucial task for the living independent. It is exceedingly difficult to create an interior navigation system for BVI. Building such systems in indoor environments are extremely challenging due to the complexity of decoration, high occlusion, inter and intra-class class variation and different lighting conditions. Understanding indoor environments is very challenging task. Persons with limited sight face different difficulties to follow visual information in indoor places. Building low cost navigation assistance systems for BVI people is urgently needed. People rely on perception and visual information particularly to identify the surrounding objects, orientations and directions. This challenging task falls under the category of wayfinding, whereas the capacity of identifying objects and avoiding obstacles falls under the category of mobility. Currently, these are few studies or navigational aids for blinds and visually impaired in new unfamiliar environments that include various decorations which make navigation in this category of spaces challenging difficult. The vision problem significantly affects the life of affected persons and makes it difficult to carry-out their daily life activities.

We propose in his work to build a new indoor wayfinding assistance system used for BVI assistance navigation and for better social integration.

The main aim from this work is to build a new wayfinding assistance technology used to support BVI persons to freely navigate in their indoor environments without being dependent to other persons. The proposed work is developed by tacking advantages of aging evolutionary algorithms.

Training and testing experiments have been performed using the proposed indoor signage dataset. The proposed dataset counts 800 images composed of 4 landmark indoor signs. The 4 signs are: WC, exit, confidence zone and disabled exit. We note that the proposed dataset is original as it covers various challenging conditions such as: different objects viewpoints, different lighting conditions, high inter and intra-class variation and so on. We note that the proposed work presents the first work evaluating the evolutionary algorithms in indoor wayfinding assistance. Another strength of the proposed work is that it provides a new indoor sign recognition system that is able to recognize new indoor signs that were not studied before by the state-of-the-art works.

Deep learning models' ability to extract high-level feature maps from input data by using satirical learning over massive amounts of data during the training process to obtain an accurate representation of the input space is the strength behind their superior performance when compared to other traditional solutions. All of these factors distinguish this method from prior ones that used feature representation created by hand. In general, the deep CNN's greater performance is the result of its high computational complexity. Due to their ability to speed up DCNN calculation, NVIDIA graphic processing units (GPUs) have become widely used for training and testing deep CNN models.

The convergence to the best neural network architecture for a particular computer vision problem was greatly improved by bio-inspired evolution neural networks. Since the creation of the NAS search space, a new category of deep learning models known as evolving Algorithms has been introduced. A meta-learning technique offered by evolutionary algorithms simply entails creating additional levels of abstraction when deep neural networks are being trained. The terms autoML and neural architecture search strategy are used in the meta-learning component. One of the most active research areas in the field of deep learning is meta learning. The evolutionary models that were utilized in this study are a part of meta-learning approaches that try to optimize the architectures of neural networks. They were trained on a particular dataset before being generalized to a different, larger dataset.

Indoor wayfinding and sign detection presents a very crucial task that can be included in various computer vision and artificial intelligence fields. Indoor sign recognition poses an important task to fully help blind and visually impaired persons (VIP) to reach their destinations.

Blindness and visual impairments pose a serious problem that affects a huge number of persons around the world. According to the world health organization (WHO) (2021), Globally, at least 2.2 billion people have a near or distance vision impairment. At least, 1billion of persons presenting vision impairments that could be prevented or has yet to be addressed and 1 billion includes persons with moderate to severe vision impairments or blindness.

Indoor objects recognition and indoor navigation in general present a major challenge for persons with visual impairments. Knowing how to move in indoor environments is very challenging for persons with disabilities especially for blind and visually impaired users. This task can be included in various computer vision tasks including indoor objects detection (Afif, 2020a, 2020b) traffic sign detection (Ayachi, 2020a,2020b) pedestrian detection (Ayachi, 2020c, 2020d), drivers fatigue detection (Ayachi, 2021), medical image processing (Fradi, 2020a, 2020b) indoor scene recognition (Afif, 2020c), indoor wayfinding assistance navigation for blind and sighted persons (Afif, 2021) and indoor sign recognition (Afif, 2020d) (Afif, 2018).

Finding an appropriate direction in an indoor environment is very crucial to move from one place to another. Actually, one of the most human activities is presented by the perception and autonomous moving in the surroundings. As persons spend a lot of their time indoors, we propose in this chapter to address the problem of indoor objects signs recognition for indoor wayfinding assistance navigation.

Since their appearance, deep learning algorithms have shown big breakthroughs on providing very new promoting solutions for various problems. Deep learning–based techniques have improved the performances of the new developed applications through providing more accurate systems in significant number of areas.

Blindness and visual impairments affect a huge number of persons all over the world. Walking confidentially, accessing the desired destinations, and avoiding obstacles present a very easy task for persons with good sight. However, it is very challenging for blind and impaired persons.

We propose in this chapter to build new indoor sign recognition system used for indoor wayfinding assistance for blind and visually impaired persons. The proposed system is able to detect a set of 4 landmark indoor signs (wc, exit, confidence zone and disabled exit) highly recommended for indoor wayfinding assistance navigation. The proposed system is developed by using deep evolutionary neural networks with aging evolution. Training and testing experiments have been conducted on the proposed indoor sign dataset which contain 800 indoor images providing four sign categories. Experiments results have shown a big efficiency and the competitive performances of the developed indoor wayfinding assistance system. The proposed work presents the following contributions:

- This paper proposes the first method for an indoor scene identification system that uses an aging evolutionary algorithm.
- High recognition accuracy was attained by the proposed indoor sign recognition system.
- In challenging input data, the proposed method attained brand-new state-of-the-art accuracies.
- The developed indoor sign recognition method was trained using input data that has not undergo any Pre-processing for the purpose of improving the image quality.
- The proposed indoor signs dataset was used to evaluate the new proposed indoor signs identification system, which obtains the highest accuracy levels on this dataset.

2. RELATED WORKS

Indoor sign recognition presents a very challenging task to be addressed. This work is important and challenging since interior environment often have complex backgrounds that make it challenging to identify these signs. The primary goal of this work is to create a sign recognition system capable of distinguishing indoor signs under challenging conditions such as varying lighting conditions, diverse image backgrounds, and inter- and intra-class variation. An important issue in the field of image and video processing is indoor sign recognition. Numerous studies have been conducted on scene recognition. For identifying indoor signs, various programs for automatically finding have developed to a sufficient level. In this research, we implement a classification application based on RGB photos for indoor signs detection.

Indoor sign recognition presents a very active research axis as it can be applied for various applications and areas. Various works have been proposed to cover this issue. Generally, indoor navigation presents a major challenge especially for persons with visual impairments, whose always lacks accessing new environments and visual cues as information signs and landmark features. In (Fusco, 2020), authors proposed to develop a new computer vision-based localization approach which can run on a real time way on a Smartphone. The developed system can widely help visually impaired persons to access new surroundings environments.

Perception presents one of the most vital senses for human being. It is essential to recognize the surrounding objects and to find its destinations. In (Sun, 2020), authors proposed to develop a new sign detection system used for accessing indoor environments which works on real time scenario. The proposed system combines a digital map of the surrounding environment with an inertial sensing system used to estimate the user's location.

Environment perception and mobility present a very serious problem for blind and visually impaired pedestrians (Golledge, 1993; Marston, 2003). A digital sign system used for indoor wayfinding for blind and visually impaired persons is proposed in (Tjan, 2005). The developed system showed high performances for detection and recognition which can cope with real world environment.

Since 2012, deep learning –based algorithms have shown an impressive progress in computer vision and artificial intelligence fields. By using deep learning and deep convolutional neural networks (DCNN), researchers have obtained very impressive results in terms of detection and recognition precisions. A new deep learning-based

framework used for indoor location recognition is proposed in (Hanni, 2017). A deep convolutional network (DCNN) is used based on transfer learning approach used for indoor scene recognition proposed in (Basu, 2020). This system is especially used to assist elderly and visually impaired persons to identify the indoor locations. The IAS system is developed based on convolutional neural networks (CNNs) algorithms.

Modern object detectors that optimize feature representation through changes to the backbone architecture and the use of a feature pyramid have demonstrated their effectiveness and performances. Network architecture search space (NAS) algorithm has shown good performances on searching for the best network architecture that fits a specific application. In (Viriyasaranon, 2022), authors proposed a new optimization for objects detectors that provides two modules: the Capsule Attention module and the NAS-gate convolutional module. The NAS-gate convolutional module uses multiple convolution conditions and differentiable architecture search cooperation to optimize conventional convolution in a backbone network to solve object scale variation issues. In order to maximize the feature representation and localization ability of the detectors, the Capsule Attention module uses the strong spatial relationship encoding capability of the capsule network to generate a spatial attention mask that emphasizes crucial features and suppresses unimportant features in the feature pyramid.

Swarm algorithms (SAs) and evolutionary algorithms (EAs) have proven beneficial in a variety of study domains for solving combinatorial and NP-hard optimization problems. But over the past ten years, relevant surveys in the field of computer vision have not been updated. In order to make up for the dearth of pertinent research in this field, a literature review that was undertaken in this regard in(Nakane, 2020). This was motivated by the recent advancement of deep neural networks in computer vision, which integrate large-scale optimization problems. This survey focuses mostly on applications linked to the genetic algorithm, differential evolution from EAs, particle swarm optimization, and colony optimization from SAs, and their variants. Swarm algorithms (SAs) and evolutionary algorithms (EAs) are effective metaheuristic tools for overcoming combinational constraints that may not contain stable solutions or for searching for solutions within a potentially enormous solution space. In order to successfully complete a variety of computer vision tasks and avoid becoming stuck in the local optima, EAs and SAs have been successfully used. A combination evolutionary search technique for circle detection termed the chaotic hybrid algorithm (CHA) was presented by Dong et al (Dong, 2012). The typical velocity and position update principles of PSO were integrated with the concepts of selection, crossover, and mutation from the GA by the authors in order to maximize the benefits of both particle swarm optimization PSO and the genetic algorithms (GA). Specifically, in each generation, the fraction of the bottom individuals goes through breeding (selection, crossover, and mutation) after the fitness values of the people are calculated. Everybody's speeds are updated, and fresh data is gathered from the population to update the position. The chosen individual is re-initialized during the mutation process using the chaotic initialization technique.

In relation to computer vision problems, various NeuroEvolution methods that optimize the DNN structure, connection weights, and hyperparameters (particularly image classification tasks) has been proposed. Image classification recently has been one of the computer vision challenges that is being researched the most, thanks to the emergence of DNNs, especially convolutional neural networks (CNNs). A standard CNN is made up of several components, and how they are arranged impacts how well it performs. Due to this property, it is challenging to implement some NAS techniques that have been effectively used with DNNs, like random search and Bayesian optimization (Sun, 2020). In this work, authors focus on research projects that use the GA and PSO to automatically construct the best DNNs for large-scale image classification benchmarks.

We propose in this chapter to develop a new indoor sign recognition system used for indoor wayfinding assistance navigation for blind and visually impaired persons (VIP) using a set of new deep learning-based architectures named evolutionary algorithms with aging evolution. The proposed system is highly recommended for blind and VIP persons assistance navigation to help them to more integrate in the daily life and to reach their desired destinations.

The reminder of this chapter is the following: section 3 provides the proposed approach adopted for indoor wayfinding assistance navigation. Section 4 details all the experiments conducted, and the results obtained, and section 5 concludes the paper.

3. PROPOSED APPROACH FOR INDOOR WAYFINDING ASSISTANCE NAVIGATION

Since their introduction, deep convolutional neural networks have completely changed the field of computer vision. Due to the strong architectures of deep learning models, they produce accurate inferences. Deep CNN presents complex designs, though, and needs strong computational resources. That indicates that these models were developed on strong machines with strong GPUs.

In several scientific domains, deep learning models have taken the lead as the most significant state-of-the-art architectures. On a variety of computer vision applications, deep convolutional neural networks have demonstrated impressive performances with high inference accuracy.

Convolution layers, pooling layers, fully connected layers, and output layers are some of the layers that define a deep CNN. Every kind of layer carries out a particular function. The input data (images, texts, videos, and audio) are subjected to various transformations by these layers before being forwarded to the following layer.

Convolution and non-linear layers are typically followed by subsampling levels and fully connected layers in deep CNN models. Convolution, nonlinear, normalizing, and subsampling layers are often found in an architecture, which is followed by a fully linked layer. All these layers are detailed in the following.

- Convolution layers: used to perform the background convolution in a deep CNN model. Kernels that are added as parameters to these layers will be convolved with the input data during the training phase. Convolution kernels are convolved with the input data with height and depth during the testing phase. A convolution volume is the outcome. The dot product between the convolution layer and the input data serves as the primary operation that makes up the convolution layer. It is possible to think of the test on the data as a matrix multiplication. Convolution layer computations are frequently accelerated on CUDA NVIDIA GPUs using the Cublas CUDA library. Convolution layer is typically followed by a non-linear function such a sigmoid, hyperbolic tangent, RELU, etc.
- Pooling layer: these subsampling layers are typically employed to decrease the computational load and the size of the feature map. In order to reduce the size of the spatial feature map, these

kinds of layers are frequently utilized between convolution layers (height and width). According to deep CNN architectures, pooling operations are carried out on local and specialized regions. According to the state-of-the-art, average and maximum pooling are the two most often utilized pooling operations.

- Normalization layer: Deep CNN typically employs one of two normalization operations: batch normalization or local response normalization (LRN) (BN). Batch normalization normalizes the input volume for each dimension throughout the testing procedure.
- Fully convolutional layer: every neuron in this layer is linked to every neuron in the layer above it. There are several parameters that impose a strain on memory storage and computational resources because of the full connection concept in these levels. It is possible to foresee these layers and get rid of them from the CNN architecture. Matrix multiplication is also used to implement the forward pass of FC layers.

Deep CNN have demonstrated very competitive results in the artificial intelligence field. These paradigms enable computers and other technology to mimic the human brain. Artificial intelligence and machine learning are subsets of deep learning.

Deep neural networks frequently use convolutional neural networks. By utilizing deeper layers in the architecture, modern deep CNN have demonstrated their finest performances for getting superior inference scores.

Each deep CNN layer produces high-level abstraction data called features maps that contain key details of the input data.

The human brain is quite good at transferring and assimilating knowledge across a variety of tasks. It approaches every task and problem in the same way. The same method is used by DCNN models to solve new computer vision algorithms by learning from completed tasks. In comparison to other conventional methods for object detection, deep convolutional neural networks show significant differences. DCNN primarily offer a deep architecture with a significant capacity to learn challenging tasks. These expressive models offer a good feature extraction method and enable powerful object representations.

Hierarchical feature representations are a key characteristic of deep learning models. In other words, features computed in the initial layers are generated and can be applied to various tasks and domains, whilst features financed by the latter layers are particular and dependent on the selected issue and the dataset being used. A DCNN's classification section (closer to the outputs) refers to the specific features generated, while the convolution part (layers closer to the input layers) refers to general features.

Generally speaking, a deep CNN model consists of two main steps:

- Convolution background: the convolution and pooling layer stack serves as this background. In order to extract features from images, DCNN uses this component.
- Classification component: often made up of layers that are completely connected. This section's goal is to categorize things seen in the photos using the previously retrieved features.

Deep learning and deep CNN models have recently experienced extraordinary success in tasks requiring object detection and recognition. More specifically, deep CNN presents the most popular deep learning architectures in many contemporary applications and is essential to the building of deep learning models. Deep CNN are the most abstract and resistant to geometric object alterations, lighting, and distortions when compared to other classic features extraction techniques.

Deep learning–based algorithms ensure a big performance for various artificial intelligence and computer vision applications. Aiming to take advantages of deep neural networks techniques, we used a new set of deep learning techniques named evolutionary algorithms with aging evolution. The network used is named "AmoebaNet-A" (Real, 2019). Aiming to fully help blind and sighted persons to reach their desired destinations, we propose in the following to develop an indoor wayfinding assistance system based on AmoebaNet-A (Real, 2019) network. We will focus in this chapter on using evolutionary algorithms. We will show in the following that the proposed work achieves very interesting results despite it was trained and tested on various challenging conditions. Evolutionary algorithms are proposed to improve neural networks topologies and architectures. They are used to discover automatically and to search for the best architectures for a specific task. To develop the proposed indoor sign recognition system, we used the evolutionary algorithm AmoebaNet-A. The following figure 1 present the search space search architecture adopted in ImageNet (Deng, 2005) dataset adopted in our work.

Figure 1. (a) NasNet search space, (b) detailed architecture with skip input

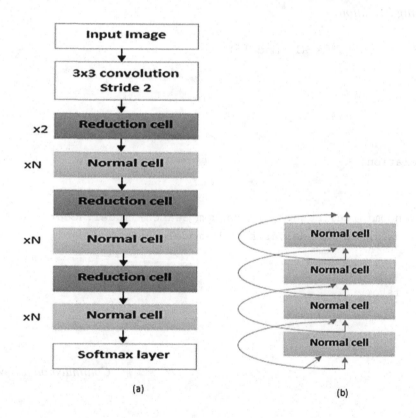

This type of architectures is especially used for classification problems. AmoebaNet family architecture is obtained by modifying the tourmenant selection evolution by adding the age property in order to favor the younger genotypes to persist more in the architecture's population. Compared to human-crafted networks, evolutionary algorithms have shown better results. To surpass the deep CNN models, AmoebaNet family introduce two main components. First it proposes to change tourmenant selection evolution and second it applies much simpler mutations in NasNet search space (Zoph, 2018). By using the aging evolution, the tourmenant selection select each genotype or architecture will be relied with an age and bias and the tourmenant selection will be charged by keeping the younger architecture: network architecture search (NAS) uses the reinforcement learning technique to optimize the network topologies. All the obtained architectures by using the NasNet search space are independent from the input image size and network depth. All the architectures obtained by NAS search space are composed of convolution layers. So, NAS search space will be charged to search for the best convolution layer or convolution cell. This fact provides two main benefits: the architecture searching process will be much faster the searching for an entire architecture and the convolution cell will be generalized to build other tasks. The stacked cells present in the obtained architectures are from two main categories: normal cells and reduction cells. These two types of cells are from the same architecture and the only difference is that after applying a reduction cell, it is followed by a stride of two which leads to reduce the feature map size. We note that the normal cells conserve the same feature map size. Algorithm 1 present all the steps used to develop the proposed indoor sign recognition system.

Algorithm 1: Aging Evolution

```
Population ←P (it contains all models)



History ← ∅



1.while |Population| <P do



model.arch← random architecture () (random search) model.accuracy← results of
train and validation of (model.arch) add model to P



add model to history



end whlile
```

Continued on following page

Algorithm 1. Continued

```
2. while|history| < C (cycle)

Samples← ∅ : Parent condidates

3.while -samples|< S do

condidates← random elements from population

add condidates to sample

end while

parent←high accuracy trained model in sample

child.arch← mutation of (parent.arch)

child.accuaracy← results of train and evaluation of (child.arch)

add child to population

add child to history

remove oldest models from population

end while return highest accuracy model in the population history (model cho-
sen to

work with)
```

So, finding the optimal architecture for the normal and reduction cell is the major goal of employing architectural search spaces. In the NasNet design, each cell has one output and two input activation tensors. The input of the second cell is made up of the outputs of the first two cells after the first cell makes two copies of the input images. The following structure is required for normal and reduction cells: the two input cells are regarded as hidden states 0 and 1. Through a process known as "pairwise combination," which entails applying operations to other hidden states already in existence and combining the results to create a new hidden state, the other hidden layers are built.

The basic idea behind the evolutionary algorithms with aging evolution is that the initial architecture population is initialized randomly and the model presenting the heights validation rate will be considered as a parent. The other architectures will be obtained using "mutation operation". Once the new architectures (child architectures) are obtained, all these models will be trained and evaluated and added to the population. This fact is named, the "tourmenant selection". The tourmenant selection will be charged by eliminating the oldest architectures present in the population. The child models are obtained by allying 3 types of mutation:

- Hidden state mutation
- Identity mutation
- Op mutation

When training the neural network, just one of these mutations is applied randomly.

The hidden state mutation initially decides whether to alter the reduction cell or the normal cell. Once the cell type has been determined, the mutation selects one pair from each of the five pairwise combinations at random. The only way the op mutation differs from a hidden state mutation is by randomly replacing the existing operation with one from a predetermined set of operations. It behaves similarly when choosing between two types of cells, one of five pairwise combinations, and one of the two elements of the pair.

The aging evolution deep learning technique was employed in our research. Because of the brief lifespans of all the models created using this method and the rapid population renewal, more model kinds are being explored. Models expire quickly, just like an aging algorithm. A model can only persist in the population for a very long time if it is passed on from parent to child through many generations.

Each inherited architecture will be retrained; if it helps produce accurate results, evolution will choose that model, else it will be eliminated from the population. Therefore, consistently doing well in retraining is the only method to ensure that a model survives in the population for a long time. Due of this aspect, we decided to use an aging algorithm in our work because it enhances the population with well-modeled designs. The population is improved by models and architectures that were taught successfully for the first time in the non-aging evolution, though.

4. EXPERIMENTS AND RESULTS

Humans are exceptionally good at accurately recognizing and classifying complicated scenes. Since convolutional neural networks excelled at recognizing scenes, we use a deep CNN architecture to create a novel program for identifying indoor scenery. Assisting in the recognition of indoor signs, which presents a simple challenge for blind and visually impaired people to explore and navigate. However, creating a new system for detecting home scenery that can discriminate various kinds of situations accurately still presents a challenging issue.

An important use of machine learning is deep neural networks. Deep CNN requires determining weight values as part of the network training process. We move on to the inference phase after the deep CNN has been trained. The neural network with weights taken from the training set is then run. Giving an input image to deep CNN prepares the inference; the result is a score vector with one vector for each class of object.

A deep CNN model can be trained in a variety of methods. In our contribution, we determined weights and bias using a fine-tuning approach. On the new job with the new dataset, the previously trained weights are used as a starting point and are then tweaked. "Transfer learning" is the name given to this idea.

When employing deep CNN models for inference (test process), we provide the model with an input, and the forward-pass result is a vector of scores, each of which is assigned to a class. The class that displays the height score denotes the object that is most likely to be in the provided image. The main goal of deep CNN model training is to compute weights and reduce the discrepancy between label and score. In other words, the goal is to decrease the scores for incorrectly categorized classes while maximizing the class score indicating the most likely class object present in the input image. We provide the deep neural network with the class label prior to training it (training set). The loss function is the difference between the actual score and the one provided by the CNN model. In order to reduce gaps over the training established by the backpropagation process, the main objective of training is to compare weights. The following is how the backpropagation operation functions: To compute how loss is achieved during the training phase, the value is sent through the deep network architecture backwards.

Our proposed system for recognizing indoor signs is constructed using neuro-evolutionary techniques. This method allows us to choose the best neural network architecture to use in our research. Gradient decent optimizer is used to acquire the weights obtained during training of the aging evolutionary neural network. AmoebaNet-free A's parameters, N and F, were as follows: N = 18 and F = 448. We use the data augmentation method to provide the model access to more training data in order to prevent overfitting.

Building new systems used for indoor signs recognition and indoor wayfinding assistance can widely help and improve the life quality for blind and visually impaired persons. To develop the proposed indoor technique which, aim to reuse the previous weights of the previous task which will be adjusted to a new task with the new dataset images. Training and testing process are conducted on the proposed dataset which is composed of 800 images containing 4 main classes highly recommended for blind and visually impaired persons indoor navigation which are (wc, exit, disabled exit and confidence zone). Each class object is presented by 200 images in the proposed dataset. Training and testing process have been conducted on a HP workstation equipped with an intel Xeon E5-2683 v4 processor with a Quadro M4000 GPU with 8 GB of graphic memory. We used the TensorFlow framework with GPU support and python 3.6 as a programming language. We note that we trained and tested the proposed work on various challenging conditions including various lighting conditions, different objects viewpoints.

The proposed indoor wayfinding assistance system is built on neuro-evolutionary method.

The dataset used in our experiments consists of 800 RGB photos divided into 4 categories and captured against various backgrounds and lighting conditions. It is very easy for a human to identify an interior scene or sign as, exit, wc, confidence zone or disabled exit, but it is exceedingly challenging for a computer to reach the same level of vision. Human perception only appears straightforward because our brains are so adept at comprehending images and the world around us. To create machines with perceptual abilities close to those of humans, massive amounts of data will be used to train models.

When using deep CNN models for inference (test process), we feed the model data and get a vector of forward-pass scores, each of which is categorized into a class. The object that is most likely to be in the provided image is indicated by the class that shows the height score. Deep CNN model training's primary objective is to compute weights and minimize the difference between label and score. In other words, the objective is to maximize the class score indicating the most likely class item existing in the input image while minimizing the scores for classes that were mistakenly classified. Prior to training, we provide the deep neural network the class label (training set).

In this regard, several tests were performed. In this work, we apply the concept of "transfer learning", which is based on an evolutionary deep CNN model that has been fully trained on a category of datasets and reused as a starting point from the existing weights, frozen as a whole model, and retrained the final layer from scratch on the new dataset for the new task.

The training set of data serves as the neural network's primary source of knowledge. It is exceedingly challenging to distinguish between these types of environments since interior areas have complicated topologies. Transfer learning will speed up the recognition process because training a deep CNN from scratch takes a long time and requires a lot of data that won't be used. It is vital to keep in mind that some photos with poor quality are utilized to test the model in order to generate ability and acquire robust recognition.

Table 1 presents all the experiments settings used during the proposed experiments.

Table 1. Experiments settings

Training steps	6000
Learning rate	0.01
Testing set	30%
Validation set	20%
Training set	50%
Train batch size	16
Validation batch size	16

In the following table 2, we provide all the per-class recognition rates obtained on the proposed dataset.

Table 2. Per-class recognition rate obtained

Class Name	Recognition Rate
Wc	94.05
Disabled exit	93.66
Exit	92.99
Confidence zone	93.14
mean	93.46

As mentioned in table 2, we obtained very encouraging recognition rates for the four indoor signs classes. We obtained 93.46% as a mean recognition rate for the four classes. Based on the obtained results, we can ensure the huge performances and the robustness of the developed wayfinding assistance system.

As far as the BVI individuals' mobility is addressed, the proposed system should provide information before the user reaches the desired objects. We assume that the optimal distance between user and object sufficient to prevent him in advance by the presence of objects is about 5 meters. We also assume that the speed of BVI person is 1.4 m/s (speed of normal person). So, the BVI person needs 3.57 s to reach the desired object. Based on all these information, the system should provide a temporal performance of 2 FPS, the proposed system achieve a processing time of 9 FPS which widely match the BVI person's needs.

5. CONCLUSION

Indoor wayfinding assistance navigation and indoor sign recognition was and still a crucial step to build various important tasks in artificial intelligence and computer vision fields. We propose in this chapter to develop a new indoor sign and wayfinding assistance system used for blind and visually impaired persons (VIP) indoor assistance navigation. To this end, we propose to use a new set of deep convolutional neural networks (DCNNs) named evolutionary algorithms with aging evolution. In order to train and test the indoor sign recognition system, we used our proposed indoor sign dataset which contain 800 images providing 4 landmark signs. The proposed work presents the first work evaluating an evolutionary algorithm with aging evolution to build such system. The developed work is especially dedicated for blind and VIP persons to fully assist them during their indoor navigation and to more participate in the daily life. Results achieved shown very encouraging performances in terms of recognition rates.

DECLARATIONS

Funding: no funding has been received.

Conflict of Interest: authors declare that there is no conflict of interest regarding the publication of this paper.

Author Contributions: All authors contributed to the study conception and design. Material preparation, data collection and analysis were performed by Mouna Afif and Riadh Ayachi. The first draft of the manuscript was written by Mouna Afif and the results evaluation and discussion has been performed by Riadh Ayachi and Yahia Said and the Mohamed Atri is the project supervisor.

Data Availability Statement: the paper does not present any associated data.

REFERENCES

Afif, M., Ayachi, R., Pissaloux, E., Said, Y., & Atri, M. (2020a). Indoor objects detection and recognition for an ICT mobility assistance of visually impaired people. *Multimedia Tools and Applications*, *79*(41), 31645–31662. doi:10.100711042-020-09662-3

Afif, M., Ayachi, R., Said, Y., & Atri, M. (2020c). Deep learning based application for indoor scene recognition. *Neural Processing Letters*, *51*(3), 2827–2837. doi:10.100711063-020-10231-w

Afif, M., Ayachi, R., Said, Y., & Atri, M. (2021). Deep learning-based application for indoor wayfinding assistance navigation. *Multimedia Tools and Applications*, *80*(18), 27115–27130. doi:10.100711042-021-10999-6

Afif, M., Ayachi, R., Said, Y., Pissaloux, E., & Atri, M. (2018). Indoor image recognition and classification via deep convolutional neural network. In *International conference on the Sciences of Electronics, Technologies of Information and Telecommunications* (pp. 364-371). Springer.

Afif, M., Ayachi, R., Said, Y., Pissaloux, E., & Atri, M. (2020b). An evaluation of retinanet on indoor object detection for blind and visually impaired persons assistance navigation. *Neural Processing Letters*, *51*(3), 2265–2279. doi:10.100711063-020-10197-9

Afif, M., Said, Y., Pissaloux, E., & Atri, M. (2020d). Recognizing signs and doors for Indoor Wayfinding for Blind and Visually Impaired Persons. In *2020 5th International Conference on Advanced Technologies for Signal and Image Processing (ATSIP)* (pp. 1-4). IEEE. 10.1109/ATSIP49331.2020.9231933

Ayachi, R., Afif, M., Said, Y., & Abdelaali, A. B. (2020c). Pedestrian detection for advanced driving assisting system: a transfer learning approach. In *2020 5th International Conference on Advanced Technologies for Signal and Image Processing (ATSIP)* (pp. 1-5). IEEE. 10.1109/ATSIP49331.2020.9231559

Ayachi, R., Afif, M., Said, Y., & Abdelali, A. B. (2020b). Traffic Sign Recognition Based On Scaled Convolutional Neural Network For Advanced Driver Assistance System. In *2020 IEEE 4th International Conference on Image Processing, Applications and Systems (IPAS)* (pp. 149-154). IEEE. 10.1109/IPAS50080.2020.9334944

Ayachi, R., Afif, M., Said, Y., & Abdelali, A. B. (2021). Drivers Fatigue Detection Using EfficientDet In Advanced Driver Assistance Systems. In 2021 18th International Multi-Conference on Systems, Signals & Devices (SSD) (pp. 738-742). IEEE. doi:10.1109/SSD52085.2021.9429294

Ayachi, R., Afif, M., Said, Y., & Atri, M. (2020a). Traffic signs detection for real-world application of an advanced driving assisting system using deep learning. *Neural Processing Letters*, *51*(1), 837–851. doi:10.100711063-019-10115-8

Ayachi, R., Said, Y., & Ben Abdelaali, A. (2020d). Pedestrian detection based on light-weighted separable convolution for advanced driver assistance systems. *Neural Processing Letters*, *52*(3), 2655–2668. doi:10.100711063-020-10367-9

Basu, A., Petropoulakis, L., Di Caterina, G., & Soraghan, J. (2020). Indoor home scene recognition using capsule neural networks. *Procedia Computer Science*, *167*, 440–448. doi:10.1016/j.procs.2020.03.253

Deng, J., Dong, W., Socher, R., Li, L. J., Li, K., & Fei-Fei, L. (2009). Imagenet: A large-scale hierarchical image database. In 2009 IEEE conference on computer vision and pattern recognition (pp. 248-255). IEEE. doi:10.1109/CVPR.2009.5206848

Dong, N., Wu, C.-H., Ip, W.-H., Chen, Z.-Q., Chan, C.-Y., & Yung, K.-L. (2012). An opposition-based chaotic GA/PSO hybrid algorithm and its application in circle detection. *Computers & Mathematics with Applications (Oxford, England), 64*(6), 1886–1902. doi:10.1016/j.camwa.2012.03.040

Fradi, M., Afif, M., & Machhout, M. (2020a). Deep learning based approach for bone diagnosis classification in ultrasonic computed tomographic images. *International Journal of Advanced Computer Science and Applications, 11*(12). doi:10.14569/IJACSA.2020.0111210

Fradi, M., Afif, M., Zahzeh, E. H., Bouallegue, K., & Machhout, M. (2020b). Transfer-deep learning application for ultrasonic computed tomographic image classification. In *2020 International Conference on Control, Automation and Diagnosis (ICCAD)* (pp. 1-6). IEEE. 10.1109/ICCAD49821.2020.9260569

Fusco, G., Cheraghi, S. A., Neat, L., & Coughlan, J. M. (2020). An indoor navigation app using computer vision and sign recognition. In *International Conference on Computers Helping People with Special Needs* (pp. 485-494). Springer. 10.1007/978-3-030-58796-3_56

Golledge, R. G. (1993). Geography and the disabled: A survey with special reference to vision impaired and blind populations. *Transactions of the Institute of British Geographers, 18*(1), 63–85. doi:10.2307/623069

Hanni, A., Chickerur, S., & Bidari, I. (2017). Deep learning framework for scene based indoor location recognition. In *2017 International Conference on Technological Advancements in Power and Energy (TAP Energy)* (pp. 1-8). IEEE

Marston, J. R., & Golledge, R. G. (2003). The hidden demand for participation in activities and travel by persons who are visually impaired. *Journal of Visual Impairment & Blindness, 97*(8), 475–488. doi:10.1177/0145482X0309700803

Nakane, T., Bold, N., Sun, H., Lu, X., Akashi, T., & Zhang, C. (2020). Application of evolutionary and swarm optimization in computer vision: A literature survey. *IPSJ Transactions on Computer Vision and Applications, 12*(1), 1–34. doi:10.118641074-020-00065-9

Real, E., Aggarwal, A., Huang, Y., & Le, Q. V. (2019). Regularized evolution for image classifier architecture search. *Proceedings of the AAAI Conference on Artificial Intelligence, 33*(01), 4780–4789. doi:10.1609/aaai.v33i01.33014780

Sun, Y., Xue, B., Zhang, M., & Yen, G. G. (2020). Evolving Deep Convolutional Neural Networks for Image Classification. *IEEE Transactions on Evolutionary Computation, 24*(2), 394–407. doi:10.1109/TEVC.2019.2916183

Tjan, B. S., Beckmann, P. J., Roy, R., Giudice, N., & Legge, G. E. (2005, September). Digital sign system for indoor wayfinding for the visually impaired. In *2005 IEEE Computer Society Conference on Computer Vision and Pattern Recognition (CVPR'05)-Workshops* (pp. 30-30). IEEE.

Viriyasaranon, T., & Choi, J. H. (2022). Object detectors involving a NAS-gate convolutional module and capsule attention module. *Scientific Reports, 12*(1), 1–13. doi:10.103841598-022-07898-7 PMID:35273256

Zoph, B., Vasudevan, V., Shlens, J., & Le, Q. V. (2018). Learning transferable architectures for scalable image recognition. In *Proceedings of the IEEE conference on computer vision and pattern recognition* (pp. 8697-8710). IEEE. 10.1109/CVPR.2018.00907

KEY TERMS AND DEFINITIONS

Assistive Technology: Present a product or a system that can be used to improve the life quality for users.

Deep Convolutional Neural Networks (DCNN): Present a type of deep learning-based models that were widely used to solve image processing issues.

Deep Learning: It is a sub-category of machine learning based on artificial neural networks.

Evolutionary Algorithms: Is an algorithm that solves tasks by modeling the behavior of life creatures using natural mechanism.

Indoor Sign Recognition: It aims to classify images that contain indoor signs.

Smart Home: A smart home is a smart environment equipped with electronic devices controlled by smartphone application.

Visually Impaired Persons (VIP): A category of persons that present van eyesight down to the normal level.

Wayfinding: An activity that aim to navigate from one place to another following a path.

Chapter 21
Artificial Intelligence Approaches in Diabetic Prediction

Sabitha E.

SRM Institute of Science and Technology, Vadapalani Campus, Chennai, India

ABSTRACT

Healthcare applications in monitoring and managing diseases have undergone rapid development in medical sectors and play an important in observing and controlling diabetes mellitus (DM). DM is a chronic infection that is caused by extreme blood sugar level. The rapid increase of DM world-wide have the effect of gaining attention to predict DM at early stage. Consequently, various technologies have been used to diagnose diabetes at an early stage to avoid major health defects. The most satisfaction in disease prediction and classification methods has been achieved through AI techniques and algorithms in healthcare. The main of the objective of the study is to provide a detail review on DM, the increase of DM around world-wide, datasets used in diabetic prediction, advance techniques and methods applied for disease prediction, and applications and its limitations used in diabetic prediction. The study also provides a detailed review on recent techniques and methods used in disease prediction, which guides the evolution of AI techniques and will provide a well-grounded knowledge of existing methods.

1. INTRODUCTION

AI has witnessed a significant increase in development in the health care sector in existing years, owing to increased consideration and its significant influence on health care provision and efficiency. AI-assisted healthcare is becoming more widespread as computational technology and algorithms improve, as well as the digitalization of massive amounts of health data. AI's advancement is reshaping how health care is individualized and distributed to patients, creating unique chances and constraints in medical care. The rapid development of computer healthcare information is outperforming human capabilities to interpret and evaluate it in ordinary medical care, which is a major concern in today's modern healthcare. Develop the existing have the option to terminate this gap while also ensuring patient safety in medical care. In

DOI: 10.4018/978-1-6684-6937-8.ch021

addition, healthcare systems are under strain from looming personnel shortages, ageing populations, and rising expenses in the face of shrinking finances. As a result, the healthcare industry is increasingly turning to AI to handle these issues, which is understandable. AI is now being used in a variety of areas in medical, from medical process automation to understanding of medical studies and forecast of healthcare results, reply to therapy, and ailment recurring. AI presents an opening for available and evidence-based decision making within the global health community given the rate at which AI algorithms are also being generated, upgraded, and used. In Medical Research, Big Data, and Autonomous Vehicles, AI has achieved some astonishing outcomes. ML, DL, and ANN are three fundamental AI ideas that aid in understanding the more complex concepts of driving software, data mining, and natural language processing. Instead of just replacing the work of members of the healthcare team, AI tools assist and improve it. AI assist healthcare team in jobs, like administration work, maintaining patient details, and patient's outreach. AI also help in areas like Image classification, medical equipment automation, and Observing patients (Chaki et al., 2020).

Most useful AI applications in healthcare are viewed from a variety of perspectives. In 2018 it is noted that AI played a major role in Organizational Systems, Image Analysis, Robotic Surgery, Simulated Assistants, and Clinical Decision Assistance (Atlas, 2015). Accenture identified the same themes in a 2018 report, as well as connected machines, Error reduction, and Cybersecurity (Marr, 2018).

AI widely used in diabetes treatment like retinal screening, risk stratification, patient management etc. Fitness trackers, mobile phones and additional gadgets have been introduced as a result of technical progressions that can assist in the constant monitoring and control of a patient's complaints and medical condition. For fast data processing and the availability of technical and gadgets for diabetes care, AI is a feasible and attractive option. For optimal diabetes treatment, doctors and medical workers can help clinicians select Automation care. Diabetic patients, medical providers, and medical systems are three primary categories in which AI can affect and improve diabetes care. AI has improved resources consumption in health care systems by presenting novel features of self-care for diabetic patients, introducing speedy and reliable decision making and flexible follow-ups for health care providers, and introducing new dimensions of self-care for diabetic patients. First the study explains the DM and its growth in world-wide in three different categories, like developed, developing and under developed country. AI in healthcare systems is also detailed in order to understand importance of AI and advance applications of AI used in healthcare. Nowadays DM became a life-threatening disease, so it is important to know the reason for the increase and also it is a responsibility to develop more applications and algorithms, that is used for early prediction of the DM, increasing day by day and also to provide clear understanding that, lacking of healthcare system is not only reason for the rise of the disease, but also the life style of human is one of the main reasons. The AI in healthcare and AI in diabetes prediction provides a knowledge on development of the advance techniques in the disease prediction.

The specific Objective of the study are as follows:

1. To understand the Diabetes Mellitus and its drastic increase over world-wide in three categories.
2. To gain knowledge in development of AI in Healthcare and most significantly in Diabetes prediction, the study also details the various applications that are employed as a prediction tools.
3. The various AI techniques is studied, to understand the existing methods and its performance based on the various metrics.
4. Limitations of AI techniques is also specified in order to improve the AI in Healthcare, so in future the applications can be implemented with required functions.

2. DIABETES MELLITUS

DM is caused due to rapid increase in blood sugar level. In other words when the pancreas quits making insulin or when the body stop using insulin effectively, diabetes develops. Insulin is a pancreas substance that facilitates the passage of glucose from the blood into human cells for energy production. Hyperglycemia is caused due to imbalance of insulin, resulting in elevated blood sugar. High blood sugar levels have been associated to long-term physical harm, as well as organ and tissue failure. Diabetes is classified like Type I, Type II and gestational diabetes. In this, TYPE II is more common, accounting for 90% of occurrences. Adults with diabetes are predicted to number 152 million by 2045, a 68 percent increase. When blood sugar levels are higher than normal, it is called prediabetes, although it is not necessarily severe enough for a doctor to diagnose diabetes. Prediabetes raises your chances of developing Type II diabetes and heart problems. Exercising and decreasing 5% to 7% of one's body weight can assist to reduce the risk of heart disease (Kalis et al., 2018).

In Health care there are plenty of algorithms and models are used implemented for various diseases prediction. A small analysis is done in order to know the growth of diabetes worldwide, that made a drastic increase in diabetes count for past few years. This is one reason for the development of the various algorithms for classification and prediction methods for the diabetes prediction. The chapter mainly focuses on diabetes prediction algorithms and techniques based on the AI by understanding its rapid growth, that leads to the other health issues. Untreated and Undiagnosed diabetes is one of the reasons of the heart disease, kidney infections and also affects the human vision. Sometimes is act like life threatening disease. According to the IDF Diabetes Atlas, in 2013, 316 million of world adult population had Impaired Glucose Tolerance (IGT), by 2035 it is expected to 50% increase in IGT (Singla et al., 2019). With increased physical activity and a nutritious diet, type 2 diabetes can be managed. The table I, II, III, IV is generated based on information gathered from IDF, the increase in diabetes is presented based on the regions from 2013 to 2035.Figure I,II,III,IV represents the pictorial of the diabetic status, that clearly present the increase of diabetic in various regions and country. By observing it is clearly stated that diabetes has shown a rapid rise across the different regions.

Table 1. Diabetes in different Regions

S. No.	Region	People With Diabetes (millions) Year	
		2013	2035
1	Europe	6.80%	7.10%
2	Africa	5.70%	6.00%
3	South East Asia	8.70%	9.40%
4	Middle East & North Africa	10.90%	11.30%
5	Western Pacific	8.10%	8.40%
6	Northern America & the Caribbean	9.60%	9.90%
7	South & Central America	8.20%	8.20%

Figure 1. Diabetes in different Region

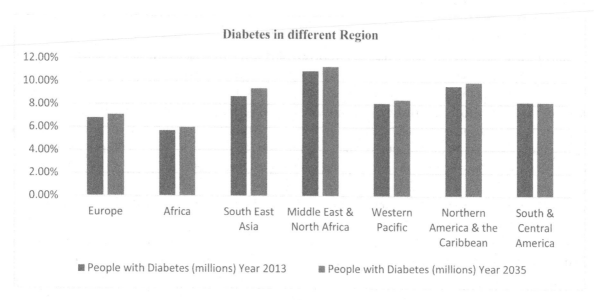

Table 2. Diabetes in Developed country

Developed Country				
S. No.	Country	2021 Population	Diabetes Rise in 1000's	
			2000	2021
1	Australia	25788.215	781.3	1,491.80
2	Belgium	11632.326	307.4	404.9
3	Canada	38067.903	1,245.50	2,974.00
4	Denmark	5813.298	561.7	309.4
5	France	65426.179	1,656.80	3,942.90
6	Germany	83900.473	2,600.00	6,199.90
7	Iceland	343.353	3.6	20.1
8	Ireland	4982.907	80.2	139.1
9	Japan	126050.804	7,113.20	11,005.00
10	Netherlands	17173.099	415.9	857
11	Russia	145912.025	0	7392.1
12	Singapore	5896.686	282.1	711.8
13	Switzerland	8715.494	199.6	389
14	United Kingdom	68207.116	1,466.80	3,996.30
15	United States	332915.073	15,280.00	32,215.30

Figure 2. Diabetes in different Region

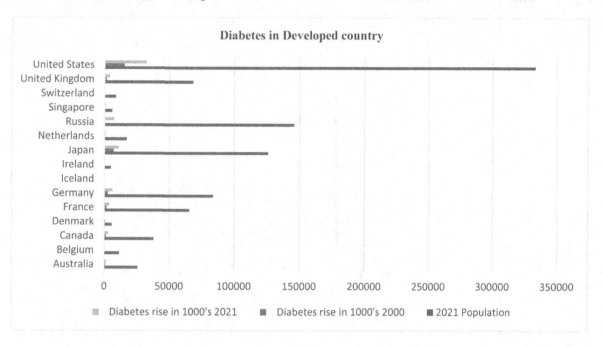

Table 3. Diabetes in Developing country

S. No.	Country	2021 Population	Diabetes Rise	
			2000	2021
1	Albania	2872.933	94.3	241.1
2	Brazil	213993.437	3310.4	15733.6
3	Bangladesh	166303.498	1759.7	13136.3
4	China	1444216.107	22564.8	140869.6
5	Indonesia	276361.783	5654.3	19465.1
6	India	1393409.038	32674.4	74194.7
7	Jordan	10269.021	194.2	866.5
8	Iran	85028.759	1323.9	5450.3
9	Kenya	54985.698	190.4	821.5
10	Pakistan	225199.937	8789.5	32964.5
11	Philippines	111046.913	1242.2	4303.9
12	South Africa	60041.994	886.4	4234
13	Sri Lanka	21497.31	335.4	1417.6
14	Thailand	69950.85	1489.1	6066.6
15	Ukraine	43466.819	1286.3	2325

Figure 3. Diabetes in Developing country

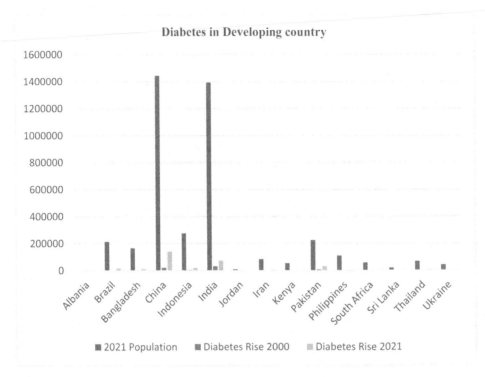

Table 4. Diabetes in Undeveloped country

Undeveloped Country				
S. No.	Country	2021 Population	Diabetes Rise	
			2000	2021
1	DR Congo	92377.993	252.6	1,908.90
2	Ethiopia	117876.227	268.1	1,920.00
3	Gambia	2486.945	2.2	18.1
4	Mali	20855.735	18.4	152.5
5	Mozambique	32163.047	117.3	349.3

Figure 4. Diabetes in Undeveloped country

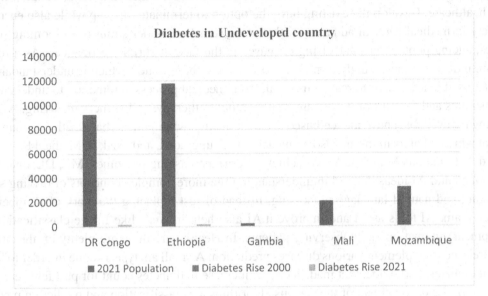

Figure 5. Role of AI in Healthcare

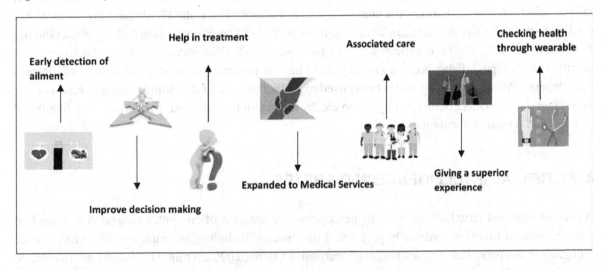

3. ARTIFICIAL INTELLIGENCE IN HEALTHCARE

AI advancement is reshaping how health care is individualized and distributed to patients, creating unique chances and constraints in medical care. Figure V express the role of AI in healthcare in different areas. Starts from detecting the ailments, improving in decision making, helping in treatment, expanding in medical services, associated in care, giving a superior experience and finally in checking health through wearable materials. The rapid development of computer healthcare information is outperforming human capabilities to interpret and evaluate it in ordinary medical care, which is a major concern in today's modern healthcare. Develop the existing have the option to terminate this gap while also ensuring patient safety in medical care. In addition, healthcare systems are under strain from looming personnel shortages, ageing populations, and rising expenses in the face of shrinking finances. As a result, the healthcare industry is increasingly turning to AI to handle these issues, which is understandable. AI is now being used in a variety of areas in medical, from medical process automation to understanding of medical studies and forecast of healthcare results, reply to therapy, and ailment recurring. AI presents an opening for available and evidence-based decision making within the global health community given the rate at which AI algorithms are also being generated, upgraded, and used. In Medical Research, Big Data, and Autonomous Vehicles, AI has achieved some astonishing outcomes. ML, DL, and ANN are three fundamental AI ideas that aid in understanding the more complex concepts of driving software, data mining, and natural language processing. Instead of just replacing the work of members of the healthcare team, AI tools assist and improve it.AI also help in areas like Image classification, medical equipment automation, and Observing patients. In Health care there are plenty of algorithms and models are used to implement various diseases prediction. A small analysis is done in order to know the growth of diabetes worldwide, that made a drastic increase in diabetes count for past few years. This is one reason for the development of the various algorithms for classification and prediction methods for the diabetes prediction.

In this chapter we mainly focus on the Early detection of DM using the AI algorithms and techniques based on the AI by understanding its rapid growth, that leads to the other health issues. Applications used to diagnosis the DM Untreated and Undiagnosed diabetes is one of the reasons of the heart disease, kidney infections and also affects the human vision. Sometimes is act like life threatening disease. According to the IDF Diabetes Atlas, in 2013, 316 million of world adult population had Impaired Glucose Tolerance (IGT), by 2035 it is expected to 50% increase in IGT. With increased physical activity and a nutritious diet, type 2 diabetes can be managed. AI has the potential to assist in the control of diseases like diabetes. Artificial intelligence is being used to predict the risk of developing diabetes based on the biological data, to detect diabetics relying on electronic health records, and to determine the likelihood of renal and retinal abnormalities.

4. ARTIFICIAL INTELLIGENCE IN DIABETES

AI is a widespread term that refers to the perception and progress of computer-generated systems that can accomplish functions ordinarily performed by humans, including as graphic observation, speech recognition, decision-making, and language translation (Team, 2020). It might be modest as "rule-based statistical approaches" or as complicated as "Data-driven statistical methods" . ML, DL, and ANN are subsets of AI that allow computers to learn and develop without being explicitly programmed (Singhal & Carlton, 2019). Artificial Intelligence tools are widely employed in all scientific sectors, and they are credited with transforming industry around the world. On the other hand, healthcare systems have been hesitant to absorb these developments and are falling far behind in this area (Kavakiotis et al., 2017).

AI has the potential to assist in the control of diseases like diabetes. AI is being used to forecast the risk of chronic diseases based on biological data, detect diabetes based on EHR data, and predict the likelihood of renal and retinal disorders (NCBI, n.d.). DM is caused due to rapid increase in blood sugar level. In other words when the pancreas quits making insulin or when the body stop using insulin effectively, diabetes develops. Insulin is a pancreas substance that facilitates the passage of glucose from the blood into human cells for energy production. Hyperglycemia is caused due to imbalance of insulin, resulting in elevated blood sugar. High blood sugar levels have been associated to long-term physical harm, as well as organ and tissue failure. Diabetes is classified like Type I, Type II and gestational diabetes. In this, TYPE II is more common, accounting for 90% of occurrences. Adults with diabetes are predicted to number 152 million by 2045, a 68 percent increase. Table V describes the aspects of diabetes care using AI/ML (Gulshan et al., 2016),in areas like diabetes prediction, Blood sugar level control, Glycemic event prediction, Complications can be predicted and Complications can be diagnosed.

Table 5. AI/ML in Diabetes Care

Area	Description
Diabetes Prediction	Algorithms have been used to find the risk of diabetes by using the genetic and clinical data. Some Algorithms assist the physicians, when they missed in finding the possibility of diabetes with help of electronic health record data.
Blood sugar level control	The Artificial Pancreas System is the main focus. Various AI algorithms use the CGM (continuous glucose monitoring) to measure the insulin rate and assist in prescribing the doses.
Glycemic event Prediction	On the basis of CGM data, it is possible to predict oncoming hypoglycemia or hyperglycemia. This method is already in use in the business world.
Complications can be predicted.	Predict the chance of retinopathy, nephropathy, neuropathy, or a cardiovascular event using baseline clinical and biochemical data.
Complications are diagnosed.	An AI/ML technique is revolutionising retinopathy identification in diabetologist's clinics by directly detecting and classifying stages based on photos generated by fundus cameras.

The Google AI research unit has already achieved great progress in the field of automated diagnosis and grading of diabetic retinopathy in partnership with a few Indian ophthalmology clinics. Adoption of these technologies can dramatically improve diabetes problem identification and management (Ellahham, 2020).

AI widely used in diabetes treatment like retinal screening, risk stratification, patient management etc. Fitness trackers, mobile phones and additional gadgets have been introduced as a result of technical progressions that can assist in the constant monitoring and control of a patient's complaints and medical condition. For fast data processing and the availability of technical and gadgets for diabetes care, AI is a feasible and attractive option. For optimal diabetes treatment, doctors and medical workers can help clinicians select Automation care. Diabetic patients, medical providers, and medical systems are three primary categories in which AI can affect and improve diabetes care. AI has improved resources consumption in health care systems by presenting novel features of self-care for diabetic patients, introducing new aspects of self-care for diabetic patients, as well as decision making and flexible follow-ups for health care providers.

Several applications were designed and developed to study the quality of food and find the nutrients and calorie value of food we consumed. These applications not only help in checking the food quality, also protect our body from many diseases that causes risk factor. Many diabetic applications are used nowadays to monitor the level of glucose that induce sugar levels, checking the physical activities and mental stress. Mostly these devices are portable and easy to use. The most important thing it reduces the frequency on going to hospital. The patient's details can be monitored by the health expert through the applications then and there instead of attending directly.

5. AI APPLICATIONS IN DIABETES

Clinical Decision Support System (CDSS)

The CDSS is an application that can be used through browser. It was designed in association with medical team for the purpose of giving data connected to diabetes that helps in providing the proper treatment and overcome the risk factors (Tcheng, 2017). The evidence of the impact of CDSS (clinical decision support system) development on healthcare processes, guidelines adoption, clinical and economic results is growing (Rollo et al., 2016). CDSS act like a guidance for the diabetes treatment for the medical expert, not only medical expert it assists the diabetes patient to take care themselves before reaching the risk factor. The goal of CDSS is to help healthcare providers by allowing them to analyse patient data and use that information to help them establish a diagnosis. It also provides information to doctors and primary care providers to help them improve the quality of treatment they provide to their patients.

Predictive Population Risk Stratification

The healthcare recommendation system (HRS) was able to anticipate the potential of a disease, including diabetes, by analysing the patient's lifestyle and monitoring the physical health component, mental health factor, and social activities. A flurry of predictive models has skipped up in response to diabetic problems. The complications of the diabetes can be control by using the predictive risk stratification, diagnosed techniques can be improved with help of advanced technology. It enables Physician to identify the right level of care and services for the distinct group of patients. Risk stratification uses a mix of objective and subjective data to assign risk levels to patients. Practices can systematically use patient risk levels to make care management decisions, such as providing greater access and resources to patients in higher risk level.

Patient Self-Management Tool

Self-awareness and attentiveness are more necessity for self-management. Thanks to AI advancements, patients may now manage and control their diabetes by monitoring metrics and becoming their own health expert. To improve alertness and understanding about day today habits and activity, web-based programmes, mobile phone and smartphone apps are now available (Carolan-Olah et al., 2015).During pregnancy helps the women to control and manage the gestational diabetes (Frøisland & Aorsand, 2015). AI allows diabetic patients to make daily food and activity decisions using self-treatment. Patients have been able to check calorie value of their meal consumption using apps. Patients' diabetes management improves when they eat a nutritious diet and exercise regularly (Seyhan & Carini, 2019).

Automated Retinal Screening

AI developed an automated diabetic retinopathy diagnostic using deep learning techniques. AI-assisted retinal screening, is a widely accepted method for diagnosing and monitoring diabetic retinopathy. Automated retina screening has 92.3 percent sensitivity and 93.7 percent specificity, respectively. 96 percent of patients are satisfied with this automated screening. Retinal Screening can monitor and detect eye damage caused by diabetes before we notice any difference within ourself.

Advanced Genomics

Recent developments in disease diagnosis and therapy include advanced genomics, molecular phenotyping, epigenetic changes, and the invention of digital biomarkers (Han & Ye, 2019). Data from the microbiome was utilised to create a database of microbiological genetic polymorphisms that can be used to predict the onset of diabetes and guide therapy in people who have already been diagnosed (Fagherazzi & Ravaud, 2019). These can be applied in diabetes, where the disease's varied character and long duration generate massive data sets.

Telehealth

Diabetes management has been transformed thanks to telehealth. Remote monitoring cuts down on continuation appointments and allows for real observation of the patient's Glycemic state and general health.70% of healthcare consultations have been replaced by virtual interaction and remote monitoring thanks to artificial intelligence (Shah & Garg, 2015)

5. DATASET

Dataset is a collection of data represented with rows and columns, with each column representing a variable and each row representing a data set record. The structure and attributes of a dataset are defined by a number of criteria. It included, for example, numerical, variable, and statistical measures. There may also be missing values, which can be compensated for in another method. There are several datasets for the disease prediction, it can be in text, images or genomic data. In particular to diabetes prediction, the more popular and used dataset is PIMA Indian Diabetes Database from UCI Machine Repository. Hasan et al.(Hasan et al., 2020),Nadeem et al.(Research Gate, n.d.),Butt et al.(Butt et al., 2021) Mujumdar et al.(Mujumdar & Vaidehi, 2019), Khanam et al.(Lai et al., 2019), Nadesh, R.K et al(Nadesh & Arivuselvan, 2020), El Jerjawi, N.S et al.(El Jerjawi & Abu-Naser, 2018), Misra, P.,et al.(Misra & Yadav, 2020) used the PIMA Indian Diabetes Database contain 768 females with both diabetic and non-diabetic. The samples are collected from the female patients at the age limit of 21 years, the samples are categorised as eight attributes and two classes. Considering the fast increase in the diabetes rate, the lifestyle is considered to be the main factor. Not only PIMA database, many researchers have collected real time data from the hospitals, to make their work more reliable and efficient. Some focus on collecting real time data's that are closely related to diabetes, depending on their life style. Table VI describes the different dataset used in the diabetic prediction. Faruque et al.(Faruque & Sarker, 2019), in this the authors collected the real time dataset from Medical Centre Chittagong (MCC), Bangladesh. The dataset contains 200 patients record set. Gill et.al (Gill & Pathwar, 2021), in this the author collected the data from Bio-statistics about 390 records out of 60 are diabetic and 330 are non-diabetic. Xu et.al (Xu et al., 2021) in this author collected 520 records from Sylhet Diabetes hospital, in the dataset there are 17 attributes from both men and women between 20 to 65 years. In Zou et.al (Zou et al., 2018) 13700 samples are randomly collected with 14 attributes. Likely Lai et.al (Lai et al., 2019) have collected approximately 255,000 records of the Canadian patients, Dinh, A., et.al (Dinh et al., 2019) from the National Health and Nutrition Examination survey, 5000 data have been used. In Hao, Y., et.al (Hao et al., 2019), the dataset is divided into four categories like without hyperlipidemia and hypertension, with hyperlipidemia but no hypertension, with hypertension but no hyperlipidemia, with both hyperlipidemia and hypertension, with both hyperlipidemia and hypertension. Data is collected from patients range from 40 to 75 years. Martinez-Vernon, A. S., et.al (Martinez-Vernon et al., 2018), dataset contains 115 urine samples, 75 of which were taken from type II diabetic patients. Hathaway, Q. A., et.al (Hathaway et al., 2019), focused on real time data, the data collected from 30 non-diabetic and 20 type II diabetes individuals and includes physiological, biochemical, and sequencing information. Ling, S. H., et.al (Ling et al., 2016), the dataset collected from 420 ECG recordings from 16 diabetic patients. Abbas, H. T., et.al (Abbas et al., 2019),1492 patients insulin concentration and plasma glucose records are included in the collection. Nguyen, B. P., et.al (Nguyen et al., 2019) comprises 9948 data from electronic health record dataset.

Table 6. Diabetes Dataset

Dataset Types	Data Description	References
PIDD	PIMA Indian diabetes dataset contain 768 females (with both diabetic and non-diabetic) at least 21 years.	Hasan et.al [25], Nadeem et al. [26], Butt et.al [27], Mujumdar et.al [28], Khanam et al.[12], Nadesh,R K.et al.[36], El Jerjawi,N.S.,et al [37], Misra, P., et.al [38]
Real time dataset from Medical centre chittagong (MCC), Bangladesh	The dataset contains 200 patients record set from MCC.	Faruque et al.[30]
Dataset from Biostatistics program at Vanderbilt.	The dataset consists of 390 records, out 390 ,60 are diabetic and 330 are non-diabetic.	Gill et al.[31]
Dataset from Sylhet Diabetes Hospital , Bangladesh	Dataset consists of 520 cases with 17 attributes from both men and women between 20 to 65 years.	Xu et al. [33]
Real time dataset from hospital Luzhou,china	Dataset contains 13700 samples randomly collected with 14 attributes.	Zou et al.[13]
Real time Dataset from Candaian Patients	Approximately 255,000 records collected from diabetic patients.	Lai et al.[29]
National Health and Nutrition Examination Survey dataset	There are 5000 data points in this dataset, which comprises clinical tests and physical examinations.	Dinh, A.,et.al [40]
Real time dataset collected from patients range from 40 to 75 years.	The dataset contains 417 records that are divided into four categories: (i) without hyperlipidemia and hypertension, (ii) with hyperlipidemia but no hypertension, (iii) with hypertension but no hyperlipidemia, (iv) with both hyperlipidemia and hypertension, and (v) with both hyperlipidemia and hypertension.	Hao, Y.,et.al [41]
Data was collected in real time from the University Hospital of Coventry and Warwickshire in the United Kingdom.	The dataset contains 115 urine samples, 75 of which were taken from type II diabetic patients.	Martinez-Vernon, A. S., et.al [42]
Real time dataset	The data was collected from 30 non-diabetic and 20 type-II diabetes individuals and includes physiological, biochemical, and sequencing information.	Hathaway, Q. A., et.al [43]
Real time dataset	The dataset contains 420 ECG recordings from 16 diabetes patients.	Ling, S. H., et.al [44]
Real time dataset	Before and after glucose ingestion, 1492 patients' insulin concentration and plasma glucose records are included in the collection.	Abbas, H. T., et.al[45]
Electronic health record dataset	The dataset comprises of 9948 diabetes patients EHR.	Nguyen, B. P., et.al [46]

6. ARTIFICIAL INTELLIGENCE TECHNIQUES IN DIABETES

Several AI techniques are used in the prediction of diabetes. Machine learning, Deep learning, Neural Networks are the part of AI, that perform through the experience and the use of data. Based on the ML, DL and NN several Classification algorithms are applied in the disease prediction. Classification is a type of Pattern Recognition that uses training data to locate a pattern that is similar to new dataset. Many researchers have conducted study in order to discover a technique that is effective and useful for forecasting diabetes in a more direct manner. The following are a few different diabetes prediction methods. Table VII describes the different classification methods, feature selection approaches, dataset and their performance metrics.

6.1. Diabetic Prediction Using Machine Learning

In the diabetic's prediction ML produces an outstanding result, traditional ML methods like support vector machine (SVM),decision tree (DT), Logistic regression (LR) and so on are recently used ML algorithms for the diabetic prediction . In (Khanam & Foo, 2021) different ML algorithms like DT, K Nearest Neighbor (KNN), Random Forest (RF), Naïve Bayes (NB), Adaboost (AB), SVM, Linear Regression (LR) are used to predict the diabetes and compared with proposed Neural Network (NN) model with different hidden layers. The DT, RF, and NN models use five-fold cross validation with feature selection methods such as Principal Component Analysis (PCA) and Minimum redundancy maximum relevance methods. In this DT have achieved better accuracy when compared with other methods (Zou et al., 2018).Likewise various algorithms are used in the diabetic's prediction in different models that improves in the performance level. Unsupervised learning is a descriptive model in which the inputs are known but the result is uncertain. Its approaches include clustering algorithms such as K-means clustering and K-clustering, Median's which are typically utilised on transactional data. On the training dataset, the semi-supervised technique uses both labelled and unlabelled data. Semi-supervised learning includes classification and regression algorithms (Swapna et al., 2018).Hasan et.al (Hasan et al., 2020) in this K-NN,DT,AB,RF,NB,XB are used to predict the diabetes using the ICA-Based feature selection, Correlation based feature selection. XB and AB methods achieved the highest accuracy when compared to other methods. Khanam et.al (Khanam & Foo, 2021) used the Pearson's correlation method as the feature selection with DT,RF,NB,LR,KNN,AB,SVM methods among them NN produced the best accuracy. Nadem et.al (Research Gate, n.d.),in this the author used the LR,KNN,RF,GD as the prediction methods, the performance of the models is measured by using the accuracy. The author used the PIMA dataset for the work. Butt et.al(Butt et al., 2021),in this author divided the model into two, one as classifier and other one is predictive model. The classifier model like RF,MLP and LR. The predictive analysis is LSTM, Logistic regression is used. Mujumdar et.al (Mujumdar & Vaidehi, 2019) used the PIMA Indian Diabetes dataset and real time data. Classification methods like LR,RF,DT,KNN,GB,AB,LDA is used, from this based on real time dataset LR achieved highest accuracy when compared to PIMA. Bhat, S. S., et.al (Bhat et al., 2022) exploiting ML Algorithms is essential if healthcare professional are able to identify disease more effectively. In this author developed a ML methodology for predicting diabetes disease risk prediction in North Kashmir. Six ML algorithms have been successfully used in experimental study, such as RF, MLP,SVM,GB,DT and LR.RF is most accurate classifier with the uppermost accuracy rate of 98% with the balanced data set.

6.2. Diabetic Prediction Using Deep Learning

Despite the fact that deep learning is a, it does not do feature extraction or categorization explicitly. All of this is done implicitly within the deep learning network's hidden layers, without involving external sources. DL techniques are used in enormous in the medical field. Many researchers had done the work to prove DL techniques provides a better outcome, with less classification error rate and robust in noise strategies. It also has capability to handle large data, solve complex problem in easy way. In DL, DNN (Deep Neural Network) which is recently very popular with its performance in disease prediction. Convolutional Neural Networks (CNN) are improvised multilayer perceptron variants. CNN used for disease prediction and drug discovery using medical images. Disease diagnosis using CNN include disease classification, segmentation and identification. In predicting Diabetic Retinopathy, CNN proved an outcome result, since CNN uses images for disease diagnosis. Like CNN, the other DL techniques that are used for disease prediction are " FCN (Fully connected network), RNN (Recurrent neural network), Dilated Convolutions, GANs(Generative Adversarial Network),AC-GAN (Auxiliary Classifier GANs),CAC -GAN (Convolutional Auxiliary Classifier GAN),Attention-based deep neural network (Attention NN),Adversarial autoencoders (AAE), GAN-AO(GAN with auxiliary output)" . Zou et.al(Zou et al., 2018) used the principal Component Analysis, Minimum Redundancy maximum relevance as feature selection method with j48,RF,NN .Gill et.al(Gill & Pathwar, 2021) used the real time data from Biostatics with ANOVA, Mutual Information, Genetic algorithm as the feature selection with LR, NB, stochastic Gradient Descent, KNN,DT,RF,SVM.RF with Genetic algorithm have achieved highest accuracy. Prabhu, Petal (Prabhu & Selvabharathi, 2019) proposed the Deep Belief Neural Network model and compared with LR,RF and SVM. The performance of the model is measured using RC,PR,FI measure. DBN model achieved highest accuracy. Xu et.al (Xu et al., 2021) in this, the author proposed IDCNN model for the diabetic prediction, and compared with NB, RF.IDCNN achieved 97% and its performance is measured by using the performance metrics like RC,PR,FI measure and accuracy. Deng, Y., et.al(Deng et al., 2021) developed a deep-Learning methods to predict patient-specific blood glucose monitoring (CGM) to predict future glucose levels in 5 min to 1hr.Two challenges are tackled like too small dataset and imbalanced hypo-and hyperglycemia episodes are usually much less common than normoglycemia. Lu, X., & Song, R. (Lu & Song, 2022) proposed a novel method to predict the Blood glucose levels for 30 min of prediction horizon(PH) with a hybrid deep learning models, integrates with the multi-layer perceptron, Bidirectional gated recurrent unit (Bi-GRU) based Recurrent Neural Network(RNN) and the attention mechanism(AM). T. R. Albi.,et.al (Albi et al., 2022) demonstrate a comparative analysis and improved performance using deep learning to classify diabetic and non-diabetic patients that will provide a feasible way to diagnosis. In this work neural network model with low variance applying synthetic minority oversampling technique is used to augment the data and improve the performance by achieving accuracy of 99% for training and 98% for validation.

6.3. Diabetic Prediction Using Artificial Neural Network

The use of data from medical institutions and data mining techniques to diagnose diabetes is believed to be an efficient and practical manner to diagnose diabetes. An ANN is the most essential technologies for diagnosing the diabetes, as it reduces classification mistakes and improves diabetes diagnostic accuracy. Diabetic diagnosis can be done through the classification problem (El Jerjawi & Abu-Naser, 2018). The Neural Network with an activation function, hidden layers are sufficient to estimate arbitrary accuracy. The feedforward neural networks are an important form of artificial neural networks that is used to diagnosis the diabetes in an efficient manner (Sim et al., 2017). ANN does not have any specific structure ; it just uses all the multiple neural layers for the prediction. Backpropagation Neural network (BPNN) is the key of neural network training, in this method weights are fine-tuned based on the error obtained from the previous epoch. Fine tuning the weights allows helps in reducing the error rate and makes model reliable .BPNN is a standard method in training the ANN. With respect to weight Gradient of a loss function can be calculated using the BPNN. MLP, CNN,RNN are the part of ANN. Using ANN many disease prediction models are designed and implemented, many research works also proved the outcome results. Many researchers focus on the feature selection methods that improve the performance of the proposed models. Feature selection enables in selecting the attributes that are highly related with the prediction approach. Sah et.al (Sah et al., 2021),used statistical feature selection method with DL and GB trees, DL performed better than the GB tree. The performance of the model is measured by AUC,PR,RC. Mizai,Z.A et.al (Miazi et al., 2021) proposed the ANN model, the PIMA dataset is used .ANN achieved 90% accuracy and its performance is measured using AUC,PR,RC .Nadesh R,K et.al (Nadesh & Arivuselvan, 2020) proposed the DNN model and used Feature Importance method as a feature selection .The model achieved 98% accuracy in 80 to 20 spilt up. EI jerjawi N.S,et.al (El Jerjawi & Abu-Naser, 2018) in this the author implemented ANN model on JNN environment, the both PIMA and real time dataset is used in this work. The model achieved 87% accuracy. The Recursive Feature Elimination method is used as feature selection method in Mersa et.al(Misra & Yadav, 2020) and Channabasavaraju .B,D et.al (Channabasavaraju & Vinayakamurthy, 2020) with cross validation and Random forest feature selection technique along LR, ANN, NB,SVM,DT,ANN with fuzzy, Fuzzy with NN .] Kowsher, M., et.al (Kowsher et al., 2021) hybridization of two or more algorithms can potentially increase the performance of the model. LSTM and BiLSTM are two excellent and widely used algorithms, still could be room for improvement in terms of accuracy via the hybridization method. In this paper proposed hybrid BiLSTM-ANN model beats all the implemented models with the most accuracy score of 93% for both validation and testing.

Table 7. Comparison of different approaches in diabetes prediction

References	Dataset	Feature selection	Methodology	Accuracy	Performance Evaluation
Hasan et.al [25]	PIMA Indian Diabetes Database	ICA-Based Feature selection , Correlation-Based Feature selection	k-NN , DT,AB, RF, NB , XB	k-NN : 92.6 % DT:91.2% AB: 94.1%RF:93.9% NB:87.9% XB:94.6%	AUC
Nadeem et al. [26]	PIMA Indian Diabetes Database	~	LR, KNN, RF, GD	LR :84%,KNN:88%,RF :98%, GD :90%	ACC
Butt et.al [27]	PIMA Indian Diabetes Database	~	Classifier :RF, MLP,LR Predictive analysis :LSTM,moving average,Logistic regression	MLP :86.083% LSTM :87.26%	RC,PR,ACC
Mujumdar et.al [28]	PIMA Indian Diabetes Database Real time dataset	~	LR,GB,LDA,AB,ET,GNB,Bagging,RF,DT,Perceptron,SVC,KNN	Using PIMA :GB,LDA,AB:77% Using real time dataset: Logistic regression :96%	ACC,Confusion matrix,F1 score,Precision,RC
Khanam et al.[12]	PIMA Indian Diabetes Database	Pearson's correlation method	DT,RF,NB,LR,KNN,AB,SVM Compared with NN model	LR:78.85% NB:78.28% RF:77.34% NN:88.57%	ACC,RC,PR,F-measure
Zou et al.[13]	Real time dataset from hospital Luzhou,china PIMA Indian Diabetes Database	Principal Component Analysis Minimum Redundancy maximum revelance	J48 ,RF,NN	Using Luzhou : RF:80.8% J48:78.5% NN:78.4% Using PIMA: RF:76.04% J48 :72.75%	SN,SP,ACC,Mathews correlation coefficient (MCC)
Lai et al.[29]	Real time Dataset from Candaian Patients	~	Gradient Boosting machine (GBM) Logistic Regression (LR)	GBM :84.7% with sensitivity :71.6%. LR:84.0% with sensitivity :73.4%	AROC
Faruque et al.[30]	Real time dataset from Medical centre chittagong (MCC), Bangladesh	~	SVM,NB,KNN,C4.5DT	C4.5 DT :73.5%	PR,RC,F-measure,ACC
Gill et al.[31]	Dataset from Biostatistics program at Vanderbilt.	ANOVA Mutual Information Genetic Algorithm	LR,NB,Stochastic Gradient Descent (SGD),KNN,DT,RF,SVM	RF with Genetic Algorithm :93.95%	ACC
Prabhu, P et al.[32]	PIMA Indian Diabetes Database	~	Proposed model:Deep Belief Neural network (DBN) Compared with : LR,RF,SVM	DBN :80.8%	RC,PR,F1 measure
Xu et al. [33]	Dataset from Sylhet Diabetes Hospital , Bangladesh	~	Proposed model :One dimensional convolutional neural network(IDCNN) Compared with : NB RF	IDCNN : 97.02%	PR,RC,F-measure,ACC
Sah et al.[34]	PIMA Indian Diabetes Database	Statistical feature selection	DL ,GB trees	DL : 90% performed better than GB trees	AUC,PR,RC,F-measure,SN,SP
Miazi, Z. A., et al.[35]	PIMA Indian Diabetes Database	~	ANN model	ANN :90.26%	ACC,PR,RC,AUC
Nadesh,R K.et al.[36]	PIMA Indian Diabetes Database	Feature Importance (FI)	DNN model	DNN :96.77% in 60-40 test spilt ratio, 97.54% in 70-30 test spilt ratio, 98.16% in 80-20 test spiltratio, 96.10% in 10 fold cross validation	ACC,SN,SP,ROC
El Jerjawi,N.S.,et al [37]	PIMA Indian Diabetes Database Real time dataset	~	ANN model implemented in JNN environment	ANN :87.3%	ACC
Misra, P., et.al [38]	PIMA Indian Diabetes Database	Recursive Feature Elimination with cross validation (RFECV)	LR,ANN,NB,SVM,DT	LR:84%	ACC,PR,RC,F1-Score
Channabasavaraju, B. D et.al [39]	PIMA Indian Diabetes Database (DD) Heart disease dataset (HD) Diabetes-Heart disease dataset (DHD)	Recursive Feature Elimination (RFE) Random Forest Feature selection technique (RFS)	ANN with fuzzy SVM Fuzzy with NN RFS-RFE	RFS-RFE :84.49 using HD	ACC,SN,SP,PR

7. PERFORMANCE METRICS

Performance metrics are the information and project specific data used to characterise and analysis the quality, capability and skills. The metrics used to predict whether the model making progress and specify it on number. All ML models, whether it is a linear regression, or other techniques need to judge the performance of the models. Diverse evaluation measures are used to evaluate various machine learning and other algorithms. A classifier, for example, is used to discriminate between photographs of various objects. Accuracy, Confusion matrix, Precision, Recall, and F1 score are the most often used performance indicators for classification problems. Mean Squared Error (MSE), Root Mean Squared Error (RMSE), and Mean Absolute Error (MAE) are some of the other error measures (MAE). The metrics are used to evaluate the model's performance in relation to the aim attained. Metrics are a type of quantitative assessment that is commonly used to compare and track a product's or service's performance.

A. Accuracy

Classification accuracy is one of the most commonly used evaluation metrics in classification tasks. It indicates how often the classifier properly predicts. The proportion of correct predictions made to the total number of forecasts is what it's called. Accuracy is beneficial when the target class is well balanced; nevertheless, it is ineffective when the target class is unbalanced. Many individuals believe that a high accuracy score is desirable, and that figures exceeding 90% are exceptional. On an unbalanced classification task, reaching 90 percent or even 99 percent classification accuracy may be a piece of cake. The classification accuracy can be enhanced by employing cross validation and cross dataset approaches. Models that are accurate and effective at generalising unknown data are better at forecasting future events and hence have more utility.

$$Accuracy = \frac{TP + TN}{TP + TN + FP + FN}$$

B. Confusion Matrix

A confusion matrix is a table that describes the performance of a classification model on a set of test data for which the true values are known. It can be used to test accuracy, precision, recall, and AUC-ROC curves.

Figure 6. Actual values

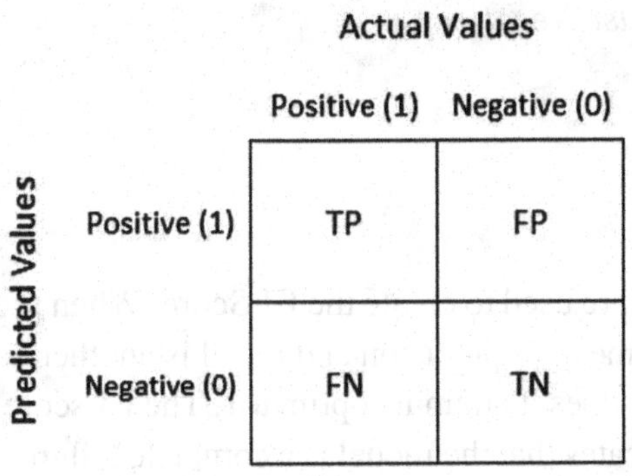

True Positive: It is predicted positive and its true, i.e., person is actually diabetic .
True Negative: It is predicted negative and its true, i.e., person is actually not diabetic and it is actually not.
False Positive: It is predicted positive and its false, i.e., person is diabetic but actually not.
False Negative: It is predicted negative and its true, i.e., person is actually not diabetic but it is true.

C. Precision

Precision is a great evaluative metric to utilise when the cost of a false positive is high and the cost of a false negative is low. The number of genuine positives divided by the number of expected positives yields precision .It also illustrates how many of the instances that were accurately predicted turned out to be positive. When the number of false positives is greater than the number of false negatives, precision is critical. When a high true positive is required for the imbalanced data, Precision is preferred because its formula contains no false negatives. The most common application of precision is in the identification of email spam. Precision is linked to a low false positive rate.

$$Precision = \frac{True\ Positive}{True\ Positive + False\ Positive}$$

D. Recall

The word recall refers to how many positive cases are accurately predicted by the model. It's a useful statistic in situations when false negatives provide a greater risk than false positives. The number of correct positive predictions made out of all possible positive predictions is measured by recall. Unlike precision, which only takes into account the correct positive predictions out of all positive predictions, recall takes into account the positive predictions that were missed. In information retrieval, a perfect precision score of 1.0 means that every search result was relevant, whereas a perfect recall score of 1.0 means that the search retrieved all relevant documents.

$$Recall = \frac{True\ Positive}{True\ Positive + False\ Negative}$$

E. F1 Score

Precision and Recall measures are used to create the F1 Score. When precision and recall are equal, it is at its optimum. The harmonic mean of precision and recall is another name for it. Only when precision and recall are both 100 percent does it attain its optimal 1. The F1 score of 1 indicates that the model is perfect, while a score of 0 indicates that the model is a complete failure. Another option to address class imbalance issues is to utilise more accurate measures, such as the F1 score, which consider not only the number of predictions mistakes produced by the model, but also the type of errors made. StandardScaler, GridSearchCV for hyperparameter tuning, and Recursive Feature Elimination can all help enhance F1 score categorization (feature selection).

$$F1 = 2.\frac{Precision \times Recall}{Precision + Recall}$$

F. AUC-ROC

The AUC (Area Under the Curve) is a measure of a classifier's ability to distinguish between classes. A probability curve depicting the TPR (True Positive Rate) vs the FPR (False Positive Rate) at different threshold values is known as a ROC. It's used to assess the accuracy of categorization models. The AUC value goes from 0.5 to 1, with 0.5 denoting a poor classifier and 1 denoting an excellent one. Highest accuracy is defined as a single cutpoint, whereas ROC tests all of the cutpoints and depicts the sensitivity and specificity. When accuracy is compared across the board, it is done so using a cutpoint. Using class weights instead of sample strategies can increase the AUC-ROC score. By increasing the cost for misclassifying underrepresented classes, bias can be reduced without overtraining on samples from underrepresented classes. ROC AUC and Precision-Recall AUC are two metrics that can be used to compare classifiers and summarise the curve. On severely imbalanced classification problems with limited samples of the minority class, ROC curves and ROC AUC can be optimistic.

Figure 7. False positive

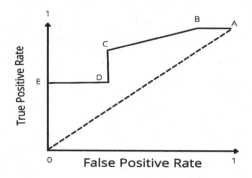

470

G. Log Loss

One of the most important performance measures for determining the performance of a classification task is Log Loss (Logistic Loss). The cross-entropy loss is another name for it. The performance of Log Loss is measured by comparing the actual class labels to the anticipated probability. Cross-entropy is used to quantify the comparison. Log Loss in binary classification refers to how close the forecast probability is to the real or true value, i.e., 0 or 1. The higher the log-loss number, the greater the difference between the expected and actual likelihood. Declaring 0.693 to be the non-informative number is a well-known metric for the log loss metric. Log loss is robust in the presence of imbalanced classes.

$$\log loss(N=1) = y\log(p) + (1-y) \log (1-p)$$

H. Sensitivity

Sensitivity is a metric that assesses a model's ability to predict true positives in each accessible category. Peoples appropriately generated positive results are tested using the sensitivity measure. A high - sensitivity test will detect almost everyone who has the disease and will not result in many false-negative results. It assesses the test's ability to detect a positive illness. Under a given set of assumptions, sensitivity determines how different values of an independent variable affect a certain dependent variable. The technique can be used to create forecasts about public company stock values or how interest rates affect bond prices. Sensitivity refers to the percentage of people who have the sickness and get a positive test result. A highly sensitive test detects the majority of individuals with the disease; when a test does an excellent job of filtering out those who don't have the ailment, it is considered to have high sensitivity. A test is considered to be low sensitivity if its sensitivity is weak.

I. Specificity

The True Negative Rate is a measure of specificity. It tells us what percentage of actual negative situations were predicted to be negative by the model. When the model's specificity is strong, it can accurately predict the true negative. The specificity of a test determines how likely it is to appropriately rule out people who do not have a condition. Validity metrics such as sensitivity and specificity aid specialists in deciding which tests to utilise. The specificity is computed by dividing the number of correctly categorised non-diseased persons by the total number of non-diseased individuals. A 90 percent specificity is obtained by multiplying 720 true negative results by 800, or all non-diseased persons, times 100.

8. LIMITATION OF ARTIFICIAL INTELLIGENCE

Generally, all the applications are developed to reduce the complexity problems. Similarly diabetic applications provide a good service in the healthcare. It helps in monitoring and controlling the sugar level by staying in their own place. If there is more advantage quite similar there will be few limitations. The limitation of AI in diabetic is given below:

8.1. Limitation of Data

The inability to create rational and accurate algorithms due to a lack of data is a prevalent problem in diabetes care. To build digital applications and uncover key answers, data sets will need to be more mature and structured. Limited data set can reduce the quality of the applications and also reduces usage of diabetic's applications.

8.2. Technical Factors

The cost, accessibility, and deployment of AI in diabetes care are the major roadblocks. Interoperability has been highlighted as a typical possible barrier to usage in diabetes care due to the rising number of devices and apps available.

8.3. Limitation of Design

Several models are designed and implemented for the disease prediction. The dataset determines the model's performance. Due to limited dataset, only few models are more familiar among the health expert. The limited data reduces the interest of designing models that can give more prominent results.

8.4. Human Factors

Some studies have looked into the factors that influence the use of AI in diabetes care. Based on expert comments, it was discovered that younger patients benefited more from diabetic smartphone apps.AI requires skilled modification on a consistent base, this might generate a malicious round of inaccuracy.

8.5 Data Bias

The AI model must be trained with a huge amount of data, such as health data or other forms of data. When the data used for training does not closely resemble the target group, or when AI models are trained with insufficient or incomplete data, this distortion might occur.

8.6 Personal

Health-care information is the most private information about another person that an individual may possess. Since confidentiality is linked to patients' rights or identity, uniqueness, and well-being, respecting an individual's privacy is a fundamental ethical principle in health care.

8.7 Ethical Double Effects

Since science is a wonder, certain findings cause damage .Sometimes this is suitable for few AI applications, the principle of ethical double effects must be strictly considered in applying AI .

8.8 Ethics Related to Research and Bio-Medicine

Bio-medical ethical principle must be obeyed in all new scientific AI techniques in health-care applications. Privacy and safety, voluntary participation, autonomous decision making should be considered and practiced in any implementation.

9. CONCLUSION

AI plays a major role in the growth of prediction methods particularly in evaluating the range of diabetes and its effects. Increase of DM around the world-wide gaining the attention on early prediction in recent years. Early prediction models for diabetic prediction are implemented based on AI techniques. The main of the objective of the study is to provide a detail review on DM, increase of DM around world-wide, datasets used in diabetic prediction, advance techniques and methods applied for disease prediction, applications and its limitations used in diabetic prediction. The study also provides a detail review on the datasets used in prediction and recent algorithms which guides the beginners focusing in the area of disease prediction with a well-grounded knowledge of existing methods. In future more real time data can be used rather using the publicly available data. The importance of performance metrics is described which to evaluate the model in terms of Accuracy, Precision, Recall, F-score, so on. AI has transformed diabetic treatment by its advance applications. Few applications are described and also the limitations, which motivates to concentrate more on the improvisation of the future prediction model with some advance datasets, algorithms and applications.

REFERENCES

Abbas, H. T., Alic, L., Erraguntla, M., Ji, J. X., Abdul-Ghani, M., Abbasi, Q. H., & Qaraqe, M. K. (2019). Predicting long-term type 2 diabetes with support vector machine using oral glucose tolerance test. *PLoS One*, *14*(12), e0219636. doi:10.1371/journal.pone.0219636 PMID:31826018

Albi, T. R., Rafi, M. N., Bushra, T. A., & Karim, D. Z. (2022). Diabetes Complication Prediction using Deep Learning-Based Analytics. *2022 International Conference on Advancement in Electrical and Electronic Engineering (ICAEEE)*, 1-6. 10.1109/ICAEEE54957.2022.9836401

Atlas, D. (2015). *International diabetes federation. In IDF Diabetes Atlas* (7th ed.). International Diabetes Federation.

Bhat, S. S., Selvam, V., Ansari, G. A., Ansari, M. D., & Rahman, M. H. (2022). Prevalence and Early Prediction of Diabetes Using Machine Learning in North Kashmir: A Case Study of District Bandipora. *Computational Intelligence and Neuroscience*, *2022*, 2022. doi:10.1155/2022/2789760 PMID:36238678

Butt, U. M., Letchmunan, S., Ali, M., Hassan, F. H., Baqir, A., & Hafiz, H. R. S. (2021). Machine Learning Based Diabetes Classification and Prediction for Healthcare Applications. *Journal of Healthcare Engineering*, *2021*, 2021. doi:10.1155/2021/9930985 PMID:34631003

Carolan-Olah, M., Steele, C., & Krenzin, G. (2015). Development and initial testing of a GDM information website for multi-ethnic women with GDM. *BMC Pregnancy and Childbirth*, *15*(1), 145. doi:10.118612884-015-0578-0 PMID:26142482

Chaki, J., Ganesh, S. T., Cidham, S. K., & Theertan, S. A. (2020). Machine learning and artificial intelligence-based Diabetes Mellitus detection and self-management: A systematic review. *Journal of King Saud University-Computer and Information Sciences*.

Channabasavaraju, B. D., & Vinayakamurthy, U. (2020). *An Analysis of Heart Disease for Diabetic Patients Using Recursive Feature Elimination with Random Forest*. Academic Press.

Deng, Y., Lu, L., Aponte, L., Angelidi, A. M., Novak, V., Karniadakis, G. E., & Mantzoros, C. S. (2021). Deep transfer learning and data augmentation improve glucose levels prediction in type 2 diabetes patients. *NPJ Digital Medicine*, *4*(1), 1–13. doi:10.103841746-021-00480-x PMID:34262114

Dinh, A., Miertschin, S., Young, A., & Mohanty, S. D. (2019). A data-driven approach to predicting diabetes and cardiovascular disease with machine learning. *BMC Medical Informatics and Decision Making*, *19*(1), 1–15. doi:10.118612911-019-0918-5 PMID:31694707

El Jerjawi, N. S., & Abu-Naser, S. S. (2018). Diabetes prediction using artificial neural network. *International Journal of Advanced Science and Technology, 121*.

Ellahham, S. (2020). Artificial intelligence: The future for diabetes care. *The American Journal of Medicine*, *133*(8), 895–900. doi:10.1016/j.amjmed.2020.03.033 PMID:32325045

Fagherazzi, G., & Ravaud, P. (2019). Digital diabetes: Perspectives for diabetes prevention, management and research. *Diabetes & Metabolism*, *45*(4), 322–329. doi:10.1016/j.diabet.2018.08.012 PMID:30243616

Faruque, M. F., & Sarker, I. H. (2019). Performance analysis of machine learning techniques to predict diabetes mellitus. In *2019 International Conference on Electrical, Computer and Communication Engineering (ECCE)* (pp. 1-4). IEEE. 10.1109/ECACE.2019.8679365

Frøisland, D. H., & Aorsand, E. (2015). Integrating visual dietary documentation in mobile-phone-based self-management application for adolescents with type 1 diabetes. *Journal of Diabetes Science and Technology*, *9*(3), 541–548. doi:10.1177/1932296815576956 PMID:25901020

Gill & Pathwar. (2021). *Prediction of Diabetes Using Various Feature Selection and Machine Learning Paradigms*. Easy Chair Preprint 6587.

Gulshan, V., Peng, L., Coram, M., Stumpe, M. C., Wu, D., Narayanaswamy, A., Venugopalan, S., Widner, K., Madams, T., Cuadros, J., Kim, R., Raman, R., Nelson, P. C., Mega, J. L., & Webster, D. R. (2016). Development and validation of a deep learning algorithm for detection of diabetic retinopathy in retinal fundus photographs. *Journal of the American Medical Association*, *316*(22), 2402–2410. doi:10.1001/jama.2016.17216 PMID:27898976

Han, W., & Ye, Y. (2019). A repository of microbial marker genes related to human health and diseases for host phenotype prediction using micro- biome data. *Pacific Symposium on Biocomputing*, *24*, 236–247. PMID:30864326

Hao, Y., Cheng, F., Pham, M., Rein, H., Patel, D., Fang, Y., Feng, Y., Yan, J., Song, X., Yan, H., & Wang, Y. (2019, April 23). A Noninvasive, Economical, and Instant-Result Method to Diagnose and Monitor Type 2 Diabetes Using Pulse Wave: Case-Control Study. *JMIR mHealth and uHealth*, *7*(4), e11959. doi:10.2196/11959 PMID:31012863

Hasan, M. K., Alam, M. A., Das, D., Hossain, E., & Hasan, M. (2020). Diabetes prediction using ensembling of different machine learning classifiers. *IEEE Access: Practical Innovations, Open Solutions*, *8*, 76516–76531. doi:10.1109/ACCESS.2020.2989857

Hathaway, Q. A., Roth, S. M., Pinti, M. V., Sprando, D. C., Kunovac, A., Durr, A. J., Cook, C. C., Fink, G. K., Cheuvront, T. B., Grossman, J. H., Aljahli, G. A., Taylor, A. D., Giromini, A. P., Allen, J. L., & Hollander, J. M. (2019). Machine-learning to stratify diabetic patients using novel cardiac biomarkers and integrative genomics. *Cardiovascular Diabetology*, *18*(1), 1–16. doi:10.118612933-019-0879-0 PMID:31185988

Kalis, B., Collier, M., & Fu, R. (2018). 10 promising AI applications in health care. *Harvard Business Review*.

Kavakiotis, I., Tsave, O., Salifoglou, A., Maglaveras, N., Vlahavas, I., & Chouvarda, I. (2017). Machine learning and data mining methods in diabetes research. *Computational and Structural Biotechnology Journal*, *15*, 104–116. doi:10.1016/j.csbj.2016.12.005 PMID:28138367

Khanam, J. J., & Foo, S. Y. (2021). *A comparison of machine learning algorithms for diabetes prediction*. ICT Express. doi:10.1016/j.icte.2021.02.004

Kowsher, M., Tahabilder, A., Sanjid, M. Z. I., Prottasha, N. J., Uddin, M. S., Hossain, M. A., & Jilani, M. A. K. (2021). LSTM-ANN & BiLSTM-ANN: Hybrid deep learning models for enhanced classification accuracy. *Procedia Computer Science*, *193*, 131–140. doi:10.1016/j.procs.2021.10.013

Lai, H., Huang, H., Keshavjee, K., Guergachi, A., & Gao, X. (2019). Predictive models for diabetes mellitus using machine learning techniques. *BMC Endocrine Disorders*, *19*(1), 1–9. doi:10.118612902-019-0436-6 PMID:31615566

Ling, S. H., San, P. P., & Nguyen, H. T. (2016). Non-invasive hypoglycemia monitoring system using extreme learning machine for Type 1 diabetes. *ISA Transactions*, *64*, 440–446. doi:10.1016/j.isatra.2016.05.008 PMID:27311357

Lu, X., & Song, R. (2022, August). A Hybrid Deep Learning Model for the Blood Glucose Prediction. In *2022 IEEE 11th Data Driven Control and Learning Systems Conference (DDCLS)* (pp. 1037-1043). IEEE. 10.1109/DDCLS55054.2022.9858348

Marr, B. (2018). How is AI used in healthcare-5 powerful real-world examples that show the latest advances. *Forbes*, (July), 27.

Martinez-Vernon, A. S., Covington, J. A., Arasaradnam, R. P., Esfahani, S., O'connell, N., Kyrou, I., & Savage, R. S. (2018). An improved machine learning pipeline for urinary volatiles disease detection: Diagnosing diabetes. *PLoS One*, *13*(9), e0204425. doi:10.1371/journal.pone.0204425 PMID:30261000

Miazi, Z. A., Jahan, S., Niloy, M. A., Shama, A., Rahman, M. Z., Islam, M. R., ... Das, S. K. (2021, July). A Cloud-based App for Early Detection of Type II Diabetes with the Aid of Deep Learning. In *2021 International Conference on Automation, Control and Mechatronics for Industry 4.0 (ACMI)* (pp. 1-6). IEEE. 10.1109/ACMI53878.2021.9528136

Misra, P., & Yadav, A. S. (2020). Improving the classification accuracy using recursive feature elimination with cross-validation. *Int. J. Emerg. Technol, 11*(3), 659–665.

Mujumdar, A., & Vaidehi, V. (2019). Diabetes prediction using machine learning algorithms. *Procedia Computer Science, 165*, 292–299. doi:10.1016/j.procs.2020.01.047

Nadesh, R. K., & Arivuselvan, K. (2020). Type 2: Diabetes mellitus prediction using deep neural networks classifier. *International Journal of Cognitive Computing in Engineering, 1*, 55–61. doi:10.1016/j.ijcce.2020.10.002

NCBI. (n.d.). https://www.ncbi.nlm.nih.gov/pmc/articles/PMC6844177/table/T1/

Nguyen, B. P., Pham, H. N., Tran, H., Nghiem, N., Nguyen, Q. H., Do, T. T., Tran, C. T., & Simpson, C. R. (2019). Predicting the onset of type 2 diabetes using wide and deep learning with electronic health records. *Computer Methods and Programs in Biomedicine, 182*, 105055. doi:10.1016/j.cmpb.2019.105055 PMID:31505379

Prabhu, P., & Selvabharathi, S. (2019). Deep Belief Neural Network Model for Prediction of Diabetes Mellitus. In *2019 3rd International Conference on Imaging, Signal Processing and Communication (ICISPC)* (pp. 138-142). IEEE. 10.1109/ICISPC.2019.8935838

Research Gate. (n.d.). https://www.researchgate.net/publication/345991601_Diabetes_prediction_using_machine_learning_algorithm

Rollo, M. E., Aguiar, E. J., Williams, R. L., Wynne, K., Kriss, M., Callister, R., & Collins, C. E. (2016). eHealth technologies to support nutrition and physical activity behaviors in diabetes self-management. *Diabetes, Metabolic Syndrome and Obesity, 9*, 381–390. doi:10.2147/DMSO.S95247 PMID:27853384

Sah, R. D., Patro, S. P., Padhy, N., & Salimath, N. (2021). Diabetics Patients Analysis Using Deep Learning and Gradient Boosted Trees. In *2021 8th International Conference on Computing for Sustainable Global Development (INDIACom)* (pp. 937-941). IEEE.

Seyhan, A. A., & Carini, C. (2019). Are innovation and new technologies in preci- sion medicine paving a new era in patients centric care? *Journal of Translational Medicine, 17*(1), 114. doi:10.118612967-019-1864-9 PMID:30953518

Shah, V. N., & Garg, S. K. (2015). Managing diabetes in the digital age. *Clinical Diabetes and Endocrinology, 1*(1), 16. doi:10.118640842-015-0016-2 PMID:28702234

Sim, L. L. W., Ban, K. H. K., Tan, T. W., Sethi, S. K., & Loh, T. P. (2017). Development of a clinical decision support system for diabetes care: A pilot study. *PLoS One, 12*(2), e0173021. doi:10.1371/journal.pone.0173021 PMID:28235017

Singhal, S., & Carlton, S. (2019). *The era of exponential improvement in healthcare.* McKinsey & Company.

Singla, R., Singla, A., Gupta, Y., & Kalra, S. (2019). Artificial intelligence/machine learning in diabetes care. *Indian Journal of Endocrinology and Metabolism, 23*(4), 495. doi:10.4103/ijem.IJEM_228_19 PMID:31741913

Swapna, G., Vinayakumar, R., & Soman, K. P. (2018). Diabetes detection using deep learning algorithms. *ICT Express, 4*(4), 243-246.

Tcheng, J. E. (Ed.). (2017). *Optimizing strategies for clinical decision support: summary of a meeting series*. National Academy of Medicine.

Team, E. (2020). What is Machine Learning? A definition-. *Expert Systems: International Journal of Knowledge Engineering and Neural Networks*.

Xu, L., He, J., & Hu, Y. (2021). Early Diabetes Risk Prediction Based on Deep Learning Methods. In *2021 4th International Conference on Pattern Recognition and Artificial Intelligence (PRAI)* (pp. 282-286). IEEE. 10.1109/PRAI53619.2021.9551074

Zou, Q., Qu, K., Luo, Y., Yin, D., Ju, Y., & Tang, H. (2018). Predicting diabetes mellitus with machine learning techniques. *Frontiers in Genetics, 9*, 515. doi:10.3389/fgene.2018.00515 PMID:30459809

478

Chapter 22
Lightweight Neural Networks for Pedestrian Detection in Intelligent Vehicles

Riadh Ayachi
University of Monastir, Tunisia

Mouna Afif
University of Monastir, Tunisia

Yahia Said
University of Monastir, Tunisia

Abdessalem Ben Abdelali
University of Monastir, Tunisia

ABSTRACT

Most actual intelligent vehicles (IV) are powered by a variety of sensors and cameras. Vision-based applications for IV mainly require visual information. In this paper, the authors introduce a pedestrian detection application used for pedestrian safety. The authors proposed a deep fully convolutional neural network (DFCNN) for pedestrian detection. The proposed model is suitable for mobile implementation. To do this, the authors propose to build lightweight blocks using convolution layers, and replace pooling layers and fully connected layers with convolution layers. Training and testing of the proposed DFCNN model for pedestrian detection were performed using the Caltech dataset. The proposed DFCNN has achieved 85% of average precision and an inference speed of 30 FPS. The reported results have demonstrated the robustness of the proposed DFCNN for pedestrian detection. The achieved performance was low computation complexity and high performance.

DOI: 10.4018/978-1-6684-6937-8.ch022

INTRODUCTION

The explosion in the number of both vehicles and pedestrians makes it hard to share the same environment safely. According to the Association for Safe International Road Travel (2019), 1.25 million persons die in a crash accident each year with an average of 3,287 deaths per day. Besides, 20-50 million persons are injured or disabled.

One of the proposed solutions is IV which is used to help the driver in a complicated situation or to perform a simple task like driving on a highway. Most IVs are equipped with the latest technologies. An IV is equipped with a big number of active sensors like ultrasonic and passive sensors like cameras. Most IV applications are based on passive sensors thanks to their low power consumption. In addition, an IV can control the vehicle through the engine, gearbox, and brakes. It can apply a set of authorized actions in case of potential danger such as a crush on another vehicle or pedestrian. A vision-based application for an IV is the most important. Many vision applications like traffic sign detection and recognition (Ayachi, 2019a), (Ayachi, 2019b), and traffic light detection (Dimian, 2019) have been stacked in IV to provide the driver with important information about the traffic environment. IV has been developed to enhance traffic security and to ensure a safer environment. Human beings, either the driver or the pedestrian, represent the most important element to focus on their safety.

Motivated by pedestrian safety, the pedestrian detection system was designed through an intelligent vision that processes camera data and localizes pedestrians automatically. A high-performance pedestrian detection system can locate pedestrians under challenging conditions such as occlusion and warn the driver to avoid potential accidents. This can help to improve driving safety in urban spaces. However, implementing an accurate pedestrian detection system on a limited computation resources device is considered a hard challenge that must be addressed. The mentioned challenge was considered a motivation for the proposed approach in addition to pedestrian safety.

With a focus on pedestrian safety, a pedestrian detection application for an IV was proposed. The main idea of the proposed application is to process the visual data and detect pedestrians while crossing the street to warn the driver. The main challenge of building a robust pedestrian detection application comes first from the limited computation resources of the platform used for IV and from the complexity of the environment because of the lighting conditions, the point of view, the complex background, and occlusion. A reliable and robust pedestrian detection application must overcome those challenges as a priority. Besides reliability, real-time operation is another challenge for pedestrian detection applications. The application must detect pedestrians even at high speed and moving pedestrians. Advances in artificial intelligence (AI) techniques have achieved great success in different fields including computer vision and its applications. Those AI techniques are considered a suitable solution for pedestrian detection in IV.

The proposed pedestrian detection application is based on a convolutional neural network (CNN) (Krizhevsky, 2012). It is a deep learning (Schmidhuber, 2015) model generally deployed to solve vision-based applications. Convolutional neural networks are inspired by the biological system (Fukushima, 1980) where the connectivity between the artificial neurons is similar to the organization of the visual cortex of an animal. This connectivity allows the building of a deep convolutional neural network (DCNN) with tens of hidden layers and enables feeding the network with a huge amount of training data without overfitting it (Zeiler, 2014). DCNN was deployed successfully to solve vision-based applications. Many DCNN models were proposed to solve vision-based applications such as object detection (Ayachi, 2020), indoor object recognition (Afif, 2018), face identification (Ranjan, 2019), and human pose estimation

(Omran, 2018). In this paper, we propose to use the DCNN for pedestrian detection applications. Although the DCNN is computationally expensive and energy intensive.

The problem that this work tries to solve is more challenging due to many reasons. First, the input data is very complex due to the complexity of the background, deformation occlusion, and many others. Second, the processing system has limited resources in terms of computation and memory. Third, real-time processing must be achieved to guarantee pedestrian safety. So, it was critical to build a high-performance detection technique that provides a balance between accuracy, processing speed, and computation complexity. The proposed model was based on DFCNN which provided the needed performance with good computation complexity.

In this work, a set of optimization techniques was proposed to make the DCNN fit into an embedded device. The first optimization is to build a custom convolution lightweight block to reduce computation complexity. The second optimization is using strided convolution layers instead of pooling layers to enhance the model precision. The third optimization is to replace fully connected layers with a convolution layer to reduce the storage memory used. So, we end up with a Deep fully convolutional neural network (DFCNN). Also, more optimizations were applied like model compression and pruning to reduce the model size in terms of memory. Also, data quantization was applied by converting the floating point to a fixed point. Thus, weights are clustered and the same number of connections can be represented using less amount of memory. The application of those optimizations results in reducing the computation effort and storage memory while getting better performance and accelerating the inference speed. In general, Deep learning models need large-scale data for training and thus to achieve high performance.

The primary aim of the proposed DFCNN is to design an efficient neural network suitable for computer vision tasks on mobile and embedded devices. In effect, the proposed model provides the best trade-off between accuracy, speed, and size. To accomplish the desired goal, we proposed to replace traditional convolution layers with lightweight convolution blocks with and without residual connections. Besides, we optimized the pedestrian detection task to a single regression problem. Through extensive experimentation, we showed that the suggested model was effective for the pedestrian detection task. by achieving impressive results in addition to the suitability for embedded implementation. The proposed DFCNN is very efficient by balancing the performance of different evaluation metrics. Most of the existing ones are optimized in one way either for high-performance or embedded implementation.

To provide training data for the proposed DFCNN, we used the Caltech dataset (Dollar, 2011). Besides, we use the same dataset for performance. The proposed model achieved 85% of average precision and an inference speed of 30 FPS when tested using an NVIDIA GTX 960 GPU. The achieved results allow for an embedded implementation with the same performance while still running in real-time.

The main contributions of this work are the followings:

- Proposing a pedestrian detection system for IV
- Proposing lightweight convolution blocks to reduce network complexity
- Proposing a DFCNN model that provides a good trade-off between network complexity and accuracy in addition to being suitable for embedded implementation.
- Performance Evaluation of the proposed DFCNN model on a challenging dataset and high performance was achieved.
- Evaluating the effect of the non-linear activation function on the performance of the model.

The rest of the paper is organized as follows, the related works and their evaluation will be presented in section 2. Section 3 will be reserved for the presentation of the proposed DFCNN model. In section 4, we will present the experimental results and discussion. The paper will be concluded in section 5.

RELATED WORKS

Pedestrian detection is a research area that attracts innovation because of its importance for many applications such as surveillance, robotic navigation, etc. The classic pedestrian detection algorithm is based on handcrafted features such as the Aggregate Channel Features (ACF) (Dollar, 2014), where individual pixel lookups are extracted from the concatenation of the LUV (Rauf, 2016), a histogram of oriented gradients (Mao, 2010), and gradient magnitude image channels (Xue, 2014). In recent years, the birth of deep learning techniques, a set of machine learning algorithms based on artificial neural networks, made it possible to reach a better performance than using handcrafted features techniques. In particular, CNN has significantly boosted state-of-the-art of pedestrian detection applications. Many works are proposed to improve the performance of the pedestrian detection application. A detailed survey (Chen, 2021) was presented to show the best deep learning-based systems for pedestrian detection in autonomous vehicles.

Mateus et al. (2019) propose to concatenate the ACF detector with a DCNN to build a pedestrian detection application. Then proposed pedestrian detection application was used for Human-Aware Navigation. The main idea was to use the pedestrian detection application for person tracking in a robot to make it able to cope with human-aware constraints. Angelova et al. (2015) proposes to cascade deep convolutional neural networks with fast features and apply them to the pedestrian detection task. Caltech dataset was used for evaluation. and a 26.2% average miss rate was achieved. The proposed approach was developed to reach real-time. Using the NVIDIA K20 Tesla GPU, 15 FPS was achieved. The proposed method was computationally extensive and requires high-performance computers.

A pedestrian detection application based on the combination of Generative Adversarial Networks (GANs) (Goodfellow, 2014) and the single-shot multi-box detector (SSD) (Lui, 2016) was proposed by Dinakaran et al. (2019). The pedestrian detection application was deployed to detect pedestrians at distance in smart cities for surveillance. The DCGAN (Radford, 2015) enhanced image resolution and thus allowed the detector to localize pedestrians of different sizes at different distances. The SSD was used to detect and identify pedestrians in the images. The proposed pedestrian detection application used the CIFAR dataset (Krizhevsky, 2009) for evaluation. it achieved a detection accuracy of 80.7%. the proposed detection method was designed to run on powerful computers and was not suitable for embedded devices.

The fusion of object detection and segmentation networks was proposed for pedestrian detection (Islam, 2022). The main idea was to fuse pair-wise features from the object detection model and the segmentation models based on a consensus scoring method. The proposed approach combined both models in an asymmetric inferencing style to solve the problem of runtime efficiency. The final accuracy of the proposed approach was boosted and the generalization power was increased.

A pedestrian detection system (Barba-Guaman, 2020) based on state-of-the-art objects detection models such as pedNet (Ullah, 2018) and SSD (Lui, 2016). The SSD model with a mobileNet v2 model (Sandler, 2018) backbone model achieved the best balance between speed and precision. The proposed models were implemented on an embedded GPU. The jetson nano was used for the evaluation of the models. The proposed models were evaluated on many benchmark datasets. A low processing speed was achieved which makes the proposed method not suitable for real use.

A pedestrian detection application using Faster R-CNN (Ren, 2015) was proposed (Zhang, 2017). The main idea was to extract features from input images using a simple convolutional neural network. The extracted features were fed to the region proposal network (RPN) to extract region proposals that might contain pedestrians. Then the proposed regions were combined with the output of the feature extractor using a spatial pooling layer. The result of this combination was sent to the classifier to identify pedestrians and to the regressor to predict bounding boxes used to locate the pedestrian. The evaluation of the proposed model on the INRIA dataset (Dalal, 2005) results in a detection accuracy of 92.7%. The achieved processing speed was too slow and cannot meet real-time processing constraints.

The YOLOv2 model was used for pedestrian detection (Said, 2019). SqueezeNet was used as a backbone. Testing on the Caltech Pedestrian Dataset achieved 75.8% of accuracy. the archived accuracy cannot guarantee pedestrian safety.

Pedestrian detection application was and still an important application for many fields. As mentioned above, many techniques were proposed for different use cases. The main inconvenience of the proposed techniques that are not suitable for embedded implementation because of the intense need for computation resources and storage memory to achieve high performance. Most of the proposed method was enhanced in one way and does not provide balanced performances. In the next section, we will provide details about the proposed pedestrian detection for IV. The proposed DFCNN used to perform pedestrian detection is suitable for embedded implementation with balanced performances.

PROPOSED METHOD

The importance of the pedestrian detection application makes it a research area that needs to be improved for better performance. Reaching a good trade-off between speed and precision is the key feature for developing the optimal pedestrian detection application. Besides, most real-world applications are implemented on embedded devices. In this section, we describe the proposed modifications made to the proposed model to make it acceptable for embedded implementation, as well as the specifics of the proposed DFCNN model utilized for the pedestrian detection application.

Traditional DCNN is composed of different layers. Convolution layers are the most important in the network since they are used to extract valuable features from the input data to learn weights. Standard convolution layers are expensive in terms of computation resources. So, lightweight convolution blocks (LCB) were built to reduce the computation effort used by convolution layers. The LCB is based on convolution and activation layers. Each block is composed of a 1x1 convolution layer followed by an expanded stage composed of 1x1 and 3x3 convolution layers and we end up with the concatenation of the output of the 1x1 and 3x3 convolution layers. Also, we add a residual connection where the input channels are equal to the output channels of the block. So, in the proposed DFCNN we used 2 types of LCB: simple LCB (SLCB) and residual LCB (RLCB) with the skip connection connecting the input to the output. Figure 1 illustrates the proposed lightweight convolution block. The first 1x1 convolution layer was used to reduce the number of input channels of the 3x3 convolution layers.

The number of parameters of a 3x3 convolution layer can be calculated as equation 1. Thus, reducing the number of input channels will result in reducing the number of parameters.

#parameters = #channels * #filters *(3*3)   (1)

Where #parameters are the number of parameters, #channels are the number of channels of the actual feature maps and #filters are the number of filters applied for generating the next feature maps.

Figure 1. Proposed lightweight convolution block

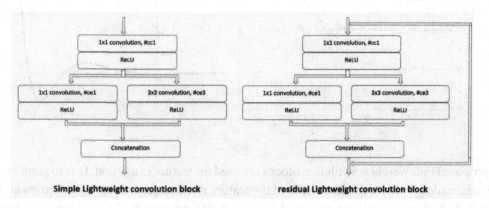

The 1x1 convolution layers at the expanded stage are used to replace the 3x3 convolution layers because 1x1 convolution has 9 times fewer parameters than 3x3 convolution. So, 1x1 convolution can run 9 times faster than 3x3 convolution. For each convolution layer, we define the number of filters (#cc1, #ce1, and #ce3) and we set #cc1 always less than the sum of #ce1 and #ce3. After each convolution, we apply an activation layer. Several nonlinear activation functions have been evaluated such as the rectified linear unit (ReLU) (Ide, 2017), Leaky ReLU (Xu, 2015), Exponential Linear Unit (ELU) (Clevert, 2015), SELU (Klambauer, 2017), SERLU (Zhang, 2018), swish (Ramachandran, 2017) and the most recent scaled polynomial constant unit (SPOCU) (Kiseľák, 2020). The curves of different activation functions are illustrated in figure 2. The main idea of using the nonlinear function for the activation layers is to allow such networks to compute nontrivial problems using only a small number of neurons. The activation function does the non-linear transformation to the input making DCNN capable of learning and performing more complex tasks than using linear functions.

Figure 2. Curves of the evaluated nonlinear activation functions

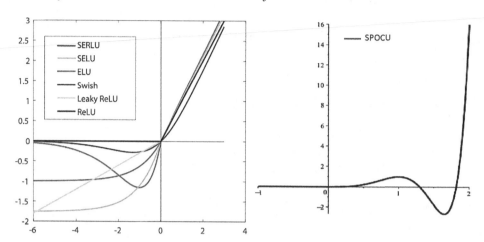

The proposed lightweight convolution blocks are used for feature extraction. Due to input high resolution, we need to downsample the dimension of the feature maps to get smaller feature maps at the output of the network. In the standard case, pooling layers are used for downsampling but many studies (Ayachi, 2018) prove that using strided convolution is more efficient than pooling layers. Besides, strided convolution can help improve the accuracy and reliability when building deep convolution neural networks for embedded divides. So, max-pooling layers were replaced by convolution layers with a stride of 2 for dimension compression. The architecture of the proposed model is illustrated in figure 3.

Figure 3. Architecture of the proposed DFCNN model

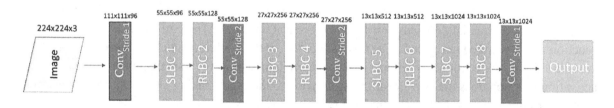

To generate predictions, standard DCNN uses fully connected layers, but in this work, we have replaced fully connected layers with 1x1 convolution layers. As known fully connected layers consume a lot of storage memory to save the network parameters. So, we can reduce memory usage by replacing the fully connected layers with the equivalent 1x1 convolution layers.

After defining the composition of the proposed model, we end up building a network using only convolution and activation layers. That's why we named the proposed model a fully deep convolutional neural network (DFCNN).

Table 1 presents proposed DFCNN configurations. The input image was fixed to 224x224x3. For all convolution layers, a 3x3 kernel size was used except for the convolution layer used for predictions.

For more optimizations to reach embedded implementation, we proposed to apply model compression and pruning techniques. The main idea of the pruning technique is to remove redundant connections and eliminate weight with very small values. Also, we apply the data quantization technique by replacing the original 32 bits floating-point representation with 16 bits fixed point. The model will lose accuracy after those optimizations. But we fine-tune the resulting model with the training data and this leads to recovering most of the initial accuracy loss.

Table 1. Configuration of the proposed DFCNN model

Layer	Size	Kernel Size	Stride	#cc1	#ce1	#ce3
Input	224x224x3					
Convolution	111x111x96	3x3	1			
SLBC 1	55x55x96		1	16	64	64
RLBC 2	55x55x128		1	16	64	64
Convolution	55x55x128	3x3	2			
SLBC 3	27x27x256		1	32	128	128
RLBC 4	27x27x256		1	32	128	128
Convolution	27x27x256	3x3	2			
SLBC 5	13x13x512		1	48	192	192
RLBC 6	13x13x512		1	48	192	192
SLBC 7	13x13x1024		1	64	256	256
RLBC 8	13x13x1024		1	64	256	256
Convolution	13x13x1024	1x1	1			

To make the proposed DFCNN useful for the pedestrian detection application, a detection technique must be defined to localize and identify pedestrians in the images. Since there is only one class to identify, the problem can be considered as a regression problem where the network must provide predictions about the parameters of the bounding box used to localize the pedestrian in the image. Pedestrian detection was solved as a simple regression problem and this will accelerate the detection process. That, in turn, will be performed with a single forward pass across the DFCNN. To generate predictions, a set of predefined anchors were tested on the output layer. In real life, pedestrians have a similar shape, which can be defined according to the dimension of the pedestrian or the distance of the detection. In effect, we define 5 anchors for pedestrian detection. To determine the dimension of the predefined anchors, we run a K-means clustering technique on the ground truth bounding boxes of the training set. We execute K-means clustering on the training data to get the centroids of the top-5 clusters in order to determine the top 5 anchors that have the best coverage for the training data. Since using the Euclidean distance as a distance metric will not be useful, IoU was used instead. The used distance metric was defined as equation 3.

$$d(box, anchor) = 1 - IOU(box, anchor) \tag{3}$$

Based on K-means clustering, we define the best 5 anchor shapes for pedestrian detection according to the different factors. To generate a prediction, we apply the different anchors on each location of the output layer. Outside, DFCNN model takes an input image with a shape of 227x227x3, 3 denotes the RGB space color, and generates an output layer with a shape of 13x13x512. The 13x13 feature map can be considered a grid. For each cell in the grid, all anchor shapes were tested and 5 parameters (x, y, w, h, c) for each bounding box were predicted. The (x, y) are coordinates of the center, h is the height, w is the width, and c is the confidence score which tells us how likely the predicted bounding box contains a pedestrian. For each tested anchor, 5 parameters were predicted $(a_x, a_y, a_w, a_h, a_c)$. Since the anchors are picked based on the IoU, the parameters are easier to learn which makes the network more stable and help to achieve higher performance. The parameters of the predicted bounding box were calculated using a sigma function on the predicted anchor parameters. Considering (c_x, c_y) are the coordinate of the top left corner of the tested anchor has a coordinate and the tested bounding box has a width w_a and a height h_a then the parameters can be calculated as equation 4.

$$x = \sigma(ax_,) + cx \tag{4}$$

$$y = \sigma(ay_,) + cy$$

$$w = w_a e^{a_w}$$

$$h = h_a e^{a_h}$$

The confidence score is determined using the sigma function on the a_c value. On the other hand, we can determine the confidence score using the IoU value. We define a p-value that accepts a value of 1 if there is a pedestrian in the expected bounding box and a value of 0 otherwise. So, the confidence score can be estimated as equation 5.

$$\sigma(ac_,) = p \times IoU \tag{5}$$

We employed the retro propagation based on the gradient descent approach to train the suggested DFCNN model. The gradient descent algorithm's main goal is to maximize a loss function that calculates the difference between the output of the network and the desired output. The basis for the loss function's optimization is the calculation of its gradient, which is subsequently used to update the network weights' value. The loss function is presented in equation 6.

$$loss = \lambda_{coord} \sum_{i=1}^{s^2} \sum_{j=1}^{k} q_{ij}^{obj} (x_i - \hat{x}_i)^2 + (y_i - \hat{y}_i)^2 + \lambda_{coord} \sum_{i=1}^{s^2} \sum_{j=1}^{k} q_{ij}^{obj} (\sqrt{w_i} - \sqrt{\hat{w}_i})^2$$
$$+ (\sqrt{h_i} - \sqrt{\hat{h}_i})^2 + \sum_{i=1}^{s^2} \sum_{j=1}^{k} q_{ij}^{obj} (c_i - \hat{c}_i)^2 + \lambda_{noobj} \sum_{i=1}^{s^2} \sum_{j=1}^{k} q_{ij}^{noobj} (c_i - \hat{c}_i)^2 \tag{6}$$

(x_i, y_i) define the *ith* center coordinate of the ground truth bounding box.

$(\hat{x}_i, \hat{y}_i)$ define the *ith* center coordinate of the predicted bounding box.

$\hat{w}_i$ is the width of the *ith* ground truth bounding box.

w_i is the width of the *ith* predicted bounding box.

$\hat{h}_i$ is the height of the *ith* ground truth bounding box.

h_i is the height of the *ith* predicted bounding box.

$\hat{c}_i$ is the confidence score of the bounding box j in cell *i*.

c_i is the target confidence score.

s is the grid size.

k is the number of the predicted bounding boxes.

The suggested model was created to be suited for embedded devices and to attain excellent performance in terms of speed and accuracy. It provides a balanced network complexity and performance. In effect, the Faster R-CNN (Ren et al., 2015) was designed to achieve high detection accuracy but low processing speed. The yolo model (Said and Barr, 2019) was proposed to achieve real-time processing but has low accuracy. The SSD model (Liu et al., 2016) has combined speed and accuracy but it was computationally extensive and required a high-performance GPU to meet real-time processing constraints.

The DFCNN building blocks were designed in a way that allows extracting more relevant features to achieve high accuracy without exploding the network complexity which results in accelerating the processing speed and reducing the model size. The combination of 1x1 and 3x3 convolution kernels at the same stage was the key to the efficiency of the lightweight convolution blocks. Furthermore, considering the detection task as a regression problem allowed us to reduce the computation complexity and accelerated the processing speed. Besides, the compression techniques have demonstrated their impact by compressing the model size and accelerating the speed without big damage to the accuracy.

EXPERIMENTS AND RESULTS

In this section, we provide details about the training and the evolution of the proposed DFCNN model and its implementation for a pedestrian detection application. To train and evaluate the proposed model, we used a desktop with an intel i7 CPU and an Nvidia GTX 690. The Nvidia GTX 690 is equipped with 1024 cores and 4 GB of memory.

The proposed DFCNN model was trained and evaluated using the Caltech Dataset (Dollar, 2011). This dataset contains 1000000 video frames where only 250000 are labeled. In this work, the labeled data were used for the training and evaluation of the proposed model. There are two types of frames: positive frames (which include pedestrians) and negative frames (frames that do not contain a pedestrian). 132000 of the frames are positive, and the rest are negative. 350000 tagged pedestrians are counted in the dataset, of which 126000 are partially obscured. There are 11 filmed sessions in the dataset. A training set and a test set were created from the dataset. Six sessions were set out for training, and five sessions for tests. This dataset is considered the best dataset for the evaluation of pedestrian detection applications for IV because the images are captured using a camera mounted on a car. So, it presents the scenario of detecting pedestrians in a road traffic environment. Figure 4 presents image samples from the Caltech dataset.

Figure 4. Images from the Caltech dataset

After preparing the data, we choose a gradient descent algorithm to optimize the loss function and train the proposed DFCNN model. In this work, Adam algorithm (Kingma and Ba, 2014) was adopted. The Adam converges faster with a better minimum. Adam assigns each set of parameters with a different learning rate for better results. Adam is based on the first moment (mean) and the second moment (uncentred variance) to adapt the learning rate for each weight of the neural network. To get the moments' estimations, Adam uses exponentially moving averages of the gradient m_t and the squared gradient v_t, computed on the gradient evaluated on a current mini-batch. The estimates of the moments can be computed as equation 7 where g is the gradient on the current mini-batch and $\beta 1$ and $\beta 2$ are 2 values close to 1. In the experiment, $\beta 1$ is equal to 0.9 and $\beta 2$ is equal to 0.999

$$mt = \beta 1 mt_{-1}(1 - \beta 1)gt$$

$$v_t = {}_{\beta}2vt - 1_{(}1 - \beta 2)gt \tag{7}$$

mt and vt are estimates of the gradient and the squared gradient. So, the expected values of the estimators should be equal to the parameter we're trying to estimate. Then, the property presented in equation 8 must be true. Based on these properties, the estimators are unbiased.

$$E[mt] = E[gt]$$

$$E\left[v_t\right] = E\left[g_t^2\right] \tag{8}$$

For estimator correction and to generate the expected values, The gradient's exponential moving average and its squared gradient both received a bias correction. The bias correction can be computed as equation 9.

$$\widehat{m_t} = \frac{m_t}{1 - \beta_1^t}$$

$$\widehat{v_t} = \frac{v_t}{1 - \beta_2^t} \tag{9}$$

After correcting the estimator, the corrected values are used for the weights updated for the network train. The weights update can be performed as equation 10. w_{t+1} is the updated weight, w_t is the current weight and α is the step size that depends on the iteration. ε is a small value equal to 10-8.

$$w_{t+1} = w_t - \frac{\alpha}{\sqrt{v_t} + \varepsilon} \widehat{m_t} \qquad (10)$$

To train the network, the weights are updated until finding the minimum difference between the output of the proposed DFCNN and the ground truth output. The curve of the loss function minimization is presented in figure 5.

Figure 5. Loss function minimization curve

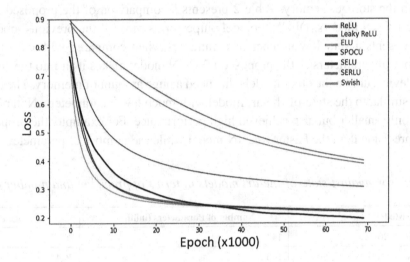

The suggested DFCNN model achieves 89% training accuracy. We opt to use precision as an evaluation parameter because accuracy can only tell us how likely the model was trained correctly. The accuracy can provide insight into how well the model performs when making real positive predictions. Precision can be calculated as equation 11.

$$precision = \frac{true\ positive}{true\ positive + false\ positive} \qquad (11)$$

On the test set of the Caltech dataset, the proposed DFCNN was assessed. and it achieved a precision of 85% using the ReLU activation function and a maximum precision of 85.86% using the SPOCU activation function. Table 2 present the achieved precision according to the used activation function.

Table 2. Achieved precision according to the used activation function

Activation Function	ReLU	Leaky ReLU	ELU	SELU	SERLU	Swish	SPOCU
Precision (%)	85	85.12	85.37	85.48	85.63	85.72	85.86

Competitive results were achieved. the proposed compression techniques were applied to reduce model size. The compression and pruning techniques cause a 1.54% loss in precision and the data quantization technique causes a loss of 2.4% of precision for the model based on the ReLU activation function. So, fine-tuning was performed using training data for 20K iterations to regain the precision. The fine-tuned model achieves a precision of 83.9%. the model based on the SPOCU activation function has achieved a slightly better precision of 83.97%. The proposed optimization results in reducing the number of parameters from 0.7 million to 0.4 million. The achieved results help to reduce the model size from 9 MB to 5 MB on the storage memory. Table 2 presents a comparison of the proposed DFCNN model against existing DCNN models. DFCNN model outperforms most of the previous models in terms of precision and presents a very low number of parameters when compared with existing models. The presented number of parameters of the proposed DFCNN model makes it fit into the small memory of the embedded device, unlike the other models that need a huge amount of memory. The proposed model has a precision similar to the state-of-the-art model with much fewer parameters. Notably, the proposed model was not only smaller but also achieved high performance. For example, the proposed model has better average precision than the Faster R-CNN model while the number of parameters is much fewer.

Table 3. Comparison against state-of-the-art models in terms of precision and number of parameters

Model	Number of Parameters (million)	Average Precision (%)
Fused DNN (Angelova, 2015)	147	89
Faster R-CNN (Zhang, 2017)	160	76.4
SSD + Squeeze Net (Verbickas, 2017)	2.5	71.6
Yolo v2 (Said, 2019)	253	75.8
DFCNN (ours)	0.7	85.86
DFCNN compressed (ours)	0.4	83.97

For an embedded implementation another factor must be respected which is real-time processing. The definition of real-time varies from one application to another. For a pedestrian detection application on an IV, we must consider the vehicle's speed, the pedestrian's movement, and the distance at which the pedestrian is visible to the camera. Yet since the speed of the vehicle is much higher than the speed of the pedestrian, we can take into account the vehicle's speed only. If we suppose that the vehicle travels with a speed of 80 KM/h, which means 22 meters/ second, and the distance separating the pedestrian and the vehicle is 30 meters. Then, to process the data and find the pedestrian, 10 frames per second will be sufficient. In this work, we tested the proposed DFCNN using an Nvidia GTX960 GPU and we got an inference speed of 30 FPS. The compressed model achieved 37 FPS. The achieved results prove the migration easily for an embedded device. Table 3 presents a comparison between the proposed DFCNN model and existing models. The proposed DFCNN model achieves the best inference speed surpassing all of the existing models by a big margin. The proposed model achieves a high balance between speed and accuracy. Additionally, it can be used for embedded implementation on edge devices. DFCNN size grants its implementation on a mobile device. In addition, the achieved processing speed allows an easy shift to the mobile device.

Table 4. Comparison with state-of-the-art models in terms of inference speed

Model	Inference Speed (FPS)
Faster R-CNN (Zhang, 2017)	21
SSD + Squeeze Net (Verbickas, 2017)	8.6
Fused DNN (Angelova, 2015)	8.15
YOLO V2 + InceptionV3	19.2
YOLO V3 +SPPnet	9.55
DFCNN (ours)	30
DFCNN compressed (ours)	37

The proposed DFCNN was implemented in pedestrian detection applications using the Nvidia GTX960 GPU and it has proved its efficiency when tested on new images. The DFCNN model presents a high generalization power. Figure 6 presents a detection example of the pedestrian detection application on images from the test set (first picture) and new images (second picture).

The proposed model has achieved a good trade-off between computation complexity and performance. The use of the lightweight convolution blocks was very effective and allowed for reducing the computation complexity and enhanced the accuracy. Besides transforming the pedestrian detection task into a regression problem has speeded up the processing speed and allowed for achieving real-time processing. The choice of the activation function is very important. The SPOCU activation function has resulted in achieving better performance compared to the use of the ReLU activation function.

The reported results prove the efficacy of the proposed model through the design of the building block and the optimization techniques. Also, considering the detection task as a regression problem has enhanced the overall performance and allowed the reaching of the desired goal. The proposed DFCNN has been validated for pedestrian detection by achieving real-time processing and high accuracy which guarantees pedestrian safety. Besides, it was suitable for embedded implementation which allows its implementation in IV perfectly.

The DFCNN was more suitable for pedestrian detection for IV due to its high performance with a low computation complexity. Higher performance with fewer layers can be achieved compared to traditional DCNN with pooling layers. Furthermore, the proposed DFCNN was very effective in detecting pedestrians under challenging conditions such as occlusion and geometric deformation. So, it can be implemented on low-power devices while assuring pedestrians' safety.

Figure 6. Detections from the pedestrian detection application

CONCLUSION

Application for pedestrian detection is crucial in many fields. In this paper, we suggested an IV application for pedestrian detection. Due to its success in resolving vision-based applications by utilizing a very deep artificial neural network, the proposed application was built on a deep convolutional neural network. The suggested DFCNN model proved appropriate for embedded implementation and provided a good trade-off between precision and speed. The proposed DFCNN has produced effective outcomes in terms of speed and precision. On the Caltech dataset's testing set, a mAP of 89% was attained. On the Nvidia GTX 960 GPU, processing speeds of 30 FPS for the base model and 37 FPS for the compressed model were attained. The performance of the proposed DFCNN model has been demonstrated through implementation in a pedestrian detection application using both new photos that are not part of the testing dataset and images from the testing dataset. In future studies, we will use an embedded device, such as an embedded GPU or an FPGA, to implement the suggested paradigm.

Disclosure of potential conflicts of interest: The authors declare that there is no conflict of interest regarding the publication of this article.

REFERENCES

Afif, M., Ayachi, R., Said, Y., Pissaloux, E., & Atri, M. (2018). Indoor image recognition and classification via deep convolutional neural network. In *International conference on the Sciences of Electronics, Technologies of Information and Telecommunications* (pp. 364-371). Springer.

Angelova, A., Krizhevsky, A., Vanhoucke, V., Ogale, A., & Ferguson, D. (2015). Real-time pedestrian detection with deep network cascades. Academic Press.

Association for Safe International Road Travel. (2019). Annual Global Road Crash Statistics. https://www.asirt.org/safe-travel/road-safety-facts/

Ayachi, R., Afif, M., Said, Y., & Atri, M. (2018). Strided convolution instead of max pooling for memory efficiency of convolutional neural networks. In *International conference on the Sciences of Electronics, Technologies of Information and Telecommunications* (pp. 234-243). Springer.

Ayachi, R., Afif, M., Said, Y., & Atri, M. (2019b). Traffic Signs Detection for Real-World Application of an Advanced Driving Assisting System Using Deep Learning. *Neural Processing Letters*, *51*(1), 837–851. doi:10.100711063-019-10115-8

Ayachi, R., Said, Y., & Atri, M. (2019a). To perform road signs recognition for autonomous vehicles using cascaded deep learning pipeline. *Artif Intell Adv*, *1*(1), 1–10. doi:10.30564/aia.v1i1.569

Ayachi, R., Said, Y., & Atri, M. (2021). A convolutional neural network to perform object detection and identification in visual large-scale data. *Big Data*, *9*(1), 41–52. doi:10.1089/big.2019.0093 PMID:32991200

Barba-Guaman, L., Eugenio Naranjo, J., & Ortiz, A. (2020). Deep learning framework for vehicle and pedestrian detection in rural roads on an embedded GPU. *Electronics (Basel)*, *9*(4), 589.

Chen, L., Lin, S., Lu, X., Cao, D., Wu, H., Guo, C., ... Wang, F. Y. (2021). Deep neural network based vehicle and pedestrian detection for autonomous driving: A survey. *IEEE Transactions on Intelligent Transportation Systems*, *22*(6), 3234–3246.

Clevert, D. A., Unterthiner, T., & Hochreiter, S. (2015). Fast and accurate deep network learning by exponential linear units (elus). arXiv preprint arXiv:1511.07289.

Dalal, N., & Triggs, B. (2005, June). Histograms of oriented gradients for human detection. In *2005 IEEE computer society conference on computer vision and pattern recognition (CVPR'05)* (Vol. 1, pp. 886-893). IEEE.

Dimian, M., Chassagne, L., Andrei, P., & Li, P. (2019). Smart Technologies for Vehicle Safety and Driver Assistance. *Journal of Advanced Transportation*, *2019*, 1–2. doi:10.1155/2019/2690498

Dinakaran, R. K., Easom, P., Bouridane, A., Zhang, L., Jiang, R., Mehboob, F., & Rauf, A. (2019). Deep learning based pedestrian detection at distance in smart cities. In *Proceedings of SAI Intelligent Systems Conference* (pp. 588-593). Springer.

Dollár, P., Appel, R., Belongie, S., & Perona, P. (2014). Fast feature pyramids for object detection. *IEEE Transactions on Pattern Analysis and Machine Intelligence*, *36*(8), 1532–1545. doi:10.1109/TPAMI.2014.2300479 PMID:26353336

Dollar, P., Wojek, C., Schiele, B., & Perona, P. (2011). Pedestrian detection: An evaluation of the state of the art. *IEEE Transactions on Pattern Analysis and Machine Intelligence*, *34*(4), 743–761. doi:10.1109/TPAMI.2011.155 PMID:21808091

Fukushima, K., & Miyake, S. (1982). Neocognitron: A self-organizing neural network model for a mechanism of visual pattern recognition. In *Competition and cooperation in neural nets* (pp. 267–285). Springer. doi:10.1007/978-3-642-46466-9_18

Goodfellow, I., Pouget-Abadie, J., Mirza, M., Xu, B., Warde-Farley, D., Ozair, S., ... Bengio, Y. (2020). Generative adversarial networks. *Communications of the ACM*, *63*(11), 139–144.

Ide, H., & Kurita, T. (2017). Improvement of learning for CNN with ReLU activation by sparse regularization. In *2017 International Joint Conference on Neural Networks (IJCNN)* (pp. 2684-2691). IEEE.

Islam, M. M., Newaz, A. A. R., & Karimoddini, A. (2022). Pedestrian Detection for Autonomous Cars: Inference Fusion of Deep Neural Networks. *IEEE Transactions on Intelligent Transportation Systems*.

Kingma, D. P., & Ba, J. (2014). Adam: A method for stochastic optimization. arXiv preprint arXiv:1412.6980.

Kiseľák, J., Lu, Y., Švihra, J., Szépe, P., & Stehlík, M. (2021). "SPOCU": Scaled polynomial constant unit activation function. *Neural Computing & Applications*, *33*(8), 3385–3401.

Klambauer, G., Unterthiner, T., Mayr, A., & Hochreiter, S. (2017). Self-normalizing neural networks. *Advances in Neural Information Processing Systems*, 30.

Krizhevsky, A., & Hinton, G. (2009). Learning multiple layers of features from tiny images. Academic Press.

Krizhevsky, A., Sutskever, I., & Hinton, G. E. (2017). ImageNet classification with deep convolutional neural networks. *Communications of the ACM*, *60*(6), 84–90. doi:10.1145/3065386

Liu, W., Anguelov, D., Erhan, D., Szegedy, C., Reed, S., Fu, C. Y., & Berg, A. C. (2016). Ssd: Single shot multibox detector. In European conference on computer vision (pp. 21-37). Springer.

Mao, L., Xie, M., Huang, Y., & Zhang, Y. (2010). Preceding vehicle detection using histograms of oriented gradients. In *2010 International Conference on Communications, Circuits and Systems (ICCCAS)* (pp. 354-358). IEEE. 10.1109/ICCCAS.2010.5581983

Mateus, A., Ribeiro, D., Miraldo, P., & Nascimento, J. C. (2019). Efficient and robust pedestrian detection using deep learning for human-aware navigation. Robotics and Autonomous Systems, 113, 23-37.

Omran, M., Lassner, C., Pons-Moll, G., Gehler, P., & Schiele, B. (2018). *Neural body fitting: Unifying deep learning and model based human pose and shape estimation. In 2018 international conference on 3D vision (3DV)*. IEEE.

Radford, A., Metz, L., & Chintala, S. (2015). Unsupervised representation learning with deep convolutional generative adversarial networks. arXiv preprint arXiv:1511.06434.

Ramachandran, P., Zoph, B., & Le, Q. V. (2017). Searching for activation functions. arXiv preprint arXiv:1710.05941.

Ranjan, R., Bansal, A., Zheng, J., Xu, H., Gleason, J., Lu, B., Nanduri, A., Chen, J.-C., Castillo, C., & Chellappa, R. (2019). A fast and accurate system for face detection, identification, and verification. *IEEE Transactions on Biometrics, Behavior, and Identity Science*, *1*(2), 82–96. doi:10.1109/TBIOM.2019.2908436

Rauf, R., Shahid, A. R., Ziauddin, S., & Safi, A. A. (2016). Pedestrian detection using HOG, LUV and optical flow as features with AdaBoost as classifier. In *2016 Sixth International Conference on Image Processing Theory, Tools and Applications (IPTA)* (pp. 1-4). IEEE. 10.1109/IPTA.2016.7821024

Ren, S., He, K., Girshick, R., & Sun, J. (2015). Faster r-cnn: Towards real-time object detection with region proposal networks. *Advances in Neural Information Processing Systems*, 28.

Said, Y. F., & Barr, M. (2019). Pedestrian detection for advanced driver assistance systems using deep learning algorithms. *IJCSNS*, *19*(10), 9–14.

Sandler, M., Howard, A., Zhu, M., Zhmoginov, A., & Chen, L. C. (2018). Mobilenetv2: Inverted residuals and linear bottlenecks. In *Proceedings of the IEEE conference on computer vision and pattern recognition* (pp. 4510-4520). IEEE.

Schmidhuber, J. (2015). Deep learning in neural networks: An overview. *Neural Networks: The Official Journal of the International Neural Network Society*, *61*, 85–117. doi:10.1016/j.neunet.2014.09.003 PMID:25462637

Ullah, M., Mohammed, A., & Alaya Cheikh, F. (2018). PedNet: A spatio-temporal deep convolutional neural network for pedestrian segmentation. *Journal of Imaging*, *4*(9), 107.

Verbickas, R., Laganiere, R., Laroche, D., Zhu, C., Xu, X., & Ors, A. (2017). SqueezeMap: fast pedestrian detection on a low-power automotive processor using efficient convolutional neural networks. In *Proceedings of the IEEE conference on computer vision and pattern recognition workshops* (pp. 146-154). IEEE.

Xu, B., Wang, N., Chen, T., & Li, M. (2015). Empirical evaluation of rectified activations in convolutional network. arXiv preprint arXiv:1505.00853.

Xue, W., Mou, X., Zhang, L., Bovik, A. C., & Feng, X. (2014). Blind image quality assessment using joint statistics of gradient magnitude and Laplacian features. *IEEE Transactions on Image Processing*, *23*(11), 4850–4862. doi:10.1109/TIP.2014.2355716 PMID:25216482

Zeiler, M. D., & Fergus, R. (2014). Visualizing and understanding convolutional networks. In *European conference on computer vision* (pp. 818-833). Springer.

Zhang, G., & Li, H. (2018). Effectiveness of scaled exponentially-regularized linear units (SERLUs). arXiv preprint arXiv:1807.10117.

Zhang, H., Du, Y., Ning, S., Zhang, Y., Yang, S., & Du, C. (2017). Pedestrian detection method based on Faster R-CNN. In 2017 13th International Conference on Computational Intelligence and Security (CIS) (pp. 427-430). IEEE.

KEY TERMS AND DEFINITIONS

Computer Vision: It is a field that studies how computers may learn to recognize digital images or video using artificial intelligence techniques. From an engineering standpoint, it tries to comprehend and automate operations that the human visual system is capable of performing.

Image Processing: It is a method of performing operations on an image in order to improve it or extract relevant information from it. It is a sort of signal processing in which the input is an image and the output can be an image or features.

Intelligent Vehicles: A vehicle that can collect and process information about its own status and the environment in order to make decisions, provide information, and react at the due time.

Lightweight Convolutional Neural Network: It is convolutional neural network with low computation complexity that is suitable for real-time application and implementation on edge devices.

Mobile Devices: It is a computation hardware system with a microprocessor that is designed to fulfill a certain purpose, either as an independent system or as part of a larger system. At the heart of the system is an integrated circuit built to perform calculation for real-time processes. It is characterized with a limited computation resources and energy based generally on battery.

Pedestrian Detection: It is an important task in many intelligent systems since it gives basic information for semantic interpretation of scenes. Because of the potential to improve safety systems, it has an apparent extension to automobile applications.

Real-Time Application: It is an application that operates in what the user perceives to be an immediate or current time frame. The latency must be shorter than a certain threshold, which is commonly measured in seconds.

Residual Connection: It is a skip connection that connects the output of one convolutional layer to the input of another convolutional layer several layers later (e.g. a number of intermediate convolutional steps are skipped). A simple sum is used to merge the mainstream model's input and the convolutional prior's input.

Chapter 23
Towards Predicting the Life of an Engine:
A Deep Learning Approach

Jayesh Soni

ⓘ https://orcid.org/0000-0002-5740-4597

Florida International University, USA

ABSTRACT

Predictive maintenance has attracted many researchers with the increased growth in the digitization of industrial, locomotive, and aviation fields. Simultaneously, extensive research in deep learning model development to its deployment has made its way to industrial applications with unprecedented accuracy. The most crucial task in predictive maintenance is to predict the machine's remaining useful life, yet the most beneficial one. In this chapter, the authors address the problem of predicting the remaining lifecycle of an engine using its sensor data. The authors provide practical implementation of predicting the RUL of an engine by proposing a deep learning-based framework on the open-source benchmark NASA's Commercial Modular Aero-Propulsion System Simulation (C-MAPSS) engine dataset, which contains sensor information of around 100 engines with 22 sensors. The proposed framework uses the bi-directional long short term memory algorithm. The authors optimize hyperparameters using advanced deep learning frameworks.

INTRODUCTION

A forecast of equipment failure requirements aids the productions team in planning equipment maintenance. With such a maintenance facility, one can avoid performing unnecessary maintenance checks, called periodical maintenance, and save a lot of energy and time. In modern factories, a huge amount of big data is captured from the sensors attached to equipment and private cloud servers (Yasumoto et al., 2016). Such sensor data contains valuable information about the behavior of equipment during its normal and failed operation. A type of sensor data analysis is termed predictive analytics and is one of the most interesting data analytics problems. A propulsion system generates a thrust for an airplane

DOI: 10.4018/978-1-6684-6937-8.ch023

to move through the air. Turbofan engines are used by modern airliners for such purposes. For aircraft maintenance, it is crucial to predict the turbofan engine's remaining useful lifecycle (RUL). This chapter analyzes the available sensor data to train a deep learning-based algorithm for predicting rul. The dataset is from NASA turbofan jet engine sensor measurements. Predictive maintenance can be performed in a classification or regression way. It predicts the likelihood of failure in subsequent n-steps in its classification approach. Predicting the remaining time left before the subsequent failure is the regression approach. Some of the real-world issues solved using data-driven approaches for RUL prediction are 1) multifaceted chronological dependencies amongst sensors: numerous modules act together with each other in myriad ways leading to complex dependencies amongst sensor readings. For example, an alteration in one sensor may lead to a variation in another sensor after an interval of a few instants. 2) fractional absence of sensor data: some data may be moderately unattainable due to reasons such as loss of communication in the network and broken or defective sensors. 3) health degradation: it is challenging to build physics-based models for complex machines with numerous constituents. 4) noisy sensor readings: varying environmental noise levels affect the sensor readings. The quantity of noise varies across sensors. Learning-based algorithms are one of the growing areas that have a high impact in the predictive maintenance domain, and that is the focus of this chapter.

BACKGROUND

Accurate prediction of the remaining useful life of an engine is one of the crucial parts of predictive maintenance (lee et al., 2017). It can be estimated through convergence rate, relative accuracy, etc. (Djeziri et al. 2020). There are three approaches for RUL prediction: data-driven, physics-based, and hybrid approach (Kim et al., 2016). When a piece of ominously precise information for fatigue crack growth is available, a physics-based approach can be employed (Byington et al. 2004, oh et al. 2010). Nonetheless, significant prior information is required. With no-fault condition data, a data-driven approach to building the model learns the normal behavior. The hybrid method is a combination of a data- and physical-based approach that can give improved results (Zhang et al., 2009; sun et al., 2019). For compound and nonlinear systems, learning-based algorithms have been used for RUL prediction. Decision tree-based Regressor, multilayer perceptron, and support vector regression are machine learning algorithms (TGS et al. 2019, Jayesh soni et al. 2019). Numerous artificial neural network and VM-based approaches are considered as black boxes since they are highly dependent on techniques required for signal processing. To mitigate this issue, several deep learning-based techniques are utilized, which do not require feature crafting from the sensors data and can extract the features automatically for further processing. For example, a recurrent neural network-based long short-term memory (LSTM) algorithm (Jayesh soni et al. 2019) is used to learn the patterns of the sequence. LSTM solves the vanishing gradient descent problem of RNN and is capable of learning the long sequences (Jayesh soni et al. 2019, 2020). LSTM does that by introducing the memory cell (Ellefsen et al., 2019; Al-dulaimi et al., 2019). An LSTM-based neural network is proposed for handling and monitoring multiple data generated from several sources for engine RUL prediction (Wu et al., 2018). With further research, the adaboost algorithm was jointly trained with LSTM for RUL estimate (Zhu et al. 2021). Yuan et al. Researched fault detection using the LSTM approach (Yuan et al., 2016). The author compared vanilla RNN, adaboost-LSTM, gated recurrent unit, and improved performance. To further increase the accuracy, bidirectional LSTM, a variant of LSTM, has been employed that can capture the long sequence dependencies in a bi-directional way and can thus learn the hidden complex patterns of the sensor signals (Huang et al., 2019). Authors (Zheng et al., 2017) use two LSTM layers followed by a feed-forward dense network and an output layer for RUL prediction. The LSTM layers capture the hidden patterns in the dataset and attain greater accuracy when matched to the hidden markov model. (Wu et al. 2018) performed a similar study. To extract new features, the authors combined LSTM with the dynamic difference method. This approach showed improved performance compared to GRU. CNN's have achieved good accuracy in object recognition (Gidaris et al., 2015) and face recognition (Li et al., 2015). For RUL predictions, CNNs can be used. (Babu et al. 2016) projected an innovative CNN method for RUL predictions. It contains two convolution layers followed by pooling layers and a dense layer. It showed improved performance compared to support vector machine (SVM) and multilayer perceptron. Several wavelet packet transformations (Bastami et al., 2019) are used to extract vibration signal features where a multilayer neural network is trained. Kong et al. trained an hybrid artificial neural network for predicting the life of coil springs (Kong et al., 2019).

TIME SERIES

Time series data is an assembly of data points acquired through repetitive measurements over a period of time. During plotting such points on a graph, time will always be on one axis. Since time is a fundamental part of discernible everything, time-series data is everywhere. With the rapid modernization of the world, sensors and complex systems are constantly generating an inflow of time series data. Various industries have numerous applications for such data. The usefulness of time series data are:

- Network logs generation
- Changes in the performance of an application over time
- Constant tracking of weather data to a minute detail
- Visualize the vitals impact of medical devices in real-time

The time-series data is of two types:

- Univariate Time-series: A univariate time series is a sequence of measurements collected at regular time intervals over a certain period for the same variable.
- Multivariate Time-series: A multivariate time series contain manifold variables where the time variable is being fixed for the whole data generation period, and another variable varies depending on specific parameters.

Time series consistently portray an association amongst two variables in which one is a quantitative value, and the other is always a time since time always acts as a positional point in such data generation. Furthermore, there does not have to be always an increase in the alteration of the variable with the change in time in the collected data points. It also shows decrement in variable time over a certain period of time. For example, the decrease or increase in the temperature value of a particular location varies and depends on many factors.

MACHINE LEARNING ALGORITHMS

Figure 1. Machine learning algorithms

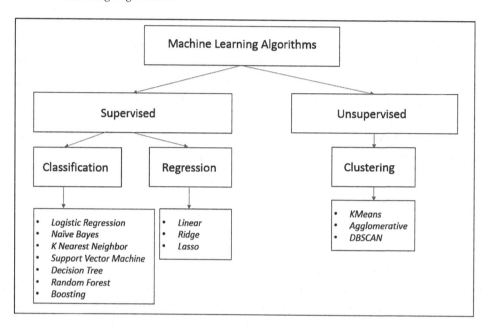

Supervised Learning

Classification and Regression are two main types of supervised learning algorithms.

Classification: Problems where the output label is categorical.

Regression: Problems where the output label is a real value.

Let us deep dive into different classification learning algorithms as mentioned in Figure 1:

Logistic Regression: It uses the features (also known as independent variables) to estimate the ground-truth value. It uses the logit function to fit the data and predict the value.

Decision Tree: It is one of the most popular machine learning algorithms used today. It uses the most relevant independent variables to split the data into two or more homogenous sets. The sets are divided until it reaches a user-specified accuracy value.

Random Forest: It is the collection of multiple decision tree algorithms. A subset of features and rows are fed as input to each decision tree. The classification is done based on the majority voting approach.

SVM (Support Vector Machine): It plots the data points into n-dimensional feature space. Furthermore, each feature value will be associated with a particular coordinate to classify the data points.

naïve Bayes: It assumes that all the features in the input data are independent of each other and that there is no correlation between them. Even if these features are interrelated, this classifier will consider each feature as a separate identity when calculating the probability value for a particular output label.

KNN (K- Nearest Neighbors): It is one of the most straightforward algorithms which uses a distance-based approach to classify new points. Given test data points, it calculates the distance to its k nearest points and further takes the majority vote. The most common class of the majority vote will be considered the output label for the test data point. Since KNN needs all the data points in memory to calculate the distance, it is computationally expensive.

Gradient Boosting and AdaBoosting: When predictions need to be made with high accuracy for big data, boosting-based algorithms are used. They are ensemble-based learning algorithms that improve robustness by training several base estimators. It builds a robust classifier by training many weak classifiers. Such boosting algorithms are used heavily in the data science competitions like Kaggle.

Now let us dive deep into different regression algorithms.

Linear Regression: It finds the weights for each feature to predict the outcome. A linear equation exemplifies it:

$$Y = a * X + b \tag{1}$$

Where,

Y: Output Variable
a: Slope
X: Feature variable
b: Intercept

The weights (coefficients) a & b are learned during the 'odel's training.

Least Absolute Shrinkage (Lasso) Regression: It is similar to linear Regression with the addition of penalties which is the sum of the absolute values of the coefficients.

Ridge Regression: It is similar to linear Regression with the addition of penalties which is the sum of the squares of the coefficients.

Unsupervised Learning

K-Means: It clusters the data into groups such that data points in the same group are similar in terms of characteristics and vice-versa. The value of K (number of clusters) has to be fed as input. The algorithm will select the K random centroids in the data space. Next, it calculates the distance between the points and the centroids. Furthermore, it will attach the data points to the nearest centroids based on the distance and update the centroid position based on the mean distance to all the data points attached. This process continues until it converges (no change in centroid position).

Density-Based Spatial Clustering of Applications with Noise (DBSCAN): It uses the criterion for a minimum number of data points and distance metric to cluster data points into groups. It takes two parameters – eps and minimum points. The distance metric is used to calculate how close the point should be to be considered as a part of a particular group. The criterion for minimum points calculates the density of the region.

Agglomerative Clustering: It is based on the Bottom-Up Approach. Here, each data point is initially considered a separate unique cluster. Next, the two nearest data points are joined together, and so on, until we get one cluster of all data points. Two nearest clusters are joined together using the linkage method. There are numerous types of linkages:

Single Linkage: Shortest distance between two points in both clusters.

Complete Linkage: Farthest distance between two points in both clusters.

Average Linkage: Average distance of every point in one cluster to every point in another cluster.

Divisive Clustering: It is the opposite of agglomerative Clustering, where all the data points are in the same groups and are divided into different clusters.

TIME SERIES ANALYSIS

Time series analysis is the statistical trend analysis technique for each data point. A time series comprises consecutive points of data that are logged at a particular time duration, where we attempt some methods to understand the behavior or make future predictions. Based on some known past results, some substantial models can forecast future values in the time-series data. The main objective of such analysis is to detect patterns such as cycles, trends, and irregular movements throughout a particular period of time. Consider an example of a restaurant, where, based on the previous occurrence of the number of customers' counts with time, the future availability on the count of the remaining tables in the restaurant can be predicted approximately.

Some of the applications of time series include inventory analysis, sales forecasting, financial analysis and forecasting, stock market analysis, etc. Furthermore, an inspection of the popularity of hashtags on social media for a specified interval can be done using time series analysis.

Algorithms for Time Series Analysis

Figure 2. Algorithms for time series analysis

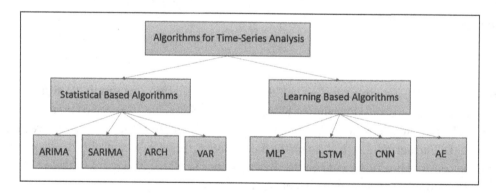

There are two types of algorithms for time-series analysis, as shown in Figure 2.

1. Statistical Based Algorithms

Statistical learning refers to a set of techniques for understanding multifaceted data. It is an established area in statistics and merges with equivalent developments in computer science.

Autoregressive integrated moving average (ARIMA) Model: It comprises three unique statistical models, namely, AR, MA, and I, where

Auto Regression (AR): It uses particular data points and some lagged data points to model the dependency relationship.

Moving Average (MA): It uses the residual error of the moving average model, which was applied to lagged observations, and models their dependency relationship.

I (Integrated): It makes the time series stationary by subtracting the current time step from the previous step.

Based on the above three combinations, the ARIMA model is fitted to the data.

SARIMA: They are the ARIMA models with a seasonal component.

Autoregressive conditionally heteroscedastic (ARCH) Model: ARCH models check the volatile variance. Such models are used in short periods where there is an increase in variation.

Vector Autoregressive (VAR) model: It captures the correlation amongst all the features as they change over a span of time.

2. Learning Based Algorithms

The field of machine learning is all about how to make computer programs that repeatedly advance with experience. One of the major advantages of using learning-based algorithms to model time series as opposed to statistical-based is that they do not make assumptions about the essential data (P. Rathore et al. 2021). There are four most relevant learning-based algorithms for time series analysis. They are:

Multi-Layer Perceptron (MLP): They are simple designs of neural networks. They entail three different components, as described in Figure 3.

The input layer: A vector of features.

The hidden layers consist of N neurons.

The output layer: Output of the network.

Figure 3. Multi-layer perceptron

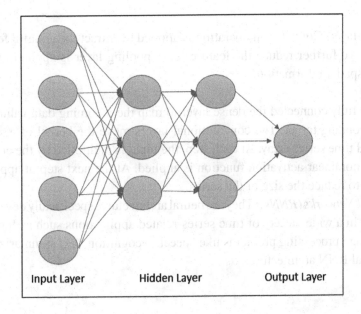

The following two steps are crucial to each node:

1. Multiplication of weights with the input and addition of the bias term to have linear transformation.
2. Since most real-world data are complex, activation functions are applied as a second step to have non-linearity functions to map the input features with the target labels.

Convolution Neural Network (CNN): They are widely used for image classification. However, such networks can be used for time series prediction after transforming the data to the proper format. Figure 4 shows the simplified version of 1D CNN.

Figure 4. Convolution neural network

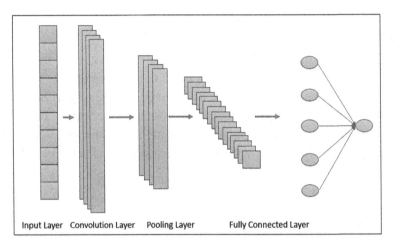

CNN has two layers:

1. Convolutional layer: Convolution operation is applied to extract meaningful features.
2. Pooling layer: To further reduce the feature set, a pooling layer is applied, which preserves the temporal and spatial information.

Finally, we have fully connected the dense layer to map the incoming data values from the pooling layer to the corresponding target. The convolutional layers move the kernel of a specific length over the one-dimensional time series array. At each step, the input is multiplied by the corresponding kernel value, and then the nonlinear activation function is applied. At the next step, it applies a pooling layer (max or average) is to reduce the size of the series.

Recurrent Neural Networks (RNNs): They are neural architectures specifically developed for sequential data. They are used in a wide variety of time series-related applications such as future forecasting and many natural language processing problems like speech recognition, text summarization, etc. Figure 5 represents the typical RNN architecture.

Figure 5. Recurrent neural network

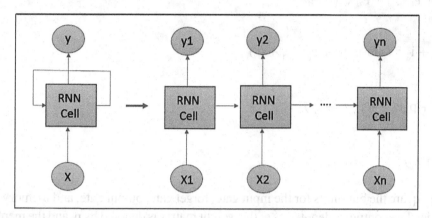

The main difference between MLP and RNN is that the former takes all the input simultaneously, whereas RNN takes one input time step sequentially. The network produces a hidden state at each step by doing the calculation on the input data with the corresponding weights. These hidden states are referred to as memory cells. This hidden state is combined with the following input value to produce the output. At the end of the sequence, the algorithm stops. Using the hidden state information, the RNN algorithm preserves the past information to co-relate with the current input value.

The same RNN cell performs all the calculations for each input, and thus all the weights and parameters are shared across all time steps. Backpropagation Through Time (BPTT) algorithm is used for training purposes where the calculation of the gradient at each step depends on the previous steps. The neural structure of such a network is unfolded by making multiple copies of neurons with recurrent connections.

RNNs have unlimited memory theoretically. Nevertheless, learning long-term dependencies is complicated through the backpropagation algorithm and creates problems such as vanishing (gradient values reach near zero) or exploding gradient (gradient values grow very large). The exploding gradient can be solved using gradient clipping, where some threshold is used to clip the gradient—the Vanishing Gradient results in small to no updates to the weights of the first few initial layers.

There are three variants of RNN to overcome that problem. They are:

Long Short-Term Memory (LSTM): They have memory cells in the form of gates. With every input, the memory is updated. The following four gates are attached to the LSTM network to mitigate the inaccuracies of the RNN.

Input gate: It regulates the updation of new memory.

Forget gate: It accounts for non-essential information removal.

Memory gate: It creates a new memory.

Output gate: It updates the hidden state with the memory cell information.

With a sample input of type $b = (b_1, b_2, b_3, b_{N-1}, b_N)$, the gates are updated as follows:

$$(b_w, e_{w-1}, s_{w-1}) \rightarrow (e_w, s_w) \tag{1}$$

$$i_w = \sigma (p_{bi}b_w + p_{ei}e_{w-1} + p_{si}z_{w-1} + q_i) \tag{2}$$

$$f_w = \sigma \ (p_{bf}b_w + p_{ef}e_{w-1} + p_{zf}z_{w-1} + q_f) \tag{3}$$

$$z_w = f_w * z_{w-1} + i_w * \tanh(p_{bz}b_w + p_{ez}e_{w-1} + q_z) \tag{4}$$

$$y_w = \sigma \ (p_{by}b_w + p_{ey}e_{w-1} + p_{zy}z_w + q_y) \tag{5}$$

$$e_w = y_w * \tanh(z_w) \tag{6}$$

where q_i, q_f, q_y, q_z are the bias units for the input gate, forget gate, output gate, and memory cell. Furthermore, the hidden layer output is denoted as e; the weight matrix is denoted by p, and the memory state is z.

Bi-Directional LSTM (Bi-LSTM): They are LSTM networks, but instead of looking only in the forward direction, they also trace the sequence from the backward direction.

Gated Recurrent Unit (GRU): GRU is also similar to LSTM but with fewer gates. Thus it is computationally faster to run but a little more inefficient than GRU.

Auto Encoders: It takes the actual input, learns a compressed representation, and reconstructs the input, as shown in Figure 6. The reconstruction error of predicted input from the actual input is used to check the validity of AE. There are numerous kinds of autoencoders with various use-case, but conceivably the collective use is automatic feature extraction or dimensionality reduction. The compressed representation of the input data is provided by the output of the model.

Figure 6. Auto encoder

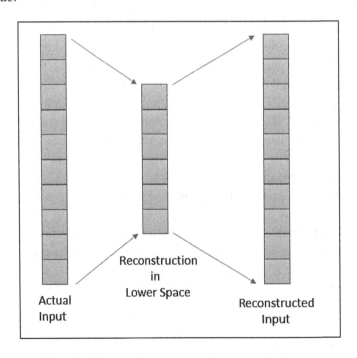

EVALUATION METRICS

Mean Absolute Error (MAE): It is a straightforward metric that estimates the absolute alteration between predicted and actual values.

$$MAE = \frac{1}{N} \sum |Y - \bar{Y}| \tag{7}$$

Where N is the total data points, Y is the actual ground-truth label, and $\bar{Y}$ is the predicted label.

Mean Squared Error (MSE): It is the same as MAE, but the only difference is that it finds the square deviations between predicted and actual values instead of taking the absolute value.

$$MSE = \frac{1}{N} \sum \left(Y - \bar{Y}\right)^2 \tag{8}$$

Root Mean Squared Error (RMSE): It is similar to MSE with the addition of the square root.

$$RMSE = \sqrt{\frac{1}{N} \sum \left(Y - \bar{Y}\right)} \tag{9}$$

R Squared (R2): It is a metric that indicates the enactment of your model rather than loss. It tells how good the trained regressor is compared to the non-trained regressor (A regressor that consistently predicts the mean value). It is also known as the Coefficient of Determination.

$$R2 \text{ Squared} = 1 - \frac{SSr}{SSm} \tag{10}$$

Where SSr is the squared sum error of the regressor line and,

SSm is the squared sum error of the mean line

If the R2 score is zero, then the trained regressor is worse than the non-trained regressor. If the R2 score is 1, then the trained regressor is good.

Adjusted R Squared: The major problem with the R2 score is that, with the addition of new features, the score will increase with the assumption that the variance increase with an increased number of features. This can create a problem when the new feature added is irrelevant. To avoid this, Adjusted R Squared is the solution.

$$\text{Adjusted R2 Squared} = 1 - \left[\left[\left(\frac{n-1}{n-k-1}\right) * \left(1 - R^2\right)\right]\right] \tag{11}$$

Where N is the number of data points and,

K is the number of features

PRACTICAL IMPLEMENTATION

This section discusses the practical implementation of predicting the Remaining Useful Life of an engine. Figure 7 shows the framework overview. It contains three stages: Data Collection, Data Preprocessing, and Algorithm Training.

Figure 7. Framework

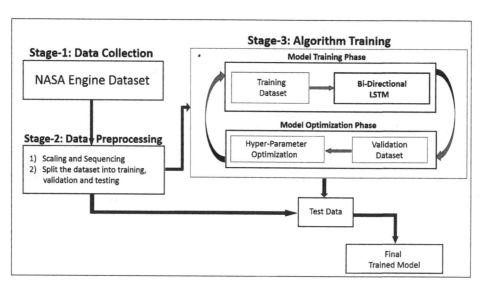

Stage 1: Data Collection

NASA's C-MAPSS dataset was used for experimentation purposes. This dataset contains information on the turbofan jet engine. This turbofan engine comprises numerous modules (compressor (low and high pressure), fan, nozzle, and combustor). The information for each of these modules is fetched using the sensors attached to the engine. The dataset contains information on 21 sensors with three operating conditions. It is the real-time illustration of the engine degradation captured through sensor measurements. Table 1 provides detailed dataset information. Some sensors contain very little info about engine enactment degradation, while others provide rich knowledge indicating a straight deterioration tendency. In real-life scenarios, human experts examine those sensors and make meaningful decisions. Each row of the dataset comprehends the following information:

1. Unit number of an engine
2. Time, in cycles

3. Three operational settings
4. 21 sensor readings

Table 1. Dataset

Dataset	Values
Number of Engines	249
Number of Training Samples	61,249
Number of Test Samples	248
Number of Sensors	26
Average Life Span	245
Operating Conditions	6

The engines in the dataset function routinely in the launch time; nonetheless, they develop a fault over time. The engines are run to failure for the training sets. Time series end before failure for the test sets. The objective is to forecast each engine's Remaining Useful Life.

Stage 2: Data Pre-processing

The following pre-processing techniques are used to clean the data:

1. Sequencing the data
2. Normalizing the data

Stage 3: Algorithm Training

We use the following libraries for training the model:

TensorFlow: TensorFlow is an open-source library from google for deep learning and Machine learning (Dillon et al., 2017).

Keras: Keras is a wrapper on Tensorflow used by many societies worldwide. The code written in Keras is internally converted to TensorFlow for further execution. It has functional API (Application Programming Interface) and Sequential API (Gulli et al., 2017).

Scikit-learn: Scikit-learn deals with a wide variety of learning-based algorithms (both supervised and unsupervised) (Pedregosa et al. 2011).

The following hyper-parameters are optimized using the validation dataset:

Epochs: Number of times models go through the training dataset.

Batch-Size: The size of the number of rows after which the weight updation is to be performed.

Sequence length: For Bi-LSTM, the number of previous sensor sequences will be fed as input to learn the future sequence.

Grid Search Algorithm with K-Fold Cross-Validation (Value of K was set to 10) is used to optimize the above parameters.

The Bi-LSTM model comprises five layers with a batch size of 256 for each epoch. To reduce overfitting, the dropout technique is used with a dropout ratio of 0.2. For optimizing the gradients, the Adam optimizer is employed with a sequence length of 15. The total epochs were set to 200 with early stopping criteria. For model evaluation, Root mean squared error (RMSE) is used. The RMSE value achieved was 12.44 for the test data. Furthermore, the final trained model can be deployed in the production line.

CONCLUSION

Predictive maintenance is a significant concern in modern machinery equipment. Global business is heavily transformed by big data and artificial intelligence technology. For any enterprise, data is the essential key, and it uses data-driven approaches for insights. This chapter studies the solicitation of learning-based algorithms for aircraft engine failure prediction. We provide in-depth detail for various statistical and learning-based algorithms useful for time series data. Furthermore, the author provided a framework describing the real-time implementation for predicting the remaining useful lifecycle using the open-source NASA turbofan jet engine dataset. The Bi-LSTM algorithm was trained in Keras, an open-source artificial neural networks API based on python programming language, with Google's TensorFlow as a backend. The efficient results from the learning-based algorithm show the value of additional consideration for application in aircraft engines.

REFERENCES

Al-Dulaimi, A., Zabihi, S., Asif, A., & Mohammadi, A. (2019). A multimodal and hybrid deep neural network model for remaining useful life estimation. *Computers in Industry*, *108*, 186–196. doi:10.1016/j.compind.2019.02.004

Babu, G. S., Zhao, P., & Li, X. L. (2016). Deep convolutional neural network based regression approach for estimation of remaining useful life. In *International Conference on Database Systems for Advanced Applications,* (pp. 214–228). Springer. 10.1007/978-3-319-32025-0_14

Bastami, R., Aasi, A., & Arghand, H. A. (2019, July). Estimation of remaining useful life of rolling element bearings using wavelet packet decomposition and artificial neural network. *Iranian Journal of Science and Technology. Transaction of Electrical Engineering*, *43*(S1), 233–245. doi:10.100740998-018-0108-y

Byington, C. S., Watson, M., Edwards, D., & Stoelting, P. (2004). A model-based approach to prognostics and health management for flight control actuators. In Proceedings of the IEEE Aerospace Conference Proceedings (IEEE Cat. No. 04TH8720), (pp. 3551–3562). IEEE. 10.1109/AERO.2004.1368172

Soni, J., Prabakar, N., Upadhyay. (2020). Comparative Analysis of LSTM Sequence-Sequence and Auto Encoder for real-time anomaly detection using system call sequences. *International Journal of Innovative Research in Computer and Communication Engineering*, 7(12), 4225–4230.

Dillon, J. V. (2017). Tensorflow distributions. arXiv:1711.10604.

Djeziri, M. A., Benmoussa, S., & Zio, E. (2020). Review on Health Indices Extraction and Trend Modeling for Remaining Useful Life Estimation. In Artificial Intelligence Techniques for a Scalable Energy Transition, (pp. 183–223). Springer. doi:10.1007/978-3-030-42726-9_8

Ellefsen, A. L. (2019). Remaining useful life predictions for turbofan engine degradation using semi-supervised deep architecture. *Reliability Engineering & System Safety, 183*, 240–251. doi:10.1016/j.ress.2018.11.027

Gidaris, S., & Komodakis, N. (2015). Object detection via a multi-region and semantic segmentation-aware cnn model. *Proceedings of the IEEE international conference on computer vision.* IEEE. 10.1109/ICCV.2015.135

Gulli, A., & Pal, S. (2017). *Deep learning with Keras.* Packt Publishing Ltd.

Huang, C.-G., Huang, H.-Z., & Li, Y.-F. (2019, November). A bidirectional LSTM prognostics method under multiple operational conditions. *IEEE Transactions on Industrial Electronics, 66*(11), 8792–8802. doi:10.1109/TIE.2019.2891463

Kim, N.-H., An, D., & Choi, J.-H. (2016). *Prognostics and Health Management of Engineering Systems: An Introduction.* Springer.

Kong, Y. S., Abdullah, S., Schramm, D., Omar, M. Z., & Haris, S. M. (2019, May). Optimization of spring fatigue life prediction model for vehicle ride using hybrid multilayer perceptron artificial neural networks. *Mechanical Systems and Signal Processing, 122*, 597–621. doi:10.1016/j.ymssp.2018.12.046

Lee, J., Jin, C., Liu, Z., & Ardakani, H. D. (2017). Introduction to data-driven methodologies for prognostics and health management. In *Probabilistic Prognostics and Health Management of Energy Systems* (1st ed., pp. 9–32). Springer. doi:10.1007/978-3-319-55852-3_2

Li, H. (2015). A convolutional neural network cascade for face detection. *Proceedings of the IEEE conference on computer vision and pattern recognition.* IEEE. 10.1109/CVPR.2015.7299170

Oh, H., Azarian, M. H., Pecht, M., White, C. H., Sohaney, R. C., & Rhem, E. (2010). Physics-of-failure approach for fan PHM in electronics applications. In Proceedings of the 2010 Prognostics and System Health Management Conference, (pp. 1–6). IEEE. 10.1109/PHM.2010.5413501

Pedregosa, F. (2011). Scikit-learn: Machine learning in Python. *Journal of Machine Learning Research, 12*, 2825–2830.

Rathore, P., Soni, J., Prabakar, N., Palaniswami, M., & Santi, P. (2021). Identifying Groups of Fake Reviewers Using a Semisupervised Approach. *IEEE Transactions on Computational Social Systems, 8*(6), 1369–1378. doi:10.1109/TCSS.2021.3085406

Soni, J., Prabakar, N., & Upadhyay, H. (2019). Deep learning approach to detect malicious attacks at the system level: poster. In *Proceedings of the 12th Conference on Security and Privacy in Wireless and Mobile Networks (WiSec '19)*, (pp. 314–315). Association for Computing Machinery. 10.1145/3317549.3326308

Soni, J., Prabakar, N., Upadhyay. (2019). Behavioral Analysis of System Call Sequences Using LSTM Seq-Seq, Cosine Similarity and Jaccard Similarity for Real-Time Anomaly Detection. *2019 International Conference on Computational Science and Computational Intelligence (CSCI)*, (pp. 214–219). IEEE. 10.1109/CSCI49370.2019.00043

Soni, J., Prabakar, N., Upadhyay. (2020). *Feature Extraction through Deepwalk on Weighted Graph.* 15th Springer International Conference on Data Science (ICDATA), Las Vegas, Nevada.

Sun, T., Xia, B., Liu, Y., Lai, Y., Zheng, W., Wang, H., Wang, W., & Wang, M. (2019). A novel hybrid prognostic approach for remaining useful life estimation of lithium-ion batteries. *Energies*, *12*(19), 3678. doi:10.3390/en12193678

T. G.S., J. Soni, K. Chandna, S. S. Iyengar, N. R. Sunitha and N. Prabakar. (2019). Learning-Based Model to Fight against Fake Like Clicks on Instagram Posts. 2019 SoutheastCon, (pp. 1-8). IEEE. doi:10.1109/SoutheastCon42311.2019.9020533. doi:10.1109/SoutheastCon42311.2019.9020533

Soni, J., Prabakar, N., Upadhyay. (2020). Visualizing High-Dimensional Data Using t-Distributed Stochastic Neighbor Embedding Algorithm. In H. Arabnia, K. Daimi, R. Stahlbock, C. Soviany, L. Heilig, & K. Brüssau (Eds.), Principles of Data Sci-ence. Transactions on Computational Science and Computational Intelligence (pp. 189–206). Springer. doi:10.1007/978-3-030-43981-1_9

Wu, Y. T., Yuan, M., Dong, S., Li, L., & Liu, Y. (2018, January). Remaining useful life estimation of engineered systems using vanilla LSTM neural networks. *Neurocomputing*, *275*, 167–179. doi:10.1016/j.neucom.2017.05.063

Yasumoto, K., Yamaguchi, H., & Shigeno, H. (2016). Survey of real-time processing technologies of IoT data streams. *Journal of Information Processing*, *24*(2), 195–202. doi:10.2197/ipsjjip.24.195

Yuan, M., Wu, Y., & Lin, L. (2016). *"Fault diagnosis and remaining useful life estimation of aero engine using LSTM neural network." 2016 IEEE international conference on aircraft utility systems (AUS).* IEEE.

Zhang, H., Kang, R., & Pecht, M. A hybrid prognostics and health management approach for condition-based maintenance. In *Proceedings of the 2009 IEEE International Conference on Industrial Engineering and Engineering Management*, (pp. 1165–1169). IEEE. 10.1109/IEEM.2009.5372976

Zheng, S. (2017). Long short-term memory network for remaining useful life estimation. 2017 IEEE international conference on prognostics and health management (ICPHM). IEEE.

Zhu, X., Zhang, P., & Xie, M. (2021, January). A joint long short-term memory and AdaBoost regression approach with application to remaining useful life estimation. *Measurement*, *170*, 108707. doi:10.1016/j.measurement.2020.108707

ADDITIONAL READING

Albawi, S., Mohammed, T. A., & Al-Zawi, S. (2017). *"Understanding of a convolutional neural network." 2017 international conference on engineering and technology (ICET).* Ieee.

Graves, A., Fernández, S., & Schmidhuber, J. (2005). Bidirectional LSTM networks for improved phoneme classification and recognition. In *International conference on artificial neural networks*. Springer., https://ti.arc.nasa.gov/tech/dash/groups/pcoe/prognostic-data-repository/ doi:10.1007/11550907_126

Louizos, C. (2015). The variational fair autoencoder. arXiv:1511.00830.

Medsker, L. R., & Jain, L. C. (2001). Recurrent neural networks. *Design and Applications, 5*, 64–67.

Ramchoun, H. (2016). Multilayer perceptron: Architecture optimization and training. Semantic Scholar.

KEY TERMS AND DEFINITIONS

API: Application Programming Interface is a list of rules and definitions for developing and integrating the application.

Encryption: It is the process of transforming the data into a secure format.

Epoch: Number of times the deep learning model goes through the dataset.

MinMaxScalar: It scales the feature value between 0 and 1.

Open Source Benchmark Dataset: Dataset available free to use for research purposes for benchmarking and validating the new proposed implementation and comparative analysis purposes.

Polymorphism: It is the concept that describes situations when there are multiple forms of the same object.

UNIX: An operating system widely used for internet servers and workstations.

Chapter 24
Nighttime Object Detection:
A Night–Patrolling Mechanism Using Deep Learning

V. Dinesh Reddy
SRM University, India

Sai Vishnu Vamsi Senagasetty
SRM University, India

Krishna Teja Vanka
SRM University, India

Mohana Vamsi Dhara
SRM University, India

Rupini Durga Puvvada
SRM University, India

Muzakkir Hussain
SRM University, India

ABSTRACT

These days, it's becoming harder to feel safer when we go out at night. So, to tackle this security problem, the authors propose a night patrolling mechanism to detect objects in low light conditions. Images taken during the nighttime have difficulties with less contrast, brightness, and noise owing to inadequate light or insufficient exposure. Deep learning-based methods accomplish end-to-end, unsupervised object recognition using convolutional neural networks, which abolishes the requirement to describe and draw out attributes separately. Despite the fact that deep learning has led to the invention of many successful object detection algorithms; many state-of-the-art object detectors, like Faster-RCNN and others, can't carry out at their best under low-light situations. Even with an extra light source, it is hard to detect the features of an item due to the uneven division of brightness. This chapter proposes a deep learning algorithm called single shot detector, with Mobilenet v2 as the backbone to tackle the issues of object detection under low-light situations.

DOI: 10.4018/978-1-6684-6937-8.ch024

1. INTRODUCTION

Object detection is the primary job in many computer vision applications because it allows more information about the identified object and the scene to be obtained. Object detection has been used in a broad range of applications, including human-computer interaction, robotics service robots, electronic goods like smartphones, security like recognition, tracking, and retrieval such as photo management, search engines, and transportation. Object localization involves locating and sizing a single object that is known to be present in the image; object presence classification involves determining whether at least one object of a given class is present in the image (without providing any information about other elements) and object recognition involves determining whether a specific object is present in the image. The fourth associated issue, view and posture estimation, requires evaluation of both the view and the location of the object. There are different types of object detection algorithms.

1.1. Coarse-to-Fine and Boosted Classifiers

Viola and Jones' enhanced cascade classifier is the most popular study in this area (2004). It operates by effectively rejecting picture patches that do not belong to the object using a series of tests and filters. The employment of cascade techniques with boosted classifiers is common for two motives: I Because boosting produces an additive classifier, it is simple to manage the complexity of each level of the cascade; (ii) boosting may also be used for feature selection during training, allowing the usage of huge (parametrized) families of data.

1.2. Dictionary Based

The Bag of Word approach (Serre et al. (2005) and Mutch & Lowe (2008)) is the greatest example in this area. This method is primarily meant to detect a single item per picture, but it can also detect the remaining objects after eliminating an identified object (Lampert et al. (2009)). This technique has two flaws: it cannot reliably handle the circumstance of two instances of the item appearing near one another, and the object's localization may be inaccurate.

1.3. Deep Learning

Convolutional neural networks are one of the first effective approaches in this class. This strategy differs from the others in that the feature representation is learned rather than defined by the user, but it comes with the disadvantage of requiring a large number of training examples to train the classifier. Deep learning is the cause of all recent developments in artificial intelligence. Self-driving cars, chatbots, Alexa and Siri would not exist without deep learning. Neural networks are the root of all these technologies.

Traditional machine learning models like SVM and Naive Bayes classifiers stop progressing beyond a saturation point, however, deep learning models tend to get more accurate with more training data.

1.4. Trainable Image Processing Architectures

The parameters of preset operators and their combinations are learned in such designs, often with an abstract notion of fitness in mind. Because they are general-purpose designs, they may be utilized to construct several modules for a larger system.

There are several limitations to existing approaches. Many applications need the detection of many object classes. When a high number of classes are discovered, processing speed, as well as the types of classes that the system can manage without losing accuracy, becomes critical. Most of the existing algorithms are designed for a single object class under a single perspective. So, they fail to handle pose variations and multiple class objects. Dealing with partial occlusions is also a significant issue for which no convincing answer exists. Further, the night patrolling system is not explored to a deep extent as there is no reliable dataset to work with. The existing algorithms are not reliable as many of them have drawbacks and have no proper dataset to work with. Hence, The discussion in the current scope covered the production of a new video dataset with roughly 60 movies depicting four meteorological and atmospheric situations.: low light, dust, rain, and fog taken from "Tripura University Video Dataset at Nighttime (TU-VDN)". To tackle these issues, this chapter proposes a deep learning algorithm called Single Shot Detector, with Mobilenet v2 as the backbone to detect objects in dimly lit areas.

2. RELATED WORK

There have been numerous proposals for scene parsing. Due to the advancement of convolutional neural networks, the layout has dramatically improved in recent years (CNNs). Wang et al.(2017) Combined superpixel-level prior position information with CNNs to better the object discrimination in scene processing. Multilevel-based methods are widely Zhang et al.(2018), Lin et al.(2017) and Cheng et al.(2019) used by studying multi level characteristics to draw out the overall context while preserving the lower-level features. Diligence-based approaches Fu et al. (2019), and Takikawa et al.(2019), have recently demonstrated promising results. Using position attention and channel attention modules, Fu et al. (2019) adaptively merged local aspects with their worldwide dependencies. To describe extended-range contextual dependencies over localized characteristic representations, Huang et al. (2019) employed a unique criss-cross attention module. Choi et al. (2020) used peak concentration to learn about many classes that are spread at various heights. The two-stream techniques were also introduced by Pohlen et al.(2017).

Takikawa et al. (2019), for example, proposed a two-stream network, one of which directly wired shape information for scene processing. Although the majority of existing works concentrate on "typical" circumstances with well-lit scenes, several works also target tough scenarios. S. Di et al.(2020) attempted to overcome the parsing challenge for wet night scenes by transferring day-time expertise. They gathered 226 photos in eight different categories. Tung et al. (2017) attempted to address this issue by presenting 95 annotated night-time photographs divided into three groups. To transform scenes under bad conditions to images with better representations for processing, Zheng et al. (2020) introduced Decoupling domain-invariant material from domain-specific style using a fork-shaped cyclic generating module. Valada et al. (2017) offered a complex blend of deep expert fusion algorithms to understand diverse and mixed adverse situations, such as rain, sunset, snow, and night scenes, amidst 13 sectors. Zendal et al. (2018) and BDD100K set out to test segmentation performance by showing 13 and 345 scenarios of night-time photos, respectively, in a variety of settings. With a limited dataset containing 151 night-time photos, Sakaridis et al.(2020) presented a guided curricular design adaptation to tackle the night-time semantic segmentation problem (NTSP). Wu et al.(2017) recently suggested an unsupervised single-stage adaptation strategy for NTSP based on antagonistic learning between a labeled daytime dataset and an unlabeled day-night aligned photo pair dataset. Unlike the research mentioned above, our solution to the NTSP problem includes a sizable collection of actual nighttime photos with semantic observations (21 sectors) and a paperback exposure-aware framework. Under image enhancement or correction, One simplistic answer to our issue is to use picture optimization on the input nighttime images and then use a daytime approach to conduct scene parsing.

Remapping the pixel values to increase the image's visibility is the goal of image enhancement techniques like those in Yan et al.(2016), Wang et al.(2013), Li et al.(2018), and Ying et al.(2017). By estimating an illumination map, Wang et al. (2019) attempted to solve the under-exposure issue. A deep picture contrast enhancer could be learned from multiple exposures of an image, according to Cai et al. (2018) In Yang et al. (2018), an end-to-end network was suggested to first transform an input LDR image to HDR in order to recover any information lost under- or over-exposure, and then reproject it back to LDR as an result while maintaining the recuperate details. To solve the practical under-exposure issue with noise, Xu et al. (2020) presented a frequency decomposition methodology. But nighttime photos frequently have areas that are both under and overexposed (with pixel values that are quite near to zero/one).The remapping procedure could fail to restore important values. As seen in our studies, our issue cannot be effectively solved by pre-processing the input photos with a cutting-edge image enhancement technique before scene parsing. One of the first methods involves histogram equalization method to improve the contrast of low-light photographs Pizer et al. (1987) It has a minimal processing complexity and is quite straightforward. However, excessive gray merging makes it easy to lose the gray levels that define image features. The γ-correction is yet another time-tested method. It is predicated on the idea that the power of the light input has an exponential relationship with the human eye's sensitivity to outside light. When illumination levels are low, it is simpler for human vision to detect differences in brightness; when gleam levels rise, it is more challenging. Gamma adjustment makes the contrast effect of image illumination more noticeable. However, it is challenging to automatically select a suitable gamma value to adjust the original photo throughout image processing.

There have been several low-illumination video enhancement algorithms presented by Malm et al. (2007), and Dong et al. (2010), many of which were inspired by the prior dark-based defogging technique He et al. (2010) For photos with low illumination and uneven illumination, Loza et al. (2013) suggested a analytical modeling technique depending on the image wavelet coefficients. Due to the popularity of deep learning approaches, low-level picture restorative research has made substantial strides in fields including deblurring, denoising, and super-resolution. Finding similar ground truth for subpar improvements is very difficult, though. Therefore, the majority of existing low-illumination improvement techniques are trained on artificial data. The first deeper auto-encoder-based technique to identify signals in low-light photographs and adaptively lighten images avoiding over-amplifying the lighter areas of the image was developed by LLNet Lore et al (2017). A two-step method to improve low-light photographs based on an atmospheric scattering illumination model was suggested by Tao et al. (2017).

Deep learning and retinex theory are frequently combined, as in LightenNet, because retinex theory is better suited to the properties of human vision. Multi-scale retinex has been shown by Shen et al. (2017) to be equivalent to a feedforward convolutional neural network with various gaussian convolutional kernels. To obtain the end-to-end mapping between the dark and light photos, they suggested using an MSR-Net. DecomNet for decomposition and EnhanceNet for illumination modification are two components of the Retinex-Net model that Wei et al. (2019) suggested. For analyzing low-light photos, Chen et al. (2017) created the first genuine low-illumination RAW dataset and an improved network SID. To address the coaching problem without poor lighting conditions image pairs, Jiang et al. (2021) presented an unsupervised fruitful adversarial network dubbed EnlightenGAN.

3. DATASET

Target detection based on videos is corresponding with photo-based object detection, removal of the background, and unfixed object categorization. In this chapter, the datasets including thermal and visual-thermal are used, publicly available datasets contain thermal infrared photos taken at night, and photographs taken in severe atmospheric conditions like low light, dust, fog, and rain are not. To the best of our perception rain, fog, and other weather conditions have not yet been reported. As a result of these flaws, object detection techniques are used. Thermal invisible images have a very damped range on weather-affected nights. The TU-VDN dataset consists of a video collection with roughly 60 videos covering four different cultures i.e., low-light, dust, drizzle, and fog characters. The motto is to design a night-time video dataset with moving objects that include footnoted ground truth in image frame sequences. The videos were recorded using a tripod stand for 2 minutes with a FLIR camera by maintaining a 2KM distance from the objects. The videos were captured in such a way that each frame contains different types of objects like bicycles, cars, buses, trains, and humans as shown in Figure 1 and Figure 2. Testing was done using TU-VDN (Xiao et al. (2020))

Figure 1. Images for 4 different light conditions

Figure 2. The data for 4 different weather conditions

There are multiple datasets that can be used for object detection during nighttime. But no other dataset provides the data for 4 different weather conditions as. TU-VDN dataset provides data for a distant variety of images, which are images of dynamic backgrounds and flat cluster backgrounds. Below mentioned few datasets are frequently used for testing the object detection algorithm.

1.   OSU-Thermal: The OTCBVS dataset adds the OSU thermal pedestrian database for testing cutting-edge computer vision algorithms. It only discusses the identification of people in outdoor settings with poor lighting, gloomy, rainy, and hazy. Only 284 frames from 10 daytime video sequences were recorded in this database. Bounding boxes are used to annotate the people who are present in a frame.

2.   BU-TIV (Thermal Infrared Video): The dataset that has addressed many visual analytic objectives, such as single or multi-view object monitoring, counting, and group actions, etc. is Thermal Infrared Video. It includes 16 video clips, totaling 63,700 frames, about a car, a bike, a motorcycle, and a bat.

3.   OSU-CT: Additionally, it is a component of the OTCBVS benchmark dataset for fusion-based color and thermal object detection. Only pedestrians are included in the OSU-CT collection, which has 17,089 frames from 6 outdoor video recordings.

4.   AIC-TV: The dataset is intended for tracking moving things like bicycles, cars, and people. It combined data from the typical thermal infrared spectrums and CCTV recordings with significant difficulties such as scale fluctuation, pitch-black night, and occlusion. A total of 2,013 frames from 6 sequences in a small indoor and outdoor dataset make up this collection.

5.   CVC-14: A current visible FIR day-and-night dataset for pedestrian detection is made up of two sets of excellent outdoor scenes consisting of a set for daytime and the other for nighttime. The bounding box approach was used to create the ground truth annotations.

6.   CDnet 2014: Low frame rate, poor weather, nocturnal sequences, and airflow instability are significant change detection issues added to CDnet 2014, which is an expansion of CDnet 2012. and 53 video segments totaling around 1,60,000 frames. The datasets have already been created to test different moving object detection techniques. While the BU-Thermal Infrared Video dataset is intended solely for visual analysis tasks, some of these datasets have been captured using thermal sensors to identify things. These datasets only comprise video clips shot throughout the day, however, the OSU Thermal dataset also includes weather data from a low-resolution thermal camera used to detect walkers exclusively. Despite the fact that it is daytime, only a minimal number of datasets, with the exception of CDNet 2014, take meteorological conditions into account. In view of the fact that above half of object-related incidents happen during night, it is challenging to assess the resilience of object recognition algorithms under atmospheric circumstances, particularly in night vision. Therefore, in order to cover numerous real-world circumstances, we have been building atmospheric weather-degraded conditions based on standard video datasets at night. Dust, fog, rain, and low light levels are taken into account as environmental conditions to maximize the benefits of the infrared sensor.

7.   OPEN IMAGES V4: Open Images is a vast image dataset that consists of approximately 9 million-image that include image-level metadata and body bounding boxes. The training set of V4 includes nearly 14 Million bounding boxes for six hundred item types on approximately 1.8M images, making it the sizable dataset which are having object position annotations. Without a predetermined list of class names, the images that were downloaded from Flickr produce natural class statistics

and remove a design phase bias.. They also have Open-Source licenses, which allow them to be shared and adapted. To make sure accuracy and consistency, the boxes were mostly drawn by expert annotators by hands. The photographs are diverse and frequently include complicated scenarios with multiple items. In addition, the set includes image-level labels for hundreds and thousands of classes.

The open images dataset can increase the speed of many tasks related to computer vision by days or months.

Table 1. Statistics of the dataset

Camera Type	Camera condition	Background	Lowlight	Rain	Fog	Dust	Total Videos
FLIR	Static	Dynamic background	8	4	6	7	25
FLIR	Static	Flat cluttered	13	4	5	6	28
FLIR	Motion	-	3	1	2	1	7
Total Videos			60				

4. BACKGROUND

The SSD model is the updated version of YOLO. YOLO identifies objects in a single pass that is present in the image. But when it comes to SSD, it uses many convolutional layers. This makes SSD an edge in adding various attribute layers at the end. The Base network of SSD predicts the balance out of the localised boxes of multiple scales and aspect ratio. SSD is able to detect around 8372 detections on average, whereas YOLO can predict only nighty eight predictions per class.

4.1 Parameters in an SSD

Grid Cell

In place of sliding windows, SSD splits images into grid cells. Every grid cell plays a role in locating the items in a particular area of the image. Object detection is all about predicting a few characteristics and placement of an object. If no object is identified in the image then a backdrop class is made up and the location is ignored. As shown in the illustration below, a 4x4 framework is used to identify the shape and position of the object.

Figure 3. Grid cell

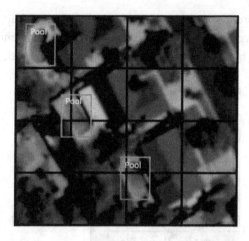

Anchor Box

Many unique anchor boxes could be assigned to every grid cell in the SSD. Each localized anchor box concludes the size and shape of a grid cell. For instance, the building in the figure below correlates to the broader box, while the swimming pool belongs to the higher anchor box.

Figure 4. Anchor box

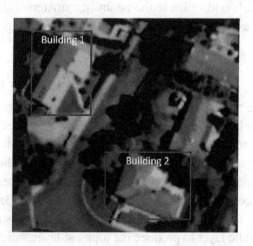

SSD performs a matching phase to match a suitable anchor box with the bounding boxes of each ground truth object within an image, a matching phase is performed by SSD while training. Basically, whichever anchor box has the highest degree of co-occurrence with an object decides the placement and class of that object. After network training, this accredit is used to predict the identified objects and their locations, this whole process is known as bounding box regression. In reality, a zoom level and aspect ratio are mainly used to define every anchor box

Aspect Ratio

Each object maintains a different shape, not only a square. Every shape has its own characteristics, angles, and many more. So, even these have to be considered by an anchor box. With the help of SSD architecture, this problem can be solved. It provides localized aspect ratios.

Figure 5. Aspect Ratio

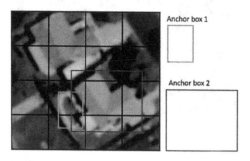

In Figure 7. Building 1 has a higher bounding box whereas building 2 has a wider bounding box.

Zoom Level

Usually, grid cells and anchor boxes have different sizes. Smaller or larger things could be discovered within a grid cell. To understand the process of scaling down or up of anchor box by comparing every grid cell, in comparison to each grid cell, use the zooms parameters. It is very similar to the example used in the anchor box while explaining. The size of the building is far greater than the size of a pool.

Receptive Field

The area that is present in the input space that a certain CNN attribute is waiting for is known as the receptive field. Here, it can be referred to as "feature" and "activation" mutually and review them as the linear amalgam of the former layer at the appropriate region, sometimes accompanied by the application of an activation function to boost nonlinearity. Attributes at multiple layers reflect varying widths of regions in the input image as a result of the convolution procedure. The size that a feature represents increases as it progresses deeper. In the below-mentioned example, we begin with the bottommost layer which is a 5x5 and then use convolution to generate the middle layer (3x3). One feature (green pixel) in the middle layer represents a 3x3 region of the input layer which is also a bottom layer. The convolution is then applied to the middle layer to produce the topmost layer which is a 2x2, where each feature corresponds to a 7x7 region on the input image.

Figure 6. Receptive field

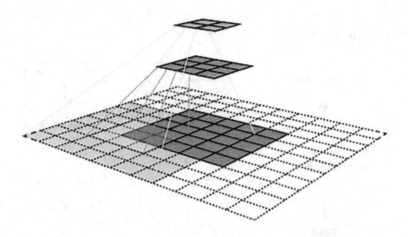

Visualisation of the Receptive Field and CNN Feature Maps

The receptive field is the central hypothesis of the SSD architecture, which allows one to recognize objects at multiple scales and output a close-fitting bounding box. The ResNet34 backbone generates feature maps with a matrix of 7x7 for an input image. If a 4x4 framework is specified, the most straightforward procedure is to simply apply convolution to the 7x7 grid and change it to 4x4. This method can only work for every possible case. By adding numerous convolutional layers to the fundamental feature map and having each of these layers produce an object recognition result, SSD goes over and above.

5. PROPOSED MODEL

The proposed paradigm for this project is a Single shot detector, where Mobilenet v2 serves as the backbone. An object detection deep learning algorithm is SSD. There are mainly two parts to an SSD. One is the SSD head and the other is the Backbone. A Backbone is an image categorization network that is pre-trained and performs the role of a feature map extractor. MobileNetV2 is a simple CNN framework that solely concentrates on performing accurately on different mobiles. MobileNetV2 is constructed on a residual structure that is bottom-sided-up where the bottleneck structures are connected by different residual connections. This framework mainly consists of a 32-filter, fully complex layer, including 19 different bottleneck layers. To refine features convolution-like lightweight depthwise is considered for an intermediary expansion layer as a source of non-linearity. Depthwise Separable Convolution, which is perfect for mobiles or any devices with limited processing capacity, was first introduced in the previous version of MobileNetV1 and has had a significant positive impact on the cost, convolution, and size of the network model. A better module with a bottom-up residual structure is added in MobileNetV2. MobileNetV2 consists of a residual structure which is inverted which makes it a convenient model. Thin layers have few non-linearities and these are removed now.

5.1 MobileNet V2 Convolutional Blocks

Figure 7. Convolutional blocks

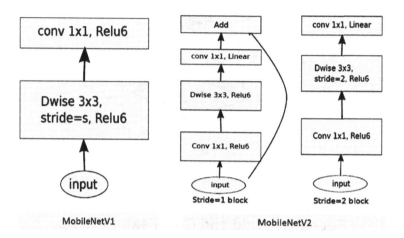

The SSD head is built on a backbone model. It is constructed from a couple of convolutional layers stocked jointly. These convolutional layers predict multiple objects in an image, bounding boxes, and categorization of objects in spatial areas are the outputs of this. SSD consists of a few final layers(blue boxes), as shown in the figure below, while the initial layers combine the backbone.

Figure 8. SSD head

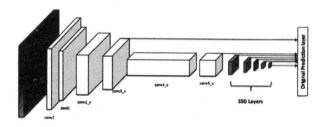

SSD first performs tasks like object locating and object classification in a single forward pass of the network (Forward pass is a process of calculating and storing the immediate variables for a neural network in a sequence from the initial layer to the target layer). After this, SSD uses a technique called Bounding box regression to perform a technique for bounding boxes for the classified objects.

5.2 Working and Analysis

In this project we used SSD, MobileNet V2 which works as a feature extractor from the images.

Step 1: Importing image
Step 2: Displaying the image to know what kind of image we are going to use to identify the objects.

Step 3: Resize the image to make better predictions.
Step 4: Converting the resized image to a JPEG format to make future analysis easy.
Step 5: Decoding the image into vectors.
Step 6: Create border margins for the identified objects in the resized image.

Resizing an image usually reduces its quality but after resizing an image we can achieve a pixelated image which makes the identification of objects in an image easy and accurate. Normally when we resize an image the image's color space would be changed. A Color Space is an organized combination of colors. The main work of a color space is converting the specific color model which turns colors into numbers. By doing this we can create border margins for the objects that will be identified in the image with ease. For resizing images we used a python imaging library named PILLOW which has all the required tools for processing an image. PILLOW supports a large number of file formats like PNG, TIFF, JPEG, and BMP and it even assists in supporting new formats in the library by creating new file decoders.

Sometimes we consider having a simple URL pattern but when we try to directly copy a link of an image from some other resource to save time. So we build the code considering these kinds of small issues included. For drawing the boundaries for the objects in the image we use the same python imaging library pillow. After resizing an image we saved the file to a jpeg format this is because we can easily convert the jpeg format to a tensor. ConversinG to tensor means simply converting the image into vectors. This makes the model recognize the dimensions of the object present in an image and assign the boundaries to the objects identified is done. For setting the boundaries we run inference using the trained model we used initially. The inference is simply a process to run data points into a machine learning model to measure the single numeric score for every output.

6. RESULTS

The model is tested with nighttime thermal images to understand the performance of our model and the accuracy rate of object detection during nighttime at different atmospheric conditions. Below mentioned images are the results we achieved. The accuracy of identifying objects varied for different objects in different scenarios. The accuracy for detecting bigger-sized objects correctly is around 30% but for the objects with the smaller size is above 12%. The model though shows lesser accuracy for detecting the objects, it can identify the objects correctly. That makes the model efficient enough to use for multiple purposes and achieve good accuracy.

The dataset, which is used for the project, has images at 4 different atmospheric conditions. And in each atmospheric condition, 2 types of images can be used for understanding the accuracy of the mode. Those are Dynamic background and Flat clustered background images.

Figure 9.

Figure 10.

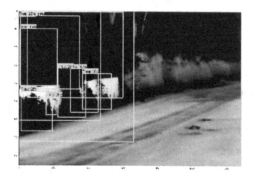

Figure 11.

Figure 12.

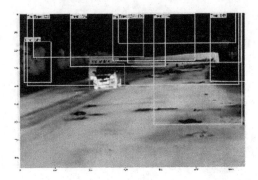

Above Figures 9,10,11,12 are images that are taken at dusk atmospheric conditions with a Dynamic Background gave a prediction accuracy of 13% - 23% for the objects in the images

Figure 13.

Figure 14.

Figure 15.

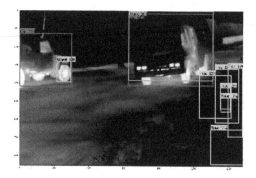

Figure 16.

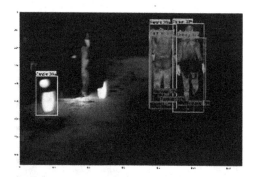

Above Figures 13,14,15,16 are images that are taken at dusk atmospheric conditions with a Flat Cluster Background gave a prediction accuracy of 16% - 30% for the objects in the images

Figure 17.

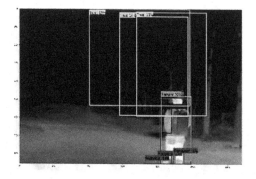

Figure 18.

Figure 19.

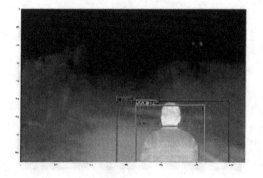

Figure 20.

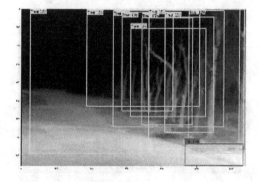

Above Figures 17,18,19,20 are images that are taken at Fog atmospheric conditions with a Dynamic Background gave a prediction accuracy of 12% - 34% for the objects in the images and detected most of the objects correctly

Figure 21.

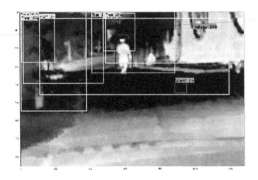

Figure 22.

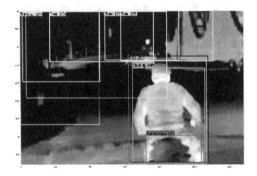

Figure 23.

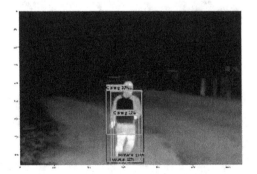

Figure 24.

Above Figures 21,22,23,24 are images that are taken at dusk atmospheric conditions with a Flat Cluster Background giving a prediction accuracy of 16% - 44% for the objects in the images. But it's not able to predict all the objects in the images accurately.

Figure 25.

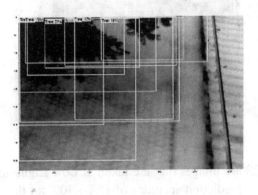

Figure 26.

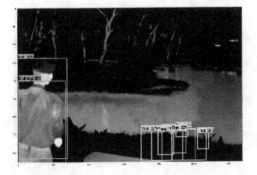

Figure 27.

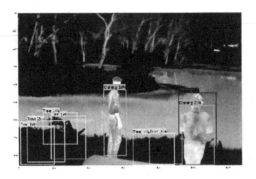

Figure 28.

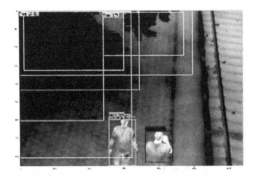

Above Figures 25,26,27,28 are images that are taken at Low Light atmospheric conditions with a Dynamic Background giving a prediction accuracy of 16% - 30% for the objects in the images and detecting most of the objects correctly.

Figure 29.

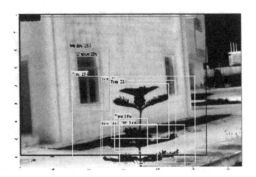

Figure 30.

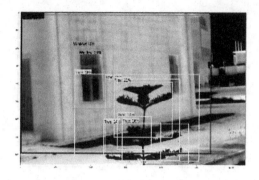

Figure 31.

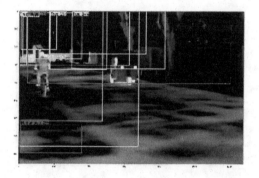

Figure 32.

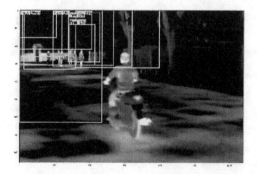

Figures 29,30,31,32 are images that are taken at Low Light atmospheric conditions with a Flat Cluster Background giving a prediction accuracy of 15% - 44% for the objects in the images. But it's not able to predict all the objects in the images accurately.

Figure 33.

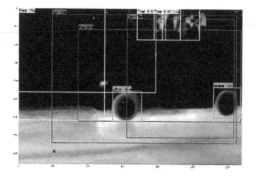

Figure 34.

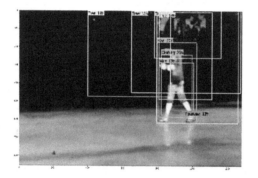

Figure 35.

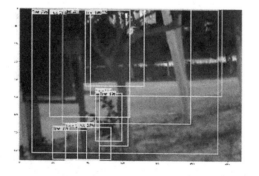

Figure 36.

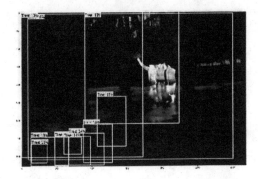

Above Figures 33,34,35,36 are images that are taken in Rain atmospheric conditions with a Dynamic Background giving a prediction accuracy of 13% - 64% for the objects in the images.

Figure 37.

Figure 38.

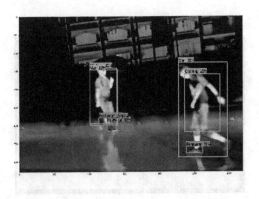

Figure 39.

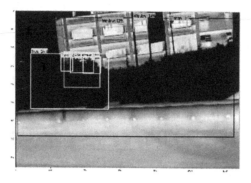

Figure 40.

Above Figures 37,38,39,40 are images that are taken at Low Light atmospheric conditions with a Flat Cluster Background giving a prediction accuracy of 17% - 30% for the objects in the images. The model can predict most of the objects in the image

Figure 41.

Figure 42.

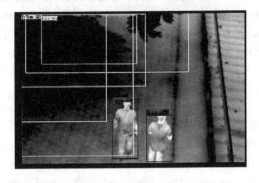

Figure 43.

Figure 44.

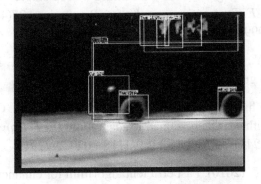

Above Figures 41,42,43,44 are considered from each atmospheric condition and these predictions were predicted by running the model on a mobile phone. And the inference time taken for the model to predict these objects in each image is less than 0.35 secs for each image. This shows that the prediction speed of this model is faster than any other existing object detection algorithms.

7. CONCLUSION

The proposed model detects objects in images efficiently under various atmospheric conditions. And there are primarily two types of images used: dynamic backgrounds and flat cluster backgrounds. The model was able to predict the majority of the objects as well as maintained prediction accuracy in the images with Dynamic backgrounds when compared with Flat cluster backgrounds. Along with the number of objects, the proposed model accurately predicted the objects. The proposed model was able to predict objects more accurately during rain conditions than any other atmospheric condition tested. The model is very faster than many other object detection algorithms and could be used even in a mobile device as the used backbone for SSD is MobileNetv2. As observed in the results, detected objects that are achieved from mobile have accurate predictions. We are planning to implement the proposed model on IoT devices and try to improve the performance of the model.

ACKNOWLEDGMENT

"The dataset of the project is provided by Tripura University (A Central University), Tripura, Suryamani-nagar-799022".

REFERENCES

Cai, J., Gu, S., Zhang, L., & Zhang, L. (2018). Learning a deep single image contrast enhancer from multi-exposure images. *IEEE Transactions on Image Processing*, 27(4), 2049–2062. doi:10.1109/TIP.2018.2794218 PMID:29994747

Cheng, B., Chen, C., Wei, Y., Zhu, Y., Huang, Z., Xiong, J., Huang, T. Hwu, W., & Shi, H. (2019). Spgnet: Semantic prediction guidance for scene parsing. In *IEEE ICCV*.

Di, S., Feng, Q., Li, C.-G., Zhang, M., Zhang, H., Elezovikj, S., Tan, C. C., & Ling, H. (2021). Rainy night scene understanding with near scene semantic adaptation. *IEEE Transactions on Intelligent Transportation Systems*, 22(3), 1594–1602. doi:10.1109/TITS.2020.2972912

Dong, X., Pang, Y., & Wen, J. (2010). Fast efficient algorithm for enhancement of low lighting video. In ACM SIGGRAPH 2010 Posters (pp. 1-1). ACM. doi:10.1145/1836845.1836920

Fu, J., Liu, J., Tian, H., Fang, Z., & Lu, H. (2019). *Dual attention network for scene segmentation*. IEEE CVPR. doi:10.1109/CVPR.2019.00326

He, K., Sun, J., & Tang, X. (2010). Single image haze removal using dark channel prior. *IEEE Transactions on Pattern Analysis and Machine Intelligence, 33*(12), 2341–2353. PMID:20820075

Huang, Z., Wang, X., Huang, L., Huang, C., Wei, Y., & Liu, W. (2019). Ccnet: Criss-cross attention for semantic segmentation. In *IEEE ICCV*.

Jiang, Y., Gong, X., Liu, D., Cheng, Y., Fang, C., Shen, X., Yang, J., Zhou, P., & Wang, Z. (2021). Enlightengan: Deep light enhancement without paired supervision. *IEEE Transactions on Image Processing, 30*, 2340–2349. doi:10.1109/TIP.2021.3051462 PMID:33481709

Li, C., Guo, J., Porikli, F., & Pang, Y. (2017). Lightennet: A convolutional neural network for weakly illuminated image enhancement. *Pattern Recognition Letters, 104*, 15–22. doi:10.1016/j.patrec.2018.01.010

Lin, G., Milan, A., Shen, C., & Reid, I. (2017). Refinenet: Multi-path refinement networks for high-resolution semantic segmentation. In *IEEE CVPR*, (pp. 1925–1934). IEEE.

Lore, K. G., Akintayo, A., & Sarkar, S. (2017). LLNet: A deep autoencoder approach to natural low-light image enhancement. *Pattern Recognition, 61*, 650–662. doi:10.1016/j.patcog.2016.06.008

Łoza, A., Bull, D. R., Hill, P. R., & Achim, A. M. (2013). Automatic contrast enhancement of low-light images based on local statistics of wavelet coefficients. *Digital Signal Processing, 23*(6), 1856–1866. doi:10.1016/j.dsp.2013.06.002

Malm, H., Oskarsson, M., Warrant, E., Clarberg, P., Hasselgren, J., & Lejdfors, C. (2007, October). Adaptive enhancement and noise reduction in very low light-level video. In *2007 IEEE 11th International Conference on Computer Vision* (pp. 1-8). IEEE. 10.1109/ICCV.2007.4409007

Pizer, S. M., Amburn, E. P., Austin, J. D., Cromartie, R., Geselowitz, A., Greer, T., ter Haar Romeny, B., Zimmerman, J. B., & Zuiderveld, K. (1987). Adaptive histogram equalization and its variations. *Computer Vision Graphics and Image Processing, 39*(3), 355–368. doi:10.1016/S0734-189X(87)80186-X

Pohlen, T., Hermans, A., Mathias, M., & Leibe, B. (2017). Full-resolution residual networks for semantic segmentation in street scenes. In *Proceedings of the IEEE conference on computer vision and pattern recognition* (pp. 4151-4160). IEEE. 10.1109/CVPR.2017.353

Sakaridis, C., Dai, D., & Van Gool, L. (2021). Map-guided curriculum domain adaptation and uncertainty-aware evaluation for semantic nighttime image segmentation. *IEEE Transactions on Pattern Analysis and Machine Intelligence*. PMID:33338013

Shen, L., Yue, Z., Feng, F., Chen, Q., Liu, S., & Ma, J. (2017). Msr-net: Low-light image enhancement using deep convolutional network. arXiv:1711.02488.

Takikawa, T., Acuna, D., Jampani, V., & Fidler, S. (2019). Gated-CNN: Gated shape CNN's for semantic segmentation. In *IEEE ICCV*.

Tao, L., Zhu, C., Song, J., Lu, T., Jia, H., & Xie, X. (2017, September). Low-light image enhancement using CNN and bright channel prior. In *2017 IEEE International Conference on Image Processing (ICIP)* (pp. 3215-3219). IEEE. 10.1109/ICIP.2017.8296876

Tung, F., Chen, J., Meng, L., & Little, J. (2017). The raincouver scene parsing benchmark for self-driving in adverse weather and at night. *IEEE Robotics and Automation Letters*, 2(4), 2188–2193. doi:10.1109/LRA.2017.2723926

Tung, F., Chen, J., Meng, L., & Little, J. J. (2017). The rain couver scene parsing benchmark for self-driving in adverse weather and at night. *IEEE Robotics and Automation Letters*, 2(4), 2188–2193. doi:10.1109/LRA.2017.2723926

Valada, A., Vertens, J., Dhall, A., & Burgard, W. (2017). Adapnet: Adaptive semantic segmentation in adverse environmental conditions. In *IEEE ICRA* (pp. 4644–4651). IEEE.

Wang, Q., Gao, J., & Yuan, Y. (2017). A joint convolutional neural networks and context transfer for street scenes labelling. *IEEE Transactions on Intelligent Transportation Systems*, 19(5), 1457–1470. doi:10.1109/TITS.2017.2726546

Wang, R., Zhang, Q., Fu, C., Shen, W., Zheng, W., & Jia, J. (2019). Underexposed photo enhancement using deep illumination estimation. In *IEEE CVPR*.

Wang, S., Zheng, J., Hu, H., & Li, B. (2013). Naturalness preserved enhancement algorithm for non-uniform illumination images. *IEEE Transactions on Image Processing*, 22(9), 3538–3548. doi:10.1109/TIP.2013.2261309 PMID:23661319

Wei, C., Wang, W., Yang, W., & Liu, J. (2018). Deep retinex decomposition for low-light enhancement. arXiv:1808.04560.

Wu, Z., Fuller, N., Theriault, D., & Betke, M. A thermal infrared video benchmark for visual analysis. In: *10th IEEE Workshop on Perception Beyond the Visible Spectrum (PBVS)*. IEEE. 10.1109/CVPRW.2014.39

Xu, K., Yang, X., Yin, B., & Lau, R. (2020). Learning to restore low-light images via decomposition-and-enhancement. In *IEEE CVPR*, (pp. 2281–2290) IEEE.

Yan, Z., Zhang, H., Wang, B., Paris, S., & Yu, Y. (2016). Automatic photo adjustment using deep neural networks. *ACM TOG*, 35(2), 1–15. doi:10.1145/2790296

Yang, X., Xu, K., Song, Y., Zhang, Q., Wei, X., & Lau, R. (2018). Image correction via deep reciprocating hdr transformation. In *IEEE CVPR*.

Ying, Z., Li, G., Ren, Y., Wang, R., & Wang, w. (2017). A new low-light image enhancement algorithm using camera response model. In *IEEE ICCV*.

Zendel, O., Honauer, K., Murschitz, M., Steininger, D., & Fernandez Dominguez, G. (2018). Wildash-creating hazard-aware benchmarks. In *ECCV*, (pp. 402–416). IEEE.

Zhang, Z., Zhang, X., Peng, C., Xue, X., & Sun, J. (2018). Exfuse: Enhancing feature fusion for semantic segmentation. In *ECCV*, pp. 269–284.

Zheng, Z., Wu, Y., Han, X., & Shi, J. (2020). Forkgan: Seeing into the rainy night. In *ECCV*.

KEY TERMS AND DEFINITIONS

Atmospheric Conditions: The elements of the atmosphere, including temperature, wind, clouds, and precipitation, that make up its current state.

Bounding Boxes: In the process of object detection, where the goal is to determine the location and nature of various items in a picture, bounding boxes are primarily used.

Deeping Learning: It is a kind of machine learning that uses artificial neural networks and numerous processing layers to extract increasingly more complex properties from data.

Feature Extraction: For the categorization of biological signals to perform better, feature extraction and dimension reduction are necessary. Finding the most condensed and informative set of features (distinct patterns) is the goal of feature extraction in order to improve the effectiveness of the classifier.

Image-Level Metadata: Image metadata is the term for the precise information and facts pertaining to a single photo file. Author, creation date, file name, themes, content, etc. are frequently included in the information.

MobileNetV2: A convolutional neural network design called MobileNetV2 aims to function well on mobile devices. It is built on an inverted residual structure where the bottleneck layers are connected by residual connections. Lightweight depthwise convolutions are used in the intermediate expansion layer as a source of nonlinearity to filter features.

Object Classification: The classification of objects is the grouping of objects into groups, each with its own set of characteristics.

Object Detection: It is a method of computer vision that enables us to find and recognize things in an image or video. Using this form of localization and identification, object detection can be used to count the items in a scene, as well as to locate and track them in real time while precisely labeling them.

Object Localization: It is a process to determine the location of an object in an image. The algorithm used for the process of localization will reveal the coordinates of the position of an object in comparison with the image.

R-CNN: It is a sort of machine learning model used for computer vision applications, particularly for object detection. The full form of R-CNN is a Region-Based Convolutional Neural Network.

Chapter 25
Identification of Avascular Necrosis or Osteoporosis Using Deep Belief Convolutional Neural Networks

Sankaragomathi B.

Sri Shakthi Institute of Engineering and Technology, India

Senthil Kumar S.

Department of Computer Science and Engineering, Amritha University, Cochin, India

ABSTRACT

Musculoskeletal impairment can be caused by Avascular Necrosis(AN). Younger people are more likely to develop it, thus early intervention and fast diagnosis are essential. The femoral bones are typically affected by this condition, which results in fractures that change the geometry of the bones. It is difficult to retrieve the AN-affected bone pictures because of the many places where the fractures are located. In this work, a useful method for retrieving AN pictures using deep belief CNN feature representation is proposed. Preprocessing is first applied to the raw dataset. In this stage, the median filter (MF) is used to reduce image noise and downsize the image. Using a deep belief convolutional neural network, features are represented (DB-CNN). The representations of the image feature data have now been converted to binary codes. Then, using the modified-hamming distance, the similarity measurement is calculated. The images are then retrieved with a focus on the similarity values. The test results demonstrated that the proposed approach is superior to the other methods now in use.

INTRODUCTION

1.2 million Australians experienced osteoporosis or AVN in 2012 (Bengio et al., 2012). The majority of them have osteoporosis, which results in fractures that cost millions of dollars to treat. Deep-seated discomfort that is present at rest, throughout exercise, and at night is experienced by the majority of

DOI: 10.4018/978-1-6684-6937-8.ch025

patients with AVN of the humeral head (Anthimopoulos et al., 2016; Giveki et al., 2015; Zhang et al., 2016). AVN denotes the femoral head's bone tissue dying from a lack of blood flow. With regular weight bearing, this condition leads to a) micro fractures in the bone, b) collapse of the subchondral bone, and c) collapse of the overlying articular cartilage surface. Younger persons are more susceptible to AVN, therefore early intervention and fast diagnosis are essential. Typically, this condition affects the femoral bones, causing fractures that change the form of the bones. Figure 1 depicts AVN.

AVN has the ability to quickly collapse the articular surface. Furthermore, this necessitates a hip replacement (Lazik et al., 2015; Tsai et al., 2013). AVN fractures with even minor minimum stress are associated with greater rates of morbidity and mortality. Figure 2 demonstrates that, despite the fact that there are more therapeutic alternatives available to control osteoporosis, under treatment is incredibly common. Only 20% of people obtain care or have a checkup for the disease.

CBIR is a frequently used IR approach in a variety of computer vision applications, such as the medical field for obtaining historical patient information, e-commerce for determining the required products, information retrieval for taking images from a large database, etc. (Subash Kumar & Nagarajan, 2018). Medical CBIR retrieves images from vast imaging archives and has been used to assist in the diagnosis of numerous comparable cases (Banerjee et al., 2018). It is possible to diagnose related lesions from photos by using a medical image. This denotes a useful aid for doctors who encounter difficult-to-diagnose conditions that could result in incorrect diagnoses (Mera et al., 2015). ConvNets have also been increasingly used because of their usefulness in a variety of fields, including image retrieval. Deep Belief CNN Feature Representation is a useful technology proposed in this chapter for retrieving AVN images (DBCNN).

Retrieving AVN Images From DBCNN

Numerous investigations have suggested brand-new IR approaches. The study in (Ashraf et al., 2018) created an automated IR mechanism and proposed a brand-new content-focused picture capturing method that relied on color characteristics. Histogram, color, and DCT analyses were used since they were reliable and required minimal processing power. The performance was compared in terms of recall, precision, retrieval speed, and feature extortion. The comparison results showed that, compared to other CBIR typical schemes, the proposed plan outperformed them all in terms of average recall and precision values. In (Jin & Shan-W, 2017), a lower-level shape-feature-focused IR system was suggested.

In this method, the salient zone was determined by looking at the image's low-level characters, and the shape attributes of that area were used to determine how similar the salient zone was to other noteworthy zones. The shape features were determined by the major axis for the proposed shape features extortion framework, and the value of each feature was denoted by several scalars. For searching and obtaining photos from a huge database, CBIR makes use of image content features.

AVN picture retrieval becomes challenging due to variations in appearance. The input images in the dataset are first preprocessed by the suggested DBCNN. In the preprocessing stage, the image is scaled and image noise is removed using the Median Filter. When extracting features from images, Deep Belief ConvNets are utilized to convert the image feature representations to binary codes. Then, using Modified Hamming Distance, the similarity assessment is assessed (MHD). The photos are then retrieved with a focus on the similarity values. In Figure 3, the DBCNN architecture is shown.

DBCNN Pre Processing

It is the first stage of DBCNN. Pre-main processing's goal is to improve the picture data by removing undesirable distortions or enhancing particular qualities that make an image valuable for future processing. The main purposes of image preprocessing are scaling and noise removal. To eliminate noise, DBCNN uses the Median Filter (MF). This filter works quite hard to keep edges sharp while removing noise. By moving across the image pixel by pixel and replacing each value with the median value of surrounding pixels, MF functions as intended. The neighbors' pattern is displayed throughout the full image in the window Ws, moving pixel by pixel across the whole thing. In order to determine the median value Ms, all of the pixel values are first sorted in the window Ws numerical order, and the middle/median pixel value Ms is then substituted. Ws allows for the computation of a median value (Eqn.1). S_1, S_2,..., S_n are the grey levels of any pixel value in any window. The photos that have been noise-filtered are then re-sized. To efficiently process the photos, the image size is changed. Images of varying sizes are therefore downsized to 256x256 pixels.

DBCNN Feature Representation

DBCNN focuses on AVN image feature representation. It is defined as the collection of a set of features or picture properties in order to effectively or meaningfully portrays the information, making the image suitable for categorization and analysis. The clarity of the images will improve IR accuracy in accordance with the feature extortion. The convolution layer (CL), max-average pooling layer, and fully connected layer are three types of layers that make up the classifier (FCL). The Multi-Learned Weight Matrices (MLWM), also known as filters or kernels that make up the convolution layer slide over the input features.

Initially the result of earlier layers, this layer is convolved to MLWM known as learned kernels or filter masks on each. The problem is then processed using a non-linear technique to produce the layer output. A stride defines how the filter convolves across the input features, and a kernel specifies the matrix that will be used to combine the features. This layer uses an equation to carry out the convolution on the coded data (Eqn. 2). A feature map is the end result of this type of convolution. "N" stands for the number of items in x, x stands for the input characteristics, and h stands for filter. The output vector denotes g, whereas the subscripts represent the nth aspect of the vector. The pooling layer is the Max-Average method for obtaining necessary features while retaining amazing features and letting go of unnecessary ones. The down-sampling layer is another name for this layer. By reducing the size of the output neurons relative to the CL, the aforementioned pooling method lowers the computational load. Typically, pooling layers are applied right after CL. The information in the CL's output is clarified by the pooling layers. Two pooling categories, average pooling and max-pooling, may be identified for the convolved matrix images with the size of u x v for each u-dimensional feature vector g_i, according to equations (3) and (4).

The characteristics of CL include data that is related to nearby features, such as position and relative position. While the distribution of the picture features is flatter and more uniform, the max-pooling function ignores the local spatial information it is connected with. It has a significant impact on the aspect of extortion and its portrayal. In that case, it is assumed that the average pooling will preserve the information that is locally related. The pooling function is then defined in the proposed method as suggested in equation (5).

A completely connected layer behaves in this case as a matrix multiplication operation, which is typically equivalent to the feature-space transformation, since $\alpha_1 + \alpha_2 = 1$. In general, it can be used for extortion and the integration of valuable information. FCL characteristics represent global information. Following many layers of pooling and convolution, the output is produced in a class-like manner. Those two layers would be capable of little more than extracting features and reducing the number of parameters used to describe the real photos.

However, an FCL must be utilised to generate an output equal to the required number of classes in order to assemble the final output. It becomes increasingly challenging to reach that number with the CL. CLs generate activation maps that show whether an image belongs to a given class. The output layer has a loss function that is used to determine the prediction error. The back-propagation procedure starts once such a forward pass is finished in order to update the biases and weights for loss and error reduction.

DBCNN Deep Binary Codes Generation

A high-response feature maps at the same index locations on the deep layer for two similar images. This perception is used to transform the visual representation into binary codes on the deep CLs. By comparing each feature map's answer to the average response across all feature maps, this binary code is created. The equation offers the activation function (Eqn. 6). Where, $\sigma\left(a_k^7 W^{HL} + b^{HL}\right)$ represents the sigmoid logistic function, which regulates the outputs between the interval (0, 1). a_k^7 denotes the output feature vectors in the FC7 layer, W^{HL} signifies the weights, and b^{HL} specifies the bias parameters in the hidden layer (HL). The Equation provides a definition of the binary coding function (Eqn.7). Figure 4 shows the multiple-scale pooling-generated deep binary code (DBC).

DBCNN Similarity Measurement

The feature vectors are converted to binary code during the HL's binary operation. The suggested strategy in IR demands picture features for the target image. Following that, binary codes are retrieved using the activation function in the HL output.

DBCNN Modified Hamming Distance

The provided Hamming distance is used to determine the degree of similarity between a given query image Q and a set of deep binary codes b_k, where k=1, 2,... L. Higher similarity indicates a lower value for the Hamming distance criterion. The HQ in DBCNN has a greater value for maximum similarity because MHD $H_Q = D - H_Q$. Here, D represents the size of b_k, and C_k represents the sorted search score that is supplied by the equation(8) and is centered on the MHD returned by b_k.

Additionally, the high scores produced by the MHD are subjected to max-min normalization so that query relevant photos provide a max-score of 1. In comparison, the offensive images receive a score of 0. An Equation measures the size of $\overline{C_k}$ an area under a curve. N stands for the first N closest neighbors found in each search result. This N parameter was created to avoid the scenario where a beneficial feature might be covered by a sorted curve due to a poor search score for a large N. The area size is controlled by this option. To select the first K higher quality features, one might use the computed area under each normalized score-curve. Each first K score is given an adjusted weight value, which is provided by equation (10). An equation is utilized to evaluate the fused search score of the higher grade DBCs (11). The dynamic score-level late fusion technique that is suggested is quite customizable. The DBC's quality is evaluated automatically and unsupervisedly. The top identical photos are then obtained on the basis of the fused score level.

DBCNN Results

In this section, the results of the suggested method are described in detail, with relevant numbers and statistics. Images that were downloaded from the RPDR database were used in the study. "Text mining" was used to extract the terms "a vascular necrosis," "AVN," and "osteonecrosis" from the RPDR database. Any reports that indicated the existence of AVN were treated as cases of AVN. All MRI findings mentioning any of these terms were evaluated. A 3x3 median filter was used to remove the speckle noise from the images, and it was implemented in MATLAB. Figure 6 lists the photos that deep belief CNN for AVN was able to recover, whereas Figure 5 shows a few typical images from the dataset.

RESULTS AND ANALYSIS

The final stage of the research employs DB-CNN to treat AVN illness. For the AVN disease-affected regions such as the femurs, humerus, and knee, data sets are gathered from the general public. The performance of the suggested DB-CNN approaches is evaluated using MATLAB software's similarity measurement for image retrieval.

Performance Analysis of the DB-CNN

A number of variables, including recall, precision, retrieval time, and retrieval accuracy, are used to control the performance analysis of the presented approaches. The input data set is chosen to represent AVN diseases that affect human body parts like the femur, hip, and knee; the results have been compared with existing methods like SIFT, SURF, and IRSFM (IR Algorithm centred on Shape Feature Matching). It has been noted that the performance indicator continues to increase over time. Each measure is covered in detail below.

Precision

The ratio of the number of photos retrieved to the total number of images retrieved is used to calculate precision(eqn.12). Figure 7 shows the performance of the DB-CNN for Precision. The values are comparatively higher than IRSFM and SS-BOVW. Femur advantages for DB-CNN are 82% higher than those for IRSFM, which are 80%. For the condition of the humerous, IRSFM scores 78%, SS-BOVW is 76%, and DB-CNN advantages are 78%. In contrast, for the sickness of the knees, IRSFM scores 70%, SS-BOVW is 75%, and DB-CNN benefits are 78%. It is evident from examining all graph values that DB-CNN performs better than other approaches.

Recall is calculated by dividing the number of relevant photos that were successfully retrieved by the total number of relevant images in the data set(Eqn.13). For the application of the disease, the values are generated separately, and the performance with the suggested DB-CNN is compared. The outcomes once more demonstrated how much more effective DB-CNN is than IRSFM and SSBOVW. The benefits for the femur are 73% for IRSFM, 70% for SSBOVW, and 80% for DB-CNN. IRSFM has a benefit rate of 74%, SSBOVW has a benefit rate of 77%, and DB-CNN has a benefit rate of 78%. Once more, DB-CNN demonstrates its effectiveness. For the knee dataset, DB-CNN demonstrates its effectiveness with a significant percentage difference from the other methods. The value for IRSFM is 69%. The value of the DB-CNN is 78%. The performance of DB-CNN is consistently superior, with a respectable margin when all the findings are considered.

Retrieval Time

It is a crucial performance indicator for image retrieval. This is obtained by multiplying the time for deep binary code creation by the time for similarity analysis. The searching time, also known as computation time, includes the feature extraction and likeness matching time, and this time has a complete impact on RT. The femur, knees, and humorous were selected for investigation as part of the research for the human body impacted by AVN. Retrieval Time is calculated by the equation 14.

In RT, the DB-CNN performs well enough, and it is ahead of IRSFM and SS BOVW. For the AVN disease affected part, femur SSBOVW shows better results with a value of 25 s, and IRSFM is 20 s, and DB-CNN 10 s. For the disease humerus, the benefits for SSBOVW are 24 s, IRSFM is 20 s, DB-CNN 9 s, Finally, for knees, the values are 18s for IRSFM, 14 s for SS-BOVW, 5 s for DB-CNN, By analyzing the results, it is concluded that the proposed methods are more suitable for medical IR. Figure 8 shows the comparison of the existing and proposed techniques in terms of retrieval time.

Retrieval Accuracy

One of the important measures is retrieval accuracy, which is determined by the proportion of relevant to irrelevant images. Retrieval Accuracy is calculated by using equation 15. The x-axis in Figure 9 represents AVN pictures, and the y-axis represents retrieval accuracy scores. The DB-CNN performs well overall for retrieval accuracy. The research was conducted using AVN illness affected sections such as the femur, humerus, and knees. The proposed approaches are compared with the traditional procedures like IRSFM and SSBOVW. Results from the Femur dataset demonstrate that DB-CNN performs better than IRSFM and SS-BOVW, with DB-CNN having an 89% RA compared to IRSFM's 82% and SS-79%. BOVW's The DB-CNN, SSBOVW, and IRSFM values for the humorous are all 94%, 86%, and 85%, respectively. IRSFM has 80% for knees, SSBOVW has 79%, and the suggested one has 86%. Overall analysis shows that the performance of the suggested system is more suitable for medical IR.

FUTURE RESEARCH DIRECTIONS

Future study should concentrate on advanced parallelization to scale the real-time response, which can be accomplished by one or more CPU or GPU. The presented approaches are not able to handle Terabyte data, which results in a decline in runtime performance.

CONCLUSION

The IRSFM and SS-BOVW techniques are contrasted with the DB-CNN method. The research was conducted using a dataset that includes images of the individual AVN-affected body components, including the femur, humerus, and knee. Calculated performance metrics include AP, AR, retrieval speed, and retrieval accuracy. Observing that the DB-CNN performs better than the other techniques The images of the knee, femur, and humorous affected by the disease vascular necrosis are utilised to evaluate the effectiveness of the proposed DB-CNN for image retrieval. The suggested DB-CNN for femur images has improved precision of 92.3%, recall of 81.56%, retrieval time of 11s, and retrieval accuracy of 90.4%. The suggested DB-CNN exhibits improved precision of 87.38%, recall of 80.23%, retrieval time of 9s, and retrieval accuracy of 95.1% for images of the humerus. The proposed DB-CNN performs better on knee pictures, with a precision of 80.5%, a recall of 79.9%, a retrieval time of 7s, and a retrieval accuracy of 88.58%. The results discussed above demonstrate that, when compared to other popular techniques, the suggested DB-CNN exhibits superior performance.

ACKNOWLEDGMENT

This research received no specific grant from any funding agency in the public, commercial, or not-for-profit sectors. The research was supported by Sri Shakthi Instiute of Engineering and Technology.

REFERENCES

Anthimopoulos, M., Christodoulidis, S., Ebner, L., Christe, A., & Mougiakakou, S. (2016). Lung Pattern Classification for Interstitial Lung Diseases Using a Deep Convolutional Neural Network. *IEEE Transactions on Medical Imaging*, *35*(5), 1207–1216. doi:10.1109/TMI.2016.2535865 PMID:26955021

Ashraf, R., Ahmed, M., Jabbar, S., Khalid, S., Ahmad, A., Din, S., & Jeon, G. (2018). Content based image retrieval by using color descriptor and discrete wavelet transform. *Journal of Medical Systems*, *42*(3), 44. doi:10.100710916-017-0880-7 PMID:29372327

Banerjee, I., Kurtz, C., Devorah, A. E., Do, B., Rubin, D. L., & Beaulieu, C. F. (2018). Relevance feedback for enhancing content based image retrieval and automatic prediction of semantic image features: Application to bone tumor radiographs. *Journal of Biomedical Informatics*, *84*, 123–135. doi:10.1016/j.jbi.2018.07.002 PMID:29981490

Bengio, Y., Courville, A. C., & Vincent, P. (2012). Unsupervised feature learning and deep learning: *A review and new perspectives. Clinical Orthopaedics and Related Research*, *1206*, 5538.

Deng, L. (2014). A tutorial survey of architectures, algorithms, and applications for deep learning. *APSIPA Transactions on Signal and Information Processing*, *3*(1), 3. doi:10.1017/atsip.2013.9

Giveki, D., Soltanshahi, A., Shiri, F., & Tarrah, H. (2015). A New Content Based Image Retrieval Model Based on Wavelet Transform. *Journal of Computer and Communications*, *3*(03), 66–73. doi:10.4236/jcc.2015.33012

Jin & Shan-W. (2017). Content-based image retrieval based on shape similarity calculation. *3D Research*, *8*(3).

Lazik, A., Landgraeber, S., Claßen, T., Kraff, O., Lauenstein, T. C., & Theysohn, J. M. (2015). Aspects of postoperative magnetic resonance imaging of patients with avascular necrosis of the femoral head, treated by advanced core decompression. *Skeletal Radiology*, *44*(10), 1467–1475. doi:10.100700256-015-2192-7 PMID:26093539

Mera, M., Roa, S. M., & González, C. (2015). Content-based image retrieval system to support the diagnosis of human papilloma virus. *Health and Technology*, *5*(3-4), 161–165. doi:10.100712553-015-0114-2

Rick, L. (2014). Stem cell therapy for the treatment of early stage avascular necrosis of the femoral head: A systematic review. *BMC Musculoskeletal Disorders*, *15*(1), 156. doi:10.1186/1471-2474-15-156 PMID:24886648

Saritha, R. R., Paul, V., & Kumar, P. G. (2018). Content based image retrieval using deep learning process. *Cluster Computing*, *1*(1), 67–78.

Subash Kumar, T. G., & Nagarajan, V. (2018). Local curve pattern for content-based image retrieval. *Pattern Analysis & Applications*, 1–10.

Tsai, A., Connolly, S., Nedder, A., & Shapiro, F. (2013). Visualization and analysis of the deforming piglet femur and hip following experimentally induced avascular necrosis of the femoral head. *IEEE Transactions on Biomedical Engineering*, *60*(6), 1742–1750. doi:10.1109/TBME.2012.2228860 PMID:23204265

Zhang, F., Song, Y., Cai, W., Hauptmann, A. G., Liu, S., Pujol, S., & Chen, M. (2016). Dictionary pruning with visual word significance for medical image retrieval. *Neurocomputing*, *177*(1), 75–88. doi:10.1016/j.neucom.2015.11.008 PMID:27688597

Compilation of References

Aaron, J. (2015). Everything You Need to Know About Artificial Neural Networks. *The Medium.* https://medium.com/technology-invention-and-more/everything-you-need-to-know-about-artificial-neural-networks-57fac18245
a1

Abbas, H. T., Alic, L., Erraguntla, M., Ji, J. X., Abdul-Ghani, M., Abbasi, Q. H., & Qaraqe, M. K. (2019). Predicting long-term type 2 diabetes with support vector machine using oral glucose tolerance test. *PLoS One, 14*(12), e0219636. doi:10.1371/journal.pone.0219636 PMID:31826018

Abdallah, F., Nassreddine, G., & Denoeux, T. (2011). A multiple-hypothesis map-matching method suitable for weighted and box-shaped state estimation for localization. *IEEE Transactions on Intelligent Transportation Systems, 12*(4), 1495–1510. doi:10.1109/TITS.2011.2160856

Abdel Baki, S. (2001). *Scientific and applied aspects of human resource management in organizations.* University house.

Abdi, H. (2007). The method of least squares. Encyclopedia of measurement and statistics, 1, 530-532.

Abdulnabi, M., Al-Haiqi, A., Kiah, M. L. M., Zaidan, A. A., Zaidan, B. B., & Hussain, M. (2017). A distributed framework for health information exchange using smartphone technologies. *Journal of Biomedical Informatics, 69*, 230–250. doi:10.1016/j.jbi.2017.04.013 PMID:28433825

Acevedo, F., Armengol, V., Deng, Z., Tang, R., Coopey, S. B., Braun, D., & Colwell, A. (2019). Pathologic findings in reduction mammoplasty specimens: A surrogate for the population prevalence of breast cancer and high-risk lesions. *Breast Cancer Research and Treatment, 173*(1), 201–207. doi:10.100710549-018-4962-0 PMID:30238276

Achsas, S. (2022). Academic Aggregated Search Approach Based on BERT Language Model. *2022 2nd International Conference on Innovative Research in Applied Science, Engineering and Technology (IRASET)*, 1–9.

Adadi, A., & Berrada, M. (2018). Peeking inside the black-box: A survey on explainable artificial intelligence (XAI). *IEEE Access: Practical Innovations, Open Solutions, 6*, 52138–52160. doi:10.1109/ACCESS.2018.2870052

Adelson, E. H., Anderson, C. H., Bergen, J. R., Burt, P. J., & Ogden, J. M. (1984). Pyramid methods in image processing. *RCA Engineer, 29*(6), 33–41.

Adusumilli, S., Bhatt, D., Wang, H., Bhattacharya, P., & Devabhaktuni, V. (2013). A low-cost INS/GPS integration methodology based on random forest regression. *Expert Systems with Applications, 40*(11), 4653–4659. doi:10.1016/j.eswa.2013.02.002

Afif, M., Said, Y., Pissaloux, E., & Atri, M. (2020d). Recognizing signs and doors for Indoor Wayfinding for Blind and Visually Impaired Persons. In *2020 5th International Conference on Advanced Technologies for Signal and Image Processing (ATSIP)* (pp. 1-4). IEEE. 10.1109/ATSIP49331.2020.9231933

Afif, M., Ayachi, R., Pissaloux, E., Said, Y., & Atri, M. (2020a). Indoor objects detection and recognition for an ICT mobility assistance of visually impaired people. *Multimedia Tools and Applications*, 79(41), 31645–31662. doi:10.100711042-020-09662-3

Afif, M., Ayachi, R., Said, Y., & Atri, M. (2020c). Deep learning based application for indoor scene recognition. *Neural Processing Letters*, 51(3), 2827–2837. doi:10.100711063-020-10231-w

Afif, M., Ayachi, R., Said, Y., & Atri, M. (2021). Deep learning-based application for indoor wayfinding assistance navigation. *Multimedia Tools and Applications*, 80(18), 27115–27130. doi:10.100711042-021-10999-6

Afif, M., Ayachi, R., Said, Y., Pissaloux, E., & Atri, M. (2018). Indoor image recognition and classification via deep convolutional neural network. In *International conference on the Sciences of Electronics, Technologies of Information and Telecommunications* (pp. 364-371). Springer.

Afif, M., Ayachi, R., Said, Y., Pissaloux, E., & Atri, M. (2020b). An evaluation of retinanet on indoor object detection for blind and visually impaired persons assistance navigation. *Neural Processing Letters*, 51(3), 2265–2279. doi:10.100711063-020-10197-9

Aggarwal, A. (2021). Beware Hype over AI-Based Healthcare in Lower-Income Countries. *FinancialTimes*. https://www.ft.com/content/f4dd834c-4835-4ee0-8737-ff98626fa010

Aggarwal, S., & Kumar, N. (2021). Blockchain 2.0: Smart contracts. *Advances in Computers*, 121, 301–322. doi:10.1016/bs.adcom.2020.08.015

Agichtein, E., Brill, E., & Dumais, S. (2006). Improving web search ranking by incorporating user behavior information. *Proceedings of the 29th Annual International ACM SIGIR Conference on Research and Development in Information Retrieval*, 19–26. ACM. 10.1145/1148170.1148177

Agostinelli, F., Hoffman, M., Sadowski, P., & Baldi, P. (2015). Learning Activation Functions to Improve Deep Neural Networks. *International Conference on Learning (ICLR)*. arXiv.

Ahmad, O. (2018). Artificial intelligence in HR. *International journal of research and analytical reviews*, 971-978.

Ahmed, N., Amin, R., Aldabbas, H., Koundal, D., Alouffi, B., & Shah, T. (2022). Machine learning techniques for spam detection in email and IoT platforms: Analysis and research challenges. *Security and Communication Networks*, 2022, 2022. doi:10.1155/2022/1862888

Ahmed, S., Bhatti, M. T., Khan, M. G., Lövström, B., & Shahid, M. (2022). Development and Optimization of Deep Learning Models for Weapon Detection in Surveillance Videos. *Applied Sciences*, 12(12), 5772. doi:10.3390/app12125772

Ainsworth, T. (2002). *Buyer beware*. Security Oz.

AirCare Access Assistance. (2022). Emergency telemedicine and mission safety support (TM), (2022). Aircare. https://www.aircareinternational.com/inflight-emergency-telemedicine

Aitzhan, N. Z., & Svetinovic, D. (2016). Security and privacy in decentralized energy trading through multi-signatures, blockchain, and anonymous messaging streams. *IEEE Transactions on Dependable and Secure Computing*, 15(5), 840–852. doi:10.1109/TDSC.2016.2616861

Akgun, S., & Greenhow, C. (2021). Artificial intelligence in education: Addressing ethical challenges in K-12 settings. *AI and Ethics*, 1–10.

Al Bitar, N., Gavrilov, A. I., & Khalaf, W. (2020). Artificial Intelligence Based Methods for Accuracy Improvement of Integrated Navigation Systems During GNSS Signal Outages: An Analytical Overview. *Gyroscopy and Navigation*, *11*(1), 41–58. doi:10.1134/S2075108720010022

Al Omar, A., Jamil, A. K., Khandakar, A., Uzzal, A. R., Bosri, R., Mansoor, N., & Rahman, M. S. (2021). A transparent and privacy-preserving healthcare platform with a ovel smart contract for smart cities. *IEEE Access: Practical Innovations, Open Solutions*, *9*, 90738–90749. doi:10.1109/ACCESS.2021.3089601

Al-Amin, M., Alam, M. B., & Mia, M. R. (2015). Detection of cancerous and non-cancerous skin by using GLCM matrix and neural network classifier. *International Journal of Computers and Applications*, *132*(8), 44–49. doi:10.5120/ijca2015907513

Alaparthi, S., & Mishra, M. (2020). Bidirectional Encoder Representations from Transformers (BERT): A sentiment analysis odyssey.

Alaskar, L., Crane, M., & Alduailij, M. (2019). Employee turnover prediction using machine learning. *In International conference on computing* (pp. 301-316). Springer.

Alauthman, M., Almomani, A., Alweshah, M., Omoush, W., & Alieyan, K. (2019). Machine learning for phishing detection and mitigation. In *Machine Learning for Computer and Cyber Security* (pp. 48–74). CRC Press. doi:10.1201/9780429504044-2

Alayan, R. M. (2007). Foundations of contemporary management (1 ed.). Dar Safaa for printing, publishing and distribution.

Albi, T. R., Rafi, M. N., Bushra, T. A., & Karim, D. Z. (2022). Diabetes Complication Prediction using Deep Learning-Based Analytics. *2022 International Conference on Advancement in Electrical and Electronic Engineering (ICAEEE)*, 1-6. 10.1109/ICAEEE54957.2022.9836401

Alcazar, C. V. (2017). Data you can trust. *Air and Space Power Journal*, *31*(2), 91–101.

Al-Dulaimi, A., Zabihi, S., Asif, A., & Mohammadi, A. (2019). A multimodal and hybrid deep neural network model for remaining useful life estimation. *Computers in Industry*, *108*, 186–196. doi:10.1016/j.compind.2019.02.004

Alex, S. A., Kumaran. U, & Santhana Mikhail Antony. S (2021) Novel Applications of Neuralink in HealthCare-An Exploratory Study, In *Proceedings of ACM/CSI/IEEE-CS Research & Industry Symposium on IoT Cloud For Societal Applications* (pp. 27-31). ACM.

Alexander, B., Ashford-Rowe, K., Barajas-Murph, N., Dobbin, G., Knott, J., McCormack, M., & Weber, N. (2019). *Horizon report 2019 higher education edition*. Horizon. https://library.educause.edu/resources/2019/4/2019-horizon-report

Alex, S. A., Nayahi, J., Shine, H., & Gopirekha, V. (2022). Deep convolutional neural network for diabetes mellitus prediction. *Neural Computing & Applications*, *34*(2), 1319–1327. doi:10.100700521-021-06431-7

Alex, S. A., Ponkamali, S., Andrew, T. R., Jhanjhi, N. Z., & Tayyab, M. (2022). Machine Learning-Based Wearable Devices for Smart Healthcare Application With Risk Factor Monitoring. In *Empowering Sustainable Industrial 4.0 Systems With Machine Intelligence* (pp. 174–185). IGI Global. doi:10.4018/978-1-7998-9201-4.ch009

Alganci, U., Soydas, M., & Sertel, E. (2020). Comparative Research on Deep Learning Approaches for Airplane Detection from Very High-Resolution Satellite Images. *Remote Sensing*, *12*(3), 458. doi:10.3390/rs12030458

Alharbi, B., & Prince, M. (2020). A hybrid artificial intelligence approach to predict flight delay. In *International Journal of Engineering Research and Technology*. *13*(4), 814-822. http://www.irphouse.com/ijert20/ijertv13n4_29.pdf

Aljihmani, L., Kerdjidj, O., Zhu, Y., Mehta, R. K., Erraguntla, M., Sasangohar, F., & Qaraqe, K. (2020). Classification of fatigue phases in healthy and diabetic adults using wearable sensor. *Sensors (Basel)*, *20*(23), 6897. doi:10.339020236897 PMID:33287112

Alkahtani, H., & Aldhyani, T. H. (2022). Artificial Intelligence Algorithms for Malware Detection in Android-Operated Mobile Devices. *Sensors (Basel)*, *22*(6), 2268. doi:10.339022062268 PMID:35336437

Almarzooqi, A. (2019). *Towards an artificial intelligence (AI)-driven government in the united arab emirates (UAE): A framework for transforming and augmenting leadership capabilities* [Thesis, Pepperdine University, USA] Proquest (2284210975). https://www.proquest.com/dissertations-theses/towards-artificial-intelligence-ai-driven/docview/2284210975/se-2

Almog, U. (2020). YOLO V3 Explained. *Towards Data Science*. https://towardsdatascience.com/yolo-v3-explained-ff5b850390f

Alpaydin, E. (2014). *Introduction to machine learning* (3rd ed.). The MIT Press.

Alshamkhany, M., Alshamkhany, W., Mansour, M., Khan, M., Dhou, S., & Aloul, F. (2020, November). Botnet attack detection using machine learning. In *2020 14th International Conference on Innovations in Information Technology (IIT)* (pp. 203-208). IEEE. 10.1109/IIT50501.2020.9299061

Alshawwa, I. A., Elkahlout, M., El-Mashharawi, H. Q., & Abu-Naser, S. S. (2019). An Expert System for Depression Diagnosis. *International Journal of Academic Health and Medical Research*, *3*(4).

Alzheimer's Society. (2022). *Facts for the media about dementia*. Alzheimer's Society. https://www.alzheimers.org.uk/about-us/news-and-media/facts-media#:~:text=How%20many%20people%20in%20the%20world%20have%20dementia%3F,to%20152.8%20million%20by%202050

Amershi, S., Weld, D., Vorvoreanu, M., Fourney, A., Nushi, B., Collisson, P., Suh, J., Iqbal, S., Bennett, P. N., & Inkpen, K. (2019). Guidelines for human-AI interaction. *Proceedings of the 2019 Chi Conference on Human Factors in Computing Systems*, 1–13. Semantic Scholar.

Amin, A., Colman, A., & Grunske, L. (2012). An approach to forecasting QoS attributes of web services based on ARIMA and GARCH models. *Proceedings - 2012 IEEE 19th International Conference on Web Services, ICWS 2012*, 74–81. IEEE. 10.1109/ICWS.2012.37

Amin, A., Grunske, L., & Colman, A. (2012). An automated approach to forecasting QoS attributes based on linear and non-linear time series modeling. *2012 27th IEEE/ACM International Conference on Automated Software Engineering, ASE 2012 - Proceedings*, 130–139. IEEE. 10.1145/2351676.2351695

Amin, S. U., Hossain, M. S., Muhammad, G., Alhussein, M., & Rahman, M. (2019). Cognitive Smart Healthcare for Pathology Detection and Monitoring. *IEEE Access: Practical Innovations, Open Solutions*, *7*, 10745–10753. doi:10.1109/ACCESS.2019.2891390

Andreas,, K. & Haenlein, M. (2019). On the interpretation, Illustrations, and implications of artificial Intelligence. *Business Horizons*, *62*(1), 15–25. doi:10.1016/j.bushor.2018.08.004

Andresen, S. L. (2002). John McCarthy: Father of AI. *IEEE Intelligent Systems*, *17*(5), 84–85. doi:10.1109/MIS.2002.1039837

Angelova, A., Krizhevsky, A., Vanhoucke, V., Ogale, A., & Ferguson, D. (2015). Real-time pedestrian detection with deep network cascades. Academic Press.

Anithadevi, N., & Sundarambal, M. (2019). A design of intelligent QoS aware web service recommendation system. *Cluster Computing*, 22(6), 14231–14240. doi:10.100710586-018-2279-8

Ankenbrand, M. J., Shainberg, L., Hock, M., Lohr, D., & Schreiber, L. M. (2021). Sensitivity analysis for interpretation of machine learning based segmentation models in cardiac MRI. *BMC Medical Imaging*, 21(1), 1–8. doi:10.118612880-021-00551-1 PMID:33588786

Anthimopoulos, M., Christodoulidis, S., Ebner, L., Christe, A., & Mougiakakou, S. (2016). Lung Pattern Classification for Interstitial Lung Diseases Using a Deep Convolutional Neural Network. *IEEE Transactions on Medical Imaging*, 35(5), 1207–1216. doi:10.1109/TMI.2016.2535865 PMID:26955021

Antoran, J., Bhatt, U., Adel, T., Weller, A., & Hernández-Lobato, J. M. (2020). Getting a CLUE: A Method for Explaining Uncertainty Estimates. International Conference on Learning Representations.

An, Y.-K., Kim, M. K., & Sohn, H. (2012). 03 30). Airplane hot spot monitoring using integrated impedance and guided wave measurements. *Structural Control and Health Monitoring*, 19(7), 592–604. doi:10.1002tc.1493

Appel, G., Grewal, L., Hadi, R., & Stephen, A. T. (2020). The Future of Social Media In Marketing. *Journal of the Academy of Marketing Science*, 48(1), 79–95. doi:10.100711747-019-00695-1 PMID:32431463

Appen. (2022). *How Artificial Intelligence Data Reduces Overhead Costs for Organizations*. From https://appen.com/blog/how-artificial-intelligence-data-reduces-overhead-costs-for-organizations/

Apte, C. (2010). *The role of machine learning in business optimization*. Semantic Scholar.

Aqle, A., Al-Thani, D., & Jaoua, A. (2018). Conceptual interactive search engine interface for visually impaired Web users. *2018 IEEE/ACS 15th International Conference on Computer Systems and Applications (AICCSA)*, 1–6. IEEE.

Archuleta, M. (2022). How Artificial Intelligence Is Transforming Healthcare. *Healthcare IT -CHIME*. https://chimecentral.org/mediaposts/how-artificial-intelligence-is-transforming-healthcare/

Arık, S. Ö., Shor, J., Sinha, R., Yoon, J., Ledsam, J. R., Le, L. T., & Epshteyn, A. (2021). A prospective evaluation of AI-augmented epidemiology to forecast COVID-19 in the USA and japan. *NPJ Digital Medicine*, 4(1), 1–18. doi:10.103841746-021-00511-7 PMID:34625656

Asaly, S., Gottlieb, L.-A., & Reuveni, Y. (2021). Using support vector machine (SVM) and Ionospheric Total Electron Content (TEC) data for solar flare predictions. *IEEE Journal of Selected Topics in Applied Earth Observations and Remote Sensing*, 14, 1469–1481. https://doi.org/10.1109/JSTARS.2020.3044470

Asano, Y. M., Rupprecht, C., Zisserman, A., & Vedaldi, A. (2021). PASS: An ImageNet replacement for self-supervised pretraining without humans. *Thirty-fifth Conference on Neural Information Processing Systems Datasets and Benchmarks Track (Round 1)*.

Asghar, R., Garzón, M., Lussereau, J., & Laugier, C. (2020). Vehicle localization based on visual lane marking and topological map matching. *IEEE International Conference on Robotics and Automation (ICRA)*, (pp. 258-264). IEEE. 10.1109/ICRA40945.2020.9197543

Ashfaq, Z., Mumtaz, R., Rafay, A., Zaidi, S. M. H., Saleem, H., Mumtaz, S., Shahid, A., Poorter, E. D., & Moerman, I. (2022). Embedded AI-based digi-healthcare. *Applied Sciences (Basel, Switzerland)*, 12(1), 519. doi:10.3390/app12010519

Ashraf, A. H., Imran, M., Qahtani, A. M., Alsufyani, A., Almutiry, O., Mahmood, A., & Habib, M. (2022). Weapons detection for security and video surveillance using cnn and YOLO-v5s. CMC-Computers. *Materials & Continua*, *70*(2), 2761–2775. doi:10.32604/cmc.2022.018785

Ashraf, R., Ahmed, M., Jabbar, S., Khalid, S., Ahmad, A., Din, S., & Jeon, G. (2018). Content based image retrieval by using color descriptor and discrete wavelet transform. *Journal of Medical Systems*, *42*(3), 44. doi:10.100710916-017-0880-7 PMID:29372327

Asim, K. M., Martínez-Álvarez, F., Basit, A., & Iqbal, T. (2017). Earthquake magnitude prediction in Hindukush region using machine learning techniques. *Natural Hazards*, *85*(1), 471–486. https://doi.org/10.1007/s11069-016-2579-3

Association for Safe International Road Travel. (2019). Annual Global Road Crash Statistics. https://www.asirt.org/safe-travel/road-safety-facts/

Aste, T., Tasca, P., & Di Matteo, T. (2017). Blockchain technologies: The foreseeable impact on society and industry. *Computer*, *50*(9), 18–28. doi:10.1109/MC.2017.3571064

Atlas, D. (2015). *International diabetes federation. In IDF Diabetes Atlas* (7th ed.). International Diabetes Federation.

Austin, University of Texas. (2022). Engineered Mattress Tricks Your Body to Fall Asleep Faster. *Medicalxpress.com*. https://medicalxpress.com/news/2022-07-mattress-body-fall-asleep-faster.html

Awujoola, O., Odion, P., Irhebhude, M., & Aminu, H. (2021). Performance evaluation of machine learning predictive analytical model for determining the job applicants employment status. *Malaysian Journal of Applied Sciences*, 67-79.

Ayachi, R., Afif, M., Said, Y., & Abdelaali, A. B. (2020c). Pedestrian detection for advanced driving assisting system: a transfer learning approach. In *2020 5th International Conference on Advanced Technologies for Signal and Image Processing (ATSIP)* (pp. 1-5). IEEE. 10.1109/ATSIP49331.2020.9231559

Ayachi, R., Afif, M., Said, Y., & Abdelali, A. B. (2020b). Traffic Sign Recognition Based On Scaled Convolutional Neural Network For Advanced Driver Assistance System. In *2020 IEEE 4th International Conference on Image Processing, Applications and Systems (IPAS)* (pp. 149-154). IEEE. 10.1109/IPAS50080.2020.9334944

Ayachi, R., Afif, M., Said, Y., & Abdelali, A. B. (2021). Drivers Fatigue Detection Using EfficientDet In Advanced Driver Assistance Systems. In 2021 18th International Multi-Conference on Systems, Signals & Devices (SSD) (pp. 738-742). IEEE. doi:10.1109/SSD52085.2021.9429294

Ayachi, R., Afif, M., Said, Y., & Atri, M. (2018). Strided convolution instead of max pooling for memory efficiency of convolutional neural networks. In *International conference on the Sciences of Electronics, Technologies of Information and Telecommunications* (pp. 234-243). Springer.

Ayachi, R., Afif, M., Said, Y., & Atri, M. (2020a). Traffic signs detection for real-world application of an advanced driving assisting system using deep learning. *Neural Processing Letters*, *51*(1), 837–851. doi:10.100711063-019-10115-8

Ayachi, R., Said, Y., & Atri, M. (2019a). To perform road signs recognition for autonomous vehicles using cascaded deep learning pipeline. *Artif Intell Adv*, *1*(1), 1–10. doi:10.30564/aia.v1i1.569

Ayachi, R., Said, Y., & Atri, M. (2021). A convolutional neural network to perform object detection and identification in visual large-scale data. *Big Data*, *9*(1), 41–52. doi:10.1089/big.2019.0093 PMID:32991200

Ayachi, R., Said, Y., & Ben Abdelaali, A. (2020d). Pedestrian detection based on light-weighted separable convolution for advanced driver assistance systems. *Neural Processing Letters*, *52*(3), 2655–2668. doi:10.100711063-020-10367-9

Ayhan, M. E., & Almuslmani, B. (2021). Positional accuracy and convergence time assessment of GPS precise point positioning in static mode. *Arabian Journal of Geosciences*, *14*(13), 1–12. doi:10.100712517-021-07428-1

Ayodele, T. O. (2010). Types of machine learning algorithms. *New Advances in Machine Learning*, *3*, 19–48.

Azaria, A., Ekblaw, A., Vieira, T., & Lippman, A. (2016). Medrec: Using blockchain for medical data access and permission management. In *Proceedings of 2nd international conference on open and big data* (pp. 25-30). IEEE. 10.1109/OBD.2016.11

Aziz, M., Ejaz, S. A., Zargar, S., Akhtar, N., Aborode, A. T., & Wani, A., T., & Akintola, A. A. (2022). Deep learning and structure-based virtual screening for drug discovery against NEK7: A novel target for the treatment of cancer. *Molecules (Basel, Switzerland)*, *27*(13), 4098. doi:10.3390/molecules27134098 PMID:35807344

Babu, G. S., Zhao, P., & Li, X. L. (2016). Deep convolutional neural network based regression approach for estimation of remaining useful life. In *International Conference on Database Systems for Advanced Applications*, (pp. 214–228). Springer. 10.1007/978-3-319-32025-0_14

Baehrens, D., Schroeter, T., Harmeling, S., Kawanabe, M., Hansen, K., & Müller, K.-R. (2010). How to explain individual classification decisions. *Journal of Machine Learning Research*, *11*, 1803–1831.

Baepler, P., & Murdoch, C. J. (2010). Academic analytics and data mining in higher education. *International Journal for the Scholarship of Teaching and Learning*, *4*(2), 1–9. doi:10.20429/ijsotl.2010.040217

Bagnell, J., Chestnutt, J., Bradley, D., & Ratliff, N. (2006). Boosting structured prediction for imitation learning. *Advances in Neural Information Processing Systems*, 19.

Bahga, A., & Madisetti, V. (2014). Internet of Things: A hands-on approach. *Pvt*.

Bahga, A., & Madisetti, V. K. (2016). Blockchain platform for the industrial internet of things. *Journal of Software Engineering and Applications*, *9*(10), 533–546. doi:10.4236/jsea.2016.910036

Baker, T., & Smith, L. (2019). *Educ-AI-tion rebooted? Exploring the future of artificial intelligence in schools and colleges*. NESTA. https://www.nesta.org.uk/report/education-rebooted/

Baker, L. (2004). *Yahoo intros new search robot – Yahoo! Slurp*. Search Engine Journal.

Ballardini, R. (2019). AI-generated content: authorship and inventorship in the age of Artificial Intelligence. In *Online Distribution of Content in the EU* (pp. 117–135). Edward Elgar Publishing. doi:10.4337/9781788119900.00015

Ball, M. J., & Lillis, J. (2001). E-health: Transforming the physician/patient relationship. *International Journal of Medical Informatics*, *61*(1), 1–10. doi:10.1016/S1386-5056(00)00130-1 PMID:11248599

Ballout, H. I. (2002). *Human resource management from a strategic perspective* (1st ed.). Arab Renaissance House for Printing, Publishing and Distribution.

Banerjee, I., Kurtz, C., Devorah, A. E., Do, B., Rubin, D. L., & Beaulieu, C. F. (2018). Relevance feedback for enhancing content based image retrieval and automatic prediction of semantic image features: Application to bone tumor radiographs. *Journal of Biomedical Informatics*, *84*, 123–135. doi:10.1016/j.jbi.2018.07.002 PMID:29981490

Banupriya, N., Saranya, S., Swaminathan, S., Harikumar, S., & Palanisamy, S. (2020). Animal Detection Using Deep Learning Algorithm. *Journal of Critical Reviews*, *7*(1), 434–439.

Bao, Y., Hilary, G., & Ke, B. (2022). Artificial intelligence and fraud detection. In *Innovative technology at the interface of finance and operations* (pp. 223–247). Springer. doi:10.1007/978-3-030-75729-8_8

Barba-Guaman, L., Eugenio Naranjo, J., & Ortiz, A. (2020). Deep learning framework for vehicle and pedestrian detection in rural roads on an embedded GPU. *Electronics (Basel), 9*(4), 589.

Barber, E. L., Garg, R., Persenaire, C., & Simon, M. (2021). Natural language processing with machine learning to predict outcomes after ovarian cancer surgery. *Gynecologic Oncology, 160*(1), 182–186. doi:10.1016/j.ygyno.2020.10.004 PMID:33069375

Barrau, A., & Bonnabel, S. (2018). Invariant Kalman filtering. *Annual Review of Control, Robotics, and Autonomous Systems, 1*(1), 237–257. doi:10.1146/annurev-control-060117-105010

Barreno, M., Nelson, B., Joseph, A. D., & Tygar, J. D. (2010). The security of machine learning. *Machine Learning, 81*(2), 121–148. doi:10.100710994-010-5188-5

Bartoletti, I. (2019a). AI in healthcare: Ethical and privacy challenges. Paper presented at the *Conference on Artificial Intelligence in Medicine in Europe*, (pp. 7-10). Springer. 10.1007/978-3-030-21642-9_2

Bashbaghi, S., Granger, E., Sabourin, R., & Parchami, M. (2019). Deep learning architectures for face recognition in video surveillance. In Deep Learning in Object Detection and Recognition, 133 - 154.

Basheer, S., Bhatia, S., & Sakri, S. B. (2021). Computational modeling of dementia prediction using deep neural network: Analysis on OASIS dataset. *IEEE Access: Practical Innovations, Open Solutions, 9*, 42449–42462. doi:10.1109/ACCESS.2021.3066213

Basri, W. (2020). Examining the impact of artificial intelligence-assisted social media marketing on the performance of small and medium enterprises: Toward effective business management in the Saudi Arabian context. *International Journal of Computational Intelligence Systems, 13*(1), 142–152. doi:10.2991/ijcis.d.200127.002

Bastami, R., Aasi, A., & Arghand, H. A. (2019, July). Estimation of remaining useful life of rolling element bearings using wavelet packet decomposition and artificial neural network. *Iranian Journal of Science and Technology. Transaction of Electrical Engineering, 43*(S1), 233–245. doi:10.100740998-018-0108-y

Bastanta, A., Nuryansyah, R., Nugroho, C. A., & Budiharto, W. (2021). Image data encryption using DES method. *2021 1st International Conference on Computer Science and Artificial Intelligence (ICCSAI), 1*, 130–135.

Basu, A., Petropoulakis, L., Di Caterina, G., & Soraghan, J. (2020). Indoor home scene recognition using capsule neural networks. *Procedia Computer Science, 167*, 440–448. doi:10.1016/j.procs.2020.03.253

Basu, P. (2020). Artificial Intelligence for digital transformation genesis, fictions, applications, and challenges. *Management Accountant., 55*(4), 1130–1141. doi:10.33516/maj.v55i4.68-72p

Bates, T. (2018, December 3). *Another perspective on AI in higher education.* Online Learning and Distance Education Resources. https://www.tonybates.ca/2018/12/02/another-perspective-on-ai-in-higher-education/

Bayne, S., & Ross, J. (2016). Manifesto Redux: making a teaching philosophy from networked learning research. In *Proceedings of the 10th international conference on networked learning. Sustainable Development Education and Research, 2*(1), 1–7.

Bayne, S. (2008). Higher education as a visual practice: Seeing through the virtual learning environment. *Teaching in Higher Education, 13*(4), 395–410. doi:10.1080/13562510802169665

BCU. (2022). *Four Ways Biomedical Engineering Has Enhanced Healthcare.* Birmingham City University. https://www.bcu.ac.uk/health-sciences/about-us/school-blog/how-biomedical-engineering-enhanced-healthcare

Beam, A. L., & Kohane, I. S. (2016). Translating artificial intelligence into clinical care. *Journal of the American Medical Association*, *316*(22), 2368–2369. doi:10.1001/jama.2016.17217 PMID:27898974

Beaumont, P. B. (1993). Human resource management: Key concepts and skills. Sage.

Bellinger, C., Sharma, S., & Japkowicz, N. (2012). One-class versus binary classification: Which and when? *In 2012 11th international conference on machine learning and applications*, (pp. 102-106). IEEE.

Bellio, M., Oxtoby, N. P., Walker, Z., Henley, S., Ribbens, A., Blandford, A., Alexander, D. C., & Yong, K. X. (2020). Analyzing large alzheimer's disease cognitive datasets: Considerations and challenges. *Alzheimer's & Dementia: Diagnosis, Assessment & Disease Monitoring*, *12*(1), e12135. doi:10.1002/dad2.12135 PMID:33313379

Bengio, Y., Courville, A. C., & Vincent, P. (2012). Unsupervised feature learning and deep learning: *A review and new perspectives*. Clinical Orthopaedics and Related Research, *1206*, 5538.

Benkedjouh, T., Medjaher, K., Zerhouni, N., & Rechak, S. (2015). Health assessment and life prediction of cutting tools based on support vector regression. *Journal of Intelligent Manufacturing*, *26*(2), 213–223. https://doi.org/10.1007/s10845-013-0774-6

Bergmeir, C., Hyndman, R. J., & Koo, B. (2018). A note on the validity of cross-validation for evaluating autoregressive time series prediction. *Computational Statistics & Data Analysis*, *120*, 70–83. doi:10.1016/j.csda.2017.11.003

Bernard, M. (2019). The Amazing Ways YouTube Uses Artificial Intelligence And Machine Learning. *Forbes*. https://www.forbes.com/sites/bernardmarr/2019/08/23/the-amazing-ways-youtube-uses-artificial-intelligence-and-machine-learning/?sh=57356eca5852

Bernard, M., & Matt, W. (2017). Artificial Intelligence In practice. Wiley & SAS business series.

Beyaz, S. (2020). A brief history of artificial intelligence and robotic surgery in orthopedics & traumatology and future expectations. *Eklem Hastaliklari ve Cerrahisi*, *31*(3), 653–655. doi:10.5606/ehc.2020.75300 PMID:32962606

Bhatele, K. R., Shrivastava, H., & Kumari, N. (2019). The role of artificial intelligence in cyber security. In *Countering Cyber Attacks and Preserving the Integrity and Availability of Critical Systems* (pp. 170–192). IGI Global. doi:10.4018/978-1-5225-8241-0.ch009

Bhat, S. S., Selvam, V., Ansari, G. A., Ansari, M. D., & Rahman, M. H. (2022). Prevalence and Early Prediction of Diabetes Using Machine Learning in North Kashmir: A Case Study of District Bandipora. *Computational Intelligence and Neuroscience*, *2022*, 2022. doi:10.1155/2022/2789760 PMID:36238678

Bhushan, S. (2021). The impact of artificial intelligence and machine learning on the global economy and its implications for the hospitality sector in India. *Worldwide Hospitality and Tourism Themes*, *13*(2), 252–259. doi:10.1108/WHATT-09-2020-0116

Bie, Y., & Yang, Y. (2021). A multitask multiview neural network for end-to-end aspect-based sentiment analysis. *Big Data Mining and Analytics*, *4*(3), 195–207. doi:10.26599/BDMA.2021.9020003

Bijan, N., Saied, P., & Somayeh, M. (2013). The effect of solar cycle's activities on earthquake: A conceptual idea for forecasting. *Disaster Advances*, *6*, 8.

Bin Sulaiman, R., Schetinin, V., & Sant, P. (2022). Review of Machine Learning Approach on Credit Card Fraud Detection. *Human-Centric Intelligent Systems*, 1-14.

Birhane, A., & Prabhu, V. U. (2021). Large image datasets: A pyrrhic win for computer vision? *2021 IEEE Winter Conference on Applications of Computer Vision (WACV)*. IEEE.

Bishop, C. M., & Nasrabadi, N. M. (2006). *Pattern recognition and machine learning (Vol. 4*, p. 738). Springer.

Bishop, C. M. (2006). *Pattern Recognition and Machine Learning*. Springer.

Boden, M. A. (2006). *Mind As Machine: A History of Cognitive Science*. Oxford University Press.

Bodnar, A., Bodnar, E., & Makerova, V. (2018). Technocratic and Humanistic Trends in Education: New Tunes. *KnE Life Sciences*, 172-181.

Boguda, S. K., & Shailaja, A. (2019). The Future of Customer Experience In The Information Age Of Artificial Intelligence-Get Ready For Change. *International Journal of Engineering Research & Technology (Ahmedabad)*, *8*, 1141–1150.

Bolstad, P. (2016). *GIS fundamentals: A first text on geographic information systems*. Eider (PressMinnesota).

Bolukbasi, T., Chang, K.-W., Zou, J. Y., Saligrama, V., & Kalai, A. T. (2016). Man is to computer programmer as woman is to homemaker? debiasing word embeddings. *Advances in Neural Information Processing Systems*, 29.

Bostrom, N. (2017). *Superintelligence: Paths, dangers, strategies*. Oxford University Press.

Bozic, J. T. (2019). Chatbot testing using AI planning. *2019 IEEE International Conference On Artificial Intelligence Testing (AITest)* (pp. 37-44). IEEE. 10.1109/AITest.2019.00-10

Braiek, H. B., Khomh, F., & Adams, B. (2018). The open-closed principle of modern machine learning frameworks. *IEEE/ACM 15th International Conference on Mining Software Repositories* (pp. 353-363). IEEE.

Brambilla, M., Ferrante, E., Birattari, M., & Dorigo, M. (2013). Swarm robotics: A review from the swarm engineering perspective. *Swarm Intelligence*, *7*(1), 1–41. doi:10.100711721-012-0075-2

Breiman, L. (2001). Random forests. *Machine Learning*, *45*(1), 5–32. https://doi.org/10.1023/A:1010933404324

Brezočnik, L., Fister, I. Jr, & Podgorelec, V. (2018). Swarm intelligence algorithms for feature selection: A review. *Applied Sciences (Basel, Switzerland)*, *8*(9), 1521. doi:10.3390/app8091521

Britting, K. (2010). *Inertial navigation systems analysis*. Artech House.

Brookings Education. (2020). *How to deal with AI-enabled disinformation*. Brookings https://www.brookings.edu/research/how-to-deal-with-ai-enabled-disinformation/

Brown, R. G., Carlyle, J., Grigg, I., & Hearn, M. (2016). Corda: an introduction. *R3 CEV, 1(15)*, 14.

Brown, L. M. (2022). Gendered Artificial Intelligence in Libraries: Opportunities to Deconstruct Sexism and Gender Binarism. *Journal of Library Administration*, *62*(1), 19–30. doi:10.1080/01930826.2021.2006979

Brownlee, J. (2019). A Gentle Introduction to Computer Vision. *Machine Learning Mastery*. https://machinelearningmastery.com/what-is-computer-vision/

Brown-Martin, G. (2017). Education and the Fourth Industrial Revolution. *Scientific Research*. https://www.scirp.org/(S(351jmbntvnsjt1aadkozje))/reference/referencespapers.aspx?referenceid=2641203

Brundage, M., Avin, S., Clark, J., Toner, H., Eckersley, P., Garfinkel, B., & Amodei, D. (2018). The malicious use of artificial intelligence: Forecasting, prevention, and mitigation.

Brunet, M.-E., Alkalay-Houlihan, C., Anderson, A., & Zemel, R. (2019). Understanding the origins of bias in word embeddings. *International conference on machine learning.* .

Brunner, G., Liu, Y., Pascual, D., Richter, O., Ciaramita, M., & Wattenhofer, R. (2019). On Identifiability in Transformers. *International Conference on Learning Representations.*

Buccio, E. D., Li, Q., Melucci, M., & Tiwari, P. (2018). Binary classification model inspired from quantum detection theory. *In Proceedings of the 2018 ACM SIGIR International Conference on Theory of Information Retrieval,* (pp. 187-190). ACM. 10.1145/3234944.3234979

Buchanan, B. G. (2005). A (very) brief history of artificial intelligence. *AI Magazine, 26*(4), 53.

Buolamwini, J., & Gebru, T. (2018). Gender shades: Intersectional accuracy disparities in commercial gender classification. Conference on fairness, accountability and transparency.

Bushkovskyi, O. (2018). 4 Types of Machine Learning Algorithms. *The App Solutions.* https://theappsolutions.com/blog/development/machine-learning-algorithm-types/

Butler-Adam, J. (2018). The Fourth Industrial Revolution and education. *South African Journal of Science, 114*(5/6), 1–2. doi:10.17159ajs.2018/a0271

Butt, U. M., Letchmunan, S., Ali, M., Hassan, F. H., Baqir, A., & Hafiz, H. R. S. (2021). Machine Learning Based Diabetes Classification and Prediction for Healthcare Applications. *Journal of Healthcare Engineering, 2021,* 2021. doi:10.1155/2021/9930985 PMID:34631003

Byington, C. S., Watson, M., Edwards, D., & Stoelting, P. (2004). A model-based approach to prognostics and health management for flight control actuators. In Proceedings of the IEEE Aerospace Conference Proceedings (IEEE Cat. No. 04TH8720), (pp. 3551–3562). IEEE. 10.1109/AERO.2004.1368172

Bzdok, D., Krzywinski, M., & Altman, N. (2018). Machine learning: Supervised methods. *Nature Methods, 15*(1), 5–6. doi:10.1038/nmeth.4551 PMID:30100821

Cain, L. N., Thomas, J. H., & Alonso, M. Jr. (2019). From sci-fi to sci-fact: The state of robotics and AI in the hospitality industry. *Journal of Hospitality and Tourism Technology, 10*(4), 624–650. doi:10.1108/JHTT-07-2018-0066

Cai, W. D., Yu, L., Wang, R., Liu, N., & Deng, E. Y. (2017). Research on blockchain-based application system development method. *Journal of Software, 28*(6), 1474–1487.

Calderon, R. (2019). *The benefits of artificial intelligence in cybersecurity.* Lasalle University.

Calvo, P., Gagliano, M., Souza, G. M., & Trewavas, A. (2020). Plants are intelligent, here's how. *Annals of Botany, 125*(1), 11–28. https://doi.org/10.1093/aob/mcz155

Calvo, R. A., Peters, D., Vold, K., & Ryan, R. M. (2020). *Supporting human autonomy in AI systems: A framework for ethical enquiry. Ethics of digital well-being.* Springer.

Campbell, D. (2018). Combining ai and blockchain to push frontiers in healthcare. Macadamian. http://www. macadamian. com/2018/03/16/combining-ai-and blockchain-in-healthcare/.

Campbell, M., Hoane, J. A. Jr, & Hsu, F.-H. (2002). Deep Blue. *Artificial Intelligence, 134*(1-2), 57–83. doi:10.1016/S0004-3702(01)00129-1

Candanedo, I. S., Nieves, E. H., González, S. R., Martín, M., & Briones, A. G. (2018). Machine learning predictive model for industry 4.0. *International Conference on Knowledge Management in Organizations* (pp. 501-510). Springer. 10.1007/978-3-319-95204-8_42

Capatina, A., Kachour, M., Lichy, J., Micu, A., Micu, A.-E., & Codignola, F. (2020). Matching the future capabilities of artificial intelligence-based software for social media marketing with potential users' expectations. *Technological Forecasting and Social Change, 151*, 151. doi:10.1016/j.techfore.2019.119794

Carleo, G., Cirac, I., Cranmer, K., Daudet, L., Schuld, M., Tishby, N., Vogt-Maranto, L., & Zdeborová, L. (2019). Machine learning and the physical sciences. *Machine learning and the physical sciences. Reviews of Modern Physics, 91*(4), 045002. doi:10.1103/RevModPhys.91.045002

Carlson, K. D., & Kavanagh, M. J. (2011). HR metrics and workforce analytics. *Human resource information systems: Basics, applications, and future directions*, 150.

Carlstdet, M. (2017). Using NLP and context for improved search result in specialized search engines.

Carolan-Olah, M., Steele, C., & Krenzin, G. (2015). Development and initial testing of a GDM information website for multi-ethnic women with GDM. *BMC Pregnancy and Childbirth, 15*(1), 145. doi:10.118612884-015-0578-0 PMID:26142482

Carrobles, M. F., Deniz, O., & Maroto, F. (2019). Gun and knife detection based on Faster R-CNN for video surveillance. *Iberian Conference on Pattern Recognition and Image Analysis*, (pp. 441 – 452). ACM.

Carter, S. M., Rogers, W., Win, K. T., Frazer, H., Richards, B., & Houssami, N. (2020). The ethical, legal and social implications of using artificial intelligence systems in breast cancer care. *The Breast, 49*, 25–32. doi:10.1016/j.breast.2019.10.001 PMID:31677530

Čartolovni, A., Tomičić, A., & Mosler, E. L. (2022). Ethical, legal, and social considerations of AI-based medical decision-support tools: A scoping review. *International Journal of Medical Informatics, 161*, 104738. doi:10.1016/j.ijmedinf.2022.104738 PMID:35299098

Castelló Ferrer, E. (2018). The blockchain: a new framework for robotic swarm systems. In *Proceedings of the future technologies conference* (pp. 1037-1058). Springer.

CBRA. (2022). *Fact Sheet New Drug Development Process.* CA Biomed. https://www.ca-biomed.org/pdf/media-kit/fact-sheets/CBRADrug Develop.pdf

CDT. (2022). *Artificial Intelligence in Healthcare Market to Witness an Explosive CAGR of 38.4% till 2030, Driven by Rising Datasets of Patient Health-Related Digital Information.* Grand View Research, Inc. https://www.thecowboychannel.com/story/46467382/artificial-intelligence-in-healthcare-market-to-witness-an-explosive-cagr-of-384-till-2030-driven-by-rising-datasets-of-patient-health-related

Cervantes, J., Garcia-Lamont, F., Rodríguez-Mazahua, L., & Lopez, A. (2020). A comprehensive survey on support vector machine classification: Applications, challenges and trends. *Neurocomputing, 408*, 189–215. doi:10.1016/j.neucom.2019.10.118

Chadalawada, S. K. (2020). *Real-Time Detection and Recognition of Construction Vehicles: Using Deep Learning Methods* [Master's Thesis, Blekinge Institute of Technology, Sweden]. https://www.diva-portal.org/smash/get/diva2:1414033/FULLTEXT 02

Chai, T., & Draxler, R. R. (2014). Root mean square error (RMSE) or mean absolute error (MAE)? – Arguments against avoiding RMSE in the literature. *Geoscientific Model Development*, *7*(3), 1247–1250. https://doi.org/10.5194/gmd-7-1247-2014

Chaki, J., Ganesh, S. T., Cidham, S. K., & Theertan, S. A. (2020). Machine learning and artificial intelligence-based Diabetes Mellitus detection and self-management: A systematic review. *Journal of King Saud University-Computer and Information Sciences*.

Chandan, G., & Jain, A., & Mohana. (2018). Real Time Object Detection and Tracking Using Deep Learning and OpenCV. *In Proceedings of the International Conference on Inventive Research in Computing Applications (ICIRCA 2018)*, (pp. 1305 – 1308). IEEE. 10.1109/ICIRCA.2018.8597266

Chander, R. (1999). Can dams and reservoirs cause earthquakes? *Resonance, 4*(11), 4–13. doi:10.1007/BF02837323

Chang, H. C., & Hawamdeh, S. (Eds.). (2020). Cybersecurity for Information Professionals: Concepts and Applications. Auerbach Publications.

Channabasavaraju, B. D., & Vinayakamurthy, U. (2020). *An Analysis of Heart Disease for Diabetic Patients Using Recursive Feature Elimination with Random Forest*. Academic Press.

Cheadle, C., Vawter, M. P., Freed, W. J., & Becker, K. G. (2003). Analysis of microarray data using Z score transformation. *The Journal of Molecular Diagnostics, 5*(2), 73–81. doi:10.1016/S1525-1578(10)60455-2 PMID:12707371

Chen, F., Yuan, S., & Mu, B. (2015). User-QoS-Based Web Service Clustering for QoS Prediction. *Proceedings – 2015 IEEE International Conference on Web Services, ICWS 2015*, 583–590. IEEE. 10.1109/ICWS.2015.83

Chen, K., Mao, H., Shi, X., Xu, Y., & Liu, A. (2017). Trust-Aware and Location-Based Collaborative Filtering for Web Service QoS Prediction. *Proceedings - International Computer Software and Applications Conference, 2*, 143–148. IEEE. 10.1109/COMPSAC.2017.8

Cheng, P., Hao, W., Yuan, S., Si, S., & Carin, L. (2020). FairFil: Contrastive Neural Debiasing Method for Pretrained Text Encoders. *International Conference on Learning Representations*.

Chen, L., Lin, S., Lu, X., Cao, D., Wu, H., Guo, C., ... Wang, F. Y. (2021). Deep neural network based vehicle and pedestrian detection for autonomous driving: A survey. *IEEE Transactions on Intelligent Transportation Systems, 22*(6), 3234–3246.

Chen, Q., Leaman, R., Allot, A., Luo, L., Wei, C.-H., Yan, S., & Lu, Z. (2021). Artificial intelligence in action: Addressing the COVID-19 pandemic with natural language processing. *Annual Review of Biomedical Data Science, 4*(1), 313–339. doi:10.1146/annurev-biodatasci-021821-061045 PMID:34465169

Chialastri, A. (2019). AF 447 as a Paradigmatic Accident: The Role of Automation on a Modern Airplane. In T. Shmelova & Yu. Sikirda (Eds.), *Automated Systems in the Aviation and Aerospace Industries* (pp. 166–192). IGI Global. doi:10.4018/978-1-5225-7709-6.ch006

Choi, W., & Hong, J. W. K. (2021). Performance Evaluation of Ethereum Private and Testnet Networks Using Hyperledger Caliper. *In Proceedings of 22nd Asia-Pacific Network Operations and Management Symposium* (pp. 325-329). IEEE. 10.23919/APNOMS52696.2021.9562684

Choi, Y., & Choi, J. (2020). A study of job involvement prediction using machine learning technique. *The International Journal of Organizational Analysis*.

Chomnunti, P., Hongsanan, S., Aguirre-Hudson, B., Tian, Q., Peršoh, D., Dhami, M. K., & Hyde, K. D. (2014). The sooty moulds. *Fungal Diversity, 66*(1), 1–36. doi:10.100713225-014-0278-5 PMID:27284275

Choudhari, K., & Bhalla, V. (2015). Video Search Engine Optimization Using Keyword and Feature Analysis. *Procedia Computer Science, 58*, 691–697. doi:10.1016/j.procs.2015.08.089

Chowdhary, K. (2020). Natural language processing. *Fundamentals of Artificial Intelligence,*, 603-649.

Chuang, C.-Y., Robinson, J., Lin, Y.-C., Torralba, A., & Jegelka, S. (2020). Debiased contrastive learning. *Advances in Neural Information Processing Systems, 33*, 8765–8775.

Chung, E., Fowers, J., Ovtcharov, K., Papamichael, M., Caulfield, A., Massengill, T., Liu, M., Lo, D., Alkalay, S., Haselman, M., Abeydeera, M., Adams, L., Angepat, H., Boehn, C., Chiou, D., Firestein, O., Forin, A., Gatlin, K. S., Ghandi, M.,, & Burger, D. (2018). Serving dnns in real time at datacenter scale with project brainwave. *IEEE Micro, 38*(2), 8–20. doi:10.1109/MM.2018.022071131

Chung, J. Y. (2020). Implementation of a precise drone positioning system using differential global positioning system. *Journal of the Korea Academia-Industrial cooperation. Society, 21*(1), 14–19.

City University of Hong Kong. (2022). Nanofiber-Based Biodegradable Millirobot That Can Release Drugs in Targeted Positions in the Intestines. Medicalxpress.com. https://medicalxpress.com/news/2022-04-nanofiber-based-biodegradable-millirobot-drugs-positions.html

Clark, K., Khandelwal, U., Levy, O., & Manning, C. D. (2019). What Does BERT Look at? An Analysis of BERT's Attention. Proceedings of the 2019 ACL Workshop BlackboxNLP: Analyzing and Interpreting Neural Networks for NLP, .

Clark, K., Luong, M.-T., Khandelwal, U., Manning, C. D., & Le, Q. V. (2019). Bam! born-again multi-task networks for natural language understanding. doi:10.18653/v1/P19-1595

Clevert, D. A., Unterthiner, T., & Hochreiter, S. (2015). Fast and accurate deep network learning by exponential linear units (elus). arXiv preprint arXiv:1511.07289.

Cloud Flare. (2021). *What is a web crawler*. Cloud Flare. https://www.cloudflare.com/en-gb/learning/bots/what-is-a-web-crawler/

Cohn, A., West, T., & Parker, C. (2016). Smart after all: Blockchain, smart contracts, parametric insurance, and smart energy grids. *Geo. L. Tech. Rev., 1*, 273.

Contact North. (2018). *Ten facts about artificial intelligence in teaching and learning*. TeachOnline. https://teachonline.ca/fr/node/101327

Content Marketing Institute. (2022). *How AI Will Power the Future of Successful Content Marketing*. Content Marketing. https://contentmarketinginstitute.com/articles/ai-content-marketing-future

Copeland, B. (2022). Artificial intelligence. *Encyclopedia Britannica*. https://www.britannica.com/technology/artificial-intelligence

Crawford, K. (2016). Artificial intelligence's white guy problem. *The New York Times, 25*(06).

Croft, W. B., Metzler, D., & Strohman, T. (2015). *Search Engines: Information Retrieval in Practice*. www.search-engines-book.com

Crosby, M., Pattanayak, P., Verma, S., & Kalyanaraman, V. (2016). Blockchain technology: Beyond bitcoin. *Applied Innovation, 2*(6-10), 71.

Crumpler, W., & Lewis, J. A. (2019). The cybersecurity workforce gap (p. 10). Center for Strategic and International Studies (CSIS).

Cui, L., & Lee, D. (2020). Coaid: Covid-19 healthcare misinformation dataset. *arXiv:2006.00885.*

Dabkowski, P., & Gal, Y. (2017). Real time image saliency for black box classifiers. *Advances in Neural Information Processing Systems*, 30.

Dahmani, K., Tahiri, A., Habert, O., & Elmeftouhi, Y. (2016,April). An intelligent model of home support for people with loss of autonomy:a novel approach. In *2016 International Conference on Control, Decisionand Information Technologies (CoDIT)* (pp. 182-185). IEEE.

Dai, J., Li, Y., He, K., & Sun, J. (2016). R-FCN: Object Detection via Region-based Fully Convolutional Networks. *Advances in Neural Information Processing Systems*, *29*, 379–387.

Daim, T., Lai, K. K., Yalcin, H., Alsoubie, F., & Kumar, V. (2020). Forecasting technological positioning through technology knowledge redundancy: Patent citation analysis of IoT, cybersecurity, and Blockchain. *Technological Forecasting and Social Change*, *161*, 120329. doi:10.1016/j.techfore.2020.120329

Dalal, N., & Triggs, B. (2005). Histograms of oriented gradients for human detection. *In 2005 IEEE computer society conference on computer vision and pattern recognition (CVPR'05), 1, 886 - 893. IEEE.*

Dalal, N., & Triggs, B. (2005, June). Histograms of oriented gradients for human detection. In *2005 IEEE computer society conference on computer vision and pattern recognition (CVPR'05)* (Vol. 1, pp. 886-893). IEEE.

Dall'Anese, D. (2020). *The impact of Artificial Intelligence on unemployment: a systematic literature review.* Università Ca' Foscari Venezia.

Dankwa-Mullan, I., Rivo, M., Sepulveda, M., Park, Y., Snowdon, J., & Rhee, K. (2019). Transforming diabetes care through artificial intelligence: The future is here. *Population Health Management*, *22*(3), 229–242.

Dao, D. V., Adeli, H., Ly, H.-B., Le, L. M., Le, V. M., Le, T.-T., & Pham, B. T. (2020). A sensitivity and robustness analysis of GPR and ANN for high-performance concrete compressive strength prediction using a monte carlo simulation. *Sustainability*, *12*(3), 830. https://doi.org/10.3390/su12030830

Das, R., Behera, K., & Shah, S. (2020). *Challenges and Role of Digital Transformation.* Omnia Health, Informa Markets. https://insights.omnia-health.com/technology/innovations-healthcare-challenges-and-role-digital-transformation?utm_source=AdWords&utm_medium=Paid+Search&utm_campaign=AEL22OMA-RK-Insights-Dynamic&utm_term=%7Bkeyword%7D&utm_content=Healthcare+technology&gclid=EAIaIQobChMIjJjtrf2n-QIVyg0rCh0ELQa6EAAYAyAAEgK3FfD_BwE

Das, S., Samui, P., Khan, S., & Sivakugan, N. (2011). Machine learning techniques applied to prediction of residual strength of clay. *Open Geosciences, 3*(4). doi:10.2478/s13533-011-0043-1

Davenport, T., & Kalakota, R. (2019). The Potential for ArtificialIntelligence in Healthcare. *Future Healthcare Journal,* *6* (2), 94–98. doi:10.7861/futurehosp.6-2-94

David, M. (2018). YouTube's AI is so good at finding offensive content that it needs more staff to keep up. *We Forum.* https://www.weforum.org/agenda/2018/04/ai-is-now-youtube-s-biggest-weapon-against-the-spread-of-offensive-videos/

Demajo, L. M., Vella, V., & Dingli, A. (2020). Explainable ai for interpretable credit scoring. *arXiv preprint arXiv:2012.03749*. doi:10.5121/csit.2020.101516

Demirkan, S., Demirkan, I., & McKee, A. (2020). Blockchain technology in the future of business cyber security and accounting. *Journal of Management Analytics*, 7(2), 189–208. doi:10.1080/23270012.2020.1731721

Deng, J., Dong, W., Socher, R., Li, L. J., Li, K., & Fei-Fei, L. (2009). Imagenet: A large-scale hierarchical image database. In 2009 IEEE conference on computer vision and pattern recognition (pp. 248-255). IEEE. doi:10.1109/CVPR.2009.5206848

Deng, L. (2014). A tutorial survey of architectures, algorithms, and applications for deep learning. *APSIPA Transactions on Signal and Information Processing*, 3(1), 3. doi:10.1017/atsip.2013.9

Deng, Y., Lu, L., Aponte, L., Angelidi, A. M., Novak, V., Karniadakis, G. E., & Mantzoros, C. S. (2021). Deep transfer learning and data augmentation improve glucose levels prediction in type 2 diabetes patients. *NPJ Digital Medicine*, 4(1), 1–13. doi:10.103841746-021-00480-x PMID:34262114

Dhurandhar, A., Chen, P.-Y., Luss, R., Tu, C.-C., Ting, P., Shanmugam, K., & Das, P. (2018). Explanations based on the missing: Towards contrastive explanations with pertinent negatives. *Advances in Neural Information Processing Systems*, 31.

Dian, J. F., Vahidnia, R., & Rahmati, A. (2020). Wearables and the Internet of Things (IoT), Applications, Opportunities, and Challenges: A Survey. *IEEE Access*, 8, 69200–69211. doi:10.1109/access.2020.2986329

Dias, J. P., & Ferreira, H. S. (2017). Automating the extraction of static content and dynamic behaviour from e-commerce websites. *Procedia Computer Science*, 109, 297–304. doi:10.1016/j.procs.2017.05.355

Digital Marketing Institute. (2017). *Grow Your Business With Social Bots*. Digital Marketing. https://digitalmarketinginstitute.com/blog/grow-your-business-with-social-bots

Dillon, J. V. (2017). Tensorflow distributions. arXiv:1711.10604.

Dilsizian, S. E., & Siegel, E. L. (2014). Artificialintelligence in medicine and cardiac imaging: Harnessing big data and advancedcomputing to provide personalized medical diagnosis and treatment. *Current Cardiology Reports*, 16(1), 1–8.

Dimian, M., Chassagne, L., Andrei, P., & Li, P. (2019). Smart Technologies for Vehicle Safety and Driver Assistance. *Journal of Advanced Transportation*, 2019, 1–2. doi:10.1155/2019/2690498

Dinakaran, R. K., Easom, P., Bouridane, A., Zhang, L., Jiang, R., Mehboob, F., & Rauf, A. (2019). Deep learning based pedestrian detection at distance in smart cities. In *Proceedings of SAI Intelligent Systems Conference* (pp. 588-593). Springer.

Ding, L., Kang, G., Liu, J., Xiao, Y., & Cao, B. (2021). QoS Prediction for Web Services via Combining Multi-component Graph Convolutional Collaborative Filtering and Deep Factorization Machine. *Proceedings - 2021 IEEE International Conference on Web Services, ICWS 2021*, 551–559. IEEE. 10.1109/ICWS53863.2021.00076

Dinh, A., Miertschin, S., Young, A., & Mohanty, S. D. (2019). A data-driven approach to predicting diabetes and cardiovascular disease with machine learning. *BMC Medical Informatics and Decision Making*, 19(1), 1–15. doi:10.118612911-019-0918-5 PMID:31694707

Dinh, T. N., & Thai, M. T. (2018). AI and blockchain: A disruptive integration. *Computer*, 51(9), 48–53. doi:10.1109/MC.2018.3620971

Dixon, L., Li, J., Sorensen, J., Thain, N., & Vasserman, L. (2018). Measuring and mitigating unintended bias in text classification. Proceedings of the 2018 AAAI/ACM Conference on AI, Ethics, and Society, 10.1145/3278721.3278729

Djeziri, M. A., Benmoussa, S., & Zio, E. (2020). Review on Health Indices Extraction and Trend Modeling for Remaining Useful Life Estimation. In Artificial Intelligence Techniques for a Scalable Energy Transition, (pp. 183–223). Springer. doi:10.1007/978-3-030-42726-9_8

Dolgikh, S. (2018). Spontaneous Concept Learning with Deep Autoencoder. [Canada.]. *International Journal of Computational Intelligence Systems*, *12*(1), 1–12. doi:10.2991/ijcis.2018.25905178

Dollár, P., Appel, R., Belongie, S., & Perona, P. (2014). Fast feature pyramids for object detection. *IEEE Transactions on Pattern Analysis and Machine Intelligence*, *36*(8), 1532–1545. doi:10.1109/TPAMI.2014.2300479 PMID:26353336

Dollar, P., Wojek, C., Schiele, B., & Perona, P. (2011). Pedestrian detection: An evaluation of the state of the art. *IEEE Transactions on Pattern Analysis and Machine Intelligence*, *34*(4), 743–761. doi:10.1109/TPAMI.2011.155 PMID:21808091

Dong, L., & Shan, J. (2013). A comprehensive review of earthquake-induced building damage detection with remote sensing techniques. *ISPRS Journal of Photogrammetry and Remote Sensing*, *84*, 85–99. https://doi.org/10.1016/j.isprsjprs.2013.06.011

Dong, N., Wu, C.-H., Ip, W.-H., Chen, Z.-Q., Chan, C.-Y., & Yung, K.-L. (2012). An opposition-based chaotic GA/PSO hybrid algorithm and its application in circle detection. *Computers & Mathematics with Applications (Oxford, England)*, *64*(6), 1886–1902. doi:10.1016/j.camwa.2012.03.040

Dornadula, V. N., & Geetha, S. (2019). Credit card fraud detection using machine learning algorithms. *Procedia Computer Science*, *165*, 631–641. doi:10.1016/j.procs.2020.01.057

DraftGlobal Strategy (2021). Digital Health 2020- 2025. *Global strategy on digital health.* https://www.who.int/docs/default-source/documents/gs4dhdaa2a9f352b0445bafbc79ca799dce4d.pdf.
</div>

Dragusin, R., Petcu, P., Lioma, C., Larsen, B., Jørgensen, H., & Winther, O. (2011). Rare disease diagnosis as an information retrieval task. *Conference on the Theory of Information Retrieval*, 356–359. Springer. 10.1007/978-3-642-23318-0_38

Draper, N. R., & Smith, H. (1998). *Applied regression analysis* (3rd ed.). Wiley.

Driver, C. N., Bowles, B. S., Bartholmai, B. J., & Greenberg-Worisek, A. J. (2020). Artificial intelligence in radiology: A call for thoughtful application. *Clinical and Translational Science*, *13*(2), 216.

Duffany, J. L. (2010). Artificial intelligence in GPS navigation systems. *2nd International Conference on Software Technology and Engineering* (pp. V1-382). IEEE.

Duffett, R. G. (2017). Influence of social media marketing communications on young consumers' attitudes. *Young Consumers*, *18*(1), 19–39. doi:10.1108/YC-07-2016-00622

Dunjko, V., & Briegel, H. J. (2018). Machine learning & artificial intelligence in the quantum domain: A review of recent progress. *Reports on Progress in Physics*, *81*(7), 074001. https://doi.org/10.1088/1361-6633/aab406

Dunphy, P., & Petitcolas, F. A. (2018). A first look at identity management schemes on the blockchain. *IEEE Security and Privacy*, *16*(4), 20–29. doi:10.1109/MSP.2018.3111247

Ebrahimi, A., Sadeghi, M., Nezhadshahbodaghi, M., Mosavi, M. R., & Abdolkarimi, E. S. (2021). Improving INS/GPS Integration with Artificial Intelligence during GPS Outage. *Electronic and Cyber Defense*, *9*(2), 143–157.

Edgley-Pyshorn, C., & Huisman, J. (2011). The role of the HR department in organisational change in a British university. *Journal of Organizational Change Management*, *24*(5), 610–625. doi:10.1108/09534811111158886

EDUCAUSE. (2018). *Horizon report: 2018 higher education edition Learning Initiative and The New Media Consortium.* Educause. https://library.educause.edu/

EDUCAUSE. (2019). *Horizon report: 2019 higher education edition.* Learning Initiative and The New Media Consortium, Educause. https://library.educause.edu/

Edward, S. (2018). Text-to-speech device for visually impaired people. *International Journal of Pure and Applied Mathematics, 119*(15), 1061–1067.

Egri, G., & Bayrak, C. (2014). The role of search engine optimization on keeping the user on the site. *Procedia Computer Science, 36,* 335–342. doi:10.1016/j.procs.2014.09.102

El Jerjawi, N. S., & Abu-Naser, S. S. (2018). Diabetes prediction using artificial neural network. *International Journal of Advanced Science and Technology, 121.*

El Massi, I., Es-Saady, Y., & El Yassa, M. (2014). Reconnaissance des épidémies agricoles causées par la mouche mineuse à base de k-means clustering et de color moments. *Research Gate.* . doi:10.13140/RG.2.1.2407.4721

El Zini, J., & Awad, M. (2022a). Beyond Model Interpretability: On the Faithfulness and Adversarial Robustness of Contrastive Textual Explanations. *Findings of the Association for Computational Linguistics: EMNLP.*

El Zini, J., Mansour, M., Mousi, B., & Awad, M. (2022). On the Evaluation of the Plausibility and Faithfulness of Sentiment Analysis Explanations. IFIP International Conference on Artificial Intelligence Applications and Innovations, 10.1007/978-3-031-08337-2_28

El Zini, J., & Awad, M. (2022b). *On the Explainability of Natural Language Processing Deep Models. ACM Computing Surveys.* CSUR.

Ellahham, S. (2020). Artificial intelligence: The future for diabetes care. *The American Journal of Medicine, 133*(8), 895–900. doi:10.1016/j.amjmed.2020.03.033 PMID:32325045

Ellahham, S., Ellahham, N., & Simsekler, M. C. E. (2020). Application of artificial intelligence in the health care safety context: Opportunities and challenges. *American Journal of Medical Quality, 35*(4), 341–348. doi:10.1177/1062860619878515 PMID:31581790

Ellefsen, A. L. (2019). Remaining useful life predictions for turbofan engine degradation using semi-supervised deep architecture. *Reliability Engineering & System Safety, 183,* 240–251. doi:10.1016/j.ress.2018.11.027

El-Rashidy, N., El-Sappagh, S., Islam, S. R., El-Bakry, H. M., & Abdelrazek, S. (2020). End-to-end deep learning framework for coronavirus (COVID-19) detection and monitoring. *Electronics (Basel), 9*(9), 1439. doi:10.3390/electronics9091439

Erabati, G. K., Goncalves, N., & Araujo, H. (2020, 07). Object Detection in Traffic Scenarios - A Comparison of Traditional and Deep Learning Approaches. *In CS & IT Conference Proceedings, 10*(9).

Ereifej, E. S., Shell, C., Schofield, J., Charkhkar, H., Cuberovic, I., Dorval, A. & Graczyk, E. (2019).Neural Engineering: The Process, Applications, and Its Role in the Future ofMedicine. *Journal of Neural Engineering, 16* (6), 063002. doi:10.1088/1741-2552/ab4869

Ertel, W. (2017). *Introduction to Artificial Intelligence.* Upgraduate Topics in Computer Science. doi:10.1007/978-3-319-58487-4

Ertel, W. (2018). *Introduction to artificial intelligence.* Springer.

Escandell-Poveda, R., Iglesias-García, M., & Papí-Gálvez, N. (2022). *From Memex to Google: The origin and evolution of search engines.* INDOCS.

Espinosa, R., Ponce, H., Gutiérrez, S., Martínez-Villaseñor, L., Brieva, J., & Moya-Albor, E. (2019). A vision-based approach for fall detection using multiple cameras and convolutional neural networks: A case study using the UP-fall detection dataset. *Computers in Biology and Medicine*, *115*, 103520. doi:10.1016/j.compbiomed.2019.103520 PMID:31698242

EUROCONTROL. (2017). Airport CDM Implementation. *Manual*, Brussels, Belgium, Available from: Eurocontrol. https://www.eurocontrol.int/sites/default/files/publication/files/airport-cdm-manual-2017.PDF

EUROCONTROL. (2018). EUROCONTROL Voluntary ATM Incident Reporting (EVAIR) *Bulletin No 19*. Eurocontrol. https://www.eurocontrol.int/sites/default/files/publication/files/evair-bulletin-19.pdf

Facebook. (2022). *Suicide Prevention*. Meta. https://www.facebook.com/safety/wellbeing/suicideprevention

Fagherazzi, G., & Ravaud, P. (2019). Digital diabetes: Perspectives for diabetes prevention, management and research. *Diabetes & Metabolism*, *45*(4), 322–329. doi:10.1016/j.diabet.2018.08.012 PMID:30243616

Fahimirad, M., & Kotamjani, S. S. (2018). A review on the application of artificial intelligence in teaching and learning in educational contexts. *International Journal of Learning and Development*, *8*(4), 106–118. doi:10.5296/ijld.v8i4.14057

Fallucchi, F., Coladangelo, M., Giuliano, R., & Luca, E. W. (2020). Predicting employee attrition using machine learning techniques. *Computers*, *9*(4), 86. doi:10.3390/computers9040086

Fang, J., Wu, W., Lu, Z., & Cho, E. (2019). Using baidu index to nowcast mobile phone sales in China. *The Singapore Economic Review*, *64*(01), 83–96. doi:10.1142/S021759081743007X

Fan, J., Fang, L., Wu, J., Guo, Y., & Dai, Q. (2020). From brain science to artificial intelligence. *Engineering*, *6*(3), 248–252. doi:10.1016/j.eng.2019.11.012

Faruk, M. J. H., Shahriar, H., Valero, M., Barsha, F. L., Sobhan, S., Khan, M. A., & Wu, F. (2021, December). Malware detection and prevention using artificial intelligence techniques. In *2021 IEEE International Conference on Big Data (Big Data)* (pp. 5369-5377). IEEE. 10.1109/BigData52589.2021.9671434

Faruque, M. F., & Sarker, I. H. (2019). Performance analysis of machine learning techniques to predict diabetes mellitus. In *2019 International Conference on Electrical, Computer and Communication Engineering (ECCE)* (pp. 1-4). IEEE. 10.1109/ECACE.2019.8679365

Fathy, C., & Saleh, S. N. (2022). Integrating deep learning-based iot and fog computing with software-defined networking for detecting weapons in video surveillance systems. *Sensors (Basel)*, *22*(14), 5075. doi:10.339022145075 PMID:35890755

Faustine, C., Dramilio, A., Sanjaya, S., & Soewito, B. (2020). The effect and technique in search engine optimization. *International Conference on Information Management and Technology*, 348-353.

Fauvel, W. (2017) Blockchain Advantages and Disadvantages. *Medium*. https://medium.com/nudjed/blockchain-advantage-and-disadvantagese76dfde3bbc0

FDA. (2018). *The drug development process*. FDA. https://www.fda.gov/patients/learn-about-drug-and-device-approvals/drug-development-process

Federal Aviation Administration. (2014). *Pilot/Controller Glossary*. FAA.

Feng, W., Sui, H., Tu, J., Huang, W., & Sun, K. (2018). A novel change detection approach based on visual saliency and random forest from multi-temporal high-resolution remote-sensing images. *International Journal of Remote Sensing*, *39*(22), 7998–8021. doi:10.1080/01431161.2018.1479794

Ferguson, R., Clow, D., Beale, R., Cooper, A. J., Morris, N., Bayne, S., & Woodgate, A. (2015) Moving through MOOCS: Pedagogy, learning design and patterns of engagement. In *European Conference on Technology Enhanced Learning*. (pp. 70-84). Springer. 10.1007/978-3-319-24258-3_6

Fidani, C. (2010). The earthquake lights (EQL) of the 6 April 2009 Aquila earthquake, in Central Italy. *Natural Hazards and Earth System Sciences*, *10*(5), 967–978. https://doi.org/10.5194/nhess-10-967-2010

Flores, A. W., Bechtel, K., & Lowenkamp, C. T. (2016). False positives, false negatives, and false analyses: A rejoinder to machine bias: There's software used across the country to predict future criminals. and it's biased against blacks. *Federal Probation*, *80*, 38.

Fradi, M., Afif, M., & Machhout, M. (2020a). Deep learning based approach for bone diagnosis classification in ultrasonic computed tomographic images. *International Journal of Advanced Computer Science and Applications*, *11*(12). doi:10.14569/IJACSA.2020.0111210

Fradi, M., Afif, M., Zahzeh, E. H., Bouallegue, K., & Machhout, M. (2020b). Transfer-deep learning application for ultrasonic computed tomographic image classification. In *2020 International Conference on Control, Automation and Diagnosis (ICCAD)* (pp. 1-6). IEEE. 10.1109/ICCAD49821.2020.9260569

Frana, P. L. (2004). Before the web there was Gopher. *IEEE Annals of the History of Computing*, *26*(1), 20–41. doi:10.1109/MAHC.2004.1278848

Francesconi, E. (2022). The winter, the summer and the summer dream of artificial intelligence in law. *Artificial Intelligence and Law*, *30*(2), 1–15. doi:10.100710506-022-09309-8 PMID:35132296

Fridgen, G., Radszuwill, S., Urbach, N., & Utz, L. (2018). Cross-organizational workflow management using blockchain technology: towards applicability, auditability, and automation. In *Proceedings of 51st Annual Hawaii International Conference on System Sciences*. Scholar Space. 10.24251/HICSS.2018.444

Frøisland, D. H., & Aorsand, E. (2015). Integrating visual dietary documentation in mobile-phone-based self-management application for adolescents with type 1 diabetes. *Journal of Diabetes Science and Technology*, *9*(3), 541–548. doi:10.1177/1932296815576956 PMID:25901020

Fukushima, K., & Miyake, S. (1982). Neocognitron: A self-organizing neural network model for a mechanism of visual pattern recognition. In *Competition and cooperation in neural nets* (pp. 267–285). Springer. doi:10.1007/978-3-642-46466-9_18

Furl, N., Phillips, P. J., & O'Toole, A. J. (2002). Face recognition algorithms and the other-race effect: Computational mechanisms for a developmental contact hypothesis. *Cognitive Science*, *26*(6), 797–815.

Fusco, G., Cheraghi, S. A., Neat, L., & Coughlan, J. M. (2020). An indoor navigation app using computer vision and sign recognition. In *International Conference on Computers Helping People with Special Needs* (pp. 485-494). Springer. 10.1007/978-3-030-58796-3_56

Fu, Z., Xian, Y., Geng, S., De Melo, G., & Zhang, Y. (2021). Popcorn: Human-in-the-loop Popularity Debiasing in Conversational Recommender Systems. Proceedings of the 30th ACM International Conference on Information & Knowledge Management, .

Gaikwad, S. K., Gawali, B. W., & Yannawar, P. (2010). A review on speech recognition technique. *International Journal of Computers and Applications*, *10*(3), 16–24. doi:10.5120/1462-1976

Gao, C., Zheng, Y. U., Li, N., Li, Y., Qin, Y., Piao, J., Quan, Y., Chang, J., Depeng, J., He, X., Li, Y., Zheng, Y., & Jin, D. (2021). Graph Neural Networks for Recommender Systems: Challenges, Methods, and Directions. *ACM Transactions on Information Systems, 1*(1), 46. doi:10.48550/arxiv.2109.12843

Garcia, M. C., Mateo, J. T., Benitez, P. L., & Gutierrez, J. G. (2021). On the Performance of One-Stage and Two-Stage Object Detectors in Autonomous Vehicles Using Camera Data. *Remote Sensing, 13*(1).

Gardner, M., Artzi, Y., Basmov, V., Berant, J., Bogin, B., Chen, S., Dasigi, P., Dua, D., Elazar, Y., & Gottumukkala, A. (2020). Evaluating Models' Local Decision Boundaries via Contrast Sets. Findings of the Association for Computational Linguistics: EMNLP 2020,

Garg, S., Perot, V., Limtiaco, N., Taly, A., Chi, E. H., & Beutel, A. (2019). Counterfactual fairness in text classification through robustness. Proceedings of the 2019 AAAI/ACM Conference on AI, Ethics, and Society

Garg, S., Sinha, S., Kar, A. K., & Mani, M. (2021). A review of machine learning applications in human resource management. *International Journal of Productivity and Performance Management.*

Gartner. (2022) *Forecasts Worldwide Artificial Intelligence.* Gartner. https://www.gartner.com/en/newsroom/press-releases/2021-11-22-gartner-forecasts-worldwide-artificial-intelligence-software-market-to-reach-62-billion-in-2022

Gatteschi, V., Lamberti, F., Demartini, C., Pranteda, C., & Santamaría, V. (2018). Blockchain and smart contracts for insurance: Is the technology mature enough?. *Future internet, 10*(2), 20.

Geffen, O., Yitzhaky, Y., Barchilon, N., Druyan, S., & Halachmi, I. (2020). A machine vision system to detect and count laying hens in battery cages. *Animal, 14*(12), 2628-2634.

Gençer, G. (2021, November 22). *How AI can improve Fraud Detection & Prevention in 2022?* AIMultiple.

Georgakopoulos, S. V., Tasoulis, S. K., Vrahatis, A. G., & Plagianakos, V. P. (2018). Convolutional neural networks for toxic comment classification. *Proceedings of the 10th hellenic conference on artificial intelligence*

Geoscience News and Information. (2021). *Plate Tectonics Map—Plate Boundary Map.* Geology.com. https://geology.com/plate-tectonics.shtml

Gerasimov, B., & Lokazyuk, V. (2007). *Intelligent Decision Support Systems: monograph.* European University Press.

Geru, M., Micu, A. E., Capatina, A., & Micu, A. (2018). Using artificial Intelligence on social media's user-generated content for disruptive marketing strategies in eCommerce. *Economics and Applied Informatics., 24*(3), 5–11.

Ghadhab, L., Jenhani, I., Mkaouer, M. W., & Ben Messaoud, M. (2021). Augmenting commit classification by using fine-grained source code changes and a pre-trained deep neural language model. *Information and Software Technology, 135*, 106566. doi:10.1016/j.infsof.2021.106566

Ghaedi, M., & Rahimi, M. reza, Ghaedi, A. M., Tyagi, I., Agarwal, S., & Gupta, V. K. (2016). Application of least squares support vector regression and linear multiple regression for modeling removal of methyl orange onto tin oxide nanoparticles loaded on activated carbon and activated carbon prepared from Pistacia atlantica wood. *Journal of Colloid and Interface Science, 461*, 425–434. doi:10.1016/j.jcis.2015.09.024

Ghafouri, H., Hashemi, M., & Hung, P. C. K. (2021). A survey on web service QoS prediction methods. In *IEEE Transactions on Services Computing.* Institute of Electrical and Electronics Engineers Inc., doi:10.1109/TSC.2020.2980793

Ghahramani, Z. (2004). Unsupervised learning. In O. Bousquet, U. von Luxburg, & G. Rätsch (Eds.), *Advanced Lectures on Machine Learning: ML Summer Schools 2003*, (pp. 72–112). Springer. doi:10.1007/978-3-540-28650-9_5

Ghandour, A., & Woodford, B. J. (2019). Ethical Issues in Artificial Intelligence in UAE. 2019 International Arab Conference on Information Technology (ACIT), (pp. 262-266). IEEE. 10.1109/ACIT47987.2019.8990997

Ghazal, T. M., Hussain, M. Z., Said, R. A., Nadeem, A., Hasan, M. K., Ahmad, M., Khan, M. A., & Naseem, M. T. (2021). Performances of k-means clustering algorithm with different distance metrics. *Intelligent Automation and Soft Computing*, *30*(2), 735–742. doi:10.32604/iasc.2021.019067

Ghobakhloo, M. (2020). Industry 4.0, digitization, and opportunities for sustainability. *Journal of Cleaner Production*, *252*, 119869. doi:10.1016/j.jclepro.2019.119869

Ghoneim, K. (2015). The olive leaf moth Palpita unionalis (Hübner) (Lepidoptera: Pyralidae) as a serious pest in the world: a review. *International Journal of Research Studies in Zoology*, *1*(2), 1–20.

Ghorbanzadeh, M., Zhang, J., & Andersson, P. (2016). Binary classification model to predict developmental toxicity of industrial chemicals in zebrafish. *Journal of Chemometrics*, *30*(6), 298–307. doi:10.1002/cem.2791

Gidaris, S., & Komodakis, N. (2015). Object detection via a multi-region and semantic segmentation-aware cnn model. *Proceedings of the IEEE international conference on computer vision.* IEEE. 10.1109/ICCV.2015.135

Giles, M. (2018). AI for cybersecurity is a hot new thing—and a dangerous gamble. *Technology Review.* https://www. technologyreview. com/s/611860/ai-for-cybersecurity-is-a-hot-new-thing-and-a-dangerous-gamble

Gill & Pathwar. (2021). *Prediction of Diabetes Using Various Feature Selection and Machine Learning Paradigms.* Easy Chair Preprint 6587.

Girshick, R., Donahue, J., Darrell, T., & Malik, J. (2014). Rich feature hierarchies for accurate object detection and semantic segmentation. *In Proceedings of the IEEE conference on computer vision and pattern recognition*, (pp. 580 – 587). IEEE. . 10.1109/CVPR.2014.81

Giveki, D., Soltanshahi, A., Shiri, F., & Tarrah, H. (2015). A New Content Based Image Retrieval Model Based on Wavelet Transform. *Journal of Computer and Communications*, *3*(03), 66–73. doi:10.4236/jcc.2015.33012

Glass, B. D. (2014). Counterfeit drugs and medical devices in developing countries. *Research and Reports in Tropical Medicine*, *5*, 11. doi:10.2147/RRTM.S39354 PMID:32669888

Golledge, R. G. (1993). Geography and the disabled: A survey with special reference to vision impaired and blind populations. *Transactions of the Institute of British Geographers*, *18*(1), 63–85. doi:10.2307/623069

Gonzalez, J. L., Zaccaro, C., Alvarez-Garcia, J. A., Morillo, L. M., & Caparrini, F. S. (2020). Real-time gun detection in CCTV: An open problem. *Neural Networks*, *132*, 297–308. doi:10.1016/j.neunet.2020.09.013 PMID:32977275

Goodfellow, I., Bengio, Y., & Courville, A. (2016). *Deep Learning.* MIT Press. https://www.deeplearningbook.org/

Goodfellow, I., Pouget-Abadie, J., Mirza, M., Xu, B., Warde-Farley, D., Ozair, S., ... Bengio, Y. (2020). Generative adversarial networks. *Communications of the ACM*, *63*(11), 139–144.

Google. (n.d.). Googlebot. *Google search Central.* https://developers.google.com/search/docs/advanced/crawling/googlebot

Graham, M. (2022).Using Natural Language Processing to Search for Textual References. In D. Hamidović, C. Clivaz, & S.B. Savant (eds.), Ancient Manuscripts in Digital Culture. (pp.115-132). Brill.

Gran, B., Booth, P., & Bucher, T. (2021). To be or not to be algorithm aware: A question of a new digital divide? *Information Communication and Society*, 24(12), 1779–1796. doi:10.1080/1369118X.2020.1736124

Graves, L. (2018). *Understanding the promise and limits of Automated Fact-Checking.* Reuters Institute. https://reutersinstitute.politics.ox.ac.uk/sites/default/files/2018-02/graves_factsheet_180226%20FINAL.pdf

Gray, A. (2016). The 10 Skills You Need to Thrive in the Fourth Industrial Revolution. *WeForum.* https://www.weforum.org/agenda/2016/01/the-10-skills-you-need-to-thrive-in-the-fourth-industrial-revolution/

Gray, C. 2022. Transforming Healthcare with Artificial Intelligence. *Technologymagazine.com.* https://technologymagazine.com/ai-and-machine-learning/transforming-healthcare-with-artificial-intelligence

Green, E., Singh, D., & Chia, R. (2022). *AI Ethics and Higher Education: Good Practice and Guidance for Educators, Learners, and Institutions.* Globethics.

Grewal, M., Andrews, A., & Bartone, C. (2020). *Global navigation satellite systems, inertial navigation, and integration.* John Wiley & Sons. doi:10.1002/9781119547860

Grgic-Hlaca, N., Zafar, M. B., Gummadi, K. P., & Weller, A. (2016). The case for process fairness in learning: Feature selection for fair decision making. NIPS symposium on machine learning and the law,

Gribbin, J. (1971). Relation of sunspot and earthquake activity. *Science*, 173(3996), 558–558. https://doi.org/10.1126/science.173.3996.558.b

Groener, A., Chern, G., & Pritt, M. (2019, 10). A Comparison of Deep Learning Object Detection Models for Satellite Imagery. *In 2019 IEEE Applied Imagery Pattern Recognition Workshop (AIPR)*, (pp. 1 – 10). IEEE.

Gudivada, V. N., Rao, D., & Paris, J. (2015). Understanding search-engine optimization. *Computer*, 48(10), 43–45. doi:10.1109/MC.2015.297

Guillemette, M. G., Laroche, M., & Cadieux, J. (2014). Defining decision making process performance: Conceptualization and validation of an index. *Information & Management*, 51(6), 618–626. doi:10.1016/j.im.2014.05.012

Gulli, A., & Pal, S. (2017). *Deep learning with Keras.* Packt Publishing Ltd.

Gulshan, V., Peng, L., Coram, M., Stumpe, M. C., Wu, D., Narayanaswamy, A., Venugopalan, S., Widner, K., Madams, T., Cuadros, J., Kim, R., Raman, R., Nelson, P. C., Mega, J. L., & Webster, D. R. (2016). Development and validation of a deep learning algorithm for detection of diabetic retinopathy in retinal fundus photographs. *Journal of the American Medical Association*, 316(22), 2402–2410. doi:10.1001/jama.2016.17216 PMID:27898976

Gumbs, A. A., Frigerio, I., Spolverato, G., Croner, R., Illanes, A., Chouillard, E., & Elyan, E. (2021). Artificial intelligence surgery: How do we get to autonomous actions in surgery? *Sensors (Basel)*, 21(16), 5526. doi:10.339021165526 PMID:34450976

Gupta, A., Puri, R., Verma, M., Gunjyal, S., & Kumar, A. (2019). Performance comparison of object detection algorithms with different feature extractors. *In 2019 6th International Conference on Signal Processing and Integrated Networks (SPIN)*, (pp. 472 – 477). Semantic Scholar.

Gupta, B. B., & Sheng, Q. Z. (Eds.). (2019). *Machine learning for computer and cyber security: principle, algorithms, and practices.* CRC Press. doi:10.1201/9780429504044

Gupta, B. B., Tewari, A., Jain, A. K., & Agrawal, D. P. (2017). Fighting against phishing attacks: State of the art and future challenges. *Neural Computing & Applications*, *28*(12), 3629–3654. doi:10.100700521-016-2275-y

Gupta, N. (2013). Artificial neural network. *Network and Complex Systems*, *3*(1), 24–28.

Hadadi, S. A. (2014). *HR Management*. University of Biskra Repository.

Haderlie, D. M., Cornelius, A., Crouch, A., Macatuno, F., Jackson, M., & Johnson, W. (2021). Understanding How Organizations Handle Cybersecurity (No. INL/EXT-21-64319-Rev000). Idaho National Lab (INL).

Haenlein, M., & Kaplan, A. (2019). A Brief History of Artificial Intelligence: On the Past, Present, and Future of Artificial Intelligence. *California Management Review*, *61*(4), 5–14. doi:10.1177/0008125619864925

Hagerty, A., & Rubinov, I. (2019). *Global AI ethics: a review of artificial Intelligence's social impacts and ethical implications*, 1-27. Cornell University.

Haid, M., Budaker, B., Geiger, M., Husfeldt, D., Hartmann, M., & Berezowski, N. (2019). Inertial-based gesture recognition for artificial intelligent cockpit control using hidden Markov models. *IEEE International Conference on Consumer Electronics (ICCE)*, (pp. 1-4). 10.1109/ICCE.2019.8662036

Hainzl, S., Kraft, T., Wassermann, J., Igel, H., & Schmedes, E. (2006). Evidence for rainfall-triggered earthquake activity. *Geophysical Research Letters*, *33*(19), L19303. https://doi.org/10.1029/2006GL027642

Haiyan, C. (2010). An impact of social media on online travel information search in China. *2010 3rd International Conference on Information Management, Innovation Management and Industrial Engineering, 3*, 509–512.

Hajian, S., Bonchi, F., & Castillo, C. (2016). Algorithmic bias: From discrimination discovery to fairness-aware data mining. *Proceedings of the 22nd ACM SIGKDD international conference on knowledge discovery and data mining*

Halaweh, M. (2018). Viewpoint: Artificial Intelligence Government (gov. 3.0): The UAE leading model. *Journal of Artificial Intelligence Research*, *62*, 269–272. doi:10.1613/jair.1.11210

Halcox, J. P., Wareham, K., Cardew, A., Gilmore, M., Barry, J. P., Phillips, C., & Gravenor, M. B. (2017). Assessment of remote heart rhythm sampling using the AliveCor heart monitor to screen for atrial fibrillation: The REHEARSE-AF study. *Circulation*, *136*(19), 1784–1794. doi:10.1161/CIRCULATIONAHA.117.030583 PMID:28851729

Halder, M., Sarkar, A., & Bahar, H. (2019). Plant disease detection by image pro-cessing: A literature review. *Image*, *1*, 3.

Halevy, M., Harris, C., Bruckman, A., Yang, D., & Howard, A. (2021). Mitigating racial biases in toxic language detection with an equity-based ensemble framework. In *Equity and Access in Algorithms* (pp. 1–11). Mechanisms, and Optimization.

Halim, Z., Yousaf, M. N., Waqas, M., Sulaiman, M., Abbas, G., Hussain, M., Ahmad, I., & Hanif, M. (2021). An effective genetic algorithm-based feature selection method for intrusion detection systems. *Computers & Security*, *110*, 102448. doi:10.1016/j.cose.2021.102448

Hamad, L. I., Ahmed, E. S. A., & Saeed, R. A. (2022). *Machine learning in healthcare: Theory, applications, and future trends. AI applications for disease diagnosis and treatment*. IGI Global.

Hamdawi, W. (2004). *HR Management*. Université 8 mai 1945 - GUELMA.

Hameed, N., Shabut, A. M., Ghosh, M. K., & Hossain, M. A. (2020). Multi-class multi-level classification algorithm for skin lesions classification using machine learning techniques. *Expert Systems with Applications*, *141*, 112961. doi:10.1016/j.eswa.2019.112961

Hamidi, H., Abdolkarimi, E. S., & Mosavi, M. R. (2020). Prediction of MEMS-based INS error using interval type-2 fuzzy logic system in INS/GPS integration. *25th International Computer Conference, Computer Society of Iran*, 1-5. IEEE. 10.1109/CSICC49403.2020.9050081

Han, S., & Cointault, F. (2013, June). Détection précoce de maladies sur feuilles par traitement d'images. In Orasis, Congrès des jeunes chercheurs en vision par ordinateur.

Han, Y. (2004). Possible triggering of solar activity to big earthquakes (Ms>8) in faults with near west-east strike in China. *Science in China Series G, 47*(2), 173. doi:10.1360/03yw0103

Hanks, H., Austin, A., & Lopez, V. (2022). *EU study into medical AI highlights they re risks and sortcoming of legal frameworks.* Freshfields Bruckhaus Deringer. .https://www.lexology.com/library/detail.aspx?g=74477d47-da0e -4cb7-b272-0134f58537de

Hanni, A., Chickerur, S., & Bidari, I. (2017). Deep learning framework for scene based indoor location recognition. In *2017 International Conference on Technological Advancements in Power and Energy (TAP Energy)* (pp. 1-8). IEEE

Han, W., & Ye, Y. (2019). A repository of microbial marker genes related to human health and diseases for host phenotype prediction using micro- biome data. *Pacific Symposium on Biocomputing, 24*, 236–247. PMID:30864326

Hao, Z. (2019). Deep learning review and discussion of its future development. In *MATEC Web of Conferences*. EDP Sciences.

Hao, Y., Cheng, F., Pham, M., Rein, H., Patel, D., Fang, Y., Feng, Y., Yan, J., Song, X., Yan, H., & Wang, Y. (2019, April 23). A Noninvasive, Economical, and Instant-Result Method to Diagnose and Monitor Type 2 Diabetes Using Pulse Wave: Case-Control Study. *JMIR mHealth and uHealth, 7*(4), e11959. doi:10.2196/11959 PMID:31012863

Harakannanavar, S. S., Rudagi, J. M., Puranikmath, V. I., Siddiqua, A., & Pramodhini, R. (2022). *Plant Leaf Disease Detection using Computer Vision and Machine Learning Algorithms.* Global Transitions Proceedings. doi:10.1016/j. gltp.2022.03.016

Harfield, H. (1982). Identity crises in letter of credit law. *Arizona Law Review, 24*, 239.

Harvard Magazine. (2019). *Artificial Intelligence and Ethics.* Harvard Press. https://www.harvardmagazine.com/2019/01/artificial-intelligence-limita-tions

Hasan, A. M., Samsudin, K., Ramli, A. R., Azmir, R. S., & Ismaeel, S. A. (2009). A review of navigation systems (integration and algorithms). *Australian Journal of Basic and Applied Sciences, 3*(2), 943–959.

Hasan, M. K., Alam, M. A., Das, D., Hossain, E., & Hasan, M. (2020). Diabetes prediction using ensembling of different machine learning classifiers. *IEEE Access: Practical Innovations, Open Solutions, 8*, 76516–76531. doi:10.1109/ ACCESS.2020.2989857

Hassan, R. (2011). A strategic approach to planning and developing human resources (1 ed.). University house for printing, publishing and distribution.

Hathaway, Q. A., Roth, S. M., Pinti, M. V., Sprando, D. C., Kunovac, A., Durr, A. J., Cook, C. C., Fink, G. K., Cheuvront, T. B., Grossman, J. H., Aljahli, G. A., Taylor, A. D., Giromini, A. P., Allen, J. L., & Hollander, J. M. (2019). Machine-learning to stratify diabetic patients using novel cardiac biomarkers and integrative genomics. *Cardiovascular Diabetology, 18*(1), 1–16. doi:10.118612933-019-0879-0 PMID:31185988

Hayes, S. (2015). *MOOCs and Quality: A Review of the Recent Literature.* QAA MOOCs.

Hay, M. C., Cadigan, R. J., Khanna, D., Strathmann, C., Lieber, E., Altman, R., Mcmahon, M., Kokhab, M., & Furst, D. E. (2008). Prepared patients: Internet information seeking by new rheumatology patients. *Arthritis Care and Research, 59*(4), 575–582. doi:10.1002/art.23533 PMID:18383399

Hazelwood, K. (2018). Applied machine learning at Facebook: A data center infrastructure perspective. *IEEE International Symposium on High-Performance Computer Architecture (HPCA)*,620-629. IEEE/

He, P., Zhu, J., Xu, J., & Lyu, M. R. (2014). A hierarchical matrix factorization approach for location-based web service QoS prediction. *Proceedings - IEEE 8th International Symposium on Service Oriented System Engineering, SOSE 2014*, 290–295. IEEE. 10.1109/SOSE.2014.41

Hearst, M. (2011). User interfaces for search, 21–55. *Modern Information Retrieval*.

He, H., Zha, S., & Wang, H. (2019). Unlearn Dataset Bias in Natural Language Inference by Fitting the Residual. Proceedings of the 2nd Workshop on Deep Learning Approaches for Low-Resource NLP (DeepLo 2019), .

Heidenreich, H. (2018, 12 4). *What are the types of machine learning?* Towards Data Science. https://towardsdatascience.com/what-are-the-types-of-machine-learning-e2b9e5d1756f

He, K., Zhang, X., Ren, S., & Sun, J. (2015). Spatial pyramid pooling in deep convolutional networks for visual recognition. *IEEE Transactions on Pattern Analysis and Machine Intelligence, 37*(9), 1904–1916. doi:10.1109/TPAMI.2015.2389824 PMID:26353135

Henzinger, M. R., Motwani, R., & Silverstein, C. (2002). Challenges in web search engines. *ACM SIGIR Forum, 36*(2), 11–22.

Henzinger, M. R. (2004). Algorithmic challenges in web search engines. *Internet Mathematics, 1*(1), 115–123. doi:10.1080/15427951.2004.10129079

Hildebrand, J. (2018). Amazon Alexa: What kind of data does Amazon get from me? | Android Central. *Aljazeera*. https://www.aljazeera.com/economy/2021/11/19/how-much-does-amazon-know-about-you

Hind, M., Wei, D., Campbell, M., Codella, N. C., Dhurandhar, A., Mojsilović, A., Natesan Ramamurthy, K., & Varshney, K. R. (2019). TED: Teaching AI to explain its decisions. Proceedings of the 2019 AAAI/ACM Conference on AI, Ethics, and Society, Intahchomphoo, C., & Gundersen, O. E. (2020). Artificial intelligence and race: A systematic review. Legal Information Management, 20(2), 74–84

Hirschberg, J., & Manning, C. D. (2015). Advances in natural language processing. *Science, 349*(6245), 261–266. doi:10.1126cience.aaa8685 PMID:26185244

Hochreiter, S., & Schmidhuber, J. (1997). Long short-term memory. *Neural Computation, 9*(8), 1735–1780. https://doi.org/10.1162/neco.1997.9.8.1735

Hölzle, K. (2010). Designing and implementing a career path for project managers. *International Journal of Project Management, 28*(8), 779–786. doi:10.1016/j.ijproman.2010.05.004

Hooker, J., & Kim, T. W. (2019). *Ethical implications of the 4th Industrial Revolution for business and society*. Emerald Publishing Limited.

Hossain, M. S., & Muhammad, G. (2018). Emotion-Aware Connected Healthcare Big DataTowards 5G. *IEEE Internet of Things Journal, 5*(4), 2399–2406. doi:10.1109/jiot.2017.2772959

Hothorn, T., Hornik, K., & Zeileis, A. (2006). Unbiased recursive partitioning: A conditional inference framework. *Journal of Computational and Graphical Statistics*, *15*(3), 651–674. https://doi.org/10.1198/106186006X133933

Huang, T. S. (1996). Computer Vision: Evolution and Promise. *CERN European Organization for Nuclear Research-Reports-CERN*, 21 - 24.

Huang, C.-G., Huang, H.-Z., & Li, Y.-F. (2019, November). A bidirectional LSTM prognostics method under multiple operational conditions. *IEEE Transactions on Industrial Electronics*, *66*(11), 8792–8802. doi:10.1109/TIE.2019.2891463

Huang, G. J., & Penson, D. F. (2008). Internet health resources and the cancer patient. *Cancer Investigation*, *26*(2), 202–207. doi:10.1080/07357900701566197 PMID:18259953

Huang, J. Y., Tsai, C. H., & Huang, S. T. (2012). The next generation of GPS navigation systems. *Communications of the ACM*, *55*(3), 84–93. doi:10.1145/2093548.2093570

Hudec, M., & Smutny, Z. (2017). RUDO: A home ambient intelligence system for blind people. *Sensors (Basel)*, *17*(8), 1926.

Hutson, M. (2018). *How Researchers Are Teaching AI to Learn Like a Child*. Science. https://www.sciencemag.org/news/2018/05/how-researchers-are-teaching-ai-learn-child

IBM. (2019). *Hardin memorial health; AI solution informs radiologists with deep patient insights*. IBM. https://www.ibm.com/case-studies/hardin-memorial-health-watson-health

Ide, H., & Kurita, T. (2017). Improvement of learning for CNN with ReLU activation by sparse regularization. In *2017 International Joint Conference on Neural Networks (IJCNN)* (pp. 2684-2691). IEEE.

IDF. (2021). *Diabetes facts & figures*. IDF. https://idf.org/aboutdiabetes/what-is-diabetes/facts-figures.html#:~:text=Almost%201%20in%202%20(240,living%20with%20type%201%20diabetes .

Iglesias, J. E., & Sabuncu, M. R. (2015). Multi-atlas segmentation of biomedical images: A survey. *Medical Image Analysis*, *24*(1), 205–219. doi:10.1016/j.media.2015.06.012 PMID:26201875

Ikada, Y. (2006). Challenges in Tissue Engineering. *Journal of the Royal Society, Interface*, *3*(10), 589–601. https://doi.org/10.1098/rsif.2006.0124

Ilyas, M., Rehman, H., & Naït-Ali, A. (2020). Detection of covid-19 from chest x-ray images using artificial intelligence: An early review. Imaging explained. https://www.nps.org.au/consumers/imaging-explained

Imamverdiyev, Y. N., & Abdullayeva, F. J. (2020). Deep learning in cybersecurity: Challenges and approaches. *International Journal of Cyber Warfare & Terrorism*, *10*(2), 82–105. doi:10.4018/IJCWT.2020040105

Institut national de la recherche scientifique (INRS). (2021). Developing Bioactive Coatings for Better Orthopaedic Implants. https://medicalxpress.com/news/2021-12-bioactive-coatings-orthopaedic-implants.html

Institute of Entrepreneurship and Development. (2022). *How is AI Transforming the Future of Digital Marketing?* From https://ied.eu/blog/how-ai-transforming-the-future-of-digital-marketing/

International Air Transport Association (IATA). (2018) Artificial intelligence (AI) in the aviation industry. https://hosteddocs.ittoolbox.com/AI-White-Paper.pdf

International Civil Aviation Organization. (2002). Human Factors Guidelines for Safety Audits Manual (1st ed.). Doc. ICAO 9806-AN/763.

International Civil Aviation Organization. (2004). *Cross-Cultural Factors in Aviation Safety: Human Factors Digest Nº 16. Circ. ICAO 302-AN/175.*

International Civil Aviation Organization. (2005). *Global Air Traffic Management Operational Concept. Doc. ICAO 9854.*

International Civil Aviation Organization. (2009). Manual on Global Performance of the Air Navigation System (PBA). Doc. 9883.

International Civil Aviation Organization. (2012a). Manual on the Approval of Training Organizations. Doc. ICAO 9841-AN/456.

International Civil Aviation Organization. (2012b). *Manual on Flight and Flow Information for a Collaborative Environment (FF-ICE). Doc. 9965.*

International Civil Aviation Organization. (2013a). Safety Management Manual (SMM) (3rd ed.). Doc. ICAO 9859-AN 474.

International Civil Aviation Organization. (2013b). *State of Global Aviation Safety.*

International Civil Aviation Organization. (2014). *Manual on Collaborative Decision-Making (CDM), Doc. 9971.*

International Civil Aviation Organization. (2015). *Manual on System Wide Information Management (SWIM) Concept,* Doc. 10039-AN/511.

International Civil Aviation Organization. (2017a). *Global Aviation Security Plan (GASP).*

International Civil Aviation Organization. (2017b). *Global Air Navigation Plan (GANP), Doc 9750 Canada.*

International Civil Aviation Organization. (2018). Potential of Artificial Intelligence (AI) in Air Traffic Management (ATM). *In: Thirteenth Air Navigation Conference ICAO,* Montréal, Canada.

International Civil Aviation Organization. (2021). Handbook for CAAs on the Management of Aviation Safety Risks related to COVID-19. Doc 10144.

Iqbal, S., Ghani Khan, M. U., Saba, T., Mehmood, Z., Javaid, N., Rehman, A., & Abbasi, R. (2019). Deep learning model integrating features and novel classifiers fusion for brain tumor segmentation. *Microscopy Research and Technique, 82*(8), 1302–1315. doi:10.1002/jemt.23281 PMID:31032544

Irfan, M. (2019). A Review on Knowledge-Based Expert System. *The International journal of analytical and experimental modal analysis, 11*(4).

Iskandar, M., & Komara, D. (2018). Application marketing strategy search engine optimization (SEO). *IOP Conference Series. Materials Science and Engineering, 407,* 012011. doi:10.1088/1757-899X/407/1/012011

Islam, Md. Milon, Ashikur Rahaman, and Md. Rashedul Islam. 2020. "Development of SmartHealthcare Monitoring System in IoT Environment." *SN Computer Science* 1(3). doi:10.1007/s42979-020-00195-y

Islam, M. M., Newaz, A. A. R., & Karimoddini, A. (2022). Pedestrian Detection for Autonomous Cars: Inference Fusion of Deep Neural Networks. *IEEE Transactions on Intelligent Transportation Systems.*

Itani, M., Itani, M. A., Kaddoura, S., & Al Husseiny, F. (2022). The impact of the Covid-19 pandemic on online examination: Challenges and opportunities. *Global Journal of Engineering Education., 24*(2), 1–16.

Izonin, I., Tkachenko, R., Shakhovska, N., Ilchyshyn, B., & Singh, K. K. (2022). A Two-Step Data Normalization Approach for Improving Classification Accuracy. In *Medical Diagnosis Domain. Mathematics, 10*(11), 1942. doi:10.3390/math10111942

Jabarulla, M. Y., & Lee, H. (2021). A blockchain and artificial intelligence-based, patient-centric healthcare system for combating the COVID-19 pandemic: Opportunities and applications. *Healthcare, 9*(8) 1019.

Jackson, P., & Moulinier, I. (2012). *Natural Language Processing for Online Applications.* Cambridge University press.

Jacobovitz, O. (2016). Blockchain for identity management. *The Lynne and William Frankel Center for Computer Science Department of Computer Science. Ben-Gurion University, Beer Sheva, 1,* 9.

Jacobs, J. P. (2012). Bayesian support vector regression with automatic relevance determination kernel for modeling of antenna input characteristics. *IEEE Transactions on Antennas and Propagation, 60*(4), 2114–2118. https://doi.org/10.1109/TAP.2012.2186252

Jain, R., & Nayyar, A. (2018). Predicting employee attrition using xgboost machine learning approach. IEEE international conference on system modeling & advancement in research trends (smart), (pp. 113-120). IEEE.

Jain, G., Sharma, M., & Agarwal, B. (2019). Optimizing semantic LSTM for spam detection. *International Journal of Information Technology, 11*(2), 239–250. doi:10.100741870-018-0157-5

Jakson, D., Paglietti, L., & Ribeiro, M. (2015). Analyse de la filière oléicole, Tunisie. *Food and Agriculture Organization of the United Nations, Report No. 17.*

Janiesch, C., Zschech, P., & Heinrich, K. (2021). Machine learning and deep learning. *Electronic Markets, 31*(3), 685–695. doi:10.100712525-021-00475-2

Janson, S., Merkle, D., & Middendorf, M. (2008). A decentralization approach for swarm intelligence algorithms in networks applied to multi-swarm PSO. *International Journal of intelligent computing and cybernetics.*

Javed, F., Luo, Q., McNair, M., Jacob, F., Zhao, M., & Kang, T. (2015). Carotene: A job title classification system for the online recruitment domain. *IEEE First International Conference on Big Data Computing Service and Applications.* IEEE. 10.1109/BigDataService.2015.61

Jawahar, G., Sagot, B., & Seddah, D. (2019). What does BERT learn about the structure of language? ACL 2019-57th Annual Meeting of the Association for Computational Linguistics, 10.18653/v1/P19-1356

Jean-Philippe, R. (2018). *Enhancing Computer Network Defense Technologies with Machine Learning and Artificial Intelligence* [Doctoral dissertation, Utica College, USA].

Jiang, W., & Luo, J. (2021). Graph Neural Network for Traffic Forecasting. *Survey (London, England).* doi:10.48550/arxiv.2101.11174

Jie, Z., Zhiying, Z., & Li, L. (2021). A meta-analysis of watson for oncology in clinical application. *Scientific Reports, 11*(1), 1–13. doi:10.103841598-021-84973-5 PMID:33707577

Jin & Shan-W. (2017). Content-based image retrieval based on shape similarity calculation. *3D Research, 8*(3).

Johnson, K. B., Wei, W., Weeraratne, D., Frisse, M. E., Misulis, K., Rhee, K., Zhao, J., & Snowdon, J. L. (2021). Precision medicine, AI, and the future of personalized health care. *Clinical and Translational Science, 14*(1), 86–93. doi:10.1111/cts.12884 PMID:32961010

Jokanoviж, V. (2022). *Artificial Intelligence.* Taylor and Francis, Boca Raton.

Jonassen, D., Davidson, M., Collins, M., Campbell, J., & Haag, B. B. (1995). Constructivism and computer-mediated communication in distance education. *American Journal of Distance Education, 9*(2), 7–26. doi:10.1080/08923649509526885

Jones, B. (1997). HR: Fated to a supporting role? *Management Review, 86*(3), 7–8.

Jones, S., & Fox, S. (2009). *Generations online in 2009*. Pew Internet & American Life Project Washington.

Joseph, S. (2016). Natural Language Processing: A Review. *International Journal of Research in Engineering and Applied Sciences, 6*(3), 207–210. http://www.euroasiapub.org

Juneja, S., Dhiman, G., Kautish, S., Viriyasitavat, W., & Yadav, K. (2021). A perspective roadmap for IoMT-based early detection and care of the neural disorder, dementia. *Journal of Healthcare Engineering, 2021*, 2021. doi:10.1155/2021/6712424 PMID:34880977

Jwa, H., Oh, D., Park, K., Kang, J. M., & Lim, H. (2019). exbake: Automatic fake news detection model based on bidirectional encoder representations from transformers (bert). *Applied Sciences (Basel, Switzerland), 9*(19), 4062. doi:10.3390/app9194062

Kaddoura, S., Alfandi, O., & Dahmani, N. (2020, September). A spam email detection mechanism for English language text emails using deep learning approach. In *2020 IEEE 29th International Conference on Enabling Technologies: Infrastructure for Collaborative Enterprises (WETICE)* (pp. 193-198). IEEE. 10.1109/WETICE49692.2020.00045

Kaddoura, S., & Al Husseiny, F. (2021). An approach to reinforce active learning in higher education for I.T. students. *Global Journal of Engineering Education, 23*(1), 43–48.

Kaddoura, S., & Al Husseiny, F. (2021). An approach to reinforce active learning in higher education for IT students. *Global Journal of Engineering Education, 23*(1), 43–48.

Kaddoura, S., & Al Husseiny, F. (2021). Online learning on information security based on critical thinking andragogy. *World Transactions on Engineering and Technology Education, 19*(2), 157–162.

Kaddoura, S., Arid, A. E., & Moukhtar, M. (2021, November). Evaluation of Supervised Machine Learning Algorithms for Multi-class Intrusion Detection Systems. In *Proceedings of the Future Technologies Conference* (pp. 1-16). Springer.

Kaddoura, S., Chandrasekaran, G., Popescu, D. E., & Duraisamy, J. H. (2022). A systematic literature review on spam content detection and classification. *PeerJ. Computer Science, 8*, e830. doi:10.7717/peerj-cs.830 PMID:35174265

Kaddoura, S., & Grati, R. (2021). Blockchain for Healthcare and Medical Systems. In *Enabling Blockchain Technology for Secure Networking and Communications* (pp. 249–270). IGI Global. doi:10.4018/978-1-7998-5839-3.ch011

Kaddoura, S., Haraty, R. A., Al Kontar, K., & Alfandi, O. (2021). A parallelized database damage assessment approach after cyberattack for healthcare systems. *Future Internet, 13*(4), 90. doi:10.3390/fi13040090

Kaggle. (2018). *2018 Kaggle Machine Learning & Data Science Survey*. Kaggle: https://www.kaggle.com/datasets/kaggle/kaggle-survey-2018

Kakulapati, V., Chaitanya, K., Chaitanya, K., & Akshay, P. (2020). Predictive analytics of HR-A machine learning approach. *Journal of Statistics and Management Systems, 23*(6), 959–969. doi:10.1080/09720510.2020.1799497

Kaku, M. (2012). *Physics of the future: the inventions that will transform our lives*. Penguin.

Kalaï, A., Zayani, C. A., Amous, I., Abdelghani, W., & Sèdes, F. (2018). Social collaborative service recommendation approach based on user's trust and domain-specific expertise. *Future Generation Computer Systems, 80*, 355–367. doi:10.1016/j.future.2017.05.036

Kalakuntla, R., Vanamala, A., & Kolipyaka, R. (2019). Cyber Security. *Holistica.*, *10*(2), 115–128. doi:10.2478/hjbpa-2019-0020

Kalis, B., Collier, M., & Fu, R. (2018). 10 promising AI applications in health care. *Harvard Business Review.*

Kanamori, H., & Brodsky, E. E. (2004). The physics of earthquakes. *Reports on Progress in Physics*, *67*(8), 1429–1496. https://doi.org/10.1088/0034-4885/67/8/R03

Kanehisa, R. F., & Neto, A. d. (2019). Firearm Detection using Convolutional Neural Networks. *Proceedings of the 11th International Conference on Agents and Artificial Intelligence (ICAART 2019)*, (pp. 707-714). Scitepress.

Kang, M., & Jameson, N. J. (2018). Machine Learning: Fundamentals. In Prognostics and Health Management of Electronics: Fundamentals, Machine Learning, and the Internet of Things, (First ed., pp. 85 - 109). John Wiley & Sons Ltd.

Kaplan, A., & Haenlein, M. (2019). Siri, Siri, in my hand: Who's the fairest in the land? On the interpretations, illustrations, and implications of artificial intelligence. *Business Horizons*, *62*(1), 15–25. https://doi.org/10.1016/j.bushor.2018.08.004

Karam, C., El Zini, J., Awad, M., Saade, C., Naffaa, L., & El Amine, M. (2021). A Progressive and Cross-Domain Deep Transfer Learning Framework for Wrist Fracture Detection. *Journal of Artificial Intelligence and Soft Computing Research*, *12*(2), 101–120. doi:10.2478/jaiscr-2022-0007

Karimi, G. (2021, 04 15). *Introduction to YOLO Algorithm for Object Detection*. Section. https://www.section.io/engineering-education/introduction-to-yolo-algorithm-for-object-detection/

Karniadakis, G. E., Kevrekidis, I. G., Lu, L., Perdikaris, P., Wang, S., & Yang, L. (2021). Physics-informed machine learning. *Physics-informed machine learning. Nature Reviews Physics*, *3*(6), 422–440. doi:10.103842254-021-00314-5

Karnouskos, S. (2020). Artificial Intelligence in digital media: The era of deep fakes. *IEEE Transactions on Technology and Society.*, *1*(3), 138–147. doi:10.1109/TTS.2020.3001312

Kashyap, R. (2019a). Artificial Intelligence Systems in Aviation. In T. Shmelova & Yu. Sikirda (Eds.), *Cases on Modern Computer Systems in Aviation* (pp. 1–26). IGI Global.

Kashyap, R. (2019b). Decision Support Systems in Aeronautics and Aerospace Industries. In T. Shmelova & Yu. Sikirda (Eds.), *Automated Systems in the Aviation and Aerospace Industries* (pp. 138–165). IGI Global. doi:10.4018/978-1-5225-7709-6.ch005

Katoch, S., Chauhan, S. S., & Kumar, V. (2021). A review on genetic algorithm: Past, present, and future. *Multimedia Tools and Applications*, *80*(5), 8091–8126. doi:10.100711042-020-10139-6 PMID:33162782

Katzman, J. L., Shaham, U., Cloninger, A., Bates, J., Jiang, T., & Kluger, Y. (2018). DeepSurv: Personalized treatment recommender system using a cox proportional hazards deep neural network. *BMC Medical Research Methodology*, *18*(1), 1–12. doi:10.118612874-018-0482-1 PMID:29482517

Kaukoranta, M. (2015). How to reach more target customers by search engine optimization (SEO) and search engine advertising (SEA), 19-33. Seinäjoki University of Applied Sciences.

Kavakiotis, I., Tsave, O., Salifoglou, A., Maglaveras, N., Vlahavas, I., & Chouvarda, I. (2017). Machine learning and data mining methods in diabetes research. *Computational and Structural Biotechnology Journal*, *15*, 104–116. doi:10.1016/j.csbj.2016.12.005 PMID:28138367

Kavitha, S., Varuna, S., & Ramya, R. (2016). A comparative analysis on linear regression and support vector regression. Online international conference on green engineering and technologies. IEEE.

Kayalvizhi, R., Malarvizhi, S., Topkar, A., Vijayakumar, P., & Choudhury, S. D. (2020). Detection of sharp objects using deep neural network-based object detection algorithm. *In 2020 4th International Conference on Computer, Communication and Signal Processing (ICCCSP)*, (pp. 1 – 5). Semantic Scholar.

Kayani, B., Konan, S., Ayuob, A., Onochie, E., Al-Jabri, T., & Haddad, F. S. (2019). Robotic technology in total knee arthroplasty: A systematic review. *EFORT Open Reviews*, 4(10), 611–617. doi:10.1302/2058-5241.4.190022 PMID:31754467

Kelly, K. (2017). *The inevitable: understanding the 12 technological forces that will shape our future*. Penguin Books.

Kena, G., Musu-Gillette, L., Robinson, J., Wang, X., Rathbun, A., Zhang, J., & Dunlop Velez, E. (2015). *The Condition of Education 2015 (NCES 2015-144)*. US Department of Education, National Center for Education Statistics.

Kenton, J. D. M.-W. C., & Toutanova, L. K. (2019). BERT: Pre-training of Deep Bidirectional Transformers for Language Understanding. Proceedings of NAACL-HLT, .

Keras. (2021). *Keras: The Python deep learning API*. Keras.https://keras.io/

Khan, M. U. H. (2019). UAE's artificial intelligence strategies and pursuits. *Defence Journal*, 23(4), 19. https://www.proquest.com/scholarly-journals/uae-s-artificial-intelligence-strategies-pursuits/docview/2358556530/se-2?accountid=15192

Khanam, J. J., & Foo, S. Y. (2021). *A comparison of machine learning algorithms for diabetes prediction*. ICT Express. doi:10.1016/j.icte.2021.02.004

Khan, S., Alourani, A., Mishra, B., Ali, A., & Kamal, M. (2022). Developing a Credit Card Fraud Detection Model using Machine Learning Approaches. *International Journal of Advanced Computer Science and Applications*, 13(3). doi:10.14569/IJACSA.2022.0130350

Khanzode, K. C., & Sarode, R. D. (2020). Advantages and Disadvantages of Artificial Intelligence and Machine Learning: A Literature Review. *International Journal of Library and Information Science*, 9(1), 3.

Kharchenko, V., Shmelova, T., & Sikirda, Y. (2012). *Decision-Making of Operator in Air Navigation System: monograph*. Kirovograd: KFA of NAU.

Kharchenko, V., Shmelova, T., & Sikirda, Y. (2016). *Decision-Making in Socio-Technical Systems: monograph*. NAU.

Khashei, M., Eftekhari, S., & Parvizian, J. (2012). Diagnosing diabetes type II using a soft intelligent binary classification model. *Review of Bioinformatics and Biometrics*, 9-23.

Kidwai, B. & Nadesh, R.K. (2020). Design and Development of Diagnostic Chabot for Supporting Primary Health Care Systems. *Procedia Computer Science 167*, 75–84. doi:10.1016/j.procs.2020.03.184

Kilbertus, N., Rojas Carulla, M., Parascandolo, G., Hardt, M., Janzing, D., & Schölkopf, B. (2017). Avoiding discrimination through causal reasoning. *Advances in Neural Information Processing Systems*, 30.

Killoran, J. B. (2013). How to use search engine optimization techniques to increase website visibility. *IEEE Transactions on Professional Communication*, 56(1), 50–66. doi:10.1109/TPC.2012.2237255

Kim, S., Petrunin, I., & Shin, H. S. (2022). A Review of Kalman Filter with Artificial Intelligence Techniques. Integrated Communication, *Navigation and Surveillance Conference* (pp. 1-12). IEEE.

Kim, Z., Araujo, A., Cao, B., Askew, C., Sim, J., Green, M., Fodiatu Yilla, N. M., & Weyand, T. (2022). Improving Fairness in Large-Scale Object Recognition by CrowdSourced Demographic Information. *arXiv e-prints*, arXiv: 2206.01326.

Kim, H., & Gelenbe, E. (2012). Reconstruction of large-scale gene regulatory networks using bayesian model averaging. *IEEE Transactions on Nanobioscience*, *11*(3), 259–265. doi:10.1109/TNB.2012.2214233 PMID:22987132

Kim, H., Park, S., Jeong, I. G., Song, S. H., Jeong, Y., Kim, C., & Lee, K. H. (2020). Noninvasive precision screening of prostate cancer by urinary multimarker sensor and artificial intelligence analysis. *ACS Nano*, *15*(3), 4054–4065. doi:10.1021/acsnano.0c06946 PMID:33296173

Kim, J., Cheon, S., & Lim, J. (2022). IoT-based unobtrusive physical activity monitoring system for predicting dementia. *IEEE Access: Practical Innovations, Open Solutions*, *10*, 26078–26089. doi:10.1109/ACCESS.2022.3156607

Kim, N.-H., An, D., & Choi, J.-H. (2016). *Prognostics and Health Management of Engineering Systems: An Introduction*. Springer.

Kim, P. (2017). *MATLAB Deep Learning: with Machine Learning, Neural Networks and Artificial Intelligence*. Apress. doi:10.1007/978-1-4842-2845-6

Kingery, K. (2021). *Antimicrobial Coating for Orthopedic Implants Prevents Dangerous Infections*. Medicalxpress.com. https://medicalxpress.com/news/2021-09-antimicrobial-coating-orthopedic-implants-dangerous.html

Kingma, D. P., & Ba, J. (2014). Adam: A method for stochastic optimization. arXiv preprint arXiv:1412.6980.

Kiseľák, J., Lu, Y., Švihra, J., Szépe, P., & Stehlík, M. (2021). "SPOCU": Scaled polynomial constant unit activation function. *Neural Computing & Applications*, *33*(8), 3385–3401.

Klambauer, G., Unterthiner, T., Mayr, A., & Hochreiter, S. (2017). Self-normalizing neural networks. *Advances in Neural Information Processing Systems*, 30.

Knowledge Insead Education. (2019). *The TikTok Strategy: Using AI Platforms to Take Over the World* Knowledge Instead. https://knowledge.insead.edu/entrepreneurship/the-tiktok-strategy-using-ai-platforms-to-take-over-the-world-11776

Köchling, A., & Wehner, M. C. (2020). Discriminated by an algorithm: A systematic review of discrimination and fairness by algorithmic decision-making in the context of HR recruitment and HR development. *Business Research*, *13*(3), 795–848. doi:10.100740685-020-00134-w

Kohavi, R., & Provost, F. (1998). Glossary of terms. *Machine Learning*, *2*(2/3), 271–274.

Kolker, E., Özdemir, V., & Kolker, E. (2016). How healthcarecan refocus on its super-customers (patients, n= 1) and customers (doctors andnurses) by leveraging lessons from Amazon, Uber, and Watson. *Omics: ajournal of integrative biology*, *20*(6), 329-333.

Kong, Y. S., Abdullah, S., Schramm, D., Omar, M. Z., & Haris, S. M. (2019, May). Optimization of spring fatigue life prediction model for vehicle ride using hybrid multilayer perceptron artificial neural networks. *Mechanical Systems and Signal Processing*, *122*, 597–621. doi:10.1016/j.ymssp.2018.12.046

Kononenko, I., & Kukar, M. (2007). *Machine learning and data mining: Introduction to principles and algorithms*. Horwood Publishing.

Koren, Y., Rendle, S., & Bell, R. (2022). Advances in Collaborative Filtering. *Recommender Systems Handbook*, 91–142. doi:10.1007/978-1-0716-2197-4_3

Koskinen, H., Tanskanen, E., Pirjola, R., Pulkkinen, A., Dyer, C., Rodgers, D., Cannon, P., Mandeville, J.-C., & Boscher, D. (2001). Space weather effects catalogue. *ESA Space Weather Study*, *2*, 11–21.

Kotsiantis, S. B. (2007). Supervised machine learning: A review of classification techniques. In I. G. Maglogiannis (Ed.), *Emerging artificial intelligence applications in computer engineering: Real word AI systems with applications in eHealth, HCI, information retrieval and pervasive technologies* (pp. 3–24). IOS Press.

Kouhizadeh, M., & Sarkis, J. (2018). Blockchain practices, potentials, and perspectives in greening supply chains. *Sustainability*, *10*(10), 3652. doi:10.3390u10103652

Kowsher, M., Tahabilder, A., Sanjid, M. Z. I., Prottasha, N. J., Uddin, M. S., Hossain, M. A., & Jilani, M. A. K. (2021). LSTM-ANN & BiLSTM-ANN: Hybrid deep learning models for enhanced classification accuracy. *Procedia Computer Science*, *193*, 131–140. doi:10.1016/j.procs.2021.10.013

Kraev, V. M., & Tikhonov, A. I. (2020). Modern recruitment approaches in personnel selection. *Revista ESPACIOS, 41*(12).

Krishna, S., Gupta, R., Verma, A., Dhamala, J., Pruksachatkun, Y., & Chang, K.-W. (2022). Measuring Fairness of Text Classifiers via Prediction Sensitivity. Proceedings of the 60th Annual Meeting of the Association for Computational Linguistics (Volume 1: Long Papers), Laugel, T., Lesot, M.-J., Marsala, C., Renard, X., & Detyniecki, M. (2017). Inverse classification for comparison-based interpretability in machine learning. *arXiv preprint arXiv:1712.08443*. 10.18653/v1/2022.acl-long.401

Krishna, M. M., Neelima, M., Harshali, M., & Rao, M. V. (2018). Image classification using Deep learning. *IACSIT International Journal of Engineering and Technology*, 7.

Kritikos, K., & Plexousakis, D. (2009). Requirements for QoS-Based Web Service Description and Discovery. *IEEE Transactions on Services Computing*, *2*(4), 320–337. doi:10.1109/TSC.2009.26

Krizanova, A., Lăzăroiu, G., Gajanova, L., Kliestikova, J., Nadanyiova, M., & Moravcikova, D. (2019). The effectiveness of marketing communication and the importance of its evaluation in an online environment. *Sustainability*, *11*(24), 1–19. doi:10.3390u11247016

Krizhevsky, A., & Hinton, G. (2009). Learning multiple layers of features from tiny images. Academic Press.

Krizhevsky, A., Sutskever, I., & Hinton, G. (2012). ImageNet classification with deep convolutional neural networks. *Advances in Neural Information Processing Systems*, *25*, 1097–1105.

Krizhevsky, A., Sutskever, I., & Hinton, G. E. (2017). ImageNet classification with deep convolutional neural networks. *Communications of the ACM*, *60*(6), 84–90. doi:10.1145/3065386

Kubicka, M., Cela, A., Mounier, H., & Niculescu, S. I. (2018). Comparative study and application-oriented classification of vehicular map-matching methods. *IEEE Intelligent Transportation Systems Magazine*, *10*(2), 150–166. IEEE. doi:10.1109/MITS.2018.2806630

Kumar, K., & Thakur, G. S. M. (2012). Advanced applications of neural networks and artificial intelligence: A review. *International journal of information technology and computer science*, *4*(6), 57.

Kumar, S., Oh, I., Schindler, S., Lai, A. M., Payne, P. R., & Gupta, A. (2021). Machine learning for modeling the progression of alzheimer disease dementia using clinical data: A systematic literature review. *JAMIA Open*, *4*(3), ooab052.

Kumar, A., Gadag, S., & Nayak, U. Y. (2021). The beginning of a new era: Artificial intelligence in healthcare. *Advanced Pharmaceutical Bulletin*, *11*(3), 414–425. doi:10.34172/apb.2021.049 PMID:34513616

Kumar, A., Singh, A. K., Ahmad, I., Kumar Singh, P., Verma, P. K., Alissa, K. A., & Tag-Eldin, E. (2022). A novel decentralized blockchain architecture for the preservation of privacy and data security against cyberattacks in healthcare. *Sensors (Basel)*, *22*(15), 5921. doi:10.339022155921 PMID:35957478

Kumar, P., & Sharma, P. (2014). 05). Artificial Neural Networks-A Study. *International Journal of Emerging Engineering Research and Technology*, 2(2), 143–148.

Kusetogullari, H., Demirel, H., Celik, T., & Bayindir, S. (2007). Real time detection and tracking of vehicles for speed measurement and licence plate detection. In *The Seventh IASTED International Conference on Visualization, Imaging and Image Processing*, (pp. 53 – 58). Research Gate.

Kuzlu, M., Fair, C. & Guler, O. (2021). Role of artificial intelligence in the inter-net of things (iot) cybersecurity. *Discover Internet of things, 1*(1). doi:10.1007/s43926-020-00001-4

Lai, H., Huang, H., Keshavjee, K., Guergachi, A., & Gao, X. (2019). Predictive models for diabetes mellitus using machine learning techniques. *BMC Endocrine Disorders*, 19(1), 1–9. doi:10.118612902-019-0436-6 PMID:31615566

Lakhani, P., Prater, A. B., Hutson, R. K., Andriole, K. P., Dreyer, K. J., Morey, J., ... Itri, J. N. (2018). Machine learning in radiology: Applications beyond image interpretation. *Journal of the American College of Radiology*, 15(2), 350–359. doi:10.1016/j.jacr.2017.09.044 PMID:29158061

Lakhani, P., & Sundaram, B. (2017). Deep learning at chest radiography: Automated classification of pulmonary tuberculosis by using convolutional neural networks. *Radiology*, 284(2), 574–582. doi:10.1148/radiol.2017162326 PMID:28436741

Lambora, A., Gupta, K., & Chopra, K. (2019, February). Genetic algorithm-A literature review. In 2019 international conference on machine learning, big data, cloud and parallel computing (COMITCon). IEEE.

Lambora, A., Gupta, K., & Chopra, K. (2019, February). *Genetic algorithm-A literature review. In 2019 international conference on machine learning, big data, cloud and parallel computing (COMITCon)*. IEEE.

Landa, J. T. (1994). *Trust, Ethnicity, and Identity: beyond the new institutional economics of ethnic trading networks, contract law, and gift-exchange*. University of Michigan Press.

Laricchia, F. (2017). *Factors surrounding preference of voice assistants over websites and applications, worldwide, as of 2017*. Statista. https://www.statista.com/statistics/801980/worldwide-preference-voice-assistant-websites-app/

Larroza, A., Bodí, V., & Moratal, D. (2016). Texture analysis in magnetic resonance imaging: review and considerations for future applications. *Assessment of cellular and organ function and dysfunction using direct and derived MRI methodologies*, 75-106.

Lasseter, R. H., & Paigi, P. (2004). Microgrid: A conceptual solution. *In Proceedings of 35th annual power electronics specialists conference* (vol. 6, pp. 4285-4290). IEEE.

Laumer, S., Maier, C., & Weitzel, T. (2022). HR machine learning in recruiting. In *Handbook of Research on Artificial Intelligence in Human Resource Management*. Edward Elgar Publishing.

Lazić. L. (2019, October). *Benefit from Ai in cybersecurity*. In The 11th International Conference on Business Information Security (BISEC-2019). *Belgrade, Serbia*.

Lazik, A., Landgraeber, S., Claßen, T., Kraff, O., Lauenstein, T. C., & Theysohn, J. M. (2015). Aspects of postoperative magnetic resonance imaging of patients with avascular necrosis of the femoral head, treated by advanced core decompression. *Skeletal Radiology*, 44(10), 1467–1475. doi:10.100700256-015-2192-7 PMID:26093539

Le Quy, T., Roy, A., Iosifidis, V., Zhang, W., & Ntoutsi, E. (2022). A survey on datasets for fairness-aware machine learning. *Wiley Interdisciplinary Reviews. Data Mining and Knowledge Discovery*, 12(3), 1452. doi:10.1002/widm.1452

Le, D.-N., Parvathy, V. S., Gupta, D., Khanna, A., Rodrigues, J., & Shankar, K. (2021). IoT Enabled Depth wise Separable Convolution Neural Network with Deep Support Vector Machine for COVID-19 Diagnosis and Classification. *International Journal of Machine Learning and Cybernetics*. https://doi.org/10.1007/s13042-020-01248-7

Lechner, M., Strittmatter, A., & Knaus, M. (2020). Heterogeneous employment effects of job search programmes: A machine learning approach. *The Journal of Human Resources*.

Ledford, J. L. (2015). *Search engine optimization bible* (Vol. 584). John Wiley & Sons.

Lee, H., Choi, T. K., Lee, Y. B., Cho, H. R., Ghaffari, R., Wang, L., & Hyeon, T. (2016). A graphene-based electrochemical device with thermoresponsive microneedles for diabetes monitoring and therapy. *Nature Nanotechnology*, *11*(6), 566–572. doi:10.1038/nnano.2016.38 PMID:26999482

Lee, H., Grosse, R., Ranganath, R., & Ng, A. Y. (2009). Convolutional deep belief networks for scalable unsupervised learning of hierarchical representations. In *Proceedings of the 26th annual international conference on machine learning*, (pp. 609 – 616). ACM.

Lee, J., Jin, C., Liu, Z., & Ardakani, H. D. (2017). Introduction to data-driven methodologies for prognostics and health management. In *Probabilistic Prognostics and Health Management of Energy Systems* (1st ed., pp. 9–32). Springer. doi:10.1007/978-3-319-55852-3_2

Lee, J., Shin, J.-H., & Kim, J.-S. (2017). Interactive visualization and manipulation of attention-based neural machine translation. Proceedings of the 2017 Conference on Empirical Methods in Natural Language Processing: System Demonstrations, .

Lee, L. (2015). New kids on the blockchain: How bitcoin's technology could reinvent the stock market. *Hastings Bus. LJ*, *12*, 81. doi:10.2139srn.2656501

Lee, M., Won, S., Kim, J., Lee, H., Park, C., & Jung, K. (2021). CrossAug: A Contrastive Data Augmentation Method for Debiasing Fact Verification Models. *Proceedings of the 30th ACM International Conference on Information & Knowledge Management*

Lee, S. B., Gui, X., Manquen, M., & Hamilton, E. R. (2019, October). Use of training, validation, and test sets for developing automated classifiers in quantitative ethnography. In *International Conference on Quantitative Ethnography* (pp. 117-127). Springer. 10.1007/978-3-030-33232-7_10

Lei, M., Liang, X., Tang, J., & Zhou, J. (2021). Multipath Error Correction Method for Slope Monitoring Based on BP Neural Network. *China Satellite Navigation Conference (CSNC 2021) Proceedings* (pp. 101-110). Springer. 10.1007/978-981-16-3138-2_11

Leo Kumar, S. P. (2019). Knowledge-based expert system in manufacturing planning: State-of-the-art review. *International Journal of Production Research*, *57*(15-16), 4766–4790. doi:10.1080/00207543.2018.1424372

Létinier, L., Jouganous, J., Benkebil, M., Bel-Létoile, A., Goehrs, C., Singier, A., ... Micallef, J. (2021). Artificial intelligence for unstructured healthcare data: Application to coding of patient reporting of adverse drug reactions. *Clinical Pharmacology and Therapeutics*, *110*(2), 392–400. doi:10.1002/cpt.2266 PMID:33866552

Lewandowski, D., & Kammerer, Y. (2021). Factors influencing viewing behaviour on search engine results pages: A review of eye-tracking research. *Behaviour & Information Technology*, *40*(14), 1485–1515. doi:10.1080/0144929X.2020.1761450

Lewis, G. (2016). *Object Detection for Autonomous Vehicles*. Stanford University. https://web.stanford.edu/class/cs231a/prev_projects_2016/object-detection-autonomous.pdf

Lexuan, Y. (2020). Improvements on Activation Functions in ANN: An Overview. *Management Science and Engineering*, *14*(1), 53–58.

Leychenko, S., Malishevskiy, A., & Mikhalic, N. (2006). *Human Factors in Aviation: monograph in two books. Book 1st.* YMEKS.

Li, H. (2015). A convolutional neural network cascade for face detection. *Proceedings of the IEEE conference on computer vision and pattern recognition*. IEEE. 10.1109/CVPR.2015.7299170

Liddy, L., Hovy, E., Lin, J., Prager, J., Radev, D., Vanderwende, L., & Weischedel, R. (2016). Natural Language Processing. *Research Gate*.

Liebowitz, J. (1988). *Introduction to Expert Systems*. Mitchell Publishing/McGraw Hill.

Liebowitz, J. (1995). Expert Systems: A Short Introduction. *Engineering Fracture Mechanics*, *50*(5), 601–607. doi:10.1016/0013-7944(94)E0047-K

Lies, J. (2019). Marketing intelligence and big data: Digital marketing techniques on their way to becoming social engineering techniques in marketing. *International Journal of Interactive Multimedia and Artificial Intelligence*, *5*(5), 134–144. doi:10.9781/ijimai.2019.05.002

Li, H. (2019). Special section introduction: Artificial Intelligence and advertising. *Journal of Advertising*, *48*(4), 333–337. doi:10.1080/00913367.2019.1654947

Lihua, M., & Wang, M. (2013). Influence of Ephemeris Error on GPS Single Point Positioning Accuracy. *Artificial Satellites*, *48*(3), 125–139. doi:10.2478/arsa-2013-0011

Li, J. H. (2018). Cyber security meets artificial intelligence: A survey. *Frontiers of Information Technology & Electronic Engineering*, *19*(12), 1462–1474. doi:10.1631/FITEE.1800573

Li, K., Fang, B., Cui, X., & Liu, Q. (2016). Research on the development of botnets. *Jisuanji Yanjiu Yu Fazhan*, *53*(10), 2189–2206.

Lin, T.-Y., Maire, M., Belongie, S., Hays, J., Perona, P., Ramanan, D., & Zitnick, L. (2014). Microsoft COCO: Common Objects in Context. *European Conference on Computer Vision*, (pp. 740-755). Springer.

Ling, S. H., San, P. P., & Nguyen, H. T. (2016). Non-invasive hypoglycemia monitoring system using extreme learning machine for Type 1 diabetes. *ISA Transactions*, *64*, 440–446. doi:10.1016/j.isatra.2016.05.008 PMID:27311357

LinkedIn Engineering. (2018). *An Introduction to AI at LinkedIn*. LinkedIn. https://engineering.linkedin.com/blog/2018/10/an-introduction-to-ai-at-linkedin#:~:text=How%20do%20we%20use%20AI,helpful%20content%20in%20the%20feed

Lin, T.-Y., Dollar, P., Girshick, R., He, K., Hariharan, B., & Belongie, S. (2017). Feature Pyramid Networks for Object Detection. *Feature pyramid networks for object detection. In Proceedings of the IEEE conference on computer vision and pattern recognition*, (pp. 2117 – 2125). IEEE.

Lin, T.-Y., Goyal, P., Girshick, R., He, K., & Dollar, P. (2020). Focal Loss for Dense Object Detection. *IEEE Transactions on Pattern Analysis and Machine Intelligence*, *42*(2), 318–327. doi:10.1109/TPAMI.2018.2858826 PMID:30040631

Litke, A., Anagnostopoulos, D., & Varvarigou, T. (2019). Blockchains for supply chain management: Architectural elements and challenges towards a global scale deployment. *Logistics*, *3*(1), 5. doi:10.3390/logistics3010005

Liu, J., Allen, P., L., B., Blickstein, D., Okidi, E., & Shi, X. (2021). A Machine Learning Approach for Recruitment Prediction. *Clinical Trial Design. arXiv.*

Liu, W., Anguelov, D., Erhan, D., Szegedy, C., Reed, S., Fu, C. Y., & Berg, A. (2016, 10). SSD: Single shot multibox detector. In *European conference on computer vision*, (pp. 21 – 37). Springer.

Liu, W., Anguelov, D., Erhan, D., Szegedy, C., Reed, S., Fu, C. Y., & Berg, A. C. (2016). Ssd: Single shot multibox detector. In European conference on computer vision (pp. 21-37). Springer.

Liu, G. H., Chen, M. Z., & Chen, Y. (2019). When joggers meet robots: The past, present, and future of research on humanoid robots. *Bio-Design and Manufacturing*, 2(2), 108–118. doi:10.100742242-019-00038-7

Liu, H., Yin, Q., & Wang, W. Y. (2019). Towards Explainable NLP: A Generative Explanation Framework for Text Classification. *Proceedings of the 57th Annual Meeting of the Association for Computational Linguistics*

Liu, L., & Özsu, M. T. (2009). *Encyclopedia of database systems* M. T. Özsu, (ed.). (Vol. 6). Springer. doi:10.1007/978-0-387-39940-9

Liu, T., Xin, Z., Ding, X., Chang, B., & Sui, Z. (2020). An Empirical Study on Model-agnostic Debiasing Strategies for Robust Natural Language Inference. *Proceedings of the 24th Conference on Computational Natural Language Learning*

Liu, Y., Fan, X., Lv, C., Wu, J., Li, L., & Ding, D. (2018). An innovative information fusion method with adaptive Kalman filter for integrated INS/GPS navigation of autonomous vehicles. *Mechanical Systems and Signal Processing*, 100, 605–616. doi:10.1016/j.ymssp.2017.07.051

Liu, Y., Jain, A., Eng, C., Way, D. H., Lee, K., Bui, P., & Gabriele, S. (2020). A deep learning system for differential diagnosis of skin diseases. *Nature Medicine*, 26(6), 900–908. doi:10.103841591-020-0842-3 PMID:32424212

Liu, Y., Luo, Q., & Zhou, Y. (2022). Deep Learning-Enabled Fusion to Bridge GPS Outages for INS/GPS Integrated Navigation. *IEEE Sensors Journal*, 22(9), 8974–8985. doi:10.1109/JSEN.2022.3155166

Liu, Y., Yu, Z., & Sun, H. (2021). Treatment effect of type 2 diabetes patients in outpatient department based on blockchain electronic mobile medical app. *Journal of Healthcare Engineering*, 2021, 1–12. doi:10.1155/2021/6693810 PMID:33728034

Li, Y., Han, Z., Xu, H., Liu, L., Li, X., & Zhang, K. (2019). YOLOv3-Lite: A Lightweight Crack Detection Network for Aircraft Structure Based on Depthwise Separable Convolutions. *Applied Sciences (Basel, Switzerland)*, 9(18), 3781. doi:10.3390/app9183781

Li, Y., Liu, Y., Jiang, Z., Guan, J., Yi, G., Cheng, S., Yang, B., Fu, T., & Wang, Z. (2009). Behavioral change related to Wenchuan devastating earthquake in mice. *Bioelectromagnetics*, 30(8), 613–620. https://doi.org/10.1002/bem.20520

Li, Z., Kang, J., Yu, R., Ye, D., Deng, Q., & Zhang, Y. (2017). Consortium blockchain for secure energy trading in industrial internet of things. *IEEE Transactions on Industrial Informatics*, 14(8), 3690–3700. doi:10.1109/TII.2017.2786307

Logpoint Team. (2021, October 13). *Cyber security: Definition, importance and benefits of cyber security.* LogPoint.

Lopezosa, C., Codina, L., Díaz-Noci, J., & Ontalba, J. (2020). SEO and the digital news media: From the workplace to the classroom. *Media Education Research Journal*, 28(63), 65-75.

Lotsch, J., Kringel, D., & Ultsch, A. (2021). Explainable Artificial Intelligence (XAI) in Biomedicine: Making AI Decisions Trustworthy for Physicians and Patients. *BioMedInformatics*, 2(1), 1–17. doi:10.3390/biomedinformatics2010001

Louis, C. (2021). 10 Ways AI And Machine Learning Are Improving Marketing In 2021. *Forbes*. https://www.forbes.com/sites/louiscolumbus/2021/02/21/10-ways-ai-and-machine-learning-are-improving-marketing-in-2021/?sh=78133b2b14c8

Loutas, T. H., Roulias, D., & Georgoulas, G. (2013). Remaining useful life estimation in rolling bearings utilizing data-driven probabilistic e-support vectors regression. *IEEE Transactions on Reliability*, *62*(4), 821–832. https://doi.org/10.1109/TR.2013.2285318

Love, J. J., & Thomas, J. N. (2013). Insignificant solar-terrestrial triggering of earthquakes: INSIGNIFICANT TRIGGERING. *Geophysical Research Letters*, *40*(6), 1165–1170. https://doi.org/10.1002/grl.50211

Lowe, D. G. (2004). Distinctive image features from scale-invariant keypoints. *International Journal of Computer Vision*, *60*(2), 91–110. doi:10.1023/B:VISI.0000029664.99615.94

Lu, X., & Song, R. (2022, August). A Hybrid Deep Learning Model for the Blood Glucose Prediction. In *2022 IEEE 11th Data Driven Control and Learning Systems Conference (DDCLS)* (pp. 1037-1043). IEEE. 10.1109/DDCLS55054.2022.9858348

Lu, Y., & Zhou, Y. (2019). A short review on the economics of artificial intelligence. *Journal of Economic Surveys*.

Lucas, Y., & Jurgovsky, J. (2020). Credit card fraud detection using machine learning. *Survey (London, England)*.

Lucieri, A., Bajwa, M. N., Braun, S. A., Malik, M. I., Dengel, A., & Ahmed, S. (2022). ExAID: A multimodal explanation framework for computer-aided diagnosis of skin lesions. *Computer Methods and Programs in Biomedicine*, *215*, 106620.

Luckin, R., Holmes, W., Griffiths, M., & Forcier, L. B. (2016). *Intelligence unleashed: An argument for AI in education*. Pearson.

Lundberg, S. M., & Lee, S.-I. (2017). A unified approach to interpreting model predictions. *Advances in Neural Information Processing Systems*, 30.

Lunenburg, F. C. (2010). The decision making process. *National Forum of Educational Administration & Supervision Journal*, *27*(4).

Lu, S., Christie, G. A., Nguyen, T. T., Freeman, J. D., & Hsu, E. B. (2022). Applications of artificial intelligence and machine learning in disasters and public health emergencies. *Disaster Medicine and Public Health Preparedness*, *16*(4), 1674–1681. doi:10.1017/dmp.2021.125 PMID:34134815

Lu, Z., Qian, P., Bi, D., Ye, Z., He, X., Zhao, Y., Su, L., Li, S., & Zhu, Z. (2021). Application of AI and IoT in clinical medicine: Summary and challenges. *Current Medical Science*, *41*(6), 1134–1150. doi:10.100711596-021-2486-z PMID:34939144

Lv, S., Yi, F., He, P., & Zeng, C. (2022). QoS Prediction of Web Services Based on a Two-Level Heterogeneous Graph Attention Network. *IEEE Access: Practical Innovations, Open Solutions*, *10*, 1871–1880. IEEE. doi:10.1109/ACCESS.2021.3138127

Magazzeni, D., McBurney, P., & Nash, W. (2017). Validation and verification of smart contracts: A research agenda. *Computer*, *50*(9), 50–57. doi:10.1109/MC.2017.3571045

Mahendran, A., & Vedaldi, A. (2016). Salient deconvolutional networks. European conference on computer vision

Maher, A. (2018). HR Management (7 ed.). University house for printing, publishing and distribution.

Mahesh, B. (2020). Machine learning algorithms-a review. *International Journal of Science and Research (IJSR).[Internet]*, *9*, 381-386.

Maier, H. R., Razavi, S., Kapelan, Z., Matott, L. S., Kasprzyk, J., & Tolson, B. A. (2019). Introductory overview: Optimization using evolutionary algorithms and other metaheuristics. *Environmental Modelling & Software*, *114*, 195–213. doi:10.1016/j.envsoft.2018.11.018

Mainkar, P.M., Ghorpade, S., & Adawadkar, M.P. (2015). Plant Leaf Disease Detection and Classification Using Image Processing Techniques. *International Journal of Innovative and Emerging Research in Engineering*.

Makhortykh, M., Urman, A., & Ulloa, R. (2021). Detecting race and gender bias in visual representation of AI on web search engines. *International Workshop on Algorithmic Bias in Search and Recommendation*, (pp. 36–50). Springer. 10.1007/978-3-030-78818-6_5

Malini, N., & Pushpa, M. (2017, February). Analysis on credit card fraud identification techniques based on KNN and outlier detection. In *2017 third international conference on advances in electrical, electronics, information, communication and bio-informatics (AEEICB)* (pp. 255-258). IEEE. 10.1109/AEEICB.2017.7972424

Mallouhy, R., Jaoude, C. A., Guyeux, C., & Makhoul, A. (2019). Major earthquake event prediction using various machine learning algorithms. *2019 International Conference on Information and Communication Technologies for Disaster Management (ICT-DM)*, 1–7. doi:10.1109/ICT-DM47966.2019.9032983

Maltarollo, V. G., Honório, K. M., & da Silva, A. B. (2013). Applications of artificial neural networks in chemical problems. *Artificial neural networks-architectures and applications*, (pp. 203 – 233). Semantic Scholar..

Mangalathu, S., Sun, H., Nweke, C. C., Yi, Z., & Burton, H. V. (2020). Classifying earthquake damage to buildings using machine learning. *Earthquake Spectra*, *36*(1), 183–208. https://doi.org/10.1177/8755293019878137

Manickam, P., Mariappan, S. A., Murugesan, S. M., Hansda, S., Kaushik, A., Shinde, R., & Thipperudraswamy, S. P. (2022). Artificial intelligence (AI) and internet of medical things (IoMT) assisted biomedical systems for intelligent healthcare. *Biosensors (Basel)*, *12*(8), 562. doi:10.3390/bios12080562 PMID:35892459

Mantripragada, M. (2020). Digging deep into YOLO V3 - A hands-on guide Part 1. *Towards Data Science*. https://towardsdatascience.com/digging-deep-into-yolo-v3-a-hands-on-guide-part-1-78681f2c7e29

Mao, L., Xie, M., Huang, Y., & Zhang, Y. (2010). Preceding vehicle detection using histograms of oriented gradients. In *2010 International Conference on Communications, Circuits and Systems (ICCCAS)* (pp. 354-358). IEEE. 10.1109/ICCCAS.2010.5581983

Ma, P., Wang, S., & Liu, J. (2020). Metamorphic Testing and Certified Mitigation of Fairness Violations in NLP Models. IJCAI, 10.24963/ijcai.2020/64

Marchitelli, V., Harabaglia, P., Troise, C., & De Natale, G. (2020). On the correlation between solar activity and large earthquakes worldwide. *Scientific Reports*, *10*(1), 11495. https://doi.org/10.1038/s41598-020-67860-3

Marco, V. (2017). What is Machine Learning? A Deinition. *Expert System*. www.expertsystem.com/machine-learning-definition/

MarketsandMarkets. (2022). *Artificial Intelligence in Healthcare Market Worth $67.4 Billion by 2027*. MarketsandMarketsTM. https://www.prnewswire.co.uk/news-releases/artificial-intelligence-in-healthcare-market-worth-67-4-billion-by-2027-exclusive-report-by-marketsandmarkets-tm--878720500.html

Markowski, M. (2018). *4 Ways AI Is Transforming the Healthcare Industry*. Herzing University. https://www.herzing.edu/blog/4-ways-ai-transforming-healthcare-industry

Marr, B. (2018*).* Artificial intelligence and Blockchain: 3 major benefits of combining these two mega-trends. *Forbes.* https:// www.forbes. com/sites/Barnard Marr/2018/03/02/artificial-intelligence and-blockchain-3-major-benefits-of combining-these-two-mega-trends/

Marr, B. (2018). How is AI used in healthcare-5 powerful real-world examples that show the latest advances. *Forbes,* (July), 27.

Marshall, S. (2016). Technological innovation of higher education in New Zealand: A wicked problem? *Studies in Higher Education, 41*(2), 288–301. doi:10.1080/03075079.2014.927849

Marston, J. R., & Golledge, R. G. (2003). The hidden demand for participation in activities and travel by persons who are visually impaired. *Journal of Visual Impairment & Blindness, 97*(8), 475–488. doi:10.1177/0145482X0309700803

Martineau, K. (2020). *Marshaling Artificial Intelligence in the Fight against Covid-19.* MIT News. https://news.mit.edu/2020/mit-marshaling-artificial-intelligence-fight-against-covid-19-0519

Martínez Torres, J., Iglesias Comesaña, C., & García-Nieto, P. J. (2019). Machine learning techniques applied to cybersecurity. *International Journal of Machine Learning and Cybernetics, 10*(10), 2823–2836. doi:10.100713042-018-00906-1

Martinez-Vernon, A. S., Covington, J. A., Arasaradnam, R. P., Esfahani, S., O'connell, N., Kyrou, I., & Savage, R. S. (2018). An improved machine learning pipeline for urinary volatiles disease detection: Diagnosing diabetes. *PLoS One, 13*(9), e0204425. doi:10.1371/journal.pone.0204425 PMID:30261000

Marwala, T., & Xing, B. (2018). Blockchain and artificial intelligence. arXiv.

Mason, M. (2010, August). Sample size and saturation in Ph.D. studies using qualitative interviews. In Forum Qualitative Sozialforschung/Forum: qualitative social research, 11(3).

Mateus, A., Ribeiro, D., Miraldo, P., & Nascimento, J. C. (2019). Efficient and robust pedestrian detection using deep learning for human-aware navigation. Robotics and Autonomous Systems, 113, 23-37.

Mathieu-Dupas, E. (2010). *Algorithme des k plus proches voisins pondérés et application en diagnostic. In 42èmes Journées de Statistique.*

Matsuzaka, Y., & Uesawa, Y. (2022). A deep learning-based quantitative Structure–Activity relationship system construct prediction model of agonist and antagonist with high performance. *International Journal of Molecular Sciences, 23*(4), 2141. doi:10.3390/ijms23042141 PMID:35216254

Mauldin, T. R., Canby, M. E., Metsis, V., Ngu, A. H., & Rivera, C. C. (2018). SmartFall: A smartwatch-based fall detection system using deep learning. *Sensors (Basel), 18*(10), 3363. doi:10.339018103363 PMID:30304768

Maulud, D., & Abdulazeez, A. M. (2020). A review on linear regression comprehensive in machine learning. *Journal of Applied Science and Technology Trends, 1*(4), 140–147. doi:10.38094/jastt1457

Ma, Y., Wang, S., Hung, P. C. K., Hsu, C. H., Sun, Q., & Yang, F. (2016). A highly accurate prediction algorithm for unknown web service QoS values. *IEEE Transactions on Services Computing, 9*(4), 511–523. IEEE. doi:10.1109/TSC.2015.2407877

McCarthy, J. (2019). *Artificial Intelligence tutorial - It's your time to innovate the future.* Data Flair. https://data-flair. training/blogs/artificial-intelligence-ai-tutorial

McGhin, T., Choo, K. K. R., Liu, C. Z., & He, D. (2019). Blockchain in healthcare applications: Research challenges and opportunities. *Journal of Network and Computer Applications, 135,* 62–75. doi:10.1016/j.jnca.2019.02.027

McHale, J. (2010). *Fundamental rights and health care* Health Rights..

McKinsey. (2015). *By 2025, Internet of Things Applications Could Have $11 Trillion Impact.* McKinsey &Company. https://www.mckinsey.com/mgi/overview/in-the-news/by-2025-internet-of-things-applications-could-have-11-trillion-impact

McNutt, S. R., & Roman, D. C. (2015). Volcanic seismicity. In The Encyclopedia of Volcanoes (pp. 1011–1034). Elsevier. https://doi.org/10.1016/B978-0-12-385938-9.00059-6.

Mehra, A. (n.d.) *Artificial Intelligence in Healthcare MarketWorth $45.2 Billion by 2026.* MarketsandMarkets. https://www.marketsandmarkets.com/PressReleases/artificial-intelligence-healthcare.asp

Mehta, S. (2020). *The Future of Artificial Intelligence (AI) in Healthcare.* Blockchain Technology, Mobility, AI and IoT Development Company. https://www.solulab.com/future-of-ai-in-healthcare/

Mehta, P., Kumar, A., & Bhattacharjee, S. (2020). Fire and Gun Violence based Anomaly Detection System Using Deep Neural Networks. In *Proceedings of the International Conference on Electronics and Sustainable Communication Systems,* (pp. 199 – 204). IEEE. 10.1109/ICESC48915.2020.9155625

Mera, M., Roa, S. M., & González, C. (2015). Content-based image retrieval system to support the diagnosis of human papilloma virus. *Health and Technology, 5*(3-4), 161–165. doi:10.100712553-015-0114-2

Mesko, B. (2017). The role of artificial intelligence in precision medicine. *Expert Review of Precision Medicine and Drug Development, 2*(5), 239–241. doi:10.1080/23808993.2017.1380516

Métivier, L., de Viron, O., Conrad, C. P., Renault, S., Diament, M., & Patau, G. (2009). Evidence of earthquake triggering by the solid earth tides. *Earth and Planetary Science Letters, 278*(3), 370–375. https://doi.org/10.1016/j.epsl.2008.12.024

Meyer-Vernet, N. (2012). *Basics of the solar wind.* Cambridge University Press. https://www.vlebooks.com/vleweb/product/openreader?id=none&isbn=9780511535765

Mhlanga, D. (2020). Industry 4.0 in finance: The impact of artificial intelligence (ai) on digital financial inclusion. *International Journal of Financial Studies, 8*(3), 45. doi:10.3390/ijfs8030045

Miazi, Z. A., Jahan, S., Niloy, M. A., Shama, A., Rahman, M. Z., Islam, M. R., ... Das, S. K. (2021, July). A Cloud-based App for Early Detection of Type II Diabetes with the Aid of Deep Learning. In *2021 International Conference on Automation, Control and Mechatronics for Industry 4.0 (ACMI)* (pp. 1-6). IEEE. 10.1109/ACMI53878.2021.9528136

Michael, A. (2019). Why Retail Is One Of The Leading Sectors Investing In AI. *Forbes.* https://www.forbes.com/sites/forbestechcouncil/2019/03/29/why-retail-is-one-of-the-leading-sectors-investing-in-ai/?sh=50914ae81b4b

Min, J., & Jeong, C. (2009). A binary classification method for bankruptcy prediction. *Expert Systems with Applications, 36*(3), 5256–5263. doi:10.1016/j.eswa.2008.06.073

Minutolo, A., Damiano, E., De Pietro, G., Fujita, H., & Esposito, M. (2022). A conversational agent for querying italian patient information leaflets and improving health literacy. *Computers in Biology and Medicine, 141*, 105004. doi:10.1016/j.compbiomed.2021.105004 PMID:34774337

Misra, P., & Yadav, A. S. (2020). Improving the classification accuracy using recursive feature elimination with cross-validation. *Int. J. Emerg. Technol, 11*(3), 659–665.

Mitrou, L. (2018). *Data protection, artificial intelligence and cognitive services: Is the general data protection regulation (GDPR) 'artificial intelligence-proof*. Artificial Intelligence and Cognitive Services.

Moayeri, M., Pope, P., Balaji, Y., & Feizi, S. (2022). A Comprehensive Study of Image Classification Model Sensitivity to Foregrounds, Backgrounds, and Visual Attributes. *Proceedings of the IEEE/CVF Conference on Computer Vision and Pattern Recognition*

Mogoane, S. N., & Kabanda, S. (2019, October). Challenges in Information and Cybersecurity program offering at Higher Education Institutions. In ICICIS (pp. 202-212).

Mohamed, A. E. (2017).. . *Comparative Study of Four Supervised Machine Learning Techniques for Classification.*, *7*(2), 14.

Mohammadi, S., & Chapon, M. (2020). Investigating the Performance of Fine-tuned Text Classification Models Based-on Bert. *2020 IEEE 22nd International Conference on High Performance Computing and Communications; IEEE 18th International Conference on Smart City; IEEE 6th International Conference on Data Science and Systems (HPCC/SmartCity/DSS)*, 1252–1257. IEEE.

Mohammed, I. A. (2020). Artificial intelligence for cybersecurity: a systematic mapping of literature. *International Journal of Innovations in Engineering RESEARCH and technology, 7*(9).

Mohapatra, M., Mohapatra, S., & Mohanti, J. (2018). Artificial Intelligence (AI)'s Role in Search Engine Optimization (SEO). *International Journal of Engineering Science Invention, 7*(5), 76–79.

Mokhov, S. A., Paquet, J., & Debbabi, M. (2014). The use of NLP techniques in static code analysis to detect weaknesses and vulnerabilities. *Canadian Conference on Artificial Intelligence*

Moles, J., & Wishart, L. (2016). Reading the map: Locating and navigating the academic skills development of pre-service teachers. *Journal of University Teaching & Learning Practice, 13*(3), 4. doi:10.53761/1.13.3.4

Monti, F., Frasca, F., Eynard, D., Mannion, D., Bronstein, M. M., Ai, F., & Lugano, U. (2019). *Fake News Detection on Social Media using Geometric Deep Learning*. arXiv. doi:10.48550/arxiv.1902.06673

Moorman, A., Boon, R. T., Keller-Bell, Y., Stagliano, C., & Jeffs, T. (2010). Effects of text-to-speech software on the reading rate and comprehension skills of high school students with specific learning disabilities. *Learning Disabilities (Pittsburgh, Pa.), 16*(1), 41–49.

Moreno, A., & Redondo, T. (2016). Text analytics: The convergence of big data and artificial intelligence. *IJIMAI, 3*(6), 57–64. doi:10.9781/ijimai.2016.369

Moreno, G., Tran, H., Chia, A. L., Lim, A., & Shumack, S. (2007). Prospective study to assess general practitioners' dermatological diagnostic skills in a referral setting. *Australasian Journal of Dermatology, 48*(2), 77–82.

Mostow, J., & Beck, J. (2006). Some useful tactics to modify, map, and mine data from intelligent tutors. *Natural Language Engineering, 12*(2), 195–208. doi:10.1017/S1351324906004153

Muhamedyev, R. (2015). Machine learning methods: An overview. *CMNT, 19*, 14–29.

Muhammad, I., & Yan, Z. (2015). Supervised Machine Learning Approaches: A Survey. *ICTACT Journal on Soft Computing, 5*(3).

Mujumdar, A., & Vaidehi, V. (2019). Diabetes prediction using machine learning algorithms. *Procedia Computer Science, 165*, 292–299. doi:10.1016/j.procs.2020.01.047

Müller, A. C., & Guido, S. (2016). *Introduction to machine learning with Python: A guide for data scientists* (1st ed.). O'Reilly Media, Inc.

Murdoch, T. B., & Detsky, A. S. (2013). The Inevitable Application of Big Data to Health Care. *Journal of the American Medical Association, 309*(13), 1351. https://doi.org/10.1001/jama.2013.393

Murwantara, I. M., Yugopuspito, P., & Hermawan, R. (2020). Comparison of machine learning performance for earthquake prediction in Indonesia using 30 years historical data. *TELKOMNIKA (Telecommunication Computing Electronics and Control), 18*(3), 1331. doi:10.12928/telkomnika.v18i3.14756

Nadesh, R. K., & Arivuselvan, K. (2020). Type 2: Diabetes mellitus prediction using deep neural networks classifier. *International Journal of Cognitive Computing in Engineering, 1*, 55–61. doi:10.1016/j.ijcce.2020.10.002

Nagy, Á., Munkácsy, G., & Győrffy, B. (2021). Pancancer survival analysis of cancer hallmark genes. *Scientific Reports, 11*(1), 1–10. doi:10.103841598-021-84787-5 PMID:33723286

Nagy, S., & Hajdú, N. (2021). Consumer acceptance of the use of artificial intelligence in online shopping: Evidence from Hungary. *Amfiteatru Economic, 23*(56), 155. doi:10.24818/EA/2021/56/155

Nair, K., & Gupta, R. (2021). Application of AI technology in the modern digital marketing environment. *World Journal of Entrepreneurship, Management and Sustainable Development, 17*(3), 318–328.

Nakane, T., Bold, N., Sun, H., Lu, X., Akashi, T., & Zhang, C. (2020). Application of evolutionary and swarm optimization in computer vision: A literature survey. *IPSJ Transactions on Computer Vision and Applications, 12*(1), 1–34. doi:10.118641074-020-00065-9

Nalini, M. (2021). Impact of Artificial intelligence on Marketing. *International Journal of Aquatic Science, 12*(2), 3159–3167.

Narejo, S., Panday, B., Vargas, D. E., Rodriguez, C., & Anjum, R. M. (2021). Weapon Detection Using YOLO V3 for Smart Surveillance System. *Mathematical Problems in Engineering, 2021*, 9. doi:10.1155/2021/9975700

NASA. (2014). *NASA/Marshall solar physics*. NASA. https://solarscience.msfc.nasa.gov/

NASA. (2021). *SPDF - OMNIWeb Service*. NASA. https://omniweb.gsfc.nasa.gov/

Nasserddine, G., & Arid, A. E. (2022). Decision Making Systems. In J. Wang (Ed.), *Encyclopedia of Data Science and Machine Learning* (Vols. 1–3). IGI Global.

National Flood Relief Commission. (1933). *Report Of The National Flood Relief Commission 1931 1932*. The Comacrib Press. https://archive.org/details/reportofthenatio032042mbp

National Geophysical Data Center / World Data Service (NGDC/WDS). (1972). *NCEI/WDS Global Significant Earthquake Database* [Data set]. NOAA National Centers for Environmental Information. doi:10.7289/V5TD9V7K

National Transportation Safety Board. (2022). *Aviation Accident Statistics*. National Transportation Safety Board (NTSB). https://www.ntsb.gov/Pages/search.aspx#k=Aviation%20Accident%20Statistics

Nayyar, A. N. A. N. D., Rameshwar, R. U. D. R. A., & Solanki, A. R. U. N. (2020). Internet of Things (IoT) and the digital business environment: a standpoint inclusive cyber space, cyber crimes, and cybersecurity. In *The Evolution of Business in the Cyber Age* (pp. 111–152). Apple Academic Press. doi:10.1201/9780429276484-6

NCBI. (n.d.). https://www.ncbi.nlm.nih.gov/pmc/articles/PMC6844177/table/T1/

Neelamegam, S., & Ramaraj, E. (2013). Classification algorithm in data mining: An overview. *International Journal of P2P Network Trends and Technology (IJPTT)*, 369-374.

Negrini, D., Padoan, A., & Plebani, M. (2021). Between Web search engines and artificial intelligence: What side is shown in laboratory tests? *Diagnosis (Berlin, Germany)*, 8(2), 227–232. doi:10.1515/dx-2020-0022 PMID:32335539

Neogy, T. K., & Paruchuri, H. (2014). Machine Learning as a New Search Engine Interface: An Overview. *Engineering International*, 2(2), 103–112. doi:10.18034/ei.v2i2.539

Newsmantraa. (2022). Global Artificial Intelligence (AI) Healthcare Market Is Expected to Grow by USD 69.2 Billion during 2022-2029, Progressing ata CAGR of 40.51% during the Forecast Period. *Digital Journal*. https://www.digitaljournal.com/pr/global-artificial-intelligence-ai-healthcare-market-is-expected-to-grow-by-usd-69-2-billion-during-2022-2029-progressing-at-a-cagr-of-40-51-during-the-forecast-period

NGDC. (2021). *Sunspot-numbers—Monthly*. NOAA. https://www.ngdc.noaa.gov/stp/space-weather/solar-data/solar-indices/sunspot-numbers/american/lists/list_aavso-arssn_monthly.txt

Nguyen, T. T., Tahir, H., Abdelrazek, M., & Babar, A. (2020). Deep learning methods for credit card fraud detection.

Nguyen, B. P., Pham, H. N., Tran, H., Nghiem, N., Nguyen, Q. H., Do, T. T., Tran, C. T., & Simpson, C. R. (2019). Predicting the onset of type 2 diabetes using wide and deep learning with electronic health records. *Computer Methods and Programs in Biomedicine*, 182, 105055. doi:10.1016/j.cmpb.2019.105055 PMID:31505379

Nguyen, Q. H., Ly, H.-B., Ho, L. S., Al-Ansari, N., Le, H. V., Tran, V. Q., Prakash, I., & Pham, B. T. (2021). Influence of data splitting on performance of machine learning models in prediction of shear strength of soil. *Mathematical Problems in Engineering*, 2021, 1–15. https://doi.org/10.1155/2021/4832864

Nick, E. (2021). How Artificial Intelligence Is Powering Search Engines. *Data Science Central*.

Nishii, R., Qin, P., & Kikuyama, R. (2020). Solar activity is one of triggers of earthquakes with magnitudes less than 6. *IGARSS 2020 - 2020 IEEE International Geoscience and Remote Sensing Symposium*, (pp. 377–380). IEEE. https://doi.org/10.1109/IGARSS39084.2020.9323381

Nishimura, T. (2017). Triggering of volcanic eruptions by large earthquakes: Triggering of Volcanic Eruptions. *Geophysical Research Letters*, 44(15), 7750–7756. https://doi.org/10.1002/2017GL074579

Nogueira, R., & Cho, K. (2019). Passage Re-ranking with BERT.

Noiret, S., Lumetzberger, J., & Kampel, M. (2021). Bias and Fairness in Computer Vision Applications of the Criminal Justice System. *2021 IEEE Symposium Series on Computational Intelligence (SSCI)*

Nomura, A., Noguchi, M., Kometani, M., Furukawa, K., & Yoneda, T. (2021). Artificial intelligence in current diabetes management and prediction. *Current Diabetes Reports*, 21(12), 1–6. doi:10.100711892-021-01423-2 PMID:34902070

Noom. (2022). Retrieved from https://www.noom.com

Nordin, N., & Norman, H. (2018). Mapping the Fourth Industrial Revolution global transformations on 21st-century education in the context of sustainable development. *Journal of Sustainable Development Education and Research, 2*(1), 1–7. doi:10.17509/jsder.v2i1.12265

Novianty, A., Machbub, C., Widiyantoro, S., Meilano, I., & Irawan, H. (2019). Tsunami potential identification based on seismic features using knn algorithm. *2019 IEEE 7th Conference on Systems, Process and Control (ICSPC)*, (pp. 155–160). IEEE. doi:10.1109/ICSPC47137.2019.9068095

Novikov, V. A., Okunev, V. I., Klyuchkin, V. N., Liu, J., Ruzhin, Y. Ya., & Shen, X. (2017). Electrical triggering of earthquakes: Results of laboratory experiments at spring-block models. *Earthquake Science, 30*(4), 167–172. doi:10.1007/s11589-017-0181-8

Novikov, V., Ruzhin, Y., Sorokin, V., & Yaschenko, A. (2020). Space weather and earthquakes: Possible triggering of seismic activity by strong solar flares. *Annals of Geophysics, 63*(5), 13. https://doi.org/10.4401/ag-7975

Nurse, J. R. (2021). Cybersecurity awareness. doi:10.1007/978-3-642-27739-9_1596-1

Ocampo, I., López, R. R., Camacho-León, S., Nerguizian, V., & Stiharu, I. (2021). Comparative evaluation of artificial neural networks and data analysis in predicting liposome size in a periodic disturbance micromixer. *Micromachines, 12*(10), 1164. doi:10.3390/mi12101164 PMID:34683215

Odintsov, S. D., Ivanov-Kholodnyi, G. S., & Georgieva, K. (2007). Solar activity and global seismicity of the earth. *Bulletin of the Russian Academy of Sciences. Physics, 71*(4), 593–595. https://doi.org/10.3103/S1062873807040466

Odintsov, S., Boyarchuk, K., Georgieva, K., Kirov, B., & Atanasov, D. (2006). Long-period trends in global seismic and geomagnetic activity and their relation to solar activity. *Physics and Chemistry of the Earth Parts A/B/C, 31*(1–3), 88–93. https://doi.org/10.1016/j.pce.2005.03.004

OECD. (2019, November 15). *Scoping the OECD AI principles.* OECD Library. https://www.oecd-ilibrary.org/science-and-technology/scoping-the-oecd-ai-principles_d62f618a-en

OFDA/CRED (2021). *International Disaster Data.* Our World in Data. https://ourworldindata.org/ofdacred-international-disaster-data

Oh, H., Azarian, M. H., Pecht, M., White, C. H., Sohaney, R. C., & Rhem, E. (2010). Physics-of-failure approach for fan PHM in electronics applications. In Proceedings of the 2010 Prognostics and System Health Management Conference, (pp. 1–6). IEEE. 10.1109/PHM.2010.5413501

Olmos, R., Tabik, S., & Herrera, F. (2018). Automatic handgun detection alarm in videos using deep learning. *Neurocomputing, 275*, 66–72. doi:10.1016/j.neucom.2017.05.012

Omoregbe, N. A., Ndaman, I. O., Misra, S., Abayomi-Alli, O. O., Damaševičius, R., & Dogra, A. (2020). Text messaging-based medical diagnosis using natural language processing and fuzzy logic. *Journal of Healthcare Engineering, 2020*, 1–14. doi:10.1155/2020/8839524

Omran, M., Lassner, C., Pons-Moll, G., Gehler, P., & Schiele, B. (2018). *Neural body fitting: Unifying deep learning and model based human pose and shape estimation. In 2018 international conference on 3D vision (3DV).* IEEE.

Ongsulee, P. (2017). Artificial Intelligence, Machine Learning and Deep Learning. *In: Fifteenth International Conference on ICT and Knowledge Engineering.* ACM.

Ongsulee, P. (2017). Artificial intelligence, machine learning and deep learning. *15th International Conference on ICT and Knowledge Engineering (ICT&KE)*, (pp. 1-6). 10.1109/ICTKE.2017.8259629

Opara, E. U., & Dieli, O. J. (2021). Enterprise cyber security challenges to medium and large firms: An analysis. *International Journal of Electronics and Information Engineering*, *13*(2), 77–85.

Optica. (2022). *NewPhotoacoustic Endoscope Fits inside a Needle*. Medicalxpress.com. https://medicalxpress.com/news/2022-07-photoacoustic-endoscope-needle.html

Orihara, Y., Kamogawa, M., & Nagao, T. (2015). Preseismic Changes of the Level and Temperature of Confined Groundwater related to the 2011 Tohoku Earthquake. *Scientific Reports*, *4*(1), 6907. https://doi.org/10.1038/srep06907

Othan, D., Kilimci, Z. H., & Uysal, M. (2019). Financial sentiment analysis for predicting direction of stocks using bidirectional encoder representations from transformers (BERT) and deep learning models. *Proc. Int. Conf. Innov. Intell. Technol.*, *2019*, 30–35.

Ou, X., Pan, W., & Xiao, P. (2014). In vivo skin capacitive imaging analysis by using grey level co-occurrence matrix (GLCM). *International Journal of Pharmaceutics*, *460*(1-2), 28–32. doi:10.1016/j.ijpharm.2013.10.024 PMID:24188984

OuYang, X., Zhu, X., Ye, L., & Yao, J. (2017). Preliminary applications of blockchain technique in large consumers direct power trading. *Zhongguo Dianji Gongcheng Xuebao*, *37*, 3672–3681.

Panarello, A., Tapas, N., Merlino, G., Longo, F., & Puliafito, A. (2018). Blockchain and iot integration: A systematic survey. *Sensors (Basel)*, *18*(8), 2575. doi:10.339018082575 PMID:30082633

Panayides, A. S., Amini, A., Filipovic, N. D., Sharma, A., Tsaftaris, S. A., Young, A., ... Kurc, T. (2020). AI in medical imaging informatics: Current challenges and future directions. *IEEE Journal of Biomedical and Health Informatics*, *24*(7), 1837–1857. doi:10.1109/JBHI.2020.2991043 PMID:32609615

Pandarinath, C., Nuyujukian, P., Blabe, C. H., Sorice, B. L., Saab, J., Willett, F. R., Hochberg, L. R., Shenoy, K. V., & Henderson, J. M. (2017). High-performance communication by people with paralysis using an intracortical brain-computer interface. *eLife*, *6*, 6. doi:10.7554/eLife.18554 PMID:28220753

Park, J., Bhat, G., Nk, A., Geyik, C. S., Ogras, U. Y., & Lee, H. G. (2020). Energy per operation optimization for energy-harvesting wearable IoT devices. *Sensors (Basel)*, *20*(3), 764. doi:10.339020030764 PMID:32019219

Patil, J. K., & Kumar, R. (2011). Advances in image processing for detection of plant diseases. *Journal of Advanced Bioinformatics Applications and Research*, *2*(2), 135–141.

Patro, B. N., Lunayach, M., Patel, S., & Namboodiri, V. P. (2019). U-cam: Visual explanation using uncertainty based class activation maps. *Proceedings of the IEEE/CVF International Conference on Computer Vision*

Pearson. (2021). *Artificial intelligence in Higher Education*. Pearson. https://www.pearson.com/uk/educators/higher-education-educators.html

Pedregosa, F., Varoquaux, G., Gramfort, A., Michel, V., Thirion, B., Grisel, O., Blondel, M., Prettenhofer, P., Weiss, R., Dubourg, V., Vanderplas, J., Passos, A., & Cournapeau, D. (2011). Scikit-learn: Machine Learning in Python. *MACHINE LEARNING IN PYTHON*, *6*.

Pedregosa, F. (2011). Scikit-learn: Machine learning in Python. *Journal of Machine Learning Research*, *12*, 2825–2830.

Penprase, B. E. (2018). The fourth industrial revolution and higher education. *Higher education in the era of the fourth industrial revolution, 10*, 978-981.

Perez, S., Massey-Allard, J., Butler, D., Ives, J., Bonn, D., Yee, N., & Roll, I. (2017). Identifying productive inquiry in virtual labs using sequence mining. In *International conference on artificial intelligence in education*. Springer. 10.1007/978-3-319-61425-0_24

Peters, G. W., Panayi, E., & Chapelle, A. (2015). *Trends in cryptocurrencies and blockchain technologies: A monetary theory and regulation perspective*. arXiv:1508.04364.

Peters, G. W., & Panayi, E. (2016). Understanding modern banking ledgers through blockchain technologies: Future of transaction processing and smart contracts on the internet of money. In *Proceedings of Banking beyond banks and money* (pp. 239–278). Springer. doi:10.1007/978-3-319-42448-4_13

Peyton Doyle. (2022). Healthcare breaches on the rise in 2022. *Tech Target*. https://www.techtarget.com/searchsecurity/news/252521771/Healthcare-breaches-on-the-rise

Pham, B. T., Qi, C., Ho, L. S., Nguyen-Thoi, T., Al-Ansari, N., Nguyen, M. D., Nguyen, H. D., Ly, H.-B., Le, H. V., & Prakash, I. (2020). A novel hybrid soft computing model using Random Forest and particle swarm optimization for estimation of undrained shear strength of soil. *Sustainability, 12*(6), 2218. https://doi.org/10.3390/su12062218

Pilkington, M. (2017). Can blockchain improve healthcare management? Consumer medical electronics and the IoT. *Consumer Medical Electronics and the IoMT*.

Ping, Z., Yu, D., & Bin, L. (2016). White paper on China's blockchain technology and application development. *Ministry of Industry and Information Technology of People's Republic of China*.

Pires, R., Goltzsche, D., Ben Mokhtar, S., Bouchenak, S., Boutet, A., Felber, P., Kapitza, R., Pasin, M., & Schiavoni, V. (2018). CYCLOSA: Decentralizing private web search through SGX-based browser extensions. *2018 IEEE 38th International Conference on Distributed Computing Systems (ICDCS)*, (pp. 467–477). IEEE.

Pitchaimani, S., Kodaganallur, V. P., Newell, C., & Kalsi, V. (2019). *U.S. Patent No. 10,491,595*. U.S. Patent and Trademark Office.

Pohjalainen, R. (2019). The benefits of search engine optimization in Google for businesses. *Semantic Scholar*.

Polak, Y. (2017). Yandex and Others: On 20 Years of Russian Search in Internet. *2017 Fourth International Conference on Computer Technology in Russia and in the Former Soviet Union (SORUCOM)*, (pp. 172–175). IEEE. 10.1109/SoRuCom.2017.00034

Pons, J. L. (2005). *Emerging actuator technologies: A micromechatronic approach*. John Wiley & Sons. doi:10.1002/0470091991

Pool, L. D., & Qualter, P. (2012). Improving emotional intelligence and emotional self-efficacy through a teaching intervention for university students. *Learning and Individual Differences, 22*(3), 306–312. doi:10.1016/j.lindif.2012.01.010

Popenici, S. (2013). *Higher Education and Affluenza*. Popenici.

Popenici, S. A., & Kerr, S. (2017). Exploring the impact of artificial intelligence on teaching and learning in higher education. *Research and Practice in Technology Enhanced Learning, 12*(1), 1–13. doi:10.118641039-017-0062-8 PMID:30595727

Poplin, R., Varadarajan, A. V., Blumer, K., Liu, Y., McConnell, M. V., Corrado, G. S., Peng, L., & Webster, D. R. (2018). Prediction of cardiovascular risk factors from retinal fundus photographs via deep learning. *Nature Biomedical Engineering*, 2(3), 158–164. doi:10.103841551-018-0195-0 PMID:31015713

Potter, S. (2020, September 15). *Solar Cycle 25 Is Here. NASA, NOAA Scientists Explain What That Means* [Text]. NASA. https://www.nasa.gov/press-release/solar-cycle-25-is-here-nasa-noaa-scientists-explain-what-that-means

Prabhu, P., & Selvabharathi, S. (2019). Deep Belief Neural Network Model for Prediction of Diabetes Mellitus. In *2019 3rd International Conference on Imaging, Signal Processing and Communication (ICISPC)* (pp. 138-142). IEEE. 10.1109/ICISPC.2019.8935838

Prajapati, H. B., Shah, J. P., & Dabhi, V. K. (2017). Detection and classification of rice plant diseases. *Intelligent Decision Technologies*, 11(3), 357–373. doi:10.3233/IDT-170301

Prasad, P. S., Gunjan, V. K., & Pathak, R., & Mukherjee, S. (2020). *Applications of Artificial Intelligence in BiomedicalEngineering*. Taylor and Francis Group. . doi:10.1201/9781003045564-6

Priest, E. (2014). Magnetohydrodynamics of the sun. Cambridge University Press. https://doi.org/10.1017/CBO9781139020732.

Priya, P., & D'souza, D. A. (2015). Study of feature extraction techniques for the detection of diseases of agricultural products. *International Journal of Innovative Research in Electrical, Electronics, Instrumentation and Control Engineering, 3*(2).

Priyadarshini, I., & Sharma, R. (Eds.). (2022). *Artificial Intelligence and Cybersecurity: Advances and Innovations*. CRC Press.

Pruksachatkun, Y., Krishna, S., Dhamala, J., Gupta, R., & Chang, K.-W. (2021). Does Robustness Improve Fairness? Approaching Fairness with Word Substitution Robustness Methods for Text Classification. Findings of the Association for Computational Linguistics: ACL-IJCNLP 2021.

Punitha, S., Al-Turjman, F., & Stephan, T. (2021). An automated breast cancer diagnosis using feature selection and parameter optimization in ANN. *Computers & Electrical Engineering*, 90, 106958. doi:10.1016/j.compeleceng.2020.106958

PwC. (2022). Capitalizingon Precision Medicine: How Pharmaceutical Firms Can Shape the Future ofHealthcare. PwC. https://www.strategyand.pwc.com/de/en/industries/health/capitalizing-precision-medicine.html

PwC. (2022). *No Longer ScienceFiction, AI and Robotics Are Transforming Healthcare*. https://www.pwc.com/gx/en/industries/healthcare/publications/ai-robotics-new-health/transforming-healthcare.html#:~:text=It%20puts%20consumers%20in%20control.

Qiang, B., Chen, R., Zhou, M., Pang, Y., Zhai, Y., & Yang, M. (2020). Convolutional Neural Networks Based Object Detection Algorithm by Jointing Semantic Segmentation for Images. *Sensors (Basel)*, 20(18), 5080. doi:10.339020185080 PMID:32906755

Quazi, S., Jangi, R., Gavas, S., & Karpinski, T. M. (2022). Artificial intelligence and machine learning in medicinal chemistry and validation of emerging drug targets. *Advancements in Controlled Drug Delivery Systems*, 27-43.

Quddus, M. A., Noland, R. B., & Ochieng, W. Y. (2008). A high accuracy fuzzy logic-based map-matching algorithm for road transport. *Journal of Intelligent Transportation Systems: Technology, Planning, and Operations*, 103-115.

Quddus, M. A. (2006). *High integrity map matching algorithms for advanced transport telematics applications.* Imperial College London.

Quddus, M., Ochieng, W., & Noland, R. (2007). Current map-matching algorithms for transport applications: State-of-the art and future research directions. *Transportation Research Part C, Emerging Technologies, 15*(5), 312–328. doi:10.1016/j.trc.2007.05.002

Rabhi, Y., Mrabet, M., & Fnaiech, F. (2018). A facialexpression controlled wheelchair for people with disabilities. *Computer Methods and Programs in Biomedicine, 165,* 89–105.

Rąb-Kettler, K., & Lehnervp, B. (2019). *Recruitment in the times of machine learning.* Management Systems in Production Engineering. doi:10.1515/mspe-2019-0018

Rácz, A., Bajusz, D., & Héberger, K. (2021). Effect of dataset size and train/test split ratios in qsar/qspr multiclass classification. *Molecules (Basel, Switzerland), 26*(4), 1111. https://doi.org/10.3390/molecules26041111

Radford, A., Metz, L., & Chintala, S. (2015). Unsupervised representation learning with deep convolutional generative adversarial networks. arXiv preprint arXiv:1511.06434.

Radford, A., Wu, J., Child, R., Luan, D., Amodei, D., & Sutskever, I. (2019). Language models are unsupervised multitask learners. *OpenAI blog, 1*(8), 9.

Raganato, A., & Tiedemann, J. (2018). An analysis of encoder representations in transformer-based machine translation. Proceedings of the 2018 EMNLP Workshop BlackboxNLP: Analyzing and Interpreting Neural Networks for NLP, 10.18653/v1/W18-5431

Rajasekharaiah, K. M., Dule, C. S., & Sudarshan, E. (2020, December). Cyber security challenges and its emerging trends on latest technologies. *IOP Conference Series. Materials Science and Engineering, 981*(2), 022062. doi:10.1088/1757-899X/981/2/022062

Raju, V. N. G., Lakshmi, K. P., Jain, V. M., Kalidindi, A., & Padma, V. (2020). Study the influence of normalization/transformation process on the accuracy of supervised classification. *2020 Third International Conference on Smart Systems and Inventive Technology (ICSSIT),* (pp. 729–735). IEEE. doi:10.1109/ICSSIT48917.2020.9214160

Ramachandran, P., Zoph, B., & Le, Q. V. (2017). Searching for activation functions. arXiv preprint arXiv:1710.05941.

Ramage, M. (2018). *From BIM to blockchain in construction: What you need to know.* Trimble Inc.

Ramzan, F., Khan, M. U. G., Iqbal, S., Saba, T., & Rehman, A. (2020). Volumetric segmentation of brain regions from MRI scans using 3D convolutional neural networks. *IEEE Access: Practical Innovations, Open Solutions, 8,* 103697–103709. doi:10.1109/ACCESS.2020.2998901

Ranjan, R., Bansal, A., Zheng, J., Xu, H., Gleason, J., Lu, B., Nanduri, A., Chen, J.-C., Castillo, C., & Chellappa, R. (2019). A fast and accurate system for face detection, identification, and verification. *IEEE Transactions on Biometrics, Behavior, and Identity Science, 1*(2), 82–96. doi:10.1109/TBIOM.2019.2908436

Rao, S., Verma, A. K., & Bhatia, T. (2021). A review on social spam detection: Challenges, open issues, and future directions. *Expert Systems with Applications, 186,* 115742. doi:10.1016/j.eswa.2021.115742

Rastogi, A., Arora, R., & Sharma, S. (2015, February). Leaf disease detection and grading using computer vision technology & fuzzy logic. In *2015 2nd international conference on signal processing and integrated networks (SPIN)* (pp. 500-505). IEEE 10.1109/SPIN.2015.7095350

Rathi, S. (2019). Generating Counterfactual and Contrastive Explanations using SHAP. *arXiv e-prints,* arXiv: 1906.09293.

Rathore, P., Soni, J., Prabakar, N., Palaniswami, M., & Santi, P. (2021). Identifying Groups of Fake Reviewers Using a Semisupervised Approach. *IEEE Transactions on Computational Social Systems, 8*(6), 1369–1378. doi:10.1109/TCSS.2021.3085406

Rauf, R., Shahid, A. R., Ziauddin, S., & Safi, A. A. (2016). Pedestrian detection using HOG, LUV and optical flow as features with AdaBoost as classifier. In *2016 Sixth International Conference on Image Processing Theory, Tools and Applications (IPTA)* (pp. 1-4). IEEE. 10.1109/IPTA.2016.7821024

Ravfogel, S., Elazar, Y., Gonen, H., Twiton, M., & Goldberg, Y. (2020). Null It Out: Guarding Protected Attributes by Iterative Nullspace Projection. Proceedings of the 58th Annual Meeting of the Association for Computational Linguistics, .

Razdan, S., & Sharma, S. (2021). Internet of medical things (IoMT): Overview, emerging technologies, and case studies. *IETE Technical Review*, 1–14.

Real, E., Aggarwal, A., Huang, Y., & Le, Q. V. (2019). Regularized evolution for image classifier architecture search. *Proceedings of the AAAI Conference on Artificial Intelligence, 33*(01), 4780–4789. doi:10.1609/aaai.v33i01.33014780

Rebecca, J. (2019). *TikTok, Explained.* Vox. https://www.vox.com/culture/2018/12/10/18129126/tiktok-app-musically-meme-cringe

Reddy, G. T., Reddy, M. P. K., Lakshmanna, K., Kaluri, R., Rajput, D. S., Srivastava, G., & Baker, T. (2020). Analysis of dimensionality reduction techniques on big data. *IEEE Access: Practical Innovations, Open Solutions, 8*, 54776–54788. https://doi.org/10.1109/ACCESS.2020.2980942

Redmayne, D. W. (1988). Mining induced seismicity in UK coalfields identified on the BGS National Seismograph Network. *Geological Society, London, Engineering Geology Special Publications, 5*(1), 405–413. doi:10.1144/GSL.ENG.1988.005.01.45

Redmond, J., & Farhadi, A. (2018). Yolov3: An incremental improvement. In Computer Vision and Pattern Recognition, 1804 - 2767.

Redmond, J. (2016). Darknet: Open Source. *Neural Networks.* https://pjreddie.com/darknet/

Redmond, J., Divvala, S., Girshick, R., & Farhadi, A. (n.d.). You Only Look Once: Unified, Real-Time Object Detection. *In Proceedings of the IEEE conference on computer vision and pattern recognition*, (pp. 779 – 788). IEEE.

Redmond, J., & Farhadi, A. (2017). YOLO9000: Better, Faster, Stronger. *2017 IEEE Conference on Computer Vision and Pattern Recognition (CVPR)*, (pp. 6517-6525). IEEE. 10.1109/CVPR.2017.690

Reinse, D., Gantz, J., & Rydning, J. (2018). *The Digitization of the World From Edge to Core* (#US44413318). Seagate IDC. https://www.seagate.com/files/www-content/our-story/trends/files/idc-seagate-dataage-whitepaper.pdf

Ren, L., & Wang, W. (2018). An SVM-based collaborative filtering approach for Top-N web services recommendation. *Future Generation Computer Systems, 78*, 531–543. doi:10.1016/j.future.2017.07.027

Ren, S., He, K., Girshick, R., & Sun, J. (2015). Faster r-cnn: Towards real-time object detection with region proposal networks. *Advances in Neural Information Processing Systems*, 28.

Research Gate. (n.d.). https://www.researchgate.net/publication/345991601_Diabetes_prediction_using_machine_learning_algorithm

Reshamwala, A. (2013). Review on natural language processing. *Research Gate.*

Rghioui, A., Lloret, J., Harane, M., & Oumnad, A. (2020). A smart glucose monitoring system for diabetic patient. *Electronics (Basel)*, *9*(4), 678. doi:10.3390/electronics9040678

Rhue, L. (2018). Racial influence on automated perceptions of emotions. *Available at SSRN 3281765*

Ribeiro, M. T., Singh, S., & Guestrin, C. (2016). Why should i trust you?" Explaining the predictions of any classifier. Proceedings of the 22nd ACM SIGKDD international conference on knowledge discovery and data mining, .

Ribera, M., & Lapedriza, A. (2019). Can we do better explanations? A proposal of user-centered explainable AI. IUI Workshops, Rogers, A., Kovaleva, O., & Rumshisky, A. (2020). A primer in bertology: What we know about how bert works. *Transactions of the Association for Computational Linguistics*, *8*, 842–866.

Rick, L. (2014). Stem cell therapy for the treatment of early stage avascular necrosis of the femoral head: A systematic review. *BMC Musculoskeletal Disorders*, *15*(1), 156. doi:10.1186/1471-2474-15-156 PMID:24886648

Ringger, E. K., Moore, R. C., Charniak, E., Vanderwende, L., & Suzuki, H. (2004). Using the Penn Treebank to Evaluate Non-Treebank Parsers. In *Language Resources and Evaluation Conference (LREC)*, Lisbon, Portugal.

Roberson, J. (2017). *A Biomedical Engineer's Role in aHealthcare Facility*. Healthcare Facilities Today. https://www.healthcarefacilitiestoday.com/posts/A-biomedical-engineers-role-in-a-healthcare-facility--14740

Rock, D. (2021). Engineering value: The returns to technological talent and investments in Artificial Intelligence. University of Pennsylvania, 1-72.

Rodriguez, R. V. (2020). The Reality About Object Detection As A Computer Vision Task. *Analytics India Magazine*. https://analyticsindiamag.com/the-reality-about-object-detection-as-a-computer-vision-task/

Rokon, M. O. F., Islam, R., Darki, A., Papalexakis, E. E., & Faloutsos, M. (2020). {SourceFinder}: Finding Malware {Source-Code} from Publicly Available Repositories in {GitHub}. In *23rd International Symposium on Research in Attacks, Intrusions and Defenses (RAID 2020)* (pp. 149-163). USENIX Association.

Rollo, M. E., Aguiar, E. J., Williams, R. L., Wynne, K., Kriss, M., Callister, R., & Collins, C. E. (2016). eHealth technologies to support nutrition and physical activity behaviors in diabetes self-management. *Diabetes, Metabolic Syndrome and Obesity*, *9*, 381–390. doi:10.2147/DMSO.S95247 PMID:27853384

Romeo, L., & Frontoni, E. (2022). A Unified Hierarchical XGBoost model for classifying priorities for COVID-19 vaccination campaign. *Pattern Recognition*, *121*, 108197. doi:10.1016/j.patcog.2021.108197 PMID:34312570

Romero, C., Ventura, S., & García, E. (2008). Data mining in course management systems: Moodle case study and tutorial. *Computers & Education*, *51*(1), 368–384. doi:10.1016/j.compedu.2007.05.016

Romero, C., Zafra, A., Luna, J. M., & Ventura, S. (2013). Association rule mining uses genetic programming to provide feedback to instructors from multiple-choice quiz data. *Expert Systems: International Journal of Knowledge Engineering and Neural Networks*, *30*(2), 162–172. doi:10.1111/j.1468-0394.2012.00627.x

Rumelhart, D. E., Hinton, G. E., & Williams, R. J. (1986). Learning representation by back-propagating errors. *Nature*, *323*(6088), 533 - 536.

Russell, S., & Norvig, P. (2010). *Artificial Intelligence A Modern Approach* (3rd ed.). Prentice Hall.

Russel, S., & Norvig, P. (2010). *Artificial intelligence - a modern approach*. Pearson Education.

Ryerkerk, M., Averill, R., Deb, K., & Goodman, E. (2019). A survey of evolutionary algorithms using metameric representations. *Genetic Programming and Evolvable Machines, 20*(4), 441–478. doi:10.100710710 019-09356-2

Saad, S., Briguglio, W., & Elmiligi, H. (2019). The curious case of machine learning in malware detection. doi:10.5220/0007470705280535

Saba, T. (2020). Recent advancement in cancer detection using machine learning: Systematic survey of decades, comparisons and challenges. *Journal of Infection and Public Health, 13*(9), 1274–1289. doi:10.1016/j.jiph.2020.06.033 PMID:32758393

Sadiku, M. N., Ashaolu, T. J., Ajayi-Majebi, A., & Musa, S. M. (2021). Artificial Intelligence in Social Media. *International Journal of Scientific Advances, 2*(1), 15–20.

Safavi, K., & Kalis, B. (2019). How AI can change the future of health care. *HBR.* https://hbr.org/ webinar/2019/02/how-ai-can-change-the-future-of-health-care

Sah, R. D., Patro, S. P., Padhy, N., & Salimath, N. (2021). Diabetics Patients Analysis Using Deep Learning and Gradient Boosted Trees. In *2021 8th International Conference on Computing for Sustainable Global Development (INDIACom)* (pp. 937-941). IEEE.

Said, Y. F., & Barr, M. (2019). Pedestrian detection for advanced driver assistance systems using deep learning algorithms. *IJCSNS, 19*(10), 9–14.

Sajjadi, N. B., Shepard, S., Ottwell, R., Murray, K., Chronister, J., Hartwell, M., & Vassar, M. (2021). Examining the Public's Most Frequently Asked Questions Regarding COVID-19 Vaccines Using Search Engine Analytics in the United States: Observational Study. *JMIR Infodemiology, 1*(1), e28740. doi:10.2196/28740 PMID:34458683

Salah, K., Rehman, M. H. U., Nizamuddin, N., & Al-Fuqaha, A. (2019). Blockchain for AI: Review and open research challenges. *IEEE Access: Practical Innovations, Open Solutions, 7,* 10127–10149. doi:10.1109/ACCESS.2018.2890507

Salem, A.-B. (Ed.). (2020). *Innovative Smart Healthcare and Bio-Medical Systems: AI, Intelligent Computing and Connected Technologies.* CRC, Press.

Salem, A.-B., & Shmelova, T. (2021). Intelligent Expert Decision Support Systems: Methodologies, Applications, and Challenges. In *Research Anthology on Decision Support Systems and Decision Management in Healthcare, Business, and Engineering* (pp. 510–531). IGI Global. doi:10.4018/978-1-7998-9023-2.ch024

Salido, J., Lomas, V., Santaquiteria, J. R., & Deniz, O. (2021, 06). Automatic Handgun Detection with Deep Learning in Video Surveillance Images. *Applied Sciences, 11,* 6085.

Salih, A. A., Ameen, S. Y., Zeebaree, S. R., Sadeeq, M. A., Kak, S. F., Omar, N., & Ageed, Z. S. (2021). Deep learning approaches for intrusion detection. *Asian Journal of Research in Computer Science,* 50-64.

Salmon, G. (2000). *E-moderating - the key to teaching and learning online* (1st ed.). Routledge.

Samuel, A. L. (1959). Some studies in machine learning using the game of checkers. *IBM Journal of Research and Development, 3*(3), 210–229. https://doi.org/10.1147/rd.33.0210

Sanchez-Gonzalez, A., Godwin, J., Pfaff, T., Ying, R., Leskovec, J., & Battaglia, P. W. (2020). Learning to Simulate Complex Physics with Graph Networks. *37th International Conference on Machine Learning, ICML 2020, PartF168147-11,* (pp. 8428–8437). 10.48550/arxiv.2002.09405

Sandler, M., Howard, A., Zhu, M., Zhmoginov, A., & Chen, L. C. (2018). Mobilenetv2: Inverted residuals and linear bottlenecks. In *Proceedings of the IEEE conference on computer vision and pattern recognition* (pp. 4510-4520). IEEE.

Santerre, R., & Geiger, A. (2018). The geometry of GPS relative positioning. *GPS Solutions, 22*(2), 1–14. doi:10.100710291-018-0713-2

Santoso, J., & Onal, C. D. (2021). An origami continuum robot capable of precise motion through torsionally stiff body and smooth inverse kinematics. *Soft Robotics, 8*(4), 371–386. doi:10.1089oro.2020.0026 PMID:32721270

Saritha, R. R., Paul, V., & Kumar, P. G. (2018). Content based image retrieval using deep learning process. *Cluster Computing, 1*(1), 67–78.

Sarker, I. H., Kayes, A. S. M., Badsha, S., Alqahtani, H., Watters, P., & Ng, A. (2020). Cybersecurity data science: An overview from machine learning perspective. *Journal of Big Data, 7*(1), 1–29. doi:10.118640537-020-00318-5

Sasank, J. S., Sahith, G. R., Abhinav, K., & Belwal, M. (2019, July). Credit Card Fraud Detection Using Various Classification and Sampling Techniques: A Comparative Study. In *2019 International Conference on Communication and Electronics Systems (ICCES)* (pp. 1713-1718). IEEE. 10.1109/ICCES45898.2019.9002289

Scarselli, F., Gori, M., Tsoi, A. C., Hagenbuchner, M., & Monfardini, G. (2009). The graph neural network model. *IEEE Transactions on Neural Networks, 20*(1), 61–80. doi:10.1109/TNN.2008.2005605 PMID:19068426

Schleicher, A. (2012). *Preparing teachers and developing school leaders for the 21st century: Lessons from around the world*. OECD Publishing.

Schmidhuber, J. (2015). Deep learning in neural networks: An overview. *Neural Networks: The Official Journal of the International Neural Network Society, 61*, 85–117. doi:10.1016/j.neunet.2014.09.003 PMID:25462637

Schölkopf, B. (2015). Learning to see and act. *Nature, 518*(7540), 486–487. doi:10.1038/518486a PMID:25719660

Schorlemmer, D., Werner, M. J., Marzocchi, W., Jordan, T. H., Ogata, Y., Jackson, D. D., Mak, S., Rhoades, D. A., Gerstenberger, M. C., Hirata, N., Liukis, M., Maechling, P. J., Strader, A., Taroni, M., Wiemer, S., Zechar, J. D., & Zhuang, J. (2018). The collaboratory for the study of earthquake predictability: Achievements and priorities. *Seismological Research Letters, 89*(4), 1305–1313. https://doi.org/10.1785/0220180053

Schweyer, A. (2018). Predictive analytics and artificial Intelligence in people management. *Incentive Research Foundation*, 1-18.

SciKit. (2021). *Supervised learning—Scikit-learn 0.24.2 documentation*. SciKit Learn. https://scikit-learn.org/stable/supervised_learning.html

SciKit. (2021). *Unsupervised learning—Scikit-learn 0.24.2 documentation*. SciKit Learn. https://scikit-learn.org/stable/unsupervised_learning.html

Searle, I. R., Ziola, S. M., & Seidel, B. (1997). Crack detection on a full-scale aircraft fatigue test. *In Smart Structures and Materials 1997. Smart Sensing, Processing, and Instrumentation, 3042*, 267–277.

Seemma, P. S., Nandhini, S., & Sowmiya, M. (2018). Overview of cyber security. *International Journal of Advanced Research in Computer and Communication Engineering, 7*(11), 125–128. doi:10.17148/IJARCCE.2018.71127

Selvaraj, S., & Sundaravaradhan, S. (2020). Challenges and opportunities in IoT healthcare systems: A systematic review. *SN Applied Sciences, 2*(1), 1–8. doi:10.100742452-019-1925-y

Serrano, W. (2016a). A big data intelligent search assistant based on the random neural network. *INNS Conference on Big Data*, (pp. 254–261). Springer.

Serrano, W. (2016b). The random neural network applied to an intelligent search assistant. *International Symposium on Computer and Information Sciences*, (pp. 39–51). Springer. 10.1007/978-3-319-47217-1_5

Setiawan, A. W. (2020, November). Image segmentation metrics in skin lesion: accuracy, sensitivity, specificity, dice coefficient, Jaccard index, and Matthews correlation coefficient. In *2020 International Conference on Computer Engineering, Network, and Intelligent Multimedia (CENIM)* (pp. 97-102). IEEE. 10.1109/CENIM51130.2020.9297970

Seyhan, A. A., & Carini, C. (2019). Are innovation and new technologies in preci- sion medicine paving a new era in patients centric care? *Journal of Translational Medicine*, *17*(1), 114. doi:10.118612967-019-1864-9 PMID:30953518

Seymour, T., Frantsvog, D., & Kumar, S. (2011). History of search engines. *International Journal of Management & Information Systems*, *15*(4), 47–58.

Shadiev, R., Hwang, W. Y., Chen, N. S., & Huang, Y. M. (2014). Review of speech-to-text recognition technology for enhancing learning. *Journal of Educational Technology & Society*, 65–84.

Shaheen, M. Y. (2021). AI in healthcare: Medical and socio-economic benefits and challenges. *ScienceOpen Preprints,* Shimoda, A., Li, Y., Hayashi, H., & Kondo, N. (2021). Dementia risks identified by vocal features via telephone conversations: A novel machine learning prediction model. *PLoS One*, *16*(7), e0253988. doi:10.1371/journal.pone.0253988 PMID:34260593

Shah, N. H., Milstein, A., & Bagley, S. C. (2019). Making machine learning models clinically useful. *Journal of the American Medical Association*, *322*(14), 1351–1352. doi:10.1001/jama.2019.10306 PMID:31393527

Shahrivari, V., Darabi, M. M., & Izadi, M. (2020). Phishing Detection Using Machine Learning Techniques. *arXiv preprint arXiv:2009.11116.*

Shah, V. N., & Garg, S. K. (2015). Managing diabetes in the digital age. *Clinical Diabetes and Endocrinology*, *1*(1), 16. doi:10.118640842-015-0016-2 PMID:28702234

Shaikh, F., Siddiqui, U. A., Shahzadi, I., Jami, S. I., & Shaikh, Z. A. (2010). SWISE: Semantic Web based intelligent search engine. *2010 International Conference on Information and Emerging Technologies*, 1–5. 10.1109/ICIET.2010.5625670

Shailaja, K., Seetharamulu, B., & Jabbar, M. A. (2018). Machine Learning in Healthcare: A Review. *Second international conference on electronics, communication and aerospace technology* (pp. 910-914). IEEE.

Shankar, S., Halpern, Y., Breck, E., Atwood, J., Wilson, J., & Sculley, D. (2017). No Classification without Representation: Assessing Geodiversity Issues in Open Data Sets for the Developing World. *stat, 1050*, 22.

Sharma, A. (2022). How the Health Sector Has Widely Implemented Artificial Intelligence. *Times of India Blog.* https://timesofindia.indiatimes.com/blogs/voices/how-the-health-sector-has-widely-implemented-artificial-intelligence/

Sharma, D., Shukla, R., Giri, A. K., & Kumar, S. (2019). A brief review on search engine optimization. *2019 9th International Conference on Cloud Computing, Data Science & Engineering (Confluence),*(pp. 687–692). Semantic Scholar.

Sharma, K. U., & Thakur, N. V. (2017). A review and approach for object detection in images. *International Journal of Computational Vision and Robotics, 7*(1 - 2), 196 - 237.

Sharma, S., & Verma, S. (2020). Optimizing website effectiveness using various SEO techniques, 918-922. IEEE.

Sharma, S., Henderson, J., & Ghosh, J. (2020). Certifai: A common framework to provide explanations and analyse the fairness and robustness of black-box models. Proceedings of the AAAI/ACM Conference on AI, Ethics, and Society, 10.1145/3375627.3375812

Sharma, Y. (2011). *Boost university-industry AI research collaboration.* University.

Shen, B., Guo, J., & Yang, Y. (2019). MedChain: Efficient healthcare data sharing via blockchain. *Applied Sciences (Basel, Switzerland), 9*(6), 1207. doi:10.3390/app9061207

Shih, F. Y. (2017). *Image processing and mathematical morphology: fundamentals and applications.* CRC press. doi:10.1201/9781420089448

Shin, S., Song, K., Jang, J., Kim, H., Joo, W., & Moon, I.-C. (2020). Neutralizing Gender Bias in Word Embeddings with Latent Disentanglement and Counterfactual Generation. Findings of the Association for Computational Linguistics: EMNLP 2020,

Shin, H., Oh, S., Hong, S., Kang, M., Kang, D., Ji, Y., & Park, Y. (2020). Early-stage lung cancer diagnosis by deep learning-based spectroscopic analysis of circulating exosomes. *ACS Nano, 14*(5), 5435–5444. doi:10.1021/acsnano.9b09119 PMID:32286793

Shmelova, T. (2019). Integration deterministic, stochastic, and non-stochastic uncertainty models in conflict situations. In CEUR Vol 2805 Workshop Proceedings (Vol. 2588). CEUR-WS.

Shmelova, T., Chialastri, A., Sikirda, Y., & Yatsko, M. (2021) Models of Decision-Making by the Pilot in Emergency "Engine Failure During Take-Off" In *CEUR.* https://ceur-ws.org/Vol-3101/Paper26.pdf

Shmelova, T., Lazorenko, V., & Burlaka, O. (2020). Unmanned Aerial Vehicles for Smart Cities: Estimations of Urban Locality for Optimization Flights. In José A.Tenedório, R.Estanqueiro & C. D. Henriques (Eds.) Methods and Applications of Geospatial Technology in Sustainable Urbanis (pp.444-477) IGI Global.

Shmelova, T., Lohachova, K., & Yatsko, M. (2022) Integration of Decision-Making Stochastic Models of Air Navigation System Operators in Emergency Situations: In *CEUR.* https://ceur-ws.org/Vol-3137/paper18.pdf

Shmelova, T., Sikirda, Y., Yatsko, M., & Kasatkin, M. (2022) Collective Models of the Aviation Human-Operators in Emergency for Intelligent Decision Support System. In *CEUR.* https://ceur-ws.org/Vol-3156/paper10.pdf

Shmelova, T., Sterenharz, A. Yu., & Dolgikh, S. (2020) Artificial Intelligence in Aviation Industries: Methodologies, Education, Applications, and Opportunities. In T.Shmelova, Yu.Sikirda., & A.Sterenharz (Eds.) Handbook of Research on Artificial Intelligence Applications in the Aviation and Aerospace Industries (pp. 1-35). IGI Global.

Shmelova, T., & Bondarev, D. (2019). Automated System of Controlling Unmanned Aerial Vehicles Group Flight: Application of Unmanned Aerial Vehicles Group. In T. Kille, P. R. Bates, & S. Y. Lee (Eds.), *Unmanned Aerial Vehicles in Civilian Logistics and Supply Chain Management* (pp. 208–242). IGI Global. doi:10.4018/978-1-5225-7900-7.ch008

Shmelova, T., Sikirda, Y., & Belyaev, Y. (2014). Informational Support of Air Navigation System's Human-Operator. *Scientific Works of the National University of Food Technologies, 20*(4), 7–18.

Shmelova, T., & Sikirda, Yu. (2019). Applications of Decision Support Systems in Socio-Technical Systems. In *Unmanned Aerial Vehicles: Breakthroughs in Research and Practice. Information Resources Management Association* (5th ed., pp. 182–214). IGI Global. doi:10.4018/978-1-5225-8365-3.ch008

Shmelova, T., & Sikirda, Yu. (2021). Applications of Decision Support Systems in Aviation. In *Encyclopedia of Information Science and Technology* (5th ed., pp. 658–674). IGI Global. doi:10.4018/978-1-7998-3479-3.ch046

Shmelova, T., Sikirda, Yu., & Jafarzade, T. R. (2019). Artificial Neural Network for Pre-Simulation Training of Air Traffic Controller. In T. Shmelova, Yu. Sikirda, & D. Kucherov (Eds.), *Cases on Modern Computer Systems in Aviation* (pp. 27–51). IGI Global. doi:10.4018/978-1-5225-7588-7.ch002

Shmelova, T., Sikirda, Yu., Salem, B., Rizun, N., & Kovalyov, Yu. (Eds.). (2018). *Socio-Technical Decision Support in Air Navigation Systems: Emerging Research and Opportunities*. IGI Global. doi:10.4018/978-1-5225-3108-1

Shmelova, T., Sikirda, Yu., & Sterenharz, A. (Eds.). (2020). *Handbook of Research on Artificial Intelligence Applications in the Aviation and Aerospace Industries*. IGI Global. doi:10.4018/978-1-7998-1415-3

Shrikumar, A., Greenside, P., & Kundaje, A. (2017). Learning important features through propagating activation differences. International conference on machine learning

Shu, F., & Shu, J. (2021). An eight-camera fall detection system using human fall pattern recognition via machine learning by a low-cost android box. *Scientific Reports*, *11*(1), 1–17. doi:10.103841598-021-81115-9 PMID:33510202

Shulman, C., & Bostrom, N. (2012). How hard is artificial intelligence? Evolutionary arguments and selection effects. *Journal of Consciousness Studies*.

Siemens, G., & Baker, R. S. D. (2012). Learning analytics and educational data mining: towards communication and collaboration. In *Proceedings of the 2nd international conference on learning analytics and knowledge*, (pp. 252-254). ACM. 10.1145/2330601.2330661

Sikirda, Yu., Kasatkin, M., & Tkachenko, D. (2019) Intelligent Automated System for Supporting the Collaborative Decision Making by Operators of the Air Navigation System During Flight Emergencies. In T.Shmelova, Yu.Sikirda., & A.Sterenharz (Eds.) Handbook of Research on Artificial Intelligence Applications in the Aviation and Aerospace Industries (pp. 66-90). IGI Global.

Sikirda, Yu., Shmelova, T., Kharchenko, V., & Kasatkin, M. (2021) *Intelligent System for Supporting Collaborative Decision Making by the Pilot/Air Traffic Controller in Flight Emergencies* In *CEUR*. https://ceur-ws.org/Vol-2853/paper12.pdf

Sikos, L. F. (Ed.). (2018). *AI in Cybersecurity* (Vol. 151). Springer.

SILSO. (2021). World Data Center for the production, preservation and dissemination of the international sunspot number. https://wwwbis.sidc.be/silso/home

Silver, D., Schrittwieser, J., Simonyan, K., Antonoglou, I., Huang, A., Guez, A., Hubert, T., Baker, L., Lai, M., & Bolton, A. (2017). Mastering the game of go without human knowledge. *nature, 550*(7676), 354-359.

Silver, D., Schrittwieser, J., Simonyan, K., Antonoglou, I., Huang, A., Guez, A., & Hassabis, D. (2017). Mastering the game of Go without human knowledge. *Nature*, *550*(7676), 354–359. doi:10.1038/nature24270 PMID:29052630

Sim, L. L. W., Ban, K. H. K., Tan, T. W., Sethi, S. K., & Loh, T. P. (2017). Development of a clinical decision support system for diabetes care: A pilot study. *PLoS One*, *12*(2), e0173021. doi:10.1371/journal.pone.0173021 PMID:28235017

Simonyan, K., Vedaldi, A., & Zisserman, A. (2013). Deep inside convolutional networks: Visualising image classification models and saliency maps. *arXiv preprint arXiv:1312.6034*.

Singh, S., Srivastava, D., & Agarwal, S. (2017, August). GLCM and its application in pattern recognition. In *2017 5th International Symposium on Computational and Business Intelligence (ISCBI)* (pp. 20-25). IEEE. 10.1109/ISCBI.2017.8053537

Singh, A. P. (2017). A study on zero-day malware attack. *International Journal of Advanced Research in Computer and Communication Engineering*, *6*(1), 391–392. doi:10.17148/IJARCCE.2017.6179

Singhal, S., & Carlton, S. (2019). *The era of exponential improvement in healthcare*. McKinsey & Company.

Singh, S., Kumar, A., Bajwa, B. S., Mahajan, S., Kumar, V., & Dhar, S. (2010). Radon monitoring in soil gas and ground water for earthquake prediction studies in north west himalayas, india. *Diqiu Kexue Jikan*, *21*(4), 685. https://doi.org/10.3319/TAO.2009.07.17.01(TT)

Singla, R., Singla, A., Gupta, Y., & Kalra, S. (2019). Artificial intelligence/machine learning in diabetes care. *Indian Journal of Endocrinology and Metabolism*, 23(4), 495. doi:10.4103/ijem.IJEM_228_19 PMID:31741913

Sirodzha, I. (2002). *Quantum Models and Methods of Artificial Intelligence for Decision Making and Management: monograph*. Naukova Dumka.

Slowik, A., & Kwasnicka, H. (2020). Evolutionary algorithms and their applications to engineering problems. *Neural Computing & Applications*, 32(16), 12363–12379. doi:10.100700521-020-04832-8

Smilkov, D., Thorat, N., Kim, B., Viégas, F., & Wattenberg, M. (2017). Smoothgrad: removing noise by adding noise. *arXiv preprint arXiv:1706.03825*.

Smith, R. G., & Eckroth, J. (2017). Building AI applications: Yesterday, today, and tomorrow. *AI Magazine*, 38(1), 6–22. doi:10.1609/aimag.v38i1.2709

Smola, A., & Vishwanathan, S. V. (2008). Introduction to machine learning. Cambridge University, 32(24), 2008.

Smola, A. J., & Schölkopf, B. (2004). A tutorial on support vector regression. *Statistics and Computing*, 14(3), 199–222. https://doi.org/10.1023/B:STCO.0000035301.49549.88

Snyder, C. F., Wu, A. W., Miller, R. S., Jensen, R. E., Bantug, E. T., & Wolff, A. C. (2011). The Role of Informaticsin Promoting Patient-Centered Care. *Cancer Journal (Sudbury, Mass.)*, 17(4), 211–218. https://doi.org/10.1097/ppo.0b013e318225ff89

So, A., Hooshyar, D., Park, K. W., & Lim, H. S. (2017). Early diagnosis of dementia from clinical data by machine learning techniques. *Applied Sciences (Basel, Switzerland)*, 7(7), 651. doi:10.3390/app7070651

Songara, A., & Chouhan, L. (2017). Blockchain: a decentralized technique for securing Internet of Things. In *Proceedings of Conference on Emerging Trends in Engineering Innovations & Technology Management*. Research Gate.

Soni, J., Prabakar, N., Upadhyay. (2019). Behavioral Analysis of System Call Sequences Using LSTM Seq-Seq, Cosine Similarity and Jaccard Similarity for Real-Time Anomaly Detection. *2019 International Conference on Computational Science and Computational Intelligence (CSCI)*, (pp. 214–219). IEEE. 10.1109/CSCI49370.2019.00043

Soni, J., Prabakar, N., Upadhyay. (2020). Comparative Analysis of LSTM Sequence-Sequence and Auto Encoder for real-time anomaly detection using system call sequences. *International Journal of Innovative Research in Computer and Communication Engineering*, 7(12), 4225–4230.

Soni, J., Prabakar, N., Upadhyay. (2020). *Feature Extraction through Deepwalk on Weighted Graph*. 15th Springer International Conference on Data Science (ICDATA), Las Vegas, Nevada.

Soni, J., Prabakar, N., Upadhyay. (2020). Visualizing High-Dimensional Data Using t-Distributed Stochastic Neighbor Embedding Algorithm. In H. Arabnia, K. Daimi, R. Stahlbock, C. Soviany, L. Heilig, & K. Brüssau (Eds.), Principles of Data Sci-ence. Transactions on Computational Science and Computational Intelligence (pp. 189–206). Springer. doi:10.1007/978-3-030-43981-1_9

Soni, J., Prabakar, N., & Upadhyay, H. (2019). Deep learning approach to detect malicious attacks at the system level: poster. In *Proceedings of the 12th Conference on Security and Privacy in Wireless and Mobile Networks (WiSec '19)*, (pp. 314–315). Association for Computing Machinery. 10.1145/3317549.3326308

Sorrell, W. H. (2016). Blockchain Technology: Opportunities and Risks. Vermont Office of the Attorney General.

Space Weather Prediction Center. (2021). *ACE real-time solar wind | NOAA / NWS space weather prediction center*. Space Weather Prediction Center. https://www.swpc.noaa.gov/products/ace-real-time-solar-wind

Specht, D. F. (1991). A general regression neural network. *IEEE Transactions on Neural Networks*, *2*(6), 568–576. doi:10.1109/72.97934 PMID:18282872

Spiess, A.-N., & Neumeyer, N. (2010). An evaluation of R2 as an inadequate measure for nonlinear models in pharmacological and biochemical research: A Monte Carlo approach. *BMC Pharmacology*, *10*(1), 6. https://doi.org/10.1186/1471-2210-10-6

Springenberg, J. T., Dosovitskiy, A., Brox, T., & Riedmiller, M. (2014). Striving for simplicity: The all convolutional net. *arXiv preprint arXiv:1412.6806*.

Srinivasu, P. N., SivaSai, J. G., Ijaz, M. F., Bhoi, A. K., Kim, W., & Kang, J. J. (2021). Classification of skin disease using deep learning neural networks with MobileNet V2 and LSTM. *Sensors (Basel)*, *21*(8), 2852. doi:10.339021082852 PMID:33919583

Stankova, E. N., Grechko, I. A., Kachalkina, Y. N., & Khvatkov, E. V. (2017). Hybrid approach combining model-based method with the technology of machine learning for forecasting of dangerous weather phenomena. *International Conference on Computational Science and Its Applications*, (pp. 495–504). Springer. 10.1007/978-3-319-62404-4_37

Steed, R., & Caliskan, A. (2021). Image representations learned with unsupervised pre-training contain human-like biases. Proceedings of the 2021 ACM conference on fairness, accountability, and transparency, .

Stock, P., & Cisse, M. (2018). Convnets and imagenet beyond accuracy: Understanding mistakes and uncovering biases. *Proceedings of the European Conference on Computer Vision (ECCV)*

Stokes, J. M., Yang, K., Swanson, K., Jin, W., Cubillos-Ruiz, A., Donghia, N. M., MacNair, C. R., French, S., Carfrae, L. A., Bloom-Ackerman, Z., Tran, V. M., Chiappino-Pepe, A., Badran, A. H., Andrews, I. W., Chory, E. J., Church, G. M., Brown, E. D., Jaakkola, T. S., Barzilay, R., & Collins, J. J. (2020). A Deep Learning Approach to Antibiotic Discovery. *Cell*, *180*(4), 688–702.e13. doi:10.1016/j.cell.2020.01.021 PMID:32084340

Stone, M., Aravopoulou, E., Ekinci, Y., Evans, G., Hobbs, M., Labib, A., & Machtynger, L. (2020). Artificial intelligence in strategic marketing decision-making: A research agenda. *The Bottom Line (New York, N.Y.)*, *33*(2), 183–200. doi:10.1108/BL-03-2020-0022

Storchak, D. A., Di Giacomo, D., Bondar, I., Engdahl, E. R., Harris, J., Lee, W. H. K., Villasenor, A., & Bormann, P. (2013). Public release of the isc-gem global instrumental earthquake catalogue(1900-2009). *Seismological Research Letters*, *84*(5), 810–815. https://doi.org/10.1785/0220130034

Strobel, V., Castelló Ferrer, E., & Dorigo, M. (2018). Managing byzantine robots via blockchain technology in a swarm robotics collective decision-making scenario.

Strobelt, H., Gehrmann, S., Behrisch, M., Perer, A., Pfister, H., & Rush, A. M. (2018). S eq 2s eq-v is: A visual debugging tool for sequence-to-sequence models. *IEEE Transactions on Visualization and Computer Graphics*, *25*(1), 353–363.

Strubhar, A. J., Tan, P., Storage, L., & Peterson, M. (2018). Concurrent validity of the VirtuSense® gait analysis system for the quantification of spatial and temporal parameters of gait. *International Journal of Exercise Science*, *11*(1), 934–940.

Subash Kumar, T. G., & Nagarajan, V. (2018). Local curve pattern for content-based image retrieval. *Pattern Analysis & Applications*, 1–10.

Subramanian, N., Elharrouss, O., Al-Maadeed, S., & Bouridane, A. (2021). Image steganography: A review of the recent advances. *IEEE Access: Practical Innovations, Open Solutions*, *9*, 23409–23423. doi:10.1109/ACCESS.2021.3053998

Subsorn, P., & Singh, K. (2020) *DSS Applications as a Business Enhancement Strategy.* Citeseerx. https://citeseerx.ist.psu.edu/viewdoc/download?doi=10.1.1.87.8235&rep=rep1&type=pdf

Su, K., Xiao, B., Liu, B., Zhang, H., & Zhang, Z. (2017). TAP: A personalized trust-aware QoS prediction approach for web service recommendation. *Knowledge-Based Systems, 115*, 55–65. doi:10.1016/j.knosys.2016.09.033

Sullivan, D. (2012). *Google: 100 billion searches per month, search to integrate Gmail, launching enhanced search app for iOS.* Search Engine Land.

Sun, C., Qiu, X., Xu, Y., & Huang, X. (2019). How to fine-tune bert for text classification? *China National Conference on Chinese Computational Linguistics*, (pp. 194–206). Springer. 10.1007/978-3-030-32381-3_16

Sunarti, S., Rahman, F. F., & Naufal, M., Risky, M., Febriyanto, K., & Masnina, R. (2021). Artificial Intelligence inHealthcare: Opportunities and Risk for Future. *Gaceta Sanitaria, 35*(1), S67–70. doi:10.1016/j.gaceta.2020.12.019

Sundararajan, M., Taly, A., & Yan, Q. (2017). Axiomatic attribution for deep networks. International conference on machine learning

Sun, H., Mao, H., Bai, X., Chen, Z., Hu, K., & Yu, W. (2017). Multi-blockchain model for central bank digital currency. In *Proceedings of 18th International conference on parallel and distributed computing, applications and technologies* (pp. 360-367). IEEE. 10.1109/PDCAT.2017.00066

Sun, T., Xia, B., Liu, Y., Lai, Y., Zheng, W., Wang, H., Wang, W., & Wang, M. (2019). A novel hybrid prognostic approach for remaining useful life estimation of lithium-ion batteries. *Energies, 12*(19), 3678. doi:10.3390/en12193678

Sun, W., Khenissi, S., Nasraoui, O., & Shafto, P. (2019). Debiasing the human-recommender system feedback loop in collaborative filtering. Companion Proceedings of The 2019 World Wide Web Conference, .

Sun, Y., Xue, B., Zhang, M., & Yen, G. G. (2020). Evolving Deep Convolutional Neural Networks for Image Classification. *IEEE Transactions on Evolutionary Computation, 24*(2), 394–407. doi:10.1109/TEVC.2019.2916183

Surati, S. B., & Prajapati, G. I. (2018). SEO-A Review. *International Journal of Research and Scientific Innovation, 5*(2), 13–17. https://www.rsisinternational.org/

Sushina, T., & Sobenin, A. (2020). Artificial Intelligence in the Criminal Justice System: Leading Trends and Possibilities. 6th International Conference on Social, economic, and academic leadership (ICSEAL-6-2019)

Sutton, R. S., & Barto, A. G. (2018). *Reinforcement learning: An introduction* (2nd ed.). The MIT Press.

Svenstrup, D., Jørgensen, H. L., & Winther, O. (2015). Rare disease diagnosis: A review of web search, social media and large-scale data-mining approaches. *Rare Diseases, 3*(1), e1083145. doi:10.1080/21675511.2015.1083145 PMID:26442199

Swan, M. (2015). Blockchain thinking: The brain as a decentralized autonomous corporation [commentary]. *IEEE Technology and Society Magazine, 34*(4), 41–52. doi:10.1109/MTS.2015.2494358

Swan, M. (2015). *Blockchain: Blueprint for a new economy.* O'Reilly Media, Inc.

Swapna, G., Vinayakumar, R., & Soman, K. P. (2018). Diabetes detection using deep learning algorithms. *ICT Express, 4*(4), 243-246.

Sytinskii, A. D. (1973). Relation between seismic activity of the earth and solar activity. *Uspekhi Fizicheskih Nauk, 111*(10), 367. doi:10.3367/UFNr.0111.197310i.0367

Szczepański, M., Choraś, M., Pawlicki, M., & Pawlicka, A. (2021). The methods and approaches of explainable artificial intelligence. *International Conference on Computational Science*, (pp. 3–17). Springer. 10.1007/978-3-030-77970-2_1

Szeliski, R. (2010). *Computer Vision: Algorithms and Applications*. Springer.

T. G.S., J. Soni, K. Chandna, S. S. Iyengar, N. R. Sunitha and N. Prabakar. (2019). Learning-Based Model to Fight against Fake Like Clicks on Instagram Posts. 2019 SoutheastCon, (pp. 1-8). IEEE. doi:10.1109/SoutheastCon42311.2019.9020533. doi:10.1109/SoutheastCon42311.2019.9020533

Tabei, F., Gresham, J., Askarian, Behnam, Jung, K., & WoonChong, J. (2020). Cuff-Less Blood Pressure Monitoring System Using Smartphones. *IEEEAccess*, *8*, 11534–45. doi:10.1109/access.2020.2965082

Taddeo, M., McCutcheon, T., & Floridi, L. (2019). Trusting artificial intelligence in cybersecurity is a double-edged sword. *Nature Machine Intelligence*, *1*(12), 557–560. doi:10.103842256-019-0109-1

Tagde, P., Tagde, S., Bhattacharya, T., Tagde, P., Chopra, H., Akter, R., Kaushik, D., & Rahman, M. (2021). Blockchain and artificial intelligence technology in e-health. *Environmental Science and Pollution Research International*, *28*(38), 52810–52831. doi:10.100711356-021-16223-0 PMID:34476701

Tahir, B., Iqbal, S., Usman Ghani Khan, M., Saba, T., Mehmood, Z., Anjum, A., & Mahmood, T. (2019). Feature enhancement framework for brain tumor segmentation and classification. *Microscopy Research and Technique*, *82*(6), 803–811. doi:10.1002/jemt.23224 PMID:30768835

Tan, C. F., Wahidin, L. S., Khalil, S. N., Tamaldin, N. H., & Rauterberg, G. W. (2016). The application of expert system: A review of research and applications. *Journal of Engineering and Applied Sciences (Asian Research Publishing Network)*, *11*(4), 2448–2453.

Tang, J., Liu, G., & Pan, Q. (2021). A review on representative swarm intelligence algorithms for solving optimization problems: Applications and trends. *IEEE/CAA Journal of Automatica Sinica*, *8*(10), 1627-1643.

Tang, M., Jiang, Y., Liu, J., & Liu, X. (2012). Location-aware collaborative filtering for QoS-based service recommendation. *Proceedings - 2012 IEEE 19th International Conference on Web Services, ICWS 2012*, 202–209. IEEE. 10.1109/ICWS.2012.61

Tang, M., Zheng, Z., Kang, G., Liu, J., Yang, Y., & Zhang, T. (2016). Collaborative Web Service Quality Prediction via Exploiting Matrix Factorization and Network Map. *IEEE eTransactions on Network and Service Management*, *13*(1), 126–137. doi:10.1109/TNSM.2016.2517097

Tang, Y., Jiang, J., Liu, J., Yan, P., Tao, Y., & Liu, J. (2022). A GRU and AKF-Based Hybrid Algorithm for Improving INS/GNSS Navigation Accuracy during GNSS Outage. *Remote Sensing*, *14*(3), 752. doi:10.3390/rs14030752

Tang, Y., Wu, Y., Wu, M., Wu, W., Hu, X., & Shen, L. (2008). INS/GNSS integration: Global observability analysis. *IEEE Transactions on Vehicular Technology*, *58*(3), 1129–1142. doi:10.1109/TVT.2008.926213

Tan, S. S.-L., & Goonawardene, N. (2017). Internet health information seeking and the patient-physician relationship: A systematic review. *Journal of Medical Internet Research*, *19*(1), e5729. doi:10.2196/jmir.5729 PMID:28104579

Tantin, A., Assi, E. B., van Asselt, E., Hached, S., & Sawan, M. (2020). Predicting urinary bladder voiding by means of a linear discriminant analysis: Validation in rats. *Biomedical Signal Processing and Control*, *55*, 101667.

Tapas, N., Longo, F., Merlino, G., & Puliafito, A. (2020). Experimenting with smart contracts for access control and delegation in IoT. *Future Generation Computer Systems*, *111*, 324–338. doi:10.1016/j.future.2020.04.020

Tapscott, D., & Tapscott, A. (2017). How blockchain will change organizations. *MIT Sloan Management Review*, *58*(2), 10.

Tarasov, V., & Gerasimov, B. (2007). Intelligent Decision Support Systems: Theory, Synthesis, Efficiency: monograph. Kyiv: International Academy of Computer Science and Systems.

Tarik Al Ani. (2008). *Réseaux de neurones avec Matlab*. Laboratoire d'Ingénierie des Systèmes de Versailles Paris.

Taunk, K., De, S., Verma, S., & Swetapadma, A. (2019, May). A brief review of nearest neighbor algorithm for learning and classification. In *2019 International Conference on Intelligent Computing and Control Systems (ICCS)* (pp. 1255-1260). IEEE. 10.1109/ICCS45141.2019.9065747

Taylor, K. (2015). *The Deloitte Centre for Health Solutions*. Deloitte. https://www2.deloitte.com/content/dam/Deloitte/uk/Documents/life-sciences-health-care/deloitte-uk-connected-health.pdf

Tcheng, J. E. (Ed.). (2017). *Optimizing strategies for clinical decision support: summary of a meeting series*. National Academy of Medicine.

Team, E. (2020). What is Machine Learning? A definition-. *Expert Systems: International Journal of Knowledge Engineering and Neural Networks*.

Tech, M. (2019). *What Is Biomedical Engineering?* Michigan Technological University. https://www.mtu.edu/biomedical/department/what-is/

Tecuci, G. (2012). Artificial Intelligence. *Wiley Interdisciplinary Reviews: Computational Statistics*, *4*(2), 168–180. doi:10.1002/wics.200

Tegmark, M. (2018). *Life 3.0: Being Human in the age of artificial intelligence*. Penguin Books.

Tenney, I., Das, D., & Pavlick, E. (2019). BERT Rediscovers the Classical NLP Pipeline. *Proceedings of the 57th Annual Meeting of the Association for Computational Linguistics*

Terasaki Institute for Biomedical Innovation. (2022). *Repairing Tendons with Silk Proteins*. Medicalxpress.com. https://medicalxpress.com/news/2022-05-tendons-silk-proteins.html

Thandekkattu, S. G., & Kalaiarasi, M. (2022). Customer-Centric E-commerce Implementing Artificial Intelligence for Better Sales and Service. *Proceedings of Second International Conference on Advances in Computer Engineering and Communication Systems*, (pp. 141–152). Springer. 10.1007/978-981-16-7389-4_14

Thanh, C. T., & Zelinka, I. (2019, December). A survey on artificial intelligence in malware as next-generation threats. In Mendel, 25(2), 27-34. doi:10.13164/mendel.2019.2.027

Thomas, T. P., Vijayaraghavan, A., & Emmanuel, S. (2020). Machine learning and cybersecurity. In *Machine Learning Approaches in Cyber Security Analytics* (pp. 37–47). Springer. doi:10.1007/978-981-15-1706-8_3

Thorndike, E. L. (2000). *Animal intelligence: Experimental studies*. Transaction Publishers.

Tian, D., Yao, J., & Wen, L. (2018). Collapse and earthquake swarm after North Korea's 3 September 2017 nuclear test. *Geophysical Research Letters*, *45*(9), 3976–3983. https://doi.org/10.1029/2018GL077649

Tihelka, D., Hanzlниek, Z., Jщzovб, M., Vнt, J., Матоиљek, J., & Grшber, M. (2018). Current state of text-to-speech system ARTIC: a decade of research on the field of speech technologies. *International Conference on Text, Speech, and Dialogue* (pp. 369-378). Springer. 10.1007/978-3-030-00794-2_40

Ting, D. S. W., Cheung, C. Y., Lim, G., Tan, G. S. W., Quang, N. D., Gan, A., & Lee, S. Y. (2017). Development and validation of a deep learning system for diabetic retinopathy and related eye diseases using retinal images from multiethnic populations with diabetes. *Journal of the American Medical Association*, *318*(22), 2211–2223. doi:10.1001/jama.2017.18152 PMID:29234807

Tixier, A. J., Hallowell, M. R., Rajagopalan, B., & Bowman, D. (2016). Automated content analysis for construction safety: A natural language processing system to extract precursors and outcomes from unstructured injury reports. *Automation in Construction*, *62*, 45–56. doi:10.1016/j.autcon.2015.11.001

Tjan, B. S., Beckmann, P. J., Roy, R., Giudice, N., & Legge, G. E. (2005, September). Digital sign system for indoor wayfinding for the visually impaired. In *2005 IEEE Computer Society Conference on Computer Vision and Pattern Recognition (CVPR'05)-Workshops* (pp. 30-30). IEEE.

Tjoa, E., & Guan, C. (2020). A survey on explainable artificial intelligence (xai): Toward medical xai. *IEEE Transactions on Neural Networks and Learning Systems*, *32*(11), 4793–4813.

Tohka, J., & Van Gils, M. (2021). Evaluation of machine learning algorithms for health and wellness applications: A tutorial. *Computers in Biology and Medicine*, *132*, 104324. doi:10.1016/j.compbiomed.2021.104324 PMID:33774270

Tsai, A., Connolly, S., Nedder, A., & Shapiro, F. (2013). Visualization and analysis of the deforming piglet femur and hip following experimentally induced avascular necrosis of the femoral head. *IEEE Transactions on Biomedical Engineering*, *60*(6), 1742–1750. doi:10.1109/TBME.2012.2228860 PMID:23204265

Tsai, C., Li, C., Lam, R. W., Li, C., & Ho, S. (2019). Diabetes care in motion: Blood glucose estimation using wearable devices. *IEEE Consumer Electronics Magazine*, *9*(1), 30–34. doi:10.1109/MCE.2019.2941461

Twesige, R. L. (2015). A simple explanation of Bitcoin and Blockchain technology.

Tzotsos, A., & Argialas, D. (2008). Support vector machine classification for object-based image analysis. In *Object-based image analysis* (pp. 663–677). Springer. doi:10.1007/978-3-540-77058-9_36

UAE Cabinet. (n.d.). *News*. UAE Cabinet. https://uaecabinet.ae/en/details/news/mohammed-bin-rashid-launches-five-decade-government-plan-uae-centennial-2071

UAE Strategy for Artificial Intelligence. (2022, February 21). *UAE strategy for Artificial Intelligence - the official portal of the UAE Government*. UAE. https://u.ae/en/about-the-uae/strategies-initiatives-and-awards/federal-governments-strategies-and-plans/uae-strategy-for-artificial-intelligence

Ujager, F. S., & Mahmood, A. (2019a). A context-aware accurate wellness determination (CAAWD) model for elderly people using lazy associative classification. *Sensors (Basel)*, *19*(7), 1613. doi:10.339019071613 PMID:30987246

Ujager, F. S., Mahmood, A., & Khatoon, S. (2019). Wellness determination of the elderly using spatio-temporal correlation analysis of daily activities. *Journal of Ambient Intelligence and Smart Environments*, *11*(6), 515–526. doi:10.3233/AIS-190538

Ullah, M., Mohammed, A., & Alaya Cheikh, F. (2018). PedNet: A spatio-temporal deep convolutional neural network for pedestrian segmentation. *Journal of Imaging*, *4*(9), 107.

UNESCO. (2019). *Artificial Intelligence in Education: Challenges and Opportunities for Sustainable Development*. United Nations Educational, Scientific and Cultural Organization.

Università della Svizzera italiana. (2022). *Mathematics Helps AI in Biomedicine.* Medicalxpress.com. https://medicalxpress.com/news/2022-02-mathematics-ai-biomedicine.html

USGS. (2021). *Usgs earthquake hazards program.* USGS. https://earthquake.usgs.gov/

Vaidya, A., Mai, F., & Ning, Y. (2020). Empirical analysis of multi-task learning for reducing identity bias in toxic comment detection. Proceedings of the International AAAI Conference on Web and Social Media, 10.1609/icwsm.v14i1.7334

Vaishnavee, K. B., & Amshakala, K. (2015). An automated MRI brain image segmentation and tumor detection using SOM-clustering and proximal support vector machine classifier. Paper presented at the *2015 IEEE International Conference on Engineering and Technology (ICETECH)*, (pp. 1-6). IEEE. 10.1109/ICETECH.2015.7275030

Vamathevan, J., Clark, D., Czodrowski, P., Dunham, I., Ferran, E., Lee, G., & Zhao, S. (2019). Applications of machine learning in drug discovery and development. *Nature Reviews. Drug Discovery, 18*(6), 463–477.

Van Couvering, E. (2008). The history of the Internet search engine: Navigational media and the traffic commodity. In *Web search* (pp. 177–206). Springer. doi:10.1007/978-3-540-75829-7_11

Van Zuylen, H. (2012). Difference between artificial intelligence and traditional methods. *Artificial Intelligence Applications to Critical Transportation Issues, 3.*

Varmedja, D., Karanovic, M., Sladojevic, S., Arsenovic, M., & Anderla, A. (2019, March). Credit card fraud detection-machine learning methods. In *2019 18th International Symposium INFOTEH-JAHORINA (INFOTEH)* (pp. 1-5). IEEE 10.1109/INFOTEH.2019.8717766

Veale, M., & Brown, I. (2020). Cybersecurity. *Internet Policy Review, 9*(4), 1–22. doi:10.14763/2020.4.1533

Veglis, A., & Geomelakis, D. (Eds.). (2021). *Search engine optimization.*

Velastin, S. A., Boghossian, B. A., & Vincencio-Silva, M. A. (2006). A motion-based image processing system for detecting potentially dangerous situations in underground railway stations. *Transportation Research Part C, Emerging Technologies, 14*(2), 96–113. doi:10.1016/j.trc.2006.05.006

Venkatesan, M., Mohan, H., Ryan, J. R., Schürch, C. M., Nolan, G. P., Frakes, D. H., & Coskun, A. F. (2021). Virtual and Augmented Reality for Biomedical Applications. *Cell Reports Medicine, 2* (7): 100348. doi:10.1016/j.xcrm.2021.100348

Verbickas, R., Laganiere, R., Laroche, D., Zhu, C., Xu, X., & Ors, A. (2017). SqueezeMap: fast pedestrian detection on a low-power automotive processor using efficient convolutional neural networks. In *Proceedings of the IEEE conference on computer vision and pattern recognition workshops* (pp. 146-154). IEEE.

Verdhan, V., & Kling, E. Y. (2020). *Supervised learning with Python: Concepts and practical implementation using Python.* Apress.

Verma, S., Sharma, R., Deb, S., & Maitra, D. (2021). Artificial Intelligence in marketing: Systematic review and future research direction. *International Journal of Information Management Data Insights, 1*(1), 1–9. doi:10.1016/j.jjimei.2020.100002

Verma, V., Chowdary, V., Gupta, M. K., & Mondal, A. K. (2018). *IoT and robotics in healthcare. Medical big data and internet of medical things.* CRC Press.

Vetter, N. (2021). The promise of artificial intelligence: A review of the opportunities and challenges of artificial intelligence in healthcare and clinical trials in skeletal dysplasia: A paradigm for treating rare diseases. *British Medical Bulletin, 139*(1), 1–3. doi:10.1093/bmb/ldab022

Compilation of References

Vig, J., & Belinkov, Y. (2019). Analyzing the Structure of Attention in a Transformer Language Model. *Proceedings of the 2019 ACL Workshop BlackboxNLP: Analyzing and Interpreting Neural Networks for NLP,* 10.18653/v1/W19-4808

Viriyasaranon, T., & Choi, J. H. (2022). Object detectors involving a NAS-gate convolutional module and capsule attention module. *Scientific Reports, 12*(1), 1–13. doi:10.103841598-022-07898-7 PMID:35273256

Viruega, J. R., & Trapero, A. (1997, September). Epidemiology of leaf spot of olive tree caused by Spilocaea oleagina in southern Spain. In *III International Symposium on Olive Growing 474* (pp. 531-534). ISHS.

Viswanathan, J., Saranya, N., & Inbamani, A. (2021). *Deep learning applications in medical imaging: Introduction to deep learning-based intelligent systems for medical applications. Deep learning applications in medical imaging.* IGI Global. doi:10.4018/978-1-7998-5071-7.ch007

Vlačić, B., Corbo, L., Costa e Silva, S., & Dabić, M. (2021). The evolving role of artificial Intelligence in marketing: A review and research agenda. *Journal of Business Research, 128,* 187–203. doi:10.1016/j.jbusres.2021.01.055

Voronin, V. (2016). The present conditions and perspectives of the humanitarianization of modern engineering education. In *INTED2017 11th International Technology Education and Development Conference,* (pp. 6323–6329). IEEE.

Vranken, H. (2017). Sustainability of bitcoin and blockchains. *Current Opinion in Environmental Sustainability, 28,* 1–9. doi:10.1016/j.cosust.2017.04.011

Walcutt, J. J., & Schatz, S. (2019). *Modernizing Learning: Building the Future Learning Ecosystem.* Advanced Distributed Learning Initiative.

Waleska, A. M. (2020). *Deepfakes and Disinformation. Friedrich Naumann Foundation for Freedom.* FNF.

Wallén, J. (2008). *The history of the industrial robot.* Linköping University Electronic Press.

Walter, A., Finger, R., Huber, R., & Buchmann, N. (2017). Smart farming is key to developing sustainable agriculture. *Proceedings of the National Academy of Sciences of the United States of America, 114*(24), 6148–6150. doi:10.1073/pnas.1707462114 PMID:28611194

Wamba-Taguimdje, S. L., Wamba, S. F., Kamdjoug, J. R. K., & Wanko, C. E. T. (2020). Influence of artificial intelligence on firm performance: The business value of AI-based transformation projects. *Business Process Management Journal, 26*(7), 1893–1924. doi:10.1108/BPMJ-10-2019-0411

Wang, F. Y., Yuan, Y., Zhang, J., Qin, R., & Smith, M. H. (2018). Blockchainized Internet of minds: A new opportunity for cyber–physical–social systems. *IEEE Transactions on Computational Social Systems, 5*(4), 897–906. doi:10.1109/TCSS.2018.2881344

Wang, G., Xu, X., Yao, Y., & Tong, J. (2019). A novel BPNN-based method to overcome the GPS outages for INS/GPS system. *IEEE Access: Practical Innovations, Open Solutions, 7,* 82134–82143. doi:10.1109/ACCESS.2019.2922212

Wang, X., He, P., Zhang, J., & Wang, Z. (2020). QoS Prediction of Web Services Based on Reputation-Aware Network Embedding. *IEEE Access: Practical Innovations, Open Solutions, 8,* 161498–161508. doi:10.1109/ACCESS.2020.3020825

Wang, Z., Hahn, K., Kim, Y., Song, S., & Seo, J. (2017). A news-topic recommender system based on keywords extraction. *Multimedia Tools and Applications, 77*(4), 4339–4353. doi:10.100711042-017-5513-0

Warsi, A., Abdullah, M., Husen, M. N., Yahya, M., Khan, S., & Jawaid, N. (2019). Gun detection system using YOLOv3. *In Proc. of the 2019 IEEE 6th International Conference on Smart Instrumentation, Measurement and Applications.* IEEE.

WebFX. (2022). Web crawlers 101: What is a web crawler and how do crawlers work? WebFX.

Wei, X., Li, J., Feng, K., Zhang, D., Li, P., Zhao, L., & Jiao, Y. (2021). A mixed optimization method based on adaptive Kalman filter and wavelet neural network for INS/GPS during GPS outages. *IEEE Access: Practical Innovations, Open Solutions*, 9, 47875–47886. doi:10.1109/ACCESS.2021.3068744

Weizenbaum, J. (1966). ELIZA—A computer program for the study of natural language communication between man and machine. *Communications of the ACM*, 9(1), 36–45. doi:10.1145/365153.365168

Welukar, J. N., & Bajoria, G. P. (2020). *Artificial Intelligence in Cyber Security-A Review*. Northeastern Illinois University.

Wen, A., Fu, S., Moon, S., El Wazir, M., Rosenbaum, A., Kaggal, V. C., Liu, S., Sohn, S., Liu, H., & Fan, J. (2019). Desiderata for delivering NLP to accelerate healthcare AI advancement and a mayo clinic NLP-as-a-service implementation. *NPJ Digital Medicine*, 2(1), 1–7. doi:10.103841746-019-0208-8 PMID:31872069

White, G., Palade, A., Cabrera, C., & Clarke, S. (2019). Autoencoders for QoS prediction at the Edge. IEEE International Conference on Pervasive Computing and Communications (PerCom), 1-9. https://doi.org/10.1109/PERCOM.2019.8767397

WHO. (2022). *Ethics and Governance of Artificial Intelligence for Health*. WHO. https://www.who.int/publications/i/item/9789240029200

Wiebe, J., Breck, E., Buckley, E., & Cardie, C. (2003). *Davis, P. Fraser, P. Litman, D., Pierce, D., Riloff, E., Wilson, T., Day, D., & Maybury, M*. Recognizing and Organizing Opinions Expressed in the World Press.

Wikipedia. (2008). *Mathematical PageRanks for a Simple Network Are Expressed as Percentages*. Wikipedia. https://en.wikipedia.org/wiki/PageRank#/media/File:PageRanks-Example.svg

Williams, K., Idowu, P. A., Balogun, J. A., & Oluwaranti, A. I. (2015). Breast cancer risk prediction using data mining classification techniques. *Transactions on Networks and Communications, 3*(2), 01.

Williamson, B. (2015). Governing software: Networks, databases and algorithmic power in the digital governance of public education. *Learning, Media and Technology, 40*(1), 83–105. doi:10.1080/17439884.2014.924527

Willmott, C., & Matsuura, K. (2005). Advantages of the mean absolute error (MAE) over the root mean square error (RMSE) in assessing average model performance. *Climate Research, 30*, 79–82. https://doi.org/10.3354/cr030079

Wilson, R. F., & Pettijohn, J. B. (2006). Search engine optimisation: A primer on keyword strategies. *Journal of Direct, Data and Digital Marketing Practice, 8*(2), 121–133. doi:10.1057/palgrave.dddmp.4340563

Wirasinghe, S. C., Caldera, H. J., Durage, S. W., & Ruwanpura, J. (2013). *Preliminary Analysis and Classification of Natural Disasters*. doi:10.13140/RG.2.1.4283.5041

Wirkuttis, N., & Klein, H. (2017). Artificial intelligence in cybersecurity. *Cyber, Intelligence, and Security, 1*(1), 103–119.

Witten, I. H., & Frank, E. (2017). *Data mining practical machine learning tools and techniques*. Elsevier Science & Technology Books.

Wolff-Mann, E. (2018). *Only good for drug dealers': More Nobel prize winners snub bitcoin*. Yahoo Finance.

Wolf, R. (1853). On the periodic return of the minimum of sun-sport; the agreement between those periods and the variations of magnetic declination. *The London, Edinburgh and Dublin Philosophical Magazine and Journal of Science, 5*(29), 67–67. https://doi.org/10.1080/14786445308646906

Wood, G. (2014). Ethereum: A secure decentralised generalised transaction ledger. *Ethereum project yellow paper, 151*, 1-32.

Wood, B., Howard, R., Thernisien, A., & Socker, D. (2009). The three-dimensional morphology of a corotating interaction region in the inner heliosphere. *The Astrophysical Journal. Letters, 708,* L89. https://doi.org/10.1088/2041-8205/708/2/L89

Woodward, B., & Cowley, A. (2011). *The Sustainable Importance of Platinum in Biomedical Applications.* Mddionline.com. https://www.mddionline.com/ivd/sustainable-importance-platinum-biomedical-applications

Woorank. (n.d). *The role of search engine crawlers.* Woorank. https://www.woorank.com/en/edu/seo-guides/search-engine-crawlers

World Health Organization. (2018). *Towards a dementia plan: A WHO guide.* WHO.

World Health Organization. (2021). *Ethics and governance of artificial intelligence for health: WHO guidance.* WHO.

WS-DREAM. (2022). *Towards Open Datasets and Source Code for Web Service Research.* WS-Dream. https://wsdream.github.io/

Wu, F., Jin, G., Gao, M., He, Z., & Yang, Y. (2019). Helmet Detection Based on Improved YOLOv3 Deep Model. *2019 IEEE 16th International Conference on Networking, Sensing and Control (ICNSC)*, (pp. 363-368). IEEE.

Wu, Q., Liu, Y., & Wu, C. (2018). An overview of current situations of robot industry development. In *ITM Web of Conferences* (Vol. 17, p. 03019). EDP Sciences. 10.1051/itmconf/20181703019

Wu, X., & Li, J. (2022). An AIoT-enabled autonomous dementia monitoring system. *arXiv:2207.00804.*

Wu, H., Yin, H., Chen, H., Sun, M., Liu, X., Yu, Y., & Zhang, J. (2020). A deep learning, image based approach for automated diagnosis for inflammatory skin diseases. *Annals of Translational Medicine, 8*(9), 581. doi:10.21037/atm.2020.04.39 PMID:32566608

Wu, J., & Tran, N. K. (2018). Application of blockchain technology in sustainable energy systems: An overview. *Sustainability, 10*(9), 3067. doi:10.3390u10093067

Wu, Y. T., Yuan, M., Dong, S., Li, L., & Liu, Y. (2018, January). Remaining useful life estimation of engineered systems using vanilla LSTM neural networks. *Neurocomputing, 275,* 167–179. doi:10.1016/j.neucom.2017.05.063

Xing, B., & Marwala, T. (2017). Implications of the Fourth Industrial Age for higher education. *Think (London, England), 73,* 10–15.

Xing, Y., Shu, H., Zhao, H., Li, D., & Guo, L. (2021). Survey on botnet detection techniques: Classification, methods, and evaluation. *Mathematical Problems in Engineering, 2021,* 2021. doi:10.1155/2021/6640499

Xin, Y., Kong, L., Liu, Z., Chen, Y., Li, Y., Zhu, H., Gao, M., Hou, H., & Wang, C. (2018). Machine learning and deep learning methods for cybersecurity. *IEEE Access: Practical Innovations, Open Solutions, 6,* 35365–35381. doi:10.1109/ACCESS.2018.2836950

Xu, B., Wang, N., Chen, T., & Li, M. (2015). Empirical evaluation of rectified activations in convolutional network. arXiv preprint arXiv:1505.00853.

Xu, L., He, J., & Hu, Y. (2021). Early Diabetes Risk Prediction Based on Deep Learning Methods. In *2021 4th International Conference on Pattern Recognition and Artificial Intelligence (PRAI)* (pp. 282-286). IEEE. 10.1109/PRAI53619.2021.9551074

Xuan, S., Liu, G., Li, Z., Zheng, L., Wang, S., & Jiang, C. (2018, March). Random forest for credit card fraud detection. In *2018 IEEE 15th international conference on networking, sensing and control (ICNSC)* (pp. 1-6). IEEE. 10.1109/ICNSC.2018.8361343

Xue, W., Mou, X., Zhang, L., Bovik, A. C., & Feng, X. (2014). Blind image quality assessment using joint statistics of gradient magnitude and Laplacian features. *IEEE Transactions on Image Processing*, 23(11), 4850–4862. doi:10.1109/TIP.2014.2355716 PMID:25216482

Xu, J., Zheng, Z., & Lyu, M. R. (2016). Web Service Personalized Quality of Service Prediction via Reputation-Based Matrix Factorization. *IEEE Transactions on Reliability*, 65(1), 28–37. doi:10.1109/TR.2015.2464075

Xu, L. D., Xu, E. L., & Li, L. (2018). Industry 4.0: State of the art and future trends. *International Journal of Production Research*, 56(8), 2941–2962. doi:10.1080/00207543.2018.1444806

Xu, S., Wang, J., Shou, W., Ngo, T., Sadick, A., & Wang, X. (2021). Computer vision techniques in construction: A critical review. *Archives of Computational Methods in Engineering*, 28(5), 3383–3397. doi:10.100711831-020-09504-3

Xu, Z., Lin, Z., Zhou, C., & Huang, C. (2016). Detecting traffic hot spots using vehicle tracking data. *2nd ISPRS International Conference on Computer Vision in Remote Sensing. 9901*, pp. 218-224. SPIE.

Yadav, N., & Binay, U. (2017). Comparative Study of Object Detection Algorithms. *International Research Journal of Engineering and Technology*, 4(11), 586–591.

Yadav, S., & Chakraborty, P. (2022). Using Google voice search to support informal learning in four to ten year old children. *Education and Information Technologies*, 27(3), 4347–4363. doi:10.100710639-021-10789-5

Yakubovich, V., & Lup, D. (2006). Stages of the recruitment process and the referrer's performance effect. *Organization Science*, 17(6), 710–723. doi:10.1287/orsc.1060.0214

Yamauchi, H., Hayakawa, M., Asano, T., Ohtani, N., & Ohta, M. (2017). Statistical Evaluations of Variations in Dairy Cows' Milk Yields as a Precursor of Earthquakes. *Animals (Basel)*, 7(12), 19. https://doi.org/10.3390/ani7030019

Yang, C., Shi, W., & Chen, W. (2017). Comparison of unscented and extended Kalman filters with application in vehicle navigation. *Journal of Navigation*, 70(2), 411–431. doi:10.1017/S0373463316000655

Yang, D., Zhao, X., Xu, Z., Li, Y., & Li, Q. (2017). Developing status and prospect analysis of blockchain in energy Internet. *Zhongguo Dianji Gongcheng Xuebao*, 37, 3664–3671.

Yang, K., Yau, J. H., Fei-Fei, L., Deng, J., & Russakovsky, O. (2022). A study of face obfuscation in imagenet. International Conference on Machine Learning, Zafar, M. B., Valera, I., Gomez-Rodriguez, M., & Gummadi, K. P. (2019). Fairness constraints: A flexible approach for fair classification. *Journal of Machine Learning Research*, 20(1), 2737–2778.

Yang, T., Guo, Q., Tai, X., Sun, H., Zhang, B., Zhao, W., & Lin, C. (2017). Applying blockchain technology to decentralized operation in future energy internet. In *Proceedings of IEEE Conference on Energy Internet and Energy System Integration* (pp. 1-5). IEEE. 10.1109/EI2.2017.8244418

Yan, Y., Zhao, J., Wen, F., & Chen, X. Y. (2017). Blockchain in energy systems: Concept, application and prospect. *Electric Power Construction*, 38(2), 12–20.

Yaseen, Q. (2021). Spam email detection using deep learning techniques. *Procedia Computer Science*, 184, 853–858. doi:10.1016/j.procs.2021.03.107

Yasumoto, K., Yamaguchi, H., & Shigeno, H. (2016). Survey of real-time processing technologies of IoT data streams. *Journal of Information Processing*, 24(2), 195–202. doi:10.2197/ipsjjip.24.195

Yi, B., Shen, X., Liu, H., Zhang, Z., Zhang, W., Liu, S., & Xiong, N. (2019). Deep Matrix Factorization With Implicit Feedback Embedding for Recommendation System. *IEEE Transactions on Industrial Informatics*, *15*(8), 4591–4601. doi:10.1109/TII.2019.2893714

Ying, R., He, R., Chen, K., Eksombatchai, P., Hamilton, W. L., & Leskovec, J. (2018). Graph convolutional neural networks for web-scale recommender systems. *Proceedings of the ACM SIGKDD International Conference on Knowledge Discovery and Data Mining*, 974–983. 10.1145/3219819.3219890

Yordanov, V. (2021). *Classification Metrics — Confusion Matrix Explained.* Retrieved from Towardsdatascience: https://towardsdatascience.com/classification-metrics-confusion-matrix-explained-7c7abe4e9543

Yu, D., Liu, Y., Xu, Y., & Yin, Y. (2014). Personalized QoS prediction for web services using latent factor models. *Proceedings - 2014 IEEE International Conference on Services Computing, SCC 2014*, 107–114. 10.1109/SCC.2014.23

Yuan, M., Wu, Y., & Lin, L. (2016). *"Fault diagnosis and remaining useful life estimation of aero engine using LSTM neural network."* 2016 IEEE international conference on aircraft utility systems (AUS). IEEE.

Yuan, S., Luo, X., Mu, B., Li, J., & Dai, G. (2019). Prediction of north atlantic oscillation index with convolutional LSTM based on ensemble empirical mode decomposition. *Atmosphere*, *10*(5), 252. https://doi.org/10.3390/atmos10050252

Yu, K., Tan, L., Lin, L., Cheng, X., Yi, Z., & Sato, T. (2021). Deep-learning-empowered breast cancer auxiliary diagnosis for 5GB remote E-health. *IEEE Wireless Communications*, *28*(3), 54–61.

Yuniarthe, Y. (2017). Application of Artificial Intelligence (AI) in Search Engine Optimization (SEO). *Proceedings - 2017 International Conference on Soft Computing, Intelligent System and Information Technology: Building Intelligence Through IOT and Big Data, ICSIIT 2017, 2018-January*, 96–101. 10.1109/ICSIIT.2017.15

Yusuf, F., Olayiwola, T., & Afagwu, C. (2021). Application of Artificial Intelligence-based predictive methods in Ionic liquid studies: A review. *Fluid Phase Equilibria*, *531*, 112898. doi:10.1016/j.fluid.2020.112898

Zadeh, M. H., & Seyyedi, M. A. (2010). Qos monitoring for web services by Time Series Forecasting. *Proceedings - 2010 3rd IEEE International Conference on Computer Science and Information Technology, ICCSIT 2010, 5*, 659–663. 10.1109/ICCSIT.2010.5563998

Zayed, A. (2006). Outstanding organizational performance. In *The way to the future organization* (2nd ed.). Arab Organization for Administrative Development.

Zednik, C. (2021). Solving the black box problem: A normative framework for explainable artificial intelligence. *Philosophy & Technology*, *34*(2), 265–288. doi:10.100713347-019-00382-7

Zeiler, M. D., & Fergus, R. (2014). Visualizing and understanding convolutional networks. European conference on computer vision, .

Zeiler, M. D., & Fergus, R. (2014). Visualizing and understanding convolutional networks. In *European conference on computer vision* (pp. 818-833). Springer.

Zhang, G., & Li, H. (2018). Effectiveness of scaled exponentially-regularized linear units (SERLUs). arXiv preprint arXiv:1807.10117.

Zhang, H., Du, Y., Ning, S., Zhang, Y., Yang, S., & Du, C. (2017). Pedestrian detection method based on Faster R-CNN. In 2017 13th International Conference on Computational Intelligence and Security (CIS) (pp. 427-430). IEEE.

Zhang, N., Wang, Y., Kang, C., Cheng, J., & He, D. (2016). Blockchain technique in the energy internet: preliminary research framework and typical applications. In *Zhongguo Dianji Gongcheng Xuebao/Proceedings of the Chinese Society of Electrical Engineering*. IEEE.

Zhang, P., Zhao, S. W., & Tan, B. (2011). Applications of Decision Support System in Aviation Maintenance. *In Tech Open*. https://www.intechopen.com/chapters/18807

Zhang, Y., Zheng, Z., & Lyu, M. R. (2011). WSPred: A time-aware personalized QoS prediction framework for Web services. *Proceedings - International Symposium on Software Reliability Engineering, ISSRE*, 210–219. IEEE. 10.1109/ISSRE.2011.17

Zhang, C., & Lu, Y. (2021). Study on artificial intelligence: The state of the art and future prospects. *Journal of Industrial Information Integration*, 23, 100224. doi:10.1016/j.jii.2021.100224

Zhang, C., & Wang, P. (2000, September). A new method of color image segmentation based on intensity and hue clustering. In *Proceedings 15th International Conference on Pattern Recognition. ICPR-2000* (Vol. 3, pp. 613-616). IEEE. 10.1109/ICPR.2000.903620

Zhang, F., Song, Y., Cai, W., Hauptmann, A. G., Liu, S., Pujol, S., & Chen, M. (2016). Dictionary pruning with visual word significance for medical image retrieval. *Neurocomputing*, 177(1), 75–88. doi:10.1016/j.neucom.2015.11.008 PMID:27688597

Zhang, H., Kang, R., & Pecht, M. A hybrid prognostics and health management approach for condition-based maintenance. In *Proceedings of the 2009 IEEE International Conference on Industrial Engineering and Engineering Management*, (pp. 1165–1169). IEEE. 10.1109/IEEM.2009.5372976

Zhang, L., Lee, B., Ye, Y., & Qiao, Y. (2019). Ethereum transaction performance evaluation using test-nets. *In Proceedings of European Conference on Parallel Processing* (pp. 179-190). Springer.

Zhang, Q., Wang, H., Dong, J., Zhong, G., & Sun, X. (2017). Prediction of sea surface temperature using long short-term memory. *IEEE Geoscience and Remote Sensing Letters*, 14(10), 1745–1749. https://doi.org/10.1109/LGRS.2017.2733548

Zhang, T., & Xu, X. (2012). A new method of seamless land navigation for GPS/INS integrated system. *Measurement*, 15(2), 691–701. doi:10.1016/j.measurement.2011.12.021

Zhang, W., & Sun, W. (2021). Research on small moving target detection algorithm based on complex scene. *Journal of Physics: Conference Series*, 1738(1), 12093. doi:10.1088/1742-6596/1738/1/012093

Zhang, X. D. (2020). *A matrix algebra approach to artificial Intelligence*. Springer Singapore. doi:10.1007/978-981-15-2770-8

Zhang, Y., Wang, Y., Foley, J., Suk, J., & Conathan, D. (2017). Tweeting Mass Shootings: The Dynamics of Issue Attention on Social Media. *Proceedings of the 8th International Conference on Social Media & Society*, (pp. 1 – 5). ACM. 10.1145/3097286.3097345

Zhao, J., Wang, T., Yatskar, M., Ordonez, V., & Chang, K.-W. (2018). Gender Bias in Coreference Resolution: Evaluation and Debiasing Methods. *Proceedings of the 2018 Conference of the North American Chapter of the Association for Computational Linguistics: Human Language Technologies*, Volume 2 (Short Papers)

Zhao, L., Qiu, H., & Feng, Y. (2016). Analysis of a robust Kalman filter in loosely coupled GPS/INS navigation system. *Measurement*, 80, 138–147. doi:10.1016/j.measurement.2015.11.008

Zhao, S., Blaabjerg, F., & Wang, H. (2020). An overview of artificial intelligence applications for power electronics. *IEEE Transactions on Power Electronics*, 36(4), 4633–4658. doi:10.1109/TPEL.2020.3024914

Zhao, Z. Q., Zheng, P., Xu, S. T., & Wu, X. (2019). Object Detection with Deep Learning: A Review. *IEEE Transactions on Neural Networks and Learning Systems, 30*(11), 3212–3232. doi:10.1109/TNNLS.2018.2876865 PMID:30703038

Zheng, C., Bouazizi, M., & Ohtsuki, T. (2022). An evaluation on information composition in dementia detection based on speech. *IEEE Access*

Zheng, S. (2017). Long short-term memory network for remaining useful life estimation. 2017 IEEE international conference on prognostics and health management (ICPHM). IEEE.

Zheng, Z., Xie, S., Dai, H., Chen, X., & Wang, H. (2017). An Overview of Blockchain Technology: Architecture, Consensus, and Future Trends. In *proceedings of IEEE International Congress on Big* Data (pp. 557-564). IEEE. 10.1109/BigDataCongress.2017.85

Zheng, Z., Ma, H., Lyu, M. R., & King, I. (2011). QoS-Aware Web Service Recommendation by Collaborative Filtering. *IEEE Transactions on Services Computing, 4*(2), 140–152. doi:10.1109/TSC.2010.52

Zheng, Z., Ma, H., Lyu, M. R., & King, I. (2013). Collaborative web service qos prediction via neighborhood integrated matrix factorization. *IEEE Transactions on Services Computing, 6*(3), 289–299. doi:10.1109/TSC.2011.59

Zheng, Z., Zhang, Y., & Lyu, M. R. (2014). Investigating QoS of Real-World Web Services. *IEEE Transactions on Services Computing, 7*(1), 32–39. doi:10.1109/TSC.2012.34

Zhou, W., Hou, J., Liu, L., Sun, T., & Liu, J. (2017). Design and simulation of the integrated navigation system based on an extended Kalman filter. *Open Physics, 15*(1), 182–187. doi:10.1515/phys-2017-0019

Zhu, X., Zhang, P., & Xie, M. (2021, January). A joint long short-term memory and AdaBoost regression approach with application to remaining useful life estimation. *Measurement, 170*, 108707. doi:10.1016/j.measurement.2020.108707

Ziakis, C., Vlachopoulou, M., Kyrkoudis, T., & Karagkiozido, M. (2019). Important factors for improving google search rank. *Future Internet. 11*(32). https://www.firstcry.ae/

Zintgraf, L. M., Cohen, T. S., Adel, T., & Welling, M. (2017). Visualizing deep neural network decisions: Prediction difference analysis. *arXiv preprint arXiv:1702.04595*

Zoph, B., Vasudevan, V., Shlens, J., & Le, Q. V. (2018). Learning transferable architectures for scalable image recognition. In *Proceedings of the IEEE conference on computer vision and pattern recognition* (pp. 8697-8710). IEEE. 10.1109/CVPR.2018.00907

Zou, Q., Qu, K., Luo, Y., Yin, D., Ju, Y., & Tang, H. (2018). Predicting diabetes mellitus with machine learning techniques. *Frontiers in Genetics, 9*, 515. doi:10.3389/fgene.2018.00515 PMID:30459809

Zuboff, S. (2019). *The Age of Surveillance Capitalism: The Fight for a Human Future at the New Frontier of Power.* Public Affairs.

Zwakman, D. S., Pal, D., & Arpnikanondt, C. (2021). Usability evaluation of artificial intelligence-based voice assistants: The case of Amazon Alexa. *SN Computer Science, 2*(1), 1–16. doi:10.100742979-020-00424-4 PMID:33458698

About the Contributors

Sanaa Kaddoura holds a Ph.D. in computer science from Beirut Arab University, Lebanon. She is currently employed as an assistant professor of Computer Science at the Department of Computing and Applied Technology, College of Technological Innovation, Zayed University, United Arab Emirates. She is also an assistant professor of business analytics for master's degree students in the UAE. She is a fellow of Higher Education Academy, Advance HE (FHEA) since 2019, which demonstrates a personal and institutional commitment to professionalism in learning and teaching in higher education. Furthermore, she is a certified specialist from Blackboard academy since November 2022. In addition to her research interests in cybersecurity, machine learning, and natural language processing, she is an active researcher in higher education teaching and learning related to enhancing the quality of instructional delivery to facilitate students' acquirement of skills and smooth transition to the workplace.

* * *

Ishrap Abdulmajeed is a master student in Business Computing school at Jinan University. She is also senior programmer and data analysis at public organisation in Iraq.

Tesfahiwet Abrham lives in Abu Dhabi, UAE is a researcher in Cyber Security related topics such as Artificial Intelligence, Machine Learning and Deep Learning in Cyber Security.

Mouna Afif received the B.Sc., M.Sc., and Ph.D. degrees in Electronics from the Faculty of Science of Monastir, Monastir University, Tunisia in 2013, 2016, and 2021 respectively. Actually she is working as an assistant professor at Faculty of Science of Monastir, Monastir University, Tunisia. His research interests are Pattern Recognition, Artificial Intelligence, Deep Learning, Convolutional Neural Networks, Image and Video Processing, Embedded Vision and FPGA implementations.

Abel Ajibesin, a strong member of NSE and IEEE STEM Champion, is currently an Associate Professor of Computer and Electrical Engineering, at the American University of Nigeria (AUN). He holds a Doctorate degree in Electrical Engineering from the University of Cape Town (UCT), South Africa, and another in Computer Science from the Modibbo Adama University of Technology, Nigeria. He is the founding Member of the Academy of Computing Sciences (FMACS), a Fellow of the African Scientific Institute, and the founding Dean, of the School of Engineering (SOE), AUN. He has supervised and graduated several graduate students and has over fifty publications in highly renowned peer-reviewed international conferences, journal articles, book chapters, and books. As a co-founder of AJISAQ Limited, he has overseen the designs, patents, and commercialization of two Engineering products that have impacted his community. He is also a consultant for many renowned organizations, including the World Bank.

Hamda Al Breiki is a PhD graduate from Khalifa University, Electrical Engineering and Computer Science department. Her thesis was about defining a trust requirements model for blockchain systems. She received a B.S. degree in Information Technology with a major in Software Engineering from UAE University, UAE, in 2007, and an M.S. degree in Information Technology with a specialization in Cyber Security from Zayed University, UAE, in 2012. She worked as an IT faculty in Higher Colleges of Technology from August 2012 to December 2015, and she taught undergraduate courses in the area of programming, software engineering, security, and web and mobile application development.

Fatima Al Husseiny is a LinkedIn content creator and is part of LinkedIn for Journalists Premium Program 2022-2023. She holds a Master's degree in Educational Management from the Lebanese International University and BA in English Language and Literature from the Lebanese University. Her research interests are related to Education, Educational Technology, AI, and Social Media. Fatima's professional goals are related to developing academic research in her fields of interest. She has been awarded two achievement awards for her contributions to Wikipedia and has various certifications from Google, Coursera, LinkedIn Learning, and Udemy. Fatima enriches her social responsibility by contributing to educational blogs in reputable media outlets (e.g. Annahar Media Group Website) and content editing in an international context, such as The International Girls Academy, NJ, USA.

Mohamed Atri is Professor in the Department of Computer Engineering at College of Computer Science, King Khalid University, Saudi Arabia. He received his Ph.D. Degree in Microelectronics from the University of Monastir, Tunisia in 2001. He has obtained the HDR degree from the University of Monastir, Tunisia in 2011. He is currently a member of the Laboratory of Electronics & Microelectronics, Faculty of Science of Monastir. His research includes Circuit and System Design, Image processing, Network Communication, IPs and SoC.

Riadh Ayachi received his Bachelor's Degree in Electronics, electro techniques, and automatic in 2015, his Master's Degree in Micro and Nanoelectronics in 2018, and his Ph.D. in 2021 from the Faculty of Sciences of Monastir. Currently, he has been working as an Assistant Professor in digital embedded electronics at the High Institute of Informatics and Mathematics of Monastir (ISIMM). His research area includes deep learning, image and video processing, autonomous systems and hardware implementation.

Sankaragomathi B. has the teaching experience of 34 years, presently working as Professor of Biomedical Engineering at Sri Shakthi Institute of Engineering and Technology, Coimbatore. 12 Research Scholars have completed their Ph.D. under her guidance. She is the Life Fellow of IETE, IE(I), Life Member of ISTE, ISOI, BMESOI, etc. Received many awards such as Women Engineer Award, Periyar Award etc.

Abdessalem Ben Abdelali received his degree in Electrical Engineering and his DEA in industrial informatics from the National School of Engineering of Sfax (ENIS), Tunisia, respectively, in 2001 and 2002. He received his PhD from ENIS and Burgundy University (BU), France, in 2007. Since 2008 he has been working as an Assistant Professor in digital embedded electronics at the High Institute of Informatics and Mathematics of Monastir (ISIMM). His current research interests include re-configurable architectures and hardware implementation of image and video processing applications.

Binish Benjamin has experience of several years in academics, research, and academic management. Her research interest includes mathematical modeling and simulation of healthcare applications, especially chemotaxis.

B. Briyolan is an Electronic and communication engineering student. Interested in article writing.

Mohana Vamsi Dhara is a student pursuing a final year in a bachelors of technology.

Doken Edgar received his Master of Science in Computer Science from the American University of Nigeria

Amal El Arid is a lab engineer and instructor in the electrical and computer engineering department at Rafik Hariri University in Lebanon. She is currently doing a lot of research on artificial intelligence, network security, and information technology in education. She earned her Master's Degree from the Electrical and Computer Engineering department at the American University of Beirut in Lebanon.

Julia El Zini is a Ph.D. candidate in the Electrical and Computer Engineering (ECE) department at the American University of Beirut (AUB). She received her B.S. and M.S. in computer science with high distinction from AUB in 2015 and 2017 respectively. Julia has over 6 years of experience in the field of Machine Learning and is interested in working on responsible AI algorithms and solutions. Her current research work focuses on fair and explainable AI from theoretical and empirical perspectives. Prior to that, she has published 10+ papers in reinforcement learning, generative adversarial networks, distributed optimization, and advanced transfer learning techniques. Julia likes to communicate AI concepts to youth, and she has been teaching programming and AI courses at AUB and delivering several workshops on different AI topics.

Mahmoud Ghorbel is a PhD researcher specialized in machine learning, deep learning, and computer vision.

Neelissetti Girish is pursuing B Tech at SRM University, AP. His research focus lies in Image processing and Machine Learning.

Rim Hamacha holds a PhD in Comparative Competition Law, an LLM in Corporate Finance Law, a fellow of the Higher Education Academy UK. She is a Fellow of the International Chamber of Commerce (France), and a Member of the Young International Arbitration Group, the London Court of International Arbitration (UK). She was awarded the Academic Staff Achievement for PhD obtained without corrections from Brunel University (UK). Rim's teaching and learning interests include Legal Research Skills, ADR and Legal Ethics, WTO Law and Policy, and the International Sale of Goods. Her research interests cover Commercial Law, Competition Law, Comparative Law, Corporate Law, and Financial Regulations.

Lubana Isaoglu is a Ph.D. student in the computer engineering department at Istanbul-Cerrahpasa university. Her main interest is working with Artificial intelligence, especially neural networks. Lubana has a long experience in the academic sector, mainly in teaching computer science in different countries: the ministry of education in Kuwait, the higher institute for telecommunications & Navigation-Kuwait University, and Ibn Haldun university in Istanbul. This diversity helped her develop various skills such as simplifying the information, delivering information with ease, and research skills.

Imen Kallel is a research member at ESSE (Advanced Electronic Systems and Sustainable Energy), ENET'COM –Tunisia. Research interests include image processing, digital watermarking and data hiding, multimedia authentication, human machine interaction (HMI), computer vision and environmental health and agriculture.

Mohamed Kallel is a research member at ESSE (Advanced Electronic Systems and Sustainable Energy), ENET'COM –Tunisia. Research interests include image processing, multimedia authentication, human machine interaction (HMI), computer vision and environmental health and agriculture.

Mzee Khamis has a Bachelor degree of Science in Computer Science at State University of Zanzibar-Tanzania 2018. Master degree of Software Engineering at University of Electronics Science and Technology of China. Research area: Intelligent Computing.

Santanu Koley has completed his Doctorate of Philosophy in the year 2013 from CSJM University Kanpur, Uttar Pradesh, India and presently he is working at Haldia Institute of Technology, Haldia, West Bengal India as a Professor in Computer Science and Engineering Department. He has more than fourteen years of research experience and more than sixteen years of teaching experience in various AICTE approved engineering colleges all over the India. He has published more than thirty research papers in various national and international Journal/conferences. Presently he is doing research works in the areas of Cloud Computing, Digital Image Processing, Artificial Intelligence and Machine Learning.

Volodymyr Kolotusha is a senior teacher of ATM personnel Training Department, Training and Certification Center Ukrainian State Air Traffic Service Enterprise. Candidate of Engineering, specialty 05.22.13 "Navigation and traffic control", Associate professor of Department of Air Navigation Systems in National Aviation University, Ukraine. Area of Scientific Interests: researches in field of professional training of air traffic controllers. Author more than 30 scientific articles, books, methodical manuals in fields of aviation, professional training of air traffic controllers. Teaching in fields of: air traffic management, human factor, aviation law, air navigation.

Simar Mansi completed a Master's degree in Information Technology topics web accessibility. A Teacher Assistant for 5 years, a Computer Science Teacher for 5 years, and a Programmer Researcher

Muzakkit Huzzain Md is working as an assistant professor in SRM University, AP. His research interest lies in resource Allocation in IoT aware Transportation/Vehicular systems and Machine learning.

Mutwalibi Nambobi is a research assistant at Motion Analysis Research Lab, Islamic University in Uganda. He is also working as the Head of Science and Technology, Labour College of East Africa. He was a research assistant in Technical and Vocational Education (TVE) department at Islamic University of Technology (IUT, 2018). He holds an MBA (Virtual University of Uganda, Muyenga, Kampala), BSc. Technical Education (Islamic University of Technology, Dhaka, Bangladesh) specializing in computer science and engineering. His research interest on Disruptive Innovations, Wargaming Strategy, Game theory, Coopetition, Blue Ocean Strategy, Blended learning, Green Skills, TVET and ICTs in a developing country. He can be reached via his website: .

Ghalia Nassreddine is an Associate Professor at the Jinan University, Lebanon. She is a Ph.D holder in information technology and systems from University of Technology of Compiegne, France since 2009. Currently, she is serving as a chairperson in the school of Business Computing in Jinan University of Lebanon. She is currently doing a lot of research in Machine Learning, education and Dempster-Shafer theory.

Mike O'Dea is a Senior Lecturer in Department of Computer Science at York St John University. He specialises in Machine Learning, Databases and Web Dev.

Semthil Kumar S. has Industrial experience of 20years and Academic experience of 10years. He has completed his Ph.D. in the area of Image Processing.

Yahia Said received the B.Sc., M.Sc., and Ph.D. degrees in Electronics from the Faculty of Science of Monastir, Monastir University, Tunisia in 2008, 2010, and 2016 respectively. He worked as an assistant professor at Faculty of Science of Monastir, Monastir University, Tunisia. Now, he is an assistant professor at Electrical Engineering Department, College of Engineering, Northern Border University, Arar, Saudi Arabia. His research interests are Pattern Recognition, Artificial Intelligence, Deep Learning, Convolutional Neural Networks, Image and Video Processing, Embedded Vision and SoC Design.

Assadig Sajo received a BSc in Electrical Engineering from the University of Blue Nile, Sudan in 2018. In 2022, Sajo received a MSc in Communication and Information Engineering from Chongqing University of Posts and Telecommunications, Chongqing, China. Sajo is currently working on a Ph.D. in Computer Science and Engineering at the University of Electronic Science and Technology of China.

Viacheslav Shkuratskyy is a research student at York St John University.

Tetiana Shmelova has a Doctorate of Science, and is a Professor of Department of Air Navigation Systems in National Aviation University (Ukraine) Areas of Scientific Interests: Artificial Intelligence; decision-making models by operators in the Air Navigation System (air traffic controller, pilot, engineer, UAV's operator), especially in an emergency; Decision Support Systems for Air Navigation System operators; research of Air Navigation system as Socio-technical system; professional effectiveness using aviation sociometry and socionics; management and marketing in aviation; problems of Human Factors in aviation. Author and editor of more than 300 scientific articles, books, methodical manuals, copyright certificates, handbook, monographs in fields of aviation, economics, mathematics, the theory of system. Teaching courses: decision making; mathematical programming; effectiveness of air traffic management; effectiveness of Unmanned Systems; Artificial Intelligence. Supervises scientific and educational courses for bachelors, masters, PhD-students of the specialty "Aviation Transport" (pilots, air traffic controller, engineers of aeronavigation system, operators of unmanned systems).

Iurii Sierostanov is an airline Captain and instructor. Sierostanov has18 years of aviation experience, 7500 total flight hours. Master's Degree 2009. FAA and ICAO ATPL. Crew Resource Management and Safety Management System specialist. https://www.linkedin.com/in/iurii-sierostanov-9540b3237.044396fa-0154-41db-b83c-5ae481ad893c

Medaramelta Sindhu is pursuing B Tech at SRM University, AP. Her research focus lies in Image processing and Machine Learning.

Jayesh Soni is a PostDoctoral researcher at Florida International University. His current research focus is on detecting anomaly at the system level by leveraging Artificial Intelligence and deep learning techniques. His project is currently funded by the Department of Defense. He also teaches machine learning, deep learning, and bigdata class.

Rajab Ssemwogerere is pursuing a Master of Science in Software engineering at the University of Electronic Science and Technology of China (UESTC) in China. He holds a postgraduate Diploma in management and teaching at higher levels of education, a B.Sc. in Computer Science (2018), and a diploma in Computer science and Information Technology (2014) from the Islamic University in Uganda. Rajab gained certificates in Introduction to cybersecurity (2018) and Introduction to the internet of things and digital transformation (2018) from CISCO Networking Academy. Currently, he works as a research assistant in the Motion Analysis Research Lab as well as a computer lab officer based at the Islamic University in Uganda. He Led a team of six that developed an autonomous smart office system that later won the Rector award at the Islamic University In Uganda (2018). He has research interests in computer vision, Artificial intelligence (IoT), and Machine learning.

Mohamed Ali Triki is Director of Research Laboratory, Genetic Ressources of Olive Tree: Caracterisation, Valorisation and Phytosanitary Protection" - Coordinator Of National Research Project: « New multidisciplinary approach for reducing uncertainties in risk assessment of Xylella fastidiosa "(Acronym: ERP-Xf) - Member (and Coordinator of the Olive Tree Institute of Tunisia) of the Federated Research Project in collaboration with the Sfax Digital Research Center (CNRNS) and the Faculty of Sciences of Sfax. Project entitled: "Multi-approach monitoring of OLIVE health in Tunisia by optical remote sensing" (2019-2021).

Farhan Sabir Ujager has several years of experience in teaching, research, and management, at different universities in Pakistan and the United Arab Emirates. He is working as a Senior Lecturer at the De Montfort University (DMU), Dubai in the faculty of Science, Engineering and Computing (SEC). His research interests include Smart and Sustainable Ambiance, Smart Healthcare, Wireless Sensor Networks, and Optical Communication. He is currently researching Context-Aware Smart ambiance and healthcare applications.

S. Uma is a Professor in the Department of Computer Science and Engineering at Hindusthan College of Engineering and Technology, Coimbatore, Tamil Nadu, India. She received her B.E., degree in

Computer Science and Engineering (CSE) in First Class with Distinction from P.S.G. College of Technology, M.S.,(By Res.,)., degree from Anna University, Chennai, Tamil Nadu. She received her Ph.D., in the faculty of Information and Communication Engineering from Anna University, Chennai with High Commendation. She has 31 years of academic experience and organized many National and International seminars, workshops and conferences. She has published more than 100 research papers in National and International Conferences, Journals, Book Chapters, Patents and Books. She is a potential reviewer of International Journals and Member of Professional Bodies like ISTE, CSI, IEEE, IAENG, etc., She is a recipient of "Bharath Jyoti", "Certificate of Excellence" and "Best Citizen of India" Awards. Her research interests are pattern recognition and analysis of nonlinear time series data, AI and digital analytics.

Aminu B. Usman is the Associate Head of Computer and Data Science, York St John University in UK. He received a Computer Science degree from Bayero Universidad, Kano, a Master's degree in Network Security from Middlesex University, London, and a Ph.D. in Network Security from Auckland University of Technology. His current research is on Security and Authentication methods, IoT, next-generation networks and security issues in wireless networks. Yang Lu is working as a lecturer in computer science at the School of Science, Technology and Health, York St John University. She received the Ph.D. degree at the University of Melbourne in 2018, and then worked at the University of Kent as a postdoctoral research fellow till 2021. Her research interests include cyber security, semantic web, machine learning, decision making, and blockchain technology.

Chilukuri Vamsee is pursuing B Tech at SRM University, AP. His research focus lies in Image processing and Machine Learning.

Krishna Teja Sri Vanka is a student in the final year at SRM University AP.

Dinesh Reddy Vemula is an assistant professor in SRM University, AP, India. He has more than 10 years of work experience which include government, industry, academia, and research careers. His research interests focus on Cloud computing, Artificial intelligence and Edge computing. He is a member of the IEEE.

Desu Yasaswini is pursuing B Tech at SRM University, AP. Her research focus lies in Image processing and Machine Learning.

Maxim Yatsko is an airline pilot, ICAO ATPL holder, current type rating is Boeing 737 300-900; Candidate of Engineering "Navigation and traffic control", associate professor of Department of Aerodynamics and Aircraft Flight Safety in National Aviation University.

Joumana Younis received her PhD degree in Information and Communication Technology, Managerial Innovation from the CNAM University France; Doctorate in Business Administration (DBA) in Human Resources at ASMP University - France. Executive Doctorate in Business Administration (EDBA) in Entrepreneurship at Montpellier University - France. Former Dean of the Faculty of Sciences at Jinan University. Actually, she is the Dean of Business Administration at Jinan University for undergraduate, graduate, and post-graduate degrees, in addition to the DBA program in partnership with ASMP- France. She is an active researcher in Business Intelligence, Machine Learning and Management Science.

Index

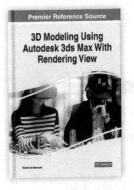

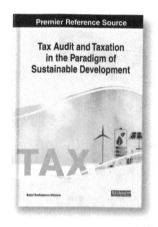   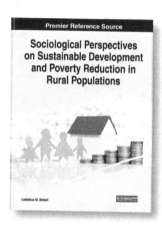